The Hoover Institution on War, Revolution and Peace, founded at Stanford University in 1919 by the late President Herbert Hoover, is a center for advanced study and research on public and international affairs in the twentieth century. The views expressed in its publications are entirely those of the authors and do not necessarily reflect the views of the Hoover Institution.

Hoover Institution Bibliographical Series 47
Standard Book Number 8179-2471-X
Library of Congress Number 71-185241
Printed in the United States of America

Hoover Bibliographical Series: 47

Please note that this is an unabridged and unedited reproduction of an original manuscript. The Hoover Institution Press is distributing the work in this form in order to make it available to scholars more promptly and economically than would otherwise be possible.

# SEMPER EX AFRICA . . .

A BIBLIOGRAPHY OF PRIMARY SOURCE FOR NINETEENTH-CENTURY

TROPICAL AFRICA AS RECORDED BY EXPLORERS, MISSIONARIES,

TRADERS, TRAVELERS, ADMINISTRATORS, MILITARY MEN,

ADVENTURERS, AND OTHERS

Robert L. Hess       and       Dalvan M. Coger

CONTENTS

# INTRODUCTION

SEMPER EX AFRICA ALIQUOD NOVI. "Always something new out of Africa," wrote Pliny the Elder in reference to the north African provinces of the Roman Empire some nineteen centuries ago. The tempestuous events of the twentieth century African political life have breathed new life into this ancient phrase. In terms of increased knowledge about Africa, however, the great century of African discovery was the nineteenth century. In that second age of exploration preceding the great wave of European imperialism that inundated the African continent and apparently submerged one African society after another more was learned about Africa than had been learned in all the centuries previous. Paradoxically, the more new information that came out of Africa from the time of Mungo Park's exploration of the Niger River in the early years of the century to the decades of the great scramble for Africa, the more Africa came to be regarded popularly as the Dark Continent, a terra incognita, a passive land without a history.

A new generation of historical scholarship has dramatically revealed that Africa has indeed a long and interesting past. While contemporary concern with the winds of change in postcolonial Africa has given rise to a vast new literature about contemporary affairs, historical research has attempted to construct a coherent and scholarly history of a continent that until recently contained only a few literature cultures. For some historians this has entailed of necessity the extensive use of nontraditional historical techniques, particularly in the gathering and examination of oral traditions, because for much of the precolonial period the historian's main repository of information -- written records -- was singularly undeveloped. This is not true for much of tropical Africa after 1800, as a cursory glance at this bibliography will indicate. The nineteenth-century history of tropical Africa, that area of the continent exclusive of the Muslim Arab North and of the Afrikaner-controlled Republic of South Africa, may be researched and written on the basis of a much larger collection of primary sources than was hitherto suspected. There is much that may be done by the historian of orthodox training who is more at ease with the written records of the past than with quasi-anthropological techniques that are not universally applicable throughout Africa.

Until relatively recently the bias of most European – and American–trained historians against African history was reflected in the secondary literature dealing with Africa and in the university curriculum, where the emphasis had long been on European overseas expansion and on the accomplishments of Europeans in Africa, rather than on the reaction of Africans to their first contacts with Europeans. Although a new generation of historians at present is attempting to rewrite African history in terms of the African, scholars have generally been handicapped by the lack of bibliographical aids like those which are taken for granted in British, American, and continental European history. The purpose of this bibliography is to give an indication of the vastness of the sources for nineteenth-century tropical Africa, to provide a useful reference work until the state of African historical bibliography attains the level of that of other fields of history, and to encourage historians to investigate the dark and unexplored areas of the primary sources of recent African history.

This work had its genesis in a graduate seminar at Northwestern University in 1964, when history students in the Program of African Studies were urged to investigate the bibliography of limited areas of the continent for the immediate precolonial period. Each student was amazed at the amount of information that was available, and the group quickly came to appreciate the potential richness of a literature that included accounts by explorers, missionaries, traders, hunters, adventurers, military men, travelers, government officials, and so on. Secondary sources were deliberately ignored. Where the primary literature had not been neglected, it was more often than not used as the basis only for European overseas history and for nonhistorical ethnographic studies. Yet it was obvious from the beginning that this literature contains a treasure of information about African societies and patterns of political and economic life for the period preceding the European conquest -- in other words, the raw materials for a new history of Africa.

It was at first hoped that this compilation would be as complete as possible. Not only were the catalogues of the African collection at Northwestern University thoroughly examined, but so were the printed catalogues of Boston University, the London School of Oriental and African Studies, the Moorland Collection of Howard University, the Library of Congress, and similar publications, as well as the numerous geographical and missionary journals which contain much long forgotten information. In order to avoid duplication with E.G. Cox's Reference Guide to the Literature of Travel for the earlier period and with the numerous bibliographies of twentieth-century African countries which have begun to make their appearance, it was decided to limit the work chronologically to the nineteenth century.

Thus the emphasis is on what Africa was like on the eve of partition and in the early years of ever intensifying contact with the European world. The rationale behind exclusion of North Africa and the Republic of South Africa will probably be readily acceptable: both areas are radically different from tropical Africa and both have received markedly greater attention than the rest of the continent .

The compilation of this bibliography proved to be a near Herculean task, for it was soon discovered that more than 3,700 Europeans and Americans had visited Africa and left a significant literary record of what they had seen and learned, to say nothing of the vast army of visitors to the continent who left behind no written account. To annotate a list of more than seven thousand entries would have meant the indefinite postponement of publication of a much needed reference work. Hopefully, the reader will find the geographic arrangement of titles, the author index, and the full presentation of often abridged titles of some use in compensation for the lack of annotation.

Much of the initial phase of this work was accomplished by the diligent research of graduate students at Northwestern University: James Graham, Isaria Kimambo, Gerald Linderman, Mary K. Mills, Samuel Nwabara, and William Pruitt. Mr. Kimambo also served in the capacity of research assistant, as did Margaret Cody Komives of Mount Holyoke College, and Judith Goldfine and Alberto Sbacchi of the University of Illinois at Chicago Circle. All put in long hours of much appreciated service at various times during the past seven years. Professor Bruce Lincoln of Northern Illinois University and Professor Michael Ihnatenko of Memphis State University were helpful in making useful suggestions in the preparation of this manuscript. We also wish to thank Dr. Peter Duignan of the Hoover Institution for his encouragement and for his many helpful suggestions of works to be included in this bibliography. Northwestern University and the University of Illinois at Chicago Circle provided research assistants for this project, and the financial assistance of the Hoover Institution and Memphis State University made possible the travel necessary to verify many of the more obscure entries in this bibliography.

Glencoe, Illinois                                            Robert L. Hess

Memphis, Tennessee                                   Dalvan M. Coger

July, 1971

PERIODICALS CONSULTED

*Académie d'Agriculture de France.*

*Académie des Sciences Coloniales. Comptes Rendus.*

*Academy* [London].

*Actas del Congreso Español de Geografica y Mercantil* [Madrid].
*Actes de la Société Philologique*
*Africa* [Naples].
*Africana Collectanea*
*African Missions* [Quebec].

*African Repository.*

*Afrika-Bote* [Trier].

*Agriculture Pratique des Pays Chauds.*

*Allgemeine Zeitung* [Munich].

*Almanach du Congo* [Brussels].

*Alpine Journal.*

*American Catholic Quarterly Review.*

*American Review: A Whig Journal.*

*Analecta Ordinis Minorum Cappoccinorum* [Rome].

*Anales de la Sociedad Española de Historia Natural* [Madrid].

*Annaes da Comissão Central Permanente de Geografia.*
*Annaes do Conselho Ultramarino*
*Annalen* [Roosendaal].

*Annalen der Afrikaansche Missiën* [Oudenbosch].

*Annalen der Hydrographic und Maritimen Meteorologie* [Hamburg].

*Annalen der Missionarissen* [Sparrendaal].

*Annalen van het Genootschap der H. Kindsheid* [Ghent].

*Annalen van Sparrendaal.*

*Annales Apostoliques* [Paris].

vii

*Annales Apostoliques C. S. Sp.*[Paris].

*Annales de Géographie*[Paris].

*Annales de la Congrégation de la Mission*[Paris].

*Annales de la Propagation de la Foi*[Lyons].

*Annales de l'Institut Colonial de Marseille.*

*Annales de Médecine et de Pharmacie Coloniales.*

*Annales de Nôtre Dame de la Salette*[Grenoble].

*Annales des Mines*[Paris].
*Annales de la Société Scientifique de Bruxelles*
*Annales des Voyages.* ⟵─────────────── ⌈*Annales de l'Université de*
*Grenoble*

*Annales d'Hygiène et de Médecine Coloniales.*

*Annales du Bureau Central Météorologique de France*[Paris].

*Annales Franciscaines*[Paris].

*Annales Maritimes et Coloniales*[Paris].

*Annales Oeuvre Ste-Enfance*[Paris].

*Annales Salésiennes.*

*Annali della Associazione del Buon Pastore*[Verona].

*Annali della Società di Maria per le Missioni Cattoliche.*

*Annali dell'Africa Italiana.*

*Annali Francescani*[Milan].

*Annuaire du Sénégal.*
*Antanarivo Annual*
*Anthropological Review.*

*Anthropologie*[Paris].

*Archives de Médecine et de Pharmacie Navales*[Paris].

*Archives des Missions Scientifiques et Littéraires*[Paris].
*Archives Israélites*
*Archiv für Religionwissenschaft.*

*Archivo per l'Antropologia e l'Etnologia*[Florence].

*Arquivo das Colonias*[Lisbon].

*Arquivos de Angola.*

*Association Internationale Africaine.*

*Athenaeum.*

*Atti Accademia di Agricoltura, Scienze et Lettere Verona.*

*Atti del R. Istituto Tecnico Industriale-Professionale e di Marina*

   *Mercantile della Privincia di Genova.*

*Atti R. Istituto Veneto di Scienze, Lettere ed Arti.*
*Atti del Terzo Congresso Geografico Internazionale*
*Aus Allen Weltteilen*[Leipzig].

*Ausland.*

*Baptist and Missions Magazine*[Boston].

*Baptist Magazine*[London].

*Belgique Coloniale*[Brussels].

*Berichte der Philogisch-Historische Klass der Koenigliche Sachische*

   *Gesellschaft der Wissenschaften.*

*Biblioteca di San Francesco Sales.*

*Blackwood's Edinburgh Magazine.*

*Blackwood's Magazine.*

*Bode van den H. Franciskus*[Antwerp].

*Bode van het H. Hart*[Alken].

*Boletim da Sociedade de Geographia de Lisboa.*

*Boletim Geral das Colónias*[Lisbon].

*Boletín de la Academia de la Historia*[Madrid].

*Boletín de la Sociedad Geográfica Nacional*[Madrid].

*Boletín de las Cámaras de Comercio, Industria y Navegación y de las Camaras Agricolas*[Madrid].

*Bollettino della Società Africana d'Italia*[Naples].

*Bollettino della Società Africana d'Italia. Sezione fiorentina*[Florence].

*Bollettino della Società Geografica Italiana*[Rome].

*Bollettino "Don Nicola Massa"*[Verona].

*Boston University Graduate Journal*.

*Bouteland, aux Bienfaiteurs de la Mission Française du Maduré*[Paris].

*Bulletin Agricole du Congo Belge*[Brussels].

*Bulletin de Géographie Historique et Descriptive*[Paris].

*Bulletin de l'Alliance Française*.

*Bulletin du Comité l'Afrique Française*.

*Bulletin de la Congrégation*[Paris].

*Bulletin de la Mission d'Afrique des Pères Blancs*[Paris].

*Bulletin de la Société Belge d'Études Coloniale*[Brussels].

*Bulletin de la Société Bretonne de Géographie*.

*Bulletin de la Société d'Anthropologie de Bruxelles*.

*Bulletin de la Société d'Anthropologie de Lyon*.

*Bulletin de la Société d'Anthropologie de Paris*.

*Bulletin de la Société de Géographie*[Paris].

*Bulletin de la Société de Géographie Commerciale de Paris*.

*Bulletin de la Société de Géographie Commercial de Bordeaux*.

*Bulletin de la Société de Géographie d'Alger et de l'Afrique du Nord*.

*Bulletin de la Société de Géographie de Aix-Marseille*.

*Bulletin de la Société de Géographie de l'Est*[Paris].

*Bulletin de la Société de Géographie de Lille.*

*Bulletin de la Société de Géographie de Lyon.*

*Bulletin de la Société de Géographie de Rochefort.*

*Bulletin de la Société de Géographie de Toulon.*

*Bulletin de la Société de Géographie de Toulouse.*

*Bulletin de la Société des Études Coloniales et Maritimes.*

*Bulletin de la Société de Topographie de France.*

*Bulletin de la Société Géographie Commercial du Havre.*

*Bulletin de la Société Géographie et d'Archeologie d'Oran.*

*Bulletin de la Société Khédivale de Géographie*[Cairo].

*Bulletin de la Société Littéraire de Strasbourg.*

*Bulletin de la Société Neuchâteloise de Géographie.*

*Bulletin de la Société Normande de Géographie*[Rouen].

*Bulletin de la Société Royale Belge de Géographie.*

*Bulletin de l'Union Géographique du Nord de la France.*

*Bulletin de l'Union Syndicale de Bruxelles.*

*Bulletin des Missions des Lazaristes Français.*

*Bulletin de la Société Royale de Géographie d'Anvers.*

*Bulletin Général Congregation Santi Spiritus*[Paris].

*Bulletin Officiel de l'État Indépendant du Congo.*

*Canadian Monthly.*

*Cape Monthly Magazine.*

*Carta Geologica d'Italia.*

*Cartas de Filipinas Cuad*[Binondo].

*Century.*

*Century Illustrated Monthly Magazine.*

*Chamber's Journal.*

*Christian Review.*

*Comptes-Rendus de la Société de Géographie*[Paris].

*Congo Illustré.*

*Congo-Indië.*

*Congrès International des Sciences Géographique.*

*Constable's Miscellany.*

*Contemporary Review.*

*Cornhill.*

*Correspondant*[Paris].

*Correspondenzblatt der Afrikanischen Gesellschaft*[Berlin].

*Cronica Naval de España*[Madrid].

*Cosmos.*

*Dépêche Coloniale Illustrée.*

*Deutsche Geographische Blätter.*

*Deutsche Kolonialzeitung.*

*Deutsche Revue.*

*Deutscher Geographentag Verhandlungen.*

*Deutsche Rundschau für Geographie und Statistik*[Vienna].

*Deutsche Weltpost.*

*Deutsche Wochenblatt.*

*Il Diritto*[Rome].

*Echo aus Africa*[Salzburg].

*Echo aus den Missionen.*

*Echo aus Knechsteden.*

*Echo de St. François*[Toulouse].

*Echo des Missions Africaines*[Lyon].

*Echo des Missions d'Afrique*[Paris].

*Echo z Afrijki*[Kraków].

*Eco Cattolico delle Glorie di S. Giuseppe*[Verona].

*Eco di S. Francesco d'Assisi*[Sorrento].

*Economiste Français*[Paris].

*Español.*

*Esploratore*[Milan].

*Études*[Paris].

*Études Franciscaines*[Paris].

*Explorateur*[Paris].

*Exploration*[Paris].

*Export*[Berlin].

*Evangelische Missions Magazine.*

*Fernschau*[Aarau, Switzerland].

*Figaro*[Paris].

*Fortnightly Review.*

*Gartanlaube*[Leipzig].

*Gazette Géographique.*

*Gazette Hebdomadaire de Médecine et de Chirurgie.*

*Gegenwart*[Berlin].

*Geographical Journal.*

*Geographical Magazine*[London].

*Géographie*[Paris].

*Geographische Nachrichten für Welthandel und Volkswirtschaft*[Berlin].

*Geographische Zeitung*[Leipzig].

*Giornale della Società di Letture e Conversazioni Scientifiche*[Genoa].

*Giornale delle Colonie*[Rome].

*Giornale Popolare di Viaggi*[Milan].

*Giro del Mondo*[Milan].

*Globus*.

*Goldthwaite's Geographical Magazine*[New York].

*Gott Will Es*[M. Gladbach].

*Grands Lacs*[Louvain].

*Graphic*[London].

*Het H. Misoffer*[Tongerloo].

*Illustrated Travels*.

*Illustration*[Paris].

*L'Indépendance Belge*.

*Indian Antiquary*.

*International Archiv für Ethnographie*.

*Iraka*[Tananarive].

*Jahresbericht das Vereins zur Unterstützung der Armen Negerkinder*[Cologne].

**Jahresbericht der Geographische Gesellschaft**[Bern].

*Jahresbericht der Geographische Gesellschaft in München*.

*Jahresbericht des Marien-Vereines zur Beforderung der Katholischen
Mission in Zentralafrika*[Vienna].

*Journal Asiatique*.

Journal de l'Agriculture[Paris].

Journal de l'Association des Anciens Élèves de l'Institut Agricole de
Gembloux[Gembloux, Belgium].

Journal des Missions Évangeliques.

Journal des Voyages et des Aventures de Terre et de Mer.

Journal of American Folklore.

Journal Officiel de la République Française.

Joural Officiel de l'A.O.F.[Dakar].

Journal of Proceedings of the Linnean Society - Botany.

Journal of the Anthropological Institute.

Journal of the Manchester Geographical Society.

Journal of the Royal African Society.

Journal of the Royal Geographical Society.

Journal of the Royal Society of Arts.

Katholischen Missionen[Freiburg].

Kleiner Herz-Jesu-Bote[Steyl].

Koloniales Jahrbuch.

Kreuz und Schwert[Münster im Wald].

Letters and Notices[Roehampton].

Lettres de Jersey.

Lettres de Mold.

Lettres de Vals[LePuy].

Lettres d'Uclès.

Lettres du Scolastical de Vals

Liberia Bulletin.

*Libertà Cattolica.*

*Lis de St-Joseph*[Grenoble].

**Littell's** *Living Age.*

*Lotos*[Prague].

*Maandelijksch Verslag der Afrikaansche Missiën*[Mechelen].

*Maria Immaculata*[Hünfeld].

*Marine Française.*

*Medicina Colonial*[Madrid].

*Mémorial de l'Artillery de la Marine*[Paris].

*Memorie della Società Geografica Italiana*[Rome].

*Mémoires de la Société d'Ethnographie*[Paris].

*Messager de St. François*[Antwerp].

*Messager des Ames du Purgatoire*[Tournai].

*Messager du Sacré-Coeur*[Toulouse].

*Meteorologisch Zeitschrift.*

*Missiën der Witte Paters*[Antwerp].

*Missionary Annals*[Rathmines].

*Missionary Herald.*

*Missionary Review of the World*[London].

*Mission de Madagascar*[Paris].

*Mission de Madagascar Central*[Paris].

*Mission Field*[London].

*Missioni Cattoliche*[Milan].

*Missioni Cattoliche Italiane*[Florence].

*Missioni Francescane*[S. M. degli Angeli].

*Missions Belges de la Compagnie de Jesus*[Brussels].

*Missions Catholiques*[Lyons].

*Missions Catholiques*[Paris].

*Missions Catholiques Françaises*[Paris].

*Missions d'Afrique*[Malines].

*Missions d'Afrique*[Paris].

*Missions d'Afrique*[Québec].

*Missions d'Alger*[Paris].

*Missions en Chine et au Congo*[Scheut].

*Missões de Angola e Congo*[Braga].

*Mitteilungen aus Justus Perthes' Geographischer Anstalt.* See,
   *Petermanns Geographische Mitteilungen.*

*Mitteilungen der Afrikanische Gesellschaft in Deutschland*[Berlin].

*Mitteilungen der Anthropologische Gesellschaft im Wien.*

*Mitteilungen der Deutscher Schutzgebiet.*

*Mitteilungen der Geographische Gesellschaft in Hamburg.*

*Mitteilungen der Gesellschaft für Thuringen.*

*Mitteilungen der K. K. Geographische Gesellschaft*[Vienna].

*Mitteilungen des Seminars für Orientalische Sprachen zu Berlin.*

*Month*[London].

*Monumenta Anastasiana*[Lucerne].

*Mouvement Antiesclavagiste Belge.*

*Mouvement des Mission Catholique au Congo.*

*Mouvement Géographique*[Brussels].

*Museo delle Missioni Cattoliche*[Turin].

*National Geographic Magazine.*

*National Review*[London].

*Natur*[Halle].

*Nature*[Paris].

*Nautical Magazine.*

*Nautical Magazine and Naval Chronicle.*

*New Review*[London].

*Nigrizia.*

*Nineteenth Century.*

*Nord und Süd*[Berlin].

*Notes, Reconnaissances et Explorations*[Tananarive].

*Nouvelle Revue*[Paris].

*Nouvelle Revue Internationale*[Paris].

*Nouvelle Annales des Voyages.*

*Nouva Antologia di Scienze, Lettere ed Arti*[Rome].

*Novo Mensageiro do Coração de Jesus.*

*Nyasa News.*

*Oeuvre de St. Augustine et de Ste.Monique.*

*Oeuvre des Écoles d'Orient*[Paris].

*Österreichische Monatsschrift für den Orient*[Vienna].

*Pêche et Pisciculture.*

*Petermanns Geographische Mitteilungen.*

*Petit Messager de St.François*[Clement-Ferrand].

*Petites Annales.*

*Portugal em Africa*[Lisbon].

*Précis Historiques*[Brussels].

*Proceedings of the Rhodesian Scientific Association.*

*Proceedings of the Royal Colonial Institute.*

*Proceedings of the Royal Geographical Society.*

*Proceedings of the Royal Society of Edinburgh.*

*Questions Diplomatiques et Coloniales*[Paris].

*Recueil de la Société Archéologique de la Province de Constantine.*

*Règne du Coeur de Jésus*[Tournai].

*Reich des Herzens Jesu*[Sittard].

*Renseignements Coloniaux.*

*Report of the South African Association for the Advancement of Science.*

*Reska*[Antananarivo].

*Revista de Geografía Colonial y Mercantil*[Madrid].

*Revista de Geografía Commercial*[Madrid].

*Revista General de la Marina Militar y Mercante Española*[Barcelona].

*Revista Portugal em Africa.*

*Revue Algerienne et Coloniale*[Paris].

*Revue Artistique*[Antwerp].

*Revue Bleue.*

*Revue Coloniale.*

*Revue Coloniale Internationale*[Amsterdam].

*Revue Congolaise.*

*Revue Contemporaine*[Paris].

*Revue d'Anthropologie*[Paris].

*Revue de France.*

*Revue de Géographie*[Paris].

*Revue de Géographie - Drapeyron*[Paris].

*Revue de l'Ethnographie.*

*Revue de l'Orient.*

*Revue de Madagascar.*

*Revue de Paris.*

*Revue des Cultures Coloniales*[Paris].

*Revue des deux Mondes.*

*Revue des Missions.*

*Revue des Questions Scientifiques*[Louvain].

**Revue du Cercle Militaire**[Paris].

*Revue du Génie Militaire.*

*Revue du Monde Catholique.*

*Revue Ethnographique.*

*Revue Française de l'Étranger et des Colonies.*

*Revue Française d'Outre-Mer.*

*Revue France.*

*Revue France Moderne.*

*Revue Générale des Sciences Pures et Appliquées.*

*Revue Géographique Internationale.*

*Revue Histoire Missions.*

*Revue Illustrée de l'Exposition Missionnaire Vaticane*[Rome].

*Revue Indigène.*

*Revue Maritime.*

*Revue Maritime et Coloniale.*

*Revue Mensuelle de l'École d'Anthropologie de Paris.*

*Revue Scientifique*[Paris].

*Revue Trimestrielle de ls Société Antiesclavagiste de France.*

*Rivista Orientale.*

*Rosario: Memorie Domenicane*[Florence].

*Rosier de St.Francois*[Chembery].

*Saint Josefs Missionsbote.*

*Saint Joseph's Advocate*[Mill Hill].

*Schorers Familienblatt*[Berlin].

*Scottish Geographical Magazine.*

*Scribner's Magazine.*

*Semaine Religieuse du Diocèse de Grenoble.*

*Sendbote des Göttlich Herzens Jesu*[Innsbruck].

*Smithsonian Report.*

*Société Nouvelle: Revue Internationale*[Brussels].

*Sommervogel*[ Brussels/Paris].

**South African Quarterly Journal.**

**Spectateur Militaire.**

*Stern der Neger.*

*Stern von Africa*[Limburg].

*Steyler Herz Jesu-Bote*[Steyl].

*Tägliche Rundschau*[Berlin].

*Tappi, Cenno Storico*[Turin].

*Textile Mercury*[Manchester].

*Tijdschrift van het K. Nederlandsch Aardrijkskundig Genootschap*[Amsterdam].

*Tour du Monde.*

*Trabalhos da Sociedade Portuguesa de Antropologia e Ethnologia*[Oporto].

*Tradition*[Paris].

*Transactions of the Bombay Royal Geographical Society.*

*Transaction of the Ethnological Society.*

*Travel.*

*Uganda Journal.*

*United Service Magazine.*

*Univers*[Paris].

*Vergissmeinnicht*[Burghausen].

*Verhandlungen der Berliner Gesellschaft für Anthropologie.*

*Verhandlungen der Deutschen-Kolonial Gesellschaft.*

*Verhandlungen der deutschen Kolonialkongresses.*

*Verhandlungen der Gesellschaft für Erdkunde zu Berlin.*

*Verslag van het Werk der Katholiche Zendingen in Congo Vrijstaat.*

*Voix du Redempteur*[Tournai].

*Voix Franciscaines*[Toulouse].

*Vom Fels zum Meer*[Stuttgart].

*Vorträge des Vereines zur Verbreitung Naturwissenschaftlicher Kenntnisse in Wien.*

*Vossiche Zeitung.*

*Walckenaer's Voyages.*

*Westermanns Monatshefte.*

*Wiener Zeitschrift für die Kund des Morgenlandes*[Vienna].

*Ymer*[Stockholm].

*Zambesi Mission Record*[London].

*Zeitschrift der Gesellschaft für Erdkunde.*

*Zeitschrift für Afrikanische Sprachen.*

*Zeitschrift für Afrikanische und Ozeanische Sprachen.*

*Zeitschrift für Ethnologie.*

# ABBREVIATIONS

ABPV  - *Annali del Buon Pastore.*

ACM   - *Annales de la Congregation de la Mission.*

AG    - *Annales de Géographie.*

AIV   - *Atti Istituto Veneto.*

APFL  - *Annales de la Propagation de la Foi.*

BGCSS - *Bulletin Général Congregatio Santi-Spiritus.*

BSAI  - *Bollettino della Società Africana d'Italia.*

BSBG  - *Bulletin de la Société Royal Belge de Géographie.*

BSGI  - *Bolletino della Società Geografica Italiana.*

BSGL  - *Boletim da Sociedade de Geographia de Lisboa.*

BSGM  - *Boletin de la Sociedad Geografica Nacional.*

BSGP  - *Bulletin de Société de Géographie.*

BSKG  - *Bulletin de la Société Khédivale de Géographie.*

BSRGA - *Bulletin de Société Royale de Géographie d'Anvers.*

CIL   - *Congo Illustre.*
CMM   - *Cape Monthly Magazine.*
CRSG  - *Comptes-Rendus de la Société de Géographie.*

DK    - *Deutsche Kolonialzeitung.*

GJ    - *Geographical Journal.*

JAI   - *Journal of the Anthropological Institute.*

JME   - *Journal des Missions Évangéliques.*

JMGS  - *Journal of the Manchester Geographical Society.*
JORF  - *Journal Officiel de la Republique Francaise.*
JRGS  - *Journal of the Royal Geographical Society.*
JRSA  - *Journal of the Royal Society of Arts.*
JVUN  - *Jahresbericht des Vereins zur Unterstützung der armen Negerkinder.*

KM    - *Katholischen Missionen.*

LSV   - *Lettres du Scolasticat de Vals.*

MAGD - *Mitteilungen der Afrikanische Gesellschaft in Deutschland.*

MCL - *Missions Catholiques* [Lyons].

MCM - *Missioni Cattoliche* [Milan].

MCP - *Missions Catholiques* [Paris].

MDS - *Mitteilungen der Deutscher Schutzgebiet.*

MG - *Mouvement Géographique.*

MH - *Missionary Herald.*

MKKG - *Mitteilungen der K. K. Geographische Gesellschaft in Wien.*

NA - *Nuova Antologia di Scienze, Lettere ed Arti.*

PM - *Petermanns Geographische Mitteilungen.*

PRGS - *Proceedings of the Royal Geographical Society.*

RFEC - *Revue Française de l'Etranger et des Colonies.*

RGCM - *Revista de Geografic Commercial* [Madrid].

RHM - *Revue Histoire Missions.*

RMC - *Revue Maritime et Coloniale.*

SGM - *Scottish Geographical Magazine.*

TM - *Tour du Monde.*

VGE - *Verhandlung der Gesellschaft für Erdkunde zu Berlin.*

ZAOS - *Zeitschrift für Afrikanische und Ozeanische Sprachen.*

ZAS - *Zeitschrift für Afrikanische Sprachen.*

ZE - *Zeitschrift für Ethnologie.*

ZGE - *Zeitschrift der Gesellschaft für Erdkunde.*

# A SELECT LIST OF BIBLIOGRAPHIES

1  *Bibliografiĩa Afriki dorevoliũtsionnaiã i sovetskaiã literatura ha russkom iãzyke original'naiã i perevoghaiã.* Moscow: Izgatel'stvo "Nauka", 1964. 276p.

2  Borchardt, P. *Bibliographie de l'Angola, 1500-1910.* Brussels: Misch, 1912. 61p.

3. Brasseur, Paule. *Bibliographie Générale du Mali (anciens Soudan français et Haut-Sénégal-Niger).* Dakar: IFAN, 1964. 416p.

4. Bridgman, Jon and Clark, David E. *German Africa: A Select Annotated Bibliography.* Stanford: The Hoover Institution, 1965. 120p.

5. British Museum. *Subject Index of the Modern Works Added to the Library of the British Museum in the Years 1881-1900.* Vol. **I**, "Africa," 15-39.

6. Brosse, Max. *Repertorium der deutsch-kolonialen Literatur, 1884-1890.* Berlin: Winckelmenn, 1891. 113p.

7. Bruel, G. *Bibliographie de l'Afrique équatoriale française.* Paris: Larose, 1914. 326p.

8. Cardinall, A. W. *Bibliography of the Gold Coast.* Accra: Government Printer, 1932. 384p.

9. Costa, M. *Bibliografia geral de Moçambique: contribução para estudo completo.* Lisbon: Agencía geral das Colonias, 1946. 359p.

10. Cox, E. G. *A Reference Guide to the Literature of Travel.* Seattle: University of Washington, 1935. I, 354-401.

11. Deutsche Kolonialgesellschaft. *Die deutsche Kolonialliteratur von 1884-95.* Berlin: Deutsche Kolonialgesellschaft, 1897. 158p.

12. Favitski de Probobysz, Cmdt. de. *Répertoire bibliographique de la littérature militaire et coloniale française depuis cent ans.* Liège: Thone, 1935. 363p.

13  Fontán Lobé, Juan. *Bibliografía colonial: contribución a un índice de publicaciones africanas*. Madrid: Dirección general de Marruecos y colonias, 1946. 669p.

14  Fumagalli, G. *Bibliografia etiopica*. Milan: Hoepli, 1893. 288p.

15  Gamble, D. P. *Bibliography of the Gambia*. London: Colonial Office, 1958. 36p.

16  Gay, Jean. *Bibliographie des ouvrages relatifs à l'Afrique et à l'Arabie*. San Remo: Gay, 1875. 312p.

17  Grandidier, G. *Bibliographie de Madagascar, 1500-1905*. 2 vols. Paris: Comité de Madagascar, 1905-1906.

18  Griffin, Appleton Prentiss Clark. *List of Books, with References to Periodicals, Relating to the Theory of Colonization, Government of Dependencies, Protectorates, and Related Topics*. 2nd ed. Washington: Library of Congress, 1900. 156p.

19  Hill, Richard L. *Bibliography of the Anglo-Egyptian Sudan from Earliest Times to 1937*. London: Luzac, 1939. 213p.

20  Ibrahim-Hilmy. [*H.H. Prince*]. *The Literature of Egypt and the Sudan from the Earliest Times to the Year 1885*. 2 vols. London: Trübner, 1886-1887.

21  Joucla, E. *Bibliographie de l'Afrique occidentale française*. Paris, 1912. 275p. 2nd ed., Paris: Société d'éditions géographiques maritimes et coloniales, 1937. 705p.

22  Kayser, Gabriel. *Bibliographie d'ouvrages ayant trait à l'Afrique en général dans ses rapports avec l'exploration et la civilisation de ces contrées*. Brussels, 1887. 176p.

23 . Lewin, Evans. *Subject Catalogue of the Library of the Royal Empire Society*, Vol. I, *The British Empire Generally, and Africa*. London: Dawsons, 1967 [1930].

24 Luke, Harry C. *A Bibliography of Sierra Leone, etc.* London: Oxford University Press, 1910. 230p. 2nd ed., Oxford University Press, 1925.

25 . Mary, G. T. *Afrika-Schrifttum. Bibliographie deutschsprachiger wissenschaftlicher Veröffentlichungen über Afrika südlich der Sahara*. Wiesbaden: Franz Steiner, 1967. 688p.

26 . Mendelssohn, Sidney. *Mendelssohn's South African Bibliography*. 2 vols. 3rd Ed. London: The Holland Press, 1968.

27 Robinson, A. M. Lewin. *A Bibliography of African Bibliographies Covering Territories South of the Sahara*. 4th ed. Cape Town: South African Public Library, 1961. 79p.

28 . Royal Commonwealth Society. *Subject Catalogue of the Library of the Royal Empire Society*. Vol. I. *The British Empire Generally and Africa*. London: Dawsons of Pall Mall, 1967. 582p.

29 Rydings, H. A. *The Bibliographies of West Africa*. Ibadan: Ibadan University Press, 1961. 36p.

30 . Santandrea, P. Stefano. *Bibliografia di studi africani della Missione dell'Africa Centrale*. Verona: Missioni Africane, 1948. 167p.

31 . Simar, T. "Bibliographie congolaise de 1895 à 1910," *Revue Congolaise*, I(1910), ?p. Also, Brussels: Vroment, 1912. 61p.

32 . Streit, R. *Die katholische deutsche Missionsliteratur. Zweite Teil: Bibliographie, 1800-1924*. Aachen: Xaverius, 1925. 278p.

33 _____ and Dindinger, J. *Bibliotheca missionum: Afrikanische Missionsliteratur, 1053-1940*. 6 vols. Freiburg: Herder, 1951-1955.

34    Tuaillon, J. L. G. *Bibliographie critique de l'Afrique occidentale française*. Paris: Lavauzelle, 1936. 50p.

35    Veth, Pieter Johannes and Kan, C. M. *Bibliographie van Nederlandsche boeken, kaarten, enz. over Africa*. Utrecht: Beijers, 1876. 99p.

36    Wauters, Alphonse Jules and Buyl, A. *Bibliographie du Congo, 1880-1895: catalogue méthodique de 3,800 ouvrages*. Brussels: Administration du Mouvement géographique, 1895. 356p.

37    Work, M. N. *Bibliography of the Negro in Africa and America*. New York: Wilson, 1928. 698p. Reprinted, New York: Octagon, 1965. 698p.

GENERAL

38 . Adler, J. B. *Afrikas Leiden und Zerfal durch den Islam.* Frankfurt and Luzern: A. Foesser Nachfolger, 1889. 28p.

39 . Agostini, Domenico. *Per la Emancipazione Degli Schiavi In Affirca. Lettera Pastorale Di S. E. Il Cardinale Domenico Agostini, Patriarca Di Venezia.* Venice: Tip. Patriarcale Ex Cordella, 1889. 10p.

40 . Alexis, M. G. *La Traite des Nègres et la Croisade Africaine.* Liège: H. Dessain, 1889. 240p.

41 . Audren, Jean-Marie. "Lettres," *Annales Apostoliques* [Paris], IV(1889), 95-103.

42 . _____. "Lettres," *Missions Catholiques* [Lyon], XXIV(1892), 490,491; XXXVII(1905), 509,510.

43 . Bacheville, Barthélemy. *Voyages des frères Bacheville. . .en Europe et en Asie après leur condamnation par la cour prévotale du Rhone en 1816.* Paris: Béchet Aîné, 1822. 434p.

44 . Baden-Powell, George Smyth. "Development of Tropical Africa,"
      *Proceedings of the Royal Colonial Institute*, XXVII(1895-1896),
      218-255.

45 . Badia y Leyblich, Domingo. *Voyages d'Ali-Bey el Abbassi* [pseud.] *en
      Afrique et en Asie pendant les années 1803, 1804, 1805, 1806 et
      1807*. 3 vols. Paris: P. Didot, 1814. English translation, 2 vols.,
      London: Longmans, 1816. Spanish translation, 3 vols. in 1,
      Barcelona: La Renaixensa, 1888.

46 . Bartholomew. [*Capt., R.N.*]. "Extracts from a 'Private Journal on Board
      H.M.S. *Leven*, When Surveying the Coast of Africa,' " *JRGS*, IV
      (1834), 220-229.

47 . Boshart, August. *Zehn Jahre afrikanischen Lebens*. Leipzig: O. Wigand,
      1898. 251p.

48 . Breher, Xavier. "Die katholischen Missionäre in Afrika als Apostel
      der Kultur. Stoffe zu Vorträgen für kirchliche Vereine, besonders
      für Afrika-Zweigvereine," *Gott will es !* V(1893), 161-163, 197-200,
      228-231, 264-268, 294-297, 327-332, 358-361, 395-402, 423-426, 460-466,
      492-495, 518-522, 549-554, 583-588, 616-620, 647-651, 681-686, 723-728.

49 . Bressi, Salvatore. "Lettere," *Annali Francescani*, XII(1881), 759,760;
      XIII(1882), 537-539.

50 . _____ . "Lettere," *Eco di S. Francesco d'Assisi*, X(1883), 570-575,
      634-639, 668-673; XI(1884), 499-509, 676-687.

51 . _____ . "Lettere," *Libertà Cattolica*, V(1882), 16; VII(1884), 2, 4.

52 . Bruce, Charles. *Round Africa: Being Some Account of the Peoples and Places of the Dark Continent*. London and New York: Cassell, Petter and Galpin, 1882. 224p.

53 . Buckley, James Monroe. *Travels in Three Continents: Europe, Africa, Asia*. New York: Hunt and Eaton, 1895. 614p.

54 . Burton, Richard Francis. *Selected Papers on Anthropology, Travel and Exploration*. . . .Ed. by N.M. Penzer. London: Philpot, 1924. 240p.

55 . Buxton, Edward North. *Two African Trips; with Notes and Suggestions on Big Game Preservation in Africa*. London: Edward Stanford, 1902. 209p.

56 . Campos, Rafael. "La Campaña contra la esclavitud y los deberes de España en Africa," *Boletín de la Sociedad Geográfica Nacional*, XXVI (1889), 271-305.

57 . Canot, Théodore. *Revelations of a Slave Trader; or, Twenty Years Adventures of Captain Canot*. London: Richard Bentley, 1854. 352p. French ed., Paris: Plon, 1931. 302p. New ed., Ed. by B. Mayer, New York: Boni, 1928. 376p.

58 . Chaillé-Long, Charles. *My Life in Four Continents*. 2 vols. London: Hutchinson, 1912.

59 . Chavanne, Josef. *Afrika im Lichte unserer Tage. Bodengestalt und geologischer Bau*. . . .Vienna: A. Hartleben, 1881. 181p.

60 . Cleve, G.L. "Zwei Zeugen versunkener Bantukultur," *Globus*, LXXVII(1900), 193-195.

61 . Cleveland, Richard Jeffry. *Voyages of a Merchant Navigator of the Days That Are Past. Compiled from the Journals and Letters of the Late Richard J. Cleveland by H.W.S.Cleveland*. New York: Harper, 1886. 245p.

62 Colville, Zelia Isabella. *Round the Black Man's Garden*. Edinburgh: Blackwood, 1893. 344p.

63 . Decle, Lionel. *Three Years in Savage Africa*. London: Methuen, 1898. 594p.

64 . Dove, Karl. *Vom Kap zum Nil. Reiseerinnerungen aus Süd-, Ost- und Nordafrika*. 2 vols. Berlin: Allgemeiner Verein für deutsche Litteratur, 1898. 319p.

65 Drake, Richard. *Revelations of a Slave Smuggler: Being the Autobiography of Capt. Richard Drake, an African Trader for Fifty Years, from 1807-1857. . . .*New York: DeWitt, 1860. 100p.

66 . Dudon, Paul. "Chronique des Missions. Afrique," *Études*, LXXXII(1900), 669-692.

67 . Dumont, Pierre Joseph. *Narrative of 34 Years Slavery and Travels in Africa*. London: Phillips, 1819. 42p.

68 . Emonet, T. R. P. "Le Rôle des Missionnaires en Afrique au double point de vue de la civilisation et de l'influence française," *Annales Apostoliques*, III(1888), 41-49.

69     Ferguson, Robert. *Harpooner. A Four-Year Voyage on the Barque Kathleen, 1880-1884*. Ed. by Leslie Dalrymple Stair. Philadelphia: University of Pennsylvania Press, 1936. 316p.

70     . Fleuriot De Langle, [*Vicomte*]. *Appendice descriptif des côtes de l'Afrique occidentale entre l'Equateur et le cap de Bonne Espérance*. Paris, 1846.

71     . Forbes, James. *Oriental Memoirs. . .Including Observations on Part of Africa. . . .* 4 vols. London: White, Cochrane, 1813.

72     . Foureau, F. *D'Alger au Congo par le Tchad. Mission Foureau-Lamy*. Paris: Masson, 1901. Also, *GJ*, XVII(1901), 135-150.

73     . Frobenius, Leo V. *Die Geheimbünde Afrikas*. Hamburg: Verlagsanstalt und Druckerei, 1894. 28p.

74     . Gandon, Antoine. *Récits du Brigadier Flageolet. Souvenirs intimes d'un vieux Chasseur d'Afrique*. 2nd ed. Paris: E. Dentu, 1859. 279p.

75     . Götzen, Gustav Adolf [*Graf*] von. *Durch Africa von Ost nach West.Resultate und Begebenheiten einer Reise von der deutsch-ostafrikanischen Küste bis zur Kongomündung in den Jahren 1893-94*. Berlin: D.Reimer, 1895. 417p.

76     Gourdault, Jules. *L'Homme blanc au pays des noirs*. Paris: Jouvet, 1885. 230p.

77     . Greenwood, James. *Curiosities of Savage Life*. 2 vols. London: Beeton, 1863-64.

78     . Grogan, Ewart Scott. *From the Cape to Cairo. The First Traverse of Africa from South to North*. London: Hurst and Blackett, 1900. 377p. Revised ed. London: Hurst and Blackett, 1902. 402 p. See also, same title, *GJ*, XVI(1900), 164-183.

79 . Harrison, Richard. *Recollections of a Life in the British Army During the Latter Half of the Nineteenth Century*. London: Smith, Elder, 1908. 382p.

80 . Hartmann, Robert. *Die Völker Afrikas*. Leipzig: Brockhaus, 1879. 341pp. French ed. Paris: G.Baillière, 1880. 158p.

81 . Hovelacque, Abel. *Les Nègres de l'Afrique sus-équatoriale (Sénégambie, Guinée, Soudan, Haut-Nil)*. Paris:Lecrosnier & Babé, 1885. 468p.

82 . Jacobs, Alfred. *L'Afrique Nouvelle; récents voyages, état moral, intellectuel et social dans le Continent Noir*.Paris: Didier, 1862. 408p.

83 . Jacobs, Eyries and Alfred. *Voyage en Asie et en Afrique*. Paris: Furne, 1859. 692p.

84 . Jedina, Leopold von. *Um Afrika, Skizzen von der Reise Sr.Majestät Corvette "Helgoland" in den Jahren 1873-75*. Vienna: A.Hartleben, 1877. 384p. French translation, *Voyage de la frégate autrichienne Helgoland autour de l'Afrique*. Paris: Dreyfous, 1878. 356p.

85 . Joanne, Adolphe Laurent. *Voyage en Afrique*. Brussels: Delevinge & Callewaert, 1850. 220p.

86 . Joest, Wilhelm. *Um Afrika*. Cologne: Dumont-Schauberg, 1885. 315p.

87 . Johnston, Harry Hamilton. *Africa, a History and Description of the British Empire in Africa*. London: National Society, 1910. 429p New York: Holt, 1910. 429p.

88 . _____. "The Commercial Prospects of Tropical Africa," *JMGS*, I(1885), 179-196.

89 . _____. *A History of the Colonization of Africa by Alien Races*.Cambridge: Cambridge University Press, 1899. 319p.

90 . _____. *The Opening up of Africa*. New York: Holt, 1911. 255p.

91 . _____. *The Story of My Life*. Indianapolis: Bobbs-Merrill, 1923. 504p.

92 . Jordan, Lewis Garnett. *Pebbles from an African Beach*. Philadelphia: Lisle-Carey, 1918. 73p.

93 . _____. *Up the Ladder in Foreign Missions*. Nashville: National Baptist Publishing Board, 1901. 263p.

94 . Keiling, Luiz Alfredo. *Quarenta anos de Africa*. Fraião: Edicão das Missões de Angola e Congo, [1934]. 192p.

95 . Krause, Gottlieb Adolf. "Beiträge zum Märchenschatz der Afrikaner," *Globus*, LXXII(1897), 229-233, 254-258.

96 . Lacour, A. *L'Esclavage africain*. Dunkirk: Michel, 1890. 66p.

97 Lacy, George. *Pictures of Travel, Sport and Adventure*. London: Pearson, 1899. 420p.

98 . Lallemand, A. "Les Missions de la Compagnie de Jésus dans l'Afrique australe," *Précis Historiques*, XXXVII(1888), 24-39, 557-578; XXXVIII(1889), 29-46; XXXIX(1890), 19-32, 117-132.

99 . Lavigerie, C. "Estensione ed errori della Schiavitù in Africa," *La Nigrizia*, VII(1889), 19-28; VIII(1890), 49-60, 81-87, 113-120, 138-151, 179-186; IX(1891), 18-21.

100 . Lenz, Oscar. *Wanderungen in Afrika: Studien und Erlebnisse.* Vienna: Literarischen Gesellschaft, 1895. 278p.

101 . Lugard, Frederick John Dealtry. *The Dual Mandate in British Tropical Africa.* Edinburgh: Blackwood, 1922. 643p.

102 . _____. "Treaty Making in Africa," *GJ*, I(1893), 53-55.

103 . Maistre, Casimir. *À travers l'Afrique centrale. Du Congo au Niger, 1892-1893.* Paris: Hachette, 1895. 302p.

104 . _____. "De l'Oubangui à la Benoué à travers l'Afrique centrale," *AG*, III(1893-1894), 64-80.

105 . _____. "La mission dans l'Afrique centrale, 1892-93," *CRSG*, XII (1893), 270.

106 . _____. "Notes sur la carte itinéraire de l'Oubangui à la Benoué," *BSGP*, 7th Ser., XV(1895), 5-8.

107 . Manning, Edward. *Six Months on a Slaver: A True Narrative.* New York: Harper, 1879. 128p.

108 . Marche, A. *Trois voyages dans l'Afrique occidentale, Sénégal, Gambie, Casamance, Gabon, Ogooué.* Paris: Hachette, 1882. 376p.

109 . Marryat, Frederick. *The Mission; or, Scenes in Africa.* 2 vols. London, 1845.

110 . Massari, A. "La traversée de l'Afrique de la mer Rouge au Golfe de Guinée," *BSBG*, VII(1883), 845.

111 . Ménégault, A. P. F. *Voyage dans l'Afrique et les deux Indes pendant les années 1809, 1810, 1811, et 1812, avec des observations sur l'état actual.* Paris: Eymery, 1814.

112 . Moister, William. *Africa, Past and Present. A Concise Account . . . by an Old Resident.* London: Hodder & Stoughton, 1879. 387p.

113 . Morphy, Michel. *Le Commandant Marchandt et ses compagnons d'armes a travers l'Afrique; histoire complète et anecdotique de la mission.* 3 vols. Paris: Geffroy, 1899-1900.

114 . Müller, John B. "Beiträge zur Afrikanischen Völkerkunde," *Globus,* XLII(1882), 317-318, 330-332.

115 . Munro, William. *Records of Service and Campaigning in Many Lands.* 2 vols. London: Hurst & Blackett, 1887.

116 . Murray, John. [*M.D.*]. *How to Live in Tropical Africa, a Guide to Tropical Hygiene and Sanitation. The Malaria Problem: the Cause, Prevention, and Cure of Malarial Fever.* London: Philips, 1895. 252p.

117 . Nachtigal, Gustav. "Reise nach dem Bahr el Ghasal, Kanem, Egai, Bodélé und Borku," *PM,* XIX(1873), 201-206.

118 . _____. *Sahara und Sudan.* 3 vols. Vol.1, *Tripolis, Fezzan, Tibesti und Bornu.* Berlin: Weidmannsche, 1879. Vol.2, *Borku, Kanem, Bornu, Bagirmi.* Berlin: Weidmannsche, 1881. Vol.3, *Wadai und Dar For.* Leipzig: Brockhaus, 1889.

119 . Negrin, Ignacia de. *Derrotero de las costas occidentales de Africa... desde Tánger hasta la bahía de Algoa.* 2 vols. Madrid: Déposito Hidrográfico, 1862-1882.

120 . Oberlander, Richard. *Deutsch-Afrika. Land und Leute. Handel und Wandel in unseren Kolonien.* Leipzig and Berlin: W. Friedrich, 1885. 176p.

121 . Owen, William FitzWilliam. *Narrative of Voyages to Explore the Shores of Africa, Arabia, and Madagascar.* 2 vols. London: Bentley, 1833. New York: Harper, 1833. See also, *JRGS,* III(1833), 199-223.

122 . Pankow, H. "Über Zwergvölker in Afrika und Asien," *ZGE*, XXVII(1892).

123 . Parke, Thomas Heazle. *Guide to Health in Africa, with Notes on the Country and Its Inhabitants.* London: S.Low & Co., 1893. 175p.

124 . Payeur-Didelot. *Trente mois au continent mystérieux: Gabon-Congo et côte occidentale d'Africa.* Paris: Berger-Levrault, 1899. 304p. Also, *Bulletin de la Société de Géographie de l'Est*, XVI(1894), 51-79, 225-262, 369-424, XVII(1895), 29-54, 99-123, 217-235, 381-405, XIX (1897), 1-17, 177-208, 397-422, XX(1898), 1-43, 223-246.

125 . Perciballi, Giovanni. *L'Europa in Africa. Ossia. Il presente progresso Africano. Alcuni appunti.* Sienna: S. Bernardino, 1900. 208p.

126 . Péron, François. *Mémoires du Capitaine Péron, sur ses voyages aux cotes d'Afrique, en Arabie, à l'île d'Amsterdam, etc.* Edited by Louis Saturnin Brissot-Thivars. 2 vols. Paris: Brissot-Thivars, 1824.

127 . Piolet, Jean-Baptiste. *La France hors de France: Notre émigration, sa nécessité, ses conditions.* Paris: n.p., 1900. 659p.

128 . Piolet, Jean-Baptiste. *Rapport sur les Missions Catholiques Françaises dressé au nom du Comité d'organisation de l'Exposition des Missions.* Paris: Téqui, 1900. 126p.

129 . Poinsard, L. *Afrique équatoriale. Ogôué, Congo, Zambèse.* Paris: Alcan, 1888.

130 . Reade, William Winwood. *The African Sketch-Book.* 2 vols. London: Smith, Elder, 1873.

131 . _____. *The Martyrdom of Man.* London, 1872. New York: Butts, 1874. 543p.

132 . _____. *Savage Africa: Being the Narrative of a Tour in Equatorial, South-western, and North-western Africa; with Notes on the Habits of the Gorilla; on the Existence of Unicorns and Tailed Men; on the Slave Trade; on the Origin, Character, and Capabilities of the Negro, and on the Future Civilization of Western Africa.* London: Smith, Elder, 1863. New York: Harper, 1864. 425p.

133. Reinecke, Paul. *Beschreibung einiger Rassenskelette aus Afrika, ein Beitrag zur Anthropologie der deutschen Schutzgebiete.* Brannschweig: Vieweg, 1898. 49p.

134. Robert, Fritz. *Afrika als Handelsgebiet: West-, Süd- und Ost Afrika.* Vienna: Gerold, 1883. 350p.

135. Rohlfs, Friedrich Gerhard. "Conference on the Races of Africa," *JAI,* XVI(1886-1887), 175.

136. _____. "Geld in Afrika," *PM,* XXXV(1889), 187.

137. _____. *Quid novi ex Afrika?* Cassel: Fischer, 1886. 288p.

138. _____. "Die Verwendbarkeit des Elephanten zur Erforschung unbekannten Gegenden," *PM,* XXXIV(1888), 138.

139. Rooney, C. J. "As missões do Congo e Angola," *Portugal em Africa,* VII (1900), 13-32, 66-85, 127-132, 176-189, 209-233, 330-335, 378-391, 433-446, 481-492, 532-554.

140. Rosel, G. *Der Feldzug gegen die Sklaverei in Afrika, dessen Nothwendigkeit, Ausführbarkeit und Organisation.* Trier: Paulinus-Druckerei, 1889. 31p.

141. Rowley, Henry. *Africa Unveiled.* London: Society for Promoting Christian Knowledge, 1876. New York: Pott, Young, 1876. 313p.

142. Saint Johnston, Alfred. *Camping Among Cannibals.* London: Macmillan, 1883. 327p.

143 . Sarzeau, J. [*Commandant*]. *Les Français aux colonies, Sénégal et Soudan français, Dahomey, Madagascar et Tunisie.* Paris: Bloud et Barral, 1897. 400p.

144 Schlauch, Lorenzo. *Due Discorsi. I. Sulla Tratta degli Schiavi in Africa. II. Sulla Quistione operaja.* Budapest: Società Franklin, 1892. 39p.

145 . Schmarda, Ludwig Karl. *Reise um die Erde in den Jahren 1853-1857.* 3 vols. Braunschweig: G. Westermann, 1861.

146 . Schweinfurth, Georg August. "Über die zivilisatorische Aufgabe in Afrika," *DK*, II(1885), 592-596.

147 . Scott, Percy Moreton. *Fifty Years in the Royal Navy.* New York: Doran, 1919. 236p. London: Murray, 1919. 358p.

148 . Seixas, Antonio José de. *A questão colonial portugueza em presença das condições de existencia da metropole.* Lisbon: Antunes, 1881. 166p.

149 . Smith, Charles Spencer. *Glimpses of Africa, West and Southwest Coast, Containing the Author's Impressions and Observations during a Voyage of Six Thousand Miles from Sierra Leone to St. Paul de Loanda and Return, Including the Rio del Ray and Cameroons Rivers, and the Congo River, from Its Mouth to Matadi.* Nashville, Tenn.: A.M.E. Publishing House, 1895. 288p.

150 . Soyaux, Herman. *Deutsche Arbeit in Afrika. Erfahrungen und Betrachtungen.* Leipzig: F. A. Brockhaus, 1888. 182p.

151 . Stanley, Henry Morton. *Africa, Its Partition and Its Future.* New York: Dodd, Mead, 1898. 263p.

152 . _____. *The Autobiography of Sir Henry Morton Stanley.* Edited by Dorothy Stanley. London: Sampson, Low, 1909. New York: Houghton Mifflin, 1909. 551p.

153 . _____. *The Exploration Diaries of H. M. Stanley.* Edited by Richard Stanley and Alan Neame. London: Kimber, [1961]. 208p.

154 . _____. "Geographical Results of the Emin Pasha Relief Expedition," *PRGS*, New Series, XII(1890), 313-328.

155 . _____. *In Darkest Africa: or, the Quest, Rescue and Retreat of Emin, Governor of Equatoria.* 2 vols. London: Sampson, Low, 1890. French ed., 2 vols. Paris: Hachette, 1890.

156 . Stanley, Henry Morton. "The Story of the Development of Africa," *Century*, LI(1895-1896), 500-509.

157 . _____. *Through the Dark Continent; or, the Sources of the Nile around the Great Lakes of Equatorial Africa and down the Livingstone River to the Atlantic Ocean.* 2 vols. New York: Harpers, 1878. French ed., 2 vols. Paris: Hachette, 1879.

158 . _____. *Unpublished Letters.* Edited by Albert Maurice. London: Chambers, 1957. 183p. New York: Philosophical Library, 1957. 190p.

159 . Staudinger, P. "Die Zähnung des Elephanten," *DK*, XII(1895), 139.

160 . Thomson, Joseph. "Note on the African Tribes of the British Empire," *JAI*, XVI(1886-1887), 182-186.

161 . Thomson, Joseph. "The Results of European Intercourse with the African," *Contemporary Review*, LVII(1890), 339-352.

162 . Tissot, Victor and Améro, Constant. *Au pays nègres: peuplades et paysages d'Afrique.* Paris: Firmin Didot, 1887. 234p.

163    . Toulotte, Joseph Anatole. "Lettere," *MCM*, XXVI(1897), 535,536.

164    . _____ . "Lettres," *Annales Oeuvre Ste Enfance*, L(1899), 20-27.

165    . _____ . "Lettres," *APFL*, LXX(1898), 74,75.

166    . _____ . "Lettres," *MCL*, XXIV(1892), 321,322; XXIX(1897), 511.

167    . _____ . "Le Paradis," *MCL*, XXV(1893), 368-372.

168    . Vandeleur, Cecil Foster Seymour. *Campaigning on the Upper Nile and Niger*. London: Methuen, 1898. 320p.

169    . Vincent, Frank. *Actual Africa: or, the Coming Continent. A Tour of Exploration*. New York: D. Appleton, 1895. 542p.

170    . Wagner, J. *Dem ganzen Deutschen Volke Gewidmet! Unsere Kolonien in West-Afrika. Kurze Darlegung des Erwerbes, der Beschaffenheit und der Aussichten sämtlicher Deutschen Besitzungen in Westafrika: Lüderitzland, kuste des Gross-Nama und Hererolandes, Kamerun- und Togogebiet*. Berlin: Engelmartt'schen Landkartenhandlung, 1884. 18p.

171    . Welles, C. M. *Three Years' Wanderings of a Connecticut Yankee in South America, Africa, Australia and California, with Descriptions of the Several Countries, Manners, Customs and Conditions of the People*. . . . New York: American Subscription Publishing House, 1859. 358p.

172    . Wilkes, Charles. *Narrative of the United States Exploring Expedition during the Years 1838, 1839, 1840, 1841, 1842*. 5 vols. Philadelphia: C. Sherman, 1844.

173    .. Woldt, A. "Deutschlands Interessen im Neger- und Kongogebiet," *Westermanns Monatshefte*, LVIII(1885).

# EASTERN AFRICA

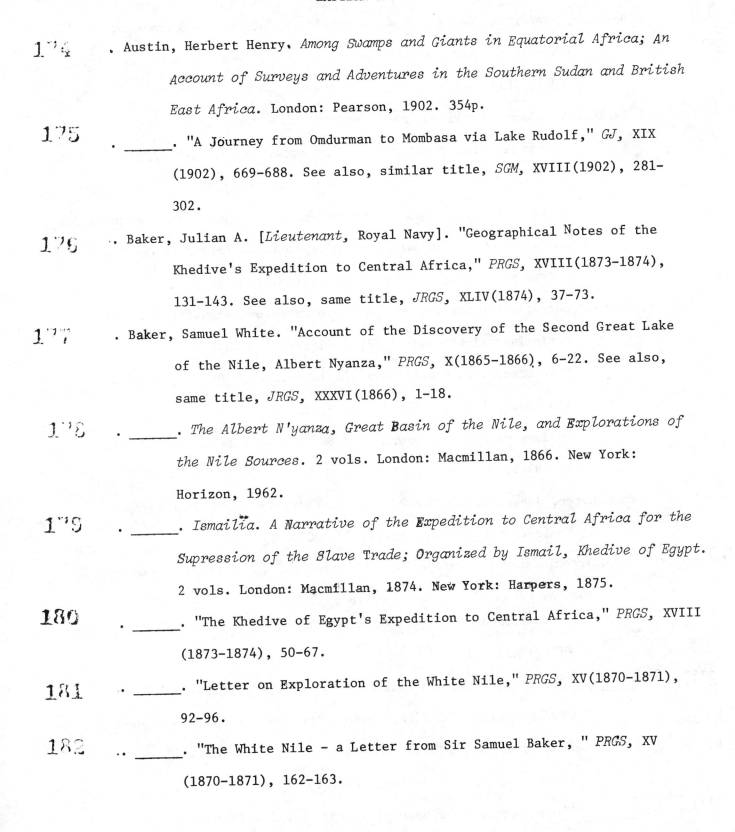

174 . Austin, Herbert Henry. *Among Swamps and Giants in Equatorial Africa; An Account of Surveys and Adventures in the Southern Sudan and British East Africa.* London: Pearson, 1902. 354p.

175 . _____. "A Journey from Omdurman to Mombasa via Lake Rudolf," *GJ*, XIX (1902), 669-688. See also, similar title, *SGM*, XVIII(1902), 281-302.

176 . Baker, Julian A. [*Lieutenant*, Royal Navy]. "Geographical Notes of the Khedive's Expedition to Central Africa," *PRGS*, XVIII(1873-1874), 131-143. See also, same title, *JRGS*, XLIV(1874), 37-73.

177 . Baker, Samuel White. "Account of the Discovery of the Second Great Lake of the Nile, Albert Nyanza," *PRGS*, X(1865-1866), 6-22. See also, same title, *JRGS*, XXXVI(1866), 1-18.

178 . _____. *The Albert N'yanza, Great Basin of the Nile, and Explorations of the Nile Sources.* 2 vols. London: Macmillan, 1866. New York: Horizon, 1962.

179 . _____. *Ismailia. A Narrative of the Expedition to Central Africa for the Supression of the Slave Trade; Organized by Ismail, Khedive of Egypt.* 2 vols. London: Macmillan, 1874. New York: Harpers, 1875.

180 . _____. "The Khedive of Egypt's Expedition to Central Africa," *PRGS*, XVIII (1873-1874), 50-67.

181 . _____. "Letter on Exploration of the White Nile," *PRGS*, XV(1870-1871), 92-96.

182 . _____. "The White Nile - a Letter from Sir Samuel Baker," *PRGS*, XV (1870-1871), 162-163.

183. Barnard, Frederick Lamport. *A Three Years' Cruise in the Mozambique Channel for the Suppression of the Slave Trade*. London: Bentley, 1848. 319p.

184. Barttelot, Edmund Musgrave. *The Life of E. M. Barttelot. . . .An Account of His Services for the Relief of Kandahar, of Gordon, and of Emin from His Letters and Diary*. London: Bentley, 1890. 413p. French translation, *Journal et corréspondance du major Edmund Musgrave Barttelot dans l'expedition Stanley à le recherche et au secours d'Émin Pasha*. Paris: Plon, Nouriet, 1891. 361p.

185. Baumann, Oscar. "Ein Bericht an die Ausfuhrungskomission der Deutschen Antisklaverei-Lotterie," *DK*, IX(1892), 163-165.

186. _____. "Die Expedition des Antisklaverei-Komitees," *DK*, IX(1892), 118-126, 153-156, 176-180; X(1893), 16-19, 33-35.

187. _____. "Reisenbriefen," *Geographische Zeitschrift*, I(1895), 409-411; II(1896), 107-109.

188. Baumgarten, Johannes. *Deutsch-Afrika und seine Nachbarn im schwarzen Erdteil*. Berlin: Dümmlers, 1887. 507p.

189. Baumgarten, Johannes. *Ostafrika, der Sudan und das Seengebiet. Land und Leute*. Gotha: F. A. Perthes, 1890. 563p.

190. Beke, Charles Tilstone. "On the Countries South of Abyssinia," *JRGS*, XIII(1843), 254-269.

191. _____. "On the Nile and Its Tributaries," *JRGS*, XVII(1847), 1-84.

192. _____. *The Sources of the Nile, Being a General Survey of the Basin of That River, and of Its Head-Streams; with the History of the Nilotic Discovery*. London: Madden, 1860. 155p.

193. _____. *Who Discovered the Sources of the Nile? A Letter to Sir Roderick I. Murchison. . .with an Appendix Containing a Letter to. . .Lord Ashburton*. London: Williams & Norgate, 1863. 16p.

194 . Berlioux, Etienne Felix. *La traite orientale. Histoire des chasses à l'homme organisées en Afrique depuis quinze ans.* Paris, 1870. 350p. English translation, abridged, *The Slave Trade in Africa in 1872.* London: Marsh, 1872. 77p.

195 . Bonchamps, de. "Rapport sur sa mission en Éthiopie et sur le Haut-Nil," *Revue Coloniale* [Paris: Ministère des Colonies], V(1889), 61-78, 122-139.

196 . Boteler, Thomas. [*Captain*, Royal Navy]. *Narrative of a Voyage of Discovery to Africa and Arabia, Performed in His Majesty's Ships Leven and Barracouta, from 1821 to 1826, under the Command of Captain F. W. Owen.* 2 vols. London: Bentley, 1835.

197 . Brard, Alphonse. "Der Victoria-Nyansa," *PM*, XLIII(1897), 77-80.

198 . Brenner, Rudolf. "Der Gallaknabe Djilo," *Globus*, XVIII(1870-1871), 161-166.

199 . Bright, R. G. T. [*Major*]. "Survey and Exploration in the Ruwenzori and Lake Region, Central Africa," *GJ*, XXXIV(1909), 128-153.

200 . Brooke, J. W. "A Journey West and North of Lake Rudolf," *GJ*, XXV(1905), 525-531.

201 . Buchta, Richard. "Meine Reise nach den Nil-Quellseen im Jahre 1878," *PM*, XXVII(1881), 81-89.

202 . Büttner, Carl G. *Anthologie aus der Suaheli-Litteratur (Gedichte und Geschichte der Suaheli.)* 2 vols. Berlin: Felber, 1894.

203 . _____. "Bilder aus dem Geistesleben der Suaheli in Ostafrika, ihrer epischen und lyrischen Dichtung entnommen," *VGE*, XX(1893), 147-160.

204 . _____. "Chuo cha Utenzi. Gedichte im alten Suahili aus den Papieren des Dr. L. Krapf," *ZAS*, I(1887-1888), 1-42, 124-137, II(1888-1889), 241-264.

205 . _____. *Lieder und Geschichten der Suaheli*. Berlin: Felber, 1894. 202p.

206 . Burgess, Ebenezer. "Probable Opening for Missionaries at Zanzibar and Accounts Received Concerning the Continental Tribes," *MH*, XXXVI(1840), 118-121.

207 . Burton, Richard Francis. *The Lake Regions of Central Africa, a Picture of Exploration*. 2 vols. New York: Harper, 1860. London: Longman, 1860. New Ed., with Introd. by Alan Moorhead, 2 vols., New York: Horizon, 1961. See also, "The Lake Regions of Central Equatorial Africa with Notices of the Lunar Mountains and the Source of the White Nile. . . ," *JRGS*, XXIX(1859), 1-454.

208 . _____. *The Nile Basin*. London: Tinsley, 1864. 195p. New edition, with introduction by Robert O. Collins, New York: De Capo Press, 1967.

209 . _____. "Notes from the Journal of the East African Expedition," *PRGS*, II(1857-1858), 52-56.

210 . _____. "On Lake Tanganyika, Ptolemy's Western Lake—Reservoir of the Nile," *JRGS*, XXXV(1865), 1-15.

211 . _____and Speke, John H. "A Coasting Voyage from Mombasa to the Pangani River; Visit to Sultan Kimwere; and Progress of the Expedition into the Interior," *JRGS*, XXVIII(1858), 188-226.

212 . _____. "Extracts from Reports by Captains Burton and Speke, of the East African Expedition, on Their Discovery of Lake Ujiji, etc., in Central Africa," *PRGS*, III(1858-1859), 111-113.

213 . Butler, William Francis. *The Campaign of the Cataracts; Being a Personal Narrative of the Great Nile Expedition of 1884-1885*. London: Sampson, Low, 1887. 389p.

214 . Cameron, Verney Lovett. "Exploration of Lake Tanganyika. Letter from Lt. V. L. Cameron, Describing the Discovery of an Outlet," *PRGS*, XIX(1874-1875), 75-77.

215 . _____. "Journal of Lt. V. L. Cameron, R.N., Commander of the Livingstone East Coast Aid Expedition," *PRGS*, XIX(1874-1875),136-155.

216 . _____. "Letters on the Progress of the Livingstone East Coast Relief Expedition," *PRGS*, XVIII(1873-1874), 69-74.

217 . _____. "On the Anthropology of Africa," *JAI*, VI(1877), 167-176.

218 . _____and Markham, C. R. "Examination of the Southern Half of Lake Tanganyika," *JRGS*, XLV(1875), 184-228.

219 . _____and others. "Death of Dr. Livingstone," *PRGS*, XVIII(1873-1874), 176-182.

220 . Cavendish, H. S. H. "Through Somaliland and Around and South of Lake Rudolph," *GJ*, XI(1898), 372-393.

221 . Chaillé-Long, Charles. *Central Africa: Naked Truths of Naked People. An Account of Expeditions to the Lake Victoria Nyanza and the Makraka Niam-Niam, West of the Bahr-el-Abiad (White Nile.)* London: Sampson, Low, 1876. 330p.

222 . Chanler, William Astor. *Through Jungle and Desert: Travel in East Africa.* London: Macmillan & Co., 1896. 535p.

223 . Chiesi, Gustavo. *La colonizzazione europea nell'Est Africa.* Turin, n.p., 1909. 814p.

224 . Christie, James [*M.D.*]. *Cholera Epidemics in East Africa: an Account of the Several Diffusions of the Disease in That Country from 1821 till 1872.* London: Macmillan & Co., 1876. 508p.

225 . Christopher, W. "Extracts from a Journal by Lt. W. Christopher, Commanding the H.C. Brig of War 'Tigris', on the East Coast of Africa," *JRGS*, XIV(1844), 76-103.

226 . Clark, George Edward. *Seven Years of a Sailors Life, a Narrative of Voyages in Merchantmen and Ships of War, Coasting, Trading and Fishing Vessels; Shipwrecks and Disasters in the Indian Ocean and the Gulf Stream; Captivity and Sufferings among the Somalies of Eastern Africa; Wanderings and Adventures in the Nubian Desert, Arabia, Hindostan, and the Indies.* Boston: Adams, 1867. 358p.

227 . Colomb, Philip Howard. *Slave-Catching in the Indian Ocean. A Record of Naval Experiences.* London: Longmans, 1873. 503p.

228 . Combes, Edmond. *Voyage en Egypt, en Nubie, dans les déserts de Beyouda, des Bicharys, et sur les côtes de la mer Rouge.* 2 vols. Paris: Desessart, 1846.

229 . Crispin, Edward S. "The 'Sudd' of the White Nile," *GJ*, XX(1902), 318-324.

230 . Crosby, Oscar T. "Notes on a Journey from Zeila to Khartoum," *GJ*, XVIII (1901), 46-61.

231 . Davis, Richard Harding. "Along the East Coast of Africa," *Scribner's Magazine*, XXIX(1901), 259-277.

232 . Debono, Andria. "Fragment d'un voyage au Saubat," *TM*, II(1860), 348-352.

233 . Decken, Carl Claus von der [*Baron*]. "Letter from the Baron. . .to Sir Roderick I. Murchison, Announcing the Departure of His New Expedition into the Interior of Eastern Africa," *PRGS*, X(1865-1866), 28-29.

234 . _____. *Reisen in Ost-Afrika in den Jahren 1859 bis 1865.* 4 vols. in 6. Leipzig: Winter, 1869-1879.

235 . Decle, Lionel. "The Watusi," *JAI*, XXIII(1893-1894), 423-426.

236 . Devereux, William Cope. *A Cruise in the "Gorgon. . .Engaged in the Suppression of the Slave Trade on the East Coast of Africa.* London: Bell & Daldy, 1869. 421p.

237 . Dundas, F. G. "Exploration of the Rivers Tana and Juba," *SGM*, IX(1893), 113-126.

238 . Eliot, C. N. E. "Notes of a Journey through Uganda, down the Nile to Gondokoro," *GJ*, XX(1902), 611-619.

239 . Elliot, George Francis Scott. *Naturalist in Mid-Africa: Being an Account of a Journey to the Mountains of the Moon and Tanganyika.* London: A. D. Innes & Co., 1896. 413p.

240 . Elton, James Frederick. *Elton and the East African Slave Trade. . .Being Extracts from the Diary of Captain James Elton.* London: Macmillan, 1952. 61p.

241 . Elton, James Frederick. *Travels and Researches among the Lakes and Mountains of Eastern and Central Africa, from the Journal of the Late J. F. E.* London, n.p., 1879. 417p.

242 Erhardt, James [*Reverend*]. "On an Inland Sea in Central Africa. Reports Respecting Central Africa, as Collected in Mambara and on the East Coast, with a New Map of the Country," *PRGS*, I(1855-1857), 8-10.

243 . Ewald, H. "Über die Völker und Sprachen südlich von Aethiopien," *Zeitschrift der Deutschen Morgenländischen Gesellschaft*, I(1847).

244 . Faulkner, Henry. *Elephant Haunts; Being a Sportsman's Narrative of the Search for Doctor Livingstone.* London: Hurst & Blackett, 1868. 325p.

245 Felkin, Robert W. "Aufzeichnungen über die Route von Ladó nach Dara," *PM*, XXVII(1881), 89-98.

246 . _____. "Journey to Victoria Nyanza and Back, via the Nile," *PRGS*, New Series, II(1880), 357-363.

247 . _____. *Über Lage und Stellung die Frau bei der Geburt auf Grund eigener Beobachtungen bein den Neger-Völkern der oberen Nil-Gegenden.* Marburg: Erhardt, 1885. 32p.

248   . Fischer, G. A. [*Dr.*]. "Am Ostufer des Victoria-Njansa," *PM*, XLI(1895),

   1-6, 42-46, 66-72.

249   . _____. "Vorläufiger Bericht über die Expedition zur Auffindung Dr.

   Junkers," *PM*, XXXII(1886), 363-369.

250   . Fitzgerald, William Walter Augustus. *Travels in the Coastlands of British*

   *East Africa and the Islands of Zanzibar and Pemba: Their Agricultural*

   *Resources and General Characteristics.* London: Chapman & Hall, 1898.

   774p.

251   . Fleuriot de Langle. [*Vicomte*]. "La traite des esclaves à la côte

   orientale d'Afrique," *RMC*, XXXVIII(1873), 785-828. See also, *TM*,

   XXIII(1872), 305-352; XXVI(1873), 353-400; XXXI(1876), 241-304.

252   . Foot, C. E. [*Capt., R.N.*]. "Transport and Trading Centres for Eastern

   Equatorial Africa," *JRSA*, XXVIII(1880), 362-369.

253   . Foster, Hubert John. *Handbook of British East Africa, Including*

   *Zanzibar, Uganda, and the Territory of the Imperial British East*

   *Africa Company.* Prepared in the Intelligence Division, War Office,

   1893. London: Her Majesty's Stationery Office, 1893.176p.

254   . Frere, Henry Bartle Edward. *East Africa As a Field for Missionary Labour:*

   *Four Letters to the Archibishop of Cantebury.* London, n.p.,

   1874. 122p.

255   . Geddie, John. *The Lake Regions of Central Africa.* London: Nelson & Sons,

   1881. 275p.

256   . Germain, Adrien. "Note sur Zanzibar et la côte orientale d'Afrique,"

   *BSGP*, 5th Series, XVI(1868), 530-559.

257 . Gibson, Henry. "Missions of the Equatorial Lakes," *Month*, LIV(1885), 491-508; LV(1885), 349-360, 504-515.

258 . Giraud, Victor. *Les lacs de l'Afrique Équatoriale. Voyage d'exploration exécuté de 1883 à 1885.* Paris: Hachette, 1890. 604p.

259 . _____. "Reise nach den innerafrikanischen Seen, 1883 bis 1885," *Globus*, L(1886), 1-7, 17-23, 33-39, 49-55, 321-328, 337-343, 353-361, 369-376, LIII(1888), 116-121, 133-138, 147-153, 164-168, 180-183, LIV(1888), 245-250, 259-265, 276-282.

260 . Gochet, Jean Baptiste. *Alexis Vrithoff, compagnon des capitains Jacques et Joubert au lac Tanganyika...sa jeunesse, son "Journal de voyage," sa mort glorieuse.* Brussels, 1893. 190p.

261 . Gommenginger, August. "Lettres," *Annales Apostoliques,* New Series, XIV (1897-1898), 334,335; XX(1904), 168.

262 . _____. "Missionsbriefe," *Echo aus Knechsteden,* V(1903-1904), 79; VI(1904-1905), 29-31; VII(1905-1906), 28, 29, 199-201.

263 . _____. "Missionsbriefe," *KM,* XXIV(1896), 183, 184; XXVI(1897-1898), 213.

264 . Gordon, Charles George. "The Khedive's Expedition to the Lake Districts," *PRGS,* XXI(1876-1877), 56-58.

265 . _____. "Observations on the Nile between Dufli and Magungo and Notes on the Victoria Nile between Magungo and Foweira," *PRGS,* XXI(1876-1877), 48-50.

266 Grant, James Augustus. "Summary of Observations on the Geography, Climate, and Natural History of the Lake Region of Equatorial Africa," *JRGS,* XLII(1872), 243-342.

267 _____. *A Walk across Africa, or, Domestic Scenes from My Nile Journal.* London: Blackwood, 1864. 452p.

268 . Grant, S. C. N. "The Anglo-Portuguese Delimitation Commission in East Africa," *SGM*, IX(1893), 337-347.

269 . Grimm, Dr. *Die Pharaonen in Ostafrika. Eine kolonialpolitische Studie.* Karlsruhe: Macklotsche, 1887. 184p.

270 . Grünenwald, Michel. "Lettres," *Le Lis de St. Joseph*, VII(1896), 182-185.

271 . _____. "Missionsbriefe," *Portugal em Africa*, IV(1897), 164-170, 382-386, 416-424.

272 . Guillain, Charles. *Documents sur l'histoire, la géographie et le commerce de l'Afrique Orientale.* 3 vols. Paris: Bertrand, 1856-57.

273 . Gwynn, C. W. [*Major*]. "Surveys on the Proposed Sudan-Abyssinian Frontier," *GJ*, XVIII(1901), 562-573.

274 . Hamilton, A. H. [*Rev.*]. "The English Church in East Africa," *West Indian Quarterly*, I(1885-1886), 248-253.

275 . Hardinge, Arthur Henry. "Legislative Methods in the Zanzibar and East African Protectorate," *Journal of the Society of Comparative Legislation*, I(1899), 1-10.

276 . Hartmann, Robert. *Abyssinien und die übrigen gebiete der Ostküste Afrikas.* Leipzig und Prague: Deutsche-Universal-Bibliothek für Gebildete, 1883. 304p. Vol. XIV, *Das Wissen der Gegenwart.*

277 . Hartmann, Robert. *Reise des Freiherren A. von Barnim durch Nord-Ost-Afrika in den Jähren 1859 und 1860.* Berlin, 1863.

278 . _____. "Untersuchungen über die Völkerschaften Nord-Ost-Afrikas," *ZE*, I(1869), 23-45, 135-158.

279 . Hedenborg, Johan. *Resa i Egypten och det Afrika, åren 1834 och 1835.* Stockholm: Hjerta, 1843.

280 . Heuglin, Martin Theodore von. "Ein arabischer Schriftsteller über die Bedja-Lander," in Bruno Hassenstein, *Ost-Afrika zwischen Chartum und dem Rothen Meere bis Suakin und Massawa.* Gotha: J. Perthes, 1861. 16p.

281    . _____. "Reise in Nordost-Afrika und längs Rothen Meeres im Jahre 1857," *PM*, VI(1860), 325-358.

282    . _____. "Zoogeographische Skizze des Nil-Gebiets und der Küstenländer des Rothen Meeres und Golfes von Aden," *PM*, XV(1869), 406-418.

283    . Hildebrandt, J. M. "Meine zweite Reise in Ostafrika," *Globus*, XXXIII (1878), 269-271, 279-281, 296-298.

284    . _____. "On His Travels in East Africa," *PRGS*, XXII(1877-1878), 446-453.

285    . Hinde, Sidney and Hildegarde. *The Last of the Masai*. London: Heinemann, 1901. 180p.

286    . Höhnel, L. Ritter von. [*K.K. Linienschiffs-Leutnant*]. "Über die hydrographische Zugehörigkeit des Rudolfsee-Gebietes," *PM*, XXXV (1889), 233-237.

287    . Hollis, Alfred Claud. *The Masai, Their Language and Folklore*. Oxford: Clarendon Press, 1905. 359p.

288    . _____. "Notes on the History of Vumba, East Africa," *JAI*, XXX(1900), 275-297.

289    . Holmwood, Frederick. "Trade between India and the East Coast of Africa," *JRSA*, XXXIII(1885), 417-429.

290    . Hutchinson, Edward. "Best Trade Route to the Lake Regions of Central Africa," *JRSA*, XXV(1877), 431-440

291    Hutchinson, Edward. "Progress of the Victoria Nyanza Expedition of the Church Missionary Society," *PRGS*, XXI(1876-1877), 498-504.

292    . Hutchinson, Edward. *The Slave Trade in Eastern Africa*. London, n.p., 1874. 96p.

293 . Isenberg, Karl Wilhelm and Krapf, Johann Ludwig. "Abstract of a Journal Kept by the Reverend Messrs. Isenberg and Krapf, on Their Route from Cairo, through Zeila to Shwá and I'fat, between the 21st of January and 12th of June, 1839," *JRGS*, X(1841), 455-468.

294 . Jackson, Frederick John. *Early Days in East Africa*. London: Arnold, 1930. 399p.

295 . _____ and Ravenstein, E. G. "Journey to Uganda via Masai-land," *PRGS*, New Series. XIII(1891), 193-206.

296 . Jannasch, Robert. *Die deutsche Handelsexpedition, 1886*. Berlin: Heymanns, 1887. 292p.

297 . Johnston, H. H. "Asiatic Colonisation of East Africa," *JRSA*, XXXVII(1889), 161-172.

298 . Johnston, Harry Hamilton. "British Interests in Eastern Equatorial Africa," *JMGS*, I(1885), 165-179. See also, same title, *SGM*, I(1885), 145-156.

299 . _____. "The People of Eastern Equatorial Africa," *JAI*, XV(1885), 3-15.

300 . Jonveaux, Émile. *Deux ans dans l'Afrique orientale*. Tours: Mame, 1871. 384p. English translation: *Two Years in East Africa: Adventures in Abyssinia and Nubia, with a Journey to the Sources of the Nile*. New York: Nelson, 1875.

301 . Junker, Wilhelm Johann. "Brief von Dr. W. Junker aus den Ländern der Niamniam," *PM*, XXVII(1881), 150-154. Also, *PRGS*, III(1881), 301-305.

302 . _____. *Reisen in Afrika, 1875-1886*. 3 vols. Vienna: Hölzel, 1889-1891. English translation, 3 vols. London: Chapman & Hall, 1890-1892.

303 . _____. "Rundreise in dem südlichen Niamniam-Lande," *PM*, XXVII(1881), 252-260.

304 . _____. "Travels in Central Africa," *SGM*, III(1887), 358-361.

305 . _____. "Von Albert Nyansa nach dem Victoria Nyansa, 1886," *PM*, XXXVII(1891), 1-8.

306 . _____. "Von Victoria Nyansa über Tabora nach Bagamojo, 1886," *PM*, XXXVII(1891), 185-191.

307 . Keane, Henry J. "An East African Waterway," *SGM*, XI(1895), 114-130.

308 . Keller, Conrad. *Reisebilder aus Ostafrika und Madagascar*. Leipzig: Winter, 1887. 341p.

309 . Kirchlechner, Theodor. "Missionsbriefe," *Echo aus Afrika*, V(1893), 94-96; VI(1894), 4, 38-40.

310 Kirk, John. "On Recent Surveys of the East Coast of Africa," *PRGS*, XXII(1873-1878), 453-455.

311 . Koettlitz, Reginald. "Journey through Somaliland and Southern Abyssinia to the Shangalla or Berta Country and the Blue Nile through the Sudan to Egypt," *SGM*, XVI(1900), 467-490, and *JMGS*, XVI(1900), 1-30.

312 _____. "Notes on the Galla of Walega and the Bertat," *JAI*, XXX(1900), 50-55.

313 . Kolb, George. "Spuren alter Kulturvölker in Ostafrika," *Jahresberichte des Vereins für Erdkunde in Metz*, XIX(1897).

314 . Krapf, Johann Ludwig. "Côte de Zanguebar,"[letter, Krapf to Barth], *JME*, XXVII(1852), 96-105.

315 . Krapf, J. L. *Reisen in Ostafrika, ausgeführt in den Jahren 1837 bis 1853*. Kornthal, 1858. 2 vols.

316 _____. "Some letters of J. L. Krapf," Edited by Norman R. Bennett. *Boston University Graduate Journal*, IX(1960), 45-58.

317 Krockow, Carl von. [*Count*]. "Exploration in East Africa between 14° to 16° North Latitude," *JRGS*, XXXVI(1866), 198-200.

318 . Leigh, T. S. "Mayotta and the Comoro Islands," *JRGS*, XIX(1849), 7-17.

319 . Lejear, *Guillaume*, "Aus Wilhelm Lejeans Reisen in Nubien und Abyssinien," *Globus*, VIII(1865), 257-264, 289-298.

320 . LeRoy, Alexandre. *Sur terre et sur l'eau. Voyage d'exploration dans l'Afrique orientale*. Tours: Alfred Mame et fils, 1898. 368p.

321 . Liebert, Major [*Generalstabe*]. "Der Wissman-Dampfer aus dem Viktoria-Nyanza," *DK*, VII(1890), 312.

322 . Liedmann, von. "Ein Besuch beim Suaheli-hauptling Futula," *DK*, VI(1889), 271-273.

323 . _____. "Von der Emin Pascha-expedition," *DK*, VI(1889), 294-296, 315-316, 328-331.

324 . Livingstone, David. "Extracts from Letters and Despatches from Dr. Livingstone," *PRGS*, XIV(1869-1870), 8-16, 38-39.

325 . _____. "Letters from Dr. Livingstone," *PRGS*, XII(1867-1868), 175-180, 182-183.

326 . _____. "Letters from the Late Explorer. . .," *PRGS*, XVIII(1873-1874), 255-281.

327 . Lugard, Frederick John Dealtry. "Characteristics of African Travel, with Notes on a Journey from the East Coast to the Albert Lake," *SGM*, VIII(1892), 625-642.

328 . _____. *The Rise of Our East African Empire. Early Efforts in Nyasaland and Uganda*. 2 vols. London: Blackwood, 1893.

329 . _____. "Slavery under the British Flag," *Nineteenth Century*, Feb., 1896, pp. 335-355.

330 . _____. "Travels from the East Coast to Uganda, Lake Albert Edward, and Lake Albert," *PRGS*, New Series. XIV(1892), 817-839.

331 . Lux, Ferdinand. "Lettres," *Annales Apostoliques*, XIV(1897-1898), 226-232; XV(1898-1899), 13-15.

332  McDermott, P. L. *British East Africa; or, Ibea. A History of the Formation and Work of the Imperial British East Africa Company.* London: Chapman & Hall, 1893. 382p.

333  . Macdonald, Duff. *Africana; or, The Heart of Heathen Africa.* 2 vols. London: Simpkin, Marshall, 1882.

334  . MacDonald, James Ronald Leslie. "East Central African Customs," *JAI*, XXII(1892), 99-122.

335  . _____. "Notes on the Ethnology of Tribes Met with During Progress of the Juba Expedition of 1897-99," *JAI*, XXIX(1899), 226-243.

336  . _____. *Soldiering and Surveying in British East Africa, 1891-1894.* London: Arnold, 1897. 333p.

337  . Mackenzie, George Sutherland. "Uganda and the East African Protectorate," *Fortnightly Review*, Dec., 1894, pp. 882-894.

338  . Marno, Ernst. "Ein Rückblick auf Samuel Baker's Expedition," *Globus*, XXIV(1873), 166-168.

339  . Martini, Gennaro. "Relazione dell'esplorazione lungo il Fiume Azurro compiuta da D. Gennaro Martini 21 settembre 1876 a maggio 1877," *ABP*, XVI(1877), 36-60.

340  . Matteucci, Pellegrino. *Spedizione Gessi-Matteucci. Sudan e Gallas.* Milano, 1879.

341  . _____. *La spedizione italiana all'Africa equatoriale.* Bologna, 1875.

342  . _____. *Viaggi africani di Pellegrino Matteucci.* [Letters and journals.] Milan, 1932. 381p.

343 . May, D. J. "The River Rovuma," *PRGS,* VI(1861-1862), 36-37.

344 . Meinecke, Gustav. *Aus dem Lande der Suaheli.* Berlin: Deutscher Kolonial-
Verlag, 1895. 194p.

345 . Meyer, Hans Heinrich Joseph. [*Dr.*]. "Briefwechsel mit einem ostafrikanischen Fürsten," *DK,* V(1888), 92-95.

346 . _____. "Die Mombassa-Kilimandscharo-Route in Britisch-Ostafrika,"
*PM,* XXXVII(1891), 257-263.

347 . Mohun, Richard Dorsey. "The Death of Emin Pasha," *Century Magazine,*
XLIX(1894-1895), 591-598.

348 . Moir, Frederick L. Maitland. "Eastern Route to Central Africa,"
*SGM,* I(1885), 95-112.

349 . Moore, J. E. S. "The Physiographical Features of the Nyasa and Tanganyika Districts of Central Africa," *GJ,* X(1897), 289-300.

350 . _____. "Tanganyika and the Countries North of It," *GJ,* XVII(1901), 1-35.

351 . _____. *To the Mountains of the Moon. Being an Account of
the Modern Aspect of Central Africa, and of Some Little Known
Regions Traversed by the Tanganyika Expedition, in 1899 and 1900.*
London: Hurst and Blackett, 1901. 350p.

352 . Munsch, Aloysius. "Missionsbriefe," *Echo aus Knechtsteden,* II(1900-1901),
45.

353 . Munzinger, Johann Albert Werner. "Der Mareb," *PM,* X(1864), 135-138.

354 . _____. *Ostafrikanische Studien.* Schaffhausen: Hurter, 1864.

355 . Neumann, Oskar. "Bericht über seine Reisen in Ost- und Central-Afrika,"
*VGE,* XXII(1895), 270-295.

356 . _____. "From the Somali Coast through Southern Ethiopia to the Sudan,"
*GJ,* XX(1902), 373-398.

357 . _____. "Von der Somali-Küste durch Süd-Äthiopien zum Sudan," *ZGE,* 4th Ser. I
(1902), 7-32.

358 . New, Charles. [*Reverend*]. "Journey from the Pangani, viâ Usambara, to Mombasa," *JRGS*, XLV(1875), 414-420.

359 . _____. "Journey from the Pangani, viâ Wadigo, to Mombasa," *PRGS*, XIX (1874-1875), 317-322.

360 . _____. *Life, Wanderings and Labours in Eastern Africa*. London: Hodder, 1873. 2nd Edition, 1874.

361 . O'Neill, Henry Edward. "The Ancient Civilization, Trade, and Commerce of East Africa," *SGM*, II(1886), 92-110.

362 . Osgood, Joseph B. T. *Notes of Travel; or, Recollections of Majunga, Zanzibar, Muscat, Aden, Mocha, and Other Eastern Ports*. Salem, Mass.: Creamer, 1845. 253p.

363 . Pearce, Francis Barrow. "Notes on the Country between Lake Chiuta and the River Luli, Central Africa," *GJ*, XV(1900), 612-619.

364 . Pease, Alfred E. "Africa North of the Equator," *Contemporary Review*, LXX(1896), 37-45.

365 . Pease, Alfred E. "Some Account of Somaliland, with Notes on Journeys through Gadabŭrsi and Western Ogaden Countries, 1896-1897," *SGM*, XIV(1898), 57-73.

366 . Peney, Alfred. *Les dernières explorations du Dr. Alfred Peney dans la région du haut fleuve Blanc*. Paris: De Martinet, 1863. 72p.

367 . Peters, Karl. Die Deutsche Emin-Pascha-Expedition; *SEE ALSO,* DK, VI(1889), 235-240, VII(1890), 2-5, 127-128. *MUNICH: R. OLDENBURG, 1891. 560 pp.*

368 . _____. "From the Mouth of the Tana to the Source-Region of the Nile," *SGM*, VII(1891), 113-123.

369 . _____. "Stanley and Emin Pasha," *Contemporary Review*, LVIII (1890), 634-638.

370 . Pfeil, Joachim [*Graf*]. "Beobachtungen während meiner letzten Reise in Ostafrika," *PM*, XXXIV(1888), 1-9.

371 . Piaggia, Carlo. "Sur le Nil Somerset et le Lac Capeke," *BSKG*, ?(1883), 185.

372 . Pogge, Paul. [*Dr.*]. "Der Reisebericht von Dr. Paul Pogge," *Globus*, XLIII(1883), 315-318, 327-329.

373 \_\_\_\_\_. "Über die Vermeidung von Elephanten bei Afrika-Reisen und Anlage von Stationen," *Globus*, XXXV(1879), 119-121.

374 . Price, Roger. *Report of the Rev. R. Price of His Visit to Zanzibar and the Coast of Eastern Africa*. London: London Missionary Society, 1876. 72p.

375 . Prideaux, William Francis. [*Lt.*]. "A Journey through the Soudan and Western Abyssinia, with Reminiscences of Captivity," *Illustrated Travels*, I(1869), 1-8, 57-63, 88-95, 110-116, 152-159, 171-178, 193-199, 248-254; 282-287.

376 . Pruen, Septimus Tristan. *The Arab and the African: Experiences in Eastern Equatorial Africa during a Residence of Three Years*. London: Seeley and Co., 1891. 338p.

377 . Purvis, John B. *Handbook to British East Africa and Uganda*. London: Swan Sonnenschein and Co., 1900. 94p.

378 . Révoil, Georges. "Voyage chez les Bénadirs, les Çomalis et les Bayouns," *TM*, IL(1895), 1-80, L(1885), 129-208. See also, *Globus*, XLVII (1885), 289 fwd., IL(1886), 145 fwd.

379 . Ritter, Carl. *Ein Blick in das Nil-Quelland*. Berlin: G. Reimer, 1844. 72p.

380 . Rohlfs, Friedrich Gerhard. *Zur Klimatologie und Hygiene Ostafrika's.* Leipzig: Hirschfeld, 1885. 15p.

381 . Rohmer, Martin. "Lettres," *Le Lis de St. Joseph,* XI(1900), 21-23; 205-206.

382 . _____. "Missionsbriefe," *Echo aus Knechtsteden,* II(1900-1901), 95; III (1901-1902), 13.

383 . _____. "Missionsbriefe," *KM,* XXVIII(1899-1900), 86, 87,

384 . Roscoe, John. *Twenty-five Years in East Africa.* Cambridge: University Press; New York: Macmillan, 1921. 288p.

385 . Sapelli, Alessandro. *Memorie d'Africa, 1883-1906.* Bologna: Zanichelli, 1935. 256p.

386 . Schanz, Moritz. *Ost- und Süd-Afrika.* Berlin: Susserott, 1902. 458p.

387 . Schlichter, H. G. "Notiz über neue afrikanische Pygmäen, östlich vom Nil," *PM,* XLII(1896), 236-237.

388 . Schmidt, K. W. "Dr. K. W. Schmidts Reisen auf den westlichen Komoren. Nach seinem Tagebuch," *PM,* XXXVI(1890), 11-15.

389 . Schnitzer, Eduard. [*Emin Pasha*]. "Journal einer Reise von Mrúli nach der Hauptstadt Unyoro's mit Bemerkungen über Land und Leute," *PM,* XXV(1879), 179-187, 220-224, 388-397.

390 . _____. "Reisen in Äquatorial-Afrika, von Dr. Emin Effendi, Chefartz der Ägyptischen Äquatorial-Provinzen, 1877," *PM,* XXIV(1878),

391 217-228.

. _____. "Reisen zwischen dem Victoria- und Albert-Nyanza, 1878," *PM.* XXVI(1880), 21-28.

392 . Schnitzer, Eduard. *Die Tagebücher von Emin Pascha.* Ed. by *F. Stuhlmann.* Braunschweig: G. Westermann, 1919-1927. 4 vols.

393. _____ and Casati, Gaetano. "The Monbuttu and Their Country," *SGM*, III (1887), 407-410.

394. Schoeller, Max. [*Dr.*] "Äequatorial-Ostafrika-Expedition 1896/97," *DK*, XV(1898), 59-63, 206-207, 232-234.

395. _____. "Die ethnologischen Verhältnisse des äquatorialen Ostafrika," *DK*, **XV(1898)**, 281-285.

396. _____. *Mitteilungen über meine Reise nach Äequatorial-Ost-Afrika und Uganda, 1896-1897.* 3 vols. Berlin, 1901-1904.

397. Schoeller, Max [*Dr.*]. "Einige wissenschaftliche Ergebnisse seiner Expedition nach Äquatorial-Ost-Afrika und Uganda 1896/97," *VGE*, XXV(1898), 251.

398. Schweinfurth, Georg August. "Der Afrikareisende Georg Schweinfurth," *Globus*, XVIII(1870-1871), 365-367, 373-375.

399. _____. "Georg Schweinfurth's Reisen in Inner-Afrika," *Globus*, XXVI (1874), 273-279, 289-294, 305-307, XXVII(1875), 81-85, 97-103, 113-117, XXVIII(1875), 257-262, 273-276, 298-299, 308-310, 324-328.

400. Schweinitz, Hans Hermann. [*Graf*]. "Aus dem Tagebuch," *DK*, IX(1892), 79-81, 96-98.

401. _____. "Zur Lage am Victoriasee," *DK*, XIII(1896), 113-114.

402. Schynse. "Pater Schynses Aufnahme des SW-Ufers des Victoria Nyansa," *PM*, XXXVII(1891), 219-220.

403. Schynse, August. "Rückreise vom Viktoria-See nach Sansibar," *PM*, XXXVI (1890), 135.

404 . Scott, Laurence. "A Holiday in East Africa," *JMGS*, IV(1888), 262-267.

405 . Seidel, August. "Die Araber in Ost- und Mittelafrika," *Globus*, LV (1889), 145-150, 168-171.

406 . _____. "Das arabische Element im Suaheli," *ZAOS*, I(1895), 9-15, 97-104.

407 . Senkovsky, Joseph De. "Fragments d'un voyage inédit en Nubie et dans l'Ethiopie septentrionale fait en 1819," *Nouvelles Annales des Voyages*, XVI(1822), 289-325.

408 . Sheldon, Mary French-. "England's Commercial and Industrial Future in Central Africa," *Journal of the Tyneside Geographical Society*, III(1897), 415-418.

409 . Sim, Arthur Fraser. *The Life and Letters of Arthur Fraser Sim, Priest in the University Mission to Central Africa*. London: Universities' Mission, 1896. 276p.

410 . Sinner, Franz. "Le tribù pagane indipendenti, intermedie fra l'Abissinia e il Sudan," *Nigrizia*, XII(1894), 158, 182, XIII(1895), 52, 85.

411 . Smith, Arthur Donaldson. [Dr.]. "An Expedition between Lake Rudolf and the Nile," *GJ*, XVI(1900), 600-624.

412 . _____. "Expedition through Somaliland to Lake Rudolf," *GJ*, VIII(1896), 120-137.

413 . _____. *Through Unknown African Countries. The First Expedition from Somaliland to Lake Lamu*. London: Arnold, 1897. 471p.

414 . Smith, C. S. "The Anglo-German Boundary in East Equatorial Africa. Proceedings of the British Comission, 1892," *GJ*, IV(1894), 424-437.

415 . Speke, John Hanning. "Extracts from a Letter by Captain Speke to Lieutenant Colonel Rigby, H.B.M.'s Consul at Zanzibar, dated Khoko
in Western Ugogo, December 12, 1860," *PRGS*, VI(1861-1862), 17-
18.

416 . _____. "Journal of a Cruise on the Tanganyika Lake, Central Africa,
and Discovery of the Victoria Nyanza Lake, the Supposed Source
of the Nile," *Blackwood's Magazine*, LXXXVI(1859), 339-357, 391-
419, 565-582.

417 . _____. *Journal of the Discovery of the Source of the Nile*. Edinburgh:
Blackwood, 1863. New York: Harper, 1864. 658p.

418 . _____. "The Upper Basin of the Nile, from Inspection and Information,
and Itineraries of a Second East African Expedition," *JRGS*,
XXXIII(1863), 322-346.

419 . _____. *What Led to the Discovery of the Source of the Nile*. Edinburgh:
Blackwood, 1864. 372p.

420 . _____ and Grant, James Augustus. "Abstracts from Letters from the East
African Expedition under Captains Speke and Grant to the
Secretary," *PRGS*, V(1860-1861), 11-16.

421 . _____ and _____. "Addresses to a Special Meeting of the Royal Geographical
Society," *PRGS*, **VII(1862-1863)**, 217-225.

422 . Spring. [*Kapitän*]. "Eine Reise nach Bukindo auf der Insel Ukerewe,"
*DK*, X(1893), 46-49.

423 . Stairs, William Grant. "From the Albert Nyanza to the Indian Ocean,"
*Nineteenth Century*, June, 1891, 953-968.

424 . Stanley, Henry Morton. *How I Found Livingstone; Travels, Adventures, and
Discoveries in Central Africa; Including Four Months' Residence
with Dr. Livingstone*. London: Sampson Low, 1872. 736p. New York:
Scribner's, 1872. 736p.

425 . _____ . "Letter on His Journey from the Albert Nyanza to the Southern Side of Victoria Nyanza," *PRGS*, New Series, XI(1889), 720-726.

426 . _____ . "Letters of Mr. H. M. Stanley on His Journey to Victoria Nyanza, and Circumnavigation of the Lake," *PRGS*, XX(1875-1876), 134-159.

427 . _____ . *My Dark Companions and Their Strange Stories*. London: Sampson Low, 1893. New York: Scribner's, 1893. 335p.

428 . _____ and Grant, James Augustus. "On Mr. H. M. Stanley's Exploration of the Victoria Nyanza," *JRGS*, XLVI(1876), 10-34.

429 . Stecker, Anton. "Dr. Anton Steckers Reisen in den Galla-Landern, 1882, nach seinen Tagebuchnotizen," *PM*, XXXVII(1891), 233-241.

430 . Steere, Edward. "East African Tribes and Languages," *JAI*, I(1871), Appendix, pp. cxliii-clv.

431 . Stevens, Thomas. *Scouting for Stanley in East Africa*. London: Cassell, 1890. 288p.

432 . Stewart, James. "Lake Nyassa, and the Water Route to the Lake Region of Africa," *PRGS*, **New Series**, III(1881), 257-274.

433 . Stigand, Chauncey Hugh. *Administration in Tropical Africa*. London: Constable, 1914. 302p.

434 . _____ . *Hunting the Elephant in Africa, and Other Recollections of Thirteen Years' Wanderings*. New York: Macmillan, 1913. 379p.

435 . _____ . *To Abyssinia Through an Unknown Land. An Account of a Journey through Unexplored Regions of British East Africa by Lake Rudolf to the Kingdom of Menelik*. London: Seeley, 1910. 352p.

436 . Stopford, J. G. B. [*Col.*]. "What Africa Can Do for White Men," *Journal of the Royal African Society*, II(1902), 50-63.

437. Strachey, R. "Meteorology of the Red Sea and Cape Guardafui," *PRGS*, New Series, X(1888), 704-708.

438. Stuhlmann, Franz [*Dr.*]. "Dr. Emin Paschas letzte Expedition, 1891," *PM*, XXXVIII(1892), 142-148.

439. _____. *Mit Emin Pascha ins Herz von Afrika. Ein Reisebericht mit Beiträgen von Emin Pascha in seinem Auftrage.* 2 vols. Berlin: Reimer, 1894.

440. Sykes, William Henry [*Colonel*]. "Notes on the Possessions of the Imam of Muscat, on the Climate and Productions of Zanzibar, and on the Prospects of African Discovery from Mombas," *JRGS*, XXIII(1853), 101-119.

441. Thomson, Joseph. "East Africa as It Was and Is," *Contemporary Review*, LV (1889), 41-51.

442. Thomson, Joseph. "East Central Africa and Its Commercial Outlook," *SGM*, II(1886), 65-78.

443. _____. "Journey of the Society's East African Expedition," *PRGS*, New Series, II(1880), 721-740.

444. _____. "Report on the Progress of the Society's Expedition to Victoria Nyanza," *PRGS*, New Series, V(1883), 544-550.

445. _____. *Through Masailand: A Journey of Exploration among the Snow-Clad Volcanic Mountains and Strange Tribes of Eastern Equatorial Africa, being the Narrative of the Royal Reographical Society's Expedition to Mount Kenya and Lake Victoria Nyanza, 1883-1884.* London: Sampson Low, 1885. Boston: Houghton Mifflin, 1885. 583p. Abridged edition, *Through Masailand with Joseph Thomson.* Edited by Roland Young, Evanston: Northwestern University Press, 1962. 218p.

456 . Wainright, Jacob. "Tagebuch von Jacob Wainright über den Transport von
Dr. Livingstone's Leiche 4. Mai 1873-18. Februar 1874," *PM*,
XX(1874), 187-193.

457 . Wakefield, Thomas. [*Reverend*]. "A Recent Journey from Lamu to Golbanti,
in the Galla Country," *JMGS*, IV(1888), 1-12.

458 . _____. "Routes of Native Caravans from the Coast to the Interior of
Eastern Africa, Chiefly from Information Given by Sa'di Bin
Ahédi, a Native of a District Near Gázi, in Udigo, a Little
North of Zanzibar," *JRGS*, XL(1870), 303-339.

459 . _____ and Ravenstein, E. G. "Somal and Galla Land," *PRGS*, New Series,
VI(1884), 255-273.

460 . Ward, Gertrude. *Letters from East Africa, 1895-1897.* 2nd ed. London:
Universities Missions to Central Africa, 1901. 227p.

461 . Weiss, Kurt. "Die Eisenbahnfrage in Ostafrika," *DK*, VIII(1891), 20-22.

462 . Wellby, Montagu Sinclair. *'Twixt Sirdar and Menelik. An Account of a
Year's Expedition from Zeila to Cairo through Unknown
Abyssinia.* London and New York: Harper, 1901. 409p.

463 . Wickenburg, Eduard von. [*Graf*]. *Wanderungen in Ost-Afrika.* Vienna:
Gerold & Co., 1899. 440p.

464 . Wilkinson, G. "Remarks on the Country between Wady Halfeh and Gebel
Berkel, in Ethiopia, with Observations on the Level of the
Nile," *JRGS*, XX(1850), 154-159.

465 . Willoughby, John Christopher. *East Africa and Its Big Game. The
Narrative of a Sporting Trip from Zanzibar to the Borders of
the Mesai.* London: Longmans, 1889. 312p.

446    . _____. *To the Central African Lakes and Back.* 2 vols. London: Sampson Low, 1881. New York: Houghton Mifflin, 1881.

447    . Tiedemann, Adolf von. *Tana-Baringo-Nil. Mit Karl Peters zu Emin Pasha.* Berlin: Walther, 1892. 332p.

448    . Torday, Emil. *Camp and Tramp in African Wilds. A Record of Adventures, Impressions and Experiences during Many Years Spent among the Savage Tribes around Lake Tanganyika and in Central Africa, with a Description of Native Life, Character and Customs.* London: Seeley, Service, 1913. 315p. Philadelphia: Lippincott, 1913. 315p.

449    . Tozer, William George. *Letters of Bishop Tozer and His Sister, together with Some Other Records of the University Mission from 1863 to 1873.* Ed. by Gertrude Ward. London: Universities' Mission to Central Africa, 1902. 304p.

450    . Trémaux, P. *Voyage en Ethiopie au Soudan oriental et dans l'Afrique septentrionale, comprenant une exploration dans les contrées inconnues de la Nigritie.* 2 vols. Paris: Hachette, 1862.

451    . Tucker, Alfred Robert. *Eighteen Years in Uganda and East Africa.* 2 vols. London: Arnold, 1908.

452    . Velten, Carl. *Prosa und Poesie der Suaheli.* Berlin, 1907. 432p.

453    . _____. *Schilderungen der Suaheli von Expeditionen von Wissmans, Dr. Bumillers, graf von Götzens, und anderer. Aus dem Munde von Suahelinegern gesammelt und übersetz.* Göttingen: Vandenhoeck & Ruprecht, 1901. 308p.

454    . _____. *Sitten und Gebräuche der Suaheli nebst einem Anhang über Rechtsgebräuche der Suaheli.* Göttingen: Venderhoeck & Ruprecht, 1903. 423p.

455    . Voeltzkow, Alfred. *Wissenschaftlichen Ergebnisse der Reisen in Madagaskar und Ostafrika in den Jahren 1889-1895.* Frankfurt: Diesterweg, 1897. 76p.

466 . Wills, J. T. "The Cape to Cairo," *Contemporary Review*, LXXV (1899), 159-168.

467 . Wilson. "Mission du Lac Nyanza," *JME*, LIII (1878), 301-308.

468 . Wilson, Charles Thomas. [*Reverend*] and Felkin, Robert William. *Uganda and the Egyptian Sudan*. 2 vols. London: Sampson Low, 1882.

469 . Würtz, Ferdinand. "Die Liongo-Sage der Ost-Afrikaner," *ZAOS*, II (1896), 88-89.

470 . Young, E. D. "Report of the Livingstone Search Expedition," *JRGS*, XXXVIII (1868), 111-118. See also, same title, *PRGS*, XII (1867-1868), 79-86.

ETHIOPIA

471  . Abargués de Sostén, Juan Víctor. "Lettres," *ACM*, XLVI(1881), 680-698.

472  . Abargués de Sostén, Juan Víctor. "Voyage en Abyssinie, dans le Zeboul et les Wollo-Gallas," *BSKG*, VI(1885), 320-324.

473  . _____. *Notas del viaje del Sr. D. J. V. Abargués de Sostén por Etiopía, Xoa, Zebul, Uolo, Galas, etc.* Madrid: Imp. de Fortanet, 1883. 93p.

474  . Abbadie, Antoine Thompson d'. *L'Abyssinie et le roi Théodore.* Paris: Douniol, 1868. Reprinted from *Le Correspondant*, LXIII(1868), 281-321.

475  . _____. *Les causes actuelles de l'esclavage en Éthiopie.* Louvain, 1877.
476  30p.

      . _____. "Conférence sur l'Éthiopie," *BSKG*, 2nd Series,  1888 , Supplement, pp. 690-692.

477  . Abbadie, Antoine d'. "Les Falacha ou Juifs de l'Ethiopie," *BSGP*, 3rd Series, IV(1845), 43-57, 65-74.

478  . Abbadie, Antoine d'. "Fr. Apollinaire," *L'Echo de St. Francois*, IV(1897), 270, 271, 316-318.

479  . _____. *Géographie de l'Éthiopie. Ce que j'ai entendu, faisant suite à ce que j'ai vu.* Paris: G. Mesnil, 1890. 457p.

480  . _____. "Idee per l'abolizione della schiavitù africana," *BSGI*, VIII(1889), 165-173.

481  . _____. "Lettre à M. le Comte de Montalembert—Saka, dans Enarya: 19 octobre 1843," *APFL*, XVII(1845), 270-285.

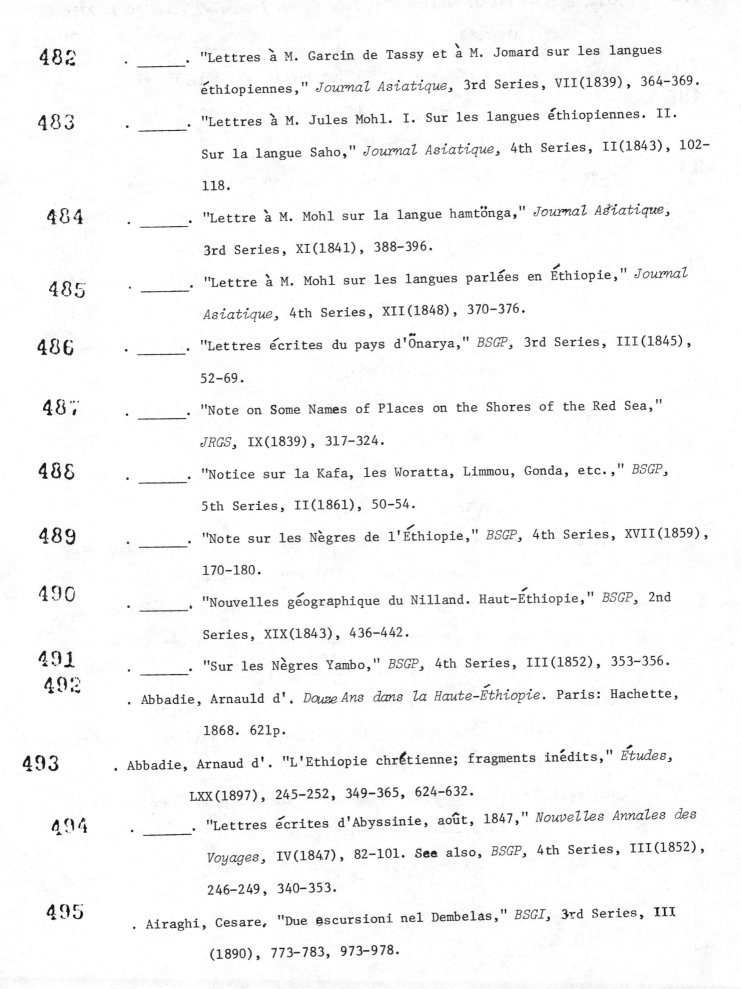

482 . _____ . "Lettres à M. Garcin de Tassy et à M. Jomard sur les langues éthiopiennes," *Journal Asiatique*, 3rd Series, VII(1839), 364-369.

483 . _____ . "Lettres à M. Jules Mohl. I. Sur les langues éthiopiennes. II. Sur la langue Saho," *Journal Asiatique*, 4th Series, II(1843), 102-118.

484 . _____ . "Lettre à M. Mohl sur la langue hamtönga," *Journal Asiatique*, 3rd Series, XI(1841), 388-396.

485 . _____ . "Lettre à M. Mohl sur les langues parlées en Éthiopie," *Journal Asiatique*, 4th Series, XII(1848), 370-376.

486 . _____ . "Lettres écrites du pays d'Önarya," *BSGP*, 3rd Series, III(1845), 52-69.

487 . _____ . "Note on Some Names of Places on the Shores of the Red Sea," *JRGS*, IX(1839), 317-324.

488 . _____ . "Notice sur la Kafa, les Woratta, Limmou, Gonda, etc.," *BSGP*, 5th Series, II(1861), 50-54.

489 . _____ . "Note sur les Nègres de l'Éthiopie," *BSGP*, 4th Series, XVII(1859), 170-180.

490 . _____ . "Nouvelles géographique du Nilland. Haut-Éthiopie," *BSGP*, 2nd Series, XIX(1843), 436-442.

491 . _____ . "Sur les Nègres Yambo," *BSGP*, 4th Series, III(1852), 353-356.

492 . Abbadie, Arnauld d'. *Douze Ans dans la Haute-Éthiopie*. Paris: Hachette, 1868. 621p.

493 . Abbadie, Arnaud d'. "L'Ethiopie chrétienne; fragments inédits," *Études*, LXX(1897), 245-252, 349-365, 624-632.

494 . _____ . "Lettres écrites d'Abyssinie, août, 1847," *Nouvelles Annales des Voyages*, IV(1847), 82-101. See also, *BSGP*, 4th Series, III(1852), 246-249, 340-353.

495 . Airaghi, Cesare. "Due escursioni nel Dembelas," *BSGI*, 3rd Series, III (1890), 773-783, 973-978.

496 . Alix, Marie-Bernard. "Lettres," *L'Echo de St. Francois*, VIII(1901), 271-291, 379, 380.

497 . Amezaga, Carlo de. "Assab," *BSGI*, 2nd Series, V(1880), 623-677.

498 . _____. "Lo Scioa e la spedizione geografica italiana," *Giornale delle Colonie* [Rome], August 16, 1879.

499 . Andree, R. *Abessinien, das Alpenland unter den Tropen und seine Grenzländer. Schilderungen von Land und Volk, vornehmlich unter König Theodoros (1855-1868)*. Leipzig: Spamer, 1869. 300p.

500 . Antinori, Orazio. "L'ambasciata in Italia del Re di Scioa," *Il Diritto* [Rome], November 9, 1872.

501 . _____. "Giornale e illustrazione dei nuovi laghi fra gli Adda Galla," *BSGI*, 2nd Series, VI(1881), 585.

502 . _____. "Relazione sommario del viaggio nel Mar Rosso," *BSGI*, 2nd Series, V(1870), 47-49.

503 . _____. "La spedizione egiziana in Abissinia," *Giornale Popolare di Viaggio* [Milan], October 13, 1872. p. 239.

504 . _____. "Sopra una colonia italiana stabilita in Sciotel nel paese dei Bogos in Abissinia," *BSGI*, III(1869), 469-474.

505 . _____. *Viaggio dei Signori O. Antinori, O. Beccari ed A. Issel nel mar Rosso, nel territorio dei Bogos e regioni circostanti durante gli anni 1870-71*. Genoa: Tip. del R. Istituto sordo-muti, 1873. 161p.

506 . _____. "Viaggio nei Bogos," *BSGI*, 2nd Series, XII(1887), 468ff., 511ff., 614ff., 668ff., 765ff. Also published as an extract, Rome: Civelli, 1887. 162p.

507 . Antonelli, Pietro. "Il primo viaggo di un Europeo attraverso l'Aussa," *BSGI*, 3rd Series, II(1889), 331-348, 526-549.

508     . _____. "Notizie del suo viaggio all'Aussa e allo Scioa, dal gennajo all'agosto 1883," *BSGI*, 2nd Series, VIII(1883), 215, 283, 395, 413, 782.

509     . _____. "Il mio viaggio da Assab allo Scioa," *BSGI*, 2nd Series, VIII(1883), 857-880.

510     . _____. "Appunti su Assab e dintorni," *BSGI*, 2nd Series, VII(1882), 463-472.

511     . _____. "Scioa e i Scioani," *BSGI*, 2nd Series, VII(1882), 69-92.

512     . Ardemanni, Ernesto. *Colonia Eritrea: Agroicolutra, Pastorizia, Sottosuolo.* Rome: G. Paravia, 1900. 67p.

513     . Ardemanni, Ernesto. *Tre pagine gloriose nella storia militare, civile, religiosa della Colonia Eritrea.* Florence: Lastrucci, 1901. 8p.

514     . Arnaud, Thomas J. "Lettre, Djeddah, 6.II.1894," *RHM*, XVI(1938), 432-434.

515     . Aubry, Alphonse. [*Ingénieur civil des mines*]. "Une mission au Choa et dans les pays Gallas," *BSGP*, 7th Series, VIII(1887), 439-485.

516     . _____. "Une mission au Choa et dans les pays Gallas," *Revue Scientifique* [Paris], 3rd Series, XI(1886), 705-717.

517     . Audon, Henry. "Voyage au Choa. (Abyssinie méridionale)," *TM*, LVIII(1889), 113-160. Italian translation, Milan: Vallardi, 1889. 52p.

518     . Avanchers, Léon des. "Esquisse géographique des pays Oromo ou Galla, des pays Soomali, et de la côte orientale d'Afrique," *BSGP*, 4th Series, XVII(1859), 153-170.

519     . _____. "Lettre," *APFL*, XXXVII(1865), 27-31.

520     . _____. "Lettre à M. A. d'Abbadie, Gera (pays Ilmorma près Kaffa), 12 juin 1861," *BSGP*, 5th Series, III(1862), 381-384.

521 . _____. "Lettre à M. A. d'Abbadie. Les pays Oromo-Sidma et le royaume de Gera," *BSGP*, 5th Series, XII(1866), 163-174.

522 . _____. "Lettre à M. A. d'Abbadie. Royaume de Gera, 20 avril 1866," *BSGP*, 5th Series, XVII(1869), 306-311.

523 . _____. "Lettre à M. Le Moyne, Massaouah, 31.XII.1851," *RHM*, XVI(1938), 585-586.

524 . _____. "Lettre à MM. les Membres des Conseils centraux, 10 septembre 1857," *APFL*, XXX(1858), 39-47.

525 . _____. "Lettera al signor Presidente della Società geografica italiana. Ghera, Galla (Alta Etiopia), 26.IV.1879," *BSGI*, XVIII(1881), 326-328.

526 . Azais, Bernardin. "Lettres," *L'Echo de St. Francois*, V(1898), 307-311, X(1902), 121-123.

527 . _____. "Lettres," *MCL*, XXXI(1899), 75, 76.

528 . _____. "Lettres," *Petit Messager de St. Francois*, VI(1901), 434-439.

529 . Baker, Samuel White. "Exploration des affluents abyssiniens du Nil, 1861-1862," *TM*, XXI(1870), 129-160.

530 . _____. "Journey to Abyssinia in 1862," *JRGS*, XXXIII(1863), 237-241.

531 . _____. "On the Tributaries of the Nile in Abyssinia," *PRGS*, X(1865-1866), 279-295.

532 . _____. *The Nile Tributaries of Abyssinia, and the Sword Hunters of the Hamran Arabs*. London: Macmillan, 1867. 596p. Philadelphia: Lippincott, 1868. 596p.

533    . Baldacci, L. "Osservazioni fatte nella Colonia Eritrea," *Carta Geologica d'Italia*[Rome], VI(1891), 110p.

534    . Barker, W. C. [*Lieutenant*]. "Extract Report on the Probable Geographical Position of Harrar; with Some Information Relative to the Various Tribes in the Vicinity," *JRGS*, XII(1842), 238-244.

535    . Barthez, Xiste. "Lettere," *MCM*, V(1876), 449-450.

536    . _____. "Lettre," *APFL*, XLVIII(1876), 453-455.

537    . _____. "Lettre," *MCL*, VIII(1876), 416-417.

538    . _____. "Lettre à M. N. à Paris, Saganaïti, 6.VIII.1871," *AGM*, XXXVII (1872), 104-112.

539    . _____. "Lettre à M. N., Alitiéne, 4.II.1876," *ACM*, XLI(1876), 458-461.

540    . Barthez, Xiste. "Lettres," *ACM*, XLVI(1881), 667-673; XLVII(1882), 246, 247; XLVIII(1883), 258-263.

541    . Baudraz, Claude-Pierre. "Lettre," *APFL*, LVIII(1886), 222-236.

542    . Beaumont, Augustinus. "Lettere," *Analecta Ordinis minorum Cappoccinorum*, X(1894), 114, 115; XI(1895), 82-89.

543    . _____. "Lettres," *Annales Franciscaines*, XVIII(1892-1894), 458, 459.

544    . _____. "Lettres," *Voix Franciscaines*, VI(1908), 453, 454.

545 . Bechtinger, J. [Dr.]. *Ost-Afrika. Erinnerungen und Miscellen aus dem abessinischen Feldzuge.* Vienna: C. Gerold's Sohn, 1869. 238p.

546 . Beillard, Chauvin. "Lettre au Ministre, Massouah, 31.V.1856," *RHM*, XVI (1938), 604.

547 . _____. "Lettre au Ministre, Massouah, 30.VI.1856," *RHM*, XVI(1938), 604-605.

548 . _____. "Lettre, Massaouah, 19.X.1857," *Revue des Missions* [Paris], XVII (1940), 36.

549 . _____. "Rapport, Massaouah, 5.VIII.1857," *Revue des Missions* [Paris], XVII (1940), 34-35.

550 . _____. "Rapport sur la Mission d'Abyssinie en 1857, Massouah, 25.IV.1857," *RHM*, XVI(1938), 606-612.

551 . Beke, Charles Tilstone. *Abyssinia. A Statement of Facts Relating to the Transactions between the Writer and the Late British Political Mission to the Court of Shoa.* London: Madden, 1845. 30p. 2nd Ed., London: Madden, 1846. 31p.

552 . _____. "Abyssinia: Being a Continuation of Routes in That Country," *JRGS*, XIV(1844), 1-64.

553 . _____. *The British Captives in Abyssinia.* London: Longmans, Green, 1865. 61p. 2nd Ed., London: Longmans, Green, 1867. 398p.

554 . _____. "Communications Respecting the Geography of Southern Abyssinia," *JRGS*, XII(1842), 84-102.

555 . _____. *An Enquiry into M. Antoine d'Abbadie's Journey to Kaffa, in the Years 1843 and 1844, to Discover the Source of the Nile.* London: Madden, 1850. 56p.

556 . _____. *The French and English in the Red Sea.* London: Taylor and Francis, 1862. 29p.

557 . _____. *Letters on the Commerce of Abessinia and Other Parts of Eastern Africa.* London: Thompson & Davidson, 1852. 51p.

558 . _____. "Map of the Route from Tajurrah to Ankobar. Letter from Dr. Beke," *JRGS*, XIII(1843), 182-183.

559 . _____. *On the Geographical Distribution of the Languages of Abyssinia and the Neighbouring Countries.* Edinburgh: Neill, 1849. 15p.

560 . _____. "Route from Ankóber to Dima," *JRGS*, XII(1842), 245-260.

561 . Bel, Louis. [*Mgr., Vicaire Apostolique d'Abyssinie*]. "Abyssinia," *APFL*, XL(1868), 73-79.

562 . _____. "Lettre à M. Etienne, Supérieur Général, Massouah, 6.I.1867," *ACM*, XXXII(1867), 547-577.

563 . _____. "Lettre à MM. les Étudiants et Séminaristes C.M., Massoua, 23.IV. 1866," *ACM*, XXXI(1866), 591-626.

564 . _____. "Lettre à Soeur N., à Paris, Massouah, 28.II.1867," *ACM*, XXXII (1867), 577-580.

565 . _____ . "Lettre au cher Frère Génin, à Paris, Hébo, 16.VIII.1867," *ACM*, XXXIII(1868), 148-150.

566 . _____ . "Lettre au cher Frère Génin, à Paris, Hébo, 11.IX.1867," *ACM*, XXXIII(1868), 171-216.

567 . Beltrame, Giovanni. *Avanti e dopo il disastro di Amba Alagi. Memoria.* Verona: Atti Accademia, 1896. 32p.

568 . _____ . *Il mio sogno sui futuri destini della Colonia Italiana Eritrea.* Venice: Atti R. Ist, 1895. 32p.

569 . Bent, James Theodore. "The Ancient Trade Route Across Ethiopia," *GJ*, II(1893), 140-146.

570 . _____ . *The Sacred City of the Ethiopians.* London: Longmans, 1893. 309p.

571 . Berghaus. "Die italienische Kolonie Eritrea," *DK*, X(1893), 142-143.

572 . Bettembourg, Nicholas. "Rapport sur les Missions," *ACM*, LIX(1894), 546-

573 . Biancheri, Lorenzo. [*Mgr.*]. "Lettre a la Soeur N., Massawah, 25.I.1860," *ACM*, XXVI(1861), 104-117.

574 . _____ . "Lettre à la Soeur N., Pays des Bogos, Karen, 5.VII.1860," *ACM*, XXVI(1861), 104-117.

575 . _____ . "Lettre à M. Delaye, Massaouah, 9.V.1854," *RHM*, XVI(1938), 597.

576 . _____ . "Lettre à M. Etienne, Supérieur-Général, Emqulo, 22.V.1854," *ACM*, XX(1855), 515-522.

577 . _____ . "Lettre à M. Poussou, Massaouah, 2.X.1854," *ACM*, XX(1855), 558-565.

578 . _____ . "Lettre à M. Poussou, Massaouah, 2.III.1855," *ACM*, XX(1855), 573-576.

579 . _____ . "Lettre à M. Sturchi, Emqulo, 6.I.1854," *ACM*, XX(1855), 495-514.

580 . _____ . "Lettre à M. Sturchi, Massaouah, 16.VI.1855," *ACM*, XX(1855), 577-582.

581 . _____ . "Lettre à M. Sturchi, Karen, pays des Bogos, 18.XI.1859," *ACM*, XXV(1860), 14-26.

582 . _____. "Lettre à M. Sturchi, Emkoullo, 26.III.1860," *ACM*, XXVI(1861), 93-96.

583 . Bianchi, Gustavo. *Alla terra dei Galla. Narrazione della spedizione Bianchi in Africa nel 1879-80.* Milan: Treves, 1884. 543p.

584 . _____. *L'ultima spedizione affricana di Gustavo Bianchi. Diari, relazioni, lettere e documenti.* Edited by Carlo Zaghi. 2 vols. Milan, 1930.

585 . Bigel, Chrysostome. "Lettres," *L'Echo de St.Francois*, II(1895), 15-17.

586
587 . _____. "Lettres," *MCL*, XXVI(1894), 559.

. Blanc, Henri Jules. "From Metemma to Damot, along the Western Shores of the Tana Sea," *JRGS*, XXXIX(1869), 36-50.

588 . _____. *Ma captivité en Abyssinie, avec des details sur l'empereur Théodoros, sa vie, ses moeurs, son peuple, son pays.* Paris: Société des Traites Religeux, 1869. 444p. English translation, *A Narrative of Captivity in Abyssinia, with Some Account of the Late Emperor Theodore, His Country and People.* London: Smith, Elder, 1868. 409p. Italian translation, *I prigionieri di Teodoro e la campagna d'Abissinia.* Milan: Treves, c.1870.

589 . _____. *Notes médicales recueillies durant une mission diplomatique en Abyssinie.* Paris: Masson, 1874. 60p. Extracted from *Gazette Hebd. de Médécine et de Chirurgie*, 1874.

590 . _____. *Story of the Captives. A Narrative of the Events of Mr. Rassam's Mission to Abyssinia. . .To Which Is Subjoined a Translation of M. Le Jean's Articles on Abyssinia and Its Monarch, from the Revue des Deux Mondes.* London: Longmans, 1868. 148p.

591 . Blundell, Herbert Weld. "Exploration in the Abai Basin, Abyssinia," *GJ*, XXVII(1906), 529-551.

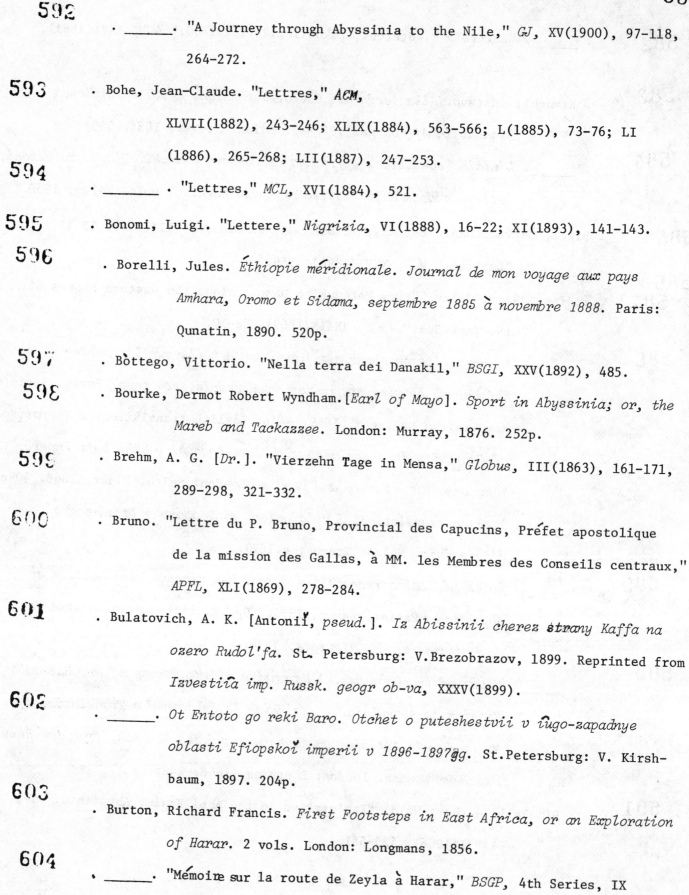

592   . _____. "A Journey through Abyssinia to the Nile," *GJ*, XV(1900), 97-118, 264-272.

593   . Bohe, Jean-Claude. "Lettres," *ACM*, XLVII(1882), 243-246; XLIX(1884), 563-566; L(1885), 73-76; LI (1886), 265-268; LII(1887), 247-253.

594   . _____ . "Lettres," *MCL*, XVI(1884), 521.

595   . Bonomi, Luigi. "Lettere," *Nigrizia*, VI(1888), 16-22; XI(1893), 141-143.

596   . Borelli, Jules. *Éthiopie méridionale. Journal de mon voyage aux pays Amhara, Oromo et Sidama, septembre 1885 à novembre 1888.* Paris: Qunatin, 1890. 520p.

597   . Bottego, Vittorio. "Nella terra dei Danakil," *BSGI*, XXV(1892), 485.

598   . Bourke, Dermot Robert Wyndham.[*Earl of Mayo*]. *Sport in Abyssinia; or, the Mareb and Tackazzee.* London: Murray, 1876. 252p.

599   . Brehm, A. G. [*Dr.*]. "Vierzehn Tage in Mensa," *Globus*, III(1863), 161-171, 289-298, 321-332.

600   . Bruno. "Lettre du P. Bruno, Provincial des Capucins, Préfet apostolique de la mission des Gallas, à MM. les Membres des Conseils centraux," *APFL*, XLI(1869), 278-284.

601   . Bulatovich, A. K. [*Antonii, pseud.*]. *Iz Abissinii cherez strany Kaffa na ozero Rudol'fa.* St. Petersburg: V.Brezobrazov, 1899. Reprinted from *Izvestiia imp. Russk. geogr ob-va*, XXXV(1899).

602   . _____. *Ot Entoto go reki Baro. Otchet o puteshestvii v iugo-zapadnye oblasti Efiopskoi imperii v 1896-1897gg.* St.Petersburg: V. Kirshbaum, 1897. 204p.

603   . Burton, Richard Francis. *First Footsteps in East Africa, or an Exploration of Harar.* 2 vols. London: Longmans, 1856.

604   . _____. "Mémoire sur la route de Zeyla à Harar," *BSGP*, 4th Series, IX (1855), 337-362.

605 . _____ . "Narrative of a Trip to Harrar," *JRGS*, XXV(1855), 136-150.

606 . Cabrouiller, Vincent. "Lettre de M. Cabrouiller à M. Pérmartin, Kéren, 20.III.1875," *ACM*, XL(1875), 417-422.

607 . Cabroulier, Vincent. "Lettere," *MCM*, X(1881), 355, 356.

608 . _____ . "Lettres," *ACM*, XLVI(1881), 579-586, 653-657; L(1885), 77, 78, 80, 81.

609 . _____ . "Lettres," *MCL*, XIII(1881), 341-343.

610 . _____ . "Missionsbriefe," *KM*, IX(1881), 194, 195.

611 . Caignard, Pierre. "Lettere," *MCM*, XIV(1885), 152-154.

612 . _____ . "Lettres," *Annales Franciscaines*, XIV(1884-1886), 114-116.

613 . _____ . "Lettres," *MCL*, XIV(1884), 605-608.

614 . Carbone, Michele. "Lettere," *Analecta Ordinis minorum Cappoccinorum*, XI(1895), 44-47; XVII(1901), 279-281.

615 . _____ . "Lettere," *Annali Francescani*, XXVI(1895), 149, 150, 430-432, 499, 500; XXIX(1898), 592-594; XXXI(1900), 186, 187; XXXII(1901), 553; XXXIII(1902), 27, 28, 81-83.

616 . _____ . "Lettere," *Eco di S. Francesco d'Assisi*, XXII(1894), 831; XXIII(1895), 39, 40, 281-283, 501-503; XXV(1897), 331, 332.

617 . _____ . "Lettere," *Missioni Francescane*, VI(1895), 495, 496.

618 . _____ . "Lettere," *MCM*, XXXIX(1910), 54, 55.

619 . _____ . "Missionsbriefe," *Echo aus Afrika*, VIII(1896), 64, 65.

620 . _____ . "Missionsbriefe," *KM*, XXVII(1898-1899), 139.

621. Cecchi, Antonio. *Da Zeila alle frontiere del Caffa.* 3 vols. Rome: Loescher, 1886-1887. German translation, *Fünf Jahre in Ostafrika; Reisen durch die südlichen Grenzländer Abessiniens von Zeila bis Kaffa.* Leipzig: Brockhaus, 1888.

622. _____. "Conferenza sui suoi viaggi in Africa," *Archivo per l'Antropologia e l'Etnologia*[Florence], XIV(1884), 420-431.

623. Cecchi, Antonio. "Missioni cattoliche a Kaffa e paesi Galla," *L'Esploratore,* V(1881), 207.

624. _____. *Relazione intorno alle ultime vicende della spedizione italiana in Africa attraverso i regni di Ghera-Gomma-Gimma-Guma.* Pesaro: Nobili, 1882. 46p.

625. _____. *L'Abissinia settentrionale e le strade che vi conducono da Massaua.* Milan: Treves, 1887. 48p.

626. _____. "Le popolazioni della regione di Assab," *NA*, 2nd Series, IL (1885), 523-532, LIII(1885), 281-293.

627. Chalais, Martial. "Les anciens missionaires Capucins de l'Ethiopie et la science," *Études Franciscaines,* V(1902), 628-642.

628. Chalais, Martial. "Les Galla ou Oromo," *Études Franciscaines,* III(1900), 20-36, 157-172, 403-423, 632-652; IV(1901), 161-184.

629. Chalais, Martial. "Mission des Gallas," *Missions Catholiques Francaises,* II(1900), 45-79.

630 . Clement, Eugene. "Lettres," *ACM*,
XLVII(1882), 250-252.

631 . Coccino, Felicissimo da Cortemiglia. "Lettres," *Annales Franciscaines*
[Paris], III(1865-1867), 213-217.

632 . Combes, Edmond and Tamisier, Maurice. *Voyage en Abyssinie, dans le pays
des Galla, de Choa et d'Ifat ... 1835-1837.* 4 vols. Paris:
Désessart, 1838.

633 . Combes, Paul. *L'Abyssinie en 1896. Le pays, les habitants, la lutte
italo-abyssine.* Paris: Andre, 1896. 179p.

634 . Cook, H. "Notes on the Climate and Geology of Abyssinia, with Table of
Heights," *PRGS*, XIV(1869-1870), 158-167.

635 . Coulbeaux, Edouard. "Au pays de Menelik," *MCL*, XXX(1898), 344-346, 357-
360, 368-372, 380-383, 393-396, 405-408, 417-420, 428-432. 437-441,
454-456, 461-464, 473-477, 487-490, 501-502, 513-515, 524-526,
532-534. See also, *MCM*, XXVIII(1899), 249-252, 261-264, 286-288,
298-300, 310-312, 318-324, 344-347, 354-357, 367-372, 381-384,
390-395.

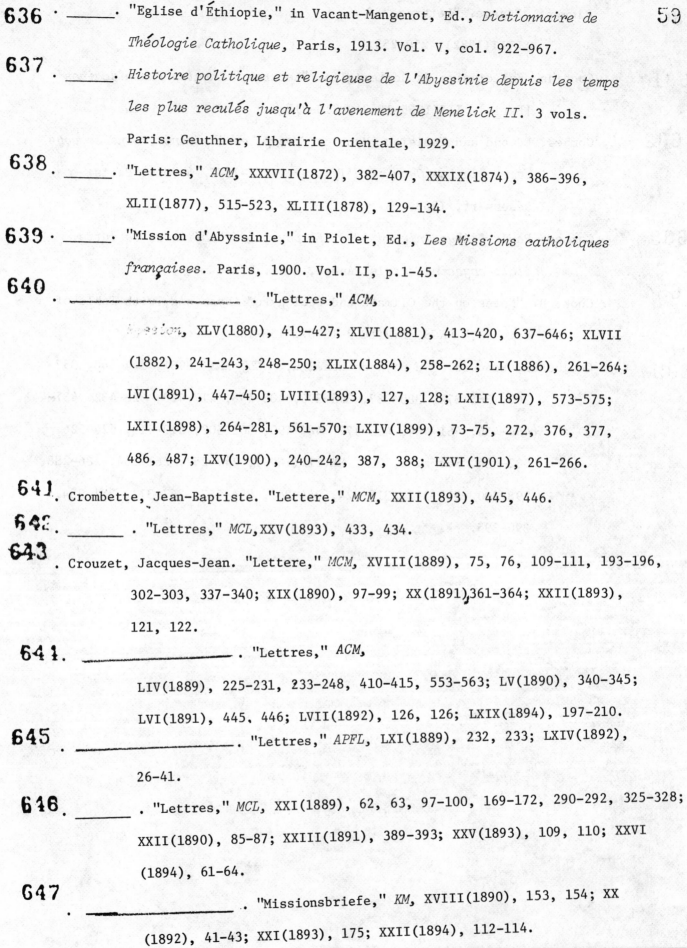

636 · ——. "Eglise d'Éthiopie," in Vacant-Mangenot, Ed., *Dictionnaire de Théologie Catholique*, Paris, 1913. Vol. V, col. 922-967.

637 . ——. *Histoire politique et religieuse de l'Abyssinie depuis les temps les plus reculés jusqu'à l'avenement de Menelick II.* 3 vols. Paris: Geuthner, Librairie Orientale, 1929.

638 . ——. "Lettres," *ACM*, XXXVII(1872), 382-407, XXXIX(1874), 386-396, XLII(1877), 515-523, XLIII(1878), 129-134.

639 · ——. "Mission d'Abyssinie," in Piolet, Ed., *Les Missions catholiques françaises.* Paris, 1900. Vol. II, p.1-45.

640 . ———————— . "Lettres," *ACM*, ......, XLV(1880), 419-427; XLVI(1881), 413-420, 637-646; XLVII (1882), 241-243, 248-250; XLIX(1884), 258-262; LI(1886), 261-264; LVI(1891), 447-450; LVIII(1893), 127, 128; LXII(1897), 573-575; LXII(1898), 264-281, 561-570; LXIV(1899), 73-75, 272, 376, 377, 486, 487; LXV(1900), 240-242, 387, 388; LXVI(1901), 261-266.

641 . Crombette, Jean-Baptiste. "Lettere," *MCM*, XXII(1893), 445, 446.

642 . ——. "Lettres," *MCL*, XXV(1893), 433, 434.

643 . Crouzet, Jacques-Jean. "Lettere," *MCM*, XVIII(1889), 75, 76, 109-111, 193-196, 302-303, 337-340; XIX(1890), 97-99; XX(1891), 361-364; XXII(1893), 121, 122.

641 . ———————— . "Lettres," *ACM*, LIV(1889), 225-231, 233-248, 410-415, 553-563; LV(1890), 340-345; LVI(1891), 445, 446; LVII(1892), 126, 126; LXIX(1894), 197-210.

645 . ———————— . "Lettres," *APFL*, LXI(1889), 232, 233; LXIV(1892), 26-41.

646 . ——. "Lettres," *MCL*, XXI(1889), 62, 63, 97-100, 169-172, 290-292, 325-328; XXII(1890), 85-87; XXIII(1891), 389-393; XXV(1893), 109, 110; XXVI (1894), 61-64.

647 . ———————— . "Missionsbriefe," *KM*, XVIII(1890), 153, 154; XX (1892), 41-43; XXI(1893), 175; XXII(1894), 112-114.

648 . _____. "Notes à M. le rapporteur de la Commission roale
d'enquête sur la colonie Erythrée," *ACM*,
LVII(1892), 616-624.

649 . _____. "Rapport adressé à S. Em. le Cardinal Préfet de la
Propagande," *ACM*,                                    LVIII(1893),
271-273.

650 . Da Offeio, Francesco. *Dal l'Eritrea: lettere sui costumi abissini*. Rome:
Tipografia della Vera Roma, 1904. 160p.

651 . _____. *I Cappuccini nella Colonia Eritrea: ricordi*. Rome:
Tipografia della SS. Concezione, 1910. 174p.

652 . De Cosson, Emilus Albert. *The Cradle of the Blue Nile. A Visit to the
Court of King John of Ethiopia*. 2 vols. London: Murray, 1877.

653 . Degoutin, A. "Lettres," *RHM*, XV(1938), 449-454, 601-606, XVI(1938), 288-
297.

654 . Delaye. "Lettres de M. Delaye à M. le Ministre, 1853-1855," *RHM*, XVI(1938),
589-602.

655 . Delmonte. "Lettres," *ACM*, XXVI(1861), 52-92, 97-103, 118-144, XXIX(1864),
147-185, XXX(1865), 61-77, 77-82, XXXI(1866), 576-590, XXXIII
(1868), 468-475, 479-494, XXXIV(1869), 116-120, 256-258.

656 . Delore, Ferdinand d'Hyères. "Lettres," *Annales Franciscaines*[Paris], IV
(1867-1868), 98-101, VII(1870-1871), 14-18, 41-43.

657 . Dimothéos, R. P. *Deux ans de séjour en Abyssinie ou vie religieuse des
Abyssiniens*. 2 vols. Jerusalem: Typographie du Couvent de Saint-
Jacques, 1871.

658 . Dove, Karl. *Kulturzonen von Nord-Abessinien*. Gotha: Petermann's
Mitteilungen, 1890. 34p.

**659** . Du Couret, L. *Les mystéres du desert, souvenirs de voyages en Asie et en Afrique.* 2 vols. Paris, 1859.

**660** . Dufey and Aubert-Roche. "Voyage dans l'Abyssinie," *Revue de l'Orient,* I(1843), 315, 435.

**661** . Duflos, Adéodat. "Lettre," *MCL*, VIII(1876), 93-97.

**662** . _____. "Lettres," *ACM*, XXXV(1870), 377-385, XXXVII(1872), 79-93, XXXIX (1874), 232-245, XL(1875), 601, XLI(1876), 549-552.

663 . Dufton, Henry. *Narrative of a Journey through Abyssinia in 1862-3. With an Appendix on "The Abyssinian Captives Question."* London: Chapman & Hall, 1867. 337p.

664 . Duno, Pasquale da. "Lettre à M. Fleury Bérard, banquier des Affaires Etrangères à Paris, Aden, 7.V.1853," *RHM*, XVI(1938), 589.

665 . _____. "Lettre au Consul Général A. Le Moyne au Cairo, Massouah, 11.IX. 1850," *RHM*, XVI(1938), 438-440.

666 . Dye, William M. *Moslem Egypt and Christian Abyssinia; or, Military Service under the Khedive, in His Provinces and Beyond Their Borders, as Experienced by the American Staff.* New York: Atkin and Prout, 1880. 500p.

667 . Englund, P. *Ett litet prof på Kunama-Språket.* Stockholm, 1873. 71p.

668 . Erlanger, Carlo von. "Bericht über meine Expedition in Nordostafrika in den Jahren 1899-1901," *ZGE*[Berlin], 1904, pp.89-117.

669 . _____. "Über die Reise Carlo Freiherr von Erlanger in den Galla-Ländern," *VGE*, XXVIII(1901), 240-248.

670 . Ernst. [*Herzog von Sachsen-Coburg-Gotha*]. "Von Mensa nach Keren im Lande der Bogos," *Globus*, II(1862), 236-239.

671 . Esteban, Joachim-Marie de Bocequillas. "Lettere," *Analecta Ordinis minorum Cappoccinorum*, VII(1891), 125-127; X(1894), 115, 116; XIV(1898), 108-117; XIX(1903), 66-70.

672 . _____. "Lettere," *Annali Francescani*, XXVIII(1897), 185; "Lettres," *Annales Franciscaines*, XVI(1888-1890), 610, 611; XVII(1890-1892), 883, 884; XVIII(1892-1894), 458.

673 . _____. "Lettres," *MCL*, XXXVII(1905), 614.

674 . Ferret, Pierre Victor Adolphe, and Galinier, Joseph Germain. *Voyage en Abyssinie, dans les provinces du Tigré, du Samen, et de l'Amhara.* 3 vols. and atlas. Paris: Paulin, 1847-1848.

675 . Flad, Johann Martin. *The Falashas (Jews) of Abyssinia.* London: W. Mackintosh, 1869. 75p.

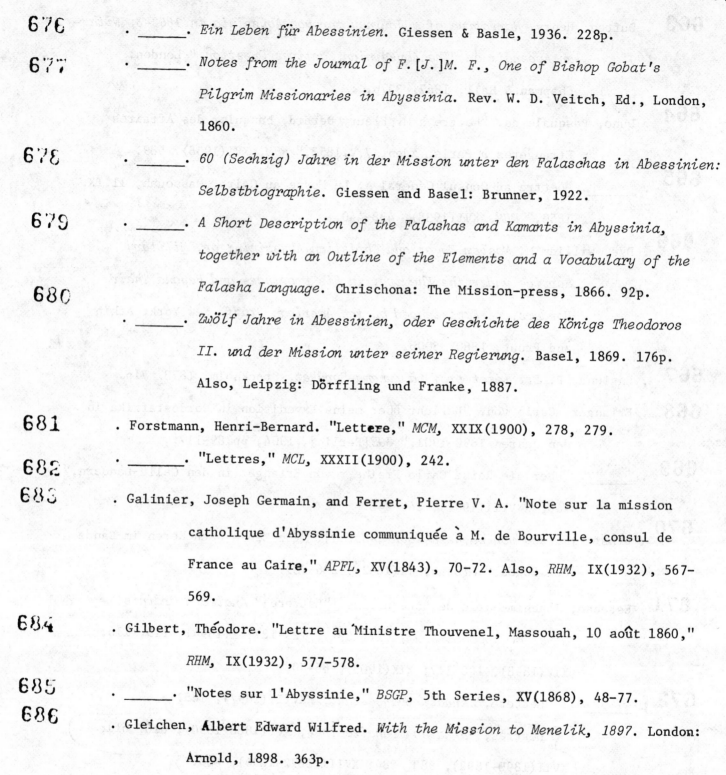

676    . _____. *Ein Leben für Abessinien.* Giessen & Basle, 1936. 228p.

677    . _____. *Notes from the Journal of F. [J.]M. F., One of Bishop Gobat's*
*Pilgrim Missionaries in Abyssinia.* Rev. W. D. Veitch, Ed., London,
1860.

678    . _____. *60 (Sechzig) Jahre in der Mission unter den Falaschas in Abessinien:*
*Selbstbiographie.* Giessen and Basel: Brunner, 1922.

679    . _____. *A Short Description of the Falashas and Kamants in Abyssinia,*
*together with an Outline of the Elements and a Vocabulary of the*

680    *Falasha Language.* Chrischona: The Mission-press, 1866. 92p.

        . _____. *Zwölf Jahre in Abessinien, oder Geschichte des Königs Theodoros*
*II. und der Mission unter seiner Regierung.* Basel, 1869. 176p.
Also, Leipzig: Dörffling und Franke, 1887.

681    . Forstmann, Henri-Bernard. "Lettere," *MCM*, XXIX(1900), 278, 279.

682    . _____. "Lettres," *MCL*, XXXII(1900), 242.

683    . Galinier, Joseph Germain, and Ferret, Pierre V. A. "Note sur la mission
catholique d'Abyssinie communiquée à M. de Bourville, consul de
France au Caire," *APFL*, XV(1843), 70-72. Also, *RHM*, IX(1932), 567-
569.

684    . Gilbert, Théodore. "Lettre au Ministre Thouvenel, Massouah, 10 août 1860,"
*RHM*, IX(1932), 577-578.

685    . _____. "Notes sur l'Abyssinie," *BSGP*, 5th Series, XV(1868), 48-77.

686    . Gleichen, Albert Edward Wilfred. *With the Mission to Menelik, 1897.* London:
Arnold, 1898. 363p.

687 . Glinskiĭ, D. *Kharar i ego obitateli*. Grodna, 1897. 36p.

688 . Gobat, Samuel. "Abyssinie," *JME*, VI(1831), 243-247, VII(1833), 49-54,

IX(1834), 235-254, XII(1837), 287-288.

689 . _____. *Journal of a Three Years' Residence in Abyssinia, in Furtherance*

*of the Objects of the Church Missionary Society*. London: Hatchard,

1834. 371p. New York: Dodd, 1850. 480p. French edition, Paris:

J. J. Risler, 1834. 438p

690 . Gondal, I. L. *Le Christianisme au pays de Menelik*. Paris: B. Bloud, 1901.

62p.

691 . Gouttes, Dominique de Castelnaudary. "Lettere," *Annali Francescani*[Milan],

IX(1878), 462-465, 695-697, XI(1880), 46-47.

692 . _____. "Lettere," *MCM*, VII(1878), 301-302, VIII(1879), 327, 568, IX(1880),

450-451, XIII(1884), 20.

693 . _____. "Lettres," *Annales Franciscaines*[Paris], IX(1874-1876), 298, X

(1876-1878), 695-697, XI(1878-1880), 271-278, 492-496.

694 . _____. "Lettres," *MCL*, I(1868), 6, VII(1875), 274-275, XI(1879), 559,

XII(1880), 426, XVI(1884), 8-9.

695 . _____. "Missionsbriefe," *KM*, VIII(1880), 40-41.

696 . Graham, Douglas Cunninghame. [*Major*]. *Glimpses of Abyssinia, or, Extracts*

*from Letters Written While on a Mission from the Government of*

*India to the King of Abyssinia in the Years 1841, 1842 and 1843*.

London: Longmans, 1867. 78p.

697 . Gruson, Charles. "Lettere," *MCM*, XXVII(1898), 242, 243; XXVIII(1899), 65
113; XXXIII(1904), 217, 218, 339, 340.

698 . _____. "Lettres," *ACM, ...les de la Congregation ... Mission*, LXV(1900),
90-93.

699 . _____. "Lettres," *APFL*, LXXIII(1901), 396-397; LXXIV(1902), 237; LXXV
(1903), 153, 154; LXXVI(1904), 314, 315, 391, 392.

700 . _____. "Lettres," *MCL*, XXX(1898), 229, 230; XXXI(1899), 89; XXXVI(1904),
193, 194, 349, 350.

701 . Gruson, Edouard. "Comment nous sommes retournes en Abyssinia en 1897,"
*Bulletin des Missions de Lazaristes Francais*, VI(1828), 39-45,
125-128, 152-156, 185-188; VII(1929), 23-27, 60-63, 105-110, 144-150,
184-190.

702 . Gruson, Edouard. "Lettere," *MCM*, XXX(1901), 289, 290, 313, 361, 362, 566.

703 . _____. "Lettres," *MCL*, XXXII(1900), 254; XXXIII(1901), 5, 277, 278, 301,
338, 542.

704 . Guiu, Exupère de Prats-de-Mollo. "Lettres," *Annales Franciscaines*[Paris],
II(1863), 69-71.

705 . Halévy, Joseph. "Excursion chez les Falacha, en Abyssinie," *BSGP*, 5th
Series, XVII(1869), 270-294.

706 . Hamilton, Charles Edward. *Oriental Zigzags, or Wanderings in Syria, Moab,
Abyssinia, and Egypt*. London: Chapman and Hall, 1875. 304p.

707 . Harris, William Cornwallis. *The Highlands of Aethiopia, Including an Account
of Eighteen Months' Residence at the Court of Shoa*. 3 vols.
London: Longmans, 1844, New York: Winchester, 1844.

708 . Harrison, James J. "A Journey from Zeila to Lake Rudolf," *GJ*, XVIII(1901),
258-275.

709 . Hartmann, Robert. "Skizzen aus Aethiopien," *Globus*, IV(1863), 202-206,
235-238.

710 . Heuglin, Martin Theodore von. "Die Habab-Länder am Rothen Meer," *PM*, IV(1858), 370-372.

711 . _____. *Reise nach Abessinien, den Gala-Ländern, Ost-Sudán und Chartum in . . .1861 und 1862.* Jena: H. Costenoble, 1868. 462p.

712 . Hildebrandt, Johann Maria. "Ausflug in die Nord-Abessinischen Grenzländer im Sommer 1872," *ZGE*, VIII(1873), 449-470.

713 . _____. "Erlebnisse auf einer Reise von Massaûa in das Gebiet der Afer und nach Aden," *ZGE*, X(1875), 1-38.

714 . Holland, Trevenen James [*Major*], and Hozier, Henry Montagne [*Capt.*]. *Record of the Expedition to Abyssinia, Compiled by Order of the Secretary of State for War.* 2 vols. London: Harrison, 1870.

715 . Hotten, John Camden. (Editor). *Abyssinia and Its People; or, Life in the Land of Prester John.* London: J. C. Hotten, 1867. 384p.

716 . Isenberg, Karl Wilhelm. *Abessinien und die evangelische Mission. Erlebnisse in Aegypten, auf und an dem Rothen Meere, dem Meerbusen von Aden und besonders in Abessinien. Tagebuch meiner dritten Missionsreise von Mai 1842 bis Dezember 1843.* 2 vols. Bonn: Marcus, 1844.

717 . _____.and Krapf, Johann Ludwig. *Journals of the Rev. Messrs. Isenberg and Krapf, Missionaries of the Church Missionary Society, Detailing Their Proceedings in the Kingdom of Shoa and Journeys in Other Parts of Abyssinia, in the Years 1839, 1840, 1841, and 1842.* London: Seeley, Burnside, and Seeley, 1843. 529p.

718 . _____. The Journals of Charles William Isenberg and J. L. Krapf detailing their proceedings in the Kingdom of Shoa and Journeys in other parts of Abyssinia in the years 1839, 1840, 1841 and 1842, to which is prefeixed a geographical memoir of Abyssinia and south-eastern Africa by James M'Queen. London: Frank Cass, 1968.

719 . Issel, Arturo. *Viaggio nel Mar Rosso e tra i Bogos.* Milan, 1872. 4th Ed.,
Milan, 1885. 213p.

720 . Jacobis, Justin de. "Lettera," *BSGI,* LIX(1922), 327-332.

721 . _____. "Lettre," *Bulletin des Missions des Lazaristes Français* [Paris],
IV(1926), 101-105.

722 . _____. "Lettres," *ACM,* IX(1843), 275-283, X(1845), 164-193, XI(1846),
59-71, XII(1847), 286-321, 478-488, 497-558, XVII(1852), 197-222,
XVIII(1853), 405-421, XX(1855), 455-494, 523-557, 586-588, XXIII
(1858), 343-353, 439-451, XXIV(1859), 65-92, XXV(1860), 5-13.

723 . _____. "Lettres," *APFL,* XV(1843), 67-70, XVI(1844), 5-12, XVII(1845), 273-
285, 422-434, XXI(1849), 327-339.

724 . _____. "Lettres," *RHM,* IX(1932), 418-436, 546-566, XV(1938), 450-451,
XVI(1938), 435-436, 584, 602-603.

725 . Jarosseau, André. "L'Apostolat catholique au Kaffa de 1861 à 1912,"
*Revue Histoire Missions,* IX(1932), 94-101.

726 . Jarosseau, André. "Descriptio physica et historica Regni Kaffa," *Analecta
Ordinis minorum Cappoccinorum,* XXII(1906), 5-15, 42-54, 74, 75.

727 . Jarosseau, André. "Deux Prêtres indigènes (Abba Elias, Abba Fessah Giogis),"
*Vois Franciscaines,* VII(1909), 333-336, 376-380.

728 . Jarosseau, André. "L'Ethiopie au Vatican; l'Apostolat du Cardinal Massaia
et de ses successeurs," *Analecta Ordinis minorum Cappoccinorum,*
XLI(1925), 57-63.

729 . Jarosseau, André. "Lettere," *Analecta Ordinis minorum Cappoccinorum,* X
(1894), 77-81; XI(1895), 89; XIX(1903), 298-303, 358; XX(1904), 10, 11.

730 . Jarosseau, André. "Lettere," *Annali Franciscani,* XXXI(1900), 343-344.

731 . Jarosseau, André. "Lettere," *MCM,* XXIX(1900), 241, 242; XXXII(1903),

229-231.

732. Jarosseau, André. "Lettres," *Annales Franciscaines,* XII(1882-1883), 649-653;

XVI(1888-1890), 705-707; XVIII(1892-1894), 459-460; XXIII(1903),

73, 406-409, 548.

733 . Jarosseau, André. "Lettres," *APFL,* LXXIII(1901), 453-467.

734. Jarosseau, André. "Lettres," *Echo de St. Francois,* I(1894), 105-108;

V(1898), 214-217; VII(1900), 363-365; IX(1902), 120, 121, 172-177,

532, 533.

735 . Jarosseau, André. "Lettres," *MCL,* XXXII(1900), 219, 220; XXXV(1903), 217-

219, 615; XXXVII(1905), 158, 159, 373, 374, 435, 436.

736 . Jarosseau, André. "Lettres," *Petit Messanger de St.François,* VIII(1903),

431, 459-461.

737 . Jarosseau, André. "Lettres," *Rosier de St. Francois,* IV(1903), 364-366.

738 . Jarosseau, André. "Lettres," *Voix Franciscaines,* I(1903), 81-83; III

(1905), 501-503.

739 . Jarosseau, André. "Missionsbriefe," *KM,* XXVIII(1899-1900), 278.

740 . Jarosseau, André. "Pie X et le Negus Ménélik: Extrait d'une relation de

Mgr. Jarosseau à Mme la contesse Ledochowska," *Petit Messager de*

*St. Francois,* XII(1907), 167-171. See also *Vois Franciscaines,*

V(1907), 202-218, and *Rosier de St. Francois,* VIII(1907), 138-149.

741 . Jarosseau, André. "Précis historique et chronologique des principaux

événements depuis la fondation de la mission des Gallas (1846)

jusqu'á nos jours," *Analecta Ordinis minorum Cappoccinorum,*

XLIII(1927), 136, 136, 149-156, 164-168, 196-205, 234-240, 288-293;

XLIV(1928), 49-55, 93-104, 259-275.

742. Jessen, B. H. "South-Western Abyssinia," *GJ*, XXV(1905), 158-171.

743. Johnston, Charles. *Travels in Southern Abyssinia, through the Country of Adel, to the Kingdom of Shoa, during the Years 1842-43*. 2 vols. London: Madden, 1844.

744. Jougla, Etienne-Sylvain. "Lettres," *Annales de la Congreg. de la Mission,* LVII(1892), 624-626; LVIII(1893), 274-280.

745. Katte, A. von. *Reise in Abyssinien im Jahre 1836*. Stuttgart and Tübingen: Cotta, 1838. 180p.

746. Kerivel, Jean de Lannion. "Lettere," *Eco di S. Francesco d'Assisi,* XI(1884), 95.

747. _____. "Lettere," *MCM*, XII(1883), 548.

748. _____. "Lettres," *Annales Franciscaines*, XIII(1882-1884), 497.

749. _____. "Lettres," *APFL*, LVI(1884), 60, 61.

750. _____. "Lettres," *MCL*, XV(1883), 531.

751. Kirk, R. "Report on the Route from Tajurra to Ankóbar Travelled by the Mission to Shwá, under Charge of Captain W. C. Harris, Engineers, 1841 (Close of the Dry Season)," *JRGS*, XII(1843), 221-238.

752. Krapf, Johann Ludwig. "Extracts from a Journal, Kept at Ankóbar from 7th June to 2nd October, 1839," *JRGS*, X(1841), 469-488.

753. _____. *An Imperfect Outline of the Elements of the Galla Language. . . Preceded by a Few Remarks Concerning the Nation of the Gallas, and an Evangelical Mission Among Them,* by C. W. Isenberg. London, 1840.

754. Krindach, F. *Russkiĭ kavalerist v Abissinii. Iz Dzhibuti v Kharar*. 2nd Ed. St. Petersburg: "Obshchestv. pol'za", 1898. 105p

755. Lagardelle. "Lettre a MM. les Etudiants de la Maison-Mère, à Paris," *ACM*, XXXVII(1872), 117-120.

756. Lasserre, Louis de Gonzague de Vézéronce. "En pays gallas," *MCL*, XX(1888), 382-384, 392-395, 405-407.

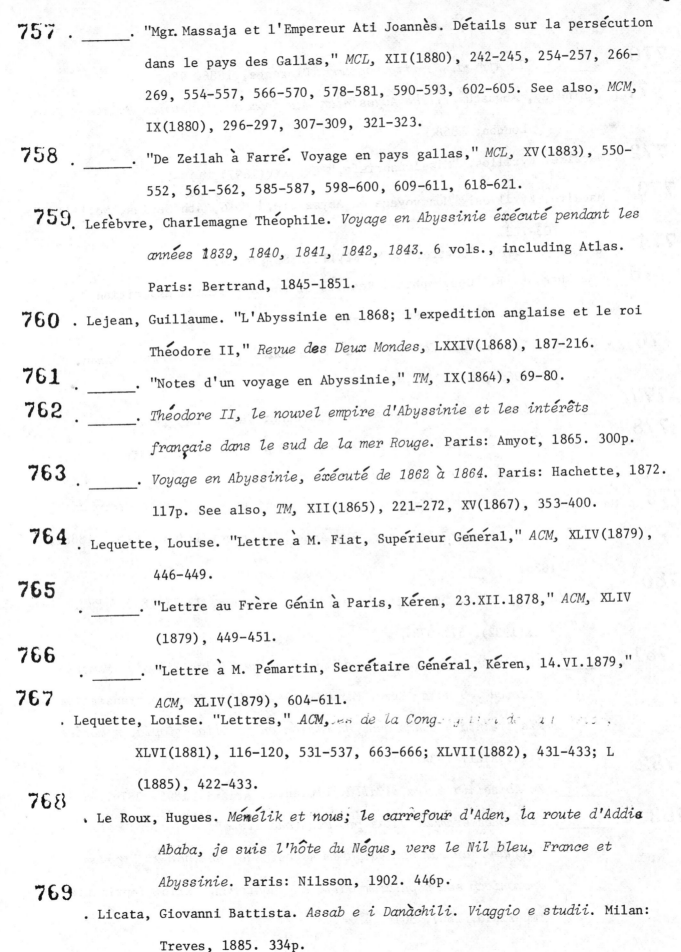

757 . _____. "Mgr. Massaja et l'Empereur Ati Joannès. Détails sur la persécution dans le pays des Gallas," *MCL*, XII(1880), 242-245, 254-257, 266-269, 554-557, 566-570, 578-581, 590-593, 602-605. See also, *MCM*, IX(1880), 296-297, 307-309, 321-323.

758 . _____. "De Zeilah à Farré. Voyage en pays gallas," *MCL*, XV(1883), 550-552, 561-562, 585-587, 598-600, 609-611, 618-621.

759 . Lefèbvre, Charlemagne Théophile. *Voyage en Abyssinie exécuté pendant les années 1839, 1840, 1841, 1842, 1843.* 6 vols., including Atlas. Paris: Bertrand, 1845-1851.

760 . Lejean, Guillaume. "L'Abyssinie en 1868; l'expedition anglaise et le roi Théodore II," *Revue des Deux Mondes*, LXXIV(1868), 187-216.

761 . _____. "Notes d'un voyage en Abyssinie," *TM*, IX(1864), 69-80.

762 . _____. *Théodore II, le nouvel empire d'Abyssinie et les intérêts français dans le sud de la mer Rouge.* Paris: Amyot, 1865. 300p.

763 . _____. *Voyage en Abyssinie, exécuté de 1862 à 1864.* Paris: Hachette, 1872. 117p. See also, *TM*, XII(1865), 221-272, XV(1867), 353-400.

764 . Lequette, Louise. "Lettre à M. Fiat, Supérieur Général," *ACM*, XLIV(1879), 446-449.

765 . _____. "Lettre au Frère Génin à Paris, Kéren, 23.XII.1878," *ACM*, XLIV (1879), 449-451.

766 . _____. "Lettre à M. Pémartin, Secrétaire Général, Kéren, 14.VI.1879," *ACM*, XLIV(1879), 604-611.

767 . Lequette, Louise. "Lettres," *ACM,*es de la Cong. . . . . . XLVI(1881), 116-120, 531-537, 663-666; XLVII(1882), 431-433; L (1885), 422-433.

768 . Le Roux, Hugues. *Méménik et nous; le carrefour d'Aden, la route d'Addia Ababa, je suis l'hôte du Négus, vers le Nil bleu, France et Abyssinie.* Paris: Nilsson, 1902. 446p.

769 . Licata, Giovanni Battista. *Assab e i Danàchili. Viaggio e studii.* Milan: Treves, 1885. 334p.

770 . _____. *In Africa. Scritto postumo.* Florence, 1886. 98p.

771 . Lindley, Augustus F. *The Abyssinian War from an Abyssinian Point of View.* London; 1868.

772 . Macaire, Kyrillos. "Missionsbriefe," *KM*, XXV(1897), 112-114.

773 . Macaire, Kyrillos. "Mon voyage en Abyssinie," *BSKG*, 4th Series, No.11(1897), 703-722.

774 . Marie. [*Sister*]. "Lettre," *ACM*, XLVIII(1883), 87-97.

775 . Markham, C. R. "Geographical Results of the Abyssinian Expedition," *JRGS*, XXXVIII(1868), 12-49.

776 . Martini, Ferdinando. *Cose affricane. Da Saati ad Abba Carima.* Milan, 1896. 344p.

777 . _____. *Il diario eritreo.* 4 vols. Florence; Vallecchi, 1947.

778 . _____. *Nell 'Africa italiana: impressioni e ricordi.* 3rd Edition. Milan: Treves, 1891. 291p.

779 . Martinis, Raffael de. "L'Impero abissino: cenni storici," *Biblioteca di San Francesco Sales*, ser. IV, Anno XIX, fasc. I(Jan,, Feb., 1888), 182p.

780 . Massaia, Guglielmo. "Extrait d'une lettre, Massowa, 23.II.1849," *RHM*, IX(1932), 571-572.

781 . _____. *I miei trentacinque anni di missione nell'alta Etiopia. Memorie storiche.* 9 vols. Rome: Manuzio, 1921-1930. Spanish translation, *Mis treinta y cinco años de misión en la Alta Etiopia, memorias.* Vigo: Rial, 1934.

782 . _____. *In Abissinia e fra i Galla.* Florence: Ariani, 1895. 387p.

783 . _____. *Lectiones Grammaticales pro missionariis qui addiscere volunt Linguam Amaricam seu vulgarem Abyssiniae, nec non et Linguam Oromonicam seu popularum Galla nuncupatorum.* Paris: Imprimérie Impériale, 1867. 501p.

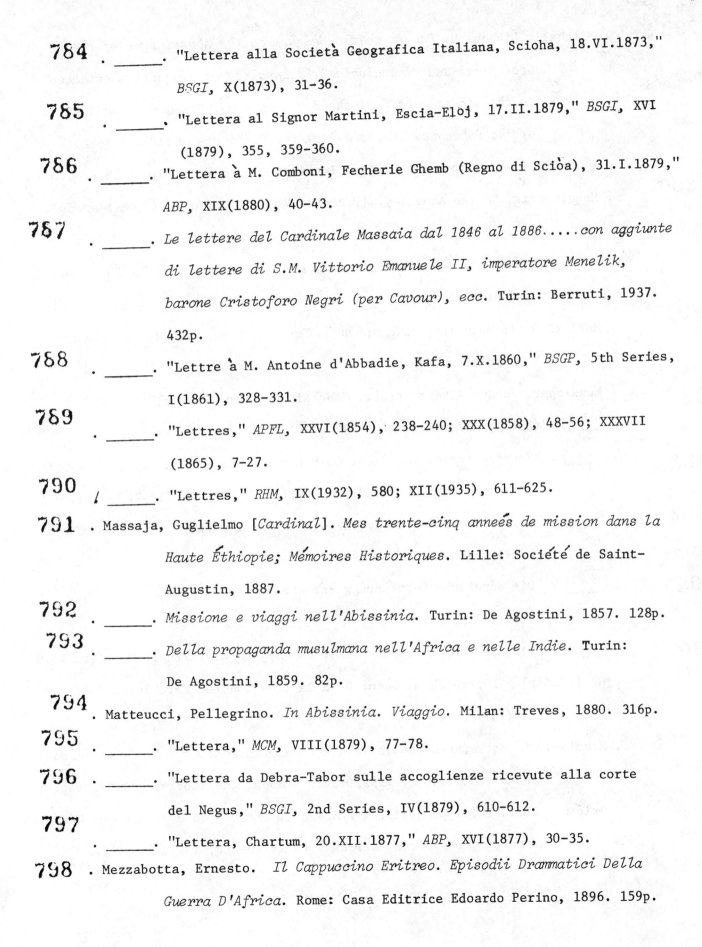

784 . _____ . "Lettera alla Società Geografica Italiana, Scioha, 18.VI.1873," *BSGI*, X(1873), 31-36.

785 . _____ . "Lettera al Signor Martini, Escia-Eloj, 17.II.1879," *BSGI*, XVI (1879), 355, 359-360.

786 . _____ . "Lettera à M. Comboni, Fecherie Ghemb (Regno di Scioa), 31.I.1879," *ABP*, XIX(1880), 40-43.

787 . _____ . *Le lettere del Cardinale Massaia dal 1846 al 1886.....con aggiunte di lettere di S.M. Vittorio Emanuele II, imperatore Menelik, barone Cristoforo Negri (per Cavour), ecc.* Turin: Berruti, 1937. 432p.

788 . _____ . "Lettre à M. Antoine d'Abbadie, Kafa, 7.X.1860," *BSGP*, 5th Series, I(1861), 328-331.

789 . _____ . "Lettres," *APFL*, XXVI(1854), 238-240; XXX(1858), 48-56; XXXVII (1865), 7-27.

790 / _____ . "Lettres," *RHM*, IX(1932), 580; XII(1935), 611-625.

791 . Massaja, Guglielmo [*Cardinal*]. *Mes trente-cinq années de mission dans la Haute Éthiopie; Mémoires Historiques.* Lille: Société de Saint-Augustin, 1887.

792 . _____ . *Missione e viaggi nell'Abissinia.* Turin: De Agostini, 1857. 128p.

793 . _____ . *Della propaganda musulmana nell'Africa e nelle Indie.* Turin: De Agostini, 1859. 82p.

794 . Matteucci, Pellegrino. *In Abissinia. Viaggio.* Milan: Treves, 1880. 316p.

795 . _____ . "Lettera," *MCM*, VIII(1879), 77-78.

796 . _____ . "Lettera da Debra-Tabor sulle accoglienze ricevute alla corte del Negus," *BSGI*, 2nd Series, IV(1879), 610-612.

797 . _____ . "Lettera, Chartum, 20.XII.1877," *ABP*, XVI(1877), 30-35.

798 . Mezzabotta, Ernesto. *Il Cappuccino Eritreo. Episodii Drammatici Della Guerra D'Africa.* Rome: Casa Editrice Edoardo Perino, 1896. 159p.

799
. Mitchell, Libbeus H. *Report on the Seizure by the Abyssinians of the Geological and Mineralogical Reconnaissance Expedition Attached to the General Staff of the Egyptian Army; Containing an Account of the Subsequent Treatment of the Prisoners and Final Release of the Commander.* Cairo: Imprimerie de l'Etat-Major, 1878. 125p.

800
. Mountnorris, George Annesley. [*Viscount Valentia, 2nd Earl Mountnorris*]. *Voyages and Travels to India, Ceylon, the Red Sea, Abyssinia, and Egypt, in the Years 1802, 1803, 1804, 1805, and 1806.* 3 vols. London: Miller, 1809.

801
. Müller, David Heinrich. *Epigraphische Denkmäler aus Abessinien.* Vienna: K. Akademie, 1894.

802
. Munzinger, Johann Albert Werner. "Abessinien. Eine Studie," *PM*, XIII (1867), 397-413.

803
. _____. "Journey Across the Great Salt Desert from Hanfila to the Foot of the Abyssinian Alps," *PRGS*, XIII(1868-1869), 219-223.

804
. _____. "Narrative of a Journey through the Afar Country," *JRGS*, XXXIX (1869), 188-232.

805
. _____. "Die nördliche Fortsetzung der Abessinischen Hochlande," *PM*, XVIII(1872), 201-206.

806
. _____. *Über die Sitten und das Recht der Bogos.* Winterthur: Wurster, 1859.

807
. N. [*Sister*]. "Lettre de ma Soeur N. à la très-honorèe Mère Juhel," *ACM*, XLIV(1879), 280-297.

808
. Nikolaev, L. *Abissinskaia missiia arkhimandrita Paiciia i N. I. Ashinova. Rasskaz uchastnika exspeditsii.* Odessa: Zhelikovskiĭ, 1889. 64p.

809
. Orléans, Henri Philippe Marie. [*Prince d'*]. *Une visite a l'empéreur Ménélick; notes et impressions de route.* Paris: Dentu, 1897. 264p.

810 . Osio, Egidio. [Capt.]. "La spedizione inglese in Abissinia:giornale di viaggio," *BSGI*, II(1869), 37-91.

811 . Paillard, Julien. "Lettere," *MCM*, XVI(1887), 477-480.

812 . Paillard, Julien. "Lettres," *ACM*, XLVIII(1883), 517-529; LII(1887), 565-573.

813 . _____ . "Lettres," *APFL*, LIX(1887), 58.

814 . _____ . "Lettres," *MCL*, XVIII(1886), 424; XIX(1887), 457-461, 477-480.

815 . _____ . "Lettres," *Oeuvre des Ecoles d'Orient*, No.156(1886), 350, 351.

816 . Paillard, Julien. "Rapport," *ACM*, (1885), 422-433.

817 . Parkyns, Mansfield. *Life in Abyssinia: Being Notes Collected during Three Years' Residence and Travels in That Country.* 2 vols. London: Murray, 1853. New York: Appleton, 1854.

818 . Paulitischke, Philipp. Viktor. "Cardinal Guglielmo Massaja," *Deutsche Rundschau für Geographie und Statistik*, X(1888), 329-331.

819 . Paulitschke, Philipp Viktor. *Dr. D. Kammel von Hardeggers Expedition in Ost-Afrika. Beiträge zur Ethnographie und Anthropologie der Somál, Galla und Harari.* Leipzig: Frohberg, 1886. 105p.

820 . _____ . *Ethnographie Nordost-Afrikas. Die materielle Cultur der Danakil, Galla und Somal.* 2 vols. Berlin: Reimer, 1893-1896.

821 . _____ . *Die geographische Erforschung der Adâl-Länder und Harâr's in Ostafrika. Mit Rücksicht auf die Expedition des Dominik Kamel.* Leipzig: Frohberg, 1884. 109p.

822 . _____ . "Harrâr," *Bulletin de la Société Bretonne de Géographie*, IX (1890), 94-101. Extracted from *Bolletino della Società Africana d'Italia*[Naples], fascicules VII, VIII, IX and X, 1888.

823 . _____ . *Harar: Forschungsreise nach den Somâl- und Galla-Ländern Ost-Afrikas.* Leipzig: Brockhaus, 1888. 557p.

824 . _____ . "Reise nach Harar und in die nördlichen Galla-Länder 1885," *PM*, XXXI(1885), 369-384, 460-474.

825 . Pearce, Nathaniel. *The Life and Adventures of Nathaniel Pearce, Written by Himself, during a Residence in Abyssinia, from the Years 1810 to 1819. Together with Mr. Coffin's Account of His Visit to Gondar.* 2 vols. London: Colburn & Bentley, 1831.

826 . Pellerin, Anastase de Pisotte. "Lettere," *Analecta Ordinis minorum Cappoccinorum,* X(1894), 116; XI(1895), 87, 88.

827 . _____ . "Lettres," *Annales Franciscaines,* XVIII(1892-1894), 459.

828 . Perini, Rufillo. "Gli idiomi parlati nella nostra colonia," *BSGI,* 3rd Series, V(1892), 54-67.

829
830 . _____ . *Di qua dal Marèb, Marèbmellàsc.* Florence, 1905. 463p.

. Petit, Antoine. "Nouveau voyage d'Abyssinie," *Nouvelles Annales des Voyages,* II(1840), 183-220.

831 . Philippe, Jean-Damascène de Pont-de-l'Arche. "D'Aden au camp du roi d'Abyssinie," *MCL,* VII(1875), 480-482, 492-494. See also, *MCM,* V(1876), 21-24, 70-71.

832 . _____ . "Lettere," *MCM,* V(1876), 195-196; VI(1877), 246-247.

833 . _____ . "Lettres," *Annales Franciscaines* [Paris], IX(1874-1876), 414-417, 441-444, 483-487, 510-512, 678-682.

834 . _____ . "Lettres," *MCL,* VIII(1876), 171-172, 465-466.

835 . _____ . "Missionsbriefe aus Afrika," *KM,* V(1877), 38-40.

836 . Picard, Pierre. "Extrait d'une lettre à M. Etienne, Supérieur général C.M. à Paris, Kéren, 8.VII.1870," *APFL,* XLIII(1871), 335-340.

837 . _____ . "Extrait d'une lettre au Frère Génin, à Paris, Kéren, 25.IV.1870," *APFL,* XLIII(1871), 331-335.

838 . _____ . "Lettere," *MCM,* IV(1875), 244-245, 542; VIII(1879), 399; XVII (1888), 76; XX(1891), 242; XXI(1892), 434-435; XXVI(1897), 137; XXVII(1898), 529-530; XXVIII(1899), 328-329; XXIX(1900), 136; XXX(1901), 146-147, 605; XXXI(1902), 206; XXXII(1903), 423.

839. _____. "Lettres," *ACM*, XXXIII(1868), 217-223, 428-435, 463-467, 476-478; XXXV(1870), 349-362, 371-376, 599-604; XXXVI(1871), 118-123; XXXVII(1872), 96-106; XXXVIII(1873), 486-496; XXXIX(1874), 246-251, 397-398; XL(1875), 85-90, 422-425; XLIV(1879), 451-456; XLV (1880), 568-573; L(1885), 72-73; LI(1886), 257-261, 575-577; LII(1887), 245-247; LIV(1889), 551-553; LV(1890), 334-337, 339-340; LVI(1891), 450-455; LVII(1892), 271-273; LIX(1894), 549-551; LXV(1900), 560-562.

840. _____. "Lettres," *APFL*, XLVII(1875), 377-379; LXIII(1891), 384-385; LXIX(1897), 317-318; LXXI(1899), 73-74; LXXV(1903), 71-72.

841. _____. "Lettres," *MCL*, VI(1874), 507-508; VII(1875), 262-263, 533-534; XI(1879), 389-392; XX(1888), 37-38; XXIII(1891), 230; XXIV(1892) 438-439; XXV(1893), 157-158; XXIX(1897), 124; XXX(1898), 494; XXXI(1899), 301-302; XXXII(1900), 112, 279; XXXIII(1901), 124; XXXIV(1902), 100, 447; XXXV(1903), 400.

842. _____. "Missionsbriefe," *KM*, XVI(1888), 87-88; XIX(1891), 178.

843. Plowden, Walter Chichele. *Travels in Abyssinia and the Galla Country, with an Account of a Mission to Ras Ali in 1848.* London: Longmans, 1868. 485p.

844. Poncins, Edmond de. [*Vicomte*]. "Voyage au Choa. Explorations au Somal et chez les Danakils," *BSGP*, 7th Series, XIX(1898), 432-488.

845. Portal, Gerald Herbert. *An Account of the English Mission to King Johannis of Abyssinia in 1887.* Winchester: Privately printed, 1888. 123p.

846. _____. *My Mission to Abyssinia.* London: Arnold, 1892. 261p.

847. Prideaux, William Francis. "An Account of the Mission and Captivity of Mr. Rassam and His Companions," in C. R. Markham, *History of the Abyssinian Expedition.* London and New York: Macmillan, 1869. 484p.

848 . Prost. [*Sister*]. "Lettres," *ACM*, L

(1885), 79, 80, 420-422.

849 . Raffray, Achille. *Afrique orientale: Abyssinie.* Paris: Plon, 1876. 396p.

850 . _____. *Les églises monolithes de la ville de Lalibéla, Abyssinie.*

Paris: A. Morel, 1882. 14p.

851 . Ragazzi, Vincenzo. "Il viaggio del dott. V. Ragazzi da Antoto ad Harar,"
*BSGI*, 2nd Series, I(1881), 57 .

852 . Rassam, Hormuzd. "Extracts from a Letter of Mr. Rassam to Colonel Play-
fair," *PRGS*, X(1865-1866), 295-299.

853 . _____. *Narrative of the British Mission to Theodore, King of Abyssinia;
with Notices of the Countries Traversed from Massowah, through the
Soodân, the Amhâra, and back to Annesley Bay, from Mâgdala.* 2 vols.

London: Murray, 1869.

854 . Reybaud, Marie Roch Louis. *La Polynésie et les îles Marquises, accompagnées
d'un voyage en Abyssinie.* Paris: Guillaumin, 1843. 507p.

855 . Reygasse. [*Sister*]. "Lettres," *ACM*,

LIV(1889), 231-233, 415-420; LIX(1894), 210-212.

856 . Rivalta, Gabriele da. "Lettera al Padre A. Hartmann, Isola di Massawah,
20.VII.1860," *Monumenta Anastasiana* [Lucerne], I(1946), 523-526.

857 . Rivoyre, Barthélémy Louis Denis de. "La baie d'Adulis et ses alentours,"
*BSGP*, 5th Series, XV(1868), 236-267.

858 . _____. *Mer Rouge et Abyssinie.* Paris: Plon, 1880. 308p.

859 . _____. *Obock, Mascate, Bouchire, Bassorah.* Paris: Plon, 1883. 292p.

860 . Robecchi-Bricchetti, Luigi. "Lingue parlate somäli, galla e harari; note
e studi raccolti ed ordinati nell'Harar," *BSGI*, 3rd Series, III
(1890), 257-271, 380-391, 689-708.

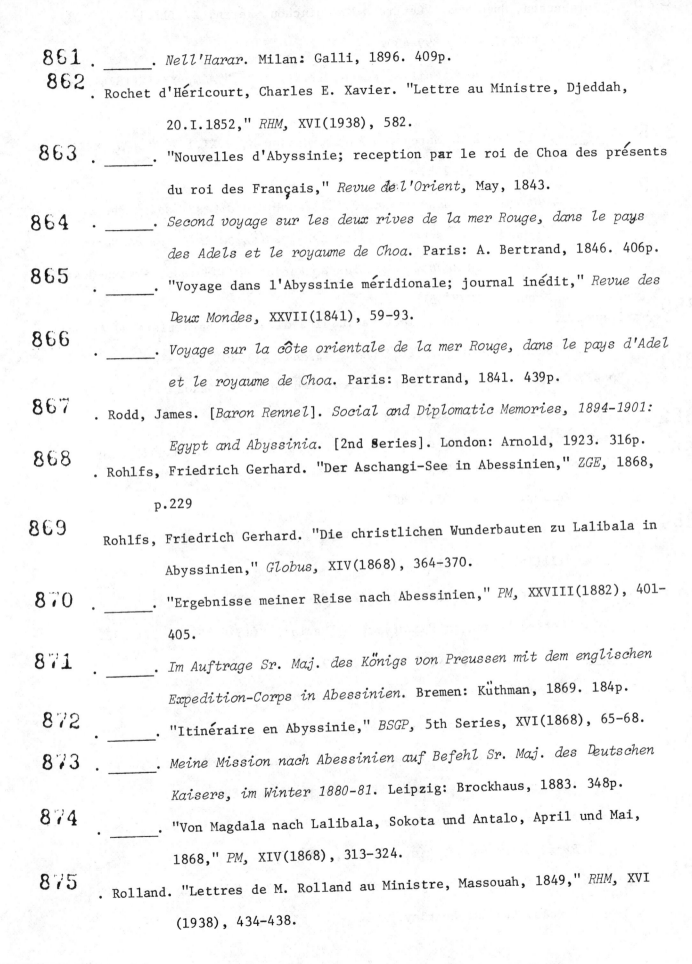

861. _____. *Nell'Harar*. Milan: Galli, 1896. 409p.

862. Rochet d'Héricourt, Charles E. Xavier. "Lettre au Ministre, Djeddah, 20.I.1852," *RHM*, XVI(1938), 582.

863. _____. "Nouvelles d'Abyssinie; reception par le roi de Choa des présents du roi des Français," *Revue de l'Orient*, May, 1843.

864. _____. *Second voyage sur les deux rives de la mer Rouge, dans le pays des Adels et le royaume de Choa*. Paris: A. Bertrand, 1846. 406p.

865. _____. "Voyage dans l'Abyssinie méridionale; journal inédit," *Revue des Deux Mondes*, XXVII(1841), 59-93.

866. _____. *Voyage sur la côte orientale de la mer Rouge, dans le pays d'Adel et le royaume de Choa*. Paris: Bertrand, 1841. 439p.

867. Rodd, James. [*Baron Rennel*]. *Social and Diplomatic Memories, 1894-1901: Egypt and Abyssinia*. [2nd Series]. London: Arnold, 1923. 316p.

868. Rohlfs, Friedrich Gerhard. "Der Aschangi-See in Abessinien," *ZGE*, 1868, p.229

869. Rohlfs, Friedrich Gerhard. "Die christlichen Wunderbauten zu Lalibala in Abyssinien," *Globus*, XIV(1868), 364-370.

870. _____. "Ergebnisse meiner Reise nach Abessinien," *PM*, XXVIII(1882), 401-405.

871. _____. *Im Auftrage Sr. Maj. des Königs von Preussen mit dem englischen Expedition-Corps in Abessinien*. Bremen: Küthman, 1869. 184p.

872. _____. "Itinéraire en Abyssinie," *BSGP*, 5th Series, XVI(1868), 65-68.

873. _____. *Meine Mission nach Abessinien auf Befehl Sr. Maj. des Deutschen Kaisers, im Winter 1880-81*. Leipzig: Brockhaus, 1883. 348p.

874. _____. "Von Magdala nach Lalibala, Sokota und Antalo, April und Mai, 1868," *PM*, XIV(1868), 313-324.

875. Rolland. "Lettres de M. Rolland au Ministre, Massouah, 1849," *RHM*, XVI (1938), 434-438.

876 . Rolshausen, Hugo von. "Lettre à M. Chinchon, Kéren, 27.III.1874," *ACM*, XXXIX(1874), 399-400.

877 . _____. "Lettre à M. Mailly, Kéren, 19.XII.1873," *ACM*, XXXIX(1874), 383-386.

878 . _____. "Lettre à M. Marcus, à Paris, Massouah, 9.XI.1873," *ACM*, XXXIX (1874), 251-255.

879 . _____. *Stimmen aus Abyssinien. Famillienbriefe eines Missionars. Hereausgegeben von einem Priester der Erzdiözese Köln zum Besten der Mission in Abyssinien.* Linz am Rhein: Rhein-Wieder Aktien-Gesellschaft, 1878. 51p.

880 . Rossetti, Carlo. "Quaranta lettere inedite di Oreste Barattiere ad Antonio Cecchi," *Annali dell'Africa Italiana*, 4(1940), 351-375.

881 . Rossi, Giacinto. *La Prefettura Eritrea.* 2nd Edition. Genoa: Tipografia Arcivescovile, 1895. 59p.

882 . Rossi, Giacinto. *Vescovo e tipografo in Africa.* Rome: G. Civelli, 1883. 9p.

883 . Roth, Johann R. *Schilderung der Naturverhältnisse in Süd-Abyssinien.* Munich: Franz, 1851. 30p.

884 . Rousseau, Alexis de Bief-du-Four. "Lettere," *Annali Francescani* [Milan], VIII(1877), 411-413, 539.

885 . _____. "Lettere," *MCM*, VI(1877), 302, 386-387.

886 . _____. "Lettre," *Annales Franciscaines* [Paris], X(1876-1878), 371-376.

887 . _____. "Lettres," *MCL*, IX(1877), 298-299, 372.

888 . Rüppell, Wilhelm Peter Eduard Simon. *Reise in Abyssinien.* 2 vols. Frankfurt am Main: Schmerber, 1838-1840.

889 . Russel, Stanislas. *Une mission en Abyssinie et dans la mer Rouge, 23 octobre 1850 - 7 mai 1860.* Paris: Plon, 1884. 306p.

890 . Salles, A. "Notes sur Massaouah en octobre 1886," *Bulletin de la Société Brettone de Géographie*, V(1886), 282-286.

891 . Salt, Henry. *Life and Correspondence of Henry Salt.* Edited by J. J. Halls, 2 vols. London: Bentley, 1834.

892 . _____. *A Voyage to Abyssinia, and Travels into the Interior of That Country, Executed under the Orders of the British Government, in the Years 1809 and 1810. In Which Are Included an Account of the Portuguese Settlements on the East Coast of Africa, Visited in the Course of the Voyage, and Some Particulars Respecting the Aboriginal African Tribes, Extending from Mozambique to the Borders of Egypt.* London: Rivington, 1814. 506p.

893 . Salvayre, Médard. "Lettre à M. Boré, Massouah, 23.II.1869," *ACM*, XXXIV (1869), 362-367.

894 . _____. "Lettre à M.Chinchon à Paris, Massouah, 7.VI.1868," *ACM*, XXXIV (1869), 106-115.

895 . _____. "Lettre à M. Etienne, Supérieur général, Massouah, 27.III.1869," *ACM*, XXXIV(1869), 356-362.

896 . _____. "Lettre à M. Hurault, Massouah, 28III.1869," *ACM*, XXXIV(1869), 593-598.

897 . Sapeto, Giuseppe. "Ambasciata mandata nel 1869 [i.e., 1859] dal governo francese a Negussié Degimatch del Tigré e del Samièn in Abissinia. (Estratta della mia opera manoscritta: Gli ultimi cento anni della Monarchia Abissinia). *BSGI*, VI(1871), 22-71. Also published as extract, Florence: Regia Tipografia, 1871. 52p.

898 . _____. *Assab e i suoi critici.* Genoa: P. Pellas, 1879. 237p.

899 . Sapeto, Giuseppe. *Etiopia: notizie raccolte dal Prof. Giuseppe Sapeto, ordinate e riassunte dal Comando del Corpo di Stato Maggiore.* Rome: C. Voghera, 1880. 436p.

900 . _____. "Etudes historiques et géographiques sur l'Abyssinie," *Annales des Voyages*, II(1845), 296ff, III(1845), 32ff.

901 . Sapeto, Giuseppe. "Gl'Italiani nell'Abissinia; Eritrea. Stato geografico, politico e sociale del paese," *Giornale della Societa di Letture e Conversazioni Scientifiche*, 2 semestre, 1885, pp. 188, 189.

902 . _____. "Mémoire sur une inscription éthiopienne d'Axoum," *Nouvelles Annales des Voyages*, II(1855), 296-310, III(1855), 32-56.

903 . _____. "Una missione commerciale italiana nel Mar Rosso," *Giro del Mondo*. [Milan], XIII(1870), 221-223.

904 . _____. *Osservazioni sulla spedizione inglese in Abissinia*. Messina: Capra, 1868.

905 . _____. "Reise in den Ländern der Mensa, Bogos und Habab," *PM*, VII(1861), 299-308.

906 . _____. "Statistica generale dell'Abissinia," *L'Exploratore*[Milan], I (1877), 65-73.

907 . _____. "Della storia de' Cussiti. Studi geografici, etnografici, linguistici, mitologici, simbolici, corografici, commerciali e storici. Divisi in due parti, anteriore e posteriore a Cristo, per servire alla storia loro dall'origine ai tempi nostri," *Atti del R. Istituto Tecnico industriale-professionale e di Marina mercantile della Provincia di Genova*, II(1868-1869), 27-156.

908 . _____. *Viaggio e missione cattolica fra i Mensa, i Bogos e gli Habab, con un cenno geografico e storico dell'Abissinia*. Rome: Propaganda Fide, 1857. 528p.

909 . _____. *Viaggi ed esplorazioni: viaggio ai Mensa, ai Bogos e gli Habab*. Rome: Istituto per gli Studi di Politica Internazionale, 1941. 258p.

910 . Schimper, Wilhelm. [*Dr.*]. *Berichte aus und über Abessinien*. Vienna: Braumüller, 1852. 15p.

911 . _____. "Geognostische Skizze der Umgegend von Axum und Adoa in Tigre," *ZGE*, IV(1869), 347-352.

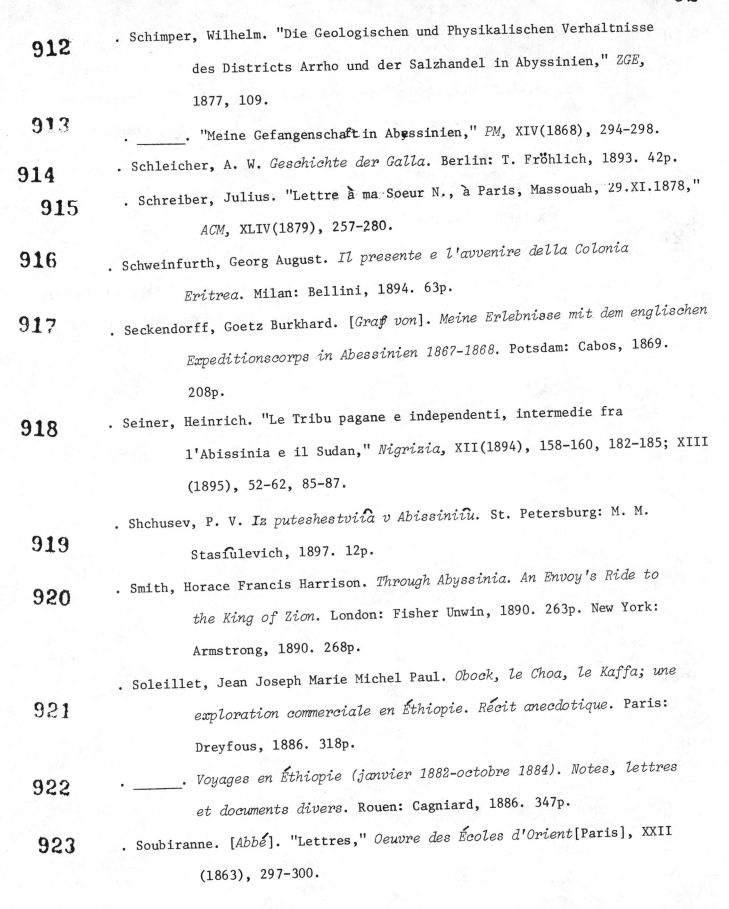

912. Schimper, Wilhelm. "Die Geologischen und Physikalischen Verhältnisse des Districts Arrho und der Salzhandel in Abyssinien," *ZGE*, 1877, 109.

913. _____. "Meine Gefangenschaft in Abessinien," *PM*, XIV(1868), 294-298.

914. Schleicher, A. W. *Geschichte der Galla*. Berlin: T. Fröhlich, 1893. 42p.

915. Schreiber, Julius. "Lettre à ma Soeur N., à Paris, Massouah, 29.XI.1878," *ACM*, XLIV(1879), 257-280.

916. Schweinfurth, Georg August. *Il presente e l'avvenire della Colonia Eritrea*. Milan: Bellini, 1894. 63p.

917. Seckendorff, Goetz Burkhard. [*Graf von*]. *Meine Erlebnisse mit dem englischen Expeditionscorps in Abessinien 1867-1868*. Potsdam: Cabos, 1869. 208p.

918. Seiner, Heinrich. "Le Tribu pagane e independenti, intermedie fra l'Abissinia e il Sudan," *Nigrizia*, XII(1894), 158-160, 182-185; XIII (1895), 52-62, 85-87.

919. Shchusev, P. V. *Iz puteshestviĭa v Abissiniĭu*. St. Petersburg: M. M. Stasĭulevich, 1897. 12p.

920. Smith, Horace Francis Harrison. *Through Abyssinia. An Envoy's Ride to the King of Zion*. London: Fisher Unwin, 1890. 263p. New York: Armstrong, 1890. 268p.

921. Soleillet, Jean Joseph Marie Michel Paul. *Obock, le Choa, le Kaffa; une exploration commerciale en Éthiopie. Récit anecdotique*. Paris: Dreyfous, 1886. 318p.

922. _____. *Voyages en Éthiopie (janvier 1882-octobre 1884). Notes, lettres et documents divers*. Rouen: Cagniard, 1886. 347p.

923. Soubiranne. [*Abbé*]. "Lettres," *Oeuvre des Écoles d'Orient*[Paris], XXII (1863), 297-300.

924 · Staff Officer. "The Egyptian Campaign in Abyssinia, from the Notes of a
Staff Officer," *Blackwood's Edinburgh Magazine*, CXXII(1877), 26-
39. Reprinted in *Littell's Living Age*, 5th Series, XIX(1877),
278-286.

925 · Stecker, Anton. "Dr. Anton Stecker's Aufnahme des Tana-Sees," *Globus*,
XL(1881), 344-347, 360-363.

926 · Stella, Giovanni. *Abissinia. Storia*. Rome: Propaganda Fide, 1850.

927 · _____. "Lettres," *ACM*, XIV(1849), 658-679; XV(1850), 542-547; XVII(1852),
226-242; XX(1855), 566-572, 583-585; XXIV(1859), 93-95, 426-429.

928 . _____. "Lettres," *RHM*, XVI(1938), 580-581, 586-587, 591-595.

929 . Stern, Henry Aaron. *The Captive Missionary: Being an Account of the Country and People of Abyssinia. Embracing a Narrative of King Theodore's Life, and His Treatment of Political and Religious Missions.* London and New York: Cassell, 1868. 398p.

930 . _____. "Lettres," *JME*, XLII(1867), 276-279, 299-303; XLIII(1868), 214-219.

931 . _____. *Wanderings among the Falasha in Abyssinia; Together with a Description of the Country and Its Various Inhabitants.* London: Wertheim, Mackintosh & Hunt, 1862. 330p.

932 . Taurin de Heubécourt Cahagne. "Autour d'Harar," *MCL*, XIV(1882), 245-246, 261-263, 270-271. See also, *Mitteilungen der Gesellschaft für Thuringen*, I(1882), 79-86.

933 . _____. "Extrait d'une correspondance à M. d'Abbadie," *CRSG*, III(1884), 171-174.

934 . _____. "Extrait des lettres à M. Antoine d'Abbadie, Lice, 12 septembre 1868," *BSGP*, 5th Series, XIX(1870), 381-382.

935 . _____. "L'Harar negli ultimi secoli," *BSGI*, XX(1883), 520-523.

936 . _____. "Lettera al P. Guido da Busseto O. Cap, Gondar, 28 Maggio 1848," in Felice da Mareto, *Missionari Cappuccini della Provincia Parmense.* Modena, 1942. pp. 87-92.

937 . _____. "Lettere," *Annali Francescani* [Milan], I(1870), 39; VIII(1877), 73-74; XI(1880), 360-362; XIII(1882), 465-466.

938 . _____. "Lettere," *MCM*, I(1872), 412-413; III(1874), 25-27; IX(1880), 50-51, 263, 385-386; X(1881), 3, 138, 229-230, 606-608; XI(1882), 89-90, 114-116, 304-305, 555; XII(1883), 313-314, 344; XIII(1884), 242-243; XIV(1885), 41-42, 112-113, 389-390; XV(1886), 150; XVI(1887), 61-63; XVII(1888), 103-104, 137, 198, 221; XIX(1890), 73, 218-219; XXI(1892), 217-218; XXIII(1894), 210.

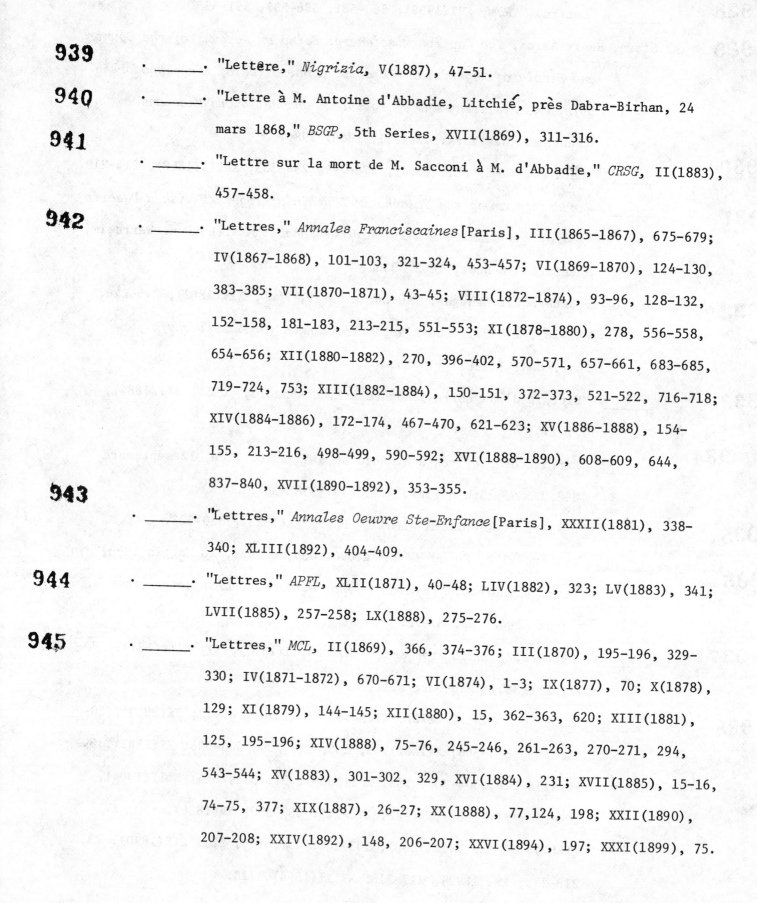

939   · _____ . "Lettère," *Nigrizia*, V(1887), 47-51.

940   · _____ . "Lettre à M. Antoine d'Abbadie, Litchié, près Dabra-Birhan, 24
941   mars 1868," *BSGP*, 5th Series, XVII(1869), 311-316.

· _____ . "Lettre sur la mort de M. Sacconi à M. d'Abbadie," *CRSG*, II(1883),
457-458.

942   · _____ . "Lettres," *Annales Franciscaines*[Paris], III(1865-1867), 675-679;
IV(1867-1868), 101-103, 321-324, 453-457; VI(1869-1870), 124-130,
383-385; VII(1870-1871), 43-45; VIII(1872-1874), 93-96, 128-132,
152-158, 181-183, 213-215, 551-553; XI(1878-1880), 278, 556-558,
654-656; XII(1880-1882), 270, 396-402, 570-571, 657-661, 683-685,
719-724, 753; XIII(1882-1884), 150-151, 372-373, 521-522, 716-718;
XIV(1884-1886), 172-174, 467-470, 621-623; XV(1886-1888), 154-
155, 213-216, 498-499, 590-592; XVI(1888-1890), 608-609, 644,
837-840, XVII(1890-1892), 353-355.

943   · _____ . "Lettres," *Annales Oeuvre Ste-Enfance*[Paris], XXXII(1881), 338-
340; XLIII(1892), 404-409.

944   · _____ . "Lettres," *APFL*, XLII(1871), 40-48; LIV(1882), 323; LV(1883), 341;
LVII(1885), 257-258; LX(1888), 275-276.

945   · _____ . "Lettres," *MCL*, II(1869), 366, 374-376; III(1870), 195-196, 329-
330; IV(1871-1872), 670-671; VI(1874), 1-3; IX(1877), 70; X(1878),
129; XI(1879), 144-145; XII(1880), 15, 362-363, 620; XIII(1881),
125, 195-196; XIV(1888), 75-76, 245-246, 261-263, 270-271, 294,
543-544; XV(1883), 301-302, 329, XVI(1884), 231; XVII(1885), 15-16,
74-75, 377; XIX(1887), 26-27; XX(1888), 77,124, 198; XXII(1890),
207-208; XXIV(1892), 148, 206-207; XXVI(1894), 197; XXXI(1899), 75.

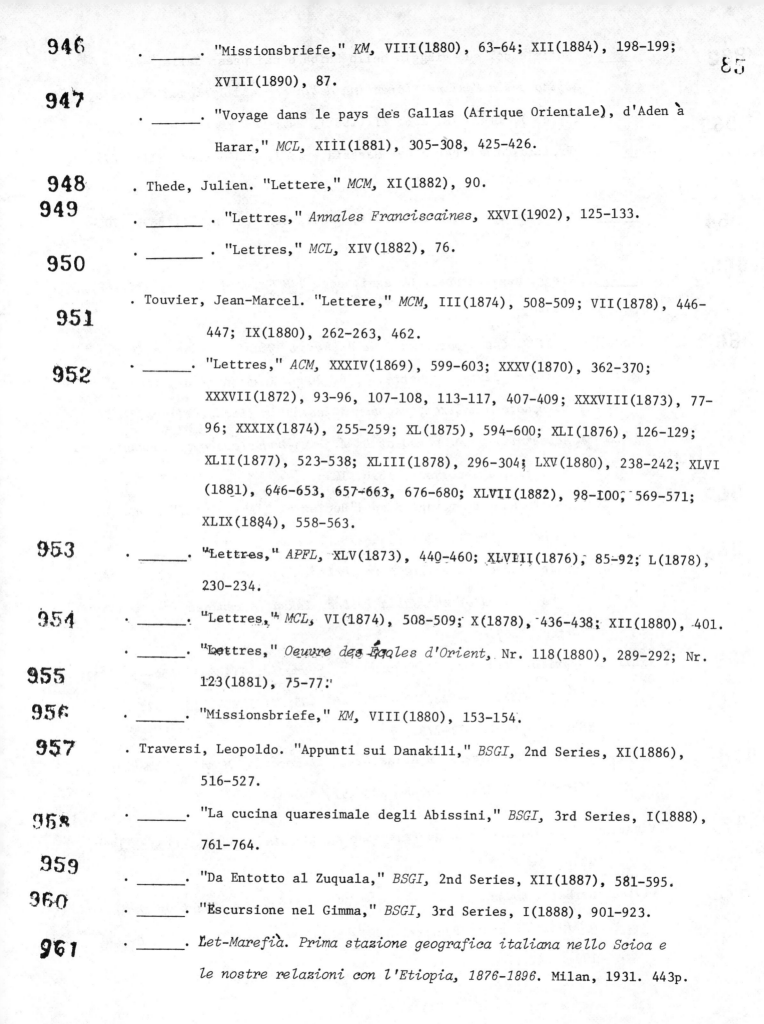

946 . _____. "Missionsbriefe," *KM*, VIII(1880), 63-64; XII(1884), 198-199; XVIII(1890), 87.

947 . _____. "Voyage dans le pays des Gallas (Afrique Orientale), d'Aden à Harar," *MCL*, XIII(1881), 305-308, 425-426.

948 . Thede, Julien. "Lettere," *MCM*, XI(1882), 90.

949 . _____. "Lettres," *Annales Franciscaines*, XXVI(1902), 125-133.

950 . _____. "Lettres," *MCL*, XIV(1882), 76.

951 . Touvier, Jean-Marcel. "Lettere," *MCM*, III(1874), 508-509; VII(1878), 446-447; IX(1880), 262-263, 462.

952 . _____. "Lettres," *ACM*, XXXIV(1869), 599-603; XXXV(1870), 362-370; XXXVII(1872), 93-96, 107-108, 113-117, 407-409; XXXVIII(1873), 77-96; XXXIX(1874), 255-259; XL(1875), 594-600; XLI(1876), 126-129; XLII(1877), 523-538; XLIII(1878), 296-304; LXV(1880), 238-242; XLVI(1881), 646-653, 657-663, 676-680; XLVII(1882), 98-100, 569-571; XLIX(1884), 558-563.

953 . _____. "Lettres," *APFL*, XLV(1873), 440-460; XLVIII(1876), 85-92; L(1878), 230-234.

954 . _____. "Lettres," *MCL*, VI(1874), 508-509; X(1878), 436-438; XII(1880), 401.

955 . _____. "Lettres," *Oeuvre des Écoles d'Orient*, Nr. 118(1880), 289-292; Nr. 123(1881), 75-77.

956 . _____. "Missionsbriefe," *KM*, VIII(1880), 153-154.

957 . Traversi, Leopoldo. "Appunti sui Danakili," *BSGI*, 2nd Series, XI(1886), 516-527.

958 . _____. "La cucina quaresimale degli Abissini," *BSGI*, 3rd Series, I(1888), 761-764.

959 . _____. "Da Entotto al Zuquala," *BSGI*, 2nd Series, XII(1887), 581-595.

960 . _____. "Escursione nel Gimma," *BSGI*, 3rd Series, I(1888), 901-923.

961 . _____. *Let-Marefià. Prima stazione geografica italiana nello Scioa e le nostre relazioni con l'Etiopia, 1876-1896.* Milan, 1931. 443p.

962 _____. "Notizie del suo viaggio nello Scioa e nei paesi Galla," *Bollettino della Sezione Fiorentina della Società Africana d'Italia,*
963    II(1886), 119, 178, 226; III(1887), 24.

_____. "Profilo da Ancober a Let-Marefia," *BSGI,* 2nd Series, XII(1887),
197-199.

964 _____. "Lo Scioa e i paesi limitrofi," *BSGI,* 3rd Series, II(1889), 703-
735.

965 _____. "Viaggi negli Arussi, Guraghi, ecc.," *BSGI,* 2nd Series, XII(1887),
267-290.

966 Vanderheym, J. G. *Une expedition avec le Négous Ménélik. Vingt mois en
Abyssinie.* Paris: Hachette, 1896. 203p. Russian translation,
*V pokhode c Menelikom, negysom Abissinskim (Dvadstat' mesîatsev
v Abissinii) Sokr. pereskaz L. A. Bich-Bogyslavskogo.* Odessa:
Izd. i tip. Iuzhnoryssk, 1896. 127p.

967 Vayssière, A. "Scènes de voyage dans l'Hedjaz el l'Abyssinie," *Revue des
Deux Mondes,* VIII(1850), 146-178.

968 Veitch, Sophie Frances Fane. *Views in Central Abyssinia. With Portraits
of the Natives of the Galla Tribes, Taken in Pen and Ink.* London:
Hotten, 1868.

969 Viallon, Cyprien. "Lettres," *L'Echo de St. François,* I(1894), 154-157, 241-
244, 286-288, 326-328, 376-379, 462-465; II(1895), 150-152, 281-
283; VII(1900), 271-273.

970 Vigna, Amedo. "I Domenicani in Abissinia," *Il Rosario, Memorie Domenicane,*
V(1888), 207-213, 242-248, 293-297, 340-343.

971 Vigneras, Sylvain. *Une mission française en Abyssinie.* Paris: Colin, 1897.
224p.

972 Vivian, Herbert. *Abyssinia. Through the Lion-Land to the Court of the Lion
of Judah.* London: Pearson, 1901. 342p. New York: Longmans, Green,
1901. 342p.

973 . Waldmeier, Theophilus. *The Autobiography of Theophilus Waldmeier, Comprising Ten Years in Abyssinia and Forty-Six Years in Syria.* London: S.W.Partridge, 1886. 339p. London: Friends' Bookshop, 1925. 317p.

974 . _____. *Erlebnisse in Abessinien in den Jahren 1858-1868.* Basel: C.F.Spitter, 1869. 139p.

975 . Wellby, M. S. "King Menelek's Dominions and the Country between Lake Gallop(Rudolf) and the Nile Valley," *GJ*, XVI(1900), 292-304.

976 . Wichmann, H. "Die Galla-Staaten im Süden von Abessinien," *PM*, XXXII(1886), 307-311.

977 . Wilkins, Henry St. Clair. *Reconnoitring in Abyssinia: A Narrative of the Proceedings of the Reconnoitring Party, Prior to the Arrival of the Main Body of the Expeditionary Field Force.* London: Smith, Elder, 1870. 409p.

978 . Wilkinson, J. Gardner. "Account of the Jimma Country," *JRGS*, XXV(1855), 206-214.

979 . Winstanley, William. *A Visit to Abyssinia. An Account of Travel in Modern Ethiopia.* 2 vols. London: Hurst & Blackett, 1881.

980 . Wylde, Augustus Blandy. *Modern Abyssinia.* London: Methuen, 1901. 506p.

981 . You, Basile. "Lettere," *MCM*, XXVII(1898), 597.

982 . _____. "Lettres," *APFL*, LXXI(1899), 153.

983 . _____. "Lettres," *MCL*, XXX(1898), 570.

984 . Zaghi, Carlo. "Italia, Francia, e Inghilterra nel Mar Rosso, dal 1880-1888, in una Memoria inedita di Cesare Nezzarini a Francesco Crispi," *Annali dell'Africa Italiana*, IV(1940), 380-400.

985 . Zichy, W. von. "Die Danakil-Küste," *PM*, XXVI(1880), 133-136.

986  . Ainsworth, John. "A Description of the Ukamba Province, East Africa
         Protectorate, and Its Progress under British Administration,"
         *JMGS*, XVI(1900), 178-196.

987  . _____. "On a Journey from Machako's to Kitwyi," *GJ*, VII(1896), 406-412.

988  . Barton, George A. "Sacrifice among the Walamba," *Journal of American
         Folklore*, XII(1899), 144-145.

989  . Bornhak, Conrad. "Die Rechtlichen Verhältnisse im Witugebiete seit Ab-
         schluss des deutsch-englischen Vertrages," *DK*, X(1893), 148-149.

990  . Broun, W. H. "A Journey to the Lorian Swamp, British East Africa," *GJ*,
         XXVII(1906), 36-51.

991  . Brutzer, Ernst. *Begegnungen mit Wakamba während meines ersten Halbjahres
         in Afrika*. Leipzig: Evangelical-Lutheran Mission, 1902. 33p.

992  . _____. *Der Geisterglaube bei den Kamba*. Leipzig: Evangelical-Lutheran
         Mission, 1903. 16p.

993  . _____. *Was Kambajungen treiben*. Leipzig: Evangelical-Lutheran Mission,
         1904. 16p.

994  . Buckley, R. B. "Colonization and Irrigation in the East African Protec-
         torate," *GJ*, XXI(1903), 349-371.

995  . Campbell, John Douglas Sutherland [*9th Duke of Argyl*]. "The British in
         East Africa," *Nineteenth Century*, Sept., 1891, pp. 341-345.

996  . Crawshay, Richard [*Major*]. "Kikuyu: Notes on the Country, People, Fauna,
         and Flora," *GJ*, XX(1902), 24-49.

997  . Denhardt, Gustav. "Bemerkungen zur Originalkarte des unteren Tana-
         Gebietes," *ZGE*, XIX(1884), 122-160, 194-217.

998  . _____. "Erkundigungen im äquatorialen Ost-Afrika," *PM*, XXVII(1881), 11-
         19, 130-143.

999  . Denhardt, Klemens. "Deutsch-Wituland," *DK*, III(1886), 428-434, 455-456,
         482-491, 516-517.

1000 . Dickson, B. [*Capt., Royal Arty*]. "The Eastern Borderlands of Kikuyu," *GJ*, XXI(1903), 36-39.

1001 . Dundas, F. G., and Gedge, Ernest. "A Recent Exploration up the River Tana to Mount Kenia," *PRGS*, New Series, XIV(1892), 515-530.

1002 . Eliot, Charles Norton Edgcumbe. *The East African Protectorate*. London: Edward Arnold, 1905. 334p. New York: Barnes and Noble, 1966.

1003 . Emery. [*Lt., R.N.*]. "Short Account of Mombasa and the Neighbouring Coast of Africa," *JRGS*, III(1833), 280-283.

1004 . Fischer, G. A. [*M.D.*]. "Die Sprachen im südlichen Gala-Lande," *ZE*, X(1878), 141-144.

1005 . Gibbons, A. St. Hill [*Major*]. "British East African Plateau Land and Its Economic Conditions," *GJ*, XXVII(1906), 242-257.

1006 . Gissing, C. E. "A Journey from Mombasa to Mounts Ndara and Kasigao," *PRGS*, New Series, VI(1884), 551-566.

1007 . Gorges, G. H. "A Journey from Lake Naivasha to the Victoria Nyanza," *GJ*, XVI(1900), 78-89.

1008 . Gregory, John Walter. "Contributions to the Physical Geography of British East Africa," *GJ*, IV(1894), 289-315, 408-424, 505-524.

1009 . _____. "Expedition in East Africa," *GJ*, I(1893), 456-457; II(1893), 326-327.

1010 . _____. "An Expedition to Mount Kenya," *Fortnightly Review*, March, 1894, 327-337.

1011 . Gregory, John Walter. *The Foundation of British East Africa*. London: Horace Marshall & Son, 1901. 271p.

1012 . _____. *The Great Rift Valley. Being the Narrative of a Journey to Mount Kenya and Lake Baringo, with Some Account of the Geology, Natural History, Anthropology, and Future Prospects of British East Africa*. London: Murray, 1896. 422p. New York: Scribners, 1896. 422p.

1013 · _____. "Mountaineering in Central Africa, with an Attempt on Mount Kenya," *Alpine Journal*, XVII(1894), 89-104.

1014 · _____. *The Rift Valleys and Geology of East Africa; an Account of the Origin and History of the Rift Valleys of East Africa and Their Relation to the Contemporary Earth-Movements Which Transformed the Geography of the World; with Some Account of the Prehistoric Stone Implements, Soils, Water Supply, and Mineral Resources of the Kenya Colony.* London: Seeley Service, 1921. 479p.

1015 · Hardwick, A. Arkell. *An Ivory Trader in North Kenia: The Record of an Expedition through Kikuyu to Galla-land in East Equatorial Africa, with an Account of the Rendili and Burkeneji Tribes.* London: Longmans, 1903. 368p.

1016 · Hauttecoeur, Célestin. "Missiensbrieve," *Annalen der Afrikaansche Missiën* [Oudenbosch], VI(1889-1890), 91-92, 166-167.

1017 · _____. "Missionsbriefe aus Afrika," *KM*, XVII(1889), 21-22; XX(1892), 177-178.

1018 · _____. "Lettere," *MCM*, XXI(1892), 313, 339-340.

1019 · _____. "Lettres," *Missions d'Afrique* [Paris], XVIII(1895-1897), 514-515.

1020 · _____. "Lettres," *Missions d'Alger* [Paris], 1879-1882, pp.542-544; 1883-1886, pp.83-84, 213-217, 404-408; 1887-1890, pp.531, 615-616, 628-629.

1021 · _____. "Lettres," *MCL*, XXIV(1892), 307, 334.

1022 · Hildebrandt, J. M. "Ethnographische Notizen über Wakamba und ihre Nachbarn," *ZE*, X(1878), 347-406.

1023 · _____. "Von Mombassa nach Kitui," *ZGE*, XIV(1879), 241-278, 321-350.

1024 · Hindlip, Charles Allsopp. "British East Africa," *Nineteenth Century*, Dec., 1903, 903-907.

1025 . Hobley, Charles William. *Bantu Beliefs and Magic, with Particular Reference to the Kikuyu Tribes of Kenya Colony*. London: Witherby, 1922. 312p.

1026 . _____. "British East Africa. Anthropological Studies in Kavirondo and Nandi," *JAI*, XXXIII(1903), 325-359.

1027 . _____. *Ethnology of A-Kamba and Other East African Tribes*. Cambridge: Archaeological and Ethnological Series, 1910. 172p.

1028 . _____. "Kavirondo," *GJ*, XII(1898), 361-372.

1029 . _____. *Kenya from Chartered Company to Crown Colony. Thirty Years of Exploration and Administration in British East Africa*. London: Witherby, 1929. 256p.

1030 . _____. "Notes on the Geography and People of the Baringo District of the East African Protectorate," *GJ*, XXVIII(1906), 471-481.

1031 . _____. "People, Places and Prospects in British East Africa," *GJ*, IV (1894), 97-123.

1032 . Höhnel, Ludwig von. *Mein Leben zur See auf Forschungsreisen und bei Hofe. . .1857-1909*. Berlin: Reimar Hobbing, 1926. 379p.

1033 . _____. *Ostäquatorial-Afrika zwischen Pangani und dem neuentdeckten Rudolph-See. Ergebnisse der Graf S. Telekischen Expedition 1887-88*. Gotha: J. Perthes, 1890. 44p.

1034 . _____. *Zum Rudolph-See und Stephanie-See. Die Forschungsreise des Grafen S. Teleki in Ost-Äquatorial Afrika, 1887-1888*. Vienna: Holder, 1892. 877p. English translation, *Discovery of Lakes Rudolf and Stefanie; A Narrative of Count Samuel Teleki's Exploring and Hunting Expedition in Eastern Equatorial Africa in 1887 and 1888*. 2 vols. London and New York: Longmans, Green, 1894.

1035 . Hofmann, J. *Geburt, Heirat und Tod bei den Wakamba*. Leipzig: Evangelical-Lutheran Mission, 1901.

1036 · Hollis, Alfred Claud. "Notes on the History and Customs of the People of Taveta," *Journal of the Royal African Society*, I(1901), 98-125.

1037 · Holst, B. "Die Kulturen der Waschambaa," *DK*, X(1893), 23-24.

1038 · Hotchkiss, Willis R. *Then and Now in Kenya Colony. Forty Adventurous Years in East Africa*. London: Oliphants, 1937. 160p. New York: Revell, 1937. 160p.

1039 · Johnstone, H. B. "Notes on the Customs of the Tribes Occupying Mombasa Sub-District, British East Africa," *JAI*, XXXII(1902), 263-272.

1040 · Kolb, George. "Von Mombasa durch Ukambani zum Kenia," *PM*, XLII(1896), 221-231.

1041 · Krapf, Johann Ludwig. "Die frühere Geschichte der Stadt und Insel Mombas(4° südlich von Aequator) in Ostafrika," *Ausland*, XXXI (1858), 849-852.

1042 · _____. "Mount Kenia," *PRGS*, New Series, IV(1882), 747-753.

1043 · Le Roy, Alexandre. "Mombase," *MCL*, XX(1888), 534-536, 547-549, 560-561. Also, *MCM*, XVII(1888), 353-356, 368-369, 380-381.

1044 · Lévesque, Auguste. "Dans l'Afrique Orientale," *Bulletin de la Société de Géographie de Lille*. IV(1885), 306-331.

1045 · _____. "Missionsbriefe," *KM*, XI(1883), 173; XII(1884), 216-219.

1046 · Linton, Andrew. *Agricultural Report on the District between Voi and Kiu in the East African Protectorate*. London: Colonial Office, 1904. 11p. [Cd. 1953].

1047 · MacDonald, James Ronald Leslie. "Uganda Railway Survey," *Journal of the Royal Engineering Institute*, XXIII(1897), 1-85.

1048 . Mackenzie, George Sutherland. *British East Africa: A Paper Read before the Royal Colonial Institute*. London: R.C.I., 1890. 47p. See also, same title, *Proceedings of the Royal Colonial Institute*, XXII (1891), 3-30.

1049 . Mackinder, Halford J. "A Journey to the Summit of Mount Kenya, British East Africa," *GJ*, XV(1900), 453-476, 480-486.

1050 . Neumann, Arthur H. *Elephant-Hunting in East Equatorial Africa; Being an Account of Three Years' Ivory-Hunting under Mount Kenia and among the Ndorobo Savages of the Lorogi Mountains, Including a Trip to the North End of Lake Rudolph*. London: Ward, 1898. 455p.

1051 . New, Charles. [*Reverend*]. "Ascent of Mount Kilima Njaro," *PRGS*, XVI (1871-1872), 167-171.

1052 . Pigott, J. R. W. "Journey to the Upper Tana, 1889," *PRGS*, New Series, XII(1890), 129-134.

1053 . Portman, Lionel. *Station Studies: Being the Jottings of an African Official*. London: Longmans and Co., 1902. 272p.

1054 . Pree, H. de. "Notes of a Journey on the Tana River, July to September, 1899," *GJ*, XVII(1901), 512-516.

1055 . Price, William Salter. *My Third Campaign in East Africa: a Story of Missionary Life in Troubled Times*. London: W. Hunt and Co., 1890. 339p.

1056 . Pringle, J. W. [*Capt., R.E.*]. "With the Railway Survey to Victoria Nyanza," *GJ*, II(1893), 112-139.

1057 · Pringle, M. A. [*Mrs.*]. *A Journey in East Africa towards the Mountains of the Moon*. Edinburgh: W. Blackwood & Sons, 1886. 386p.

1058 · Rabenhorst, Rudolph. "Deutsch-Wituland," *DK*, IV(1887), 237-241; V(1888), 19-20.

1059 · Schmidt, A. R. [*Leutnant*]. "Deutsch-Wituland," *DK*, V(1888), 405-409, 418-421.

1060 · _____. "Deutsch-Witu-Land," *Globus*, LIV(1888), 129-134, 145-147, 173-175, 188-190.

1061 · Sheldon, Mary French. "Customs among the Natives of East Africa, from Teita to Kilimegalia, with Special Reference to Their Women and Children," *JAI*, XXI(1892), 358-390.

1062 · Sheldon, Mary French-. *Sultan to Sultan. Adventures among the Masai and other Tribes of East Africa*. London: Saxon, 1892. 435p.

1063 · Smith, G. E. "Road-Making and Surveying in British East Africa," *GJ*, XIV(1899), 269-289.

1064 · Toeppen, Kurt, "Aus Deutsch Witu-Land," *DK*, VI(1889), 325-328.

1065 · Wakefield, Thomas [*Reverend*]. "Fourth Journey to the Southern Galla Country, in 1877," *PRGS*, New Series, IV(1882), 368-372.

1066 · Würtz, Ferdinand. "Lieder der Wa-Pokomo," *ZAOS*, I(1895), 324-328.

# SOMALIA[1]

1067 . Barker. [*Lt.*]. "On Eastern Africa," *JRGS*, XVIII(1848), 130-136.

1068 . Berghold, Kurt. "Somalia-Studien," *ZAOS*, III(1897), 1-16. See also, *Wiener Zeitschrift fur die Kunde des Morgenlandes*, XIII(1899), 123-198.

1069 . Bottego, Vittorio. *L'esplorazione del Giuba e dei suoi affluenti compiuta dal cap V. Bottego durante gli anni 1891-1893*. Genoa, 1895. 558p.

1070 . _____. *Viaggio di scoperta nel cuore dell'Africa. Il Giuba esplorato*. Rome: Loescher, 1895. 537p.

1071 . Boucher, R. "Lettre sur la colonie d'Obock," *Bulletin de la Société Bretonne de Géographie*, III(1884), 228-231.

1072 . Cox, Percy Zachariah and Abud, Henry Mallaby. *Genealogies of the Somál, Including Those of the Aysa and the Gadabürsi*. London: Eyre and Spottiswoode, 1896. 47p.

1073 . Cruttenden, Charles J. *Memoir on the Western or Edoor Tribes, Inhabiting the Sonali Coast of N.-E. Africa, with the Southern Branches of the Family of Darrood, Resident on the Banks of the Webbe Shebeyli, Commonly Called the River Webbe*. Bombay: Times Press, 1848. Also, Aden: Bombay Geographical Society, 1848. Also, *JRGS*, XIX(1849),
1074 49- 76.

. _____. "On Eastern Africa," *JRGS*, XVIII(1848), 136-139.

. _____. "Report on the Mijjertheyn Tribe of Somalis Inhabiting the District
1075 Forming the North East Point of Africa," *Transactions of the Bombay Royal Geographical Society*, VII(1846),111-126.

1076 . Dundas, F. G. "Expedition up the Jub River through Somali-Land, East Africa," *GJ*, I(1893), 209-222.

[1] Including the French territory of the Afar and Issa.

1077   • Edye, John Simpson. *Sport in India and Somalia Land with Hints to Young Shikaries*. London: Gale and Polden, 1895. 170p.

1078

1078   • Francis, John Cyril. *Three Months' Leave in Somali Land*. London: Porter, 1895. 96p.

1079   • Ghika, Nicolas [*Prince*]. *Cinq mois au pays des Somalis*. Geneva, n.p., 1898. 223p.

1080   • Gouttes, Dominique de Castelnaudary. "Étude sur les Somalis (Afrique orientale)," *MCL*, XII(1880), 443-444, 453-454. See also, *MCM*, IX(1880), 537-539, 550-551. See also, *KM*, IX(1881), 133-139.

1081   • Heinitz, W. "Vorläufige Bemerkungen über die Somali," *ZE*, VII(1875).

1082   • Heuglin, Martin Theodore von. "Reise Längs der Somáli-Küste im Jahre 1857," *PM*, VI(1860), 418-437.

1083   • Hildebrandt, Johann Maria. "Vorläufige Bemerkungen über die Somal," *ZE*, VII(1875), 1-16.

1084   • Hirsch, L. "Einiges von den Somalis," *DK*, VI(1899), 285-287.

1085   • Hoyos, Ernst. [*Graf*]. *Reise- und Jagderlebnisse im Somalilande*. Vienna: Gerold, 1895. 192p.

1086   • James, Frank Linsly. "A Journey through the Somali Country to the Webbe Shebeyli," *PRGS*, New Series, VII(1885), 625-646.

1087   • _____. *The Unknown Horn of Africa. An Exploration from Berbera to the Leopard River*. London: Philip, 1888. 344p. 2nd Ed. London: Philip, 1890. 273p.

1088 . Karr, Heywood Walter Seton-. "Discovery of Evidences of the Palaeolithic Stone Age in Somalia," *JAI*, XXV(1896), 270-275; XXVII(1898), 93-95.

1089 . Keller, Conrad. [*Dr.*]. "Reise Studien in den Somaliländern," *Globus*, LXIX(1896), 181-186, 203-208, 361-367, LXX(1896), 158-162, 170-173, 331-334, 349-352.

1090 . King, James Stewart. [*Captain*]. "Somali As a Written Language," *Indian Antiquary*, XVI(1887), 242-243, 285-287, XVII(1888), 48-50, XVIII (1889), 116-120.

1091 . Kirk, John. "Visit to the Coast of Somali-land," *PRGS*, XVII(1872-1873), 340-342.

1092 . Lallemand, M. "Obock, possession française dans la mer Rouge," *Bulletin de la Société Bretonne de Géographie*, III(1884), 63-72.

1093 . Lambert, Henri. "Voyages de M. Henri Lambert," *TM*, VI(1862), 65-80.

1094 . Lowther, Henry Cecil [*Maj. Gen.*]. "Lion Hunting beyond the Haud," *Nineteenth Century*, Sept., 1895, pp. 474-493.

1095 . M'Hardy, R. A. "Somaliland," *SGM*, XX(1904), 225-234.

1096 . Melliss, Charles John [*Maj. Gen.*]. *Lion-Hunting in Somali-Land, also an Account of Pig-Sticking the African Wart-Hog*. London: Chapman and Hall, 1895. 186p.

1097 . Menges, Josef. "Ausflug in das Somali-Land," *PM*, XXX(1884), 401-410.

1098 . _____. "Streifzüge in dem Küstenlande der Habr Auel," *PM*, XL(1894), 227-234.

1099 . _____. "Von der Somaliküste," *DK*, II(1885), 351-355.

1100 . _____. "Zweite Reise in das Somaliland und Besteigung des Gan-Libach," *PM*, XXXI(1885), 449-457.

1101 . Miles, Samuel Barrett. "On the Somali Country," *PRGS*, XVI(1871-1872), 149-157.

1102 . Nurse, Charles G. "A Journey through Part of Somali-land, between Zeila and Bulhar," *PRGS*, New Series, XIII(1891), 657-663.

1103 . Parc, C. du. "Les dépendances d'Obock," *Bulletin de la Société Bretonne de Géographie*, IV(1885), 563-568.

1104 . Parkinson, F. B. and Brander-Dunbar. [Lt.]. "Two Recent Journeys in Northern Somaliland," *GJ*, XI(1898), 15-48.

1105 . Paulitschke, Philipp Viktor. "Prähistorische Funde aus dem Somaliland," *Mitteilungen der Anthropologische Gesellschaft im Wien*, XXVIII (1898).

1106 . Pearce, Francis Barrow. *Rambles in Lion Land: Three Months' Leave Passed in Somaliland*. London: Chapman & Hall, 1898. 260p.

1107 . Peel, Charles Victor Alexander. *Somaliland: Being an Account of Two Expeditions into the Far Interior*. London: Robinson, 1900. 345p.

1108 . Pluvy. ["*Évangéliste*"]. "Au pays des Somalis," *Bulletin de la Société de Géographie de Lyon*, XIV(1896), 550-552.

1109 . Potocki, Józef. *Notatki myśliwskie z Afyrki. Somali*. Warsaw, 1897. 134p.

1110 . Révoil, Georges. *Faune et flore des pays Çomalis*. Paris: Challamel ainé, 1882. 15p.

1111 . _____. "Journey into the South Somali Country," *PRGS*, New Series, V(1883), 717-719.

1112 . _____. *Voyages au Cap des aromates, Afrique orientale.* Paris: Dentu, 1880. 299p.

1113 . _____. *Voyage aux pays Çomalis, Afrique orientale; la vallée du Darror.* Paris: Challamel, 1882. 388p.

1114 . Robecchi-Bricchetti, Luigi. "L'exploration. . .au pays des Somalis," *Bulletin de la Société Bretonne de Géographie,* X(1891), 7-28.

1115 . _____. *Nel paese degli aromi; diario di una esplorazione da Obbia ad Aula.* Milan: Cogliati, 1903. 633p.

1116 . _____. *Somalia e Benadir. Viaggio di esplorazione nell 'Africa Orientale; prima traversata della Somalia compiuta per incarico della Società Geografica Italiana.* Milan: Carlo Aliprandi, 1899. 726p.

1117 . Smith, Arthur Donaldson. "Expedition in Somaliland," *GJ,* IV(1894), 528-531, V (1895), 124-127.

1118 Smith, Arthur Donaldson. *Through Unknown African Countries: The First Expedition from Somaliland to Lake Lamu.* London and New York: Arnold, 1897. 471p.

1119 . Sorrentino, Giorgio. *Ricordi del Benadir.* Naples: Trani, 1912. 441p.

1120 . Swayne, Harald George Carlos. *Seventeen Trips through Somaliland. A Record of Exploration and Big Game Shooting, 1885 to 1893.* London: Ward, 1895. 386p.

1121 . Teyssier, Eustache. "Lettres," *Petit Messager de S. François*, II(1897), 148-150.

1122 . Vesme, Baudi di. "Exploration au pays Somali," *Bulletin de la Société Bretonne de Géographie*, XI(1892), 281-293.

1123 . Wolverton, Frederick Glyn. *Five Months' Sport in Somali Land*. London: Champman & Hall, 1894. 108p.

1124 . X.Y.Z. "Die Benadirkuste," *DK*, III(1886), 135-144.

1125 . Zaytoun, Fred S. "Cape Juby," *SGM*, XIII(1897), 113-120.

1126 . Abbadie, Antoine T. and Abbadie, Arnauld d'. "Notes sur le haut fleuve Blanc," *BSGP*, 3rd Series, XII(1849), 144-161.

1127 . Abbate, Onofrio. [*Pasha*]. *De l'Afrique centrale, ou voyage de S.A. Mohammed Saïd Pasha dans ses provinces ou Soudan.* Paris: H. Plon, 1858.

1128 . _____. *Le Soudan sous le règne du Khédive Ismail; notes d'une décade historique, 1868-1878.* Cairo, 1905.

1129 . Alfani, A. "La Scuola orfanotrofio di Luqsor," *Religione e Civiltà* (1894), 104-108.

1130 . Alford, Henry Stamford Lewis and Sword, William Dennistoun. *The Egyptian Soudan: Its Loss and Recovery.* London and New York: Macmillan, 1898. 336p.

1131 . Ampère, J. J. *Voyage en Égypte et en Nubie.* Paris: Lévy frères, 1868. 577p.

1132 . An Officer. *Sudan Campaign, 1896-99.* London: Chapman & Ha 1, 1899. 261p.

1133 Antinori, Orazio and Beltrame, Giovanni. "Sulla parola Niam-Niam," *BSGI*, I(1868), 157-165, 298-305.

1134 Antoni, Karl. "Missionsbriefe," *Stern der Neger*, I(1898), 68-71, 133; 134; II(1899), 163-166, 181-186, 189-192.

1135 . Athanasi, Giovanni d'. *Brief Account of the Researches and Discoveries in Upper Egypt Made under the Direction of Henry Salt.* London: John Hearne, 1836. 161p.

1136 . Atteridge, Andrew Hilliard. *Towards Khartoum; the Story of the Soudan War of 1896.* London: Innes, 1897. 357p.

1137 . Austin, H. H. [*Major*]. "Survey of the Sobat Regions," *GJ*, XVII(1901), 495-512.

1138 · Avanchers, Léon des. "Lettere," *ABPV*, (1881), No. 26, 15-19.

1139 · Baker, Samuel White. "Experiences in Savage Warfare," *Royal United Service Institute*, XVII(1873), 904-921.

1140 · _____. "Extracts from a Letter of Samuel W. Baker, Esq., F.R.G.S., to Rear-Admiral the Hon. Henry Murray, Khartum, 24th Nov., 1862," *PRGS*, VII(1862-1863), 78-80.

1141 · _____. "Latest Intelligence from Mr. Baker in a Letter to J. Arrowsmith, Esq., Khartoum, 8th Nov., 1862," *PRGS*, VII(1862-1863), 46-48.

1142 · Banholzer, W. "Missionsfahrten auf dem weissen Nil," *Stern der Neger*, 1902, 227-230, 259-265, 295-301, 329-334.

1143 · _____. "Von Assuan nach Omdurman und zuruck," *JVUN*, II(1899), 10-100. See also, *Stern der Neger*, 1900, 6-13, 60-63, 78-83, 105-113, 147-158.

1144 · Beduschi, Giuseppe. "Lettere," *Nigrizia*, XV(1897), 37-40, 51-54; XVI (1898), 163-167; XVII(1899), 188, 199; XVIII(1900), 7, 8, 71-74, 84-88, 115-121.

1145 · _____. "Gli orrori della Schiavitù," *Nigrizia*, XIX(1901), 9-14, 33-35, 44-46, 63-66, 95-98, 125-129, 140-144.

1146 · Beltrame, Giovanni. "Gli Akka del Miani," *BSGI*, XVI(1879), 65-66.

1147 · _____. "Brevi cenni sui Denca e sulla loro origine," *Rivista Orientale*, VIII(1867), 791-806. See also, same title, Florence, 1867. 32p.

1148 · _____. "Un capitolo dell'opera inedita dell'Al. Prof. Beltrame (1'arrivo à Singe)," *BSGI*, XVI(1879), 65-66.

1149 · _____. "Un capitolo dell'opera inedita (viaggio ai Sciangalla)," *BSGI*, XVI(1879), 151-167. See also, *Cosmos*, V(1878-1879), 404-410.

1150 · _____. "Causa della barbarie da cui fu sempre dominata l'Africa e specialmente la parte centrale—Condizione intellettuale e morale dei Negri..," *AIV*, 5th Series, V(1879), 889-911.

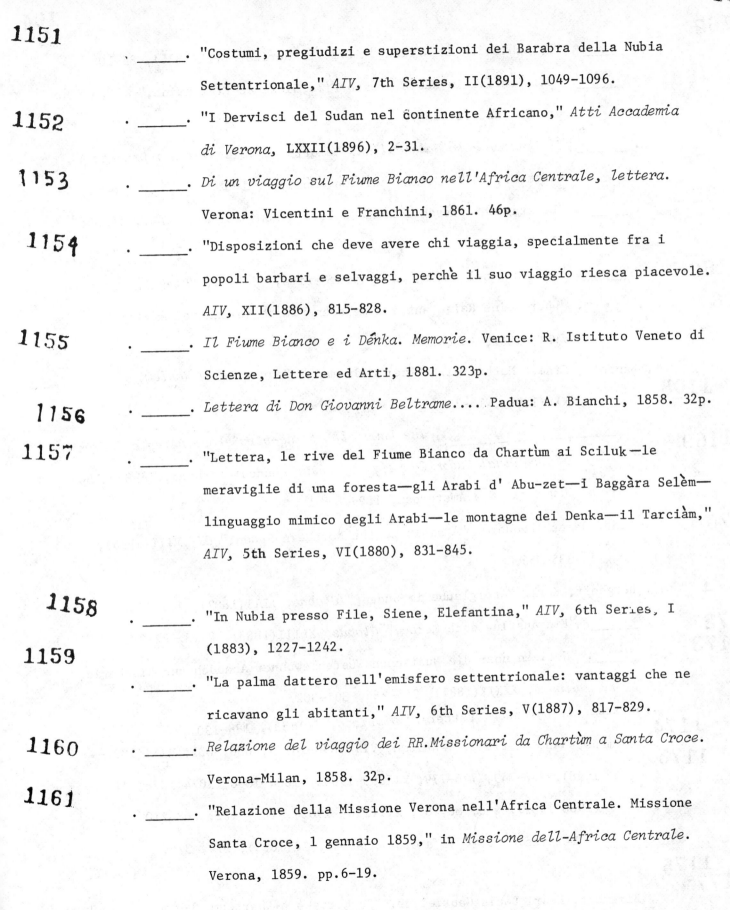

1151   . _____ . "Costumi, pregiudizi e superstizioni dei Barabra della Nubia
Settentrionale," *AIV*, 7th Series, II(1891), 1049-1096.

1152   . _____ . "I Dervisci del Sudan nel continente Africano," *Atti Accademia
di Verona*, LXXII(1896), 2-31.

1153   . _____ . *Di un viaggio sul Fiume Bianco nell'Africa Centrale, lettera.*
Verona: Vicentini e Franchini, 1861. 46p.

1154   . _____ . "Disposizioni che deve avere chi viaggia, specialmente fra i
popoli barbari e selvaggi, perchè il suo viaggio riesca piacevole.
*AIV*, XII(1886), 815-828.

1155   . _____ . *Il Fiume Bianco e i Dénka. Memorie.* Venice: R. Istituto Veneto di
Scienze, Lettere ed Arti, 1881. 323p.

1156   . _____ . *Lettera di Don Giovanni Beltrame....* Padua: A. Bianchi, 1858. 32p.

1157   . _____ . "Lettera, le rive del Fiume Bianco da Chartùm ai Sciluk—le
meraviglie di una foresta—gli Arabi d' Abu-zet—i Baggàra Selèm—
linguaggio mimico degli Arabi—le montagne dei Denka—il Tarciàm,"
*AIV*, 5th Series, VI(1880), 831-845.

1158   . _____ . "In Nubia presso File, Siene, Elefantina," *AIV*, 6th Series, I
(1883), 1227-1242.

1159   . _____ . "La palma dattero nell'emisfero settentrionale: vantaggi che ne
ricavano gli abitanti," *AIV*, 6th Series, V(1887), 817-829.

1160   . _____ . *Relazione del viaggio dei RR.Missionari da Chartùm a Santa Croce.*
Verona-Milan, 1858. 32p.

1161   . _____ . "Relazione della Missione Verona nell'Africa Centrale. Missione
Santa Croce, 1 gennaio 1859," in *Missione dell-Africa Centrale.*
Verona, 1859. pp.6-19.

1163 ._____. "La schiavitù in Africa," *AIV*, 7th Series, VIII(1896), 85-102.

1163 ._____. "Gli Schiavi in Nubia presso File,Siene ed Elefantina," *AIV*, 6th Series, II(1884).

1164 ._____. *Il Sènnaar e lo Sciangàllah. Memorie.* 2 vols. Verona: Drucker & Tedeschi, 1879. German edition, Münster, 1882.

1165 ._____. "Le stagioni presso i Denca e loro denominazioni," *BSGI*, I(1868), 294-298.

1166 ._____. "I Turchi nel Sudan," *AIV*, 5th Series, V(1879), 904-911.

1167 ._____. "Über seine Reise auf den weissen Flusse in Central Afrika," *JVUN*, 1861, 14-46.

1168 . Bennett, Ernest Nathaniel. "After Omdurman," *Contemporary Review,* LXXV(1899), 18-33.

1169 ._____. *The Downfall of the Dervishes: Being a Sketch of the Final Sudan Campaign of 1898.* London: Methuen, 1898. 255p. New York: New Amsterdam, 1899.

1170 . Bent, James Theodore. "A Visit to the Northern Sudan," *GJ*, VIII(1896), 335-356.

1171 . Berghoff, Karl. "Aberglaube im Sudan," *Globus*, XLII(1882), 157-158.

1172 ._____. "Ein Ausflug nach Meroe," *Globus*, XLIII(1883), 8-13, 22-27.

1173 ._____. "Notizen über die Nubischen Wüstenbewohner Ababdeh und Bischarib," *Globus*, XXXIX(1881), 285-286, 301-302.

1174 . Bertrocchi, Lorenzo. "Lettere," *Nigrizia,* I(1883), 188-190.

1175 . Biermans, Jan. "Lettres," *Annalen,* VII(1896-1897), 650, 651; VIII(1897-1898), 746-749, 776-779; X(1899-1900), 1004-1006, 1074-1076; XI (1900-1901), 6-8, 88, 89; XII(1901-1902), 161, 162, 208-210.

1176 ._____. "Lettres," *St. Josefs-Missionsbote,* IV(1899), 374, 375.

1177 . Bizemont, Henri Louis Gabriel de. "De Korosko à Khartoum. Lettres à M. le marquis de Chasseloup-Laubat, président de la Société de Géographie," *BSGP*, 6th Series, I(1871), 120-130, 218-246.

1178 . Blank, Heinrich. "Missionsbriefe," *Stern der Neger*, III(1900), 141-144.

1179 . Bolognesi, A. "Voyage au fleuve des Gazelles," *TM*, V(1862), 385-397.

1180 . Bonola, F. "Monseigneur Comboni et les Missions chrétiennes en Afrique," *BSKG*, Series II, VI(1885), 283-288.

1181 . Bonomi, Luigi. "Brano di lettera di D. Luigi Bonomi, Obeid, 5.I.1879," *ABPV*, XXI(1882), 58-60.

1182 . _____. "Corrispondenza di D. L. Bonomi, prigioniero del Mahdi," *MCL*, XV(1883), 241-245. See also, *APFL*, II(1883), 334-340.

1183 . _____. "Cose della Missione dei Nuba," *ABPV*, XIII(1874), 28-41.

1184 . _____. "L. Bonomi, Briefe aus El-Obeid," *JVUN*, XXIII(1876), 55-68.

1185 . _____. "Memorie per servire alla storia dell' insurrezione Mahdista," *Nigrizia*, IV(1886), 166-175, V(1887), 16,72, 112, 153, 166, VI(1888), 26, 52, VII(1889), 12, VIII(1890), 9, 76, 102, 174. See also, "Beiträge zur Geschichte der Mahdi-wirren in Sudan," in *JVUN*, 1888, 25-101.

1186 . _____. "Relazione del M.R.P.L. Bonomi à S.E.R. Mons. Sogaro," *MCL*, XVII(1885), 461-462, 476-478, 483-485. See also *KM*, XIV(1886), 12-15, 25-29, and *APFL*, V(1886), 28-50.

1187 . _____. "Stazione di el Obeid," *ABPV*, XIV(1875), 14-35. See also, *JVUN*, XXIII(1876), 55-68.

1188 . _____. "Sul Kordofan," *ABPV*, XXIV(1885), 25-33.

1189 . Bosco, Alessandro dal. "Lettera di D. Alessandro dal Bosco a Don Nicola Mazza, Chartum, 27.X.1858," in Antonio Spagnole, *Di Don Nicola Mazza e della Ia Missione Italiana dell'Africa Centrale*. Verona, 1910. 97-111.

1190 . Bouchard, Arturo. "Lettere," *ABPV*, No. 25 (1881), 48-51; No. 29(1882), 48-59.

1191 . _____. "Lettere," *MCM*, XIV(1885), 137, 138.

1192 . _____. "Lettere," *Nigrizia*, III(1885), 30-36, 47-49.

1193 . _____. "Lettres," *Annales Oeuvre Ste-Enfance*, XXXIII(1882), 199-204.

1194 . _____. "Lettres," *MCL*, XVII(1885), 101.

1195 . _____. "Missionsbriefe," *KM*, XIII(1885), 110.

1196 . Brackenbury, Henry. *The River Column: a Narrative of the Advance of the River Column of the Nile Expeditionary Force and Its Return down the Rapids.* Edinburgh: Blackwood and Sons, 1885. 291p.

1197 . Brehm, Alfred. "Chartum," *Globus*, III(1863), 247-251, 273-276.

1198 . _____. "Chartum und seine Bewohner," *Zeitschrift fur allgemeine Erdkunde*, I, No. 6 (1856), 27, 92, 208.

1199 . Bressers, Richard. "Letters," *St. Joseph's Advocate*, III(1895-1900), 201.

1200 . Buchta, Richard. *Der Sudan unter Ägyptischer Herrschaft; Rückblicke auf der letzen sechzig Jahre.* Leipzig: Brockhaus, 1888. 228p.

1201 . Buijsrogge, Piet. "Lettres," *Annalen*, VIII(1897-1898), 728, 759, 760; IX(1898-1899), 879-881, 908-910; X(1899-1900), 978, 979; XI(1900-1901), 56, 57.

1202 . _____. "Lettres," *St. Josefs-Missionsbote*, V(1900), 35.

1203 . Burkhardt, John Lewis. *Travels in Nubia.* London: Murray, 1819. 543p.

1204 . Burleigh, Bennet. *Desert Warfare. Being the Chronicle of the Eastern Soudan Campaign.* London: Chapman and Hall, 1884. 320p.

1205 . _____. *Khartoum Campaign, 1898; or, the Re-conquest of the Soudan.* London: Chapman and Hall, 1899. 340p. New York: Scribner's, 1899. 340p.

1206 . _____. *Sirdar and Khalifa; or, the Re-conquest of the Soudan, 1898.* London: Chapman and Hall, 1898. 305p. New York: Scribner's, 1898. 305p.

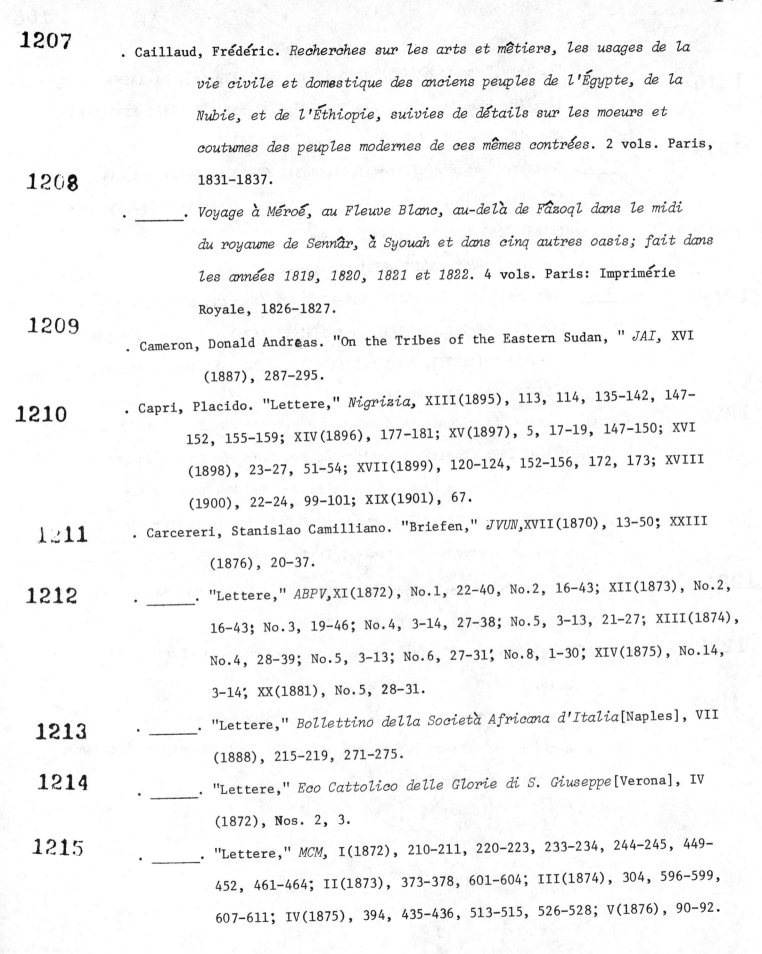

1207  . Caillaud, Frédéric. *Recherches sur les arts et métiers, les usages de la vie civile et domestique des anciens peuples de l'Égypte, de la Nubie, et de l'Éthiopie, suivies de détails sur les moeurs et coutumes des peuples modernes de ces mêmes contrées.* 2 vols. Paris,

1208  1831-1837.

. _____. *Voyage à Méroé, au Fleuve Blanc, au-delà de Fâzoql dans le midi du royaume de Sennâr, à Syouah et dans cinq autres oasis; fait dans les années 1819, 1820, 1821 et 1822.* 4 vols. Paris: Imprimérie Royale, 1826-1827.

1209  . Cameron, Donald Andreas. "On the Tribes of the Eastern Sudan, " *JAI*, XVI (1887), 287-295.

1210  . Capri, Placido. "Lettere," *Nigrizia*, XIII(1895), 113, 114, 135-142, 147-152, 155-159; XIV(1896), 177-181; XV(1897), 5, 17-19, 147-150; XVI (1898), 23-27, 51-54; XVII(1899), 120-124, 152-156, 172, 173; XVIII (1900), 22-24, 99-101; XIX(1901), 67.

1211  . Carcereri, Stanislao Camilliano. "Briefen," *JVUN*, XVII(1870), 13-50; XXIII (1876), 20-37.

1212  . _____. "Lettere," *ABPV*, XI(1872), No.1, 22-40, No.2, 16-43; XII(1873), No.2, 16-43; No.3, 19-46; No.4, 3-14, 27-38; No.5, 3-13, 21-27; XIII(1874), No.4, 28-39; No.5, 3-13; No.6, 27-31; No.8, 1-30; XIV(1875), No.14, 3-14; XX(1881), No.5, 28-31.

1213  . _____. "Lettere," *Bollettino della Società Africana d'Italia*[Naples], VII (1888), 215-219, 271-275.

1214  . _____. "Lettere," *Eco Cattolico delle Glorie di S. Giuseppe*[Verona], IV (1872), Nos. 2, 3.

1215  . _____. "Lettere," *MCM*, I(1872), 210-211, 220-223, 233-234, 244-245, 449-452, 461-464; II(1873), 373-378, 601-604; III(1874), 304, 596-599, 607-611; IV(1875), 394, 435-436, 513-515, 526-528; V(1876), 90-92.

**1216** . _____ . "Lettere," *Museo delle Missioni Cattoliche*[Turin], XI(1868), No.9, 129-140, 145-156; XV(1872), 501-505, 531-538, 583-588; XXVI(1883), 308-310, 324-325, 350-351, 359-360, 381-383.

**1217** . _____ . "Lettere," *Nigrizia*[Verona], I(1883), 62-73, 114-127, 135-145, 165; II(1884), 19-26, 82-85, 149-153, 184-189; III(1885), 92-100, VI (1888), 180-185; VII(1889), 89-94.

**1218** . _____ . "Lettres," *APFL*, XLIV(1872), 26-43.

**1219** . _____ . "Lettres," *MCL*, IV(1872), 469-471, 481-483, 494-497, 685-688, 697-700, 708-710; V(1873), 362-364; VI(1874), 488-490, 499-501, 514-515; VII(1875), 430; VIII(1876), 68-70, 317-318; XV(1883), 448-452, 463-464, 486-488.

**1220** . Casati, Gaetano. *Dieci anni in Equatoria e ritorno con Emin Pascià*. 2 vols. Milan, 1891. English translation, *Ten Years in Equatoria and the Return with Emin Pasha*. 2 vols. London and New York: Warne, 1891. French translation, *Dix années en Equatorie. Le retour d'Emin-Pacha et l'expedition Stanley*. Paris: Didot, 1892. 498p.

**1221** . Cavedon, Emilio. "Lettere," *Nigrizia*, XVI(1898), 78, 79, 95, 96, 135-138, 170-173; XVII(1899), 86-90, 147-152.

**1222** . Chaillé-Long, Charles. *L'Égypte et ses provinces perdues*. Paris, 1892. 327p.

**1223** . _____ . *The Three Prophets: Chinese Gordon, Mohammed-Ahmed(El Mahdi), Arabi Pasha. Events before and after the Bombardment of Alexandria*. New York: Appleton, 1884. 235p.

1224  Chenivesse, Emile. "Lettres," *Missions d'Afrique*, (1895-1897), 327, 328.

1225  . _____. "Lettres," *Missions d'Alger*, (1887-1890), 717-721.

1226  . _____. "Missionsbriefe," *Afrika-Bote*, II(1896), 124, 125.

1227  . Chesnais, René de. "Les stations catholiques dans la Nigritie orientale,"
*Bulletin de la Société de Géographie de Lille*, II(1883), 73-82.

1228  . Churchill, Winston L. S. *The River War: An Historical Account of the
Reconquest of the Soudan*. 2 vols. London: Longmans and Co., 1899.

1229  . Colborne, John [Col.]. *With Hicks Pasha in the Soudan. Being an Account of
the Senaar Campaign in 1883*. London: Smith, Elder and Co., 1884.
288p.

1230  . Colombaroli, Angelo. "Lettere," *Nigrizia*, XVI(1898), 17-21; XVIII(1900),
3, 4.

1231  . Colston, R.E. [Colonel ]. "Itinerary from Debbé to El Obeyad, on the Upper
Nile, with Details of Places of Most Importance," *PRGS*, XX
(1875-1876), 357-362.

1232  _____. "The Land of the False Prophet," *Century*, XXIX(1885),
643-662.

1233  _____. *Report on Northern and Central Kordofan*. Cairo:
Egyptian General Staff, 1878. 95p.

1234  . Comboni, Daniele. "Bianca Lemuna: Biographie eines Negermadchens,"
*JVUN*, XXVIII(1881), 53-63. Also, *ABPV*, (1881), No. 25, 36-47.

1235  _____. *La carestia e pestilenza dell-Africa Central nel 1878-79*.
Verona: Tipografia S. Giuseppe Di A. Merlo, 1880. 62p.

1236  _____. *Historische Übersicht und Schilderung des
Zustandes des apostolisches Vicariates von Central-Africa und der
apostolischen Gründungen in demselben*. Vienna: F. Eigeldauer, 1878.
108p.

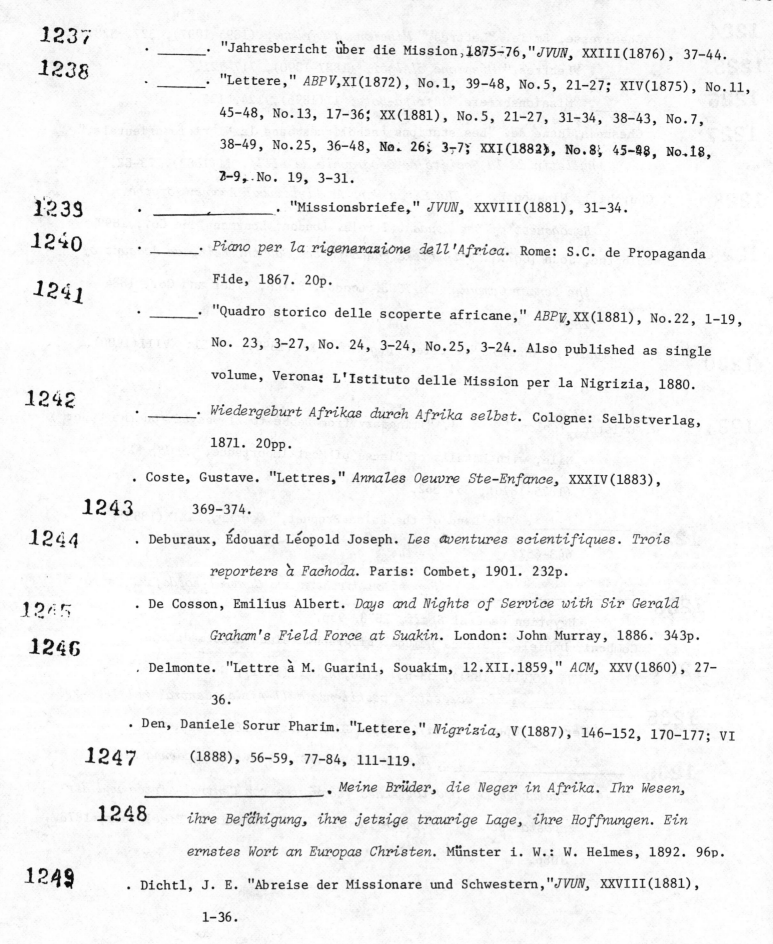

1237 · _____. "Jahresbericht über die Mission,1875-76,"*JVUN*, XXIII(1876), 37-44.

1238 · _____. "Lettere," *ABPV*,XI(1872), No.1, 39-48, No.5, 21-27; XIV(1875), No.11, 45-48, No.13, 17-36; XX(1881), No.5, 21-27, 31-34, 38-43, No.7, 38-49, No.25, 36-48, No. 26, 3-7; XXI(1882), No.8, 45-48, No.18, 3-9, No. 19, 3-31.

1239 · _____. "Missionsbriefe," *JVUN*, XXVIII(1881), 31-34.

1240 · _____. *Piano per la rigenerazione dell'Africa*. Rome: S.C. de Propaganda Fide, 1867. 20p.

1241 · _____. "Quadro storico delle scoperte africane," *ABPV*,XX(1881), No.22, 1-19, No. 23, 3-27, No. 24, 3-24, No.25, 3-24. Also published as single volume, Verona: L'Istituto delle Mission per la Nigrizia, 1880.

1242 · _____. *Wiedergeburt Afrikas durch Afrika selbst*. Cologne: Selbstverlag, 1871. 20pp.

· Coste, Gustave. "Lettres," *Annales Oeuvre Ste-Enfance*, XXXIV(1883), 1243    369-374.

1244 · Deburaux, Édouard Léopold Joseph. *Les aventures scientifiques. Trois reporters à Fachoda*. Paris: Combet, 1901. 232p.

1245 · De Cosson, Emilius Albert. *Days and Nights of Service with Sir Gerald Graham's Field Force at Suakin*. London: John Murray, 1886. 343p.

1246 · Delmonte. "Lettre à M. Guarini, Souakim, 12.XII.1859," *ACM*, XXV(1860), 27-36.

· Den, Daniele Sorur Pharim. "Lettere," *Nigrizia*, V(1887), 146-152, 170-177; VI 1247    (1888), 56-59, 77-84, 111-119.

1248 _____. *Meine Brüder, die Neger in Afrika. Ihr Wesen, ihre Befähigung, ihre jetzige traurige Lage, ihre Hoffnungen. Ein ernstes Wort an Europas Christen*. Münster i. W.: W. Helmes, 1892. 96p.

1249 · Dichtl, J. E. "Abreise der Missionare und Schwestern,"*JVUN*, XXVIII(1881), 1-36.

_____. "Da Cairo a Chartum; descrizione," *ABPV*, (1881), No. 25,

1250    68-71; No. 26, 41-48.

1251    . _____. *Der Sudan*. Graz, 1884. 452p. Also, *JVUN*, XXXI(1884), 6-176; XXXII

(1885), 5-173.

. Dittmar, August. "Missionsbriefe," *KM*, XII(1884), 199.

1252

. Drontmann, Herman. "Letters," *St. Joseph's Advocate*, III(1895-1900), 504,

1253    505; IV(1901-1906), 543.

. _____. "Lettres," *Annalen*, X(1899-1900), 1083, 1084; XII(1901-1902), 163,

1254    164, 238, 239.

1255    . Dutau, P. Adolphe. "Fragment d'un récit de voyage dans la Haut-Nubie,"

*Études religieuses, historiques et littéraires*, April 15, 1868,

433-481.

1256    . Ehrenberg, Christian-Gottfried. *Naturgeschichtliche Reise in Ägypten*

*Dongola, Syrien, Arabien, und Habessinien von 1820-1825*. Berlin,

1828.

1257    . English, George Bethune. *A Narrative of the Expedition to Dongola and*

*Sennar under the Command of His Excellency Ismael Pasha by an*

*American in the Service of the Viceroy*. London: Murray, 1822.

232p. Boston: Wells & Lilly, 1823. 232p.

1258    . Ensor, F. Sidney. *Incidents on a Journey through Nubia to Darfoor*. London:

Allen, 1881. 225p.

1259    . Falkonberg, B. E. *Desert Life; Recollections of an Expedition in the*

*Soudan*. London: Allen, 1880. 382p.

1260 Fechet, Oscar E. *Journal of the March of an Expedition in Nubia between Assouan and Abouhamed. . .1873*. Cairo: Egyptian General Staff, 1878.

1261 Felkin, Robert William. "Notes on the For Tribe of Central Africa," *Proceedings of the Royal Society of Edinburgh*, XIII(1885), 205-265.

1262 _____. "The Soudan Question," *Contemporary Review*, LXXIV (1898), 482-497.

1263 Fraccaro, Giovanni Battista. "Lettere," *ABPV*, XVIII(1879), No.18, 58-63; No. 19, 44-54; XXI(1882), No. 18, 61-63.

1264 _____. "Lettere," *MCM*, IX(1880), 3-4.

1265 _____. "Lettres," *MCL*, XI(1879), 619-620.

1266 Franceschini, Giuseppe Camillo. "Lettere," *ABPV*, XIII(1874), No. 6, 3-15.

1267 _____. "Lettres," *MCL*, V(1873), 578-579.

1268 _____. "Progressi della Missione in Kordofan," *ABPV*, XX(1881), No.6, 3-14.

1269 Franzoj, Augusto. *Aure Africane*. Milan: Galli, 1892. 149p.

1270 _____. *Continente nero, note di viaggio*. Turin: Roux & Favale, 1885. 350p.

1271 Frobenius, Herman. *Die Erdgebäude im Sudan*. Hamburg, 1897. 36p.

1272 Galloway, William. *The Battle of Tofrek Fought near Suâkin, March 22, 1885, under Sir John Carstairs McNeill*. London: Allen, 1887. 399p.

1273 Ganzenmüller, Konrad. [Dr.]. "Sennaar," *Globus*, XLV(1884), 119-123, 135-139, 152-156.

1274 Gatacre, W. [Major General]. "After the Atbara and Omdurman," *Contemporary Review*, LXXV(1899), 299-304.

1275 . Gatta, L. *Da Massaua a Chartum per Keren e Cassala*. Rome, n.p., 1885. 38p.

1276 . Gessi, Romolo. *Sette anni nel Sudan egiziano, esplorazioni, caccie e guerra contro i negrieri*. Milan: C. Chiesa, 1891. 489p. English translation, *Seven Years in the Soudan; Being a Record of Explorations, Adventures, and Campaigns against the Arab Slave Hunters*. London: Sampson Low, 1892. 467p. New York: Scribner's, 1892.

1277 Geyer, Francis X. "Aus dem Lande der Bedja," *JVUN*, XXXVII(1890), 56-58.

1278 . _____. "Aberglaube im Niltale," *Stern der Neger*, I(1898), 29-34, 53-55, 87-94, 115-120, 128-133, 187-190, 213-216.

1279 . _____. "Aus dem Leben der Barabra in Nubien," *Stern der Neger*, V(1902), 143-147.

1280 . _____. "Aus dem Leben der Kinder im Sudan," *JVUN*, XLII(1895), 27-48. See also *Stern der Neger*, VIII(1905), 270-280.

1281 . _____. "Die Barbara in Nubien," *Stern der Neger*, IV(1901), 289-293, 305-307, 330-334, 369-371.

1282 . _____. "Christenthum, Islam und Sklaverei in Afrika," *JVUN*, XXXVII(1890), 30-56.

1283 . _____. "Colonialpolitik und Christenthum in Afrika," *Stern der Neger*, I(1898), 7-11. Also, *BNC*, XLIX(1902), 51-63.

1284 . _____. "Credenze religiose dei Neri pagani nel Sudan," *Nigrizia*, XIV(1896), 115-118, 138-140, 175, 176, 183-186.

1285 . _____. "Da Suakim a Tokar," *Nigrizia*, XI(1893), 175-182; XII(1894), 7-14, 36-39.

1286 —————. *Durch Sand, Sumpf und Wald. Missionsreisen in Zentral Afrika*. Freiburg, 1912. 555p.

1287 —————. "Erinnerungen an eine Reise im Roten Meer," *Stern der Neger*, III (1900), 21-24, 41-42, 89-91, 119-120, 137-140, 164-167, 186-192, 206-207.

1288 —————. "Etwas über Charakter und Anlage des Negers," *JVUN*, XLII (1895), 61-76.

1289 —————. "Favole e racconti del Sudan," *Nigrizia*, IX(1891), 131-138, 166-170.

1290 —————. "Favole nel Sudan," *Nigrizia*, X(1892), 20-22.

1291 —————. "Eine Gerichtssitzung im Lande der Barabra," *JVUN*, XLIV(1897), 62-70.

1292 —————. "Gewerbe und Industrie im Sudan," *Stern der Neger*, IV(1901), 105-110.

1293 —————. *Handbuch für die Missionäre des Ap. V. Khartoum*, Khartoum, 1914. 270p.

1294 —————. "L'islamismo e i negri nella nostra Missione," *Nigrizia*, XI(1893), 110-116, 152-154.

1295 —————. "Ist der Islam geeignet Naturvölker zu bilden ?" *Stern der Neger*, IV (1901), 43-46, 80-85.

1296 —————. "Khartoum," *Stern der Neger*, X(1907) 169-177, 193-204, 217-223.

1297 —————. "Mission und Kultur," *Stern der Neger*, V(1902) 150-155, 196-201. 235-240, 279-286.

1298 —————. "Missionsbriefe," *Echo aus Afrika*, II(1890-1891), 7; III (1891), 20, 21, 40, 41, 64, 65; IV(1892), 21-24, 51, 52, 57, 58, 83-86, 103, 104, 119, 132, 133; V(1893), 3, 4, 9, 19, 20, 34, 35, 67, 68, 86-88; VI(1894), 19-21, 85, 86; VII(1895), 53, 54.

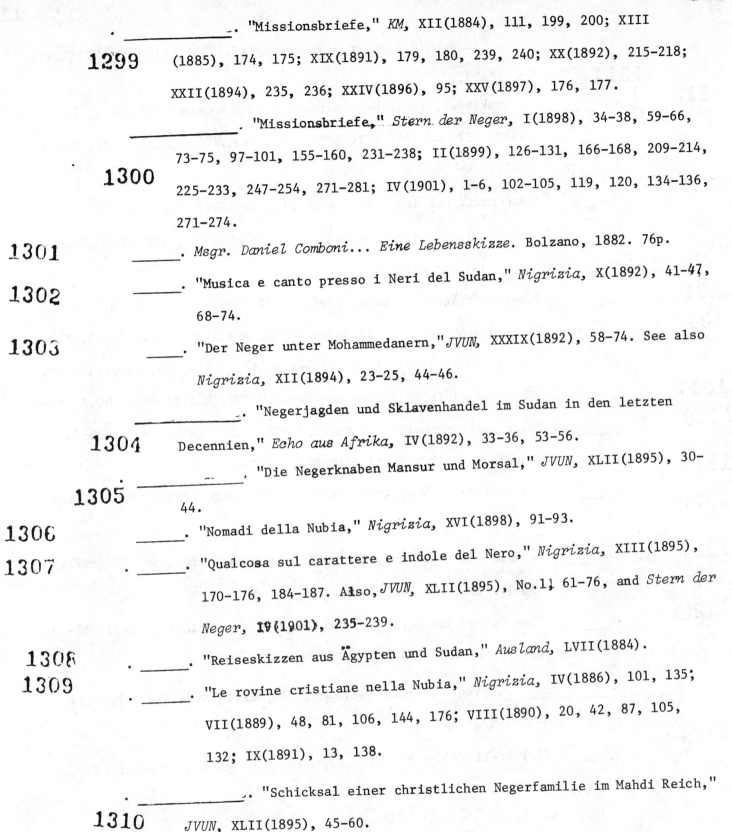

_____. "Missionsbriefe," *KM*, XII(1884), 111, 199, 200; XIII

1299    (1885), 174, 175; XIX(1891), 179, 180, 239, 240; XX(1892), 215-218;

XXII(1894), 235, 236; XXIV(1896), 95; XXV(1897), 176, 177.

_____. "Missionsbriefe," *Stern der Neger*, I(1898), 34-38, 59-66,

73-75, 97-101, 155-160, 231-238; II(1899), 126-131, 166-168, 209-214,

1300    225-233, 247-254, 271-281; IV(1901), 1-6, 102-105, 119, 120, 134-136,

271-274.

1301    _____. *Msgr. Daniel Comboni... Eine Lebensskizze*. Bolzano, 1882. 76p.

1302    _____. "Musica e canto presso i Neri del Sudan," *Nigrizia*, X(1892), 41-47,

68-74.

1303    _____. "Der Neger unter Mohammedanern," *JVUN*, XXXIX(1892), 58-74. See also

*Nigrizia*, XII(1894), 23-25, 44-46.

_____. "Negerjagden und Sklavenhandel im Sudan in den letzten

1304    Decennien," *Echo aus Afrika*, IV(1892), 33-36, 53-56.

_____. "Die Negerknaben Mansur und Morsal," *JVUN*, XLII(1895), 30-

1305    44.

1306    _____. "Nomadi della Nubia," *Nigrizia*, XVI(1898), 91-93.

1307    _____. "Qualcosa sul carattere e indole del Nero," *Nigrizia*, XIII(1895),

170-176, 184-187. Also, *JVUN*, XLII(1895), No.1, 61-76, and *Stern der*

*Neger*, IV(1901), 235-239.

1308    _____. "Reiseskizzen aus Ägypten und Sudan," *Ausland*, LVII(1884).

1309    _____. "Le rovine cristiane nella Nubia," *Nigrizia*, IV(1886), 101, 135;

VII(1889), 48, 81, 106, 144, 176; VIII(1890), 20, 42, 87, 105,

132; IX(1891), 13, 138.

_____. "Schicksal einer christlichen Negerfamilie im Mahdi Reich,"

1310    *JVUN*, XLII(1895), 45-60.

1311 ._____. "Da Suakim a Tokar," *Nigrizia*, XI(1893), 175-181; XII(1894), 7-13, 36-39.

1312 ._____. "I suakimesi, le tribu limitrofe e loro usanze," *Nigrizia*, VI (1888), 22, 40, 74; VII(1889), 44. Also, *JVUN*, XXXIX(1892), No.2, 53-57.

1313 _____. "Superstizioni dei Neri," *Nigrizia*, XV(1897), 21, 40.

1314 ._____. "Le superstizioni nel Sudan," *Nigrizia*, XII(1894), 70-74, 110-116, 151-157, 186-189.

1315 ._____. "Über Blutrache im Sudan,"*JVUN*, XLIII(1896), No.2, 72-78.

1316 ._____. "Über den Aberglauben im Sudan,"*JVUN*, XL(1893), No.1, 74-93; XLI (1894), No.1, 37-64. Also, *Nigrizia*, XII(1894), 70, 110, 151, 186.

1317 ._____. "Über religiöse Ansichten der Neger,"*JVUN*, XLIII(1896), No.1, 46-57.

1318 ._____. "Über Zeiteintheilung im Sudan,"*JVUN*, XLIII(1896), No.2, 65-72.

1319 ._____. "Unsere Neger,"*JVUN*, XXXVI(1889), 23-75.

1320 ._____. "Verschiedenes über Afrika und seine Bewohner,"*JVUN*, XXXVIII(1891), 68-120.

1321 ._____. "Viaggio di esplorazione sul Fiume Bianco," *Nigrizia*, XV(1897), 46, 76, 104, 156; XVI(1898), 28, 45, 60.

1322 _____. "Von Cairo nach Chartum," *Stern der Neger*, II(1899), 26-31, 61-69, 82-92, 115-120, 154-163, 187-189, 200-208.

1323 _____. "Von Suez nach Dschedda," *KM*, XXVI(1897-1898), 169-174, 203-207, 223-227.

1324 ._____. "Zur Stellung der Frau in Ägypten und im Sudan," *Stern der Neger*, I (1898), 244-248.

1325 . Gidrol, Marcellin. "Lettere," *MCM*, XXVIII(1899), 553–557.

1326 . _____. "Lettres," *APFL*, LXXII(1900), 207–216.

1327 . _____. "Lettres," *MCL*, XXXI(1899), 529–532.

1328 . _____. "Lettres," *Petites Annales*, X(1900), 305–312.

1329 . Gleichen, Albert Edward Wilfred [Ed.]. *The Anglo-Egyptian Sudan. A Compendium Prepared by Officers of the Sudan Government.* London: His Majesty's Stationery Office, 1905, 1906. 2 vols.

1330 — _____. *A Guardsman's Memoirs. A Book of Recollections.* Edinburgh and London: Blackwood, 1932. 396p.

1331 . _____. *Report on the Nile and Country between Dongola, Suakin, Kassala, and Omdurman.* London: Harrison, 1898. 338p.

1332 . _____. *With the Camel Corps up the Nile.* London: Chapman & Hall, 1888. 320p.

1333 . Godio, Guglielmo. *Vita africana. Ricordi d'un viaggio nel Sudan orientale.* Milan: Vallardi, 1885. 231p.

1334 . Gordon, Charles George. *Colonel Gordon in Central Africa, 1874–79. From Original Letters and Documents.* Edited by G. Birkbeck Hill. London: De la Rue, 1881. 456p. New York: Macmillan, 1899. 456p.

1335 . _____. *Equatoria under Egyptian Rule. The Unpublished Correspondence of Colonel, Afterwards Major-General, C. G. Gordon with Ismaïl, Khedive of Egypt and the Sudan, during the Years 1874–1876.* Cairo: Cairo University Press, 1953. 478p.

1336 . _____. *The Journals of Major-General C. G. Gordon, C.B., at Kartoum.* London: Kegan Paul, 1885. 587p. Boston: Houghton Mifflin, 1885. 479p. French edition, *Journal du général Gordon-Pascha. Siège de Khartoum.* Paris, 1886. 454p.

1337 . _____. *Letters of General C. G. Gordon to His Sister, M. A. Gordon.* London: Macmillan, 1888. 404p.

1338     . \_\_\_\_\_. "Notes to Accompany a Survey of the White Nile from Lardo to Nyamyungo," *JRGS*, XLVI(1876), 431-432.

1339     . \_\_\_\_\_. "Unpublished Letters of Colonel C. G. Gordon," *Sudan Notes and Records*, 1927, 1-59.

1340     . Gordon, John. *My Six Years with the Black Watch, 1881-1887*. Boston: Usher, 1929. 362p.

. Graham, Gerald [*Lt. Gen.*]. *Life, Letters and Diaries of Lt. General Sir Gerald Graham*. [Compiled by Col. R. H. Vetch]. Edinburgh: Blackwood & Sons, 1901. 492p.

1341

1342     . Grant, James Augustus. *Khartoum as I Saw It in 1863*. Edinburgh: Blackwood, 1885. 38p.

1343     . \_\_\_\_\_. "Route March, with Camels, from Berber to Korosko in 1863," *PRGS*, New Series, VI(1884), 326-335.

. Grimshaw, Edmund. "Letters," *St. Joseph's Advocate*, III(1895-1900), 472, 473; IV(1901-1906), 55, 56, 138, 294, 295, 563, 564.

1344

1345     . Hanlon, Henry. "Lettere," *MCM*, XXV(1896), 530; XXVII(1898), 159.

1346     . \_\_\_\_\_. "Letters," *St. Joseph's Advocate*, III(1895-1900), 61, 62, 100 - 102, 234, 300, 328, 329, 376, 409, 422; IV(1901-1906), 90, 91, 173, 255.

1347     . \_\_\_\_\_. "Lettres," *Annalen*[Roosendaal], VI(1895-1896), 475, 476, 501-503, 521-524; VII(1896-1897), 557-559, 593, 594, 607-609; VIII(1897-1898), 730, 731, 758, 759; X(1899-1900), 985-988; XII(1901-1902), 229, 230.

1348     . \_\_\_\_\_. "Lettres," *APFL*, LXIX(1897), 73, 74.

1349     . \_\_\_\_\_. "Lettres," *MCL*, XXVIII(1896), 507.

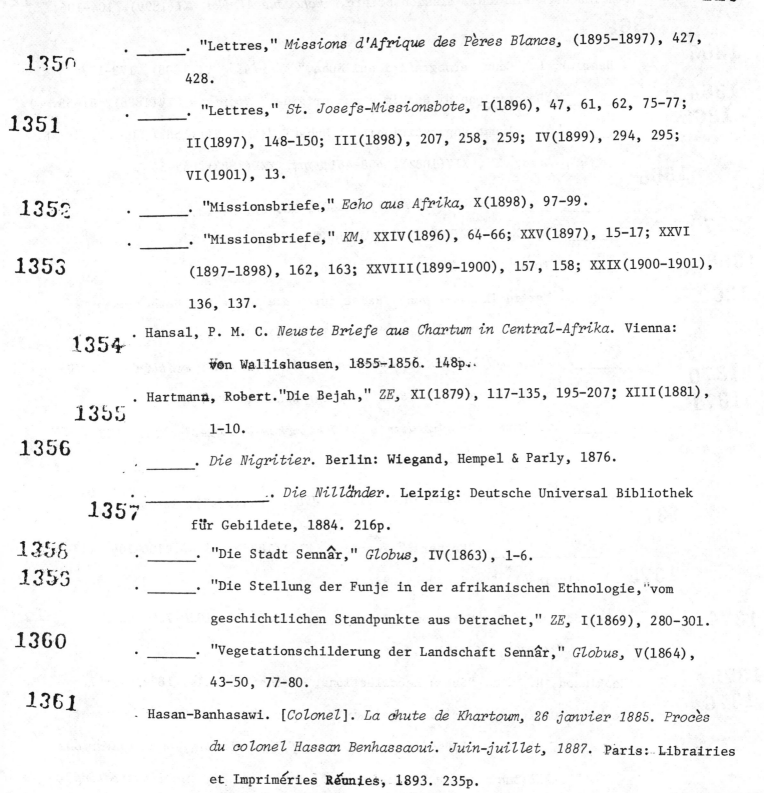

1350    . _____. "Lettres," *Missions d'Afrique des Pères Blancs,* (1895-1897), 427, 428.

1351    . _____. "Lettres," *St. Josefs-Missionsbote,* I(1896), 47, 61, 62, 75-77; II(1897), 148-150; III(1898), 207, 258, 259; IV(1899), 294, 295; VI(1901), 13.

1352    . _____. "Missionsbriefe," *Echo aus Afrika,* X(1898), 97-99.

1353    . _____. "Missionsbriefe," *KM,* XXIV(1896), 64-66; XXV(1897), 15-17; XXVI (1897-1898), 162, 163; XXVIII(1899-1900), 157, 158; XXIX(1900-1901), 136, 137.

1354    . Hansal, P. M. C. *Neuste Briefe aus Chartum in Central-Afrika.* Vienna: Von Wallishausen, 1855-1856. 148p.

1355    . Hartmann, Robert. "Die Bejah," *ZE,* XI(1879), 117-135, 195-207; XIII(1881), 1-10.

1356    . _____. *Die Nigritier.* Berlin: Wiegand, Hempel & Parly, 1876.

1357    . _____. *Die Nilländer.* Leipzig: Deutsche Universal Bibliothek für Gebildete, 1884. 216p.

1358    . _____. "Die Stadt Sennâr," *Globus,* IV(1863), 1-6.

1359    . _____. "Die Stellung der Funje in der afrikanischen Ethnologie," vom geschichtlichen Standpunkte aus betrachet," *ZE,* I(1869), 280-301.

1360    . _____. "Vegetationschilderung der Landschaft Sennâr," *Globus,* V(1864), 43-50, 77-80.

1361    . Hasan-Banhasawi. [*Colonel*]. *La chute de Khartoum, 26 janvier 1885. Procès du colonel Hassan Benhassaoui. Juin-juillet, 1887.* Paris: Librairies et Impriméries Réunies, 1893. 235p.

Heimanns, Heinrich. "Missionsbriefe," *Echo aus Afrika*, XI(1899), 104-106.

1362

1363    Henriot, L. "Cenni etnografici sui Nuba," *Nigrizia*, VI(1888), 173-177.

1364    _____. "Descrizione di Suakim e sua origine," *Nigrizia*, IV(1886), 51-58.

1365    _____. "Di alcune superstizioni dei Nubani,"*ABPV*, XIX(1882), No.29, 38-48.

   Also, *MCL*, XIV(1882), 458-461,*JVUN*, XXX(1883), 45-54.

1366    _____. "Lettere," *ABPV*, (1880), No. 21, 33-43.

1367    _____. "Sui Nuba," *ABPV*,XIX(1880), No.21, 33-44.

1368    _____. "Tokar," *Nigrizia*, IX(1891), 38-44.

1369    Heuglin, Martin Theodore von. "Reise durch die Wüste von Berber nach Suakin, September 1864," *PM*, XII(1866), 165-171.

1370    _____. *Reisen in das Gebiet des weissen Nil und seiner westlichen Zuflüsse, in den Jahren 1862-1864.* Leipzig: Winter, 1869. 382p.

1371    _____. *Die Tinne'sche Expedition im Westlichen Nil-Quellgebiet 1863 und 1864.* Gotha: J.Perthes, 1855.

Heymans, Franz. "Bekehrung in Gesirah," *JVUN*, XLII(1895), 24-29.

1372

_____. "Lettere," *Nigrizia*, XIII(1895), 41-46, 106-108, 115-117;

1373    XIV(1896), 59-62, 70-74, 93, 94.

1374    Holroyd, Arthur T. "Notes on a Journey to Kordofán in 1836-7," *JRGS*, IX(1839), 163-191.

1375    Hopkinson, H. C. B. "Sudan Recollections," *Cornhill*, July, 1899, 47-57.

1376    Hoskins, George Alexander. *Travels in Ethiopia above the Second Cataract of the Nile, Exhibiting the State of That Country, and Its Various Inhabitants under the Dominion of Mohammed Ali, and Illustrating the Antiquities, Arts, and History of the Ancient Kingdom of Meroe.* London: Longmans, 1835. 367p.

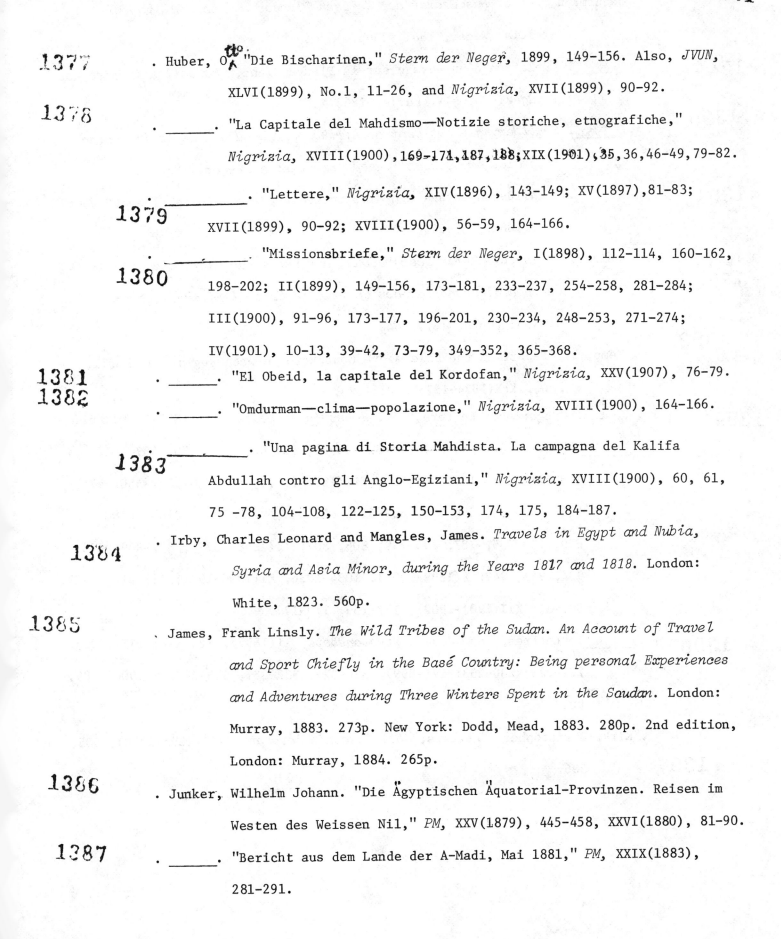

1377 . Huber, O. "Die Bischarinen," *Stern der Neger*, 1899, 149-156. Also, *JVUN*, XLVI (1899), No.1, 11-26, and *Nigrizia*, XVII (1899), 90-92.

1378 . _____. "La Capitale del Mahdismo—Notizie storiche, etnografiche," *Nigrizia*, XVIII (1900), 169-171, 187, 188; XIX (1901), 35, 36, 46-49, 79-82.

1379 . _____. "Lettere," *Nigrizia*, XIV (1896), 143-149; XV (1897), 81-83; XVII (1899), 90-92; XVIII (1900), 56-59, 164-166.

1380 . _____. "Missionsbriefe," *Stern der Neger*, I (1898), 112-114, 160-162, 198-202; II (1899), 149-156, 173-181, 233-237, 254-258, 281-284; III (1900), 91-96, 173-177, 196-201, 230-234, 248-253, 271-274; IV (1901), 10-13, 39-42, 73-79, 349-352, 365-368.

1381 . _____. "El Obeid, la capitale del Kordofan," *Nigrizia*, XXV (1907), 76-79.

1382 . _____. "Omdurman—clima—popolazione," *Nigrizia*, XVIII (1900), 164-166.

1383 . _____. "Una pagina di Storia Mahdista. La campagna del Kalifa Abdullah contro gli Anglo-Egiziani," *Nigrizia*, XVIII (1900), 60, 61, 75 -78, 104-108, 122-125, 150-153, 174, 175, 184-187.

1384 . Irby, Charles Leonard and Mangles, James. *Travels in Egypt and Nubia, Syria and Asia Minor, during the Years 1817 and 1818*. London: White, 1823. 560p.

1385 . James, Frank Linsly. *The Wild Tribes of the Sudan. An Account of Travel and Sport Chiefly in the Basé Country: Being personal Experiences and Adventures during Three Winters Spent in the Saudan*. London: Murray, 1883. 273p. New York: Dodd, Mead, 1883. 280p. 2nd edition, London: Murray, 1884. 265p.

1386 . Junker, Wilhelm Johann. "Die Ägyptischen Äquatorial-Provinzen. Reisen im Westen des Weissen Nil," *PM*, XXV (1879), 445-458, XXVI (1880), 81-90.

1387 . _____. "Bericht aus dem Lande der A-Madi, Mai 1881," *PM*, XXIX (1883), 281-291.

1388 . Kaufmann, Anton. *Das Gebiet des Weissen Flusses und dessen Bewohner.* Brescia: Weger, 1861. 206p.

1389 . _____. "Relation d'un voyage sur le Fleuve Blanc," *Nouvelles Annales des Voyages.* Vol. IV. Paris, 1863.

1390 . _____. *Schilderungen aus Central-Afrika oder Land und Leute im oberen Nilgebiet am Weissen Flusse.* Brescia: A. Weger, 1862. 208p.

1391 . _____. "Schilderungen aus dem Missionsgebiete aus weissen Flusse," *JVUN,* VIII(1861), 46-86.

1392 . Keller, Gherardus. *Kurze Beschreibung der Reise nach Jerusalem, Nazareth und von Alessandria nach Chartum in Central-Afrika.* Bolzano: J. Wohlgemuth, 1870. 44p.

1393 . Kemp, J. "Report on the Nile above Gondokoro between Regiaf and Dufli," *PRGS,* XIX(1874-1875), 324-325.

1394 . Kesten, Gregorius. "Letters," *St. Joseph's Advocate,* III(1895-1900), 61.

1395 . _____. "Lettres," *Annalen,* VI(1895-1896), 421-429, 478-480, 487-491, 495-501, 511-513, 524, 525; VII(1896-1897), 534-538, 547-550, 571, 572, 582-584, 594-596, 609-612, 651-655; VIII(1897-1898), 678, 679, 733-735, 787, 794-799, 806, 807; IX(1898-1899), 837-839, 928-934, 941, 942; X(1899-1900), 1034-1036; XI(1900-1901), 17-21, 25-29, 80, 81; XII(1901-1902), 157-159, 170-174.

1396 . _____. "Lettres," *St. Josefs-Missionsbote,* II(1897), 123-126; III(1898), 222-226, 230-233; IV(1899), 320-324, 332-337, 378-380; V(1900), 89, 90.

1397 . Kirk, Christopher. "Letters," *St. Joseph's Advocate,* III(1895-1900), 505, 506.

1398 . Klodt, Karl. "Missionsbriefe," *Stern der Neger*, IV(1901), 277, 278.

1399 . Knight, Edward Frederick. *LLetters from the Sudan by the Special Correspondent of the Times. (Reprinted from The Times of April to October, 1896.)* London: Macmillan, 1897. 325p.

1400 . Knoblecher, Ignaz. "Bericht an das Central-Comité des Marien-Vereines," *Jahresbericht des Marien-Vereines*, I(1852), 12-33.

1401 _____. "Lettera," *Museo delle Missioni Cattoliche*, V(1862), 1-3.

1402 . _____. *Notizie storiche sulla recente missione nell'Africa Centrale.* Padua, 1851. 18p.

1403 . _____. *Reise auf dem weissen Nil.* Ljubljana: V.F.Klun, 1851. 2nd Edition. 1952.

1404 . _____. *Das apostolische Vicariat in Central-Africa.* Vienna, 1850. 11p.

1405 . Kobinger, Johann. "Missionsbriefe," *Stern der Neger*, II(1899), 140-142.

1406 . Kocijančič, Johann. "Fahrt des Missionsschiffes Stella Matutina von Korosko bis Dongola," *Jahresbericht des Marien-Vereines*, I(1852), 33-39.

1407 Legh, Thomas. *Narrative of a Journey in Egypt and the Country beyond the Cataracts.* London, 1816. 157p. 2nd Edition, London: Murray, 1817. 297p.

1408 Lejean, GUILLAUME. "Excursion aux environs de Gondokoro," *TM*, VIII(1863), 199-200.

1409 . _____. "Gondokoro," *TM*, V(1862), 397-400.

1410 . _____. "Voyage au Kordofan," *TM*, VII(1863), 24-32.

1411 . _____. "Voyage au Taka," *TM*, XI(1865), 97-160.

1412 . _____. *Voyage aux deux Nils (Nubie, Kordofan, Soudan oriental.)* Paris: Hachette, 1865. 192p.

1413 _____. "Voyage dans l'Afrique orientale," *TM*, II(1860), 97-103; III(1861), 139-144; V(1862), 177-192.

1414 Lenard, L. "Ein Blick auf die Bodenbeschaffenheit Centralafrikas," *Stern der Neger*, II(1899), 195-200; 219-223.

1415    . Lesbros, Etienne. "Lettres," *Missions d'Afrique*, (1901-1902), 295, 296.

1416    . Linant, M. Adolphe. "Journal of a Voyage on the Bahr-Abiad or White Nile, with Some General Notes on That River, and Some Remarks on the District of Atbara, Made in a Tour from Hartoum," *JRGS*, II(1832), 171-190.

1417    Loring, William Wing. *A Confederate Soldier in Egypt*. New York: Dodd, Mead, 1884. 450p.

1418    Losi, Giovanni. "Cronaca della Missione," *ABPV*,XXI(1882), No.8, 8-43.

1419    . _____. "Lettere," *ABPV*,(1881),No.5,21-30;(1882),No.18,14-28,No.23,60-64,No.26,13-14.

1420    . _____. "Missione di Gebel Nuba," *ABPV*,XXI(1882), No.19, 54-63, and *Museo delle Missioni Cattoliche*[Turin], XXIII(1880), No.3, 37-40.

1421    . _____. "La Missione in El Obeid," *ABPV*,XIV(1875), No.10, 3-22, and *JVUN*, XII(1875), 8-46.

1422    . _____. "Relazione del viaggio dal Cairo a Chartum," *ABPV*,XXI(1882), No.7, 21-30; No.8, 31-43.

1423    . _____. "Viaggio fra i Nuba nei pressi di Delen," *ABPV*,XVII(1878), No.18, 14-28.

1424    . Lucas, Louis. "On the Natives of Suakin, and Bishareen Vocabulary," *JAI*, VI(1877), 191-194.

1425    . Lupton, Frank. [Lupton *Bey*]. "Geographical Observations in the Bahr-el-Ghazal Region," *PRGS*, New Series, VI(1884), 245-253.

1426    . Macdonald, Alexander. *Too Late for Gordon and Khartoum: the Testimony of an Independent Eye-Witness*. London: Murray, 1887. 359p.

1427    . _____. *Why Gordon Perished, or, The Political and Military Causes which Led to the Sudan Disasters. By a War Correspondent Who Accompanied the Nile Expedition*. London: Allen, 1896. 318p.

1428 . Macdonald, James Ronald Leslie. "Journeys to the North of Uganda," *GJ*, XIV(1899), 129-152.

1429 . Madox, John. *Excursion in the Holy Land, Egypt, Nubia, Etc.* 2 vols. London, 1834.

1430 Marno, Ernst. "Der Bahr Seraf; Reisebriefe, Dezember 1871 bis September 1872," *PM*, XIX(1873), 130-136.

1431 _____. *Reisen im Gebiet des blauen und weissen Nil, im ägyptischen Sudan und den angrenzenden Negerländern, in den Jahren 1869 bis 1873.* Vienna: Gerold, 1874.

1432 _____. *Reise in der ägyptischen Äquatorial-Provinz und in Kordofan in den Jahren 1874-1876.* Vienna: Hölder, 1878.

1433 _____. "Reisen in Hoch Sennaar, 1870-71," *PM*, XVIII(1872), 450-456; XIX (1873), 246-252.

1434 _____. "Die Sumpfregion des aquatorialen Nilsystem und deren Grasbarren," *PM*, XXVII(1881), 411-426.

1435 _____. "Die Verlegungen im Bahr-el-Ghasal und deren Beseitigung im April bis Juni 1881," *PM*, XXVIII(1882), 121-129.

1436 . Martini, Gennaro. "Ancora dei Nuba," *ABPV,* XIV(1875), No.13, 3-17. See also, *Museo delle Missioni Cattoliche,* XVIII(1875), 698-702, 713-721, *MCL,* VII(1875), 503-5, 518-519.

1437 _____. "Bericht über die Mission in den Nubaländern," *JVUN,* XXIII(1876), 1-19.

1438 _____. "Missione a Gedaref," *ABPV,* (1880), No.19, 15-35; No.20, 35-39. Also, *Museo delle Missioni Cattoliche,* XXIII(1880), 193-198, 209-213, 225-229; *MCL,* XII(1880), 133-137, 146-147.

1439 _____. "Relazione del viaggio dell'ultima carovana da Cairo a Khartum," *ABPV,* XIV(1875), No.11, 3-41.

1440 . Martonne, Edward Guillaume de. "Dongola," *AG,* V(1896), 436-438.

1441 . Marzano, Vincenzo. "Lettere," *ABPV*, (1880), No. 22, 20-27; (1881), No. 25, 52-59; No. 26, 26-35; No. 28, 30-33.

1442 _____. "Lettere," *MCM*, X(1881), 377, 378.

1443 . _____. "Nuova Chiesa di N. S. del S. Cuore Regina della Nigrizia in El-Obeid, capitale del Cordofan," *ABPV*, (1881), No. 25, 52-59.

1444 . _____. "Piccolo cenno sull'ultimo viaggio di Mons. Daniele Comboni attravero i Monti di Dar-Nuba," *ABPV*, (1881), No. 26, 26-35.

1445 . Mason, Alexander McComb. [Mason-*Bey*]. "Dar-For," *PM*, XXVI(1880), 377-381.

1446 . Matthews, Thomas. "Letters," *St. Joseph's Advocate*, III(1895-1900), 60, 61, 108-110, 135, 192, 301, 409, 410, 498, 499; IV(1901-1906), 178.

1447 . _____. "Lettres," *Annalen*, VII(1896-1897), 594.

1448 . _____. "Missionsbriefe," *Echo aus Afrika*, IX(1897), 34-36.

1449 . Mauro, Salvatore. "Lettere," *ABPV*, XII(1873), No.3, 15-18; XIV(1875), No.6, 16-20; No.13, 22-24; XV(1876), No.14, 36-46.

1450 . _____. "Relazione del S. Mauro, Obeid, 15.VIII.1873," *ABPV*, XX(1881), No.5, 15-20.

1451 . Maxse, F. I. [*Col.*]. "Last of the Dervishes," *National Review*, Jan., 1900, pp. 683-695.

1452 . Mayr, Heinrich von. *Malerische Ansichten aus dem Orient, gesammelt auf der reise des Herzog Maximilian in Bayern nach Nubien, Aegypten, Palästina, Syrien und Malta im Jahre 1838*. Munich: Weigel, 1839, 1840.

1453 . Meignan, Victor. *Après bien d'autres. Souvenirs de la Haute-Égypte et de la Nubie.* Paris, 1873.

1454 . Melly, George. *Khartoum and the Blue and White Niles.* 2 vols. London, 1851.

1455 . Melotto, Angelo. "Zibaldone [diario] di Don Angelo Melotto del'Istituto di Don Mazza, Missionario in Africa," *Bollettino "Don Nicola Mazza"* [Verona], 1935, pp. 118-123, 245-247; 1936, pp. 297-298, 309-312, 345-348, 373-377; 1937, pp. 2-4, 33-35.

1456 . Menges, Josef. "Die Karwanenstrassen zwischen Suakin und Kassala," *PM*, XXIII(1887), 97-101.

1457 . _____. "Reisen zwischen Kassala und dem Setit," *PM*, XXXIV(1888), 65-67.

1458 . Meyer, P. C. "Erforschungsgeschichte und Staatenbildung im Sudan," *PM*, 1897, Ergänzungsheft 121.

1459 . Milne, Arthur Dawson. "Life on the Nile South of Fashoda," *Nineteenth Century*, Aug., 1899, 273-281.

1460 _____ "Notes from the Equatorial Province," *SGM*, XV(1899), 480-483.

1461 . Mitterrutzner, Johann Chrysostomus. *Ein Blatt der Erinnerung an die Missionare aus Tirol in Centrale-Afrika.* Brixen: A. Weger, 1890. 21p.

1462 . _____. *Dr. Ignaz Knoblecher, apostolischer Provikar der Katholischen Mission in Central-Afrika. Eine Lebensskizze.* Brixen, 1869.

1463 . _____. *Kurze Lebensbeschreibung des Hochwürdigen Herrn A. Haller, apostolischen Missionärs zu Chartum in Central-Afrika.* Innsbruck, 1855.

1464 . _____. *Ein Palmenzweig auf das Grab des Hochw. Johann Ev. Dichtl.* Vienna, 1899. 20p. See also, *Stern der Neger*, 1901, 257-260, 294-298, and *JVUN*, XXXV(1889), 15-22, and "Una palma sulla tomba del R. P. Giovanni Dichtl," *Nigrizia*, VII(1889), 55-64.

1465 . Montuori. "Lettre," *ACM*, VIII(1843), 291-315.

1466 . Morlang, F. "Missionsreise," *Jahresbericht des Marien-Verein*[Vienna], IX (1860), 30-43.

1467 . Moschonas, Demetrius. "Les Hadendowas et les traces chez eux de la langue et des moeurs de l'antique Égypte," *BSKG*, VIII(1883).

1468 . Mounteney Jephson, A. J. *Emin-Pacha et la rébellion à l'équateur. Neuf mois d'aventures dans la plus reculée des provinces soudanaises.* Paris: Hachette, 1891. 350p.

1469 . Müller, John W. von.[Baron]. "Extracts from Notes Taken during His Travels in Africa in the Years 1847-8-9," *JRGS*, XX(1850), 275-289.

1470 _____. "Kartographische Arbeiten des ägyptischen Generalstabs im östlichen Sudan," *PM*, XXIX(1883), 293-294.

1471 . Münch, Josef. "Missionsbriefe," *Stern der Neger*, I(1898), 23, 24, 46, 47, 71, 72, 85, 86, 121, 122, 182-187, 194-198, 227, 228, 258-264, 282, 283.

1472 . _____. "Der Sudan," *Stern der Neger*, II(1899), 92-94, 134-136, 223, 224.

1473 . _____ "Die Tiroler Missionäre in Zentralafrika," *Stern der Neger*, II(1899), 3-8, 38-42, 54-57.

1474 . _____. "Zur Afrikanischen Volks- und Länderkunde," *Stern der Neger*, V(1902), 212-218.

1475 . Muḥammad ibn ʿUmar, Al-Tūnusī. *Voyage au Darfour par le cheykh Mohammed Ebn-Omar El-Tounsy.* Paris: Jomard, 1845. English translation, *Travels of an Arab Merchant in Soudan (the Black Kingdom of Central Africa).* London, 1854.

1476 . Munzinger, Werner. "Bericht über seine und Th. Kinzelbach's Reise nach El Obed, 1862," *PM*, IX(1863), 183-190.

1477 . _____. "Bericht über den Tod Eduard Vogel's," *Globus*, II(1862), 338-341.

1478 . Myers, Arthur Bowen Richards. *Life with the Hamran Arabs. An Account of a Sporting Tour of Some Officers of the Guards in the Soudan during the Winter of 1874-75.* London, 1876.

1479 . Nachtigal, Gustav. "Dar Fōr, die neue Ägyptische Provinz, und Dr. Nachtigal's Forschungen zwischen Kuka und Chartum," *PM*, XXI(1875),

1480 281-286.

. _____. "Dr. Gustav Nachtigal und seine neueste Reise im Sudan," *Globus*, XXIII(1873), 375-378.

1481 . _____. "Handel im Sudan," *Mitteilungen der geographischen Gesellschaft in Hamburg*, I(1876/1877), 305.

. Neufeld, Carl. *A Prisoner of the Khaleefa: Twelve Years' Captivity at Omdurman.* London: Chapman & Hall, 1899. 365p. New York: Putnam,

1482 1899. German translation, *In Ketten des Kalifen: zwölf Jahre Gefangenschaft in Omdurman.* Berlin & Stuttgart, 1899. 316p.

1483 . Ohrwalder, Joseph. *Auffstand und Reich des Mahdi im Sudan und meine zehnjährige Gefangenschaft dortselbst.* Innsbruck: Rauch, 1892. English translation, *Ten Years' Captivity in the Mahdi's Camp, 1882-1892.* London: Sampson Low, 1892. 460p. New York: Scribner's, 1893.

1484 . _____. "Da Assuan a Chartum," *Nigrizia*, XVII(1899), 161-170.

1485 . _____. "La condizione degli schiavi negli stati del Mahdi," *Nigrizia*, XII(1894), 19-20.

1486 . _____. "La condizione degli schiavi nell'antico Sudan Egiziano," *Nigrizia*, XI(1893), 184-185.

1487 . _____. "Das Gefängnis in Der Mahdia," *DK*, XV(1898), 326-328.

1488 . _____. "Im Lande der Schilluk," *Stern der Neger*, 1901, pp.327-329.

1489 . Oliphant, Laurence. *The Land of Khemi. Up and Down the Middle Nile.* Edinburgh: Blackwood & Sons, 1882. 260p.

1490 . Pallme, Ignatius. *Beschreibung von Kordofan und einigen angränzenden Ländern.* Stuttgart: Cotta, 1843. English translation, *Travels in Kordofan, Embracing a Description of that Province of Egypt, and of Some of the Bordering Countries.* London: J. Madden, 1844. 356p.

1491 . Parkyns, Mansfield. "The Kubbabish Arabs between Dongola and Kordofan," *JRGS*, XX(1850), 254-275.

1492 . Paulitschke, Philipp Viktor. *Die Sudanländer nach dem gegenwärtigen Stande der Kenntnis.* Freiburg im Bresgau and St.Louis, Mo.: Herder, 1885. 311p.

1493 . Percy, Algernon. [*4th Duke of Northumberland*]. "Extracts from Private Memoranda Kept by Lord Prudhoe on a Journey from Cairo to Sennar, in 1829, Describing the Peninsula of Sennar," *JRGS*, V(1835), 38-58.

1494 . Perron, Nicoles. [*Dr.*]. "Lettre sur le Darfour," *Journal Asiatique*, 3rd Series, VIII(1839), 177-206.

1495 . Petherick, John. *Egypt, the Soudan and Central Africa, with Explorations from Khartoum on the White Nile, to the Regions of the Equator: Being Sketches from Sixteen Years' Travel.* Edinburgh: Blackwood, 1861.

1496 . _____. "Land Journey Westward of the White Nile, from Abu Kuka to Gondokoro," *JRGS*, XXXV(1865), 289-300.

1497 . _____. "Memorandum of a Journey from Khartum by the White Nile, Bahr el Gazal, and in the Interior of Central Africa, during the Years 1857 and 1858," *PRGS*, V(1860-1861), 27-39.

1498 . _____. "Sources of the Nile. A Letter from Consul Petherick," *PRGS*, IV (1859-1860), 223-225.

1499    ._____and Petherick, Katherine. "Report of Expedition up the White Nile,"
        *PRGS*, VIII(1863-1864), 122-148.

1500    ._____. *Travels in Central Africa, and Explorations of the Western Nile*
        *Tributaries*. 2 vols. London: Tinsley, 1869.

1501    . Pimazzoni, Francesco. "Lettere," *ABPV*, (1880), No. 20, 35-39; (1881), No. 24,
        39-53; (1882), No. 27, 63, 64; No. 30, 17-25.

1502    ._____. "Lettere," *MCM*, XII(1883), 65, 66.

1503    ._____. "Lettere," *Nigrizia*, I(1883), 17-23, 38, 39.

1504    ._____. "Spedizione di missionari nell'Africa Centrale,"
        *ABPV*, (1880), No. 20, 15-34.

1505    . Polinari, Domenico. "Lettere," *Nigrizia*, II(1884), 38, 39.

1506    . Poncet, Jules. *Le fleuve Blanc. Notes géographiques et ethnologiques, et*
        *chasses a l'éléphant dans le pays des Dincha et des Djour.* Paris:
        Bertrand, c.1868.

1507    ._____. "Notice géographique et ethnologique sur la région du fleuve Blanc
        et sur ses habitants," *Nouvelles Annales des Voyages*, 6th Series,
        IV(1863), 5-62.

1508    ._____and Poncet, Ambrose. "Les pays situés a l'ouest du haut-fleuve-Blanc,"
        *BSGP*, 5th Series, XV(1868), 445-453.

1509    . Poussou. "Lettres," *ACM*, XVII(1852), 130-195.

1510    . Power, Frank. *Letters from Khartoum, Written during the Siege.* London:
        Sampson Low, 1885. 119p.

1511 . Prendergast, James. "Letters," *St. Joseph's Advocate,* III(1895-1900), 62-64, 102-106, 110-113, 142, 143; 300, 301, 313, 376, 377.

1512 . _____. "Lettres," *Annalen,* VI(1895-1896), 476-478, 513, 514.

1513 . Proctor, John. "Letters," *St. Joseph's Advocate,* III(1895-1900), 473, 474, 513; IV(1901-1906), 163, 196.

1514 . Prout, Henry G. [*Major*]. *General Report on the Province of Kordofan.* Cairo: Egyptian General Staff, 1877. 212p.

1515 . Prudhoe, Algernon Percy [*Duke of Northumberland*]. "Extracts from Private Memoranda Kept on a Journey from Cairo to Sennar, in 1829, Describing the Peninsula of Sennar," *JRGS,* V(1835), 35--58.

1516 . Quenedey, L. *En passant le Nil-Khartoum: Notes de voyage.* Paris: n.p., 1901. 174p.

1517 . Resener, Hans. "Der ägyptische Sudan als neues Absatzgebiet," *DK,* XVI (1899), 101-102.

1518 . _____. "Der Sudanfeldzug," *DK,* XIII(1896), 402-404.

1519 . Rivoyre, Barthélémy Louis Denis de. *Aux pays du Soudan, Bogos, Mensah, Souakim.* Paris: Plon, 1885. 292p.

1520 . Robinson, Phil. "In Osman Digna's Garden," *Contemporary Review,* IL (1886), 849-862.

1521 . Rokeby, Langham and Parry, Francis. "Narrative of an Expedition from Suakin to the Soudan, Compiled from the Journal of the Late Capt. L. R. by Francis Parry," *JRGS,* XLIV(1874), 152-163.

1522 . Rolleri, Bartolomeo. "Briefe," *KM,* I(1873), 68.

1523 . _____. "Chartum e costumi del Sudan," *ABPV,* XX(1881), No.26, 19-26, No.28, 33-39.

1524 . _____. "Lettere," *ABPV,* XII(1873), No.3, 23-27, XIV(1875), No.10, 33-35.

1525 . _____. "Lettere," *MCM*, II(1873), 378, 423, III(1874), 16, 78, 231, 280-281, 305, IV(1875), 41-42, 149, VII(1878), 78, 231, 280-281, 305, IV(1875), 41-42, 149, VII(1878), 197, VIII(1879), 136, 196.

1526 . _____. "Lettres," *MCL*, V(1873), 149, 258, 364, VI(1874), 52, 224, 277, VII(1875), 19-20, 124, 161, X(1878), 184, XI(1879), 114-115, 175.

. _____ . "Processione del Corpus Domini a Chartum," *ABPV*,
1527 (1881), No. 26, 35-41.

. _____ . "Stazione di Chartoum," *ABPV*, (1881), No. 24, 35-38.
1528

1529 . Rosignoli, P. *I miei dodici anni di prigionia in mezzo ai dervisci del Sudan.* Mondovì: Tipografia Graziano, 1898. 268p.

. Roveggio, Antonio. "Berichte," *JVUN*, XLII(1895), 7-23.
1530

1531 . _____ . "Lettere," *MCM*, XVIII(1889), 486, 487; XIX(1890), 67, 68; XXI(1892), 186, 187; XXX(1901), 313-315, 422, 423, 471.

. _____ . "Lettere," *Missioni Cattoliche Italiane*, (1901),
1532 16-27.

. _____ . "Lettere," *Nigrizia*, VII(1889), 129-132; VIII
1533 (1890), 5-9, 165-168; IX(1891), 9-11; X(1892), 36-40; XII(1894), 162-169; XIII(1895), 11-24, 27-31, 106-109, 115-117, 145-147, 181-184; XVI(1898), 3-7; XVII(1899), 17-21, 33-35; XVIII(1900), 5, 6, 41, 42; XIX(1901), 4, 5, 39, 40, 54-60.

. _____ . "Lettere," *Tappi, Cenno Storico*, (1894), 145-151.
1534

. _____ . "Lettres," *APFL*, LXXIII(1901), 361-368.
1535

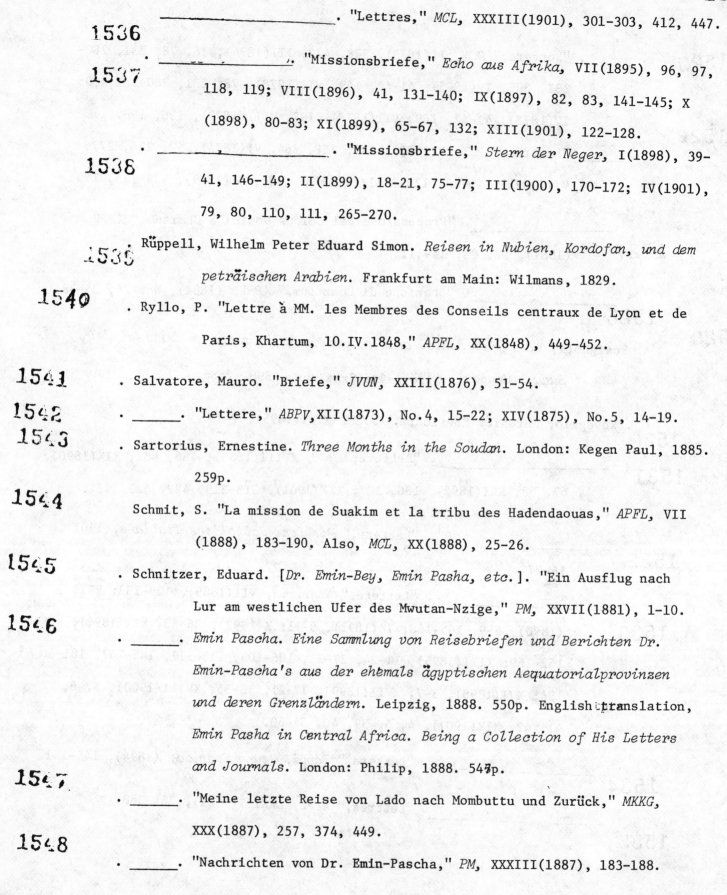

1536 _____. "Lettres," *MCL*, XXXIII(1901), 301-303, 412, 447.

1537 _____. "Missionsbriefe," *Echo aus Afrika*, VII(1895), 96, 97, 118, 119; VIII(1896), 41, 131-140; IX(1897), 82, 83, 141-145; X (1898), 80-83; XI(1899), 65-67, 132; XIII(1901), 122-128.

1538 _____. "Missionsbriefe," *Stern der Neger*, I(1898), 39-41, 146-149; II(1899), 18-21, 75-77; III(1900), 170-172; IV(1901), 79, 80, 110, 111, 265-270.

1539 Rüppell, Wilhelm Peter Eduard Simon. *Reisen in Nubien, Kordofan, und dem peträischen Arabien*. Frankfurt am Main: Wilmans, 1829.

1540 Ryllo, P. "Lettre à MM. les Membres des Conseils centraux de Lyon et de Paris, Khartum, 10.IV.1848," *APFL*, XX(1848), 449-452.

1541 Salvatore, Mauro. "Briefe," *JVUN*, XXIII(1876), 51-54.

1542 _____. "Lettere," *ABPV*, XII(1873), No.4, 15-22; XIV(1875), No.5, 14-19.

1543 Sartorius, Ernestine. *Three Months in the Soudan*. London: Kegen Paul, 1885. 259p.

1544 Schmit, S. "La mission de Suakim et la tribu des Hadendaouas," *APFL*, VII (1888), 183-190. Also, *MCL*, XX(1888), 25-26.

1545 Schnitzer, Eduard. [*Dr. Emin-Bey, Emin Pasha, etc.*]. "Ein Ausflug nach Lur am westlichen Ufer des Mwutan-Nzige," *PM*, XXVII(1881), 1-10.

1546 _____. *Emin Pascha. Eine Sammlung von Reisebriefen und Berichten Dr. Emin-Pascha's aus der ehemals ägyptischen Aequatorialprovinzen und deren Grenzländern*. Leipzig, 1888. 550p. English translation, *Emin Pasha in Central Africa. Being a Collection of His Letters and Journals*. London: Philip, 1888. 547p.

1547 _____. "Meine letzte Reise von Lado nach Mombuttu und Zurück," *MKKG*, XXX(1887), 257, 374, 449.

1548 _____. "Nachrichten von Dr. Emin-Pascha," *PM*, XXXIII(1887), 183-188.

1549 . _____. "Reisen im Osten des Bahr-el-Djebel, März bis Mai 1881," *PM*, XXVIII(1882), 259-272, 321-327.

1550 . _____. "Reisen im Westen des Bahr-el-Djebel, Oktober-Dezember 1882," *PM*, XXIX(1883), 415-428.

1551 . _____. "Rundreise durch die Mudirië Rohl," *PM*, XXIX(1883), 260-268, 323-340.

1552 . _____. "Die Strombarren des Bahr-el-Djebel," *PM*, XXV(1879), 273-274.

1553 . _____. "Von Dufilé nach Fatiko, 27.Dezember 1878 bis 8.Januar 1879," *PM*, XXVI(1880), 210-217.

1554 . _____. "Voyage dans l'Afrique équatoriale en 1877," *RMC*, XLV(1880).

1555 . _____, Lupton, Frank and Junker, Wilhelm. "Eine Post aus dem ägyptischen Sudan, Briefe von Dr. Emin-Bey, F. Lupton-Bey und Dr. W. Junker," *PM*, XXVIII(1882), 422-428.

1556 . Schroer, C. "Einiges über die Schillukneger und ihre Einrichtunger," *JVUN*, XLVIII(1901), No.2, 47-57.

1557 . _____. "Reiseskizzen," *JVUN*, XLVIII(1901), No.1, 29-42; No.2, 8-45.Also, *Stern der Neger*, **1902**, pp.38-42, 65-69, 100-105, 130-135.

1558 . Schuver, Juan María. *Reisen im oberen Nilgebiet. Erlebnisse und Beobachtungen auf der Wasserscheide zwischen Blauen und Weissen Nil und in den ägyptisch-abessinischen Grenzländern 1881 und 1882*. Gotha: Perthes, 1883. 95p.

1559 . _____. "Von Cairo nach Fádassi, 1.Januar bis 12.Juli 1881," *PM*, XXVIII (1882), 1-4.

1560 . Schweinfurth, Georg August. *Afrikanisches Skizzenbuch. Verschollene Merkwürdigkeiten*. Berlin: Deutsche Buchgemeinschaft, 1925. 313p.

1561 . _____. "Am westlichen Rande des Nilthals zwischen Farschut und Kom Ombo," *PM*, XLVII(1901), 1-10.

1562 . _____. *Artes Africanae. Abbildungen und Beschreibungen von Erzeugnissen des Kunstfleisses central afrikanischer Völker.* Text in German and English. Leipzig: Brockhaus; London: Low, Marston, Low & Searles, 1875. 42p.

1563 . _____. *Georg Schweinfurth. Lebensbild eines Afrikaforschers; Briefe von 1857-1925.* Edited by Konrad Guenther. Stuttgart: Wissenschaftliche Verlagsgesellschaft, 1954. 341p.

1564 . _____. *Im Herzen von Afrika. Reisen und Entdeckungen im centralen Aequator-ial-Afrika während der Jahre 1868 bis 1871.* 2 vols. Leipzig: Brockhaus, 1874. English translation, *The Heart of Africa. Three Years' Travels and Adventures in the Unexplored Regions of Central Africa, from 1868 to 1871.* 2 vols. London: Low, Marston, Low & Searle, 1873. French translation, *Au coeur de l'Afrique, 1866-1871. Voyages et découvertes dans des régions inexplorées de l'Afrique centrale.* 2 vols. Paris: Hachette, 1875. Also, *TM*, XXVII(1874), 273f

1565 . _____. "Linguistiche Ergebnisse einer Reise nach Central Afrika," *ZE*, IV(1872), Supplement, 82p. Also, Berlin: Wiegandt & Hempel, 1873.

1566 . _____. "Pflanzengeographische Skizze des gesammten Nil-Gebiets und der uferländer des Rothen Meeres," *PM*, XIV(1868), 244-248.

1567 . _____. "Völkerskizzen aus dem Gebiet der Bahr el Ghasal," *Globus*, XXII (1872), 74-77, 88-90, 225-228, XXIII(1873), 1-6, 23-25, 39-41.

1568 . Seiner, Heinrich. "Lettere," *MCM*, XXIII(1894), 487-488.

1569 . _____. "Lettere," *Nigrizia*, XVIII(1900), 101-103, 111; XIX(1901), 150-152.

1570 . _____. "Missionsbriefe," *Echo aus Afrika*, XIII(1901), 103-105.

1571 . _____. "Missionsbriefe," *Stern der Neger*, I(1898), 239-240, 283-284; II (1899), 131-134; III(1900), 37-41; IV(1901), 23-24, 281-288, 335-338.

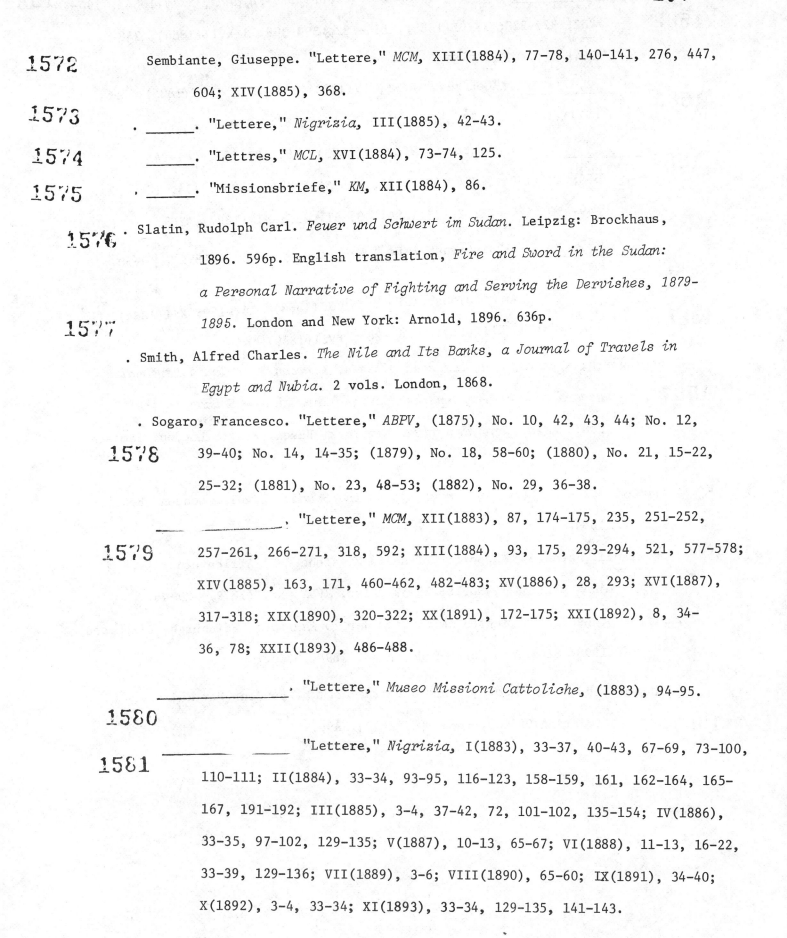

1572     Sembiante, Giuseppe. "Lettere," *MCM*, XIII(1884), 77-78, 140-141, 276, 447, 604; XIV(1885), 368.

1573     . _____. "Lettere," *Nigrizia*, III(1885), 42-43.

1574     _____. "Lettres," *MCL*, XVI(1884), 73-74, 125.

1575     . _____. "Missionsbriefe," *KM*, XII(1884), 86.

1576     . Slatin, Rudolph Carl. *Feuer und Schwert im Sudan*. Leipzig: Brockhaus, 1896. 596p. English translation, *Fire and Sword in the Sudan: a Personal Narrative of Fighting and Serving the Dervishes, 1879-1895*. London and New York: Arnold, 1896. 636p.

1577     . Smith, Alfred Charles. *The Nile and Its Banks, a Journal of Travels in Egypt and Nubia*. 2 vols. London, 1868.

     . Sogaro, Francesco. "Lettere," *ABPV*, (1875), No. 10, 42, 43, 44; No. 12,
1578     39-40; No. 14, 14-35; (1879), No. 18, 58-60; (1880), No. 21, 15-22, 25-32; (1881), No. 23, 48-53; (1882), No. 29, 36-38.

     _____. "Lettere," *MCM*, XII(1883), 87, 174-175, 235, 251-252,
1579     257-261, 266-271, 318, 592; XIII(1884), 93, 175, 293-294, 521, 577-578; XIV(1885), 163, 171, 460-462, 482-483; XV(1886), 28, 293; XVI(1887), 317-318; XIX(1890), 320-322; XX(1891), 172-175; XXI(1892), 8, 34-36, 78; XXII(1893), 486-488.

     _____. "Lettere," *Museo Missioni Cattoliche*, (1883), 94-95.

1580

     _____. "Lettere," *Nigrizia*, I(1883), 33-37, 40-43, 67-69, 73-100,
1581     110-111; II(1884), 33-34, 93-95, 116-123, 158-159, 161, 162-164, 165-167, 191-192; III(1885), 3-4, 37-42, 72, 101-102, 135-154; IV(1886), 33-35, 97-102, 129-135; V(1887), 10-13, 65-67; VI(1888), 11-13, 16-22, 33-39, 129-136; VII(1889), 3-6; VIII(1890), 65-60; IX(1891), 34-40; X(1892), 3-4, 33-34; XI(1893), 33-34, 129-135, 141-143.

1582 _____. "Lettres," *Annales Oeuvre Ste-Enfance,* XXXV(1884), 194–202, 327–328; XXXVI(1885), 130–132, 393–398; XXXVII(1886), 248–264; XL(1889), 43–57.

1583 _____. "Lettres," *APFL,* LV(1883), 334–340; LVII(1885), 256; LVIII(1886), 28–50, 118, 322–323; LIX(1887), 320–321.

1584 _____. "Lettres," *MCL,* XV(1883), 78, 181–182, 241–245, 316, 353; XVI(1884), 284, 434, 511, 565–566; XVII(1885), 124, 164, 327, 449–450, 475–476; XVIII(1886), 8, 51, 293; XIX(1887), 269.

1585 _____. "Missionsbriefe," *Echo aus Afrika,* IV(1892), 49–50.

1586 _____. "Missionsbriefe," *KM,* XI(1883), 147–150; XII(1884), 86, 179–180; XIII(1885), 260–263; XVII(1889), 46–47.

1587 Southworth, Alvan S. *Four Thousand Miles of African Travels: A Personal Record of a Journey up the Nile and Through the Soudan to the Confines of Central Africa.* New York: Baker, Pratt; London: Sampson, Low, 1875.

1588 Speedy, Cornelia Mary. *My Wanderings in the Soudan.* 2 vols. London: Bentley, 1884.

1589 Squaranti, Antonio. "Rapporto.... sulla Missione dell'Africa centrale," *ABPV,* XXI(1882), No.18, 29–59. Also, *JVUN,* XXVI(1879), 29–43.

1590 Steevens, George Warrington. *With Kitchner to Khartoum.* Edinburgh: Blackwood, 1898. 326p. New York: Dodd, Mead, 1898. 326p.

1591 Stewart, D. H. [*Lt. Col.*]. *Report on the Soudan.* London: Her Majesty's Printing Office, 1883. [c. 3670]. 39p.

1592 . Stoppani, Antonio. "Lettere," *Nigrizia*, XVIII(1900), 12-14, 46-48; XIX (1901), 182-184.

1593 . Stoppani, A. "La musica degli Arabi," *Nigrizia*, XVIII(1900), 46-48.

1594 . Stutfield, Hugh E. M. "The Experiences of an African Trader," *Macmillan's Magazine*, LXV(1891-1892), 110-120.

1595 . Sykes, Clement Arthur [*Brig. Gen.*]. *Service and Sport on the Tropical Nile. Some Records of the Duties and Diversion of an Officer among Natives and Big Game during the Reoccupation of the Nilotic Province.* London: John Murray, 1903. 306p.

1596 . Tappi, Carlo. "A Sud di Chartum," *Nigrizia*, XVII(1899), 68-71.

1597 . _____. "Gli abitatori del Nilo," *Nigrizia*, XVI(1898), 10-12, 38-40. Also *JVUN*, XLV(1898), 21-30.

1598 . _____. "La capitale del Sudan," *Nigrizia*, XVI(1898), 180-186.

1599 . _____. *Cenno Storico della Missione dell'Africa Centrale dal suo principio fino ad oggi.* Turin: Tipografia Salesiana, 1894. 192p.

1600 . _____. "Civilizzazione dei Neri," *Nigrizia*, XIV(1898), 157-160, 170-173.

1601 . _____. "Come si fanno gli sposalizi tra i Sudanesi," *Nigrizia*, XII(1894), 145-149.

1602 . _____. "Come si fanno i balli tra i Sudanesi," *Nigrizia*, XVI(1898), 42, 56, 106.

1603 . _____. "Un'escursione sul Basso Sobat," *BSGI*, XXXIV(1901), 930-940.

1604 . _____. "Feticci e feticismo," *Nigrizia*, XIX(1901), 76-79.

1605 . _____. "Il fiume delle Gazelle," *Nigrizia*, XVII(1899), 8-10.

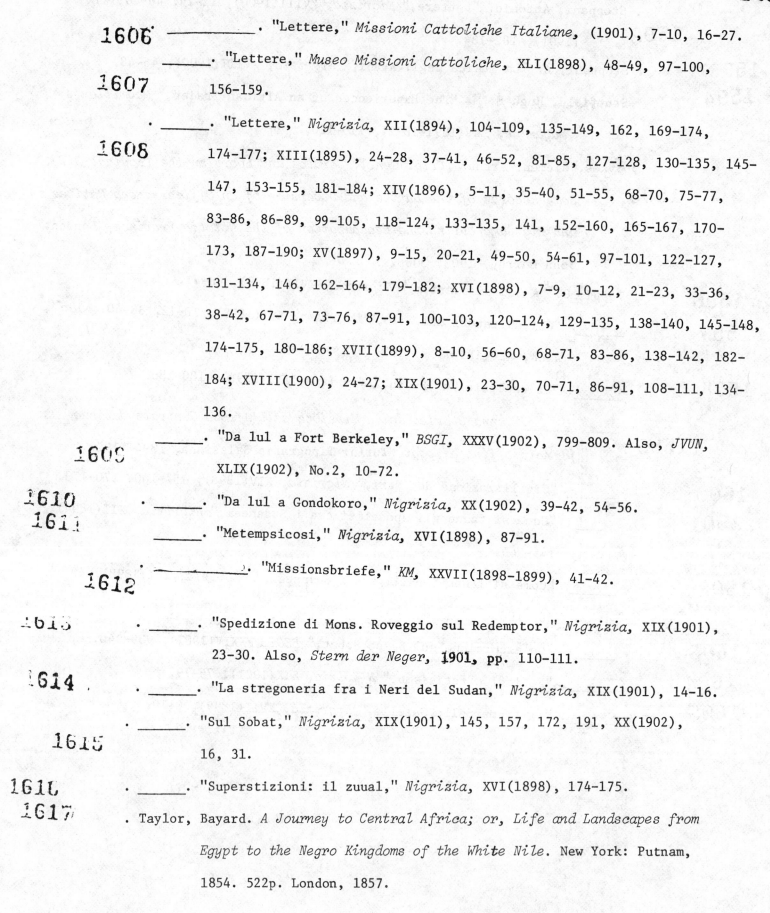

1606 ————. "Lettere," *Missioni Cattoliche Italiane*, (1901), 7-10, 16-27.

1607 ————. "Lettere," *Museo Missioni Cattoliche*, XLI(1898), 48-49, 97-100, 156-159.

1608 ————. "Lettere," *Nigrizia*, XII(1894), 104-109, 135-149, 162, 169-174, 174-177; XIII(1895), 24-28, 37-41, 46-52, 81-85, 127-128, 130-135, 145-147, 153-155, 181-184; XIV(1896), 5-11, 35-40, 51-55, 68-70, 75-77, 83-86, 86-89, 99-105, 118-124, 133-135, 141, 152-160, 165-167, 170-173, 187-190; XV(1897), 9-15, 20-21, 49-50, 54-61, 97-101, 122-127, 131-134, 146, 162-164, 179-182; XVI(1898), 7-9, 10-12, 21-23, 33-36, 38-42, 67-71, 73-76, 87-91, 100-103, 120-124, 129-135, 138-140, 145-148, 174-175, 180-186; XVII(1899), 8-10, 56-60, 68-71, 83-86, 138-142, 182-184; XVIII(1900), 24-27; XIX(1901), 23-30, 70-71, 86-91, 108-111, 134-136.

1609 ————. "Da lul a Fort Berkeley," *BSGI*, XXXV(1902), 799-809. Also, *JVUN*, XLIX(1902), No.2, 10-72.

1610 ————. "Da lul a Gondokoro," *Nigrizia*, XX(1902), 39-42, 54-56.

1611 ————. "Metempsicosi," *Nigrizia*, XVI(1898), 87-91.

1612 ————. "Missionsbriefe," *KM*, XXVII(1898-1899), 41-42.

1613 ————. "Spedizione di Mons. Roveggio sul Redemptor," *Nigrizia*, XIX(1901), 23-30. Also, *Stern der Neger*, 1901, pp. 110-111.

1614 ————. "La stregoneria fra i Neri del Sudan," *Nigrizia*, XIX(1901), 14-16.

1615 ————. "Sul Sobat," *Nigrizia*, XIX(1901), 145, 157, 172, 191, XX(1902), 16, 31.

1616 ————. "Superstizioni: il zuual," *Nigrizia*, XVI(1898), 174-175.

1617 Taylor, Bayard. *A Journey to Central Africa; or, Life and Landscapes from Egypt to the Negro Kingdoms of the White Nile*. New York: Putnam, 1854. 522p. London, 1857.

1618 . Thibaut [called "Ibrahim Effendi"]. *Expédition à la recherche des sources du Nil (1839-1840). Journal de M. Thibaut.* Paris: A. Bertrand, 1856. 101p.

1619 . Tiedemann, Adolf von. *Mit Lord Kitchner gegen den Mahdi. Erinnerungen eines preussischen Generalstabsoffiziers an den englischen Sudan-Feldzug.* Berlin: Schwetschke, 1906. 206p.

. Titz, Carlo. "Lettere," *Nigrizia*, XV(1897), 84, 85.

1620 ____. "Missionsbriefe," *Stern der Neger*, II(1899), 21-24, 47-48.

1621
1622 . Tonolli, Roberto. *Un Missionario Trentino fra i Selvaggi dell'Africa tenebrosa.* Trent: Tipografia Artigianelli, 1899. 388p. Also, *Nigrizia*, IV(1886) through XII(1894).

1623 . Trail, Henry Duff. *From Cairo to the Soudan Frontier.* London: Lane, 1896. 256p. Chicago: Way & Williams, 1896.

1624 . Trémaux, Pierre. "Notes sur la localité où sont situées les principales mines d'or du Soudan oriental, et observations critiques sur le récit du colonel Kovalevski relatif à cette meme contrée," *BSGP*, 3rd Series, XIII(1850), 201-232.

1625 ____. "Voyage au Soudan oriental," *TM*, XIV(1866), 161-192.

1626 ____. *Voyage au Soudan orientale, dans l'Afrique septentrionale et dans l'Asie Mineure, exécute de 1847 à 1854, comprenant une exploration dans l'Algérie, la Régence de Tunis, le Tripoli, l'Asie mineure, l'Egypte, la Nubie, les déserts, l'île de Méroé, le Sennaar, le Fa-Zogl, et dans les contrées inconnues de la Nigritie.* Paris: Borrani, 1859.

1627 . Twyford, A. W. "Notes Relative to the Late Proposed Expedition to Discover the Sources of the White Nile," *PRGS*, I(1855-1857), 503-508.

. Van Agt, Frans. "Lettres," *Annalen*, XI(1900-1901), 37, 38.

1628

_____. "Lettres," *St. Josefs-Missionsbote*, VI(1901), 32.

1629

Van den Bergh, Leonard. "Letters," *St. Joseph's Advocate*, III(1895-1900),

1630    200, 213-215, 377-378, 392-393; IV(1901-1906), 53, 54, 441.

. _____. "Lettres," *Annalen*, VIII(1897-1898), 726-728, 746; IX(1898-

1631    1899), 848, 942-943; X(1899-1900), 999-1001, 1058-1062; XI(1900-

1901), 44-45; XII(1901-1902), 164-165.

. _____. "Lettres," *St. Josefs-Missionsbote*, II(1897), 133-134; IV(1899),

1632    354-356.

. Van der Kallen, Lambertus. "Lettres," *Annalen*, XI(1900-1901), 50-53, 80,

1633    92-93.

. Van de Walle, Théophile. "Lettres," *Maandelijksch Verslag der Afrikaansche

1634    Missiën*, XI(1890), 215-219.

. Van Term, Antonius. "Letters," *St. Joseph's Advocate*, III(1895-1900), 198-

1635    199, 200-201, 212-213, 230-233, 423-424, 488-489, 503; IV(1901-

1906), 52-53.

. _____. "Lettres," *Annalen*, VII(1896-1897), 650-651; VIII(1897-1898), 725-

1636    726; IX(1898-1899), 853-856, 871-872, 892-894, 958-959; X(1899-

1900), 962-964, 1077-1078.

_____. "Lettres," *St. Josefs-Missionsbote*, II(1897), 119-122; III(1898),

1637    205-207, 266, 278-280; V(1900), 64.

. Verner, William Willoughby Cole. *Sketches in the Soudan*. London: Porter,

1638    1885.

1639 . Vianello, Federico. "Lettere," *Nigrizia*, XV(1897), 165-170; XVI(1898), 13-15.

1640 . Vicentini, Domenico. "L'Insurrezione mahadista nella Provincia di Dongola," *BSGI*, XXII(1885), 351-367, 438-454. Also, *Nigrizia*, III (1885), 109-122, 161-164, 174-193; IV(1886), 11-19.

1641 . _____. "Lettere," *BSGI*, XXVI(1889), 86-88, 134-135.

1642 . _____. "Lettere," *MCM*, XII(1883), 208-210; XIII(1884), 100-102, 186; XVIII(1889), 487-488.

1643 . _____. "Lettere," *Nigrizia*, I(1883), 51-56, 180-188; II(1884), 15-17, 31-32, 48-50, 62-63, 64, 70-75, 96, 167-169, 170-173; III(1885), 6-13, 13-30, 43-46, 154-156; IV(1886), 38-40; V(1887), 129-131; VI(1888), 137-139; VII(1889), 137-140; VIII(1890), 33-34.

1644 . _____. "Missionsbriefe," *KM*, XII(1884), 85-86, 154-155; XIV(1886), 19.

1645 . _____. "La prima Cateratta del Nile presso Assuan," *Nigrizia*, II(1883), 129-143.

1646 . _____. "La schiavitù in Africa," *Nigrizia*, VII(1889), 71-78, 112-120, 149-150, 154, 168-176; VIII(1890), 13-20.

1647 . _____. "Da Suakin," *Bollettino della Società Africana d'Italia*[Naples], VIII(1889), 86-88, 134-135.

1648 . Villiers, Frederick. "My Recent Journey from the Nile to Suakim," *JRSA*, XLVI(1898), 233-241.

1649 . Vinco, Angelo. "Extrait d'une lettre à M. Brun Rollet, Bellenia, 2.IV. 1851," *BSGP*, 4th Series, III(1852), 32.

1650 . _____. *Reisebericht des hochwürdigen apostolischen Missionärs, Herrn Angelo Vinco, niedergeschrieben auf einer Reise in den Gebieten der verschiedenen Aequatorial-Stämme am weissen Flusse, vom Januar 1851 angefangen bis zur Hälfte des Jahres 1852.* Vienna: Kaiserlich-Königlichen Hof- und Staatsdruckerei, 1853. 24p.

1651 . _____. "Relazione del viaggio del Reverendo Sacerdote Don Angelo Vinco, Missionario Apostolico, fra le varie tribù equatoriali del Fiume Bianco dal principio dell'anno 1851 fino alla metà del 1852," *Annali della Società di Maria per le Missioni Cattoliche*, II (1853), 3-48.

1652 . _____. "Riposte a un questionario di Antonio d'Abbadie, inoltratogli a mezzo di Alessandria Vaudey," *BSGP*, 4th Series, IV(1852), 525-535.

1653 . Waddington, G. and HANBURY, Bernard. *Journal of a Visit to Some Parts of Ethiopia.* London: Murray, 1822. 333p.

1654 . Watkins, Owen Spencer. *With Kitchner's Army, Being a Chaplain's Experiences with the Nile Expedition of 1898.* London: S. W. Partridge & Co., 1899. 276p.

1655 . Watson, C. M. [*Lt. Royal Eng.*]. "Notes to Accompany a Traverse Survey of the White Nile, from Khartoum to Rigaf, 1874," *JRGS*, XLVI(1876), 412-427.

1656 . _____. "The Suakin-Berber Route to the Sudan," *JMGS*, X(1894), 107-119.

1657 . _____. "Trade Prospects with the Sudan," *JMGS*, III(1887), 170-180.

1658    . Werne, Ferdinand. *Expedition zur Entdeckung der Quellen des Weissen Nil (1840-1841)*. Berlin, 1848. English translation, *Expedition to Discover the Sources of the White Nile, in the Years 1840, 1841*. 2 vols. London: Bentley, 1849.

1659    . _____. *Feldzug von Sennar nach Taka, Basa und Beni-Amer, mit besonderem Hinblick auf die Völker von Bellad-Sudan*. Stuttgart: Cotta, 1851. English translation, *African Wanderings, or an Expedition from Sennaar to Taka, Basa, aand Beni-Amer; with a Particular Glance at the Races of Bellad Sudan*. London: Longman, Brown, Green & Longmans, 1852. 267p.

1660    . _____. *Reise durch Sennaar nach Mandera, Nasub, Cheli, im Lande zwischen dem blauen Nil und dem Atbara*. Berlin: Ducker, 1852.

1661    . Williams, Josiah. *Life in the Soudan: Adventures amongst the Tribes, and Travels in Egypt, in 1881 and 1882*. London: Remington, 1884. 338p.

1662    . Wills, J. T. "The Cultivable Area of the Egyptian Sudan," *SGM*, II(1886), 411-415.

1663    . Wilson, Charles William. *From Korti to Khartum. A Journal of the Desert March from Korti to Gubat, and of the Ascent of the Nile in General Gordon's Steamers*. London: Blackwood, 1886. 313p.

1664    . _____. "Tribes of the Nile Valley, North of Khartúm," *JAI*, XVII(1887), 3-23.

1665    . Wilson, H. H. "A Trip up the Khor Felus, and Country on the Left Bank of Sobat," *GJ*, XX(1902), 401-405.

1666    . Wingate, Francis Reginald. *Mahdiism and the Egyptian Soudan*. London: Macmillan, 1891. 617p.

1667 . Wortley, Edward James Montagu Stuart-. "With the Sirdar," *Scribner's Magazine*, Jan., 1899, pp. 118-122.

1668 . Wouters, Willem. "Lettres," *Annalen der Afrikaansche Missiën*, XV(1898-1899), 86-89, 119-120.

1669 . Wright, H. C. Seppings. *Soudan '96: The Adventures of a War Artist.* London: Cox, 1897. 108p.

1670 . Wylde, Augustus Blandy. *'83 to '87 in the Soudan. With an Account of Sir William Hewett's Mission to King John of Abyssinia.* 2 vols. London: Remington, 1888.

1671 . Zebehr Pasha, and Shaw, Flora. "The Story of Zebehr Pasha," *Contemporary Review*, LII(1887), 333-349, 568-585, 658-682.

1672 . Zurbuchen, J. [*Dr.*]. "Reise nach Chartum, durch Kordofan und Darfur, 1879. Tagebuchblätter von Dr. J. Zurbuchen," *PM*, XXX(1884), 443-454.

TANZANIA

1673    . Abbott, W. L. "Ethnological Collections in the U. S. National
Museum from Kilima-Njaro, East Africa," *Smithsonian Report,*
XLVI(1891), 381-427.

. Acker, Amand. *Die Aufgabe der katholischen Mission in den Kolonien.* Essen:
1674    G. D. Baedecker, 1909. 16p.

1675    . _____. "Lettere," *MCM,* IX(1880), 337-339, 361-366.

1676    . _____. "Lettres," *MCL,* XII(1880), 314-315, 337-344.

1677    . _____. "Missionsbriefe," *Echo aus Afrika,* IV(1892), 113-115; V(1893), 53-54,
109; X(1898), 18-20.

1678    _____. "Missionsbriefe," *KM,* IX(1881), 46-50.

. ____ _____. "Über einige Mittel zur allmählichen Abschaffung der
Sklaverei," *Verhandlungen des deutschen Kolonialkongresses,* 1902,
1673    453ff.

. Adams, Alfons. *Im Dienste des Kreuzes. Erinnerungen aus Meinem Missionsleben
in Deutsch-Ostafrika.* Augsburg: M.Huttler, 1899. 154p.
1680

. Adams, P. *Lindi und sein Hinterland.* Berlin: Reimer, 1903. 71p.
1681
1682    . Aga Khan. "Zur Inderfrage in Deutsch-Ostafrika," *DK,* XVII(1900),
96, 110.

. Alexis, M. G. *Alexis Vrithoff, Compagnon des Capitaines Jacques et Joubert
1683    au Lac Tanganika.* Tournai: Société de Saint-Augustin, 1893. 192p.

1684 · Allgeyer, Emil. "Lettere," *MCM*, XXIX(1900), 609-610.

1685 · _____. "Lettres," *Annales Apostoliques*, XVI(1900-1901), 56-60.

1686
1687 · _____. "Lettres," *Bulletin de la Congrégation*, XX(1899-1900), 49-51, 85.

· _____. "Lettres," *MCL*, XXXI(1899), 610; XXXII(1900), 230.

1688 · _____. "Missionsbriefe," *Echo aus Afrika*, XII(1900), 5-7.

1689 · _____. "Missionsbriefe," *Echo aus Knechtsteden*, III(1901-1902), 117-118.

1690 · Anonymous. "Sketches of Zanzibar: Written during a Sojourn on That Island, from May 20th to August 10th, 1843," *The American Review: A Whig Journal*, II(Aug., 1845), 154-162.

1691 · Arning, Wilhelm. "Die Wahehe," *MDS*, IX(1896), 233-246, X(1897), 46-60.

1692 _____. *Deutsch-Ostafrika gestern und heute*. Berlin, 1936. 338p.

1693 · Avon, Théophile. "Lettere," *MCM*, XXVIII(1899), 37-39.

1694 · _____. "Lettres," *Annalen der Afrikaansche Missiën*, XVI(1899-1900), 9-14.

1695 · _____. "Lettres," *Annales Oeuvre Ste-Enfance*, L(1899), 84-90.

1696 · _____. "Lettres," *MCL*, XXXI(1899), 25-27.

1697 · _____. "Lettres," *Missiën der Witte Paters*, XX(1899), 79-83, 188-192.

1698 · _____. "Lettres," *Missions d'Afrique*, XX(1899), 65-71, 136-140.

1699 · _____. "Lettres," *Missions d'Afrique*[Paris], (1895-1897), 175-176, 451-454; (1897-1900), 542-545, 606-611, 850-858.

1700 · _____. "Missionsbriefe," *Afrika-Bote*, II(1896), 27, 28; III(1897), 27-29; V(1899), 165-169; VI(1899-1900), 253-258; VII(1900-1901), 159-162, 277-281.

1701 · _____. "Missionsbriefe," *Echo aus Afrika*, XI(1899), 139-140.

1702 . _____. "De Ngil of Afrikaansche Toovenaar," *Annalen der Afrikaansche Missiën*, XV(1898-1899), 107-114, 142-148, 176-182, 239-245, 275-279, 301-306, 327-332, 364-367; XVI(1899-1900), 14-19.

1703 . Barth, C. G. "Die ersten Lebensjahre unserer deutschen Schule in Tanga, Ostafrika," *DK*, XII(1895), 90-93.

1704 . Bateman, George W. *Zanzibar Tales: Told by Natives of the East Coast of Africa*. Chicago: McClurg, 1901. 224p.

1705 . Baumann, Oscar. *Afrikanische Skizzen*, Berlin: D. Reimer, 1900. 119p.

1706 . _____. *Durch Massailand zur Nilquelle. Reisen und Forschungen der Massai-Expedition des deutschen Antisklaverei-Komite in den Jahren 1891-1893*. Berlin: D. Reimer, 1894. 385p.

1707 . _____. "Gottesurteile bei den Swahili," *Globus*, LXXVI(1899), 371-372.

1708 . _____. *In Deutsch-Ostafrika während des Aufstandes*. Vienna & Olmutz, 1890. 224p. Berlin: D. Reimer, 1900. 119p.

1709 . _____. *Die kartographischen Ergebnisse der Massai-Expedition des deutschen Antisklaverei-Comités*. Gotha: Petermanns, 1894. 56p.

1710 . _____. "Ostafrikanische Schulen," *DK*, XI(1894), 56-57.

1711 . _____. *Der Sansibar-Archipel. Ergebnisse einer mit Unterstützung des Vereins für Erdkunde zu Leipzig 1895-96 ausgeführten Forschungreise*. Leipzig: Duncker & Humboldt, 1896. 101p.

1712 . _____. "Der Unterlauf des Pangani-Flusses," *PM*, XLII(1896), 59-62.

1713 . _____. "Usambara," *PM*, XXXV(1889), 41-47.

1714 . _____. *Usambara und seine Nachbargebiete*. Berlin: Reimer, 1891. 375p.

1715 . Baumstark, Paul. "Die Warangi," *MDS*, XIII(1900), 45-60.

1716 . Baur, Étienne. "Lettere," *MCM*, II(1873), 74-75, 339-340; III(1874), 424, 436; IV(1875), 529-531; XI(1882), 217-218.

1717 . _____. "Lettres," *Annales Oeuvre Ste-Enfance*, XXXIV(1883), 107-115; XXXV (1884), 328-341.

1718 . _____. "Lettres," *APFL*, LIV(1882), 354-373.

1719 . _____. "Lettres," *MCL*, V(1873), 521-522; XIV(1882), 194-195.

1720 . _____. "Missionsbriefe," *KM*, IV(1876), 22; X(1882), 174.

1721 . _____. *Voyage dans l'Oudoé et l'Ouzigoua(Zanguebar)*. Lyon: Mougin-Rusand, 1882. 95p. Also, *MCL*, XIV(1882), 342ff; *MCM*, XII(1883), 10ff.

1722 . _____ and Le Roy, A. *À travers le Zanguebar*. Tours: Mame, 1886. 568p.

1723 . Beardall, William. "Exploration of the Rufiji River under the Orders of the Sultan of Zanzibar," *PRGS*, New Series, III(1881), 641-656.

1724 Beerwald, K. "Am Kilimandscharo," *DK*, XV(1898), 391-394.

1725 . Behr, H. F. von. "Am Rowuma," *DK*, IX(1892), 66-67, 93-96, 108-110.

1726 . _____. "Am Rufiji," *DK*, IX(1892), 139-143.

1727 . _____. "Geographische und ethnographische Notizen aus dem Flussgebiet des Rovuma," *MDS*, V(1892), 15-20.

1728 . _____. *Kriegsbilder aus dem Araberaufstand in Deutsch-Ostafrika*. Leipzig, 1891. 343p.

1729 . _____. "Die Völker zwischen Rufiji und Rovuma," *MDS*, VI(1893), 69-87.

1730 . Bellville, Alfred. " Journey to the Universities Mission Station of Magila, on the Borders of the Usambara Country," *PRGS*, XX(1875-1876), 74-78.

1731 . _____. "A Trip round the South End of Zanzibar Island," *PRGS*, XX(1875-1876), 69-74.

1732 . Berg. "Das Bezirksamt Mikindani. Bericht des Bezirksamtmanns," *MDS*, X (1897), 206-222.

1733 . Beringer, Otto L. "Notes on the Country between Lake Nyasa and Victoria Nyanza," *GJ*, XXI(1903), 25-36.

Bernhard, Louis. "Lettres," *Lis de St-Joseph*, X(1899), 301-302.

**1734**

Bertram, Otto. "Lettres," *Het H. Misoffer*, III(1900), 241-245; IV(1901),

**1735**    13-18, 36-40, 81-84, 98-104, 173-176, 191-196, 204-207, 229-233.

**1736**    Bockelmann, A. von. "Die Regierungsschulen in Deutsch-Ostafrika," *DK*,

XVI(1899), 346-347.

**1737**    Boddaert, Ernest. "Lettres," *Missions d'Afrique*, (1895-1897), 359-362.

**1738**    _____. "Lettres," *Missions d'Alger*, (1893-1894), 229.

**1739**    _____. "Missionsbriefe," *Africa-Bote*, II(1896), 167-169.

**1740**    Böcking, G. "Sagen der Wa-Pokomo," *ZAOS*, II(1896), 33-39.

**1741**    Böckner, C. "Die wichtigsten Kultur- und Nutzpflanzen Deutsch-Ostafrikas,"

*Koloniales Jahrbuch*, 1891, 100-117.

**1742**    Böhm, Richard. "Bericht aus Rakoma," *MAGD*, III(1881-1883).

**1743**    _____. "Reise nach Urambo und Besuch beim Häuptling Mirambo," *MAGD*,

III(1881-1883), 275.

**1744**    _____. *Von Sansibar zum Tanganjika. Briefe aus Ostafrika*. Leipzig:

Brockhaus, 1888. 171p.

**1745**    _____ and Kaiser, E. "Reise nach dem Tanganjika," *MAGD*, III(1881-1883),

181-209.

**1746**    _____ and Reichard, P. "Bericht über die Befahrung des Wala," *MAGD*,

III(1881-1883).

**1747**    _____. "Bericht uber die Befahrung des Wala," *MAGD*, III(1881-1883).

**1748**    _____. "Ergänzungen zu früheren Berichten," *MAGD*, IV(1883-1885).

**1749**    Boileau, F. F. R. and Wallace, L. A. "The Nyasa-Tanganyika Plateau," *GJ*,

XIII(1899), 577-621.

**1750**    Bornhardt, Friedrich Wilhelm Conrad Eduard. *Zur Oberflächengestaltung

und Geologie Deutsch-Ostafrikas*. Berlin, 1900. 595p.

1751     . Boyer, Adrien. "Lettres," *MCL*, XXXIII(1901), 438-441.

1752     . _____. "Lettres," *Missions d'Afrique*[Paris], (1897-1900), 197-198, 426-428.

1753     . _____. "Missionsbriefe," *Afrika-Bote*, V(1899), 105-106; VII(1900-1901), 262-272.

1754     . Brard, Alphonse and Dromaux. "Die Missionen der 'Weissen Vater' in Deutsch-Ostafrika," *KM*, XXV(1897), 49-52, 80-83. See also, *Afrika-Bote*, III(1897), 51-56, 67-69, 83-87.

1755     . Brehme. "Bericht über das Kulturland des Kilimandjaro und dessen Klimatische und Gesundheitliche Verhältnisse," *MDS*, VII(1894), 106.

1756     . Brenner, Laurentius. "Missionsbriefe," *Missionsblätter*, IV(1900), 105.

1757     . Brichaux, J. B. [*Fr.Mattheus*]. "Lettres," *Maandelijksch Verslag de Afrikaansche Missiën*, XIX(1898), 71-72.

1758     . Bridoux, Léonce. [*Msgr.*]. "Une première tournée pastorale au Tanganika," *MCL*, XXII(1890), 471-472, 488-490, 500-502, 512-515, 519-521, 536-538, 548-550, 562-563, 573-576.

1759     . _____ _____. "Lettere," *MCM*, XIX(1890), 32-33.

1760     _____. "Lettres," *Annalen der Afrikaansche Missiën*, VI(1899-1890), 6-9, 243-246; VII(1890-1891), 235-236, 271-275; VIII(1891-1892), 10-15.

1761     _____. "Lettres," *Annales Oeuvre Ste-Enfance*, XLII(1891), 383-403; XLIII (1892), 20-31.

1762     _____. "Lettres," *APFL*, LXIII(1891), 267-278.

1763     . _____. "Lettres," *Maandelijksch Verslag der Afrikaansche Missiën*, XII (1891), 105-110, 183-185.

1764     . _____. "Lettres," *MCL*, XXI(1889), 619.

1765     . _____. "Lettres," *Missions d'Alger*, (1887-1890), 345-347, 511-514, 638-641, 881-882; (1891-1892), 62-69, 247-250.

1766     _____. "Missionsbriefe," *Echo aus Afrika*, III(1891), 33-36, 45-48.

1767 . Bringuier, Joseph. "Lettres," *Missions d'Afrique*, XIX(1898), 332-335.

1768 . Bronsart von Schellendorff, Fritz. *Strausse, Zebras und Elephanten. Die Bedeutung eingeborener Thiere für die wirtschaftliche Entwickelung Deutsch-Ostafrikas*. Berlin: Walther, 1898. 52p.

1769 . _____. *Thierbeobachtungen und Jagdgeschichten aus Ostafrika*. Berlin: Deutscher Kolonialverlag, 1900. 155p.

1770 . Browne, James Ross. *Etchings of a Whaling Cruise, with Notes of a Sojourn on the Island of Zanzibar*. New York: Harper, 1846. 580p.

1771 . Broyon-Mirambo, Philippe. "Description of Unyamwesi, the Territory of King Mirambo, and the Best Route Thither from the East Coast," *PRGS*, XXII(1877-1878), 28-36.

1772 . Bülow, Frieda Friederike Louise von.[*Baroness*]. *Reiseskizzen und Tage-buchblätter aus Deutsch-Ostafrika*. Berlin: Walther & Apolant, 1889. 196p.

1773 . Büttner, Carl G. "Das deutsch-evengelische Hospital in Sansibar," *DK*, V(1888), 157-158, 363.

1774 . Burton, Richard Francis. "On the Ukara, or the Ukerewe Lake of Equatorial Africa," *PRGS*, XVI(1871-1872), 129-130.

1775 . _____. *Zanzibar: City, Island and Coast*. 2 vols. London: Tinsley, 1872.

1776 . Cameron, Verney Lovett. "England and Germany in East Africa," *Fortnightly Review*, New Series, XLVIII(1890), 129-143.

1777 . _____. "Zanzibar: Its Past, Present and Future," *Revue Coloniale Internationale*, I(1885), 417-430.

1778 . Capelle. [*Fr. Stephanus*]. "Lettres," *Maandelijksch Verslag der Afrikaansche Missiën*, XII(1891), 303-306; XV(1894), 239-241; XVII(1896), 36-38.

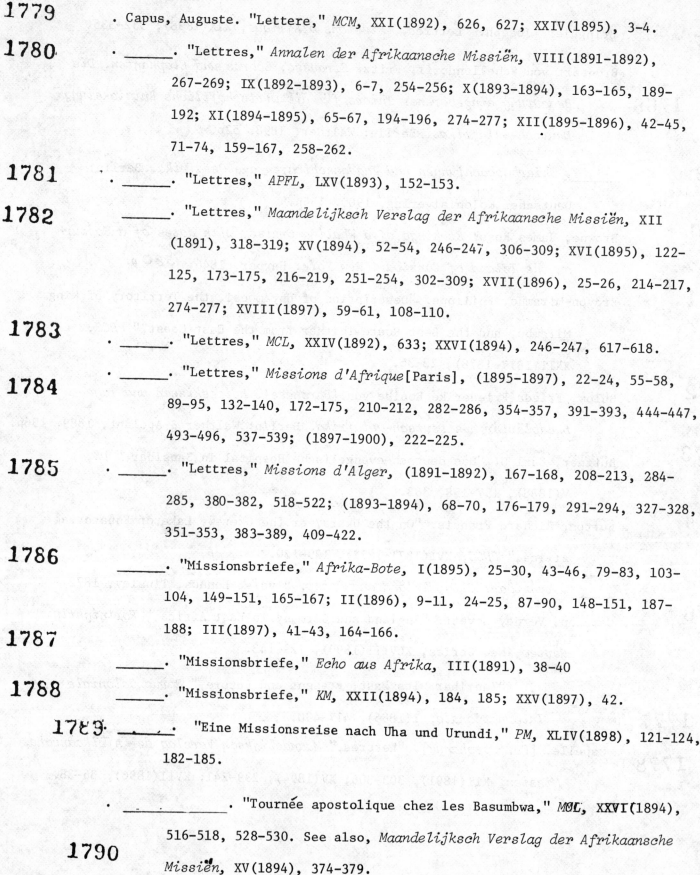

1779    . Capus, Auguste. "Lettere," *MCM*, XXI(1892), 626, 627; XXIV(1895), 3-4.

1780    . _____. "Lettres," *Annalen der Afrikaansche Missiën*, VIII(1891-1892), 267-269; IX(1892-1893), 6-7, 254-256; X(1893-1894), 163-165, 189-192; XI(1894-1895), 65-67, 194-196, 274-277; XII(1895-1896), 42-45, 71-74, 159-167, 258-262.

1781    . _____. "Lettres," *APFL*, LXV(1893), 152-153.

1782    _____. "Lettres," *Maandelijksch Verslag der Afrikaansche Missiën*, XII (1891), 318-319; XV(1894), 52-54, 246-247, 306-309; XVI(1895), 122-125, 173-175, 216-219, 251-254, 302-309; XVII(1896), 25-26, 214-217, 274-277; XVIII(1897), 59-61, 108-110.

1783    . _____. "Lettres," *MCL*, XXIV(1892), 633; XXVI(1894), 246-247, 617-618.

1784    . _____. "Lettres," *Missions d'Afrique*[Paris], (1895-1897), 22-24, 55-58, 89-95, 132-140, 172-175, 210-212, 282-286, 354-357, 391-393, 444-447, 493-496, 537-539; (1897-1900), 222-225.

1785    . _____. "Lettres," *Missions d'Alger*, (1891-1892), 167-168, 208-213, 284-285, 380-382, 518-522; (1893-1894), 68-70, 176-179, 291-294, 327-328, 351-353, 383-389, 409-422.

1786    _____. "Missionsbriefe," *Afrika-Bote*, I(1895), 25-30, 43-46, 79-83, 103-104, 149-151, 165-167; II(1896), 9-11, 24-25, 87-90, 148-151, 187-188; III(1897), 41-43, 164-166.

1787    _____. "Missionsbriefe," *Echo aus Afrika*, III(1891), 38-40

1788    _____. "Missionsbriefe," *KM*, XXII(1894), 184, 185; XXV(1897), 42.

1789    _____. "Eine Missionsreise nach Uha und Urundi," *PM*, XLIV(1898), 121-124, 182-185.

. _____. "Tournée apostolique chez les Basumbwa," *MCL*, XXVI(1894), 516-518, 528-530. See also, *Maandelijksch Verslag der Afrikaansche Missiën*, XV(1894), 374-379.

1790

1791 . Castelyn, Gustave. "Lettere," *MCM*, XXIV(1895), 399-400.

1792 . _____. "Lettres," *MCL*, XXVII(1895), 387.

1793 . Charbonnier, Jean-Baptiste. "Lettere," *MCM*, XV(1886), 243-244, XVI(1887), 123-126, 148-150.

1794 . _____. "Lettres," *APFL*, LIX(1887), 253-254.

1795 . _____. "Lettres," *MCL*, XVIII(1886), 219-220, XIX(1887), 87-89, 110-112.

1796 . _____. "Missiensbrieve," *Annalen der Afrikaansche Missiën*, III(1886-1887), 154-159, IV(1887-1888), 45-47, 81-93, 143, V(1888-1889), 59-60.

1797 . Cleve, G. L. [*Missionary*]. "Die Auffassung der Neger Deutsch-Ostafrikas von den krankheitszuständen," *DK*, XVI(1899), 48-50.

1798 . Codrington, Robert. "A Voyage on Lake Tanganyika," *GJ*, XIX(1902), 598-603.

1799 . Cole, H. "Notes on the Wagogo of German East Africa," *JAI*, XXXII(1902), 305-338.

1800 . Conradt, L. "Die Eingeborenen in der umgebung der Station Johann-Albrechts-Höhe," *DK*, XVII(1900), 33-36.

1801 . Cotterill, H B. "On the Nyassa and a Journey from the North End to Zanzibar," *PRGS*, XXII(1877-1878), 233-249.

1802 . Coulbois, François. *Dix années au Tanganyika*. Limoges: Impr. P. Dumont, 1901. 304p.

1803 . _____ "Lettere," *MCM*, XIV(1884), 419-420; XV(1886), 470-471; XVII(1888), 349-352.

1804 . _____. "Lettres," *Annalen der Afrikaansche Missiën*, III(1886-1887), 71-77; V(1888-1889), 67-68.

1805 . _____. "Lettres," *Maandelijksch Verslag der Afrikaansche Missiën*, XV(1894), 108-111, 131-136; XVI(1895), 60-62.

1806 . _____. "Lettres," *MCL*, XVII(1885), 408; XVIII(1886), 446-448; XX(1888), 325-328.

1807  · _____. "Lettres," *Missions d'Algers* (1883-1886), 85-88, 143-145, 341-345, 451-455; (1887-1890), 306-307, 544-547.

1808  · _____. "Missionsbriefe," *KM*, XIV(1886), 257-258; XVII(1889), 257-258.

1809  · _____. "L'Esclavage au Zanguebar," *Annales Apostoliques*, VII(1892), 4-15.

1810  · _____. "Lettere," *MCM*, XVII(1888), 25-26, 475; XVIII(1889), 37-41, 49-50, 73-75, 121-124, 205-206, 241-246, 349-351, 597-598, 606-607; XX(1891), 169-171, 339-341; XXII(1893), 301-302, 409-410; XXIV(1895), 90; XXVII(1898), 370-372.

1811  · _____. "Lettres," *Annales Apostoliques*, IV(1889), 6-14, 41-53; V(1890), 79-80; VI(1891), 41-44; IX(1894), 81-86; XI(1896), 67-71.

1812  · _____. "Lettres," *Annales Oeuvre Ste-Enfance*, XXXVI(1885), 316-339; XXXVIII(1887), 91-107.

1813  · _____. "Lettres," *APFL*, LXI(1889), 47-63, 304-306.

1814  · _____. "Lettres," *Echo des Missions d'Afrique*, II(1885), 227-236.

1815  · _____. "Lettres," *MCL*, XIX(1887), 613-614; XX(1888), 449; XXI(1889), 25-29, 39-40, 63-64, 109-112, 181-182, 229-233, 337-339, 582-583, 598-599; XXII(1890), 421-423; XXIII(1891), 13-15, 53; XXV(1893), 289-290, 386-388; XXVII(1895), 64; XXX(1898), 46-47.

1816  · _____. "Missionsbriefe," *Echo aus Afrika*, III(1891), 62; IV(1892), 38, 67-68, 98-99; VIII(1896), 137.

1817  · _____. "Missionsbriefe," *KM*, XVII(1889), 86-89, 108-110, 219-220, 242-243; XIX(1891), 88-91, 108-110.

1818  · _____. *Notre-Dame des Anges ou un hôpital a Zanzibar*. Lyon: Imprimerie Catholique, 1885. 39p. 2nd Ed., 1886. 32p. Also, *MCL*, XVII(1885), 378-380, 389-391, 401-405; and, *MCM*, XV(1886), 248-251, 256-259.

1819    _____. "Seconde tournée dans le Vicariat Apostolique du Zanguebar," *MCL*, XVIII(1886), 594-597, 604-605, 615-620. Also, *MCM*, XVI(1887), 221-224, 237-238, 248-252.

1820    _____. "Le Sultanat du Zanguebar," *MCL*, XVIII(1886), 382-384, 393-395, 404-406, 412-414.

1821    _____. "Une tournée dans le Vicariat Apostolique de Zanguebar Oct.-Nov. 1884," *MCL*, XVII(1885), 462-466, 485-489, 497-502, 512-515, 521-525, 536-538, 545-548. Also, *MCM*, XV(1886), 331-347, 353-356, 370-372, 382-384, 394-396, 404-406.

1822    Cross, D. Kerr. "Geographical Notes of the Country Between Lakes Nyasa, Rukwa, and Tanganyika," *SGM*, VI(1890), 281-293.

1823    Dahlgruen, H. "Heiratsgebräuche der Schambaa," *MDS*, XVI(1903), 219-230.

1824    Dale, Godfrey. " An Account of the Principal Customs and Habits of the Natives Inhabiting the Bondei Country, Compiled Mainly for the Use of European Missionaries in the Country," *JAI*, XXV(1896), 181-239.

1825    _____. *The Peoples of Zanzibar, Their Customs and Religious Beliefs*. Westminister: Universities' Mission to Central Africa, 1920. 124p.

1826    Dantz, K. "Vorläufiger Bericht über Seine Reisen in Deutsch-Ostafrika," *Zeitschrift der deutschen geologischen Gesellschaft*, 1900, p.41.

1827    Daull, Emile. "Lettres," *Maandelijksch Verslag van de Afrikaansche Missiën*, XIX(1898), 280-283.

1828    _____. "Lettres," *Missions d'Afrique*, XIX(1898), 267-271; XX(1899), 306-311, 330-335; XXII(1901), 70-75.

1829    _____. "Missionsbriefe," *Afrika-Bote*, VI(1899-1900), 203-205; VII(1900-1901), 80-82, 131-133; VIII(1901-1902),185-188.

1830    _____. "Missionsbriefe," *Echo aus Afrika*, XI(1899), 179-182.

1831    Debaize, Alexandre. [*Abbé*]. "Lettre," *Bulletin de la Société de Géographie de Aix-Marseille*, III(1879), 44-47, 48-52; IV(1880), 156-166.

1832

. Decken, Carl Claus von der. [Baron]. "Geographical Notes of an Expedition
to Mount Kilima-ndjaro in 1862-63," *JRGS*, XXXIV(1864), 1-6.

1833

. Decle, Lionel. "The Tanganyika Railway," *Fortnightly Review*, Jan.,
1899, pp. 25-33.

1834

. Delaunay, Henri. "Fondation d'une nouvelle Mission au Massanze, Tanganyka,"
*Exploration*, XII(1881), 594-598.

1835

. _____. "Lettere," *MCM*, X(1881), 351-354.

1836

. _____. "Lettres," *Missions d'Alger*[Paris], (1879-1882), 388-394. See also
*Missions d'Afrique*, (1919), 66-67.

1837

. _____. "Lettres," *MCL*, XIII(1881), 253-256; LI(1919), 194.

1838

. Delpuech, Emmanuel. "Lettres," *Annales Apostoliques*, VI(1891), 25-27; IX
(1894), 68-72.

1839

. Deniaud, Pierre. "Lettres," *Annales Oeuvre Ste. Enfance*, XXXI(1880), 49-60.

1840

. _____. "Lettres," *Oeuvre de St. Augustin et de Ste. Monique*, No.28(1878),
425-426.

1841

. _____. "Lettres," *Missions d'Alger*, (1879-1882), 172-177, 181-183, 250-
252, 254-255, 316, 354-355, 476-477.

1842

. Depaillat, Julien. "Lettres," *Missions d'Afrique*, (1897-1900), 146-158.

1843

. _____. "Missionsbriefe," *Afrika-Bote*, III(1897), 179-186.

1844

. Desoignies, Charles. "Lettere," *MCM*, XXIII(1894), 253-255.

1845

. _____. "Lettres," *Annalen der Afrikaansche Missiën*, X(1893-1894), 4-6;
XI(1894-1895), 192-194; XIV(1897-1898), 293-297.

1846

. _____. "Lettres," *Maandelijksch Verslag der Afrikaansche Missiën*, XV
(1894), 244-246; XVI(1895), 6-8.

1847

. _____. " Lettres," *MCL*, XXVI(1894), 245-246.

1848

. _____. "Lettres," *Missions d'Afrique*[Malines], XIX(1898), 198-203.

1849

. _____. "Lettres," *Missions d'Afrique*[Paris], (1895-1897), 447-450; (1897-
1900), 714-717, 783-786.

1850

. _____. "Lettres," *Missions d'Alger*, (1893-1894), 54-58, 229, 325-327.

1851

. _____. "Missionsbriefe," *Afrika Bote*, III(1897), 43-45; IV(1898), 148-150.

1852 . Diesing, Ernst. "Eine Reise in Ukongo (Deutsch-Ostafrika)," *Globus*, VC(1909), 309-312, 325-328.

1853 . Dietlin, Achilles. "Lettere," *MCM*, XXVII(1898), 605.

1854 . _____. "Lettres," *APFL*, LXXI(1899), 154.

1855 . Dixon, J. W. "Mikindani Bay, East Coast of Africa," *Nautical Magazine*, XLIII(1874), 840-841.

1856 . Döring, P. Paul. *Lehrungsjahre eines Jungen Missionars in Deutsch-Ostafrika*. Berlin: Warnecke, 1900. 86p.

1857 . _____. *Morgendämmerung in Deutsch Ostafrika. Ein Rundgang durch die Ostafrikan*. Berlin, 1900. 191p.

1858 . Dromaux, Théophile. "Durchquerung von Deutsch-Ostafrika: Bagamojo, Kiwele, Karema. Mit Benutzung brieflicher Mitteilungen des Reisenden," *PM*, XLV(1899), 1-4.

1859 . _____. "Lettere," *MCM*, XVII(1888), 109-112; XXI(1892), 62-63.

1860 . _____. "Lettres," *APFL*, LXVI(1894), 316-317.

1861 . _____. "Lettres," *MCL*, XX(1888), 73-76; XXIV(1892), 50-51; XXVI(1894), 176.

1862 . _____. "Missionsbriefe," *Annalen der Afrikaansche Missiën*, II(1885-1886), 105-108; IX(1892-1893), 87-91; X(1893-1894), 200.

1863 · _____. "Missionsbriefe aus Afrika," *KM*, VIII(1880), 172; XIV(1886), 110.

1864 · _____. "De Zanzibar à Ujiji. Les Bords du Tanganika; de Karema à Zanzibar par le Zambèze," *Bulletin de la Société de Géographie de Lille*, XXVI(1896), 339-350.

1865 · Eberstein, von. "Über die Rechtsanschauungen der Küstenbewohner des Bezirks Kilwa," *MDS*, IX(1896).

1866 · Ehlers, Otto E. "Meine Besteigung des Kilima Ndscharo," *PM*, XXXV(1889), 68-71.

1867 · Eiffe, F. "Reiseskizzen aus Deutsch-Ostafrika," *DK*, XIV(1897), Beilage Nr. XI, 47-48.

1868 · "Einem Deutschen Kaufmann." "Die Deutsch-Ostafrikanische Kolonie," *DK*, II(1885), 246-249.

1869 · Eitner, M. *Berliner Mission im Njassa-Lande(Deutsch-Ostafrika)*. Berlin: Evangelical Missionsgesellschaft, 1897. 102p.

1870 · Elliott, George Francis Scott. "Expedition to Ruwenzori and Tanganyika," *GJ*, VI(1895), 301-317.

1871 · Elton, James Frederick. "On the Coast Country of East Africa, South of Zanzibar," *JRGS*, XLIV(1874), 227-252.

1872 · Falkenhorst, C. *Der Ostafrikaner*. Stuttgart: Union, 1890. 284p.

1873 · _____. *Schwarze Fürsten. Bilder aus der Geschichte des dunklen Weltteils*. 2 vols. Leipzig, 1891, 1892.

1874 · _____. *Der Zauberer vom Kilimandjaro. Adlers Kriegs- und Jagdabenteuer in Ostafrika*. Leipzig, 1888. 145p.

1875 · Farler, John Prediger. "England and Germany in East Africa," *Fortnightly Review*, New Series, XLV(1889), 157-165.

_____. "Native Routes in East Africa from the Pangani to the Masai Country and the Victoria Nyanza," *PRGS*, New Series, IV(1882), 730-742.

_____. "The Usambara Country in East Africa," *PRGS*, New Series, I (1879), 81-97.

_____. *The Work of Christ in Central Africa. A Letter to the Reverend H. P. Liddon.* London, 1878.

Faure, Julien. "Lettres," *Missions d'Alger*, (1883-1886), 114-118, 244-247, 374-380.

Fava, M. "Extrait d'une lettre de M. Fava, vice-préfet apostolique du Zanguebar, à MM. les Présidents des Conseils de l'Oeuvre, Île Zanzibar: 12 août 1862," *APFL*, XXXV(1863), 124-141.

_____. "Lettres," *APFL*, XXXV(1863), 8-48, 257-277.

Ferstl, Basilius. "Missionsbriefe," *Echo aus Afrika*, VIII(1896), 57-58.

_____. "Missionsbriefe," *Missionsblätter*, I(1897), 53-56, 66-70, 103-110, 129-140, 163-176, 193-208, 225-238, 267-276, 293-298, 349-350.

Firminger, Walter Keller. "The Protectorate of Zanzibar," *British Empire Series*, II(1899), 259-278.

Fischer, G. A. "Journey in the Masai Country," *PRGS*, New Series, VI(1884), 76-83.

_____. *Das Massai-Land (Ost-Aequatorial-Afrika). Bericht über die im Auftrage der Geographischen Gesellschaft in Hamburg ausgeführte Reise von Pangani bis zum Naiwascha-See.* Hamburg, 1885. 155p.

_____. *Mehr Licht im dunklen Weltteil. Betrachtungen über die Kolonisation des tropischen Afrika, unter besonderer Berücksichtigung des Sansibar-Gebiets.* Hamburg, 1885. 130p.

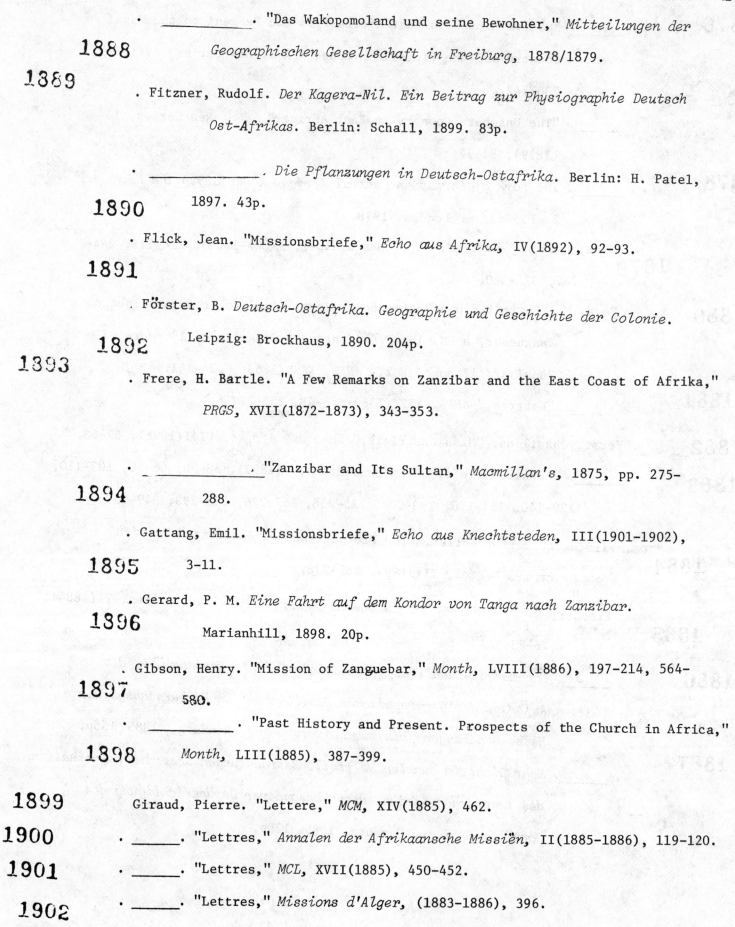

1888

1389

· _____. "Das Wakopomoland und seine Bewohner," *Mitteilungen der Geographischen Gesellschaft in Freiburg*, 1878/1879.

· Fitzner, Rudolf. *Der Kagera-Nil. Ein Beitrag zur Physiographie Deutsch Ost-Afrikas*. Berlin: Schall, 1899. 83p.

1890

· _____. *Die Pflanzungen in Deutsch-Ostafrika*. Berlin: H. Patel, 1897. 43p.

· Flick, Jean. "Missionsbriefe," *Echo aus Afrika*, IV(1892), 92-93.

1891

· Förster, B. *Deutsch-Ostafrika. Geographie und Geschichte der Colonie*. Leipzig: Brockhaus, 1890. 204p.

1892

1393

· Frere, H. Bartle. "A Few Remarks on Zanzibar and the East Coast of Afrika," *PRGS*, XVII(1872-1873), 343-353.

· _____. "Zanzibar and Its Sultan," *Macmillan's*, 1875, pp. 275-288.

1894

· Gattang, Emil. "Missionsbriefe," *Echo aus Knechtsteden*, III(1901-1902), 3-11.

1895

· Gerard, P. M. *Eine Fahrt auf dem Kondor von Tanga nach Zanzibar*. Marianhill, 1898. 20p.

1896

· Gibson, Henry. "Mission of Zanguebar," *Month*, LVIII(1886), 197-214, 564-580.

1897

· _____. "Past History and Present. Prospects of the Church in Africa," *Month*, LIII(1885), 387-399.

1898

1899    Giraud, Pierre. "Lettere," *MCM*, XIV(1885), 462.

1900    · ____. "Lettres," *Annalen der Afrikaansche Missiën*, II(1885-1886), 119-120.

1901    · ____. "Lettres," *MCL*, XVII(1885), 450-452.

1902    · ____. "Lettres," *Missions d'Alger*, (1883-1886), 396.

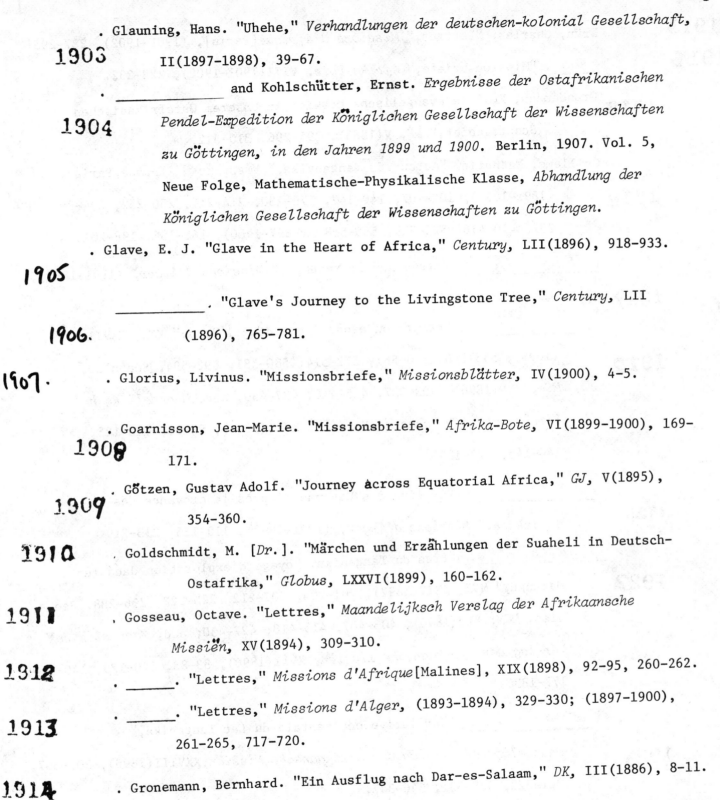

. Glauning, Hans. "Uhehe," *Verhandlungen der deutschen-kolonial Gesellschaft,* II(1897-1898), 39-67.

. _____ and Kohlschütter, Ernst. *Ergebnisse der Ostafrikanischen Pendel-Expedition der Königlichen Gesellschaft der Wissenschaften zu Göttingen, in den Jahren 1899 und 1900. Berlin, 1907. Vol. 5,* Neue Folge, Mathematische-Physikalische Klasse, *Abhandlung der Königlichen Gesellschaft der Wissenschaften zu Göttingen.*

. Glave, E. J. "Glave in the Heart of Africa," *Century,* LII(1896), 918-933.

_____. "Glave's Journey to the Livingstone Tree," *Century,* LII (1896), 765-781.

. Glorius, Livinus. "Missionsbriefe," *Missionsblätter,* IV(1900), 4-5.

. Goarnisson, Jean-Marie. "Missionsbriefe," *Afrika-Bote,* VI(1899-1900), 169-171.

. Götzen, Gustav Adolf. "Journey across Equatorial Africa," *GJ,* V(1895), 354-360.

. Goldschmidt, M. [*Dr.*]. "Märchen und Erzählungen der Suaheli in Deutsch-Ostafrika," *Globus,* LXXVI(1899), 160-162.

. Gosseau, Octave. "Lettres," *Maandelijksch Verslag der Afrikaansche Missiën,* XV(1894), 309-310.

. _____. "Lettres," *Missions d'Afrique*[Malines], XIX(1898), 92-95, 260-262.

. _____. "Lettres," *Missions d'Alger,* (1893-1894), 329-330; (1897-1900), 261-265, 717-720.

. Gronemann, Bernhard. "Ein Ausflug nach Dar-es-Salaam," *DK,* III(1886), 8-11.

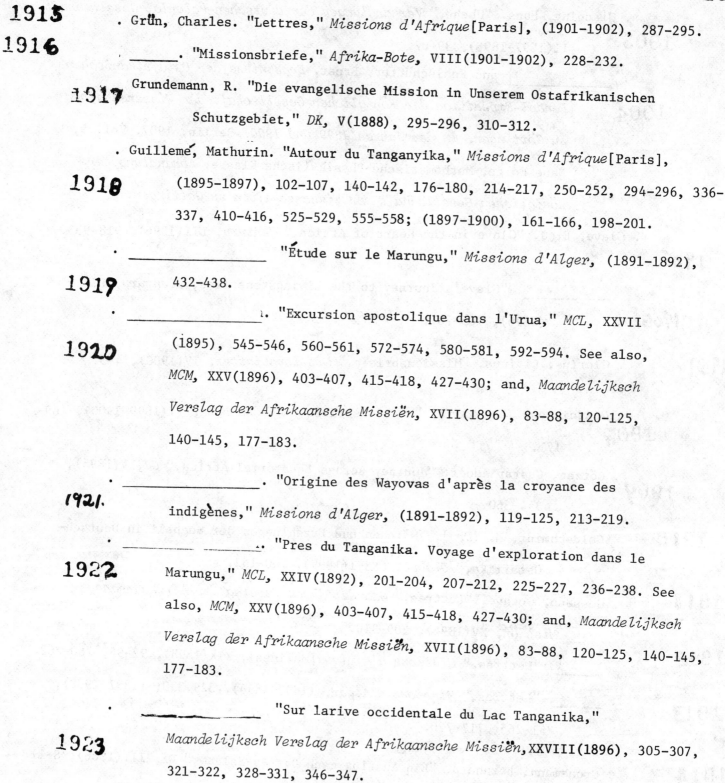

Grün, Charles. "Lettres," *Missions d'Afrique*[Paris], (1901-1902), 287-295.

_____. "Missionsbriefe," *Afrika-Bote*, VIII(1901-1902), 228-232.

Grundemann, R. "Die evangelische Mission in Unserem Ostafrikanischen Schutzgebiet," *DK*, V(1888), 295-296, 310-312.

Guillemé, Mathurin. "Autour du Tanganyika," *Missions d'Afrique*[Paris], (1895-1897), 102-107, 140-142, 176-180, 214-217, 250-252, 294-296, 336-337, 410-416, 525-529, 555-558; (1897-1900), 161-166, 198-201.

_____ "Étude sur le Marungu," *Missions d'Alger*, (1891-1892), 432-438.

_____ "Excursion apostolique dans l'Urua," *MCL*, XXVII (1895), 545-546, 560-561, 572-574, 580-581, 592-594. See also, *MCM*, XXV(1896), 403-407, 415-418, 427-430; and, *Maandelijksch Verslag der Afrikaansche Missiën*, XVII(1896), 83-88, 120-125, 140-145, 177-183.

_____. "Origine des Wayovas d'après la croyance des indigènes," *Missions d'Alger*, (1891-1892), 119-125, 213-219.

_____ "Pres du Tanganika. Voyage d'exploration dans le Marungu," *MCL*, XXIV(1892), 201-204, 207-212, 225-227, 236-238. See also, *MCM*, XXV(1896), 403-407, 415-418, 427-430; and, *Maandelijksch Verslag der Afrikaansche Missiën*, XVII(1896), 83-88, 120-125, 140-145, 177-183.

_____ "Sur larive occidentale du Lac Tanganika," *Maandelijksch Verslag der Afrikaansche Missiën*, XXVIII(1896), 305-307, 321-322, 328-331, 346-347.

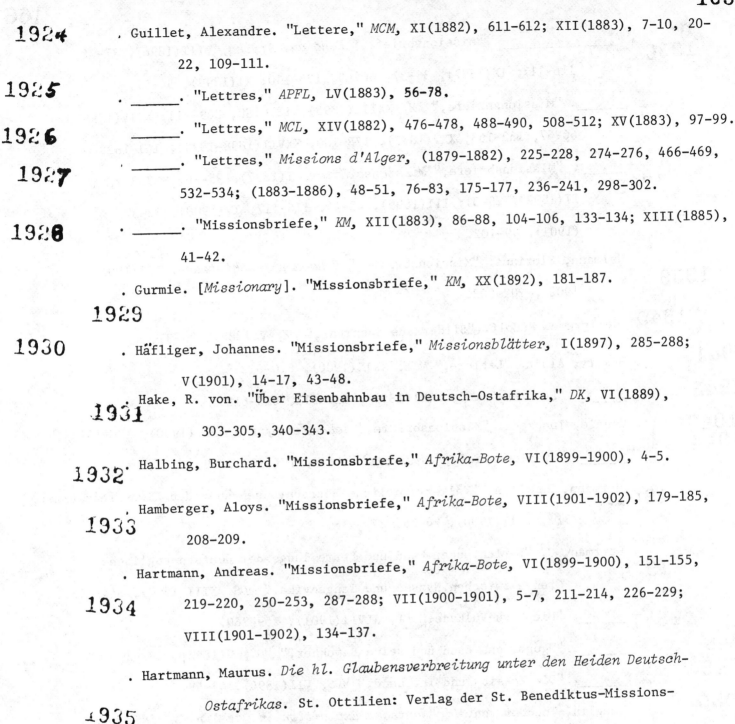

. Guillet, Alexandre. "Lettere," *MCM*, XI(1882), 611-612; XII(1883), 7-10, 20-22, 109-111.

. _____. "Lettres," *APFL*, LV(1883), **56-78**.

. _____. "Lettres," *MCL*, XIV(1882), 476-478, 488-490, 508-512; XV(1883), 97-99.

. _____. "Lettres," *Missions d'Alger*, (1879-1882), 225-228, 274-276, 466-469, 532-534; (1883-1886), 48-51, 76-83, 175-177, 236-241, 298-302.

. _____. "Missionsbriefe," *KM*, XII(1883), 86-88, 104-106, 133-134; XIII(1885), 41-42.

. Gurmie. [*Missionary*]. "Missionsbriefe," *KM*, XX(1892), 181-187.

. Häfliger, Johannes. "Missionsbriefe," *Missionsblätter*, I(1897), 285-288; V(1901), 14-17, 43-48.

. Hake, R. von. "Über Eisenbahnbau in Deutsch-Ostafrika," *DK*, VI(1889), 303-305, 340-343.

. Halbing, Burchard. "Missionsbriefe," *Afrika-Bote*, VI(1899-1900), 4-5.

. Hamberger, Aloys. "Missionsbriefe," *Afrika-Bote*, VIII(1901-1902), 179-185, 208-209.

. Hartmann, Andreas. "Missionsbriefe," *Afrika-Bote*, VI(1899-1900), 151-155, 219-220, 250-253, 287-288; VII(1900-1901), 5-7, 211-214, 226-229; VIII(1901-1902), 134-137.

. Hartmann, Maurus. *Die hl. Glaubensverbreitung unter den Heiden Deutsch-Ostafrikas*. St. Ottilien: Verlag der St. Benediktus-Missionsgenossenschaft, 1894. 23p.

1936 ——————. "Missionsbriefe," *Echo aus Afrika*, VIII(1896), 77-78, 116-117; IX(1897), 36-37, 66-69, 125-130; XI(1899), 54-57.

1937 ——————. "Missionsbriefe," *KM*, XXIII(1895), 187-188, 209-211; XXIV(1896), 66-67, 162-163; XXV(1897), 178-180; XXVII(1898-1899), 161-162.

1938 ——————. "Missionsbriefe," *Missionsblätter*, I(1897), 95-96, 337-342; II(1898), 25-31; III(1899), 43-44, 116-117; IV(1900), 33-37; V(1901), 99-102.

1939 Heimann, Florinus. "Missionsbriefe," *Echo aus Knechtsteden*, III(1901-1902), 202-203.

1940 Hellgrewe, Rudolf. "Bilder aus Sansibar," *DK*, V(1888), 36-37, 54.

1941 Hémery, Alain. "Lettere," *MCM*, XXIX(1900), 610-612.

1942 ——————. "Lettres," *MCL*, XXXI(1899), 610-612, 615-618.

1943 Hendle, Innozenz. "Missionsbriefe," *Echo aus Afrika*, XII(1900), 136-137.

1944 ——————. "Missionsbriefe," *Missionsblätter*, IV(1900), 18.

1945 Hermann, Rudolf A. "Völkerrechtliche Betrachtungen über den Kiwu-Grenzstreit," *DK*, XVII(1900), 24-25, 37.

1946 Herrman, C. "Bericht über Land und Leute längs der deutsch-englischen Grenze zwischen Nyassa und Tanganyika," *MDS*, XIII(1900), 344-346.

1947 ——————. "Die Kivu-Vulkane," *PM*, XLVII(1901), 259-260.

1948 ——————. "Ugogo, das Land und seine Bewohner," *MDS*, V(1892), 191-203.

1949 ——————. "Die Wassiba und ihr Land," *MDS*, VII(1894), 43-59.

1950 Heuglin, Theodor von. *Die deutsche Expedition in Ost-Afrika, 1861 und 1862*. Gotha: Justus Perthes, 1864. 46p.

1951 Hill, Clement H. "Boat Journey up the Wami River," *PRGS*, XVII(1872-1873), 337-340.

1952 . Hirzlin, François-Antoine. "Lettres," *Annales Apostoliques*, III(1888), 86-93.

1953 . Hobley, Charles William. "Upon a Visit to Tsavo and the Taita Highlands," *GJ*, V(1895), 545-561.

1954 . Höhnel, L. Ritter von. "Die Chanler-Expedition in Ostafrika," *PM*, XXXIX(1893), 120-122, 146-148.

1955 . Hofbauer, Severin. "Missionsbriefe," *Missionsblätter*, I(1897), 255-256; II(1898), 4-6.

1956 . Hofer, Michael. "Missionsbriefe," *Missionsblätter*, I(1897), 285-286; V (1901), 4-5, 103-104.

1957 . Hoffmann. [*Kommandant "Möwe"*]. "Die Küste des Sultanats Sansibar von Tonghi bis Sadaani," *DK*, III(1886), 539-541.

1958 . Holmwood, F. "The Kingani River, East Africa," *JRGS*, XLVII(1877), 253-267.

1959 . Holst, Carl. "Der Landbau der Eingeborenen von Usambara," *DK*, X(1893), 113-114, 128-130.

1960 . Hore, Annie Boyle. *To Lake Tanganyika in a Bath Chair*. London: Sampson, Low, 1886. 217p.

1961 . Hore, Edward Coode. "Lake Tanganyika," *PRGS*, New Series, IV(1882), 1-25; XI(1889), 581-595.

1962 . _____. "Stone Implements," *PRGS*, New Series, IV(1882), 7.

1963 . _____. *Tanganyika: Eleven Years in Central Africa*. London: Stanford, 1892. 306p.

1964 . _____. "The Twelve Tribes of Tanganyika," *JAI*, XII(1883), 2-20.

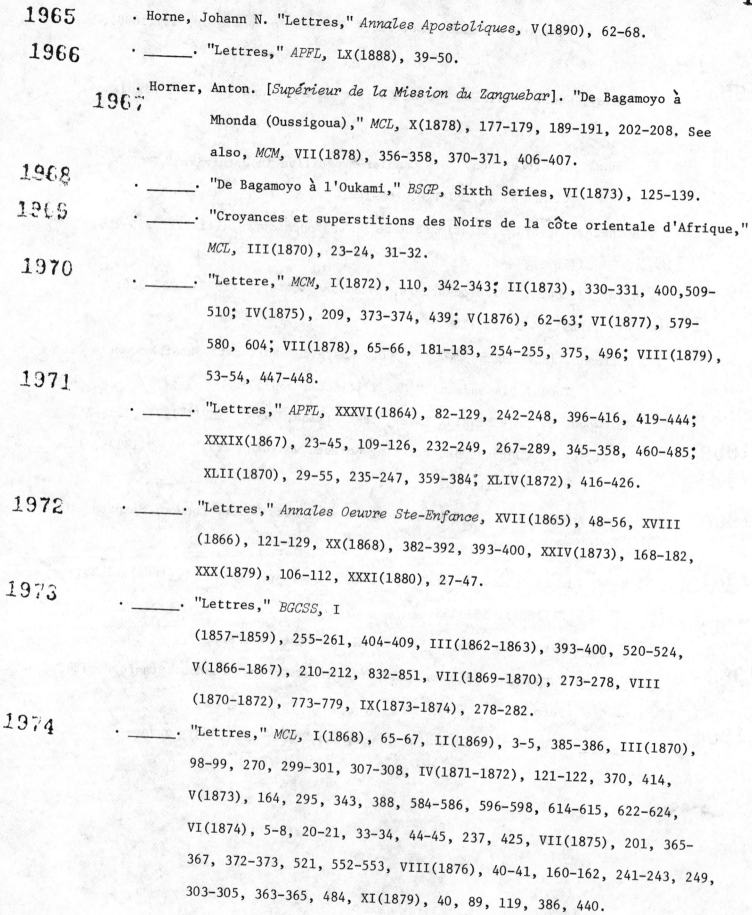

1965    . Horne, Johann N. "Lettres," *Annales Apostoliques*, V(1890), 62-68.

1966    . _____. "Lettres," *APFL*, LX(1888), 39-50.

1967    . Horner, Anton. [*Supérieur de la Mission du Zanguebar*]. "De Bagamoyo à Mhonda (Oussigoua)," *MCL*, X(1878), 177-179, 189-191, 202-208. See also, *MCM*, VII(1878), 356-358, 370-371, 406-407.

1968    . _____. "De Bagamoyo à l'Oukami," *BSGP*, Sixth Series, VI(1873), 125-139.

1969    . _____. "Croyances et superstitions des Noirs de la côte orientale d'Afrique," *MCL*, III(1870), 23-24, 31-32.

1970    . _____. "Lettere," *MCM*, I(1872), 110, 342-343; II(1873), 330-331, 400,509-510; IV(1875), 209, 373-374, 439; V(1876), 62-63; VI(1877), 579-580, 604; VII(1878), 65-66, 181-183, 254-255, 375, 496; VIII(1879), 53-54, 447-448.

1971    . _____. "Lettres," *APFL*, XXXVI(1864), 82-129, 242-248, 396-416, 419-444; XXXIX(1867), 23-45, 109-126, 232-249, 267-289, 345-358, 460-485; XLII(1870), 29-55, 235-247, 359-384; XLIV(1872), 416-426.

1972    . _____. "Lettres," *Annales Oeuvre Ste-Enfance*, XVII(1865), 48-56, XVIII (1866), 121-129, XX(1868), 382-392, 393-400, XXIV(1873), 168-182, XXX(1879), 106-112, XXXI(1880), 27-47.

1973    . _____. "Lettres," *BGCSS*, I (1857-1859), 255-261, 404-409, III(1862-1863), 393-400, 520-524, V(1866-1867), 210-212, 832-851, VII(1869-1870), 273-278, VIII (1870-1872), 773-779, IX(1873-1874), 278-282.

1974    . _____. "Lettres," *MCL*, I(1868), 65-67, II(1869), 3-5, 385-386, III(1870), 98-99, 270, 299-301, 307-308, IV(1871-1872), 121-122, 370, 414, V(1873), 164, 295, 343, 388, 584-586, 596-598, 614-615, 622-624, VI(1874), 5-8, 20-21, 33-34, 44-45, 237, 425, VII(1875), 201, 365-367, 372-373, 521, 552-553, VIII(1876), 40-41, 160-162, 241-243, 249, 303-305, 363-365, 484, XI(1879), 40, 89, 119, 386, 440.

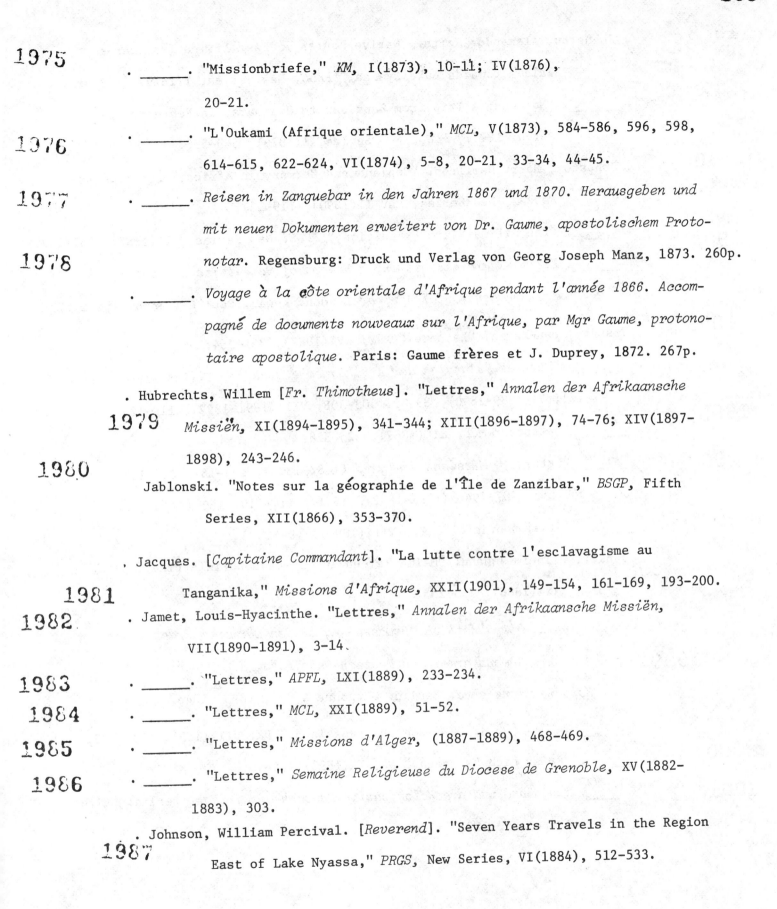

. _____. "Missionbriefe," *KM*, I(1873), 10-11; IV(1876), 20-21.

. _____. "L'Oukami (Afrique orientale)," *MCL*, V(1873), 584-586, 596, 598, 614-615, 622-624, VI(1874), 5-8, 20-21, 33-34, 44-45.

. _____. *Reisen in Zanguebar in den Jahren 1867 und 1870. Herausgeben und mit neuen Dokumenten erweitert von Dr. Gaume, apostolischem Protonotar.* Regensburg: Druck und Verlag von Georg Joseph Manz, 1873. 260p.

. _____. *Voyage à la côte orientale d'Afrique pendant l'année 1866. Accompagné de documents nouveaux sur l'Afrique, par Mgr Gaume, protonotaire apostolique.* Paris: Gaume frères et J. Duprey, 1872. 267p.

. Hubrechts, Willem [*Fr. Thimotheus*]. "Lettres," *Annalen der Afrikaansche Missiën*, XI(1894-1895), 341-344; XIII(1896-1897), 74-76; XIV(1897-1898), 243-246.

. Jablonski. "Notes sur la géographie de l'île de Zanzibar," *BSGP*, Fifth Series, XII(1866), 353-370.

. Jacques. [*Capitaine Commandant*]. "La lutte contre l'esclavagisme au Tanganika," *Missions d'Afrique*, XXII(1901), 149-154, 161-169, 193-200.

. Jamet, Louis-Hyacinthe. "Lettres," *Annalen der Afrikaansche Missiën*, VII(1890-1891), 3-14.

. _____. "Lettres," *APFL*, LXI(1889), 233-234.

. _____. "Lettres," *MCL*, XXI(1889), 51-52.

. _____. "Lettres," *Missions d'Alger*, (1887-1889), 468-469.

. _____. "Lettres," *Semaine Religieuse du Diocese de Grenoble*, XV(1882-1883), 303.

. Johnson, William Percival. [*Reverend*]. "Seven Years Travels in the Region East of Lake Nyassa," *PRGS*, New Series, VI(1884), 512-533.

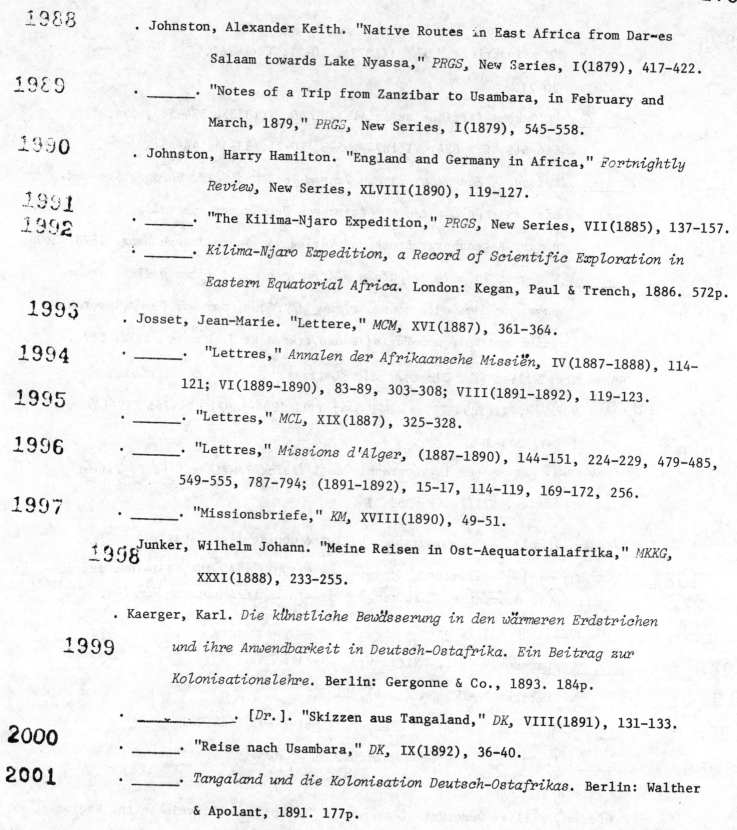

1988 . Johnston, Alexander Keith. "Native Routes in East Africa from Dar-es Salaam towards Lake Nyassa," *PRGS*, New Series, I(1879), 417-422.

1989 . _____. "Notes of a Trip from Zanzibar to Usambara, in February and March, 1879," *PRGS*, New Series, I(1879), 545-558.

1990 . Johnston, Harry Hamilton. "England and Germany in Africa," *Fortnightly Review*, New Series, XLVIII(1890), 119-127.

1991
1992 . _____. "The Kilima-Njaro Expedition," *PRGS*, New Series, VII(1885), 137-157.

. _____. *Kilima-Njaro Expedition, a Record of Scientific Exploration in Eastern Equatorial Africa.* London: Kegan, Paul & Trench, 1886. 572p.

1993 . Josset, Jean-Marie. "Lettere," *MCM*, XVI(1887), 361-364.

1994 . _____. "Lettres," *Annalen der Afrikaansche Missiën*, IV(1887-1888), 114-121; VI(1889-1890), 83-89, 303-308; VIII(1891-1892), 119-123.

1995 . _____. "Lettres," *MCL*, XIX(1887), 325-328.

1996 . _____. "Lettres," *Missions d'Alger*, (1887-1890), 144-151, 224-229, 479-485, 549-555, 787-794; (1891-1892), 15-17, 114-119, 169-172, 256.

1997 . _____. "Missionsbriefe," *KM*, XVIII(1890), 49-51.

1998 Junker, Wilhelm Johann. "Meine Reisen in Ost-Aequatorialafrika," *MKKG*, XXXI(1888), 233-255.

. Kaerger, Karl. *Die künstliche Bewässerung in den wärmeren Erdstrichen und ihre Anwendbarkeit in Deutsch-Ostafrika. Ein Beitrag zur Kolonisationslehre.* Berlin: Gergonne & Co., 1893. 184p.

1999

. _____. [*Dr.*]. "Skizzen aus Tangaland," *DK*, VIII(1891), 131-133.

2000 . _____. "Reise nach Usambara," *DK*, IX(1892), 36-40.

2001 . _____. *Tangaland und die Kolonisation Deutsch-Ostafrikas.* Berlin: Walther & Apolant, 1891. 177p.

2002 . Kaiser, E. "Reise von Iganda zum Kilwa, September-Oktober 1882," *MAGD*, IV(1883-1885).

2003 . _____and Reichard, P. "Bericht aus Kakoma," *MAGD*, III(1881-1883).

2004 . _____; Reichard, P.; and Bohm, B. "Berichte über die Station Gonda, Besucht bei Mirambo, projektirte Reise nach den Moero-See," *MAGD*, III (1881-1883), 261-286.

2005 . Kallenberg, Friedrich. *Auf dem Kriegspfad gegen die Massai. Eine Frühlingsfahrt nach Deutsch-Ostafrika.* Munich, 1892. 200p.

2006 . Kannenberg, Carl. "Durch die Marénga Makàli," *MDS*, XIII(1900), 3-17.

2007 . _____. "Reise durch die hamitischen Sprachgebiete um Kondoa," *MDS*, XIII (1900), 144-172.

2008 Karst, Joseph. "Lettres," *APFL*, LXIII(1891), 33-43.

2009 . Kersten, Otto. "Otto Kersten in Sansibar," *Globus*, XXI(1872), 22-26.

2010 . Kirk, John. "Notes on Two Expeditions up the River Rovuma, East Africa," *JRGS*, XXXV(1865), 154-167. Also, *PRGS*, IX(1864-1865), 284-288.

2011 . _____. "On a New Harbour Opposite Zanzibar," *PRGS*, XI(1866-1867), 35-36.

2012 Kohler, J. "Das Banturecht in Ostafrika," *Zeitschrift für Vergleichende Rechtswissenschaft*, XV(1902).

2013 . Kohlschütter, E. "Die Grabenländer im nördlichen Deutsch-Ostafrika," *ZGE*, 1901, p. 152.

2014 . Kollmann, Paul. *Auf deutschem Boden in Afrika. Ernste und heitere Erlebnisse.* Berlin, 1901. 383p.

2015 . _____. *Der Nordwesten unserer ostafrikanischen Kolonie. Eine Beschreibung von Land und Leuten am Victoria-Nyanza, nebst Aufzeichungen einiger daselbst gesprochenen Dialekte.* Berlin, 1898. 191p. English translation, *The Victoria Nyanza, the Land, the Races, and Their Customs, with Specimens of Some of the Dialects.* London: Swann Sonnenschein, 1899. 254p.

2016 Koolen, Petrus. "Lettres," *Annalen des Afrikaansche Missiën*, XV(1898-1899), 126-130, 266-269; XVI(1899-1900), 52-56.

2017 . Kornmann, Joseph. "Lettres," *Annales Apostoliques*, XI(1896), 116-120.

2018 . Krenzler, Eugen. *Ein Jahr in Ost-Afrika im Auftrag der Deutsch-Ostafrikanischen Gesellschaft*. Ulm: Ebner, 1888. 124p.

2019 Kröhling, Mauritius. "Missionsbriefe," *Missionsblätter*, IV(1900), 9-11; V(1901), 69.

2020 . Lang, Leo. "Missionsbriefe," *Missionsblätter*, V(1901), 102-103.

2021 Langhans, Paul. "Mgr. Lechaptois' Reisen auf der Ufipa-Hochfläche und im Rikwa-Graben," *PM*, XLV(1899), 225-229.

2022 _____ "Zur Hydrographie des Batanga-Landes," *PM*, XXXIII(1887), 81.

2023 . Langheld, Wilhelm. "Bericht des Hauptmanns Langheld über seine Expedition nach Unyamwesi," *Deutsches Kolonialblatt*, VIII(1897), 511-512.

2024 . _____. *Zwanzig Jahre in deutschen Kolonien*. Berlin: Marine und Kolonial Verlag, 1909. 431p.

2025 . Last, J. T. "A Journey into the Nguru Country from Mamboia, East Central Africa," *PRGS*, New Series, IV(1882), 148-157.

2026 . _____. "A Visit to the Masai People Living beyond the Borders of the Nguru Country," *PRGS*, New Series, V(1883), 517-538.

2027 . _____. "A Visit to the Wa-itumba Iron-Workers and the Mangaheri, near Mamboia, in East Central Africa," *PRGS*, New Series, V(1883), 581-592.

2028   . Lechaptois, Adolphe. "Lettres," *Annalen der Afrikaansche Missiën,* VI
(1889-1890), 204-209, 232-238; VII(1890-1891), 237; IX(1892-1893),
21-22; XI(1894-1895), 67-72; XIII(1896-1897), 158-161.

2029   . _____. "Lettres," *Annales Oeuvre Ste-Enfance,* XXXIX(1888), 308-323; XLI
(1890), 106-120; XLVI(1895), 103-110; XLIX(1898), 395-400.

2030   . _____. "Lettres," *Maandelijksch Verslag der Afrikaansche Missiën,* XV
(1894), 77-81, 370-373; XVII(1896), 362-363.

2031   . _____. "Lettres," *MCL,* XXVIII(1896), 471.

2032   . _____. "Lettres," *Missions d'Afrique*[Malines], XX(1899), 325-330; XXII
(1901), 5.

2033   . _____. "Lettres," *Missions d'Afrique*[Paris], (1895-1897), 317-319;
(1897-1900), 601-606.

2034   . _____. "Lettres," *Missions d'Alger,* (1887-1890), 514-520, 884; (1891-
1892), 236-237; (1893-1894), 100-114, 251-256, 395-397, 408.

2035   . _____. "Missionsbriefe," *Afrika-Bote,* I(1895), 13-14; II(1896), 133-135;
VI(1899-1900), 27-31, 52-53, 71.

2036   . _____. "Missionsbriefe," *KM,* XXVIII(1899-1900), 64-65.

2037   . Leconte, Paul. "Lettres," *APFL,* LXXI(1899), 353-357.

2038   . _____. "Missionsbriefe," *KM,* XXVIII(1899-1900), 39-41.

2039   . Ledonné, Désiré. "Lettres," *Annales Apostoliques,* VIII(1893), 94-97; IX
(1894), 72-80.

2040   . Ledoulx, Charles. "Explorateurs et missionaires francais dans l'Afrique
orientale," *CRSG,* III(1884), 307-309, 515-519; IV(1885), 11-13,
183-184, 211, 357-358.

2041 _____. "Les missions catholiques dans l'Afrique orientale," *BSGP*, 7th Series, I(1881), 488-490.

2042 Lent, Carl. [*Dr.*]. "Aus dem Tagebuch des Dr. Lent," *DK*, XI(1894), 38-41, 67-68, 168-170.

2043 _____. "Ein Ausflug nach Taweta," *DK*, X(1893), 165-170.

2044 _____. "Die katholische Mission am Kilimandscharo," *DK*, XI(1894), 6-8.

2045 _____. *Tagebuch-Berichte der Kilimanjaro-Station.* 6 vols. Berlin: C. Heyman, 1894.

2046 Léonard, Henri. "Lettres," *Maandelijksch Verslag der Afrikaansche Missiën*, XVIII(1897), 85-88, 275-278.

2047 _____. "Lettres," *Missions d'Afrique*, (1897-1900), 777-781.

2048 Lepelletier, Ludovic. "Lettres," *Maandelijksch Verslag der Afrikaansche Missiën*, XVI(1895), 285-286; XVII(1896), 23-25.

2049 _____. "Lettres," *Missions d'Afrique*, (1895-1897), 96-97, 205-207; (1897-1900), 560-562.

2050 _____. "Lettres," *Afrika-Bote*, I(1895), 105-106; II(1896), 26-27; V (1899), 182-183.

2051 Le Roy, Alexandre. "A bord du 'Nyanza'," *MCL*, XIV(1882), 242-245, 254-257.

2052 _____. "À la decouverte," *MCL*, XIX(1887), 293-296, 308-312, 320-322, 330-334, 341-344, 353-356, 365-367, 381. Also, *MCM*, XVII (1888), 130-131, 138-141, 148-151, 162-165, 177-179, 189-190, 200-201, 215-216.

2053 _____. *À travers le Zanguebar.* Lyon: Missions Catholiques, 1884. 202p. Also, *MCL*, XVI(1884), 16ff; *MCM*, XIII(1884), 243ff.

2054       ————————. *D'Aden a Zanzibar*. Tours: Alfred Mame et fils, 1899. 364p.

2055       . ——————. *Au Kilima-Ndjaro*. Paris: L. de Soye, 1893. 469p. Also, *MCL*, XXIV(1892), 369ff.

2056       . ————————————. "Au Zanguebar anglais," *MCL*, XXII(1890), 435-439, 448-451, 461-465, 472-477, 484-488, 496-499, 508-512, 522-525, 532-536, 545-548, 567-573, 580-586, 593-598, 604-608, 616-620, 628-634. Also, *MCM*, XX (1891), 202ff, and, *KM*, XIX(1891), 120ff.

2057       . ————————————. "Un coin de l'Arabie heureuse," *MCL*, XVII(1885), 115-118, 125-128, 136-139, 149-152, 176-178, 190-192, 197-200, 209-213, 221-224, 232-236. Also, *MCM*, XV(1886), 11-12, 19-22, 29-31, 44-48, 53-55, 64-69, 83-84, 91-94.

2058       . ———————————— "Dari-Salama," *MCL*, XVIII(1886), 512-527. Also, *MCM*, XVI(1887), 555-558, 568-569.

2059       . ————————————. "Lettere," *MCM*, XIII(1884), 584; XVI(1887), 279; XVIII(1889), 414-416; XIX(1890), 169-170; XXIV(1895), 97-100, 505-507.

2060       . ———————. "Lettres," *APFL*, LVI(1884), 42-59; LVIII(1886), 186-198; LIX(1887), 394-395; LXV(1893), 394; LXVIII(1896), 38-50, 200-220.

2061       . ———————. "Lettres," *MCL*, XVI(1884), 567; XIX(1887), 256; XXI(1889), 317-319; XXII(1890), 157-158; XXV(1893), 280-281; XXVI(1894), 85-87; XXVII(1895), 85-88, 493-496.

2062       ————————————. "Le long des côtes. De Zanzibar à Lamo," *MCL*, XXI (1889), 8-12, 18-21, 30-33, 40-44, 53-56, 65-70, 77-81, 89-92, 101-104, 114-117, 129-132. Also, *MCM*, XVIII(1889), 333-336, 358-359, 370-371, 379-380, 390-392, 405-408, 418-420, 427-430, 440-443, 450-452, 463-466, 475-478.

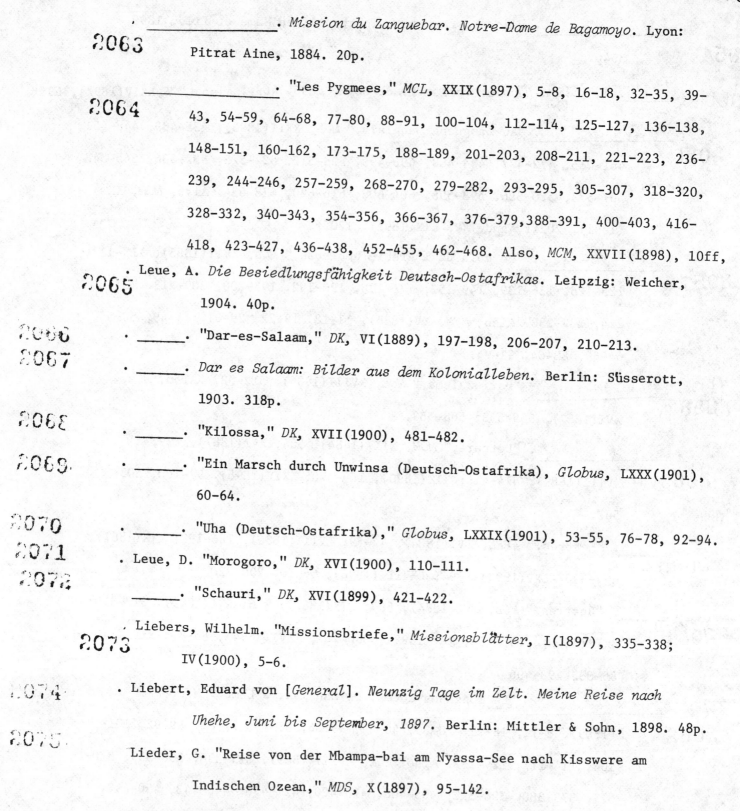

2063     _____. *Mission du Zanguebar. Notre-Dame de Bagamoyo.* Lyon: Pitrat Aine, 1884. 20p.

2064     _____. "Les Pygmees," *MCL*, XXIX(1897), 5-8, 16-18, 32-35, 39-43, 54-59, 64-68, 77-80, 88-91, 100-104, 112-114, 125-127, 136-138, 148-151, 160-162, 173-175, 188-189, 201-203, 208-211, 221-223, 236-239, 244-246, 257-259, 268-270, 279-282, 293-295, 305-307, 318-320, 328-332, 340-343, 354-356, 366-367, 376-379,388-391, 400-403, 416-418, 423-427, 436-438, 452-455, 462-468. Also, *MCM*, XXVII(1898), 10ff,

2065     Leue, A. *Die Besiedlungsfähigkeit Deutsch-Ostafrikas.* Leipzig: Weicher, 1904. 40p.

2066     _____. "Dar-es-Salaam," *DK*, VI(1889), 197-198, 206-207, 210-213.

2067     _____. *Dar es Salaam: Bilder aus dem Kolonialleben.* Berlin: Süsserott, 1903. 318p.

2068     _____. "Kilossa," *DK*, XVII(1900), 481-482.

2069     _____. "Ein Marsch durch Unwinsa (Deutsch-Ostafrika), *Globus*, LXXX(1901), 60-64.

2070     _____. "Uha (Deutsch-Ostafrika)," *Globus*, LXXIX(1901), 53-55, 76-78, 92-94.

2071     Leue, D. "Morogoro," *DK*, XVI(1900), 110-111.

2072     _____. "Schauri," *DK*, XVI(1899), 421-422.

2073     Liebers, Wilhelm. "Missionsbriefe," *Missionsblätter*, I(1897), 335-338; IV(1900), 5-6.

2074     Liebert, Eduard von [*General*]. *Neunzig Tage im Zelt. Meine Reise nach Uhehe, Juni bis September, 1897.* Berlin: Mittler & Sohn, 1898. 48p.

2075     Lieder, G. "Reise von der Mbampa-bai am Nyassa-See nach Kisswere am Indischen Ozean," *MDS*, X(1897), 95-142.

2076 . _____ "Zur Kenntnis der Karawanenwege im südlichen Theile des östafrikanischen Schutzgebiets," *MDS*, VII(1894), 277.

2077 . Lishout, E. van [*Fr. Egidius*]. "Lettres," *Annalen der Afrikaansche Missiën*, XIV(1897-1898), 67-69; XV(1898-1899), 54-56.

2078 . Lombard, Joseph-Henri. "Lettres," *Annalen der Afrikaansche Missiën*, X (1893-1894), 244-248.

2079 . _____. "Lettres," *Maandelijksch Verslag der Afrikaansche Missiën*, XV (1894), 115-119.

2080 . _____. "Lettres," *Missions d'Alger*, (1887-1890), 49; (1891-1892), 474-478.

2081 . Lucas, Alexander [*Kommerzienrat*]. "Zur Inderfrage in Deutsch-Ostafrika," *DK*, XVI(1899), 275.

2082 . Luschan, Felix von. "Beiträge zur Ethnographie des Abflusslosen Gebietes in Deutsch-Ost-Afrika," C. W. Werther's *Die mittleren Hochländer des nördlichen Deutsch-Ost-Afrika*. Berlin: H. Paetel, 1898, pp. 323-381.

2083 . McClounie, J. "A Journey Across the Nyika Plateau," *GJ*, XXII(1903), 423-437.

2084 . Machon, Pierre. "Lettre," *Annales Apostoliques*[Paris], XI(1896), 76-79.

2085 . _____. "Lettre," *Annales Oeuvre Ste-Enfance*[Paris], XXV(1874), 315-320.

2086 . _____. "Lettre," *Echo aus Afrika*[Salzburg], V(1893), 16-17, 74-75, 107-108.

2087 . Maples, Chauncy. "Masasi and the Rovuma District in East Africa," *PRGS*, New Series, II(1880), 337-350.

2088 . Marno, Ernst. "Bericht über eine Excursion von Zanzibar (Saadani) nach Koa-Kiora," *MKKG*, XXI(1878), 353.

2089    • Martin, Ernst. "Lettres," *Annalen der Afrikaansche Missiën*, XIV(1897-1898), 297-301.

2090    • _____. "Missionsbriefe," *Afrika-Bote*, IV(1898), 28-29, 71-73, 108-109, 133-135; V(1899), 125-126.

2091    • Matthias, Nicolaus. "Lettres," *Annalen der Afrikaansche Missiën*, XII (1895-1896), 263-265; XVI(1899-1900), 43-51.

2092    • Maximini, Wunibald. "Missionsbriefe," *Vergissmeinnicht*, XIX(1901), 18.

2093    • Mayer, Ambrosius. "Missionsbriefe," *Missionsblätter*, I(1897), 87-89, 237-240; II(1898), 32-34, 35-37; III(1899), 20-24; IV(1900), 13-14, 38-39, 79-88; V(1901), 5, 35.

2094    • Meinecke, Gustav. *Deutsche Kultivation in Ostafrika und der Kaffeebau.* Berlin: Heymann, 1892. 42p.

2095    _____. "Die erste Kulturzone Ostafrikas," *DK*, IX(1892), 110-112, 127-128, 136-137.

2096    • _____. "Pangani," *DK*, XI(1894), 154-155.

2097    • _____. "Plantagen-Kultivation, das erste Erfordernis rationeller Wirtschaftpolitik," *Koloniales Jahrbuch*, 1892, p. 1.

2098    • _____. "Tanga," *DK*, XI(1894), 140-141.

2099    • _____. "Wirtschaftliche Untersuchungen in Ostafrika," *DK*, XII(1895), 129-132, 154-156, 162-165.

2100    Ménard, François. "Lettres," *Missions d'Afrique*, (1897-1900), 629-632, 740-743.

2101    • _____. "Missionsbriefe," *Afrika-Bote*, VI(1899-1900), 84-87.

2102    • Merensky, Alexander. *Deutsche Arbeit am Njasza, Deutsch-Ostafrika.* Berlin: Berliner Evangelische Missionsgesellschaft, 1894. 368p.

2103 . _____. "Konde-Land und Konde-Volk in Deutsch-Ostafrika auf Grund eigener Beobachtungen," *VGE*, XX(1893), 385.

2104 . _____. "The Konde Country," *GJ*, II(1893), 321-323.

2105 . Merker, M. *Die Masai. Ethnographische Monographie eines ostafrikanischen Semitenvolkes*. Berlin: Reimer, 1904. 421p.

2106 . _____. "Rechtsverhältnisse und Sitten der Wadschagga," *PM*, XXX(1902), Supplementary No. 138, 41p.

2107 _____. "Religion und Tradition der Masai," *ZE*, XXXV(1903), 733-744.

. Mertz, G. [*Br. Gerard*]. "Lettres," *Annalen der Afrikaansche Missiën*, II (1885-1886), 34-44, 53-59; III(1886-1887), 57-62; VI(1889-1890), 37-42.

2108

2109 . Mesters, Mathieu. "Lettres," *Missiën der Witte Paters*, XXII(1901), 220-221.

2110 . _____. "Lettres," *Missions d'Afrique*, XXII(1901), 190-191.

2111 . Metzger, E. "Einige Betrachtungen über Kultivation in den Tropen," *DK*, II(1885), 611.

. Mével, Jean-Marie. "Lettere," *MCM*, XXIII(1894), 115-118.

2112 . _____. "Lettres," *Annales Apostoliques*, II(1887), 3-10; VI(1891), 105-107; VIII(1893), 121-128; X(1895), 64-71.

2113

2114 . _____. "Lettres," *APFL*, LXV(1893), 204-217; LXVI(1894), 17-31; LXVII (1895), 277-288.

2115 . _____. "Lettres," *MCL*, XXV(1893), 400-403.

2116 . Meyer, Hans Heinrich Joseph. [*Dr.*]. "Ascent to the Summit of Kilimanjaro," *PRGS*, New Series, XII(1890), 331-344.

2117 . _____. "Das Bergland Ugueno und der westliche Kilimandscharo," *PM*, XXXVI(1890), 46-48.

2118 . _____. "Die Besteigung des Kilimandscharo," *PM*, XXXVI(1890), 15-22.

2113 · _____ . *Das deutsche Kolonialreich. Eine Länderkunde der deutschen Schutzgebiet.* 2 vols. Leipzig and Vienna: Bibliographische Institute, 1909-1910.

2120 · _____ . *Die Eisenbahnen im tropischen Afrika.* Leipzig: Duncher & Humbolt, 1902. 186p.

2121 · _____ . *Ergebnisse einer Reise durch das Zwischenseegebiet Ostafrika, 1911.* Berlin, 1913. 127p.

2122 · _____ . "Ergebnisse meiner vierten ostafrikanischen Reise," *Globus*, LXXIV(1898), 265-266.

2123 · _____ . "Die Ersteigung des Kilimandjaro," *VGE*, XVII(1890), 90-102.

2124 · _____ . "Die Gletscher des Kilimandjaro," *Geographische Zeitung*[Leipzig], V(1899), 209-226.

2125 · _____ . *Der Kilimandjaro. Reisen und Studien.* Berlin: Reimer, 1900. 436p.

2126 · _____ . *Ostafrikanische Gletscherfahrten; Forschungsreisen im Kilimanjaro Gebiet.* Leipzig: Duncker & Humbolt, 1890.376p. English translation, *Across East African Glaciers.* London: Philip, 1891. 404p.

2127 · _____ . "Die Schneeverhältnisse am Kilimandscharo im Sommer 1887," *Mitteilungen des Vereins für Erdkunde*, 1887, 277.

2128 · _____ . "Uber seine neue Kilima-Ndscharo-Expedition," *VGE*, XXVI(1899), 88.

2129 · _____ . "Vorläufiger Bericht uber meine Besteigung des Kilimandscharo, Juli 1887," *PM*, XXXIII(1887), 353-355.

2130 · _____ . "Zur Anlage neuer stationen in Njika- und Burndali-Land im November 1898," *PM*, XLV(1899), 166-167.

2131 Mohun, R. Dorsey. "Bombardment of Zanzibar," *Cosmopolitan Magazine*, June, 1898, pp. 157-164.

2132 Moncet, Auguste. "Lettera," *MCM*, XV(1886), 239-240.

2133 _____. "Lettre," *Missions d'Afrique*, (1890).

2134 _____. "Lettre," *MCL*, XVIII(1886), 192.

2135 Mondières, A. T. "Les douz tribus du lac Tanganyika," *Revue d'Anthropologie*, XII(1883), 117.

2136 Moore, John Edward S. *The Tanganyika Problem: An Account of the Researches Undertaken Concerning the Existence of Marine Animals in Central Africa*. London: Hurst & Blackett, 1903. 371p.

2137 Müller, Franz. "Lettres," *Missions d'Afrique*, (1895-1897), 358-359.

2138 _____. "Missionsbriefe," *Afrika-Bote*, II(1896), 152-153; III(1897), 90-93; IV(1898), 26-28, 69-71, 105-108, 117-119; V(1899), 26-29; VI(1899-1900), 6-10, 33-37, 53-60, 81-84, 108-112, 136-138, 147-151, 174-177, 177-179; VII(1900-1901), 50-55, 127-131, 154-159, 194, 218-221.

2139 Newman, Henry Stanley. *Banani: the Transition from Slavery to Freedom in Zanzibar and Pemba*. London: Headley, 1898. 216p.

2140 Oechelhaeuser, Wilhelm. *Die Deutsch-Ostafrikanische Centralbahn*. Berlin: J. Springer, 1899. 119p.

2141 Ovir, Ewald. "Märchen und Räthsel der Wamadschame," *ZAOS*, III(1897), 65-84.

2142 Pascal, Joachim. "Lettera," *MCM*, VII(1878), 389-390.

2143 _____. "Lettres," *MCL*, X(1878), 379, 522-523; XI(1879), 104-105,

2144 . Paul. *Deutsch-Ostafrika*. Leipzig: F. Richter, 1900. 352p. Vol. II of author's *Die Mission in unsern kolonien*.

2145 . Pearce, Francis Barrow. *Zanzibar, the Island Metropolis of Eastern Africa*. London: Fisher, Unwin, 1920. 431p.

2146 . Peters, Karl Friedrich Hubert. *Afrikanische Köpfe. Charakterskizzen aus der neueren Geschichte Afrikas*. Berlin, Vienna: Ullstein, 1915. 267p.

2147 . _____. *British Prevarication*. Translated by J. W. van Eyndhoven. n.p., n.d., 8p.

2148 . _____. *Die deutsch-ostafrikanische Kolonie in ihrer Entstehungsgeschichte und wirtschaftlichen Eigenart*. Berlin, 1889. 44p.

2149 . _____. *Das deutsch-ostafrikanische Schutzgebiet*. Munich: Oldenbourg, 1895. 467p.

2150 . _____. *Door Afrika's Wildernissen*. 3 vols. Leiden: A. W. Sijthoff, 1891.

2151 . _____. *Gesammelte Schriften*. 3 vols. Munich and Berlin: C. H. Beck, 1943-1944.

2152 . _____. *Die Gründung von Deutsch-Ostafrika*. Berlin: C. A. Schwetschke, 1906. 276p.

2153 . _____. "Letters from German East Africa," *DK*, V(1888), 18-19.

2154 . _____. *New Light on Dark Africa*. London and New York: Wark, Lock, 1891. 597p.

2155 . _____. *Wie Deutsch-Ostafrika Entstand!* Leipzig: Koehler & Voigtländer, 1940. 172p.

2156 . _____. *Zur Weltpolitik*. Berlin: K. Siegismund, 1912. 383p.

2157 . Pfeil, Joachim [*Graf*]. "Uhehe," *DK*, VIII(1891), 157 XV(1898), 132-133.

2158 . _____. "Uhehe in Deutsch-Ostafrika," *Globus*, LXXIII(1898), 37-43.

2159 . _____. *Vorschläge zur praktischen Kolonisation in Ost-Afrika*. Berlin: Rosenbaum & Hart, 1888. 79p.

2160 . _____. *Zur Erwerbung von Deutsch-Ostafrika. Ein Beitrag zu seiner Geschichte*. Berlin: K. Curtius, 1907. 232p.

**2161** Picardo, Cado. "Autour de Mandera. Notes sur l'Ouzigoua, l'Oukwere et l'Oudoe," *MCL*, XVIII(1886), 184-189, 197-201, 208-211, 225-228, 234-237, 246-249, 258-261, 269-274, 281-285, 294-297, 322-324, 332-334, 342-346, 356-357, 365-369. Also, *MCM*, XVI(1887), 19-23, 29-33, 44-48, 52-57, 66-68, 77-82, 88-92, 104-106, 116-117, 127-128, 142-144, 154-155, 164-166.

**2162** _____. "Lettere," *MCM*, XIV(1885), 99-104, 218-219.

**2163** . _____. "Lettres," *Annales Apostoliques*, I(1886), 13-29.

**2164** . _____. "Lettres," *Annales Oeuvre Ste-Enfance*, XXXV(1884), 400-413.

**2165** . _____. "Lettres," *Echo des Missions d'Afrique*, I(1884), 171-183; II(1885), 154-159.

**2166** _____. "Lettres," *MCL*, XVI(1884), 505-509; XVII(1885), 195.

**2167** . Pogge, Paul. "Bericht über die Reise von Mukenge nach Nyangwe und zurück," *MAGD*, IV(1883-1885), 179, 205.

**2168** . Porter, William Carmichael. "The Magwangwara," *JMGS*, II(1886), 265-282.

**2169** . Prager, M. [*Kapitän*]. "Die Volksstämme im deutschen Gebiet am Nyassasee, ihre Sitten und Gebräuche," *DK*, XIII(1896), 186-188.

**2170** . Préville, de. "Extrait d'une lettre," *Bulletin Société Bretonne de Géographie*, II(1883), 211-212.

**2171** . Quass, E. "Stadt und Hafen Zanzibar," *Zeitschrift für Allgemeine Erdkunde*, New Series, VIII(1860), 177.

**2172** . Raffray, Achille. "Voyage chez les Ouanika, sur la Côte du Zanguebar," *TM*, XXXV(1878), 289-304.

**2173** . Ramsay, S. [*Hauptmann*]. "Uha, Urundi und Ruanda," *MDS*, X(1897), 177-181.

2174 . Randabel, Camille. "Lettres," *Annalen der Afrikaansche Missiën*, V(1888-1889), 68-69; VI(1889-1890), 42-48; XI(1894-1895), 190-192.

2175 . _____. "Lettres," *Grands Lacs*, LII(1935-1936), 204-207.

2176 . _____. "Lettres," *Maandelijksch Verslag der Afrikaansche Missiën*, XV (1894), 369-370.

2177 . _____. "Lettres," *Missions d'Alger*, (1883-1886), 21-25; (1887-1890), 307-308, 547-549; (1891-1892), 431; (1893-1894), 389-390.

2178 . _____. "Missionsbriefe," *KM*, XI(1883), 199-200.

2179 . Rankin, L. K. "The Elephant Experiment in Africa; A Brief Account of the Belgian Elephant Expedition on the March from Dar-es-Salaam to Mpwapwa," *PRGS*, New Series, IV(1882), 273-289.

2180 . Raum, Johannes. "Blut- und Speichelbünde bei den Wadschagga," *Archiv für Religionwissenschaft*, X(1907), 269-294.

2181 . _____. "Einige Masai-Märchen in Kimadschame," *ZAOS*, IV(1898), 124-132.

2182     .  _____ . "Die Religion der Landschaft Moschi am Kilimandjaro," *Archiv für Religionswissenschaft*, XIV(1911), 159-211.

2183     .  _____ . "Über angeblicke Götzen am Kilimandscharo, nebst Bemerkungen über die Religion der Wadschagga und Bantuneger überhaupt," *Globus*, LXXXV(1904), 101-105.

2184     . Reichard, Paul. "Afrikanische Diplomatie," *DK*, IX(1892), 15-17.

2185     .  _____ . "Das Afrikanische Elfenbein und sein Handel," *Deutsche Geographische Blätter*, XII(1888), 132-168.

2186     .  _____ . "Die Bedeutund von Tabora für Deutsch-Ostafrika," *DK*, VI(1890), 67-68.

2187     .  _____ . "Bericht über seine Reisen in Ostafrika und das Quellgebiet des Kongo," *VGE*, XII(1886), 107.

2188     .  _____ . *Deutsch-Ostafrika. Das Land und seine Bewohner, seine politische und wirtschaftliche Entwickelung.* Leipzig: O. Spamer, 1891. 524p.

2189     .  _____ . "Fünf Jahre verschollen. Reise-Erlebnisse in Ost- und Central-Afrika," *Deutsche Weltpost*[Berlin], IV(1886), No. 2.

2190     .  _____ . "Gebärden und Mienenspiel des Negers," *Ausland*, LXIII(1890), 381-385, 425-428.

2191     .  _____ . "Hexenprozesse in Afrika." *DK*, VI(1889), 172-174, 179-180.

2192     .  _____ . "Land und Leute in Ostafrika." *DK*, III(1886), 57-64.

2193     .  _____ . "Die Mahähä," *DK*, VIII(1891), 161-164.

2194     .  _____ . "Die Manjamuesi," *DK*, VII(1890), 228-230, 239-241, 263-265, 276-278.

2195     .  _____ . "Reise von Karema nach Kapampa und durch Marungu nach Mpala," *MAGD*, IV(1883-1885), 159-170.

2196     .  _____ . "Die Station Mpala. Reise in Marungu, juli-juni 1883," *MAGD*, IV(1883-1885), 99-159.

2197 · _____. "Vorschläge zu eine Reiseausrüstung für Ost- und Centralafrika," *ZGE*, XXIV(1889), 1-82.

2198 · _____. "Die Wanjamuesi," *ZGE*, XXIV(1889), 246-260, 304-331, XXV(1890), 228-230, 239-241, 263-265, 276-288.

2199 · _____. "Was ich in Afrika gegessen habe," *Deutsche Wochenblatt*, 1888, pp. 381-384.

2200 · Richter, Franz. "Der Bezirk Bukoba," *MDS*, XII(1899), 67-105.

2201 · _____. "Einige weitere ethnographische Notizen über den Bezirk Bukoba," *MDS*, XIII(1900), 61-75.

2202 · Rigby, C. P. "Das Gebiet von Zanzibar," *PM*, VII(1861), 249-261.

2203 · Rindermann, Josef. "Die Kampfe bei Tabora," *DK*, IX(1892), 126-127, 134-135.

2204 · _____. "Die Station Bukoba," *DK*, X(1893), 101-102.

2205 · Roos, Joseph. "Missionsbriefe," *Afrika-Bote*, VIII(1901-1902), 218-222, 272-273.

2206 Rothbletz, Adelhard. "Missionsbriefe," *Echo aus Knechtsteden*, II(1900-1901), 41-43, 87-89.

2207 · Ruedel, Anton [*Missionary*]. "Schauri," *DK*, XV(1898), 106-108, 134-135, 262-263.

2208 · _____. "Missionsbriefe," *Echo aus Afrika*, XII(1900), 55-56; XIII (1901), 34-35, 202-205.

2209 · _____. "Missionsbriefe," *Missionsblätter*, I(1897), 89-92, 151-154, 216-217, 367-378; II(1898), 12-18, 38-43; III(1899), 45-46, 90, 118; IV (1900), 6-7, 70-74, 102-104, 110-114; V(1901), 3-4, 8-14, 40-41.

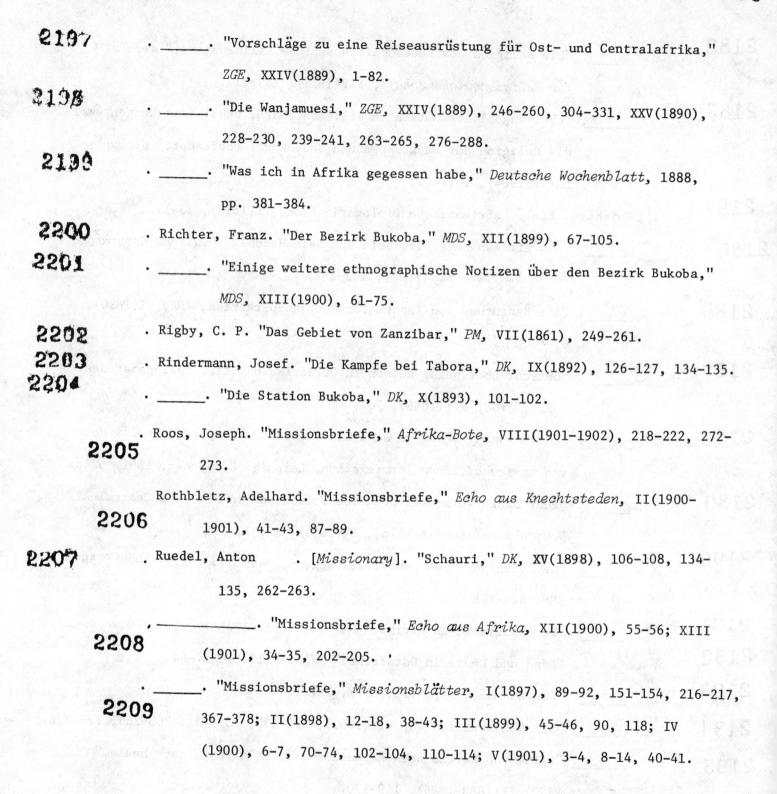

2210 . Ruete, Emily. *Memorien einen arabischen Prinzessin.* 2 vols. Berlin, 1886.

English translation, *Memoirs of an Arabian Princess. An autobiography.*

New York: Appleton, 1888. 307p. New York: Doubleday, Page, 1907.

227p.

2211 . Ruschenberger, William S. W. *A Voyage around the World. . .in 1835, 1836,*

*and 1837.* Philadelphia: Carey, Lea & Blanchard, 1838. 559p. Also,

2 vols, London: Bentley, 1838.

. Samassa, Paul [Dr.]. *Die Besiedlung Deutsch-Ostafrikas.* Berlin: W. Weicher,

2212 1909. 313p.

2213 . Schellendorff, F. Bronsart von. "Zebrafang bei Mbuguni (Kilimandscharo),"

*DK,* XIV(1897), Beilage Nr. XIII, 53-55.

2214 . Scheuermann, Antoine. "Lettera," *MCM,* III(1874), 503-504.

2215 . _____. "Lettre," *BGCSS,* X(1874-1875), 208-211.

2216 . _____. "Lettre," *MCL,* VI(1874), 442.

2217 . Schlobach, Gaston. "Die Volksstämme der deutschen Ostküste des Victoria-

Nyansa," *MDS,* XIV(1901), 183-193.

2218 . Schloifer, Otto. *Bana Uleia, ein Lebenswerk in Afrika; aus den Tagebüchern*

*eines alten Kolonial-pioniers.* Berlin: D. Reimer, 1939. 342p.

2219 . _____. "Die Tanganyika-Dampfer-Expedition," *DK,* XVI(1899), 238-240.

2220 . Schmidt, Karl Wilhelm. *Sansibar: Ein ostafrikanisches Kulturbild.*

Leipzig, 1888. 184p.

2221 . Schmidt, Rochus. *Aus kolonialer Frühzeit.* Berlin: Safari-Verlag, 1922.

222p.

2222 . _____. *Deutschlands koloniale Helden und Pioniere der Kultur im schwarzen*

*Kontinent.* 2 vols. Braunschweig: A. Limbach, 1896.

2223 . _____. *Kolonialpioniere; persönliche Erinnerungen aus kolonialer*

*Frühzeit.* Berlin: Safari-Verlag, 1938. 302p.

2224 . _____. "Die südliche Grenzdistrikt Deutsch-Ostafrikas," *DK,* X(1893), 138-

140.

2225 Schneider, Dekan. *Die Sklavenfrage in Ostafrika*. Stuttgart: "Deutsches Volksblatt", 1888. 14p.

2226 . Schneider, Gebhard. *Die katholische Mission von Zanguebar*. Regensburg: Manz, 1877. 324p.

2227 . Schneider, Theophil. *Auf dem Missionspfade in Deutsch-Ostafrika. Von Sansibar zum Kilimandscharo, Reise-Bericht gewidmet den deutschen Katholiken*. Münster i. W.: Heinrich Schöningh, 1899. 115p.

2228 Schulze. "Berichte, Aug. bis Dec., 1884," *MAGD*, IV(1883-1885), 274-291.

2229 Schweiger, Ivo. "Missionsbriefe," *Missionsblätter*, IV(1900), 18.

2230 . Schynse, A. *Mit Stanley und Emin Pascha durch Deutsch-Ostafrika. Tage-buch herausgegeben von Karl Hespers*. Cologne: Bachem, 1890.

2231 . Seidel, A. "Beiträge zur Charakteristik des ostafrikanischen Negers," *Kolonial Jahrbuch*, 1892, pp. 41-58.

2232 . Semler, H. *Die tropische Agrikultur. Ein Handbuch für Pflanzer und Kaufleute*. 3 vols. Wismar: Hinstorff, 1886-1893.

2233 . _____. "Zur Kaffeekultur. I. Die Baumschule. II. Die Anpflanzung," *DK*, III(1886), 242, 735.

2234 . Sigiez, Jean. "Lettres," *Missions d'Afrique*, (1895-1897), 393-402; (1897-1900), 390-393.

2235 . _____. "Missionsbriefe," *Afrika-Bote*, II(1896), 181-186; IV(1898), 186-189.

2236 . Smith, G. E. [*Capt., Royal Eng.*]. "From the Victoria Nyanza to Kiliman-jaro," *GJ*, XXIX(1907), 249-269.

2237 . Smith, John. [*M.D.*]. "A mi-chemin du Lac Nyanza," *JME*, LII(1877), 308-312.

2238 . Smoor, Corneille. "Lettres," *Annalen der Afrikaansche Missiën*, XVI(1899-1900), 138-142, 284-290; XVII(1900-1901), 31-35, 100-105, 206-211, 295-301, 371-377; XVIII(1901-1902), 85-87, 116-118, 151-153, 202-204.

2239 . _____. "Missionsbriefe," *Afrika-Bote*, VII(1900-1901), 273-276.

2240 . Southon, Ebenezer J. "Notes of a Journey through Northern Ugogo, in East Central Africa, in July and August, 1879," *PRGS*, New Series, III (1881), 547-553.

2241 . Spiss, Cassian. "Missionsbriefe," *Echo aus Afrika*, XI(1899), 99-101; XII(1900), 9-11.

2242 . _____. "Missionsbriefe," *Missionsblätter*, II(1898), 34-35, 101-110; III (1899), 17-18, 46-50, 81-85, 118-121; IV(1900), 15-18, 40-43, 74-75; V(1901), 6-8.

2243 . Stadlbaur. [*Leutnant*]. "Tutu," *MDS*, X(1897), 169-176.

2244 . Stairs, W. E. "De Zanzibar au Katanga: journal," *CIL*, II(1893), 5.

2245 . Storch. "Sitten, Gebräuche und Rechtspflege bei den Bewohnern Usambaras und Pares," *MDS*, VIII(1895), 310-331.

2246 . Storms. [*Lt.*]. "Le Tanganika. Quelques particularités sur les moeurs africaines," *BSBG*, X(1886), 169-200.

2247 . Stuhlmann, Franz. "Bericht über das deutsch-portugiesische Grenzgebiet am Ruvuma," *MDS*, X(1897), 182-190.

2248 . _____. "Forschungsreisen in Usaramo," *MDS*, VII(1894), 225-232.

2249 . _____. "Über die Uluguruberge in Deutsch-Ostafrika," *MDS*, VIII(1895), 209-226.

2250 . _____. *Die wirtschaftliche Entwicklung Deutsch-Ostafrikas*. Berlin: D. Reimer, 1898. 158p.

2251 . Sullivan, George L. "Survey of the Lower Course of the Rufiji River," *JRGS*, XLV(1875), 364-367.

2252 · Thomé, Anton. "Missionsbriefe," *Echo aus Knechtsteden*, II(1900–1901), 131–138, 146–149.

2253 · _____ "Die Götzen am Kilimandscharo," *Globus*, LXXXIII(1903), 231–235.

2254 · Thomson, Joseph. "Notes on the Basin of the River Rovuma, East Africa," *PRGS*, New Series, IV(1882), 65–79.

2255 · _____. "Notes on the Geology of Usambara," *PRGS*, New Series, I(1879), 558–564.

2256 · _____. "Notes on the Route Taken by the Royal Geographical Society's East African Expedition from Dar-es-Salaam to Uhehe; May 19th to August 29th, 1879," *PRGS*, New Series, II(1880), 102–122.

2257 · _____. "Progress of the East African Expedition; Mr. Thomson's Report on his Journey from Lake Nyasa to Lake Tanganyika," *PRGS*, New Series, II(1880), 209–212.

2258 · _____. "Through the Masai Country to Victoria Nyanza," *PRGS*, New Series, VI(1884), 690–713.

2259 · Thornton, Richard. "Expedition to Kilimanjaro (in Company with the Baron von der Decken)," *PRGS*, VI(1861–1862), 47–49.

2260 · _____. "Notes on a Journey to Mount Kilimandjaro," *JRGS*, XXXV(1865), 15–21.

2261 · Toeppen, Kurt. "Aus Sansibar," *DK*, IV(1887), 554–559.

2262 · _____. "Eigene Beobachtungen und Erkundigungen in den deutschen Schutzgebieten Ostafrikas," *DK*, III(1886), 518–523.

2263 · Toeppen, Olga. "Erzählungen der Suaheli-Neger in Zansibar," *Globus*, LIV (1888), 60–61, LV(1889), 42–45.

. Trossmann, Simon. "Missionsbriefe," *Missionsblätter*, IV(1900), 51-53.

2264

2265 . Trotha, L. von. *Meine Bereisung von Deutsch-Ostafrika*. Berlin: Brigl, 1897.

2266 96p.

. Ursel, H. d'. [*Comte*]. *Les Belges au Tanganika*. Brussels: Vanderauwera,

1893. 24p. Extracted from *BSBG*, XVII(1893).

. Van Aken, Antoon. "Lettres," *Annalen der Afrikaansche Missiën*, XVIII

2267 (1901-1902), 93-95, 213-215.

. Van den Biesen, Joseph. **"Lettres,"** *Annalen der Afrikaansche Missiën*, XIII

2268 (1896-1897), 31-40, 97-105, 167-176, 186-191, 215-217, 302-311; XIV

(1897-1898), 32-37, 61-67, 93-97, 127-131, 260-264; XV(1898-1899),

64-73.

. "Lettres," *Maandelijksch Verslag der Afrikaansche Missiën*, XVII

2269 (1896), 366-374; XVIII(1897), 88-90, 116-124, 281-287, 305-311,

311-312, 341-345; XIX(1898), 151-155.

2270 . "Lettres," *Missions d'Afrique*, (1897-1900), 381-389.

2271 . "Missionsbriefe," *Afrika-Bote*, V(1899), 8-13.

. Van den Eynde, Felix. "Lettres," *Missiën der Witte Paters*, XXII(1901),

2272 189-190, 369-373.

2273 . Van der Bom, Theodore. "Lettere," *MCM*, XXV(1896), 555.

2274 . "Lettres," *Annalen der Afrikaansche Missiën*, VII(1890-1891),

146-148, 179-183, 238-239; VIII(1891-1892), 49-52; XI(1894-1895),

306-307; XII(1895-1896), 38-41, 228-232; XIII(1896-1897), 50-54;

XVI(1899-1900), 134-136, 167-169; XVII(1900-1901), 130-134.

2275 . "Lettres," *Maandelijksch Verslag der Afrikaansche Missiën*, XVI

(1895), 20-26; XVII(1896), 348-349.

2276 . "Missionsbriefe," *Afrika-Bote*, VI(1899-1900), 62-63.

2277 · Van der Jeught, Ernest. "Lettres," *Maandelijksch Verslag der Afrikaansche Missiën*, XV(1894), 346-350.

2278 · Van der Straeten, Camille. "Lettres," *Annalen der Afrikaansche Missiën*, IV(1887-1888), 135-140, 152-156, 156-158; V(1888-1889), 142-146, 174-176; VII(1890-1891), 183-188, 205-212, 246-252.

2279 · _____. "Lettres," *Maandelijksch Verslag der Afrikaansche Missiën*, XI (1890), 45-51, 107-112, 153-163; XI(1891), 18-21, 39-41, 381-382.

2280 · Van der Wee, Antonius Joannes. "Lettres," *Annalen der Afrikaansche Missiën*, XI(1894-1895), 272-274; XII(1895-1896), 280-289; XIII(1896-1897), 46-50, 195-200; XIV(1897-1898), 80-83, 301-305; XV(1898-1899), 48-53, 79-86, 160-165, 217-220, 322-327, 348-352; XVI(1899-1900), 171-177, 303-308, 335-339, 365-369; XVII(1900-1901), 62-70, 287-291, 291-294.

2281 · _____. "Lettres," *Maandelijksch Verslag der Afrikaansche Missiën*, XVII (1896), 277-278; XVIII(1897), 40-44, 247-249.

2282 · _____. "Lettres," *Missiën der Witte Paters*, XXI(1900), 254-255.

2283 · _____. "Lettres," *Missions d'Afrique*, (1895-1897), 357-358.

2284 · _____. "Missionsbriefe," *Afrika-Bote*, II(1896), 151-152; VI(1899-1900), 10-16.

2285 · Van Waesberghe, August. "Lettres," *Annalen der Afrikaansche Missiën*, XII(1895-1896), 330-335, 355-359; XIII(1896-1897), 19-23, 54-58, 106-111, 311-317, 346-352; XIV(1897-1898), 19-24, 177-183, 200-206, 357-362; XV(1898-1899), 37-41; XVI(1899-1900), 221-226; XVIII(1901-1902), 227-230.

2286 · _____. "Lettres," *Maandelijksch Verslag der Afrikaansche Missiën*, XVIII (1897), 250-254.

2287 · _____. "Lettres," *Missiën der Witte Paters*, XXI(1900), 258-261.

2288 · _____. "Lettres," *Missions d'Afrique*, (1897-1900), 786-788.

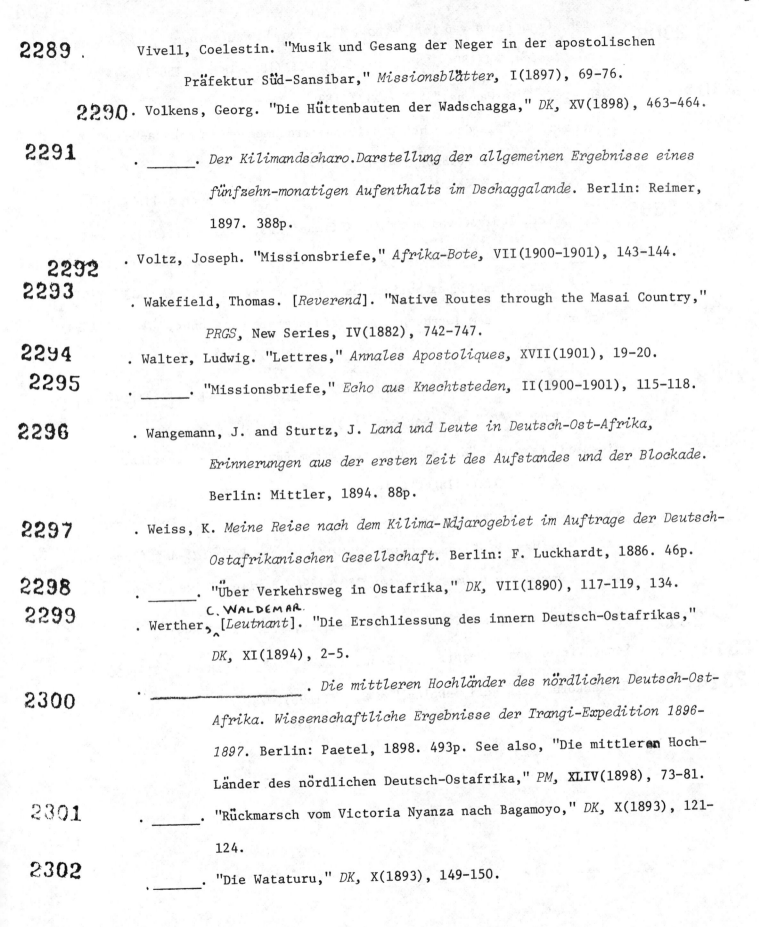

2289 . Vivell, Coelestin. "Musik und Gesang der Neger in der apostolischen Präfektur Süd-Sansibar," *Missionsblätter*, I(1897), 69-76.

2290 . Volkens, Georg. "Die Hüttenbauten der Wadschagga," *DK*, XV(1898), 463-464.

2291 . _____. *Der Kilimandscharo.Darstellung der allgemeinen Ergebnisse eines fünfzehn-monatigen Aufenthalts im Dschaggalande*. Berlin: Reimer, 1897. 388p.

2292 . Voltz, Joseph. "Missionsbriefe," *Afrika-Bote*, VII(1900-1901), 143-144.

2293 . Wakefield, Thomas. [*Reverend*]. "Native Routes through the Masai Country," *PRGS*, New Series, IV(1882), 742-747.

2294 . Walter, Ludwig. "Lettres," *Annales Apostoliques*, XVII(1901), 19-20.

2295 . _____. "Missionsbriefe," *Echo aus Knechtsteden*, II(1900-1901), 115-118.

2296 . Wangemann, J. and Sturtz, J. *Land und Leute in Deutsch-Ost-Afrika, Erinnerungen aus der ersten Zeit des Aufstandes und der Blockade*. Berlin: Mittler, 1894. 88p.

2297 . Weiss, K. *Meine Reise nach dem Kilima-Ndjarogebiet im Auftrage der Deutsch-Ostafrikanischen Gesellschaft*. Berlin: F. Luckhardt, 1886. 46p.

2298 . _____. "Über Verkehrsweg in Ostafrika," *DK*, VII(1890), 117-119, 134.

2299 . Werther, C. WALDEMAR. [*Leutnant*]. "Die Erschliessung des innern Deutsch-Ostafrikas," *DK*, XI(1894), 2-5.

2300 . _____. *Die mittleren Hochländer des nördlichen Deutsch-Ost-Afrika. Wissenschaftliche Ergebnisse der Irangi-Expedition 1896-1897*. Berlin: Paetel, 1898. 493p. See also, "Die mittleren Hoch-Länder des nördlichen Deutsch-Ostafrika," *PM*, **XLIV**(1898), 73-81.

2301 . _____. "Rückmarsch vom Victoria Nyanza nach Bagamoyo," *DK*, X(1893), 121-124.

2302 . _____. "Die Wataturu," *DK*, X(1893), 149-150.

2303 · Wetten, Franciscus van [*Fr. Wiro*]. "Lettres," *Annalen der Afrikaansche Missiën*, XI(1894-1895), 304-306; XIII(1896-1897), 156-158.

2304 Weule, K. "Die Wahehe," *VGE*, XXIII(1896), 467-492.

2305 · Wichmann, H. "Die deutschen Missionsunternehmungen im Njassa-Gebiet," *PM*, XXXVIII(1892), 249-256.

2306 · Widenmann, A. "Bericht über die Klimatischen und gesundheitlichen Verhältnisse von Moshi am Kilimandjaro," *MDS*, VIII(1895), 283.

2307 · _____ "Die Kilimandscharo-Bevölkerung; anthropologisches und ethnographisches Notizen aus dem Dschaggalande," *PM*, XLV(1899).

2308 · Wiener, J. "Aus dem Tagebuch des Forstassessors J. Wiener," *DK*, XI(1894), 21-22.

2309 · Wilson, Charles Thomas. [*Reverend*]. "A Journey from Kagéi to Tabora and Back," *PRGS*, New Series, II(1880), 616-620.

2310 · Wissmann, Hermann. "Ein neues Kultursystem für Deutsch-Ostafrika," *DK*, XIV(1897), Beilage, 1-3.

2311 · Wohltmann, Ferdinand. *Deutsch-Ostafrika. Bericht über die Ergebnisse seiner Reise, ausgeführt im Auftrage der Kolonial-Abteilung des Auswärtigen Amtes, Winter 1897-1898*. Berlin: Telge, 1898. 92p.

2312 · Zache, H. "Sitten und Gebräuche der Suaheli," *ZE*, XXXI(1899).

2313 · Zech, Victor von. [*Graf*]. "Die Station Kwai," *DK*, XV(1898), 141-143.

2314 Ziegenkorn. "Das Rufiyi-Delta," *MDS*, IX(1896), 78.

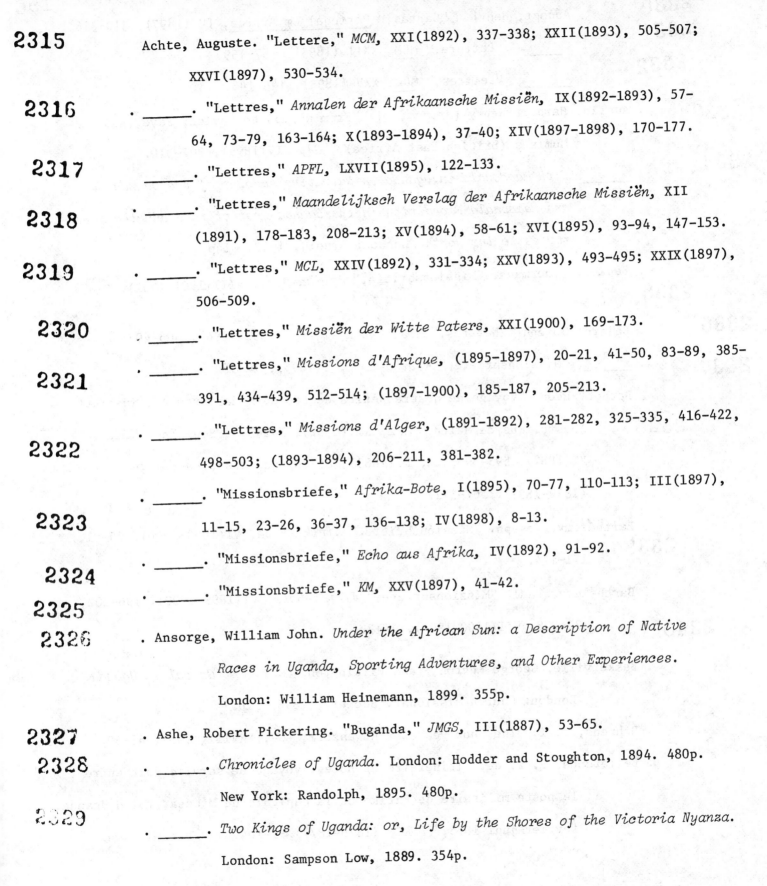

2315    Achte, Auguste. "Lettere," *MCM*, XXI(1892), 337–338; XXII(1893), 505–507; XXVI(1897), 530–534.

2316    . _____. "Lettres," *Annalen der Afrikaansche Missiën*, IX(1892–1893), 57–64, 73–79, 163–164; X(1893–1894), 37–40; XIV(1897–1898), 170–177.

2317    . _____. "Lettres," *APFL*, LXVII(1895), 122–133.

2318    . _____. "Lettres," *Maandelijksch Verslag der Afrikaansche Missiën*, XII (1891), 178–183, 208–213; XV(1894), 58–61; XVI(1895), 93–94, 147–153.

2319    . _____. "Lettres," *MCL*, XXIV(1892), 331–334; XXV(1893), 493–495; XXIX(1897), 506–509.

2320    . _____. "Lettres," *Missiën der Witte Paters*, XXI(1900), 169–173.

2321    . _____. "Lettres," *Missions d'Afrique*, (1895–1897), 20–21, 41–50, 83–89, 385–391, 434–439, 512–514; (1897–1900), 185–187, 205–213.

2322    . _____. "Lettres," *Missions d'Alger*, (1891–1892), 281–282, 325–335, 416–422, 498–503; (1893–1894), 206–211, 381–382.

2323    . _____. "Missionsbriefe," *Afrika-Bote*, I(1895), 70–77, 110–113; III(1897), 11–15, 23–26, 36–37, 136–138; IV(1898), 8–13.

2324    . _____. "Missionsbriefe," *Echo aus Afrika*, IV(1892), 91–92.

2325    . _____. "Missionsbriefe," *KM*, XXV(1897), 41–42.

2326    . Ansorge, William John. *Under the African Sun: a Description of Native Races in Uganda, Sporting Adventures, and Other Experiences.* London: William Heinemann, 1899. 355p.

2327    . Ashe, Robert Pickering. "Buganda," *JMGS*, III(1887), 53–65.

2328    . _____. *Chronicles of Uganda.* London: Hodder and Stoughton, 1894. 480p. New York: Randolph, 1895. 480p.

2329    . _____. *Two Kings of Uganda: or, Life by the Shores of the Victoria Nyanza.* London: Sampson Low, 1889. 354p.

2330
2331
2332

. Aucopt, Henri. "Cartas," Portugal em Africa, IV (1897), 310-316.

. _____. "Lettere," MCM, XXII (1893), 157-159.

. _____. "Lettres," MCL, XXV (1893), 145-146.

2333

. Austin, Herbert Henry [Brigadier]. "From Njemps to Marich, Save, and Mumia's (British East Africa)," GJ, XIV(1899), 307-310.

2334

. _____. With Macdonald in Uganda. A Narrative Account of the Uganda Mutiny and Macdonald Expedition in the Uganda Protectorate and the Territories to the North. London: Arnold, 1903. 314p.

2335

. Backhove, Hermann. "Missionsbriefe," Afrika-Bote, VIII(1901-1902), 3-6.

2336

. Bajard, Joseph. "Lettres," Missions d'Alger, (1893-1894), 405-407.

2337

. _____. "Missionsbriefe," Afrika-Bote, I(1895), 12-13.

2338

. Barbot, Léon. "Voyage de quatre petits nègres de M'dabourou à l'Institut Apostolique de Malte," MCL, XIV(1882), 542-545. See also, MCM, XI.(1882), 593-595; KM, XI(1883), 85-86; and Missions d'Alger, (1879-1882), 567-571.

2339

. Barthélemy, Joseph. "Missionsbriefe," Afrika-Bote, VI(1899-1900), 75-81, 171-174.

2340

. Barthélemy, Paul. "Missionsbriefe," Afrika-Bote, VI(1899-1900), 196-202, 221-228; VII(1900-1901), 7-12.

2341

. Baskerville, George Knyton, and Pilkington, G. L. The Gospel in Uganda. London: Church Missionary Society, 1896. 52p.

2342
2343

. Behrens, T. T. "The Snow-Peaks of Ruwenzori," GJ, XXVIII(1906), 43-50.

. Bellefonds, E. L. de. "Itinéraire et notes; voyage de service fait entre le poste militaire de Fatiko et la capitale de M'tesa, roi d'Uganda, février-juni 1875," BSKG, (1876-1877), 1-104.

2344 . Blanc, Leonard. "Lettres," *Missions d'Alger*, (1879-1882), 574-575; (1883-1886), 27-29, 281-283.

2345 . _____. "Missionsbriefe," *KM*, XIII(1885), 155-156.

2346 Brard, Alphonse. "Lettres," *Annalen der Afrikaansche Missiën*, IX(1892-1893), 96-100, 164-166.

2347 . _____. "Lettres," *APFL*, LXVIII(1896), 89-97.

2348 . _____. "Lettres," *Maandelijksch Verslag der Afrikaansche Missiën*, XV (1894), 241-242; XVII(1896), 147-151.

2349 _____. "Lettres," *Missions d'Afrique*, XIX(1898), 312-318.

2350 . _____. "Lettres," *Missions d'Afrique*[Paris], (1895-1897), 277-282, 351-353; (1897-1900), 371-377, 809-816; (1901-1902), 7-13, 121-125.

2351 . _____. "Lettres," *Missions d'Alger*, (1891-1892), 282-284, 405-409, 503-518; (1893-1894), 95-96, 217-222, 382-383.

2352 . _____. "Missionsbriefe," *Afrika-Bote*, II(1896), 70-74, 137-139; IV(1898), 89-90; V(1899), 5-7, 23-25, 153-154; VI(1899-1900), 221; VII(1900-1901), 98-100, 122-126.

2353 . _____. "Missionsbriefe," *Echo aus Afrika*, IX(1897), 78-80; XI(1899), 68-71; XII(1900), 117-119; XIV(1902), 4-5, 67-68, 84-86.

2354 . _____. "Missionsbriefe," *KM*, XXIV(1896), 231-233.

2355 . _____. "Die Sesse-Inseln," *PM*, XLI(1895), 169.

2356 . Braun, Antoon [*Fr. Philippus*]. "Lettres," *Annalen der Afrikaansche Missiën*, XIV(1897-1898), 103-106.

2357 . Bresson, Eugène. "Lettres," *Missions d'Afrique*, (1895-1897), 426; (1897-1900), 781-783.

2358 _____. "Missionsbriefe," *Afrika-Bote*, I(1895), 38.

2359 . Bright, R. G. T. [*Major*]. "Uganda-Congo Boundary Commission," *GJ*, XXXII (1908), 488-493.

2360 . Brökling, Herman [*Fr. Raphaël*]. "Lettres," *Annalen der Afrikaansche Missiën*, XV(1898-1899), 296-301.

2361 . Burlaton, Louis. "Lettres," *Annalen der Afrikaansche Missiën*, X(1893-1894), 154-159.

2362 _____. "Lettres," *Missions d'Alger*, (1893-1894), 166-171.

2363 . Cabon, Alexandre. "Lettres," *Missions d'Afrique*, (1897-1900), 847-850.

2364 . Chaillé-Long, Charles. "Mission to King M'tesa," *PRGS*, XIX(1874-1875), 107-110.

2365 . Chevalier, Claude. "Lettres," *Annalen der Afrikaansche Missiën*, VI(1889-1890), 263-269.

2366 _____. "Lettres," *Maandelijksch Verslag der Afrikaansche Missiën*, XI (1890), 66-74.

2367 _____. "Lettres," *Missions d'Alger*, (1897-1890), 669-674.

2368 . Chippindall, William Harold. [*Lieutenant*]. "Journey beyond the Cataracts of the Upper Nile towards the Albert Nyanza," *PRGS*, XX(1875-1876), 67-69.

2369 . Chomérac, Georges. "Lettres," *Missions d'Afrique*, (1897-1900), 709-713.

2370 . Claes, Louis [*Fr. Victor*]. "Lettres," *Annalen der Afrikaansche Missiën*, IX(1892-1893), 27-28; X(1893-1894), 305-311.

2371 . _____. "Lettres," *Maandelijksch Verslag der Afrikaansche Missiën*, XI (1890), 272-284, 305-309; XII(1891), 329-340; XV(1894), 25-27, 233-237, 237-238; XVI(1895), 273-275, 345-346; XVII(1896), 189-191, 360-362.

2372 . _____. "Lettres," *Missiën der Witte Paters*, XXI(1900), 60-62.

2373 . Classe, Léon. "Du lac Nyanza au lac Kivou," *MCL*, XXXIV(1902), 136-139, 152-154, 161-166. See also, *MCM*, XXXI(1902), 594-595, 611-612.

2374 . _____. "Lettres," *Missions d'Afrique*, (1901-1902), 377-394, 409-423.

2375 . Colville, Henry Edward. *The Land of the Nile Springs. Being Chiefly an Account of How We Fought Kabarega*. London: Arnold, 1895. 312p.

2376 . Cook, Albert Ruskin. *A Doctor and His Dog in Uganda. From the Letters and Journals of A. R. Cook*. Edited by Mrs. H. B. Cook. London: Religious Tract Society, 1903. 162p.

2377 . _____. "Journey to Uganda in 1896," *Uganda Journal*, I(April, 1934), 83-95.

2378 . Couffignal, Pierre. "Lettres," *Missions d'Afrique*, (1897-1900), 775-777; (1901-1902), 13-16.

2379 . _____. "Missionsbriefe," *Afrika-Bote*, VII(1900-1901), 100-103.

2380 . _____. "Missionsbriefe," *KM*, XXIX(1900-1901), 158-159.

2381 . Couillaud, Jóseph. "Lettere," *MCM*, XX(1891), 171-172.

2382 . _____. "Lettres," *Annalen der Afrikaansche Missiën*, V(1888-1889), 176-184.

2383 . _____. "Lettres," *MCL*, XXII(1890), 531-532.

2384 . _____. "Lettres," *Missions d'Alger*, (1887-1890), 427-442, 846-851; (1891-1892), 204, 368-369.

2385  Cunningham, James Francis. *Uganda and Its Problems: Notes on the Protectorate of Uganda, Especially the Anthropology and Ethnology of Its Indigenous Races.* London: Hutchinson and Co., 1905. 370p.

2386  Delmé-Radcliffe, C. [*Lt.Col.*]. "Surveys and Studies in Uganda," *GJ*, XXVI (1905), 481-497, 616-632.

2387  Denoit, Camille. "Les derniers événements de l'Afrique équatoriale," *MCL*, XXI(1889), 136-140, 153-155, 166-168, 178-180, 189-191, 201-203. See also, *MCM*, XVIII(1889), 145-148, 157-159, 169-171, 184-186, 196-198, 219-223; and *KM*, XVII(1889), 130-133, 151-154, 173-176, 198-199.

2388  _____. "Lettere," *MCM*, XVI(1887), 526-528; XVII(1888), 76-78.

2389  _____. "Lettres," *Annalen der Afrikaansche Missiën*, IV(1887-1888), 109-113, 145-149; V(1888-1889), 52-58, 112-114; VI(1889-1890), 20-27, 49-52, 77-79, 103-105, 128-131, 160-163, 185-190, 219-221, 238-243, 281-284; VII(1890-1891), 263-264; IX(1892-1893), 94-96.

2390  _____. "Lettres," *MCL*, XIX(1887), 505-507; XX(1888), 38-39.

2391  _____. "Lettres," *Missions d'Alger*, (1887-1890), 140-144, 187-190, 249-255, 358-360, 403-405.

2392  _____. "Missionsbriefe," *KM*, XVI(1888), 18-19, 88-89.

2393  Dominikus, Jan-Baptist D'Hooge. "Lettres," *Maandelijksch Verslag der Afrikaansche Missiën*, XI(1890), 272-284, 305-309; XV(1894), 28-29.

2394  Dupoint, Joseph. "Lettres," *Missions d'Afrique*, (1895-1897), 25-34, 286-290, 523-524, 550-552; (1897-1900), 159-161.

2395  _____. "Lettres," *Missions d'Alger*, (1891-1892), 299-302, 479; (1893-1894), 33-35, 181-182, 256-257, 330-331, 353-359, 362-363, 422-423, 424-428.

2396 . Elliott, G. F. Scott. "The Best Route to Uganda," *Contemporary Review*, LXVIII(1895), 15-20.

2397 . Embil, Lauréano. "Lettres," *Missions d'Afrique*, (1901-1902), 351-354.

2398 . Esser, Hubert. "Lettres," *Annalen der Afrikaansche Missiën*, XIV(1897-1898), 195-199, 255-259; XV(1898-1899), 42-47, 74-79, 139-141, 225-230, 293-295; XVI(1899-1900), 37-43, 86-89, 196-201, 230-237; XVII(1900-1901), 81-85, 150-156, 266-269, 380-384; XVIII(1901-1902), 113-116, 125-128.

2399 . Facq, Louis. "Lettres," *Missions d'Afrique*, XXII(1901), 375-377.

2400 . Fauconnier, Ambroise. "Lettres," *Missions d'Afrique*, (1901-1902), 125-127.

2401 . Felkin, Robert William. [*M.D.*]. "Notes on the Waganda Tribe of Central Africa," *Proceedings of the Royal Society of Edinburgh*, XIII(1886), 699-770.

2402 _____. "Uganda," *SGM*, II(1886), 208-226.

2403 . Ferryman, Augustus F. Möckler [*Lt. Col.*]. "Story of the Uganda Mutiny," *Macmillan's Magazine*, Aug., 1898, pp. 308-320.

2404 . Fischer, Nikolaus. "Missionsbriefe," *Afrika-Bote*, VIII(1901-1902), 55-62, 127-134, 153-158, 175-178, 205-207, 235-238, 250-253, 274-281.

2405 . Gâcon, Jean. "Lettere," *MCM*, XXIII(1894), 522-523.

2406 . _____. "Lettres," *MCL*, XXVI(1894), 488.

2407 . Gaudibert, Henri. "Lettres," *Annalen der Afrikaansche Missiën*, XII (1895-1896), 16-17.

2408 . _____. "Lettres," *Maandelijksch Verslag der Afrikaansche Missiën*, XVI (1895), 271-273.

2409 . _____. "Lettres," *Missions d'Afrique*, (1895-1897), 485-488.

2410 . _____. "Lettres," *Missions d'Alger*, (1893-1894), 289-291.

2411 . _____. "Missionsbriefe," *Echo aus Afrika*, III(1891), 38.

2412 . Geerts, Henri[*Fr. Wenceslaus*]. "Lettres," *Annalen der Afrikaansche Missiën*, XVI(1899-1900), 363-365.

2413. Gessi, Romolo. "On the Circumnavigation of the Albert Nyanza," *PRGS*, XXI(1876-1877), 50-56. See also, "Gessi's Umschiffung des Albert Nyanza," *Globus*, XXX(1876), 249-251.

2414 . Giacomelli, Casimiro. "Lettere," *MCM*, XIX(1890), 170-171, 580-581; XX (1891), 592-593.

2415 . _____. "Lettere," *Nigrizia*, IV(1886), 142-145; VII(1889), 6-7, 52-55, 101-104; VIII(1890), 161-165; IX(1891), 161-164; XI(1893), 68-69, 162-171.

2416 . _____. "Lettres," *APFL*, LXVI(1894), 73.

2417 . _____. "Lettres," *MCL*, XXV(1893), 508.

2418 . _____. "Missionsbriefe," *Stern der Neger*, I(1898), 228-231.

2419 . Girault, Ludovic. "Lettere," *MCM*, XVI(1887), 559-560.

2420 . _____. "Lettres," *Annalen der Afrikaansche Missiën*, II(1885-1886), 117-118; IV(1887-1888), 104-106.

2421 . _____. "Lettres," *MCL*, XIX(1887), 528.

2422 . _____. "Lettres," *Missions d'Alger*, (1879-1882), 350-352, 541-542; (1883-1886), 146-148, 241-244, 310-315, 394-396; (1887-1890), 111-113, 138-140, 191-192, 485-491.

2423 . Gorju, Julien-Louis. "Lettres," *Missions d'Afrique*, XIX(1898), 138-147.

2424 Grove-Rasmussen, Andreas Christian Ludwig. *Uganda, et Kristnet Land i Kjertet af Afrika*. Odense: Milo, 1894. 95p.

2425 . Guillermain, Antonin. "Lettere," *MCM*, XX(1891), 397-399; XXII(1893), 31-32; XXIII(1894), 49-54; XXV(1896), 67.

2426 . _____. "Lettere," *Nigrizia*, XI(1893), 148-151.

2427 . _____. "Lettres," *Annalen der Afrikaansche Missiën*, IX(1892-1893), 31-34, 151-162, 178-187, 212-222; XI(1894-1895), 247-252; XII(1895-1896), 188-202, 341-343.

2428 . _____. "Lettres," *APFL*, LXVIII(1896), 156-157.

2429 . _____. "Lettres," *Maandelijksch Verslag der Afrikaansche Missiën*, XII (1891), 271-276; XV(1894), 300-306, XVIII(1897), 81-85.

2430 . _____. "Lettres," *MCL*, XXIII(1891), 375-377, XXIV(1892), 271-272; XXV (1893), 13-14; XXVI(1894), 25-29; XXVIII(1896), 41.

2431 . _____. "Lettres," *Missions d'Afrique*, (1895-1897), 65, 265-266, 302-303, 478-484.

2432 . _____. "Lettres," *Missions d'Alger*, (1891-1892), 368; (1893-1894), 23-33, 98-100, 238-248, 323-324, 344-350.

2433 . _____. "Missionsbriefe," *Afrika-Bote*, II(1896), 101-102, 115-116.

2434 . _____. "Missionsbriefe," *Echo aus Afrika*, V(1893), 33-34; VIII(1896), 3-4.

2435 . _____. "Missionsbriefe," *KM*, XXI(1893), 66, 110-111; XXII(1894), 86-88, 114-115; XXIV(1896), 231.

2436 . Hall, Martin John. *Through My Spectacles in Uganda, or, the Story of a Fruitful Field*. **London**: Church Missionary Society, 1898. 104p.

2437 . Hanlon, HENRY [Bishop]. "Letter from Uganda," *JMGS*, XII(1896), 79-81.

2438 . Hannington, James. *The Last Journals of Bishop Hannington, from August 1st, 1885 to . . .October 29th, 1885.* London: Church Missionary Society, 1886. 24p. See also, **E. C.** Dawson, **Editor,** *The Last Journals of Bishop Hannington.* London: Seeley, 1888. 239p.

2439 . Hespers, Karl. *P. Schynse's letzte Reisen. Brief und Tagebuchblätter.* Cologne: Verlag J. P. Bachem, 1892. 100p.

2440 . Heurtebise, Valentin, "Lettres," *Annalen der Afrikaansche Missiën,* IX (1892-1893), 102-104.

2441 . Hirth, Jean-Joseph [*Msgr.*]. *Affaire de l'Ouganda. Enquête ouverte par le capitaine Macdonald, Ingénieur.* Paris: A la Procure des Missions d'Afrique, 1893. 30p.

2442 . _____. "Enquête ouverte par le capitaine Macdonald, ingénieur, au nom du gouvernement britannique," *Missions d'Alger,* (1893-1894), 129-154.

2443 . Hobley, Charles William. *Eastern Uganda, an Ethnological Survey.* London: Anthropological Institute, 1902. 95p.

2444 . _____. "Notes on a Journey Round Mount Masawa, or Elgon," *GJ,* IX(1897), 178-185.

2445 . Huwiler, Burkard. "Missionsbriefe," *Afrika-Bote,* IV(1898), 121-122; V (1899), 25.

2446 Johnston, Harry Hamilton. *The Uganda Protectorate: An Attempt to Give Some Description of the Physical Geography, Botany, Zoology, Anthropology, Languages and History of the Territories under British Protection in East Central Africa.* 2 vols. London: Hutchinson, 1902.

2447 _____. "The Uganda Protectorate, Ruwenzori, and the Semliki Forest," *GJ,* XIX(1902), 1-40.

. Kock, Hermann. "Missionsbriefe," *Afrika-Bote*, VI(1899-1900), 162-163.

2448

. Kreijns, Hubert. "Oeganda en de Bagandas," *Annalen der Afrikaansche Missiën*,

2449    XV(1898-1899), 57-61, 89-93, 121-126, 151-156, 182-189, 245-250, 306-

310, 338-341, 367-371; XVI(1899-1900), 27-31, 56-61, 89-94, 122-126,

154-158, 185-189. 215-219, 276-281, 308-312, 339-343, 370-375. See also,

*Maandelijksch Verslag der Afrikaansche Missiën*, XIX(1898), 346-350;

and, *Missiën der Witte Paters*, XX(1899), 59-64, 109-113, 222-224, 312-

315.

2450    . Laane, Joseph. "Lettres," *Annalen der Afrikaansche Missiën*, XIII(1896-1897),

6-17, 161-167; XIV(1897-1898), 102-103, 132-135, 158-165, 289-292,

330-336, 352-357; XV(1898-1899), 256-266; XVI(1899-1900), 257-259,

313-323; XVII(1900-1901), 257-266; XVIII(1901-1902), 81-83.

2451    . _____. "Lettres," *APFL*, LXXI(1899), 38-51.

. _____, "Lettres," *Maandelijksch Verslag der Afrikaansche Missiën*, XVI

2452    (1895), 327-328; XVII(1896), 195-206; XVIII(1897), 5-11, 233-237,

339-341; XIX(1898), 90-93, 211-217, 244-250, 284-287.

2453    . _____. "Lettres," *Missiën der Witte Paters*, XX(1899), 56-59, 97-109;

XXI(1900), 181-191; XXII(1901), 97-106.

2454    . _____. "Lettres," *Missions d'Afrique*[Malines], XIX(1898), 292-299, 342-347,

376-379; XX(1899), 71-83.

2455    . _____. "Lettres," *Missions d'Afrique*[Paris], (1895-1897), 342-346;

(1897-1900), 183-185, 568-578.

2456    . _____. "Missionsbriefe," *Afrika-Bote*, II(1896), 153-158.

2457    . _____. "Missionsbriefe," *KM*, XXIV(1896), 184-187, 254-255.

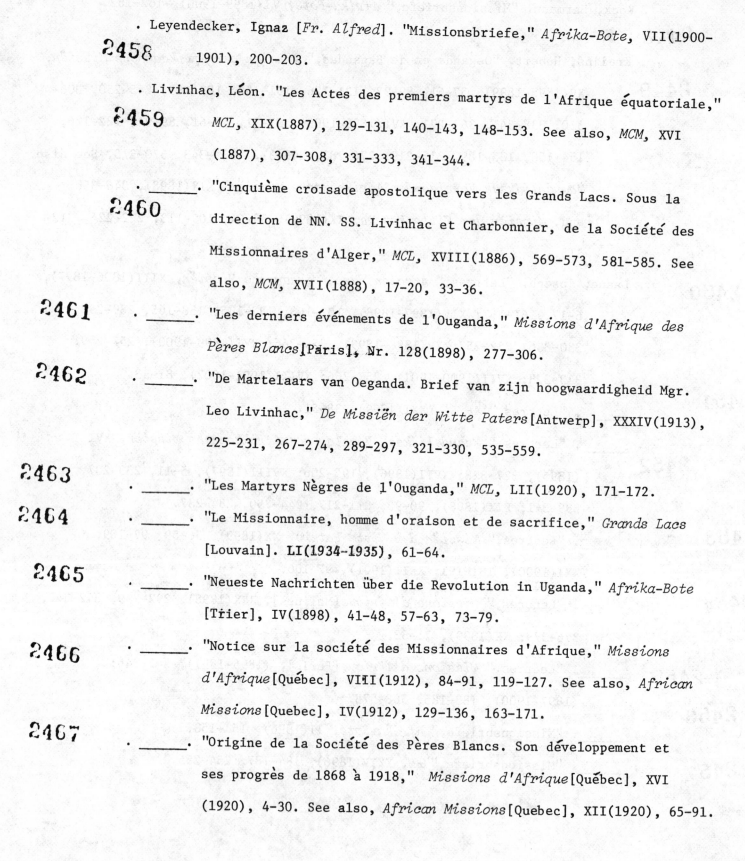

2458 . Leyendecker, Ignaz [*Fr. Alfred*]. "Missionsbriefe," *Afrika-Bote*, VII(1900-1901), 200-203.

2459 . Livinhac, Léon. "Les Actes des premiers martyrs de l'Afrique équatoriale," *MCL*, XIX(1887), 129-131, 140-143, 148-153. See also, *MCM*, XVI (1887), 307-308, 331-333, 341-344.

2460 . _____. "Cinquième croisade apostolique vers les Grands Lacs. Sous la direction de NN. SS. Livinhac et Charbonnier, de la Société des Missionnaires d'Alger," *MCL*, XVIII(1886), 569-573, 581-585. See also, *MCM*, XVII(1888), 17-20, 33-36.

2461 . _____. "Les derniers événements de l'Ouganda," *Missions d'Afrique des Pères Blancs*[Paris], Nr. 128(1898), 277-306.

2462 . _____. "De Martelaars van Oeganda. Brief van zijn hoogwaardigheid Mgr. Leo Livinhac," *De Missiën der Witte Paters*[Antwerp], XXXIV(1913), 225-231, 267-274, 289-297, 321-330, 535-559.

2463 . _____. "Les Martyrs Nègres de l'Ouganda," *MCL*, LII(1920), 171-172.

2464 . _____. "Le Missionnaire, homme d'oraison et de sacrifice," *Grands Lacs* [Louvain]. LI(1934-1935), 61-64.

2465 . _____. "Neueste Nachrichten über die Revolution in Uganda," *Afrika-Bote* [Trier], IV(1898), 41-48, 57-63, 73-79.

2466 . _____. "Notice sur la société des Missionnaires d'Afrique," *Missions d'Afrique*[Québec], VIII(1912), 84-91, 119-127. See also, *African Missions*[Quebec], IV(1912), 129-136, 163-171.

2467 . _____. "Origine de la Société des Pères Blancs. Son développement et ses progrès de 1868 à 1918," *Missions d'Afrique*[Québec], XVI (1920), 4-30. See also, *African Missions*[Quebec], XII(1920), 65-91.

2468      . _____ . "Près des Grands Lacs. Le Nyanza," *MCL*, XVII(1885), 140-141, 153-155, 166-168, 178-180, 195-197, 213-214, 238-240. See also, *MCM*, XIV(1885), 501-503, 514-516, 526-527, 538-539, 551-552, 564, 575-576, 586-588, 597-598.

2469      . _____ . "Un protecteur des Missionnaires d'Afrique, le Cardinal Rampolla (1843-1913]," *Grands Lacs* [Louvain], LII(1935-1936), 247-255.

2470      . _____ . "La sainteté de l'apôtre," *Grands Lacs* [Louvain], LII(1935-1936), 461-464.

2471      . _____ . "De Saint-Joseph de Kipalapala (Ounyanyembé) à Notre-Dame de Kamoga (Boukoumbi), Février-Mars 1886," *MCL*, XVIII(1886), 591-593, 608-612, 620-623, 628-632. See also, *MCM*, XVII(1888), 285-287, 299-300, 311-312, 321-324, 331-335.

Loonus, Marie Louis. *Lebensskizze und Briefe des Hochw. Herrn P. Marie*

2472      *Louis Loonus*. Luxemburg: St. Paulus-Gesellschaft, 1899. 35p.

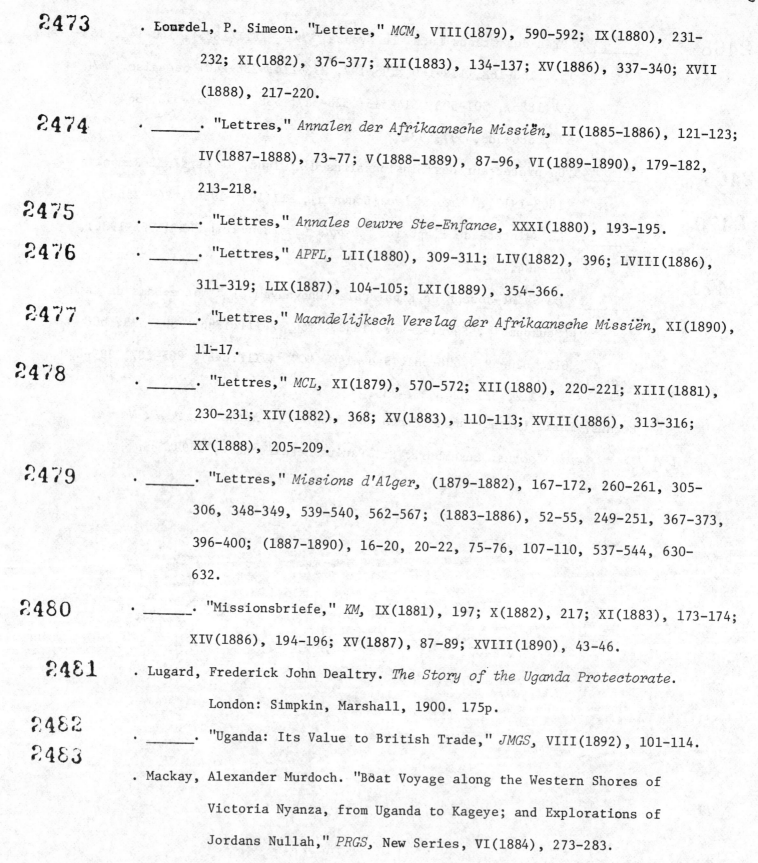

2473 . Lourdel, P. Simeon. "Lettere," *MCM*, VIII(1879), 590-592; IX(1880), 231-232; XI(1882), 376-377; XII(1883), 134-137; XV(1886), 337-340; XVII (1888), 217-220.

2474 . _____. "Lettres," *Annalen der Afrikaansche Missiën*, II(1885-1886), 121-123; IV(1887-1888), 73-77; V(1888-1889), 87-96, VI(1889-1890), 179-182, 213-218.

2475 . _____. "Lettres," *Annales Oeuvre Ste-Enfance*, XXXI(1880), 193-195.

2476 . _____. "Lettres," *APFL*, LII(1880), 309-311; LIV(1882), 396; LVIII(1886), 311-319; LIX(1887), 104-105; LXI(1889), 354-366.

2477 . _____. "Lettres," *Maandelijksch Verslag der Afrikaansche Missiën*, XI(1890), 11-17.

2478 . _____. "Lettres," *MCL*, XI(1879), 570-572; XII(1880), 220-221; XIII(1881), 230-231; XIV(1882), 368; XV(1883), 110-113; XVIII(1886), 313-316; XX(1888), 205-209.

2479 . _____. "Lettres," *Missions d'Alger*, (1879-1882), 167-172, 260-261, 305-306, 348-349, 539-540, 562-567; (1883-1886), 52-55, 249-251, 367-373, 396-400; (1887-1890), 16-20, 20-22, 75-76, 107-110, 537-544, 630-632.

2480 . _____. "Missionsbriefe," *KM*, IX(1881), 197; X(1882), 217; XI(1883), 173-174; XIV(1886), 194-196; XV(1887), 87-89; XVIII(1890), 43-46.

2481 . Lugard, Frederick John Dealtry. *The Story of the Uganda Protectorate*. London: Simpkin, Marshall, 1900. 175p.

2482 . _____. "Uganda: Its Value to British Trade," *JMGS*, VIII(1892), 101-114.
2483

. Mackay, Alexander Murdoch. "Böat Voyage along the Western Shores of Victoria Nyanza, from Uganda to Kageye; and Explorations of Jordans Nullah," *PRGS*, New Series, VI(1884), 273-283.

. Mackenzie, G. S. "Troubles in Uganda," *National Review*, July, 1892, 92-104.

2484. Malcolm, Neill [*Maj. Gen.*]. "On Service in the Uganda Protectorate,"

2485    *Blackwood's Magazine*, Nov., 1899, 631-643.

. Manceau, Jean-Baptiste. "Lettres," *Missions d'Afrique*, (1901-1902), 89-93.

2486

2487 . Marcou, Jean. "Lettres," *Annalen der Afrikaansche Missiën*, X(1893-1894),
   282-285; XI(1894-1895), 308-314; XII(1895-1896), 75-79; XIII(1896-
   1897), 69-73, 135-137, 233-237, 292-297.

2488 . _____. "Lettres," *Maandelijksch Verslag der Afrikaansche Missiën*, XV
   (1894), 111-114; XVI(1895), 92-93, 177-182, 210-214, 368-369; XIX(1898),
   188-191, 218-220, 250-254.

2489 . _____. "Lettres," *MCL*, XXVIII(1896), 483.

2490 . _____. "Lettres," *Missions d'Afrique*[Malines], XIX(1898), 110-113, 153-158,
   182-186, 218-222.

2491 . _____. "Lettres," *Missions d'Afrique*[Paris], (1895-1897), 15-19, 77-83,
   160-161, 193-205, 243-245, 272-275, 314-316; (1897-1900), 221, 253-256.

2492 . _____. "Lettres," *Missions d'Alger*, (1893-1894), 249-251.

2493 . _____. "Missionsbriefe," *Afrika-Bote*, I(1895), 52-55, 106-108, 181-182;
   II(1896), 12-14, 28-29, 43-46, 57-60, 74-76, 90-93, 105-107; IV
   (1898), 132-133.

2494 . _____. "Missionsbriefe," *KM*, XXII(1894), 115-116; XXIII(1895), 263-264.

2495 . Mason, Alexander McComb. [*Colonel Mason-Bey*]. "Report of a Reconnaissance
   of Lake Albert," *PRGS*, XXII(1877-1878), 225-228.

2496 . Maxse, F. I. [*Col.*]. "Soldiering in Uganda," *National Review*, Aug., 1903, pp. 1002-1016.

2497 . Ménandais, Jacques. "Lettres," *Missions d'Afrique*, (1895-1897), 350.

2498 . _____. "Missionsbriefe," *Afrika-Bote*, II(1896), 166-167.

2499 . Mercui, Joseph. *L'Ouganda. La mission catholique et les agents de la compagnie anglaise.* Paris: La Procure des Missions d'Afrique, 1893. 326p.

2500 . Moffat, Hilda V. "Recollections of Uganda Housekeeping," *Cornhill*, New Series, XXIII(1907), 514-528.

2501 . Molinier, Louis. "Lettere," *MCM*, XXX(1901), 172-173.

2502 . _____. "Lettres," *APFL*, LXXIII(1901), 312-313.

2503 . _____. "Lettres," *MCL*, XXXIII(1901), 146-147.

2504 . Moullée, Simon. "Lettres," *APFL*, LXIX(1897), 27-44.

2505 . _____. "Lettres," *Maandelijksch Verslag der Afrikaansche Missiën*, XVI (1895), 153-156; XVIII(1897), 105-107, 216-222.

2506 . _____. "Lettres," *Missions d'Afrique*, (1895-1897), 50-54, 439-443, 489-491, 504-512; (1897-1900), 256-260, 531-541, 706-709; (1901-1902), 423-428.

2507 . _____. "Lettres," *Missions d'Alger*, (1893-1894), 93-95.

2508 . _____. "Missionsbriefe," *Afrika-Bote*, I(1895), 77-79; III(1897), 45-48, 117-120, 133-136; V(1899), 156-162.

2509 . Mulders, Gerard. [*Fr. Jacobus*]. "Lettres," *Annalen der Afrikadsnche Missiën*, XIV(1897-1898), 273-275; XV(1898-1899), 120.

2510 . Murrer, Lucien. "Lettres," *Annalen der Afrikaansche Missiën*, XVII (1900-1901), 85-90; XVIII(1901-1902), 132-135.

2511 . Nicq, Chanoine Augustin [*Abbé*]. *Vie du R.P.Siméon Lourdel, de la congrégation des Pères blancs de Notre-Dame d'Afrique, premier missionnaire catholique de l'Ouganda (Afrique équatoriale).* Paris: C. Poussielgue, 1896. 675p. 2nd Ed., 1906, 627p.

2512    . Parke, Thomas Heazle. "Uganda," *Journal of the Tyneside Geographical Society*, II(1893), 174-182.

2513    . Phalip, Victor. "Lettres," *Annalen der Afrikaansche Missiën*, XIII (1896-1897), 143-146.

2514    . _____. "Lettres," *Maandelijksch Verslag der Afrikaansche Missiën*, XVII (1896), 151-152.

2515    . _____. "Lettres," *Missions d'Afrique*, (1895-1897), 170-171, 276; (1897-1900), 191-197.

2516    . _____. "Missionsbriefe," *Afrika-Bote*, II(1896), 11-12, 93-94.

2517    . Pluijm, A. v. d. [*Fr. Felix*]. "Lettres," *Annalen der Afrikaansche Missiën*, XI(1894-1895), 156-158; XVIII(1901-1902), 128-129.

2518    . Portal, Gerald Herbert. *The British Mission to Uganda in 1893*. London: Arnold, 1894. 351p.

2519    . Pouget, Justin. "Lettres," *Missions d'Afrique*, (1901-1902), 354-356.

2520    Powell-Cotton, P. H. G. [*Major*]. "Journey through Northern Uganda," *GJ*, XXIV(1904), 56-65.

2521    Purvis, John Bremmer. *Through Uganda to Mount Elgon*. London: Fisher Unwin, 1909. 371p.

2522    . Reichard, Paul. "Meine Erwerbung des Landes Ugunda," *DK*, VI(1890), 77-79.

2523    . Richter, Julius. *Uganda. Ein blatt aus der Geschichte der evangelischen Mission und der Kolonialpolitik in Centralafrika*. Gütersloh: C. Bertelsmann, 1893. 268p.

2524 . Roche, Pierre. "Lettres," *Annalen der Afrikaansche Missiën*, XII(1895-1896), 297-302.

2525 . _____. "Lettres," *Missions d'Afrique*, (1895-1897), 162-167, 167-170, 443-444.

2526 . _____. "Missionsbriefe," *Afrika-Bote*, I(1895), 182-185; III(1897), 26-27.

2527 . Roscoe, John. "Further Notes on the Manners and Customs of the Baganda," *JAI*, XXXII(1902), 25-80.

2528 . _____. "Notes on the Manners and Customs of the Baganda," *JAI*, XXXI (1901), 117-130.

2529 . Roussez, Léon. "Lettres," *Missions d'Afrique*[Malines], XIX(1898), 55-62; XX(1899), 131-136.

2530 . _____. "Lettres," *Missions d'Afrique*[Paris], (1897-1900), 377-381, 597-601, 738-740; (1901-1902), 93-102.

2531 . Salle, Antoine. "Lettres," *Maandelijksch Verslag der Afrikaansche Missiën*, XVII(1896), 271-273.

2532 . _____. "Lettres," *Missions d'Afrique*, (1895-1897), 347-349.

2533 . _____. "Missionsbriefe," *Afrika-Bote*, II(1896), 164-166.

2534 . Schmier, Louis. "Lettres," *Annalen der Afrikaansche Missiën*, VII(1890-1891), 100-102, 113-118, 223-231, 284-291, 309-316; VIII(1891-1892), 15-18, 35-42, 77-83, 123-132, 180-197, 287-299; IX(1892-1893), 134-142, 188-198, 237-247.

2535 . Schmitt, Seraphim. "Lettere," *MCM*, XV(1886), 568; XVI(1887), 152; XVII (1888), 61-63; XVIII(1889), 256.

2536 . _____. "Lettere," *Nigrizia*, V(1887), 97-99; VII(1889), 7-8, 66-67.

2537 . _____. "Lettres," *APFL*, LIX(1887), 113-114, 256-257; LX(1888), 183-190.

2538 . _____. "Lettres," *MCL*, XVIII(1886), 541-542; XIX(1887), 113; XX (1888), 25-27.

2539 . _____. "Missionsbriefe," *KM*, XV(1887), 46-47.

2540 . Smith, F. C. "Uganda," *JMGS*, XII(1896), 65-73.

2541 . _____. "The Uganda Experiences of Mr. F. C. Smith ("Simisi')," *JMGS*, X(1894), 222-226.

2542 . Stairs, W. E. "Ascent of Ruwenzori," *PRGS*, New Series, XI(1889), 726-730.

2543 . Stanley, Henry Morton. "Letter on His Journey from Yambuya Camp to the Albert Nyanza," *PRGS*, New Series, XI(1889), 261-272.

2544 . Stock, Sarah Geraldina. *The Story of Uganda and the Victoria Nyanza Mission.* London: Religious Tract Society, 1892. 223p. New York: Revell, 1892. 223p.

2545 . Streng. [*Fr. Adrianus*]. "Lettres," *Annalen der Afrikaansche Missiën*, X (1893-1894), 98-103; XVIII(1901-1902), 13-15.

2546 . Stuhlmann, FRANZ [*Dr.*]. "Essai d'ethnographie des pays situés a l'ouest du Nyanza," *Missions d'Alger*, (1893-1894), 61-66.

2547 . Sweens, Joseph. "Lettres," *Annalen der Afrikaansche Missiën*, XVIII(1901-1902), 87-89, 122-124, 141-146, 204-206.

2548 . Sylvester. "Missionsbriefe," *Afrika-Bote*, VI(1899-1900), 155-162; VII (1900-1901), 103-105.

2549 . Tauzin, J. M. [*Thimothée*]. "Lettres," *APFL*, LXX(1898), 113-120.

2550 . _____. "Lettres," *Missions d'Afrique*, (1897-1900), 214-220, 806-809.

2551 . _____. "Missionsbriefe," *KM*, XXVIII(1899-1900), 228-230; XXIX(1900-1901), 42.

2552 . Thomson, Joseph. "The Uganda Problem," *Contemporary Review*, LXII(1892), 786-796.

2553
2554 . Thuet, Joseph. "Missionsbriefe," *Afrika-Bote*, I(1895), 38-39, 163-164.

. _____. "Missionsbriefe," *Echo aus Afrika*, VI(1894), 84-85; VII(1895), 31-32.

2555 Thurston, Arthur Blyford. *African Incidents: Personal Experiences in Egypt and Unyoro.* London: Murray, 1900. 331p.

2556 . Toulze, Jean. "Lettere," *MCM*, XXII(1893), 423.

2557 . _____. "Lettres," *MCL*, XXV(1893), 377.

2558 . _____. "Lettres," *Missions d'Afrique*, (1897-1900). 141-145.

2559 . Tucker, Alfred Robert. *African Sketches, or Uganda and the Way Thither.* London: Church Missionary Society, 1892.

2560 . Tucker, Alfred Robert [*Bishop*]. "Bishop Tucker on the State of Uganda," *Church Missionary Intelligencer*, Oct., 1898, pp. 748-752.

2561 .. _____. *Toro. Visits to Ruwenzori, "Mountains of the Moon."* London: Church Missionary Society, 1899. 51p.

2562. . Vandaele, Arsenius. "Lettres," *Missiën der Witte Paters*, XX(1899), 348-350.

2563 . Vandeleur, C. F. S. "Two Years' Travel in Uganda, Unyoro, and on the Upper Nile," *GJ*, IX(1897), 369-391.

2564 . Van Oost, Achille. "Lettres," *Annalen der Afrikaansche Missiën*, VIII(1891-1892), 214-217; X(1893-1894), 192-199.

2565 . _____. "Lettres," *Maandelijksch Verslag der Afrikaansche Mi   iën*, XII (1891), 346-349.

2566 . _____. "Lettres," *Missions d'Alger*, (1883-1886), 321-325; (1891-1892), 109-110, 382-385, 386-389; (1893-1894), 35-36.

2567 . Van Thiel, Henri. "Lettres," *Annalen der Afrikaansche Missiën*, X(1893-1894), 214-220, 302-305; XVI(1899-1900), 226-230.

2568 . Van Wees, Pierre. "Lettres," *Annalen der Afrikaansche Missiën*, XIII (1896-1897), 317-325, 342-346; XIV(1897-1898), 54-56, 98-101, 231-234.

2569 . _____. "Lettres," *Maandelijksch Verslag der Afrikaansche Missiën*, XVIII (1897), 299-300.

2570 . Varangot, Adolphe. "Lettres," *Maandelijksch Verslag der Afrikaansche Missiën*, XVIII(1897), 373-377.

2571 . _____. "Lettres," *Missions d'Afrique*, (1897-1900), 188-190, 615-628.

2572 . _____. "Missionsbriefe," *Afrika-Bote*, I(1895), 38.

2573 . Vekemans, Piet. "Lettres," *Annalen der Afrikaansche Missiën*, XVIII (1901-1902), 105-107, 146-150, 166-168, 210-213.

2574 . Weiler, Josef. "Lettere," *MCM*, XXIX(1900), 193-194.

2575 . _____. "Lettere," *Nigrizia*, XVI(1898), 152-157; XVIII(1900), 18-22, 38-41.

2576 . _____. "Lettres," *APFL*, LXXII(1900), 319.

2577 . _____. "Lettres," *MCL*, XXXII(1900), 170-171.

2578 . _____. "Missionsbriefe," *Echo aus Afrika*, XII(1900), 38-40.

2579 . _____. "Missionsbriefe," *Stern der Neger*, I(1898), 17-23, 41-46, 55-59, 79-84, 107-111, 123-126, 179-182, 190-191, 204-205, 205-213, 248-253, 272-276; III(1900), 64-72; IV(1901), 164-165, 372-375.

2580  . Williams, [*Captain, Royal Engineers*]. "Uganda and Its People," *JMGS*, VIII (1892), 278-282.

2581  Wilson, Charles Thomas. "Uganda and the Victoria Lake," *PRGS*, New Series, II(1880), 353-357.

2582  Wollaston, A. F. R. and Freshfield, Douglas W. "Ruwenzori and the Frontier of Uganda," *GJ*, XXVIII(1906), 481-483.

2583  . Woodward, Edward Mabbott [*Maj. Gen.*]. *Précis of Information Concerning the Uganda Protectorate*. London: War Office, 1902. 159p.

2584  . Woosnam, R. B. "Ruwenzori and Its Life Zones," *GJ*, XXX(1907), 616-629.

2585 . Abinal, Antoine. "Lettres," *Lettres de Vals*, July, 1863, 1-5; July, 1864, 3-7; Dec., 1864, 15-18; Sept., 1865, 17-22, March, 1866, 9, 10; May, 1866, 1-8; Nov., 1867, 25-33; Nov., 1868, 63, 64; Aug., 1873, 18-20; Dec., 1873, 31-34; Oct., 1874, 16-20.

2586 . _____. "Missionsbriefe," *KM*, XX(1892), 132-134.

2587 . _____. *Vingt ans à Madagascar. Colonisation, traditions historiques, moeurs et croyances, d'après les notes du P. Abinal et de plusieurs autres missionnaires de la Compagnie de Jésus.* [Compiled by Jules de Le Vaissiere.] Paris: Victor Lecoffre, 1885. 363p.

2588 . Aigouy, Paul. "Lettres," *MCL*, XXIV(1892), 585.

2589 . Ailloud, Laurent. "Lettere," *MCM*, I(1872), 448; II(1873), 242; III(1874), 496-497; IV(1875), 341; VI(1877), 65, 327.

2590 . _____. "Lettres," *APFL*, XXXIX(1867), 69-73; XLVII(1875), 148-149.

2591 . _____. "Lettres," *LSV*, Feb., 1859, p.16; Jan.,1864, p.5,6; Dec., 1864, 13-15; March, 1865, p.18-20; Nov., 1868, p.64-67; Oct., 1874, p.2, 3, 13, 14.

2592 . _____. "Lettres," *Messager du Sacré-Coeur*[Toulouse], XVIII(    ), 99.

2593 . _____. "Lettres," *MCL*, IV(1871-1872), 707-708; V(1873), 230-231; VI(1874), 497-498; VII(1875), 333-334; VIII(1876), 245-246, 569; IX(1877), 325.

2594 . _____. "Missionsbriefe," *KM*, II(1874), 19-20.

2595 . Allen-Collier. "Lettre," *APFL*, XVII(1845), 273-285, 422-434.

2596 . Andebert, J. "Bei den Valadé auf Madagaskar," *Globus*, XLIV(1883), 122-124, 198-201, 215-218, 265-268, 282-285, 295-298.

2597 . _____. "Im Lande der Voilakertra auf Madagaskar," *Globus*, XLII(1882), 295-298, 312-315, 328-330, 343-346.

2598 . Attwell. [*Mrs.*] "Madagascar," *JME*, XXXXVIII(1873), 355-358.

2599 . Audebert, L. *Madagaskar und das Hovareich*. Berlin: Dümmler's Verlag, 1883. 64p.

2600 . _____ . "Über die wilden Volksstämme Madagaskars," *VGE*, X(1883).

2601 . Baker. "Letter," *MH*, XXIX(1833), 377-378.

2602 . Barbe, Firmin. "Lettres," *MCL*, II(1869), 39; III(1870), 236; VI(1873), 538-539.

2603 . _____ . "Missionsbriefe," *KM*, VII(1879), 142-143.

2604 . Bardon, Louis. "Lettere," *MCM*, XXIII(1894), 313-315; XXVI(1897), 530; XXVII(1898), 403.

2605 . _____ . "Lettres," *Lettres de Vals*, Aug., 1901, 74-76.

2606 . _____ . "Lettres," *MCL*, XXII(1890), 400; XXVI(1894), 293-295; XXX(1898), 390.

2607 . Bareyt, Jean-Baptiste. "Lettres," *Annales Oeuvre Ste-Enfance*, XXXIX(1888), 302-308.

2608 . Barker, E. "Progrès de la Bible dans l'île de Madagascar," *JME*, VI(1831), 216-220.

2609 . Batut, Alexandre. "Lettres," *Lettres de Vals*, Aug., 1901, 13-16.

2610 . _____ . "Lettres," *Notes, Reconnaissances et Explorations*, (1899), 395-398.

2611 . Batz, Gaston de. "Lettres," *LSV*, Oct., 1877, p.59-69; April, 1880, p.56-58.

2612 . Berbizier, François. "Lettres," *Lettres d'Uclès*, (1886), 104, 105; 2nd Series, III(1895), 253, 254, 256-258.

2613 . Berthieu, Jaques. "Lettere," *MCM*, XV(1886), 434, 435.

2614 . _____ . "Lettres," *Bouteland, aux Bienfaiteurs de la Mission française du Maduré*, (1896), 33, 34.

2615 . _____ . "Lettres," *Lettres d'Uclès*, 2nd Series, IV(1896), 62-64.

2616 . _____ . "Lettres," *MCL*, XVIII(1886), 410, 411.

2617 . Biron, Jean. "Lettres," *LSV*, Jan., 1861, p.13,14; Feb., 1863, p.5,6.

2618 . Bory de Saint-Vincent, Jean Baptiste Généviève Marcellin. *Voyage dans les quatre principales îles des mers d'Afrique, fait par ordre du gouvernement. . .en 1801 et 1802.* 3 vols. Paris, 1804. English translation, abridged, *Voyage to, and Travels through the Four Principal Islands of the African Seas.* London: Phillips, 1805. 212p.

. Boudou, Adrien. *Le Père Jacques Berthieu de la Compagnie de Jésus,*

2619 *missionnaire à Madagascar.* Tananarive: Imprimerie Catholique, 1933. 17p.

2620 . Boy-Mellis, Andrea. "Lettres," *LSV*, June, 1862, p.18-20; Feb., 1864, p.7,8.

. Braud, Justin. "Lettres," *L'Iraka*, No. 38 (1898), 299, 300.

2621

2622 . Brégère, Hippolyte. "Lettere," *MCM*, II(1873), 254-255; III(1874), 604-605; IV(1875), 320-322; V(1876), 99-100, 531-532; VIII(1879), 357, 466-468; XIX(1890), 74-75; XXVIII(1899), 495.

2623 . _____. "Lettres," *Annales Oeuvre Ste. Enfance* [Paris], XXX(1879), 52-62; XLIX(1898), 303-308.

2624 . _____. "Lettres," *APFL*, XLVII(1875), 379-383; LI(1879), 385-387; LXI(1889), 261-271.

2625 . _____. "Lettres," *LSV*, Oct., 1904, p.4-9; Feb., 1906, p.22-25.

2626 . _____. "Lettres," *MCL*, IV(1871-1872), 67-68; V(1873), 254-256; VI(1874), 6; VII(1875), 310-312; VIII(1876), 75-76, 510; XI(1879), 276-285, 455-457; XXII(1890), 62-63; XXXI(1899), 472-473.

2627 . _____. "Lettres," *Mission de Madagascar* [Paris], II(1913-1915), 163-164.

2628 . _____. "Missionsbriefe," *KM*, III(1875), 192. IV(1876), 86-87, 255; V(1877), 152-154; XVIII(1890), 177-178.

2629 . Brossard de Corbigny, Charles Paul [*Baron*]. *Un voyage à Madagascar, janvier 1862.* Paris: Challamel, 1862. 53p.

2630    Brucker, Joseph. *La Liberté réligieuse a Madagascar*. Amiens: Yvert & Tellier, 1897. 17p.

2631    Burleigh, Bennet. *Two Campaigns: Madagascar and Ashantee*. London: Unwin, 1897. 555p.

2632    Cadet, Ambroise. "Lettere," *MCM*, XIX(1890), 75, 76.

2633    _____. "Lettres," *MCL*, XXII(1890), 63, 64; XXIII(1891), 61-65.

2634    _____. "Missionsbriefe," *KM*, XIX(1891), 175-178.

2635    Calemard, François. "Lettere," *MCM*, XVII(1888), 601-603.

2636    _____. "Lettres," *MCL*, XX(1888), 578-580.

2637    Callet, François. "Lettres," *Annales Oeuvre Sainte-Enfance*[Paris], XVII (1865), 317-328.

2638    _____. "Lettres," *APFL*, XLII(1870), 29-55, 235-247, 359-384.

2639    _____. "Lettres," *LSV*, Nov., 1857, p.18; Sept., 1865, p.11-18; Nov., 1868, p.37-42; May, 1870, p.4-6; Jan., 1872, p.13-15.

2640    Camboué, Paul. "Deux Bombyciens sericigènes de Madagascar," *MCL*, XVI (1884), 287, 288.

2641    _____. "Faune de Madagascar. L'araignée 'Vancoho' ou 'Menavody' (Latrodectus Menavody)," *MCL*, XVIII(1886), 166-168. Also, *MCM*, XV (1886), 540, 551, 552.

2642    _____. "Faune de Madagascar. L'Halabe (Epeira Madagascariensis, Vins)," *MCL*, XXI(1889), 565, 566. Also, *MCM*, XXIV(1895), 500.

2643 _____ _____. "Lettere," *MCM*, XV(1886), 254; XXII(1893), 217-219; XXIII (1894), 601, 602; XXIV(1895), 118-120; XXV(1896), 300, 361-363, 448, 472; XXVI(1897), 21.

2644 . _____. "Lettres," *Annales Oeuvre Ste-Enfance*, XLVIII(1897), 8-35.

2645 . _____. "Lettres," *APFL*, LXV(1893), 272-292; LXIX(1897), 151, 152.

2646 _____. "Lettres," *MCL*, XVIII(1886), 230; XXV(1893), 205-207; XXVI(1894), 581, 582; XXVII(1895), 11, 12, 22, 23, 239, 240; XXVIII(1896), 325, 337-339, 603.

2647 . _____. "Missionsbriefe," *KM*, XIII(1885), 89, 90; XIV(1886), 171, 172; XXI(1893), 175, 176.

2648 . _____. *Madagascar: Etablissements des Missionnaires Français. Pourquoi et comment ils doivent être secondés.* Paris, 1893. 32p.

2649 Campbell, Belle McPherson. *Madagascar.* Chicago: Women's Presbyterian Board of Missions of the Northwest, 1889. 80p.

2650 . Campenon, Pierre. "Les cultures à Madagascar," *Revue des Cultures Coloniales,* (1897), 259-262.

2651 _____ _____. "Lettere," *MCM*, IX(1880), 445-447.

2652 _____. "Lettres," *MCL*, XII(1880), 421-423; XXVIII(1896), 531.

2653 _____. "Lettres," *Revue Trimestrielle de la Société Antiesclavagiste de France,* (1902), 144-146.

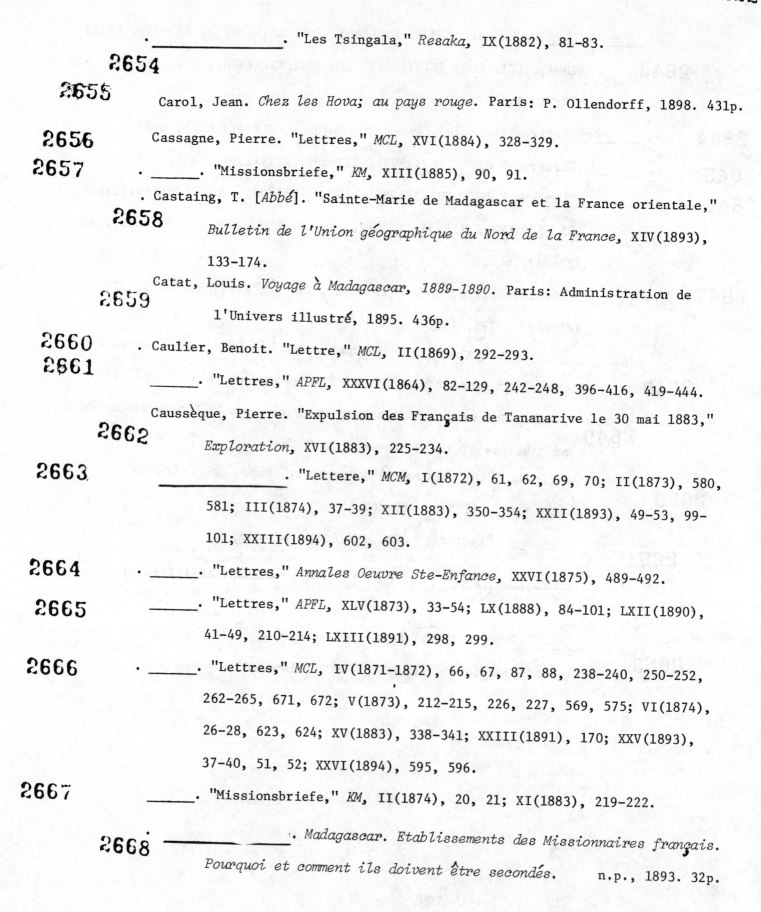

. _____. "Les Tsingala," *Resaka*, IX(1882), 81-83.

2654

2655      Carol, Jean. *Chez les Hova; au pays rouge*. Paris: P. Ollendorff, 1898. 431p.

2656      Cassagne, Pierre. "Lettres," *MCL*, XVI(1884), 328-329.

2657      . _____. "Missionsbriefe," *KM*, XIII(1885), 90, 91.

. Castaing, T. [*Abbé*]. "Sainte-Marie de Madagascar et la France orientale,"

2658      *Bulletin de l'Union géographique du Nord de la France*, XIV(1893),

133-174.

Catat, Louis. *Voyage à Madagascar, 1889-1890*. Paris: Administration de

2659      l'Univers illustré, 1895. 436p.

2660      . Caulier, Benoit. "Lettre," *MCL*, II(1869), 292-293.

2661      _____. "Lettres," *APFL*, XXXVI(1864), 82-129, 242-248, 396-416, 419-444.

Caussèque, Pierre. "Expulsion des Français de Tananarive le 30 mai 1883,"

2662      *Exploration*, XVI(1883), 225-234.

2663      _____. "Lettere," *MCM*, I(1872), 61, 62, 69, 70; II(1873), 580,

581; III(1874), 37-39; XII(1883), 350-354; XXII(1893), 49-53, 99-

101; XXIII(1894), 602, 603.

2664      . _____. "Lettres," *Annales Oeuvre Ste-Enfance*, XXVI(1875), 489-492.

2665      _____. "Lettres," *APFL*, XLV(1873), 33-54; LX(1888), 84-101; LXII(1890),

41-49, 210-214; LXIII(1891), 298, 299.

2666      . _____. "Lettres," *MCL*, IV(1871-1872), 66, 67, 87, 88, 238-240, 250-252,

262-265, 671, 672; V(1873), 212-215, 226, 227, 569, 575; VI(1874),

26-28, 623, 624; XV(1883), 338-341; XXIII(1891), 170; XXV(1893),

37-40, 51, 52; XXVI(1894), 595, 596.

2667      _____. "Missionsbriefe," *KM*, II(1874), 20, 21; XI(1883), 219-222.

2668      _____. *Madagascar. Etablissements des Missionnaires français.*

*Pourquoi et comment ils doivent être secondés.*    n.p., 1893. 32p.

2669 _____. "Madagascar. Statistiques et légendes d'après les documents officiels," *Études*, LVIII(1893), 34-55.

2670 Cazeaux, François. "Lettere," *MCM*, I(1872), 254-255.

2671 _____. "Lettres," *APFL*, XLIII(1871), 40-48, 108-123, 208-224, 328-340, 436-456.

2672 _____. "Lettres," *Bulletin de la Société de Géographie de Lyon*, VII(1887), 407-410; VIII(1889), 83-84.

2673 _____. "Lettres," *Lettres d'Uclès*, XIII(1877), 89-93.

2674 _____. "Lettres," *LSV*, Jan., 1871, p.23-24; Jan., 1873, p.27-30; Jan., 1877, p. 27-29.

2675 _____. "Lettres," *MCL*, IV(1871-1872), 514-516.

2676 _____. "Quelques notes sur la géographie agricole de Madagascar," *Études*[Paris], LXX(1897), 17-33.

2677 _____. "Les Sakalaves et leur pays," *Bulletin de la Société de Géographie Commerciale de Bordeaux*, 1888, p. 299-303.

2678 _____. "La vigne à Madagascar," *Bulletin de la Société de Géographie Commerciale de Bordeaux*, 1887, p.289-293.

2679 . Cazet, Jean-Baptiste. "Lettere," *MCM*, I(1872), 23, 24, 157-159; IV(1875), 2, 3, 424, 425; VII(1878), 100; VIII(1879), 42; IX(1880), 41, 325-327, 424; XI(1882), 111; XIII(1884), 325-327; XIV(1885), 362-365; XV(1886), 301, 302; XVI(1887),289, 290; XVII(1888), 557; XIX(1890), 146; XX(1891), 73-77; XXIII(1894), 315, 316, 602; XXIV(1895), 25, 26; XXV(1896), 314-316, 399, 541, 542; XXVI(1897),181, 182, 529, 530; XXVII(1898), 141, 142, 411, 412; XXVIII(1899), 280, 281; XXXII (1903), 580.

2680 _____. "Lettres," *Annales Oeuvre Ste-Enfance*, XXX(1879), 196-211, 397-402; XXXI(1880), 34, 35; XXXIV(1883), 46-52; XLV(1894), 321-328; L(1899), 183-186, 242-245.

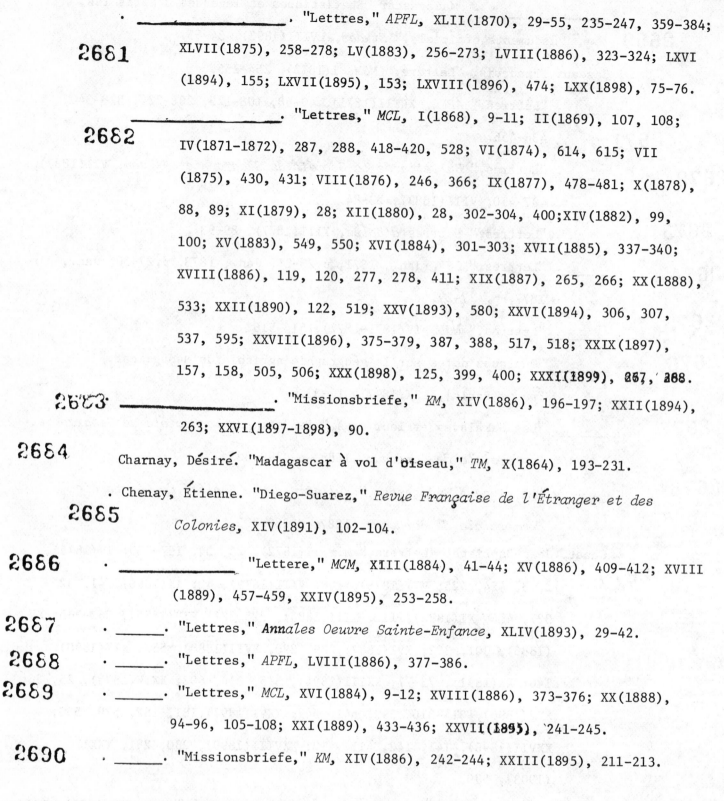

2681 ————————. "Lettres," *APFL*, XLII(1870), 29-55, 235-247, 359-384; XLVII(1875), 258-278; LV(1883), 256-273; LVIII(1886), 323-324; LXVI (1894), 155; LXVII(1895), 153; LXVIII(1896), 474; LXX(1898), 75-76.

2682 ————————. "Lettres," *MCL*, I(1868), 9-11; II(1869), 107, 108; IV(1871-1872), 287, 288, 418-420, 528; VI(1874), 614, 615; VII (1875), 430, 431; VIII(1876), 246, 366; IX(1877), 478-481; X(1878), 88, 89; XI(1879), 28; XII(1880), 28, 302-304, 400;XIV(1882), 99, 100; XV(1883), 549, 550; XVI(1884), 301-303; XVII(1885), 337-340; XVIII(1886), 119, 120, 277, 278, 411; XIX(1887), 265, 266; XX(1888), 533; XXII(1890), 122, 519; XXV(1893), 580; XXVI(1894), 306, 307, 537, 595; XXVIII(1896), 375-379, 387, 388, 517, 518; XXIX(1897), 157, 158, 505, 506; XXX(1898), 125, 399, 400; XXXI(1899), 267, 268.

2683 ————————. "Missionsbriefe," *KM*, XIV(1886), 196-197; XXII(1894), 263; XXVI(1897-1898), 90.

2684 Charnay, Désiré. "Madagascar à vol d'oiseau," *TM*, X(1864), 193-231.

2685 Chenay, Étienne. "Diego-Suarez," *Revue Française de l'Étranger et des Colonies*, XIV(1891), 102-104.

2686 ————————. "Lettere," *MCM*, XIII(1884), 41-44; XV(1886), 409-412; XVIII (1889), 457-459, XXIV(1895), 253-258.

2687 ————————. "Lettres," *Annales Oeuvre Sainte-Enfance*, XLIV(1893), 29-42.

2688 ————————. "Lettres," *APFL*, LVIII(1886), 377-386.

2689 ————————. "Lettres," *MCL*, XVI(1884), 9-12; XVIII(1886), 373-376; XX(1888), 94-96, 105-108; XXI(1889), 433-436; XXVII(1895), 241-245.

2690 ————————. "Missionsbriefe," *KM*, XIV(1886), 242-244; XXIII(1895), 211-213.

2691 . _____. "La Mission de Fort-Dauphin," *MCL*, XXV(1893), 596-599, 604-606. Also, *MCM*, XXIV(1895), 32-35, 45-47.

2692 . Chervalier, Alphonse. "Lettere," *MCM*, XIV(1885), 404, 405.

2693 . _____. "Lettres," *MCL*, XVII(1885), 208, 209.

2694 . Clinch, B. J. "Roman Catholic Missions in Madagascar," *American Catholic Quarterly Review*, XVIII(1893), 392 fwd.

2695 . Coignet, F. "Excursion sur la côte nord-est de l'île de Madagascar," *BSGP*, 5th Series, XIV(1867), 253-295, 334-367.

2696 . Colson, Pierre Louis. *Guide de Madagascar*. Paris: Lavauzelle, 1895. 220p.

2697 . Combet, Joachim. "Lettres," *LSV*, June, 1862, p.16-17.

2698 . Compagnie de Madagascar. *Documents sur la Compagnie de Madagascar, précédés d'une notice historique*. Paris: Challamel, 1867. 430p.

2699 . Copland, Samuel. *A History of the Island of Madagascar, Comprising a Political Account of the Island, the Religion, Manners, and Customs of the Inhabitants, and Its Natural Production; with an Appendix Containing a History of Several Attempts to Introduce Christianity into the Island*. London, 1822.

2700 . Cornish, Robert Kestell. *Journal of a Tour of Exploration in the North of Madagascar by the Right Reverend Bishop Kestell-Cornish, June 15-October 22, 1876*. London: Society for the Propagation of the Gospel in Foreign Parts, 1877. 55p.

2701 . Cotain, P. "Lettres," *APFL*, XVIII(1846), 157-173; XXVI(1854), 94-108.

2702 . Cousins, G. "Une dédicace de temple," *JME*, XLII(1867), 271-276.

2703 . _____. "Lettre," *JME*, XLIII(1868), 434-438.

2704 · Cousins, William Edward. *Madagascar of Today, a Sketch of the Island with Chapters on Its Past History and Present Prospects*. London: Religious Tract Society, 1895. 159p.

2705 · _____. *Malagasy Customs: Native Accounts of the Circumcision, the Tangena, Marriage, and Burial Ceremonies*. Antananarivo: L.M.S. Press, 1876. 56p.

2706 · Cowan, William Deans. [*Rev.*]. *The Bara Land: a Description of the Country and People*. Antananarivo: L.M.S. Press, 1881. 72p.

2707 · _____. "Geographical Excursions in South Central Madagascar," *PRGS*, New Series, IV(1882), 521-534.

2708 · _____. *The Tanala*. Faravohitra: Friends' Foreign Mission Association, 1881. 14p.

2709 · _____. "Travels in Eastern and South-Central Madagascar," *SGM*, II(1886), 321-337.

2710 · Crancq, Jean-Marie. "Lettere," *MCM*, XXVII(1898), 173, 174.

2711 · _____. "Lettres," *MCL*, XXX(1898), 160.

2712 · Dahle, Lars Nielsen. *Madagaskar og dets beboere*. 2 vols. Christiania, 1876-1877.

2713 · _____. *Overrigt over Det norske Missionsselskabs historie hjemml og ude 1842-93*. Stavanger: Nye missionstraktater, 1894. 32p.

2714 · _____. *Specimens of Malagasy Folk-Lore*. Antananarivo: A. Kingdom, 1877. 457p.

2715 · Dalmond. "Extrait d'un Mémoire présenté à MM. les membres des Conseils Centraux de l'Oeuvre par m. Dalmond, Préfet apostolique de Madagascar," *APFL*, XVIII(1846), 146-156.

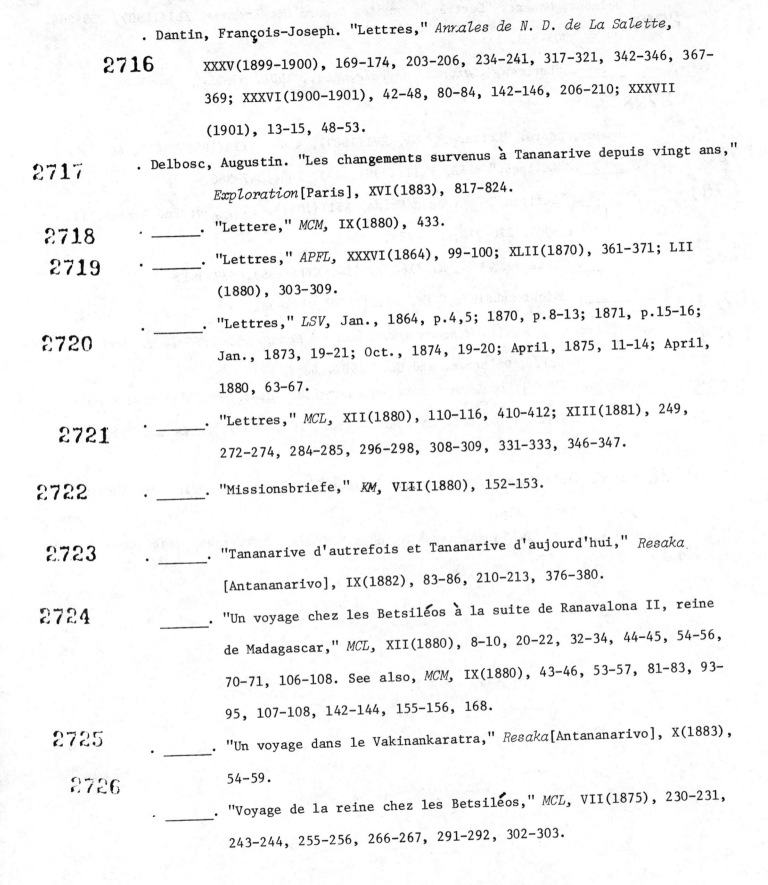

. Dantin, François-Joseph. "Lettres," *Annales de N. D. de La Salette,*

2716     XXXV(1899-1900), 169-174, 203-206, 234-241, 317-321, 342-346, 367-

369; XXXVI(1900-1901), 42-48, 80-84, 142-146, 206-210; XXXVII

(1901), 13-15, 48-53.

2717   . Delbosc, Augustin. "Les changements survenus à Tananarive depuis vingt ans,"

*Exploration*[Paris], XVI(1883), 817-824.

2718   . _____. "Lettere," *MCM,* IX(1880), 433.

2719   . _____. "Lettres," *APFL,* XXXVI(1864), 99-100; XLII(1870), 361-371; LII

(1880), 303-309.

. _____. "Lettres," *LSV,* Jan., 1864, p.4,5; 1870, p.8-13; 1871, p.15-16;

2720     Jan., 1873, 19-21; Oct., 1874, 19-20; April, 1875, 11-14; April,

1880, 63-67.

. _____. "Lettres," *MCL,* XII(1880), 110-116, 410-412; XIII(1881), 249,

2721     272-274, 284-285, 296-298, 308-309, 331-333, 346-347.

2722   . _____. "Missionsbriefe," *KM,* VIII(1880), 152-153.

2723   . _____. "Tananarive d'autrefois et Tananarive d'aujourd'hui," *Resaka*

[Antananarivo], IX(1882), 83-86, 210-213, 376-380.

2724   . _____. "Un voyage chez les Betsiléos à la suite de Ranavalona II, reine

de Madagascar," *MCL,* XII(1880), 8-10, 20-22, 32-34, 44-45, 54-56,

70-71, 106-108. See also, *MCM,* IX(1880), 43-46, 53-57, 81-83, 93-

95, 107-108, 142-144, 155-156, 168.

2725   . _____. "Un voyage dans le Vakinankaratra," *Resaka*[Antananarivo], X(1883),

2726     54-59.

. _____. "Voyage de la reine chez les Betsiléos," *MCL,* VII(1875), 230-231,

243-244, 255-256, 266-267, 291-292, 302-303.

2727 · Delmont, Mamert. "Lettres," *Annales Oeuvre Ste-Enfance*, XLI(1890), 259-264, 305-333.

2728 · _____. "Lettres," *Lettres de Vals*, Aug., 1901, 57-61.

2729 · Denjoy, André. "Lettere," *MCM*, XVI(1887), 434; XVIII(1889), 601, 602.

2730 · _____. "Lettres," *APFL*, LXII(1890), 145, 146, 347-360.

2731 · _____. "Lettres," *Lettres d'Uclès*, XIII(1887), 149, 150; 2nd Series, III (1895), 270-276, 284-286, 320-328.

2732 · _____. "Lettres," *MCL*, XIX(1887), 414; XXI(1889), 579-581.

2733 · _____. "Missionsbriefe," *KM*, XVII(1889), 579-581.

2734 · Desmarquest, Joseph. *Mission Apostolique à Madagascar 1890-1900*. Paris: Desclée, De Brower and Co., 1901. 63p.

2735 · Dupont. [*Mme.*]. *La Lorraine au pays Betsileo (district d'Ambohimahasoa): Mission apostolique a Madagascar (1890-1900)*. Paris and Lille; 1900. 63p.

2736 · Dupré, Marie Jules. *Trois mois de séjour à Madagascar*. Paris: The Author, 1863. 281p.

2737 · Dupuy, P. J. "De Tananarive à Majunga," *Etudes*, LXIV(1895), 534-544.

2738    . Elie, Colin. "Lettere," *MCM*, XXIV(1895), 277-280, 585-588; XXV(1896),

454-456.

2739    . _____. "Lettres," *APFL*, LXXII(1900), 156.

2740    . _____. "Lettres," *MCL*, XXVII(1895), 265-268, 285-288; XXVIII(1896), 10-12;

XXXII(1900), 5.

2741    . Elliott, George Francis Scott. "Notes on a Botanical Trip in Madagascar,"

*PRGS*, New Series, XIII(1891), 158-163.

2742    . Ellis, William. *History of Madagascar. Comprising also the Progress of the*

*Christian Mission.* 2 vols. London: Fisher, 1838.

2743    . _____. "Lettres," *JME*, XXXVII(1862), 151-154, 375-380, 427-429, 459-465;

XXXVIII(1863), 142-147, 309-312; XLI(1866), 250-260.

2744    _____. *Madagascar Revisited.* London: J. Murray, 1867. 502p.

2745    . _____. "Madagascar, une nouvelle visite aux chrétiens de cette île,"

*JME*, XXX(1855), 54-59.

2746    . _____. *The Martyr Church, a Narrative of the Introduction, Progress, and*

*Triumph of Christianity in Madagascar. With Notices of Personal*

*Intercourse and Travel in That Island.* London, 1870.

2747    . _____. *Three Visits to Madagascar during the Years 1853, 1854 and 1856,*

*Including a Journey to the Country and the Present Civilisation*

*of the People.* London, 1858. Philadelphia: Bradley, 1859. 426p.

2748    _____ and Cameron, James. "Christianity in Madagascar," *MH*, L(1854), 54-56.

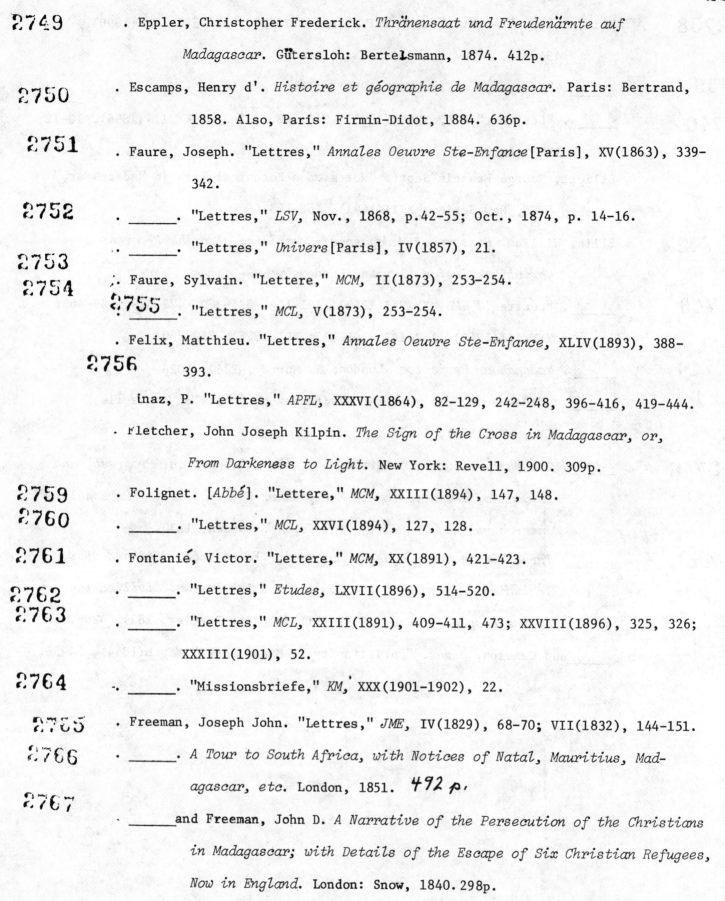

2749 . Eppler, Christopher Frederick. *Thränensaat und Freudenärnte auf Madagascar*. Gütersloh: Bertelsmann, 1874. 412p.

2750 . Escamps, Henry d'. *Histoire et géographie de Madagascar*. Paris: Bertrand, 1858. Also, Paris: Firmin-Didot, 1884. 636p.

2751 . Faure, Joseph. "Lettres," *Annales Oeuvre Ste-Enfance* [Paris], XV(1863), 339-342.

2752 . _____. "Lettres," *LSV*, Nov., 1868, p.42-55; Oct., 1874, p. 14-16.

2753 . _____. "Lettres," *Univers* [Paris], IV(1857), 21.

2754 . Faure, Sylvain. "Lettere," *MCM*, II(1873), 253-254.

2755 . _____. "Lettres," *MCL*, V(1873), 253-254.

. Felix, Matthieu. "Lettres," *Annales Oeuvre Ste-Enfance*, XLIV(1893), 388-393.

2756 . inaz, P. "Lettres," *APFL*, XXXVI(1864), 82-129, 242-248, 396-416, 419-444.

. Fletcher, John Joseph Kilpin. *The Sign of the Cross in Madagascar, or, From Darkness to Light*. New York: Revell, 1900. 309p.

2759 . Folignet. [*Abbé*]. "Lettere," *MCM*, XXIII(1894), 147, 148.

2760 . _____. "Lettres," *MCL*, XXVI(1894), 127, 128.

2761 . Fontanié, Victor. "Lettere," *MCM*, XX(1891), 421-423.

2762 . _____. "Lettres," *Etudes*, LXVII(1896), 514-520.

2763 . _____. "Lettres," *MCL*, XXIII(1891), 409-411, 473; XXVIII(1896), 325, 326; XXXIII(1901), 52.

2764 . _____. "Missionsbriefe," *KM*, XXX(1901-1902), 22.

2765 . Freeman, Joseph John. "Lettres," *JME*, IV(1829), 68-70; VII(1832), 144-151.

2766 . _____. *A Tour to South Africa, with Notices of Natal, Mauritius, Madagascar, etc.* London, 1851. *492 p.*

2767 . _____ and Freeman, John D. *A Narrative of the Persecution of the Christians in Madagascar; with Details of the Escape of Six Christian Refugees, Now in England*. London: Snow, 1840. 298p.

2768 Gachet, Célestin. "Lettres," *Annales de N. D. de La Salette*, XXXVI (1900-1901), 327-331, 365-368; XXXVII(1901), 74-79.

2769 . Gallichet, Henri. *La guerre à Madagascar. Histoire anecdotique des expeditions françaises de 1885 à 1895*. 2 vols. Paris: Garnier, 1897.

2770 . Galliéni, Joseph Simon. "Extrait du rapport de M. le général Gallièni," *Revue Coloniale* [Paris: Ministère des colonies], V(1899), 280-284.

2771 _____. *Lettres de Madagascar, 1896-1905*. Paris, 1928.

2772 . Gardes, Henri. "Lettere," *MCM*, XXVII(1898), 253-255; XXX(1901), 538-540.

2773 . _____. "Lettres," *Iraka*, (1898), 205-208.

2774 . _____. "Lettres," *LSV*, Aug., 1901, 40-45.

2775 . _____. "Lettres," *MCL*, XXX(1898), 241-243; XXXII(1900), 29, 266, 423-426.

2776 . Gauchy, Louis. "Lettere," *MCM*, IX(1880), 447, 448.

2777 . _____. "Lettres," *MCL*, XII(1880), 424, 425.

2778 . _____. "Lettres," *Resaka*, IX(1882), 204-206.

2779 . Gautier, E. F. "Lettre sur les récents progrès de notre connaissance de "L'Oeuvre scolaire à Madagascar," *Revue de Madagascar*, II(1900), 27-42.

2780 _____. "Rapport sur l'enseignement à Madagascar," *Bulletin de l'Alliance française*, XV(1898), 13-24.

2781 . Gibson, Henry. "The Mission of Madagascar," *Month*, LVI(1886), 221-238, 385-405; LVII(1886), 62-77, 226-245.

2783
. Gindre, Henri. *En Afrique australe et à Madagascar*. Paris: A. Challamel, 1897. 49p.

2784
. Grandidier, Alfred. *Histoire physique, naturelle et politique de Madagascar*. 39 vols. Paris: Imprimérie nationale, 1892-1901

2785
Grosclaude, Étienne. *Un Parisien à Madagascar. Aventures et impressions de voyage*. Paris: Hachette, 1898. 368p.

2786
. Guerret. [*Abbe*]. "Trois mois autour de Madagascar en 1859-1860," *Bulletin de l'Union Géographique du Nord de la France*, III(1882), 429-483.

2787
. Guillain, Charles. *Documents sur l'histoire, la géographie et le commerce de la partie occidentale de l'île de Madagascar*. Paris: Imprimérie royale, 1845. 376p.

2788
. Gunst. [*Dr.*]. "On a Visit to Unexplored Parts in the North of Madagascar," *PRGS*, IX(1864-1865), 289-292.

2789
. Hartman, Robert. *Madagaskar und die Inseln Seychellen, Aldabra, Komoren und Maskarenen*. Leipzig: Freytag, 1886. 151p.

2790
. Hastie, James and others. "Île de Madagascar, description, caractère des Malagaches, etc.," *JME*, XX(1845), 381-395, 419-433.

2791
. Hildebrandt, Johann Maria. "Ausflug zum Ambergebirge in Nord-Madagaskar," *ZGE*, 1880, p. 263.

2792
. Hildebrandt, Johann Maria. "West-Madagaskar," *ZGE*, 1880, p. 81.

2793
. Holding, John. [*Rev.*]. "Notes on the Province of Tanibé, Madagascar," *PRGS*, XIV(1869-1870), 359-372.

2794 . Jalabert, Emile. "Lettere," *MCM*, XII(1883), 469-473.

2795 . _____. "Lettres," *MCL*, XV(1883), 457-461.

2796 . Jean, Celestin. "Lettere," *MCM*, XIII(1884), 256-260; XVI(1887), 138, 139.

2797 . _____. "Lettres," *LSV*, Aug., 1901, 38, 39.

2798 . _____. "Lettres," *MCL*, XVI(1884), 241-244; XIX(1887), 90-92.

2799 . Joannis, Joseph de. "Observatoire royale de Madagascar," *Etudes*, LV (1892), 159-162.

2800 . Jorgensen, S. G. "Zur Ethnographie Madagaskars," *DK*, IV(1887), 305-307.

2801 . Jouen, Louis. "Le Christianisme à Madagascar," *Revue de l'Orient*, XII (1852), 41.

2802 . _____. "Extrait d'un rapport à MM. les Membres des Conseils centraux," *APFL*, XLI(1869), 43-77.

2803 . _____. "Lettres," *APFL*, XXI(1849), 272-281; XXV(1853), 441-450; XXVII (1855), 121-142; XXXIV(1862), 257-261; XXXV(1863), 81-123; XXXVI(1864), 396-416;XLIII(1871), 436-451.

2804 . _____. "Missions Malgaches. Coup d'oeil historique sur l'île de Mada- gascar," *APFL*, XLI(1869), 36-42.

2805 . _____. *Rapport sur les Missions Catholiques de Madagascar*. Tananarivo: Imprimérie de la Mission Catholique, 1862. 59p.

2806 . _____. "Résumé de quinze années de la Mission de Madagascar," *APFL*, XXXIII(1861), 81-102, 257-281.

2807 . Jouga, Guillaume. "Lettre," *Annales Oeuvre Ste-Enfance* [Paris], XXIII (1871-1872), 541-543.

2808 . _____. "Lettre," *BGCSS*, VII(1869-1870), 154-156.

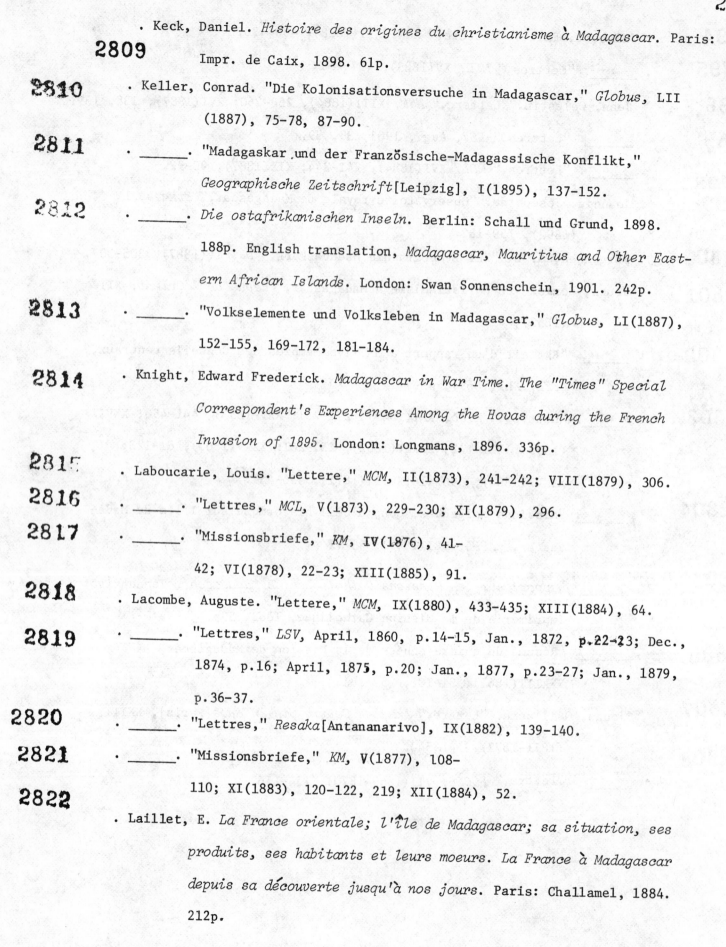

2809 . Keck, Daniel. *Histoire des origines du christianisme à Madagascar*. Paris: Impr. de Caix, 1898. 61p.

2810 . Keller, Conrad. "Die Kolonisationsversuche in Madagascar," *Globus*, LII (1887), 75-78, 87-90.

2811 . _____. "Madagaskar und der Französische-Madagassische Konflikt," *Geographische Zeitschrift*[Leipzig], I(1895), 137-152.

2812 . _____. *Die ostafrikanischen Inseln*. Berlin: Schall und Grund, 1898. 188p. English translation, *Madagascar, Mauritius and Other Eastern African Islands*. London: Swan Sonnenschein, 1901. 242p.

2813 . _____. "Volkselemente und Volksleben in Madagascar," *Globus*, LI(1887), 152-155, 169-172, 181-184.

2814 . Knight, Edward Frederick. *Madagascar in War Time. The "Times" Special Correspondent's Experiences Among the Hovas during the French Invasion of 1895*. London: Longmans, 1896. 336p.

2815 . Laboucarie, Louis. "Lettere," *MCM*, II(1873), 241-242; VIII(1879), 306.

2816 . _____. "Lettres," *MCL*, V(1873), 229-230; XI(1879), 296.

2817 . _____. "Missionsbriefe," *KM*, IV(1876), 41-42; VI(1878), 22-23; XIII(1885), 91.

2818 . Lacombe, Auguste. "Lettere," *MCM*, IX(1880), 433-435; XIII(1884), 64.

2819 . _____. "Lettres," *LSV*, April, 1860, p.14-15, Jan., 1872, p.22-23; Dec., 1874, p.16; April, 1875, p.20; Jan., 1877, p.23-27; Jan., 1879, p.36-37.

2820 . _____. "Lettres," *Resaka*[Antananarivo], IX(1882), 139-140.

2821 . _____. "Missionsbriefe," *KM*, V(1877), 108-110; XI(1883), 120-122, 219; XII(1884), 52.

2822 . Laillet, E. *La France orientale; l'île de Madagascar; sa situation, ses produits, ses habitants et leurs moeurs. La France à Madagascar depuis sa découverte jusqu'à nos jours*. Paris: Challamel, 1884. 212p.

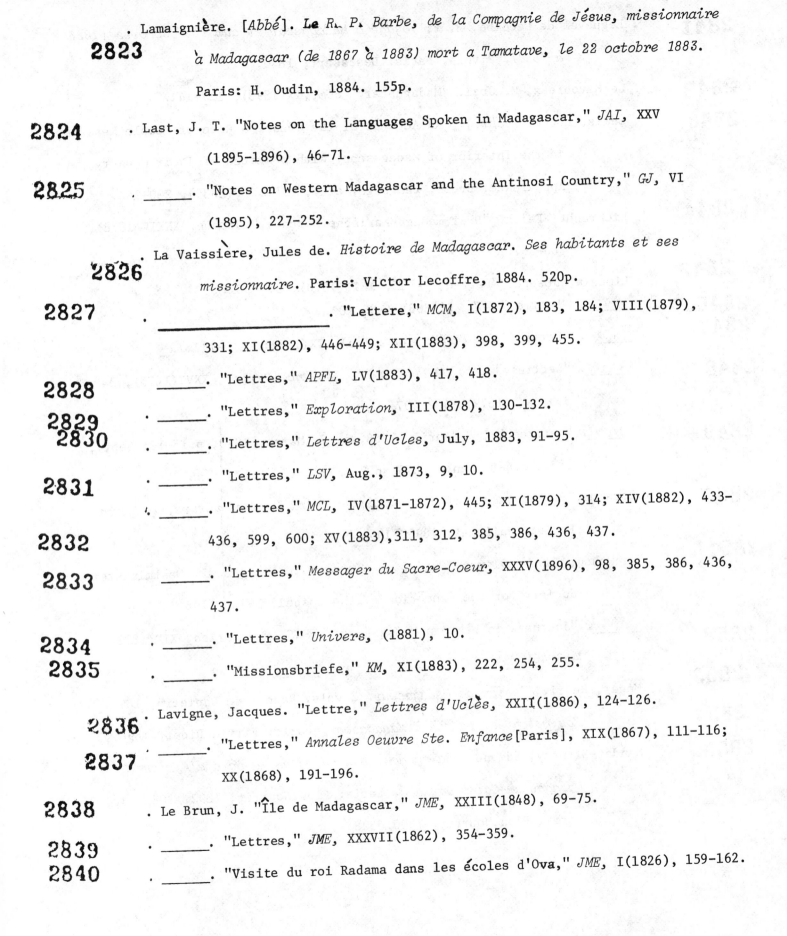

2823 . Lamaignière. [Abbé]. *Le R. P. Barbe, de la Compagnie de Jésus, missionnaire à Madagascar (de 1867 à 1883) mort a Tamatave, le 22 octobre 1883.* Paris: H. Oudin, 1884. 155p.

2824 . Last, J. T. "Notes on the Languages Spoken in Madagascar," *JAI*, XXV (1895-1896), 46-71.

2825 . _____. "Notes on Western Madagascar and the Antinosi Country," *GJ*, VI (1895), 227-252.

2826 . La Vaissière, Jules de. *Histoire de Madagascar. Ses habitants et ses missionnaire.* Paris: Victor Lecoffre, 1884. 520p.

2827 . _____. "Lettere," *MCM*, I(1872), 183, 184; VIII(1879), 331; XI(1882), 446-449; XII(1883), 398, 399, 455.

2828 . _____. "Lettres," *APFL*, LV(1883), 417, 418.

2829 . _____. "Lettres," *Exploration*, III(1878), 130-132.

2830 . _____. "Lettres," *Lettres d'Ucles*, July, 1883, 91-95.

2831 . _____. "Lettres," *LSV*, Aug., 1873, 9, 10.

2832 . _____. "Lettres," *MCL*, IV(1871-1872), 445; XI(1879), 314; XIV(1882), 433-436, 599, 600; XV(1883),311, 312, 385, 386, 436, 437.

2833 . _____. "Lettres," *Messager du Sacre-Coeur*, XXXV(1896), 98, 385, 386, 436, 437.

2834 . _____. "Lettres," *Univers*, (1881), 10.

2835 . _____. "Missionsbriefe," *KM*, XI(1883), 222, 254, 255.

2836 . Lavigne, Jacques. "Lettre," *Lettres d'Uclès*, XXII(1886), 124-126.

2837 . _____. "Lettres," *Annales Oeuvre Ste. Enfance*[Paris], XIX(1867), 111-116; XX(1868), 191-196.

2838 . Le Brun, J. "Île de Madagascar," *JME*, XXIII(1848), 69-75.

2839 . _____. "Lettres," *JME*, XXXVII(1862), 354-359.

2840 . _____. "Visite du roi Radama dans les écoles d'Ova," *JME*, I(1826), 159-162.

2841  . Leguével de Lacombe, B. F. *Voyage à Madagascar et aux îles Comores (1823 à 1830)*. 2 vols. Paris: Desessart, 1840.

2842  . Le Savoureux, M. Joel. "Madagascar," *SGM*, IX(1893), 127-141.

2843  . Lewis, Locke. [*Capt.*]. "An Account of the Ovahs, a Race of People Residing in the Interior of Madagascar: with a Sketch of Their Country, Appearance, Dress, Language, etc.," *JRGS*, V(1835), 230-242.

2844  . Liebrecht, Felix. "Drei madagaskarische Märchen," *Globus*, XXXIV(1878), 366-367.

2845  . Limozin, Joseph. "Lettre," *APFL*, XLII(1870), 379-381.

2846  . _____. "Lettre," *MCL*, I(1868), 188-189.

2847  . _____. "Lettre," *Resaka*[Antananarivo], IX(1882), 110-111.

2848  . _____. "Lettres," *Annales Oeuvre Ste. Enfance*[Paris], XXVI(1875), 349-355; XXX(1879), 402-407.

2849  . _____. "Lettres," *LSV*, April, 1868, p. 7; March, 1870, p.15-17; Sept., 1871, p.6-8; Jan., 1873, p.25-27; Oct., 1877, p.55-59.

2850  . Locamus, P. *Madagascar et ses richesses; bétail, agriculture, industrie*. Paris: Challamel, 1896. 195p.

2851  . MacMahon, Edward Oliver. *Christian Missions in Madagascar*. Westminister: Society for the Promotion of the Gospel, 1914. 179p.

2852  . _____. "Journeys in Western Madagascar," *PRGS*, New Series, XIV(1892), 463-464.

2853  . Mager, Henri. *Mission de Madagascar*. 2 vols. Rouen: de Lapierre, 1897.

2854  . _____. *Nos colonies. La vie à Madagascar*. Paris: Firmin-Didot, 1898. 330p.

2855  . Mandat-Grancey, Edmond. [*Baron de*]. *Souvenirs de la côte d'Afrique, Madagascar-Saint-Barnabé*. Paris: Plon,Nourrit, 1892. 308p. 3rd Ed. Paris: Plon,Nourrit, 1900. 308p.

2856 . Manifatra, Venance. "Lettres," *APFL*, LIX(1887), 114, 115.

2857 . _____. "Lettres," *MCL*, XVIII(1886), 591.

2858 . Marseille, Eugène. "Lettera," *MCM*, I(1872), 460-461.

2859 . _____. "Lettres," *LSV*, March, 1870, p.12-13; April, 1870, p.31-32.

2860 . _____. "Lettres," *MCL*, III(1870), 245; IV(1871-1872), 722-723.

2861 . Matthews, Thomas Trotter. *Notes of Nine Years' Mission Work in the Province of Vonizongo, North West Madagascar, with an Historical Introduction*. London: Hodder and Stoughton, 1881. 164p.

2862 . _____. *Thirty Years in Madagascar*. London: Religious Tract Society, 1904. 384p. New York: Armstrong, Doran, 1904. 384p.

2863 . Maude, Francis Cornwallis. *Five Years in Madagascar, with Notes on the Military Situation*. London: Chapman and Hall, 1895. 285p. New York: Scribner's, 1896.

2864 . Maundrell, H. [*Rev.*]. "A Visit to the North-East Province of Madagascar," *JRGS*, XXXVII(1867), 108-116. See also *PRGS*, XI(1866-1867), 50-51.

2865 . Maupoint, Armand-René. *Madagascar et ses deux premiers evêques*. 2nd Ed., 2 vols. Paris: C. Dillet, 1864.

2866 . Maynard, J. Howard. "Journey from Antananarivo to Mojunga," *PRGS*, XX (1875-1876), 110-114.

2867 . Mears, John William. *The Story of Madagascar*. Philadelphia: Presbyterian Board of Publications, 1873. 313p.

2868 . Michel, Antonin. "Lettres," *LSV*, April, 1879, p. 27-35.

2869 . Michel, Louis. "Lettres," *LSV*, Aug., 1901, 12, 13, 16, 17, 32-37.

2870 Miramont, J. T. de. *André Denjoy, soldat et apôtre, aumônier militaire à Madagascar*. Paris: Librairie de l'Oeuvre de Saint-Paul, 1897. 326p.

2871 . Montaut, Victor. "Lettere," *MCM*, XVIII(1889), 293, 294.

2872 . _____. "Lettres," *MCL*, XXI(1889), 280.

2873 . Montgomery. "Les prédicateurs indigènes," *JME*, XLVII(1872), 29-31.

2874 . Mullens, Joseph. "On the Central Provinces of Madagascar," *JRGS*, XLV (1875), 128-152. See also, *PRGS*, XIX(1874-1875), 182-202.

2875 _____. "On the Origin and Progress of the People of Madagascar," *JAI*, V(1876), 181-196.

2876 . _____. *Twelve Months in Madagascar*. London and Edinburgh, 1875. New York: Carter, 1876.

2877 . _____ and others. "Recent Journeys in Madagascar," *JRGS*, XLVII(1877), 47-72. See also, *PRGS*, XXI(1876-1877), 155-173.

2878 . Murat, Chanoine. "Lettere," *MCM*, XXI(1892), 451; XXIV(1895), 6, 7.

2879 . _____. "Lettres," *APFL*, LXVII(1895), 153, 154.

2880 . _____. "Lettres," *MCL*, XXIII(1891), 181, 182; XXIV(1892), 452, 453; XXV (1893), 376, 377; XXVI(1894), 619.

2881 . Neuling. [*Dr.*]. "Dr. C. Rutenberg's Reisen in Südafrika und Madagaskar," *Globus*, XXXV(1879), 299-304.

2882 . Oliver, Samuel Pasfield. *Les Hovas et autres tribus caractéristiques de Madagascar*. Guernesey, 1869. 36p.

2883 . _____. *Madagascar. An Historical and Descriptive Account of the Island and Its Former Dependencies*. 2 vols. London and New York: Macmillan, 1886.

2884 . _____. *Madagascar and the Malagasy, with Sketches in the Provinces of Tamatave, Betanimena and Ankova*. London: Day, 1866. 105p.

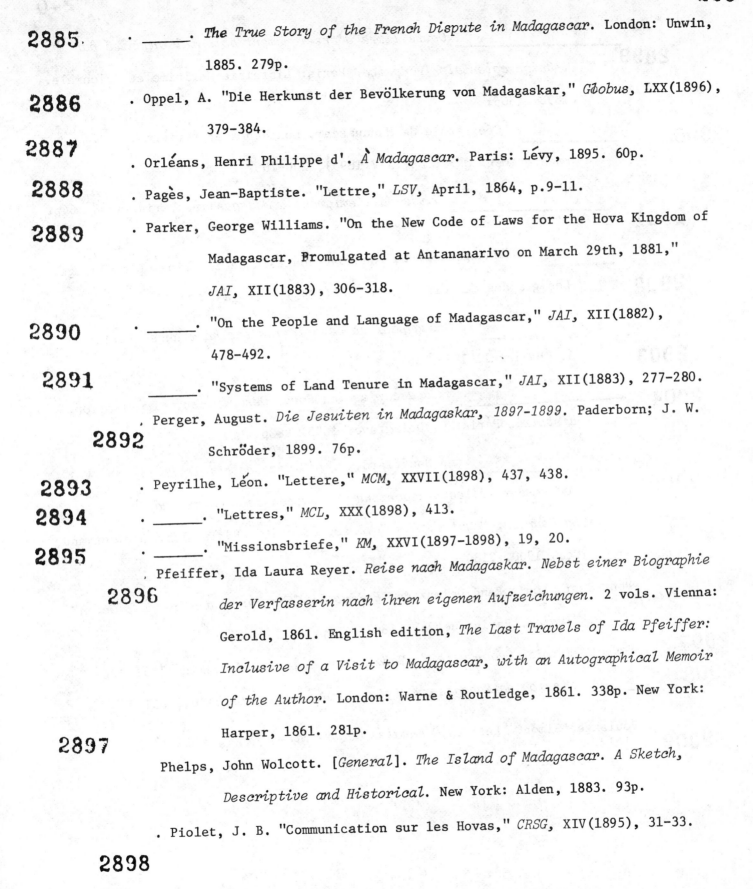

2885. _____. *The True Story of the French Dispute in Madagascar*. London: Unwin, 1885. 279p.

2886. Oppel, A. "Die Herkunst der Bevölkerung von Madagaskar," *Globus*, LXX(1896), 379-384.

2887. Orléans, Henri Philippe d'. *À Madagascar*. Paris: Lévy, 1895. 60p.

2888. Pagès, Jean-Baptiste. "Lettre," *LSV*, April, 1864, p.9-11.

2889. Parker, George Williams. "On the New Code of Laws for the Hova Kingdom of Madagascar, Promulgated at Antananarivo on March 29th, 1881," *JAI*, XII(1883), 306-318.

2890. _____. "On the People and Language of Madagascar," *JAI*, XII(1882), 478-492.

2891. _____. "Systems of Land Tenure in Madagascar," *JAI*, XII(1883), 277-280.

2892. Perger, August. *Die Jesuiten in Madagaskar, 1897-1899*. Paderborn; J. W. Schröder, 1899. 76p.

2893. Peyrilhe, Léon. "Lettere," *MCM*, XXVII(1898), 437, 438.

2894. _____. "Lettres," *MCL*, XXX(1898), 413.

2895. _____. "Missionsbriefe," *KM*, XXVI(1897-1898), 19, 20.

2896. Pfeiffer, Ida Laura Reyer. *Reise nach Madagaskar. Nebst einer Biographie der Verfasserin nach ihren eigenen Aufzeichungen*. 2 vols. Vienna: Gerold, 1861. English edition, *The Last Travels of Ida Pfeiffer: Inclusive of a Visit to Madagascar, with an Autographical Memoir of the Author*. London: Warne & Routledge, 1861. 338p. New York: Harper, 1861. 281p.

2897. Phelps, John Wolcott. [*General*]. *The Island of Madagascar. A Sketch, Descriptive and Historical*. New York: Alden, 1883. 93p.

2898. Piolet, J. B. "Communication sur les Hovas," *CRSG*, XIV(1895), 31-33.

2899 _____. *Cours libre d'enseignement colonial organisé par l'Union coloniale française.* Paris: Librairie Maritime et Coloniale, 1898. 436p.

2900 _____. "Géographie de Madagascar, montagnes et rivières," *Enseignement chrétien,* XIV(1895), 200-206.

2901 _____. *Guide de l'emigrant à Madagascar.* Paris, 1898. 64p.

2902 _____. "Madagascar. La Fandroana ou Bain de la Reine. L'esclavage. Les grandes cultures," *RFEC,* XX(1895), 129-143.

2903 _____. *Madagascar sa description ses habitants.* Paris: A. Challamel, 1895. 587p.

2904 _____. *Madagascar et les Hova. Description, organisation, histoire.* Paris: C. Delagrave, 1895. 283p.

2905 _____ and Noufflard, C. *L'Empire coloniale de France.* Vol. I, *Madagascar et les possessions françaises de l'océan indien: La Réunion, Mayotte, Les Comores, Dijbouti.* Paris: Firmin Didot and Co., 1900. 218p.

2906 Pont-Jest, Louis René Delmas de. *Bolino le Négrier: souvenirs de l'Océan Indien.* Paris: Hetzel, 1862. 324p.

2907 Pouget, Firmin. *Géographie de Madagascar.* Lyon: de Naegelin, 1851. 12p.

2908 _____. *Mission de Magascar.* Lyon: Lithographie Naegelin, 1851. 83p.

2909 Poulange, Simon. "Lettres," *Annales Oeuvre Ste-Enfance,* XLII(1891), 257-259, 311-317.

2910 . Pra, François. "Lettres," *Annales de N. D. de La Salette*, XXXVI(1900-1901), 113-115, 146-148, 170-173, 274-277.

2911 . Rahidy, Basilide-Marie. "Lettres," *LSV*, May, 1866, p.18-20; March, 1870, p.13-15.

2912 _____. "Le Père Rahidy, premier prêtre indigène de Madagascar," *MCL*, XV(1883), 311, 312. Also, *MCM*, XII(1883), 334, 335.

2913 . Ransome, L. H. "The River Antanambalana, Madagascar," *PRGS*, New Series, XI(1889), 295-305.

2914 . Regnon, P. de. "Lettre," *APFL*, XXXVI(1864), 93-96.

2915 . Richardson. "Madagascar," *JME*, LIII(1878), 114-118.

2916 . Rooke, W. [*Capt.*]. "A Boat-Voyage Along the Coast-Lakes of East Madagascar," *JRGS*, XXXVI(1866), 52-64.

2917 . Royon, Régis. "Lettres," *LSV*, Aug., 1901, 18-25.

2918 . Ryan, Vincent William. *Mauritius and Madagascar: Journals of an Eight Years' Residence in the Diocese of Mauritius, and of a Visit to Madagascar*. London: Seeley, Jackson and Halliday, 1864. 340p.

2919 . Santini de Riols, Emmanuel-Napoléon. *La guerre de Madagascar, anciennement France orientale, historique complet de l'expédition de 1895*. Paris: O. Bornemann, 1896. 108p.

2920 . Shufeldt, Mason A. "La Question Malagache," *The United Service*, IX (1883), 453-460.

2921 _____ _____. "To, about, and across Madagascar," *The United Service*, XII(January-June, 1885), 1, 506, 691; XIII(July-December, 1885), 79, 203.

2922 Sewell, M. "Madagascar," *JME*, XLVII(1872), 305-308.

2923 Shaw, George A. *Madagascar and France with Some Account of the Island, Its People, Its Resources and Development*. London: Religious Tract Society, 1885. 320p.

2924 _____. *Madagascar of Today. An Account of the Island, Its People*. London: Religious Tract Society, 1886. 190p.

2925 Sibree, James Jr. "Curious Words and Customs Connected with Chieftainship and Royalty among the Malagasy," *JAI*, XXI(1891-1892), 215-229.

2926 _____. "Decorative Carving on Wood, Especially on Their Burial Memorials by the Bètsilèo Malagasy," *JAI*, XXI(1891-1892), 230-244.

2927 _____. *Fifty Years in Madagascar. Personal Experiences of Mission Life and Work*. London: Allen & Unwin, 1924. 359p. Boston: Houghton Mifflin, 1924. 359p.

2928 _____. *The Great African Island. Chapters on Madagascar*. London: Trübner, 1880. 372p.

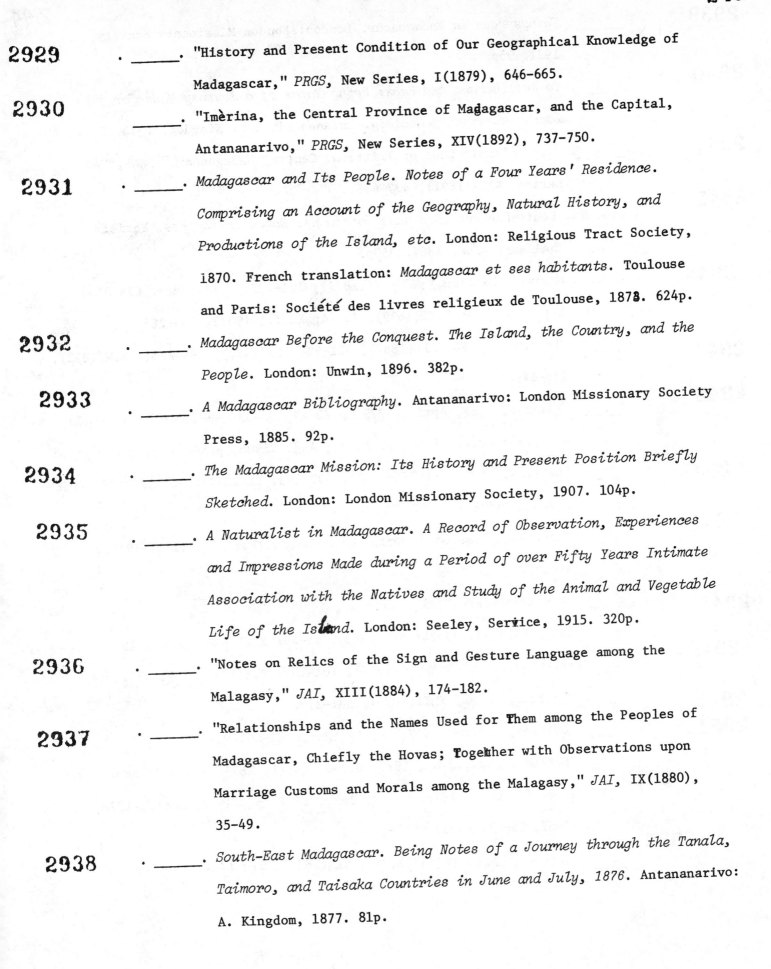

2929 . _____ . "History and Present Condition of Our Geographical Knowledge of Madagascar," *PRGS*, New Series, I(1879), 646-665.

2930 . _____ . "Imèrina, the Central Province of Madagascar, and the Capital, Antananarivo," *PRGS*, New Series, XIV(1892), 737-750.

2931 . _____ . *Madagascar and Its People. Notes of a Four Years' Residence. Comprising an Account of the Geography, Natural History, and Productions of the Island, etc.* London: Religious Tract Society, 1870. French translation: *Madagascar et ses habitants.* Toulouse and Paris: Société des livres religieux de Toulouse, 1873. 624p.

2932 . _____ . *Madagascar Before the Conquest. The Island, the Country, and the People.* London: Unwin, 1896. 382p.

2933 . _____ . *A Madagascar Bibliography.* Antananarivo: London Missionary Society Press, 1885. 92p.

2934 . _____ . *The Madagascar Mission: Its History and Present Position Briefly Sketched.* London: London Missionary Society, 1907. 104p.

2935 . _____ . *A Naturalist in Madagascar. A Record of Observation, Experiences and Impressions Made during a Period of over Fifty Years Intimate Association with the Natives and Study of the Animal and Vegetable Life of the Island.* London: Seeley, Service, 1915. 320p.

2936 . _____ . "Notes on Relics of the Sign and Gesture Language among the Malagasy," *JAI*, XIII(1884), 174-182.

2937 . _____ . "Relationships and the Names Used for Them among the Peoples of Madagascar, Chiefly the Hovas; Together with Observations upon Marriage Customs and Morals among the Malagasy," *JAI*, IX(1880), 35-49.

2938 . _____ . *South-East Madagascar. Being Notes of a Journey through the Tanala, Taimoro, and Taisaka Countries in June and July, 1876.* Antananarivo: A. Kingdom, 1877. 81p.

2939 · _____. *Things Seen in Madagascar.* London: London Missionary Society, 1921. 95p.

2940 · _____. *To Antsihanaka and Back: Being Notes of a Journey Made for the London Missionary Society.* Antananarivo: A. Kingdom, 1874. 29p.

2941 · _____. "The Volcanic Lake of Tritriva, Central Madagascar," *PRGS,* New Series, XIII(1891), 477-483.

2942 · Simonin, Louis-Laurent. *Les pays lointains. Notes de voyages.* Paris: Challamel aîné, 1867. 350p.

2943 · Taix, Alphonse. "Lettere," *MCM,* VI(1877), 101-102; XVII(1888), 614-615; XX(1891), 423; XXXI(1899), 73-74; XXXIII(1901), 265-266.

2944 · _____. "Lettres," *APFL,* LIX(1887), 321-322; LX(1888), 294-298; LXIV(1892), 148-149.

2945 · _____. "Lettres," *LSV,* April, 1879, p.23-27, 36-38; Aug., 1901, p. 39-40, 45-47, 50-51; Oct., 1904, p. 18-24; Aug., 1906, p.46.

2946 · _____. "Lettres," *MCL,* IV(1871-1872), 692-693; IX(1877), 80; XX(1888), 256-257; XXIII(1891), 200-202.

2947 · _____. "Lettres," *Mission de Madagascar Central*[Paris], I(1911-1912), 27-29.

2948 · _____. "Missionsbriefe," *KM,* II(1874), 147-150; VI(1878), 23-24; XVI(1888), 43-44; XXVI(1897-1898), 19.

2949 · Taix, Henri. "Lettere," *MCM,* VI(1877), 101-102; XVI(1887), 194-195.

2950 · _____. "Lettres," *APFL,* XLII(1870), 371-379.

2951 · _____. "Lettres," *Lettres d'Uclès,* IV(1896), 64-65, 95-97.

2952 · _____. "Lettres," *LSV,* Jan., 1873, p.2-6; April, 1875, p.15-19; Nov., 1875, p. 64-69; Oct., 1876, p. 27; Jan., 1877, p. 21-22; April, 1878, p. 41-57, 58-69; April, 1879, p.27.

2953 · _____. "Lettres," *MCL,* IX(1877), 81; XIX(1887), 170-171.

2954 . Talazac, Stanislas. "Excursion chez les Tanala indépendants," *Bulletin de la Société de Géographie de Lyon*, XII(1893-1894), 495-499.

2955 . _____ . "Lettere," *MCM*, XX(1891), 253-256.

2956 . _____ . "Lettres," *MCL*, XXIII(1891), 349-351.

2957 . Thiénard, Albert. "Lettres," *Annales Apostolique C. S. Sp.*, (1901), 101-107.

2958 . Vigroux, Germain. "Lettere," *MCM*, XXIV(1895), 387-390.

2959 . _____ . "Lettres," *Annales Oeuvre Ste-Enfance*, XXXV(1884), 247-259; XXXVIII(1887),311-323.

2960 . _____ . "Lettres," *Lettres d'Uclès*, (1886), Nr.2, 210-212; (1887), Nr. 1, 85-93; (1889), Nr. 1, 138, 139; 2nd Series, I(1893), 163-165; II (1894), 315-353; III(1895), 261-266, 299-304; IV(1896), 60, 61, 65-68, 513-515.

2961 . _____ . "Lettres," *LSV*, Oct., 1879, 32-39.

2962 . _____ . "Lettres," *MCL*, XXVII(1895), 375, 376.

2963 . Villèle, Joseph de. "Lettres," *LSV*, Aug., 1901, 29-32.

2964 . _____ . "Lettres," *MCL*, XXII(1891), 17.

2965 . Vinson, Auguste. *Voyage à Madagascar au couronnement de Radama II*. Paris and Saint-Cloud, 1865. 575p.

2966 . Voeltzkow, Alfred. "Besuch des Kinkoni-Gebietes in West-Madagaskar," *ZGE*, 1891, p. 65.

2967 . _____ . "Von Beseva nach Soala. Reiseskizze aus West-Madagaskar," *ZGE*, 1893, p. 137.

2968 —————————. "Vom Morondaua zum Mongóky, Reiseskizze aus West-Madagaskar," *ZGE*, 1896, p. 105.

2969 —————————. "West-Madagaskar auf Grund eigener Anschauung," *VGE*, XXIII(1896), 170.

2970 . Wilkinson, T. "Journey from Tamatave to the French Island Colony of St. Mary, Madagascar," *PRGS*, XIV(1869-1870), 372-377.

2971 Wilson, J. C. [*Capt., RN*]. "Notes on the West Coast of Madagascar," *JRGS*, XXXVI(1866), 244-246.

## CENTRAL AND SOUTHERN AFRICA

2972 . Anderson, Andrew A. "Notes on the Geography of South Central Africa," *PRGS*, New Series, VI(1884), 19-36.

2973 _____ and Wall, Alfred H. *A Romance of N'Shabé. Being a Record of Startling Adventures in South Central Africa.* London: Chapman & Hall, 1891. 366p.

2974 . Andersson, C.J. "On South Africa," *PRGS*, IV(1859-1860), 63-66.

2975 Arnot, Frederick Stanley. *Bihé and Garenganze, or Four Years' Further Work and Travel in Central Africa.* London: Hawkins, 1893. 150p.

2976 . _____. *From Natal to the Upper Zambesi. Extracts from Letters and Diaries of F.S.Arnot.* Edited by H.Groves. Glasgow, 1883. 70p.

2977 . _____. *Garenganze, or Seven Years' Pioneer Mission Work in Central Africa.* London: Hawkins, 1889. 276p.

2978 . _____. "Journey from Natal to Bihé and Benguella and Thence Across the Central Plateau of Africa to the Sources of the Zambesi and Congo," *PRGS*, New Series, XI(1889), 65-82.

2979 . _____. *Missionary Travels in Central Africa.* Bath: Echoes of Service, 1914. 159p.

2980 . _____. *Six Months More among the Garenganze, Sept.,1886 to March, 1887.* London: Hawkins, 1887-1888. 24p.

2981 . Baines, Thomas. *Explorations in South-West Africa.* London: Longmans, Green, 1864. 535p.

2982 . Baines, Thomas. "Scenes on the Zambesi," *CMM*, VIII(1860), 289-299.

2983 . Baldwin, William Charles. "Chasses en Afrique: de Port-Natal aux chutes du Zambèse," *TM*, VIII(1863), 369-416.

2984 . Barrow, John. *An Account of Travels into the Interior of Southern Africa in the Years of 1797 and 1798.* 2 vols. London: Cadell & Davis, 1801.

2985 . _____. *An Auto-Biographical Memoir of Sir John Barrow, Bart., Late of the Admiralty, Including Reflections, Observations, and Reminiscences at Home and Abroad, from Early Life to an Advanced Age.* London: Murray, 1847. 515p.

2986 . Bates, Laura H. "The American Board's Work in Africa," *MH*, XCII(1896), 144-146.

2987 . Brode, Heinrich. *Tippu Tip. Lebensbild eines zentralafrikanischen Despoten.* Berlin: E. Nagel, 1905. 167p. English translation, *Tippoo Tib: the Story of His Career in Central Africa; Narrated from His Own Account.* London: Edward Arnold, 1907. 254p.

2988 . Bunker, Fred R. "Matebele and Gaza lands," *MH*, LXXXVIII(1892), 401-403.

2989 . Burchell, William John. *Travels in the Interior of South Africa.* 2 vols. London: Longmans, 1822-1824. New edition, ed. by I.Schapera, London: Batchworth Press, 1953.

2990 . Caddick, Helen. *A White Woman in Central Africa.* London: Fisher Unwin, 1900. 242p. New York: Cassell, 1900.

2991 . Cameron, Verney Lovett. *Across Africa.* 2 vols. London: Daldy, Isbister, 1877. French edition, *A travers l'Afrique, voyage de Zanzibar à Benguela.* Paris: Hachette, 1878. 559p. Also published in *TM*, XXXIII(1877), 1-80, XXXIV(1877), 65-160.

2992 . _____. "Cameron's Brief über seine Reise quer durch Afrika," *Globus*, XXIX(1876), 89-93.

2993 . _____. "Letters Detailing the Journey of the Livingstone East Coast Expedition from Lake Tanganyika to the West Coast of Africa," *PRGS*, XX(1875-1876), 118-127.

2994 . _____. "On His Journey across Africa, from Bagamoyo to Benguela," *PRGS*, XX(1875-1876), 304-325.

2995 . Cameron, V. L. "Trade of Central Africa, Present and Future," *JRSA*, XXV(1877), 162-171.

2996 . Campbell, Dugald. *In the Heart of Bantuland, a Record of Twenty-Nine Years Pioneering in Central Africa among the Bantu Peoples, with a Description of Their Habits, Customs, Secret Societies, and Languages*. Philadelphia: Lippincott, 1922. 313p. London: Seeley, Service, 1922. 313p.

2997 . _____. *Wanderings in Central Africa*. London: Seeley, Service, 1929. 284p.

2998 . Capello, Hermenegildo Carlos Brito, and Ivens, Roberto. *De Angola á contra-costa, descripção de uma viagem atravez do continente africano*. 2 vols. Lisbon: Impr. nacional, 1886.

2999 . Chapman, James. "Notes on South Africa," *PRGS*, V(1860-1861), 16-18.

3000 _____ ___. *Travels in the Interior of South Africa, Comprising Fifteen Years' Hunting and Trading; with Journeys across the Continent from Natal to Walvisch Bay, and Visits to Lake Ngami and the Victoria Falls*. 2 vols. London: Bell and Daldy, 1868.

3001 . Coillard, F. "Expédition missionaire du Zambeze," *JME*, LIV(1879), 9-13, 41-59, 163-177, 286-302; LV(1880), 48-50, 92-96, 168-176.

3002 . _____. "Une nouvelle exploration," *JME*, LIII(1878), 321-336.

3003  . Colrat de Montrozier, Raymond. *Deux ans chez les anthrophages et les sultans du centre africain.* Paris: Plon, Nourrit, 1902. 326p.

3004  . Crouch, Archer Philip. *On a Surf-Bound Coast; or, Cable-Laying in the African Tropics.* London: Low, Marston, Searle and Rivington, 1887. 338p.

3005  . Currie, Donald. *Thoughts upon the Present and Future of South Africa, and Central and Eastern Africa.* London, 1877. 54p.

3006  . Deckert, Emil. "Die wissenschaftlichen Ergebnisse der Stanley'schen Expedition," *Globus*, LVII(1890), 336-342, 363-365.

3007  . Delhaise-Arnould, M. L. "Le problème de la Lukuga. Notes sur les différences de niveau du lac Tanganika avant et après 1880 et sur les origines de la Lutengar, déversoir des eaux du lac dans le fleuve Congo," *BSBG*, XXXII(1908), 228-236.

3008  . Depelchin, Henri, and Croonenberghs, Charles. *Trois ans dans l'Afrique australe. Le pays des Matabélés. Debuts de la mission au Zambèze. Lettres des pères H. D. et C. C.*, *1879-1881*. 2 vols. Brussels: Polleunis, Cauterick & Lefèbvre, 1882-1883.

3009  . Donat, Emil. *Kreuz und Quer durch Süd-Afrika. Reiseskizzen und Bilder.* Aarau: Emil Wirz, 1899. 280p.

3010 . Dutrieux, Pierre Joseph. *Souvenirs d'une exploration médicale dans l'Afrique intertropicale*. Paris: Carré, 1885. 146p.

3011 . Elton, Frederick [*Capt.*]. "Journal of an Exploration of the Limpopo River," *JRGS*, XLII(1872), 1-49. Also, *PRGS*, XVI(1871-1872), 89-99.

3012 . Erskine, St. Vincent. "Exploration of Part of South East Africa," *PRGS*, XVII(1872-1873), 297-298.

3013 . _____. "Remarks on the Line of Inland Telegraph Suggested in the African Exploration Committee's Circular," *PRGS*, XXII(1877-1878), 224-225.

3014 . Foa, Édouard. *À travers l'Afrique centrale. Du Cap au Lac Nyassa*. Paris: Plon-Nourrit, 1897. 382p.

3015 . _____. *After Big Game in Central Africa. Records of a Sportsman from August 1894- November 1897*. London: A.&C. Black, 1899. 330p.

3016 . _____. "Coup de l'Afrique Equatoriale du Sud-Est au Nord-Ouest (Zambèze-Congo)," *Géographie*, II(1900), 19-122.

3017 . _____. *De l'Océan indien à l'Océan atlantique. La traversée de l'Afrique du Zambèze au Congo français*. Paris: Plon-Nourrit, 1900. 323p.

3018 . _____. *Résultats scientifiques des voyages en Afrique d'Édouard Foa*. Paris: Plon, 1908. 742p.

3019 . _____. "Traversée de l'Afrique Equatoriale de l'embouchure du Zambèze a celle du Congo par les grands lacs, 1894-1897," *CRSG*, XVII(1898), 108-131.

3020 . Frere, H. Bartle. "On Systems of Land Tenure among Aboriginal Tribes in South Africa," *JAI*, XII(1883), 258-272.

3021 . Gamitto, Antonio Candido Pedroso. *O Muâta Cazembe e os Povos Maraves, Chévas, Muizas, Muembas, Lundas e outros da Africa austral. Diario da Expedição portuguesa comandada pelo Major Monteiro, 1831-1832.* 2 vols. Lisbon, 1884. Also, Lisbon: Agencia Geral das Colonias, 1937. English translation, *King Kazembe and the Marave, Cheva, Bisa, Bemba, Lunda, and Other Peoples of Southern Africa; Being the Diary of the Portuguese Expedition to That Potentate in the Years 1831 and 1832.* Translated by Ian Cunnison. 2 vols. Lisbon, 1960.

3022 . Gillmore, Parker. *Days and Nights in the Desert.* London: Kegan Paul, 1888. 234p.

3023 . Giraud, Victor. "Attempt to Cross Africa from Lake Bangweolo and the Upper Congo," *PRGS*, New Series, VII(1885), 332-337.

3024 _____. "Explorations in the Lake Region of Central Africa," *PRGS*, New Series, VII(1885), 603-607.

3025 . Guyot, Paul. *Voyage au Zambèse.* Nancy: Berger-Levrault, 1889. 326p.

3026 . Hahn, Theophilus. "Die Buschmänner," *Globus*, XVIII(1870-1871), 65-68, 81-85, 102-105, 120-123, 140-143, 153-155.

3027 . Halle, Ernst von. "Das Britisch-Zentralafrikanische Schutzgebiet," *DK*, XVI(1899), 353-354.

3028 . Herhallet, C. P. *Instructions nautiques sur la côte occidentale d'Afrique, comprenant: la côte du Congo; la côte d'Angola, la côte de Benguela et la colonie du Cap.* Paris, 1870. 406p.

3029 . Holub, Emil. *Sieben Jahre in Süd-Afrika. Erlebnisse, Forschungen und Jagden auf meinen Reisen.* 2 vols. Vienna: Hölder, 1881. English translation, *Seven Years in South Africa, Travels, Researches and Hunting Adventures.* 2 vols. London: Sampson, Low, 1881. See also, "Au pays des Marutsés. Episodes de voyages sur la haut Zambèse," *TM*, XLV (1883), 1-80.

3030 . _____. *Von der Capstadt ins Land der Maschukulumbe. Reisen im südlichen Afrika in den Jahren 1883-1887.* 2 vols. Vienna, 1890.

3031 . Hübner, Adolf. "Aus den Briefen Adolf Hübner's über Südafrika. Unter den Matabelekaffern. Misslungener Versucht, die Wasserfalle des Sambesi zu erreichen," *Globus*, XXIII(1873), 249-251, 266-267.

3032 . Hutchinson, Edward. "Development of Central Africa," *JRSA*, XXIV(1876), 689-704.

3033 . Hutchinson, George Thomas. *From the Cape to the Zambezi.* London: Murray, 1905. 205p.

3034 . Jalla, Louis. "Bonnes nouvelles de Sesheke," *JME*, LXIII(1888), 472-478.

3035 . _____. "Lettres," *JME*, LXII(1887), 63-67, 104-107, 191-192, 219-220, 336-346, 425-429; LXIII(1888), 20-23, 101-102.

3036 . Johnston, H. H. "Commercial Development of Central Africa and Its Beneficent Results on the Slave Traffic," *Journal of the Tyneside Geographical Society*, III(1894), 31-39.

3037 . _____. "England's Work in Central Africa," *Liberia Bulletin*, X(1897), 16-24.

3038 . _____. "Journey North of Lake Nyassa and Visit to Lake Leopold," *PRGS*, New Series, XII(1890), 225-227.

3039 . _____. "On the Races of the Congo and the Portuguese Colonies in Western Africa," *JAI*, XIII(1883), 461-478.

3040 . Johnston, James [*M.D.*]. *Reality vs Romance in South Central Africa. An Account of a Journey across the Continent from Benguella on the West to the Mouth of the Zambesi on the East Coast.* London: Hodder & Stoughton, 1893. New York: Revell, 1893. 353p.

3041     Junker, Wilhelm Johann. *Bei meinen Freunden den Menschenfressern.*
Leipzig: Brockhaus, 1926. 159p.

3042     • _____. "Explorations in Central Africa," *PRGS*, New Series, IX(1887), 399-417.

3043     • _____. *Wissenschaftliche Ergebnisse von Dr. W. Junkers Reisen in Zentral-Afrika, 1880-1885.* Gotha: Perthes, 1889. 114p.

3044     • Kemp, Sam, and Marsh, Howard R. *Black Frontiers. Pioneer Adventures with Cecil Rhodes in Africa.* New York: Brewer, Warren & Putnam, 1931. 288p.

3045     • Kerr, Walter Montagu. *The Far Interior; a Narrative of Travel and Adventure from the Cape of Good Hope across the Zambesi to the Lake Regions of Central Africa.* 2 vols. Boston: Mifflin, 1886. London: Sampson, Low, 1886.

3046     • _____. "A Journey from Cape Town Overland to Lake Nyassa," *PRGS*, New Series, VIII(1886), 65-85.

3047     • _____. "The Upper Zambesi Zone," *SGM*, II(1886), 385-402.

3048     • Kerr Cross, David. "Notes on the Country Lying between Lakes Nyassa and Tanganyika," *PRGS*, New Series, XIII(1891), 86-99.

3049     • Kirk, John. "Examination of the Lufigi River Delta, East Africa," *PRGS*, XVIII(1873-1874), 74-76.

3050     • _____. "Notes on the Gradient of the Zambesi, on the Level of Lake Nyassa, on the Murchison Rapids, and on Lake Shirwa," *JRGS*, XXXV(1865), 167-169.

3051     • Lacerda e Almeida, Francisco José Maria de. *Diarios de viagem de Francisco José de Lacerda e Almeida.* Rio de Janeiro: Imprense Nacional, 1944. 266p.

3052     • _____. *Diario de viagem de Moçambique para os rios de Sena.* Lisbon: Imprensa Nacional, 1889. 31p.

3053 . _____. *Travessia de África. Edição acrescida do Diário da viagem de Moçambique para os rios de Sena e do diario do regresso a Sena, pelo padre Francisco João Pinto.* Lisbon: Agencia geral das colónias, 1936. 411p.

3054 . Laporte, Francis L. de. *Renseignements sur l'Afrique Centrale, et sur une nation d'hommes à queue qui s'y trouverait, d'après le rapport des nègres du Soudan, esclaves à Bahia.* Paris: Bertrand, 1851. 62p.

3055 . Leclercq, Jules Joseph. *À travers l'Afrique australe.* Paris: Plon, Nourrit, 1895. 312p.

3056 . Leyland, J. *Adventures in the Far Interior of South Africa.* London: Routledge, 1866.

3057 . Livingstone, David. *Africa Journal, 1853-1856.* Edited by I. Schapera. 2 vols. London: Chatto & Windus, 1963.

3058 . _____. *Cambridge Lectures.* Cambridge, 1858.

3059 . _____. *Explorations in Africa.* Chicago: Union Publishing Co., 1872.

3060 . _____. "Explorations from Interior of Africa to W. Coast," *PRGS,* I (1855-1857), 6-7.

3061 . _____. "Explorations into the Interior of Africa," *JRGS,* XXIV(1854), 291-306; XXV(1855), 218-237; XXVI(1856), 78-84; XXVII(1857), 349-387.

3062 . _____. "Exploration to the West of Lake Nyassa in 1863," *JRGS,* XXXIV (1864), 245-251.

3063 . _____. "Extracts from the Despatches of Dr. David Livingstone. . .to Lord Malmesbury and Lord John Russell," *JRGS,* XXXI(1861), 256-296.

3064   · _____. *The Last Journals of David Livingstone in Central Africa*. 2 vols. London; 1874. French translation, *Dernier journal, relatant sas explorations et découvertes de 1866 à 1873, suivi du récit de ses derniers moments et du transport de ses restes*. 2 vols. Paris: Hachette, 1876.

3065   · _____. "Latest Explorations into Central Africa beyond Lake Ngami," *JRGS*, XXII(1852), 163-174.

3066   · _____. "Letters to Sir Thomas Maclear," *PRGS*, **XVII**(1872-1873), 67-73.

3067   · _____. *Missionary Correspondence, 1841-1856*. London: Chatto and Windus, 1961.

3068   · _____. *Missionary Travels and Researches in South Africa*. London: Murray, 1857. 786p. New York: Harpers, 1858.

3069   · _____. *Narrative of an Expedition to the Zambesi and Its Tributaries, and of the Discovery of Lakes Shirwa and Nyassa, 1858-1864*. London: Murray, 1865. 608p.

3070   · _____. *Private Journals, 1851-1853*. Edited by I. Schapera. London: Chatto & Windus, 1960. 341p.

3071   · _____. "Second Visit to the South African Lake, Ngami," *JRGS*, XXI(1851), 18-24.

3072   · _____. *Some Letters from Livingstone, 1840-1872*. Edited by David Chamberlain. London and New York: Oxford University Press, 1940. 280p.

3073   · _____. *Travels and Researches in South Africa; Including a Sketch of Sixteen Years' Residence in the Interior of Africa, and a Journey from the Cape of Good Hope to Loanda on the West Coast, Thence across the Continent, down the River Zambezi, to the Eastern Ocean*. Philadelphia: Bentley, 1861. French translation, *Exploratations dans l'intérieur de l'Afrique australe et voyages à travers le continent de Saint-Paul de Loanda à l'embouchure du Zambèze, de 1840-à 1856*. Paris: Hachette, 1877. 688p.

3074 . _____. *The Zambezi Expedition of David Livingstone, 1858-1863*. 2 vols. London: Chatto & Windus, 1956.

3075 . Lloyd, Albert Bushnell. *In Dwarf Land and Cannibal Country. A Record of Travel and Discovery in Central Africa*. London: Unwin, 1899. 385p.

3076 . McClure. [*Capt.*]. *With Stanley in Africa*. New York: Worthington, 1891.

3077 . Magyar, László. "Extracts from the Letters of an Hungarian Traveller in Central Africa," *JRGS*, XXIV(1854), 271-275.

3078 . Mackenzie, John. "Bechuanaland, with Some Remarks on Mashonaland and Matebeleland," *SGM*, III(1887), 291-315.

3079 . Madinier, Paul. *Projet d'une expédition française dans l'Afrique centrale*. Paris: Rouvier, 1856. 14p.

3080 . Manheimer, Émile. *Du Cap au Zambèze. Notes de voyage dans l'Afrique du Sud*. Geneva: Haden, 1884. 195p.

3081 . Maples, Chauncy. *Journals and Papers*. Edited by Ellen Maples. London: Longmans, 1899. 278p.

3082 . Mendonça, João de. *Colonias e possessões portuguezas*. Lisbon: Verde, 1877. 119p.

3083 . Middletown, W. H. *An Account of an Extraordinary Living Hidden City in Central Africa, and Gatherings from South Africa*. London: Kell, Sell & Railton [c.1894]. 135p.

3084 . Moffat, Robert. *African Scenes, or, Incidents in the Life of the Rev. Robert Moffat*. Birmingham: Showell, 1842. 28p.

3085 . Mohr, Eduard. *Nach den Viktoriafällen des Zambesi.* Leipzig: Hirt & Sohn, 1875. 2 vols. Eng. trans., *To the Victoria Falls of the Zambesi.* London: Sampson Low, Marston, Searle and Rivington, 1875. 462p.

3086 . _____. "Von Bremen nach dem Mosiwatunja, den Victoria-Fällen des Zambesi," *Elfter Jahresbericht des Vereins von Freunden der Erdkundenzu Leipzig,* (1872), 31-56.

3087 . Moir, Jane. *A Lady's Letters from Central Africa.* New York: Macmillan, 1891. Glasgow: Maclehose, 1891. 91p.

3088 . Monteiro, Joaquim John. *Angola and the River Congo.* 2 vols. London, 1875. New York: Macmillan, 1876. 354p.

3089 . Mullens, Joseph. "A New Route and a New Mode of Travelling into Central Africa, Adopted by the Rev. Roger Price in 1876," *PRGS,* XXI (1876-1877), 233-244.

3090 . Pogge, Paul [*Dr.*]. *Im Reiche des Muata-Jamwo. Tagebuch meiner im Auftrage der Deutschen Gesellschaft zur Erforschung Aequatorial-Afrika's.* Berlin: Reimer, 1880. 246p. See also, *Globus,* XXXII(1877), 14-15, 28-31.

3091 . _____. "Von der Pogge-Wissmann'schen Expedition," *Globus,* XLII(1882), 167-169.

3092 . Rankin, Daniel J. "Explorations in the Loangwa-Zambesi Basin," *SGM,* VIII (1892), 569-579.

3093 . _____. "The Peoples and Commercial Prospects of the Zambesi Basin," *SGM,* IX(1893), 225-240.

3094 . _____. *The Zambezi Basin and Nyasaland.* Edinburgh and London: Blackwood, 1893. 277p.

3095 . Robertson, Patrick. "The Commercial Possibilities of British Central Africa," *SGM,* XVI(1900), 235-245.

3096     . Rohlfs, Gerhard. "Pfahlbauten der Neger in Centralafrika," *Globus*, XVIII
                (1870-1871), 358-359.

3097     . Rose, Cowper. *Four Years in Southern Africa*. London: Colburn and Bentley,
                1829.

3098     . Schlichter, Henry [*Dr.*]. "The Pygmy Tribes of Africa," *SGM*, VIII(1892),
                289-301, 345-357.

3099     . Schulz, Aurel, and Hammar, August. *The New Africa. A Journey up the Chobe
                and Down the Okovanga Rivers. A Record of Exploration and Sport*.
                London: Heinemann, 1897. New York: Scribner's, 1897. 406p.

3100     . Selous, Frederick Courtenay. *African Nature Notes and Reminiscences*.
                London: Macmillan, 1908. 356p.

3101     . _____. *A Hunter's Wanderings in Africa; Being a Narrative of Nine Years
                Spent amongst the Game of the Far Interior of South Africa*.
                London: Bentley, 1881. 455p.

3102     . _____. "Journeys in the Interior of South Central Africa," *PRGS*, New
                Series, III(1881), 169-175.

3103     . _____, Millais, J. G. and Chapman, A. *The Big Game of Africa and Europe*.
                London: London and Counties Press Association, 1914. 408p.

3104     . Serpa Pinto, Alexandre Alberto da Rocha de. *Como eu atravessei a Africa do
                Atlantico ao Mar Indico. Viagens de Benguella á Contracosta*. . . .
                2 vols. London: Sampson and Low, 1881. English translation, *How
                I Crossed Africa; from the Atlantic to the Indian Ocean, through
                Unknown Countries; Discovery of the Great Zambesi Affluents, etc.*

3105                 2 vols. Philadelphia: Lippincott, 1881. London: Sampson and Low, 1881.
    . _____. "Journey across Africa," *PRGS*, New Series, I(1879), 481-489.

3106. Sharpe, Alfred. "Central African Trade and the Nyasa Waterway," *Blackwood's Magazine*, Feb., 1892, 319-325.

3107. _____. "Journey from Karonga (Nyassa) to Katanga (Msidi's Country) via the Northern Shore of Lake Mwero," *PRGS*, New Series, XIII(1891), 423-427.

3108. _____. "A Journey from the Shire River to Lake Mweru and the Upper Luapula," *GJ*, I(1893), 524-533.

3109. Silva Porto, Antonio Francisco Ferreira da. *Silva Porto e a travessia de continente africano*. Lisbon: Divisão de publicaçoes e biblioteca, Agencia geral das Colónias, 1938. 166p.

3110. _____. *Os ultimos dias de Silva Porto(extracto do seu diario)*. Lisbon: Typ. do Commercio de Portugal, 1891. 15p.

3111. Smith, Andrew. *The Diary of Dr. Andrew Smith, Director of the Expedition for Exploring Central Africa, 1834-1836*. 2 vols. Cape Town: Van Riebbeck Society, 1939.

3112 . \_\_\_\_\_. "Report of the Expedition for Exploring Central Africa," *JRGS*, VI(1836), 394-413.

3113 . Stanley, Henry Morton. "Central Africa and the Congo Basin," *SGM*, I(1885), 1-16. See also, *JMGS*, I(1885), 6-25.

3114 . \_\_\_\_\_. *My Kalulu, Prince, King and Slave: a Story of Central Africa.* London, 1873. New York: Scribner, Armstrong, 1874.

3115 . \_\_\_\_\_. *Through South Africa.* New York: Scribner's, 1898. 140p.

3116 . \_\_\_\_\_. *Wonders of the Tropics.* London, Ontario: McDermid and Logan, 1889.

3117 . Stevenson, James. *The Arabs in Central-Africa and at Lake Nyassa.* Glasgow: J. Maclehose and Sons, 1888. 25p. See also, *JMGS*, IV(1888), 72-84.

3118 . Swann, Alfred James. *Fighting the Slave-Hunters in Central Africa. A Record of Twenty-Six Years of Travel and Adventure Round the Great Lakes and of the Over-throw of Tip-pu-Tib, Rumaliza, and Other Great Slave-Traders.* London: Seeley, 1910. 358p. Philadelphia: Lippincott, 1910.

3119 . Thomas, Thomas Morgan. *Eleven Years in Central South Africa.* London: John Snow and Co., 1872. 418p.

3120 . Thornton, Richard. "Notes on the Zambesi and the Shiré," *JRGS*, XXXIV(1864), 196-199.

3121 . Trivier, E. *Mon voyage au continent noir. La "Gironde" en Afrique.* Paris: Firmin-Didot, 1891. 386p.

3122 . Verner, Samuel Phillips. *Pioneering in Central Africa.* Richmond: Presbyterian Committee of Publication, 1903. 500p.

3123 . Waddell, Hope Masterton. *Twenty-Nine Years in the West Indies and Central Africa: a Review of Missionary Work and Adventure, 1829-1858.* London: Nelson, 1863.

3124 . Walmsley [Capt.] and Walmsley, Hugh Molleneux. *The Ruined Cities of Zululand*. 2 vols. London: Chapman and Hall, 1869.

3125 . Watson, A. Blair. "Lake Mweru and the Luapula Delta," *GJ*, IX(1897), 58-60.

3126 . Wauters, A. J. *Les Belges dans l'Afrique centrale. Le capitaine Cambier au Tanganika*. Bruxelles: Muquardt, 1881. 36p.

3127 . _____. "Du Congo au Chari. Découverte du Chari supérieur," *MG*, X(1893),1.

3128 . Weld, Alfred. *Mission of the Zambesi*. Liverpool: Rockliff Brothers, 1878. 22p. London: Burns and Oates, 1878. Dublin: M.H.Gill, 1878. See also, *KM*, VII(1879), 173-176.

3129 . _____. *The Suppression of the Society of Jesus in the Portuguese Dominions*. London: Burns and Oates, 1877. 384p.

3130 . Wilkinson, Edward. "Notes on a Portion of the Kalahari," *GJ*, I(1893), 324-338.

3131 . Wissmann, Hermann von. "Journey across Africa," *PRGS*, New Series, V(1883), 163-165.

3132 . _____. *Meine zweite Durchquerung Äquatorial-Afrikas vom Congo zum Zambesi wahrend der Jahre 1886 und 1887*. Frankfort am Oder; 1890. 261p. English translation, *My Second Journey through Equatorial Africa, from the Congo to the Zambesi, in the Years 1886 and 1887*. London: Chatto & Windus, 1891. 326p.

3133 . _____. *Unter deutscher Flagge:Quer durch Afrika von West nach Ost, 1880-1883*. Berlin: Walther und Apolant, 1889. 444p.

3134 . _____. "Von San-Paulo de Loanda nach Zanzibar," *MKKG*, XXVI(1883), 97-103.

3135 . Younghusband, Francis [Capt.]. *South Africa of To-Day*. London: Macmillan, 1898. 177p.

3136  . Abreu e Lima, Luís António de. [*Visconde de Carreira*]. *Memoria sobe as colónias de Portugal, situadas na costa occidental d'Africa, mandada ao governo pelo antigo governador de Angola, Antonio de Saldanha da Gama, en 1814*. **Paris**, 1839.

3137  . Albuquerque, Affonso de. "**Cartas**" *Portugal em Africa*, IV(1897), 71-74.

3138  . Amaral, F. and Ferreira d'Almeida, J. B. "Apontamentos para a historia do estabelecimento da colonia agricola 'S. Januario,'" *BSGL*, II(1880-1881), 304-317, 456-467.

3139  . André, Lourenço. "Cartas," *Portugal em Africa*, V(1898), 351-354; VII (1900), 34.

3140  . Antunez, José Maria. "Cartas," *Portugal em Africa*, I(1894), 110-112, 128-130; II(1895), 534-537.

3141  . _____. "Lettres," *Annales Apostoliques*, I(1886), 113, 114; VII(1892), 113-115; IX(1894), 121-126; XIV(1897-1898), 66, 67, 307-309; XV(1898-1899), 23, 24.

3142  . _____. "Lettres," *Annales Oeuvre Ste-Enfance*, XXXVI(1885), 260-267; XXXVII(1886), 264-267; XLVII(1896), 307-313.

3143  . _____. "Relatorio do superior da missão do real padroado na Huilla," *BSGL*, VII(1887), 383-394.

3144  . Arnot, Frederick Stanley. "Journal at Bailundu," *MH*, LXXXI(1885), 149-152.

3145  . ____ and others. "News from the West Central African Missions," *MH*, LXXXII(1886), 19, 106-107, 142-143, 189, 190, 228-229, 348-349, 452-453, 508-509.

3146  . Azerado, José Pinto de. *Ensaios sobre algumas enfermidades d'Angola*. Lisbon: R. Officina Typografica, 1799. 149p.

3147 . Bagster, William W. and others. "Letters from the West Central Africa Mission," *MH*, LXXVII(1881), 97-100, 125-128, 144-145, 310-313, 352-353, 500-502; LXXVIII(1882), 28-30, 70-72, 101-104, 213-217.

3148 . Baracho, Dantas. *Alguns documentos sobre a minha missão na Africa.* Lisbon: Minerva Central, 1892. 89p.

3149 . Barros e Sousa de Mesquita de Macedo Leitão e Carvalhosa, Manoel Francisco de. [*Visconde de*]. *Demonstração dos direitos que tem a corôa de Portugal sobre os territorios situados na costa occidental d'Africa entre 05° grau e 12 minutos e 08° de latitude meridional e por consequinte aos territorios de Molembo, Cabinda e Ambriz.* Lisbon: Imprensa Nacional, 1855. 40p.

3150 . Barros Gomes, Henrique de. *Missões en Africa.* Lisbon: Imprensa Nacional, 1893. 41p.

3151 . Barth, Heinrich. "Exploraçao geológica na Angola. Part I: Primeiro relatiorio do comissario encarregado de exploraçao geológica da provinça de Angola," *Annaes da Comissão Central Permanente de Geografia,* (1876), 35-37.

3152 . Bast, Joseph. "Missionsbriefe," *Maria Immaculata,* VII(1899-1900), 112, 113; VIII(1900-1901), 11.

3153 . Bastian, Adolf. *Ein Besuch in San Salvador der Haupstadt des Königs-reichs Congo. Ein Beitrag zur Mythologie und Psychologie.* Bremen: Strack, 1859. 365p.

3154 . _____. *Die deutsche Expedition an der Loango-Küste, nebst älteren Nachrichten über die zu erforschenden Länder.* 2 vols. Jena: Costenoble, 1874.

3155 . _____. "Die Loango Küste," *ZGE*, 3rd Series, VIII(1873), 125-140.

3156 . Bell, Sarah and others. "Letters from the West Central African Mission," *MH*, LXXXVII(1891), 63-65, 157-159, 197-199, 247-248, 334-335, 422-424; LXXXVIII(1892), 20-21, 115-117, 156-159, 240-241, 330-331, 468-470, 528-529.

20378. Boavida, António José. *Annales das Missões Portuguezas.* Lisbon: Typographia

3157       Nacional, 1889. 166p.

3158   . Botelho, Eduardo Rodrigues Vieira da Costa. "Agricultura no districto

de Benguella" *BSGL*, VIII(1888-1889), 239-263.

3159   . _____. "O planalto de Caconda e a Bacia do Lubango. Sob o ponto de vista

da colonisação europea e aptião agricola dos seus terrenos,"

*BSGL*, X(1891), 209-228.

3160   . _____. "Terrenos e agricultura no districto de Mossamedes," *BSGL*,

IX(1890), 579-634.

3161   . Bowdich, Thomas Edward. *An Account of the Discoveries of the Portuguese*

*in the Interior of Angola and Mozambique, to which Is Added a*

*Note by the Author on a Geographical Error of Mungo Park, in*

*His Last Journal into the Interior of Africa.* London: Booth, 1824. 186p.

3162   . Braga, Eduardo. *Caminho de ferro de Benguella ao Bihé.* Lisbon: Moreira,

1899. 23p.

3163   . Braz, Manuel Gonçalves. "Cartas" *Portugal em Africa*, V(1898), 502-507;

IX(1902), 288-290.

3164   . Büchner, Max. *Recepçao e conferência do Exmo. Dr. Max Buchner, explorador*

*alemão.* Luanda: Sociedade de Propaganda de Conhecimientos

Geográficos Africanos, 1881.

3165   . _____. "Reise in Angola," *Globus*, XXXV(1879), 330-334.

3166   . Büttner. [*Dr.*]. "Von der Deutschen Westafrikanischen Expedition,"

*Globus*, XLVII(1885), 378-380.

3167   . Capello, Hermenegildo Carlos Brito; and Ivens, Roberto. *De Benguella ás*

*terras de Iácca. Descripção de uma viagem na Africa Central e*

*Occidental.* . . . .2 vols. Lisbon, 1881. English translation, *From*

*Benguella to the Territory of Yacca. Description of a Journey*

*into Central and West Africa.* 2 vols. London: Sampson Low, 1882.

3168   . Cardoso, F. *Memorias contendo a descripçao geográfica dos Reinos de*

*Angola e de Benguella.* Paris, 1825.

**3169** . Carneiro, João. "Cartas." *Portugal em Africa*, II(1895), 1079-1082.

3170 . Carvalho e Menzes, Joaquim Antonio de. *Memoria geografica e politica das possessoes portuguezas n'Africa occidental, que diz respeito aos reinos de Angola. Benguela e suas dependencias.* Lisbon: Typ. Carvalhense, 1834. 41p.

**3171** . Carvalho e Menzes, Vasco Guedes de. *Apontamentos para a historia d'Angola.* Funchal, 1882. 30p.

**3172** . Chatelain, Aida. *Héli Chatelain, l'ami de l'Angola, fondeteur de la mission philafricaine (1895-1908).* Lausanne: Secretariat de la Mission philafricaine, 1918.

**3173** . Chatelain, Héli. *Folk-Tales of Angola. Fifty Tales, with Ki-Mbundu Text, Literal English Translation, Introduction and Notes.* Boston: Houghton, Mifflin, 1894. 315p.

**3174** . Chavanne, J. [*Dr.*]. "Reisen im Gebiet des Muschi-Congo im portugieschen Westafrika," *PM*, XXXII(1886), 97- 106.

. Coinet, Narcisse. "Lettres," *Annales Apostoliques*, I(1886), 149-151.

**3175**

**3176** . Coquilhat, [*Capt.*]. "The Bangala," *JMGS*, III(1887), 239-243.

**3177** . Cordeiro, Luciano. *Viagens, explorações e conquistas dos Portuguezes; collecção de documentos.* Lisbon: Imprensa Nacional, 1881.

**3178** . Cunha, P. A. da. "Expedição ao sul de Angola, 1839," *BSGL*, VI(1886), 249-255.

**3179** . Cunninghame, Boyd A. "A Pioneer Journey in Angola," *GJ*, XXIV(1904), 153-168.

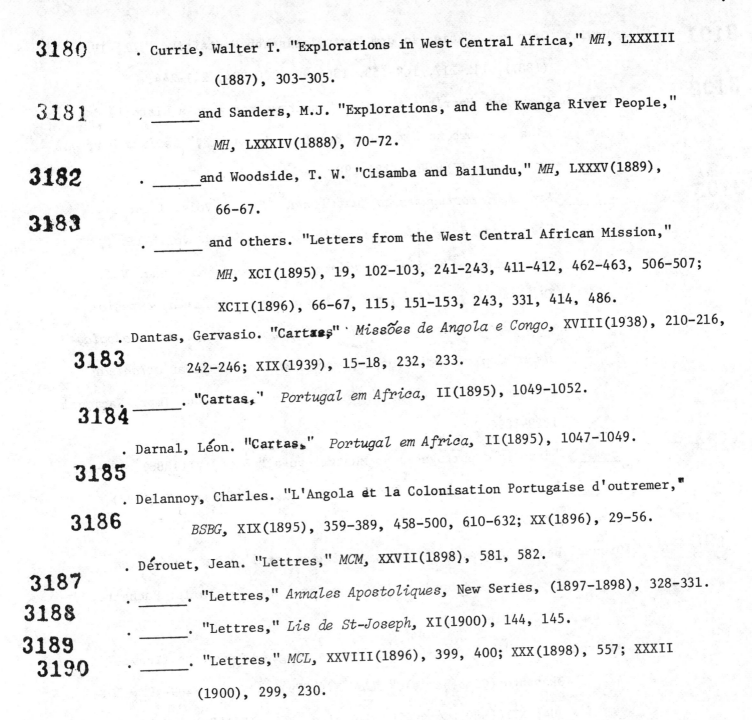

3180    . Currie, Walter T. "Explorations in West Central Africa," *MH*, LXXXIII (1887), 303-305.

3181    . _____and Sanders, M.J. "Explorations, and the Kwanga River People," *MH*, LXXXIV(1888), 70-72.

3182    . _____and Woodside, T. W. "Cisamba and Bailundu," *MH*, LXXXV(1889), 66-67.

3183    . _____ and others. "Letters from the West Central African Mission," *MH*, XCI(1895), 19, 102-103, 241-243, 411-412, 462-463, 506-507; XCII(1896), 66-67, 115, 151-153, 243, 331, 414, 486.

3183    . Dantas, Gervasio. "Cartas," *Missões de Angola e Congo*, XVIII(1938), 210-216, 242-246; XIX(1939), 15-18, 232, 233.

3184    . "Cartas," *Portugal em Africa*, II(1895), 1049-1052.

3185    . Darnal, Léon. "Cartas," *Portugal em Africa*, II(1895), 1047-1049.

3186    . Delannoy, Charles. "L'Angola et la Colonisation Portugaise d'outremer," *BSBG*, XIX(1895), 359-389, 458-500, 610-632; XX(1896), 29-56.

3187    . Dérouet, Jean. "Lettres," *MCM*, XXVII(1898), 581, 582.

3188    . _____. "Lettres," *Annales Apostoliques*, New Series, (1897-1898), 328-331.

3189    . _____. "Lettres," *Lis de St-Joseph*, XI(1900), 144, 145.

3190    . _____. "Lettres," *MCL*, XXVIII(1896), 399, 400; XXX(1898), 557; XXXII (1900), 299, 230.

3191 . Dewitz, Otto von. "Reise in dem Portugiesischen Westafrika," *DK*, IV (1887), 112-117, 149-153, 186-190, 200-204, 241-244.

3192 . Dias de Carvalho, Henrique Augusto. "Apontamentos para a história das minas de ouro no Lombinge, Province de Angola," *Revista Portugal em Africa*, IV(1896), 184-190.

3193 . _____. *Expedição portugueza ao Muatiãnvua, 1884-8. Vols. I and II. Descripçao da viagem a Mussumba do Muatiãnvua. Vol. III. Ethnografia e história tradicional dos povos da Lunda. Vol. IV. Methodo practico para fallar a léngua de Lunda contento narrações historicas dos diversos povos. Vol. V. Meteorologia, climatologia e coloniçaçao, modo practice de facer colonisar com vantagem as terras de Angola.* 5 vols. Lisbon: Impr. Nacional, 1889-1894.

3194 . _____. "Expedição portugueza ao Muatyan-vu-a," *BSGL*, VI(1886), 133-162.

3195 . _____. "Luanda portugueza," *Revista Portugal em Africa*, III(1895), 517-526.

3196 . Drouet, Henri. *Sur terre et sur mer. Excursion d'un naturaliste en France, aux Açores, à la Guyane et à Angola.* Paris: Hachette, 1870. 301p.

3197 . Duparquet, Charles-Victor-Albert. "Notes géographiques. Le fleuve Okavango (Cimbébasie)," *MCL*, XI(1879), 477-481, 489-492, 501-504; XII(1880), 454-456. See also, *MCM*, IX(1880), 20-24, 29-34, 57-58, 71-72; X(1881), 211-214.

3198 . _____. "Voyage en Cimbébasie. Journal," *MCL*, XII(1880), 367-370, 278-382, 404-407, 416-418, 426-431; XIII(1881), 476-477, 484-486, 500-501, 514, 515, 524-525, 538-539, 559-561, 568-571, 580-581, 597-599, 606-610. *MCM*, XI(1882), 275-276, 281-284, 295-296, 308-310, 331-332.

3199   . Duparquet, M. P. "État commercial de la côte du Loango et du Congo," *Missions Catholiques*, III(1875).

3200   . Falcão, Joaquim José. "Instrucãoes com que veiu o Senhor Governador Geral Lourenzo Germack Possolo. --Secretaria d'Estado dos Negocios da Marinha e Ultramar: 28 de Novembro de 1843," *Arquivos de Angola*, II(1936), 695-713.

3201   . Fay, William E. "Maps of the West Central African Mission," *MH*, LXXXI (1885), 183-186.

3202   . _____. "Our West Central African Mission," *MH*, LXXXIV(1888), 292-294.

3203   . _____. "A Revolution at Bihe," *MH*, LXXXV(1889), 242-243.

3204   . _____ and Sanders, W. H. "The Trip to Bihe," *MH*, LXXX(1884), 180-182, 313-315, 349-351, 504-507, 509-514.

3205   . Fernandes das Neves, Diocleciano. "Exploração do rio Bembe," *BSGL*, III(1882), 336-347.

3206   . Ferreira, João Antonio das Neves. "Benguella," *BSGL*, V(1885), 92-100.

3207   . Ferreira da Silva Porto, Antonio Francisco. "Novas Jornadas nos sertões Africanos," *BSGL*, V(1885), 3-36, 145-172, 569-586, 603-642; VI (1886), 56-62, 189-194, 255-258, 307-322, 441-452, 537-540.

3208   . Ferreira do Amaral, Francisco Joaquín. "O caminho de ferro de Ambaca," *BSGL*, III(1882), 143-160.

3209   . Filliung, Joseph. "Missionsbriefe," *Maria Immaculata*, IV(1896-1897), 206-209; VI(1898-1899), 15-17, 35-38, 40, 41; X(1902-1903), 166, 167.

3210    Fischer, Thomas, "Lettres," *Lis de St-Joseph*, VI(1895), 165.

3211   . François, Curt von. "Reise von Hamburg nach Malange," *Globus*, LV (1889), 33-36, 49-53, 65-70.

3212 · Génié, Etienne. "Cartas," *Portugal em Africa*, III(1896), 389-395.

3213 · _____. "Lettres," *Annales Oeuvre Ste-Enfance*, XXXIX(1888), 99-112; XLV
(1894), 8-20.

3214 · _____. "Lettres," *MCL*, XVIII(1886), 542, 543.

3215 · Giraul. [*Visconde de*]. "Ideas geraes sobre a colonizaçao europea da
provincia de Angola," *BSGL*, XVIII(1900), 611-642.

3216 · Göpp, Joseph. "Lettres," *Annales Apostoliques*, XVII(1901), 133-135.

3217 · Guilmin, H. "Dans le Mossamedes. Province d'Angola," *Bulletin de la
Société de Géographie Commerciale*, XVII(1895), 318-335.

3218 · Hall, Wilburn. "Capture of the Slave Ship *Cora*," *Century*, XLVIII(1894),
115-129.

3219 · Havenith, Gerhard. "Missionsbriefe," *Maria Immaculata*, VII(1899-1900),
227-230.

3220 · Heinrichs, Hubert. "Missionsbriefe," *Maria Immaculata*, VIII(1900-1901),
131-134.

3221 · Jaeger, Franz. "Lettres," *Petites Annales*, XI(1901), 71.

3222 · _____. "Missionsbriefe," *Maria Immaculata*, VIII(1900-1901), 134, 135.

3223 · Kambo, Charles. "Lettres," *Annales Apostoliques*, IX(1894), 21, 22.

3224 · Keiling, Luiz-Alfredo. "Lettere," *MCM*, XXV(1896), 149, 150.

3225 · _____. "Lettres," *MCL*, XXVIII(1896), 125.

3226 · Kieffer, André. "Lettere," *MCM*, XXVII(1898), 185, 186.

3227 · _____. "Lettres," *MCL*, XXX(1898), 173.

3228 . Kieger, Josef. "Lettere," *MCM*, XXX(1901), 446, 447.

3229 . _____. "Lettres," *MCL*, XXXIII(1901), 422, 423.

3230 . _____. "Lettres," *Petites Annales*, VIII(1898), 331, 332.

3231 . _____. "Missionsbriefe," *Maria Immaculata*, V(1897-1898), 93, 94, 316, 317; VI(1898-1899), 19, 57-60, 83-86, 91, 92; IX(1901-1902), 92, 93.

3232 . Kipper, Jakob. "Missionsbriefe," *Maria Immaculata*, VI(1898-1899), 184-186; VII(1899-1900), 282, 283.

3233 . Krafft. [*Rev.*]. "Landana e Malange," *BSGL*, XI(1892), 617-632.

3234 . Lacerda e Almeida, Francisco José Maria de. *Exame das viagens do doutor Livingstone*. Lisbon, 1867. 635p.

3235 . _____. *The Land of Cazembe*. [Translated by Sir Richard Francis Burton]. *Journey of the Pombeiros*. *Resumé of the Journey of Monteiro and Gamitto*. London: Royal Geographical Society, 1873.

3236 . _____. *Portuguese African Territories*. *Reply to Dr. Livingstone's Accusations and Misrepresentations*. London: Edward Stanford, 1865. 40p.

3237 . Lang, J. C. "O petroleo do Dande, 1839," *BSGL*, VI(1886), 240-249.

3238 . Lecompte, Ernest. "A travers la Haute-Cimbébasie," *MCL*, XXXIII(1901), 569-572, 581-584, 597-599, 610-612. See also, *MCM*, XXXI(1902), 437-439, 452-456, 466, 467, 475-479.

3239 . _____. "A travers la Haute-Cimbébasie, Afrique occidentale," *MCL*, XXVI(1894), 236-238, 253-255, 262-265, 271-274, 285, 286. See also, *MCM*, XXIV(1895), 293-296, 318-321, 340-343, 352-354, 367, 368.

3240   ———————. "Cartas," *Portugal em Africa*, I(1894), 162-172, 183-205, 290-295; II(1895), 1055-1059; III(1896), 131-134, 223-229; IV(1897), 283-284, 453-455; V(1898), 223-224; VI(1899), 41-44, 264-265; VII (1900), 629-631; VIII(1901), 224-228, 685-687.

3241   ———————. [*Rev.*]. "**Entre o Cunene e o Zambeze**," *BSGL*, XIII (1894), 1163-1165.

3242   ———————. "Lettere," *MCM*, XIV(1885), 507-509; XXII(1893), 157-159; XXVII(1898), 390; XXX(1901), 471-472.

3243   ———. "Lettres," *Annales Apostoliques*, XI(1896), 125-135; New Series, (1897-1898), 273-275; XVI(1900-1901), 148-151; XVII(1901), 45, 135-137, 139-141.

3244   ———. "Lettres," *Annales Oeuvre Ste-Enfance*, XLV(1894), 329-336.

3245   ———. "Lettres," *APFL*, LIX(1887), 254-255, 274-281; LXXIII(1901), 266-273.

3246   ———. "Lettres," *Bulletin de la Congrégation*, VIII(XXI), (1901-1902), 114-115.

3247   ———. "Lettres," *Lis de St-Joseph*, XII(1901), 215-216.

3248   ———. "Lettres," *MCL*, XVII(1885), 470-471; XXV(1893), 145-146, 147; XXX(1898), 375-376; XXXIII(1901), 436.

3249   ———. "Missionsbriefe," *KM*, XIV(1886), 67-68; XV(1887), 258-259; XXII (1894), 266-267; XXV(1897), 43-45.

3250   Lecompte, Ernest. "La Mission de Sainte-Marie de Bailoundo," *MCL*, XXVIII (1896), 486-491. See also, *MCM*, XXVI(1897), 209-211, 221, 222.

3251   ———. "No Cubango," *BSGL*, VIII(1888-1889), 345-358.

3252 _____. "Novo methodo para aprender e ler e a escrever o Ganguella," *Portugal em Africa*, V(1898), 224-226.

3253 _____. "Plan'alto do sul de Angola: missões portuguezas—Caconda, Catoco, Bihe e Bailundo," *BSGL*, XVI(1897), 223-248.

3254 _____. "Voyage au pays des Amboëllas," *Annales Apostoliques*, III(1888), 5-29.

3255 _____. Leuper, Johann. "Missionsbriefe," *Maria Immaculata*, VII(1899-1900), 210-212.

3256 _____. Livingstone, David. "On the Province of Angola," *JRGS*, XXV(1855), 229-235.

3257 _____. Lopes, David de Mello. *Textos em aljamia portuguesa, documentos para a historia do dominio português em Safim, extrahidos dos originaes da Torre do Tombo*. Lisbon: Imprensa Nacional, 1897. 161p.

3258 _____. Lopes de Calheiros e Meneses, Sebastião. "Relatório do Governador Geral da Província de Angola [1861]," *Boletim Geral das Colónias*, LII(1929), 111.

3259 _____. Lülsdorf, Casimir. "Missionsbriefe," *Echo aus Knechtsteden*, II(1900-1901), 25-29, 43-45, 61, 62, 78, 92-94, 108-110, 122-126, 139-141, 152-158, 170-172, 183-188.

3260 _____. Luna de Carvalho, Joaquim Maria. "Expedição ao Humbe," *BSGL*, XII(1893), 121-138.

3261 _____. Lur. [*Oberleutnant*]. "Unter den Bangelas in Westafrika," *Globus*, XXXV(1879), 182-185.

3262 _____. Lux, Anton E. "Reise van Malange bis Kimbundu und zurück," *VGE*, III (1876), 33.

3263 _____. "Reiseberichte," *Corresvondenzblatt der Afrikanischen Gesell-schaft*, II(1873-1877), 78, 127.

3264    . _____. *Von Loanda nach Kimbundu; Ergebnisse der Forschungsreise im*
        *Äquatorialen West Afrika, 1875-1876.* Vienna: E. Hölzel, 1880.
        219p.

3265    . Lynch, Joseph-Antoine. "Lettres," *L'Echo des missions d'Afrique*, II(1885),
        172, 173.

3266    . _____. "Missionsbriefe," *KM*, X(1882), 108-110.

3267    . Magyar, László. *Reisen in Sud-Afrika, 1847-1857*. Pest and Leipzig:
        Lauffer und Stolp, 1859. 450p.

3268    . Marques, Agostinho Sisenando. *Expedição portugueza ao Muata-Ianvo. Os*
        *climas e os producções das terras de Malange á Lunda.* Lisbon:
        Imprensa Nacional, 1889. 128p.

3269    . Matasse, Basile. "Cartas," *Portugal em Africa*, I(1894), 373-377, 418-425.

3270    . _____. "Lettres," *Annales Apostoliques*, XV(1898-1899), 54, 55.

3271    . Mello, Miguel Antonio de. "Angola no começo do Seculo, 1802," *BSGL*,
        V(1885), 548-564.

3272    . _____. "Angola no fim do seculo XVIII. Documentos: Relação do D.
        Miguel Antonio de Mello. S. Paulo da Assumpção, 3.II.1800,"
        *BSGL*, VI(1886), 274-307.

3273    . Meyer, Charles. "Missionsbriefe," *Echo aus Afrika*, X(1898), 61-63.

. Meyer, Peter. "Missionsbriefe," *Maria Immaculata*, VII(1899-1900), 132-134.

3274

3275 . Miller, Samuel T. and Nichols, Francis O. "Letters from Bailunda," *MH*, LXXVIII(1882), 383-384.

3276 . Möller, P. "Fran Kongo utefter Kusten af Angola," *Ymer*, IX(1889), 30-46.

3277 . _____. *Resa i Afrika genom Angola, Ovampo och Damaraland*. Stockholm: W. Billes, 1899. 226p.

3278 . Monteiro, A. C. P. *O Muata Cazembe e os povos*. Lisbon, 1854.

3279 . Monteiro, Joaquim John. "On the Quissama Tribe of Angola," *JAI*, V(1876), 198-201.

3280 . Moraes, J. A. da Cunha. *Africa occidental; album photographico e descriptivo*. 4 vols. Lisbon: Corazzi, 1885-1888.

. Morvan, Yves-Marie. "Lettres," *Annales Apostoliques*, XVI(1900-1901), 157-163.

3281

3282 . Motta Feo, Luiz da. "Officio do Governador para o Conde da Barca sobre a reedificacao da Se Velha, S. Paulo d'Assumpcao, 20.5.1817," *Arquivos de Angola*, II(1936), 675-676.

3283 . _____. "Officio do Governador para o Conde dos Arcos, communicando a transferencia da Se Cathedral para a Igreja do Convento de Sam Jose, S. Paulo d'Assumpcao, 16.5.1818," *Arquivos de Angola*, II(1936), 683-684.

3284 . _____. "O Vice-Almirante Luiz da Motta Feo Governador e Capitao General, aos Habitantes do Reino de Angola, S. Paulo de Assumpcao de Loanda, 1.1.1818," *Arquivos de Angola*, II(1936), 677-682.

3285 . Müller, Auguste. "Lettres," *APFL*, LXX(1898), 450-461.

3286 . Muraton, Louis. "Cartas," *Portugal em Africa*, I(1894), 130-138, 228-237, 258-266.

3287 . —————. "Lettere," *MCM*, XXI(1892), 241-243; XXXII(1903), 89, 90.

3288 . —————. "Lettres," *Annales Apostoliques*, VII(1892), 149-152; IX(1894), 8-17; XI(1896), 100-115, 136-144.

3289 . —————. "Lettres," *APFL*, LXV(1893), 471, 472; LXVI(1894), 97-110; LXVIII(1896), 444-467.

3290 . —————. "Lettres, *Lis de St-Joseph*, IV(1893), 269, 270.

3291 . —————. "Lettres," *MCL*, XXIV(1892), 229-231, 535, 536, 632, 633; XXV(1893), 340, 376; XXXV(1903), 64, 65.

3292 . —————. "Missionsbriefe," *Echo aus Knechtsteden*, IV(1902-1903), 161-163.

3293 . Nichols, F. O. and others. "Letters from Bailunda," *MH*, LXXIX(1883), 29-30, 151-152, 189-190, 228-230, 272, 301-302, 338-339, 489-490; LXXX(1884), 55-56, 103-104, 145-146.

3294 . Nogueira, Antonio Francisco. *Povos e campanhas d'Africa; a expedicao aos Gambos em 1856*. Lisbon: Ferin, 1898. 19p.

3295 . Padrel, Lourenco Justiniano. "Expedicao ao Humbe," *BSGL*, XI(1892), 811-847.

3296 . Paiva, Artur de. "A expedição ao Cubango, 1885-86," *BSGL*, VII(1887), 97-142.

3297 . _____. "Expedição ao Cubango, 1889," *BSGL*, IX(1890), 253-293.

3298 . _____. "Da exploração do Cunene," *BSGL*, XLII(1923-1924), 162-173.

3299 . Paiva Couceiro, Henrique de. *Relatorio de viagem entre Bailundo e as terras do Mucusso*. Lisbon: Imprensa Nacional, 1892. 215p.

3300 . Pedroso, Antunes a Fernando de Almeida. "Africa occidental Portugueza: a fronteira do Sul," *BSGL*, IV(1883), 470-476.

3301 . Pereira, Carlos Augusto. "Cartaes," *Portugal em Africa*, VII(1900), 617, 618.

3302 . Pereira de Sampaio Forjas de Serpa Pimentel, J. *Un anno no Congo. Apreciações sobre o districto do Congo...Traços generaes d'una administração ultramarina*. Lisbon, 1899. 274p.

3303 . Pereira do Nascimento, José. *O districto de Mossamedes*. Lisbon: Typo. do Jornal as Colonias portuguezas, 1892. 172p.

3304 . _____. *Exploração geographica e mineralogica no districto de Mossamedes em 1894-1895*. Lisbon, 1898.

3305 . Pignol, Léon. "Lettres," *Annales Apostoliques*, XVI(1900-1901), 151-154.

3306 . Pinto, Francisco Antonio. *Angola e Congo*. Lisbon: Ferreira, 1888. 419p.

3307 . Poussot, Jean-Joseph. "Congo. Extraits d'une lettre à MM. le Membres des Conseils centraux, Ambriz, 15.2.1867," *APFL*, XL(1868), 143-161.

3308 . Puts, Hroznata. "Lettres," *Het H. Misoffer*, II(1899), 90, 91.

3309    Rascalou, Camille. "Lettres," *Annales Apostoliques*, XVI(1900-1901), 194-197.

3310    . Read, Frank W. and others. "Letters from the West Central African Mission," *MH*, XCV(1899), 73-74, 114-115, 203-204, 239, 289-290, 365-366, 536-537; XCVI(1900), 24, 65, 109-111, 155-156, 197-198, 284-286, 324, 402-403, 524-526; XCVII(1901), 19-20, 113-114, 204-206, 283-284, 374-375, 416-417.

3311    . Richard, Victor. "Lettres," *Annales Apostoliques*, VII(1892), 148, 149.

3312    . _____. "Lettres," *MCL*, XXIV(1892), 559.

3313    . Riedlinger, Emile. "Lettres," *Annales Apostoliques*, XVII(1901), 137-139.

3314    . _____. "Lettres," *Annales Oeuvre Ste-Enfance*, LI(1900), 242-249.

3315    . _____. "Lettres," *Missões de Angola e Congo*, VII(1927), 216-218; VIII (1928), 133-135.

3316    . _____. "Lettres," *Portugal em Africa*, IX(1902), 153, 154.

3317    . _____. "Missionsbriefe," *KM*, XXVI(1897-1898), 138, 139.

3318    : Rippon, Joseph. "The Portuguese Possessions of the South-West Coast of Africa, and Particularly of Angola," *JMGS*, V(1889), 359-364.

3319    . Rolle, Albert. "Lettres," *Lis de St-Joseph*, XI(1901), 17-19.

3320    . Romme, Augustinus. "Lettres," *Het H. Misoffer*, III(1900), 167, 168.

3321 . Roupnel, Julien. "Lettere," *MCM*, XXII(1893), 157-159.

3322 . _____. "Lettres," *Lis de St-Joseph*, VI(1895), 166, 167.

3323 . _____. "Lettres," *MCL*, XXV(1893), 145, 146.

3324 . Saldanha da Gama, Antonio de. "Cartas do Gobernador de Angola António de Saldanha da Gama, 1807," *Arquivos de Angola*, IV(1938), 41-106.

3325 . _____. *Memoria sobre as colonias de Portugal situadas na costa occidental d'Africa, mandada ao governo pelo antigo governador e Capitão General do reino de Angola, Antonio de Saldanha da Gama, em 1814.* Paris: Casimir, 1839. 60p.

3326 . Sanders, M. J. "The New King of Bihé," *MH*, LXXXIV(1888), 18-19.

3327 . Sanders, W. H. "Letters," *MH*, LXXVIII(1882), 261-263, 488-489, 526-529.

3328 . _____. "Visit to Bihé," *MH*, LXXVIII(1882), 349-351.

3329 . _____. "West Central African Mission: The End of the War," *MH*, LXXXI (1885), 355-356.

3330 . _____ and Arnot, F. S. "Letters from Angola," *MH*, LXXXI(1885), 25-26.

3331 . _____ and Sanders, Mary J. "The War in Bihé," *MH*, LXXXVII(1891), 108-111.

3332 . _____ and Walter, F. A. "The West Central African Mission," *MH*, LXXXI (1885), 194-195, 240-242, 278-279, 397-399, 465-467, 523.

3333 . Santa Brigida de Sousa, Rodolpho de. "Mossamedes," *BSGL*, VII(1887), 396-414.

3334 . Santos, Ignacio dos. "Lettres," *Portugal em Africa*, V(1898), 400-404, 450-454, 495-502; VIII(1901), 684, 685.

3335 . Sarmento, Alfredo de. *Os sertões d'Africa (apontamentos de viagem).* Lisbon: da Silva, 1880. 231p.

3336 . Schaller. [*Rev.*]. "La Mission de Cassinga," *BSGL*, X(1891), 51-61.

3337 . Schneider, Jean. "Missionsbriefe," *KM*, XXVI(1897-1898), 187-189.

3338 . Schütt, Otto. "Der Kaiserin-Augusta-Fall in Westafrica," *Globus*, XXXVII(1880), 295-297.

3339 . _____. "Reise von Malange zum Luba-Häuptling Mai und zurück," *Globus*, XXXVI(1879), 358-361; XXXVII(1880), 11-13, 30-31, 59-62.

3340 . Serpa Pimental, Antonio de. "O Congo portuguez. Relatorio sobre as feiboras do Zaire, seu commercio," *BSGL*, VII(1887), 269.

3341 . Serpa Pinto da Ruy, Alexandre Alberto. "Prehistoria angolense," *Trabalhos da Sociedade Portuguesa de Antropologia e Etnologia*, IV(1922), fasc. 2.

3342 . Silva, José Severino da. "Cartas," *Portugal em Africa*, IV(1897), 213-222; V(1898), 151-154, 227-230, 266-268, 397-399; VI(1899), 44, 45, 163-169, 227, 228, 316, 317, 500-505; VII(1900), 321-329; VIII(1901), 31-39, 108-110, 543, 544.

3343 . Silva Gil, Francisco da. *Relatorio da administração do Correio Central de Loanda*. Loanda, 1881.

3344 . Silva Leitão e Castro, António Tomás da. *Pro Patria. Diocese de Angola e Congo. Carta . . .a Luciano Cordeiro, Secretario Perpetuo da mesma Sociedade*. Lisbon: Typographia Portugueza, 1889. 19p.

3345 . Siméon, Jules. "Missionsbriefe," *Echo aus Afrika*, VII(1895), 75, 76.

3346 . Sousa, Manuel José de. "Lettres," *Portugal em Africa*, I(1894), 324-328.

3347 . Sousa Brum, A. J. de, and Pereira, S. J. "No Congo, trabalhos da missão portugueza de Salvador," *BSGL*, V(1885), 36.

3348 . Soyaux, Hermann. "Angola. Ein Stüch Culturgeschichte in Afrika," *Gegenwart*, II(1877), 148-151.

3349 . Stover, Bertha D. "An African Superstition," *MH*, LXXXII(1886), 215-217.

3350 . _____. "The Daydawn in Bailundu," *MH*, LXXXIII(1887), 205-208.

3351 . _____. "King Kwikwi of Bailundu," *MH*, LXXXIV(1888), 346-348.

3352 . Stover, Wesley M. "Christmas at Bailunda, West Central Africa," *MH*, LXXX(1889), 203-206.

3353 . _____ and Stover, Bertha D. "Letters," *MH*, LXXXIII(1887), 26-28.

3354 . _____ and others. "Notes on the West Central African Mission," *MH*, LXXXIII(1887), 105-108, 184-187, 310-313, 359-361, 396-398, 463-464, 530-531.

3355 . Tams, Georg. *Die portugiesischen Besitzungen in Süd-West-Afrika. Ein Reisebericht.* Hamburg: Kittler, 1845. English translation, *Visit to the Portuguese Possessions in South-Western Africa.* 2 vols. London: T.C.Newby, 1845. Portuguese translation, *Visita as possessoes portuguezas na costa occidental d'Africa.* Oporto, 1850.

3356 . Teixeira de Vasconcellos, Antonio Augusto. *Carta acerca do trafico dos escravos na provincia de Angola.* Lisbon: Silva, 1853. 15p.

3357 . Tils, Theodor. "Lettres," *Het H. Misoffer*, IV(1901), 18-20, 79-81; V(1902), 156-160.

3358 . Vermeulen, Engelbertus. "Lettres," *Het H. Misoffer*, II(1899), 73-76, 95-100, 113-119, 132-135, 149-152, 165-170, 170-173, 185-189, 210-214.

3359 . Veth, Daniel. *Daniël Veth's Reizen in Angola*. Edited by Pieter Johannes Veth. Haarlem: Willink, 1887. 430p.

3360 . Victoria Pereira, Albino Estevão. *Uma exploração africana; a Nova Lisboa*. Marinha Grande: Empresa typographica, 1890. 256p.

3361 . Vidal, Manuel Bernardo. *Exame dos actos do ex-governador geral de Angola*. Lisbon: Typ. de H.A.d.V., 1839. 59p.

3362 . Walter, Margaret D. and Sanders, W. H. "Journey to Bailunda," *MH*, LXXVIII(1882), 222-227.

3363 . Webster, A. H. and others. "Letters," *MH*, LXXXIV(1888), 113-114, 161-162, 257-258, 352, 445-446; LXXXV(1889), 110-111, 192-193, 287-289, 366-369, 412; LXXXVI(1890), 20-21, 66-67, 113-114, 238-239, 290-292, 320-323, 373-374, 475-476.

3364 . Wellman, F. C. [*Dr.*]. and others. "Letters," *MH*, XCIII(1897), 20-21,
69-70, 109-110, 152, 195-197, 234, 393-394, 511; XCIV(1898),
22-23, 108-110, 144-146, 191-193, 311-312, 349-350, 398-400,
504-505.

3365 . _____. "Some Native Evangelists in Central Africa," *MH*, XCVI(1900),
421-424.

3366 . Welwitsch. "Die Pedras Negras von Pungo Anpongo in Angola," *PM*, XIV
(1868), 260-264.

3367 . Wolff, W. "Berichte über die Kongo-Expedition," *MAGD*, IV(1884-1885).

3368 . _____. "Reise von San Salvador zum Quango," *ZGE*, XXI(1886),

3369 . _____. "Reise zum Kiamvo Kassongo," *MAGD*, IV(1885), 362. See also,
*VGE*, XIII(1886), 46.

3370 . _____. *Von Banana zum Kiamvo*. Oldenburg and Leipzig: Schulze, 1889.
248p.

3371 . Woodside, Thomas W. "The Death of King Kwikwi," *MH*, LXXXIX(1893),
324-326.

3372 . _____. "King Kwikwi's 'War'," *MH*, LXXXV(1889), 534-536.

3373 . _____. "The Ombala at Bailundu," *MH*, LXXXVIII(1892), 290-291.

3374 . _____ and others. "Letters," *MH*, LXXXIX(1893), 26-27, 65-67, 112,
194-195, 238-240, 324, 367-368, 411-412, 524-526; XC(1894), 24-
25, 115-116, 160-161, 210-211, 252-253, 339-340, 387-388, 427,
490-491, 523-524.

## THE CONGO BASIN
### (Central African Republic, Congo-Brazzaville, and Congo-Kinshasa)

3375   . Abruzzi, Duke of the. "The Snows of the Nile. Being an Account of the Exploration of the Peaks, Passes and Glaciers of Ruwenzori," *GJ*, XXIX(1907), 121-147.

3376   . Adams, C. "Cannibals," *Goldthwaite's Geographical Magazine*, I(1891).

3377   Alexis, F. *Soldats et missionnaires au Congo*. Brussels: Société de Saint-Augustin, n.d.. 240p.

3378   . Alexis, M. G. *La barbarie africaine et l'action civilisatrice des missions catholiques au Congo et dans l'Afrique équatoriale*. Liège: H. Dessain, 1889. 208p.

3379   _____. *Les Congolais, leurs moeurs et usages*. Liège: H. Dessain, 1890. 192p.

3380   . Alis, Harry. "Les Bayagas, petits hommes de la grande forêt équatoriale," *CRSG*, IX(1890), 548-554.

3381   . Allaire, Olivier. "Lettres," *Annales Apostoliques*, V(1890), 121-130; XI (1896), 15-35, 153-156.

3382   . _____. "Lettres," *APFL*, LXV(1893), 253-270; LXVIII(1896), 98-112, 154-156.

3383   . _____. "Lettres," *MCL*, XXIII(1891), 209, 210, 223-225; XXVIII(1896), 30.

3384   . _____. "Missionsbriefe," *Annalen der Afrikaansche Missiën*, XIII (1896-1897), 40-46.

3385 . Allart, J. B. *Rapport commercial concernant l'État indépendant du Congo.* Brussels: Weissenbruch, 1893. 44p.

3386 . _____. *Rapport sur l'État indépendant du Congo.* Brussels: Weissenbruch, 1891. 49p.

3387 . Andrade-Cordeiro Luciano, José Baptista de. "No Zaire[1853-1869]," *BSGL*, III(1882), 387-425.

3388 . Andriessen, W. F. "De afrikaansche Dwergvolken," *Tijdschrift van het Nederlandsch Aardrijkskundig Genootschap*, IV(1887), 516.

3389 . Annoni, Antonio. *Le imprese agricole, industriali e commerciali dei Belgi nel Congo ed il Congo all' Esposizione di Anversa 1894.* Milan: P. B. Bellini, 1895. 31p. See also, *Bollettino della Società di Esplorazione commerciale in Africa di Milano*, X(1895).

3390 . Anon. ["i."]. "Letters from the Congo," *DK*, II(1885), 656-658; III(1886), 91-92, 122-123, 190-192, 223.

3391 . Augouard, J. De. "Les anthropophages au Congo," *Nouvelle Revue*, 1st Series, VIII(1893), 595.

3392 . _____. "Colonisation. Lettre de l'Evêque du Haut Congo français," *Dépêche Coloniale Illustrée*, III(1902), March 25-27.

3393 . _____. *Les Missions de l'Oubanghi.* Poitiers: Oudin, 1890. 54p.

3394 . _____. "Missions et expéditions au Congo," *Correspondant*, Feb., 1892.

3395 . _____. *Les origines du Congo belge.* 2nd Ed. Paris: Plon-Nourrit, 1916.

3396 _____. "À la suite de Stanley et de Brazza," *MCL*, XV(1883), 37-42.

3397 _____. "L'Anthropophagie dans le bassin de l'Oubanghi," *Annales Apostoliques*, V(1890), 85-102.

3398 _____. "Au coeur de l'Afrique," *MCL*, XXIX(1897), 537-539, 551, 552, 558-561, 569-573, 582-585, 594-597. See also *MCM*, XXVII(1898), 286, 296-298, 311, 312, 322-324, 330-334, 344-347, 368-370.

3399 _____. "Au coeur du continent noir," *MCL*, XXXI(1899), 16-18, 28-31, 44-46, 52-55; XXXII(1900), 52-54, 68, 69, 81-84, 106, 107, 116-118, 129-131. See also *MCM*, XXIX(1900), 10-12, 21-24, 30, 31, 41-44.

3400 _____. "Dans le Haut-Oubanghi," *MCL*, XXVII(1895), 449-451, 464-468, 478-480, 489-491, 502, 503.

3401 _____. "Dans le Haut-Oubanghi. Fondation de Saint-Paul des Rapides," *MCL*, XXVII(1895), 514-516, 527, 528, 538-540.

3402 _____. "De Brazzaville à l'équateur," *MCL*, XVIII(1886), 10-12, 17-21, 28, 29, 56, 57, 69-71, 80-83, 93-96, 103-106. See also *MCM*, XV(1886), 527, 528, 538-540, 548, 572-575, 579-583, 617-622.

3403 _____. "De Loango à l'Oubanghi," *MCL*, XXII(1890), 365-368, 377-379, 391-393, 400-402, 414-417, 428-430. See also *MCM*, XX(1891), 395, 396, 403-406, 417-420, 426-429, 439-443.

3404 _____. *Dernier voyage dans l'Oubanghi et l'Alima*. Liguge: M. Bluté, 1899. 30p.

3405 _____. "A Escravatura (Apontamentos)," *Portugal em Africa*, II(1895), 527-533.

3406 _____. "A escravatura e a anthropophagia na Africa. Conferencia," *Portugal em Africa*, IV(1897), 49-62.

3407 ───────────────. "Lettere," *MCM*, X(1881), 567-570; XI(1882), 509; XIII(1884), 614, 615; XIV(1885), 253-256; XVI(1887), 110-112, 135, 136; XVIII(1889), 386, 387; XXI(1892), 470, 471; XXII(1893), 374-376; XXIII(1894), 41, 42, 145, 146; XXIV(1895), 425, 426; XXVI (1897), 245, 246; XXVII(1898), 68, 505, 506; XXVIII(1899), 217-219; XXX(1901), 255, 459, 460; XXXII(1903), 221, 222, 556, 592, 593.

3408 ───────────────. "Lettres," *Annales Apostoliques*, IV(1889), 81-84; VII(1892), 41-49, 131-134; VIII(1893), 76, 77; IX(1894), 87-96; X(1895), 16-24, 41-52; XII(1897-1898), 74, 75, 141-143, 175-178.

3409 ───────────────. "Lettres," *Annales Oeuvre Ste-Enfance*, XXXIII (1882), 320-323; XLVI(1895), 53-62.

3410 ───────────────. "Lettres," *APFL*, LII(1880), 118-133, LVI(1884), 297-318; LVII(1885), 355-370; LXII(1890), 332-346; LXVI(1894), 318, 396, 397, 426-450; LXXI(1899), 111-117, 279-290; LXXII(1900), 450-457; LXXIII(1901), 313, 314.

3411 ───────────────. "Lettres," *Bulletin de la Congregation*, VI (1898-1899), 569, 570; VII(1899-1900), 470-475.

3412 ───────────────. "Lettres," *Correspondant*, XII(1894), 25.

3413 ───────────────. "Lettres," *L'Echo des Missions d'Afrique*, I (1884), 98-105, 127-131; II(1885), 103-110, 186-192, 223-226.

3414 ───────────────. "Lettres," *Lis de St-Joseph*, V(1894), 41, 42, 275-278; VI(1895), 399-402; XI(1900), 335-338.

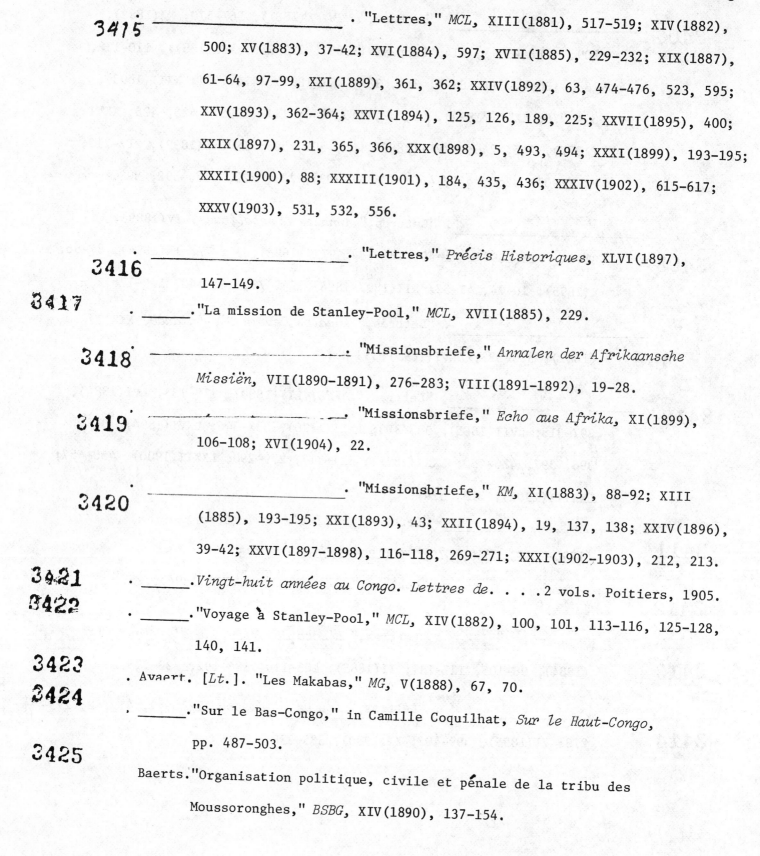

3415 ————————————. "Lettres," *MCL*, XIII(1881), 517-519; XIV(1882),
500; XV(1883), 37-42; XVI(1884), 597; XVII(1885), 229-232; XIX(1887),
61-64, 97-99, XXI(1889), 361, 362; XXIV(1892), 63, 474-476, 523, 595;
XXV(1893), 362-364; XXVI(1894), 125, 126, 189, 225; XXVII(1895), 400;
XXIX(1897), 231, 365, 366, XXX(1898), 5, 493, 494; XXXI(1899), 193-195;
XXXII(1900), 88; XXXIII(1901), 184, 435, 436; XXXIV(1902), 615-617;
XXXV(1903), 531, 532, 556.

3416 ————————————. "Lettres," *Précis Historiques*, XLVI(1897),
147-149.

3417 ——————. "La mission de Stanley-Pool," *MCL*, XVII(1885), 229.

3418 ————————————. "Missionsbriefe," *Annalen der Afrikaansche
Missiën*, VII(1890-1891), 276-283; VIII(1891-1892), 19-28.

3419 ————————————. "Missionsbriefe," *Echo aus Afrika*, XI(1899),
106-108; XVI(1904), 22.

3420 ————————————. "Missionsbriefe," *KM*, XI(1883), 88-92; XIII
(1885), 193-195; XXI(1893), 43; XXII(1894), 19, 137, 138; XXIV(1896),
39-42; XXVI(1897-1898), 116-118, 269-271; XXXI(1902-1903), 212, 213.

3421 ——————. *Vingt-huit années au Congo. Lettres de. . . .*2 vols. Poitiers, 1905.

3422 ——————. "Voyage à Stanley-Pool," *MCL*, XIV(1882), 100, 101, 113-116, 125-128,
140, 141.

3423 Avaert. [*Lt.*]. "Les Makabas," *MG*, V(1888), 67, 70.

3424 ——————. "Sur le Bas-Congo," in Camille Coquilhat, *Sur le Haut-Congo*,
pp. 487-503.

3425 Baerts. "Organisation politique, civile et pénale de la tribu des
Moussoronghes," *BSBG*, XIV(1890), 137-154.

3426    . Baesten, V. "La nouvelle Mission Belge de la Compagnie de Jésus dans l'État indépendant du Congo," *Précis Historiques*, XLI(1892), 193-202.

3427    . Bailey, Henry ["Bula N'Zan," *pseud*.]. *Travels and Adventures in the Congo Free State and Its Big Game Shooting*. London: Chapman and Hall, 1894. 336p.

3428    . Balat. [*Commandant*]. "Les Sakaras et leur Sultan Bangasso," *CIL*, IV(1895), 154-156.

3429    . Baltus, Nicolaus. "Lettres," *Missions en Chine et au Congo*, (1892-1894), 474, 475; (1895-1897), 74-76; (1898-1900), 75-78. See also, *Missiën in China en Congo*, **same period**.

3430    . "La maladie du sommeil," *Belgique Coloniale*, IV(1898), 305-307.

3431    . "La maladie du sommeil a Berghe-Sainte-Marie," *BSBG*, XXII(1898), 341, 342.

3432    . Bas, François de. *Avis impartial dans la question du Congo*. Schiedam: Roelants, 1890. 20p.

3433     . _____. "Een Nederlandsche reiziger aan den Congo," *Tijdschrift van het Nederlandsch Aardrijksundig Genootschap*, III(1886), 339, XII(1895), 353-571, 657-726.

3434     . Bastian, Adolf. *Afrikanische Reisen*. Bremen: H. Strack, 1859. 365p.

3435     . _____. "Les Ba-Kongo," *ZE*, VI(1874).

3436     . _____. "Bericht über seine Reise nach den Congo-ländern," *Correspondenzblatt der Afrikanischen Gesellschaft*, I(1873), 66.

3437     . _____. "Pflanzenweldt der Loango-Küste," *Lotos*, XXIV(1875), 229.

3438     . _____. "Reiseberichte," *Correspondenzblatt der Afrikanischen Gesellschaft*, I(1873), 34, 39, 50, 57.

3439     . _____. "Zum Westafrikanischen Fetischdienst," *ZE*, VI(1874), 1, 80.

3440     . Bateman, Charles Somerville Latrobe. *The First Ascent of the Kasaï: Being Some Records of Serivce under the Lone Star*. New York: Dodd, Mead, 1889. London: Philip & Son, 1889. 192p.

3441     . Baumann, Oscar [*Dr.*]. "An der Küste des Kongostaates," *Deutsche Geographische Blatter*, XI(1888), 320.

3442     . _____. "Die Araber, and den Stanley-Fällen des Congo," *Globus*, LII (1887), 145-148.

3443     . _____. "Ausflug nach Siwa-Siwas Dorf," *MKKG*, XXX(1887), 167.

3444     . _____. *Beiträge zur Ethnographie des Kongo*. Vienna: Hölder, 1887. 22p. See also, *Mitteilungen der Anthropologische Gesellschaft in Wien*, XVII(1887).

3445     . _____. "Beiträge zur physischen Geographie des Kongo," *MKKG*, XXX(1887), 513.

3446    . _____. "Between Victoria-Nyanza and Tanganyika," *GJ*, I(1893), 180.

3447    . _____. "Handel und Plantagenbau im tropischen Afrika," *Österreichische Monatsschrift für den Orient*[Vienna], XIV(1889), 1-7.

3448    . _____. "Handel und Verkehr am Kongo," *Revue coloniale internationale* [Amsterdam], V(1887), 223.

3449    . _____. "Höhenmessungen auf der Route Brazzaville-M'Boma," *MKKG*, XXXI (1887), 529.

3450    . _____. "Österreichische Kongo-Expedition," *MKKG*, XXIX(1886),

3451    . _____. "La station des Stanley-Falls. Description du pays et des habitants de la septième cataracte des Stanley-Falls sur le Congo," *BSBG*, XII(1887), 1-27. See also, *MKKG*, XXIX(1886), 647; XXX(1887), 65, 86, 219.

3452    . _____. *Die Umgebung von Ango-Ango am untern Kongo*. Vienna: Holzel, 1886. 15p. See also, *MKKG*, XXIX(1886), 129-133.

3453    Beck, Henry. "Lettres," *Précis Historiques*, XLVI(1897), 433-435.

3454    . Becker, Jerome Jacques. *La troisième expédition belge au Pays Noir*. Brussels: J. Lebegue, 1889. 313p.

3455    . _____. *La vie en Afrique, ou, trois ans dans l'Afrique.centrale*. 2 vols. Paris. J. Lebèque, 1887.

3456    . Bellet, D. "Une culture coloniale: le kola," *Journal de l'agriculture*, XXIX(1894),

3457    . Bellingham, William. *The Diary of a Working Man in Central Africa, December 1884-October 1887*. London: Society for Promoting Christian Knowledge; New York: Young, 1890. 141p.

3458    . Bennett, Albert L. "Ethnographical Notes on the Fang," *JAI*, XXIX(1899), 66-97.

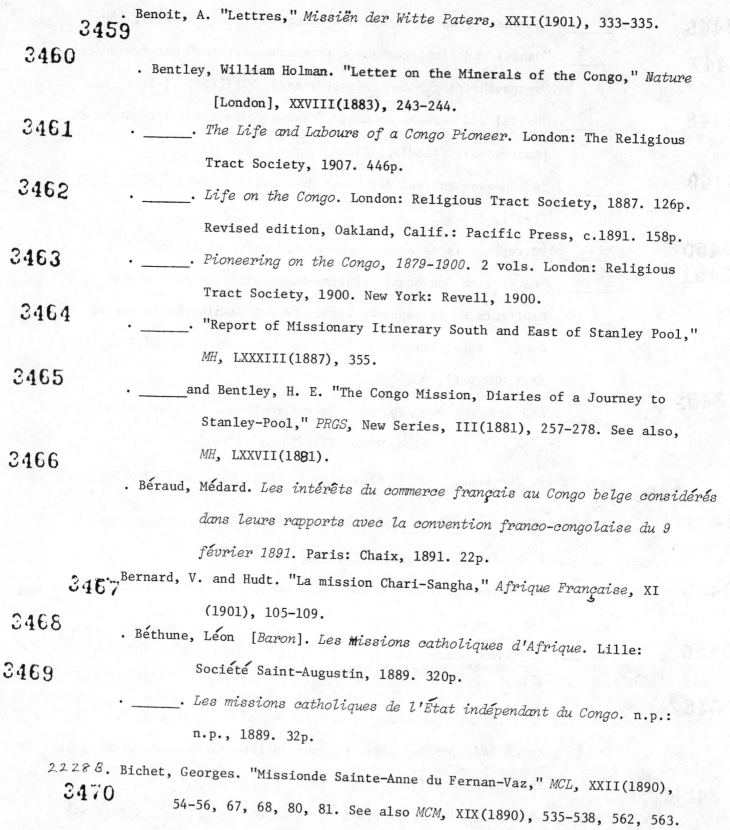

3459 . Benoit, A. "Lettres," *Missiën der Witte Paters*, XXII(1901), 333-335.

3460 . Bentley, William Holman. "Letter on the Minerals of the Congo," *Nature* [London], XXVIII(1883), 243-244.

3461 . _____. *The Life and Labours of a Congo Pioneer*. London: The Religious Tract Society, 1907. 446p.

3462 . _____. *Life on the Congo*. London: Religious Tract Society, 1887. 126p. Revised edition, Oakland, Calif.: Pacific Press, c.1891. 158p.

3463 . _____. *Pioneering on the Congo, 1879-1900*. 2 vols. London: Religious Tract Society, 1900. New York: Revell, 1900.

3464 . _____. "Report of Missionary Itinerary South and East of Stanley Pool," *MH*, LXXXIII(1887), 355.

3465 . _____ and Bentley, H. E. "The Congo Mission, Diaries of a Journey to Stanley-Pool," *PRGS*, New Series, III(1881), 257-278. See also, *MH*, LXXVII(1881).

3466 . Béraud, Médard. *Les intérêts du commerce français au Congo belge considérés dans leurs rapports avec la convention franco-congolaise du 9 février 1891*. Paris: Chaix, 1891. 22p.

3467 Bernard, V. and Hudt. "La mission Chari-Sangha," *Afrique Française*, XI (1901), 105-109.

3468 . Béthune, Léon [*Baron*]. *Les missions catholiques d'Afrique*. Lille: Société Saint-Augustin, 1889. 320p.

3469 . _____. *Les missions catholiques de l'État indépendant du Congo*. n.p.: n.p., 1889. 32p.

2228 B. 3470 Bichet, Georges. "Missionde Sainte-Anne du Fernan-Vaz," *MCL*, XXII(1890), 54-56, 67, 68, 80, 81. See also *MCM*, XIX(1890), 535-538, 562, 563.

. Billiau, Joseph. "Lettres," *Voix du Rédempteur*, VIII(1899), 284, 285.

3471

3472 . Bizemont, H. de. "La dernière expédition française dans l'Afrique équatoriale," *Revue maritime et coloniale*[Paris], XLIV(1879),

3473 . _____. "Une nouvelle expédition dans l'Afrique équatoriale," *Revue maritime et coloniale*[Paris], XLIV(1879),

3474 . Blanquart de Bailleul. *Mission commercial au Congo français. (mai à septembre 1891)*. Rouen: L. Brière, 1892. 28p.

3475 . Blinck, H. [*Dr.*]. *Het Kongo-Land en zijne bewoners in betrekking tot de Europeesche Staatkunde en den Handel*. Haarlem: H. D. Tjeenk, Willinck, 1891. 195p.

3476 . Bodeven, Joachim. "Lettere," *MCM*, XXV(1896), 292.

3477 . _____. "Lettres," *MCL*, XXVIII(1896), 269.

3478 . Bodson, L. "Exploration du Lokepo," *MG*, VII(1890), 13.

3479 . Böhm, R. "Reise von Karema nach Mpala," *MAGD*, IV(1884), 170-179.

3480 . _____; Kaiser, E.; and Reichard, P. "Begrundung der Belgischen Station Mpala. Reise in Marungu, April-Juni 1883," *MAGD*, IV(1884), 79-108, 179-183.

3481 Boel, Alphonse. "Lettres," *Missiën der Witte Paters*, XXII(1901), 294-299, 336-339.

3482 Boghemans, Audomarus. "Lettres," *Missions en Chine et au Congo*, XIII(1901), 169-172.

3483 . Bohl, J. *Nederlands Congobelang*. Amsterdam: Brinckman, 1890. 24p.

3484 . Boshart, August. *Mitteilungen über Stanley's Expedition am Congo*. Munich, 1885.

3485 · Boucherie, Nestor. "Lettres," *Mouvement Antiesclavagiste Belge*, XII(1900), 283; XIV(1902), 272, 273.

3486 · _____. "Lettres," *Verslag van het Werk der katholiche zendingen in Congo Vrijstaat*, III(1900), 175, 176.

3487 · Bouchout, Moretus. "Lettres," *Mouvement Antiesclavagiste Belge*, XIII(1901), 25-29; XIV(1902), 370.

3488 · Bouleuc, Georges. "Lettres," *Annales Apostoliques*, XV(1899-1900), 275, 276.

3489 · Bourdarie, P. "La récolte du caoutchouc," *MG*, XII(1895), 225.

3490 · Bourke, Dermot Robert Wyndham. [*Earl of Mayo*]. *De rebus Africanis. The Claims of Portugal to the Congo and Adjacent Littoral, with Remarks on the French Annexation*. London: W. H. Allen, 1883. 63p.

3491 · Bouysson, J. "L'agriculture au Congo-français," *Revue des Cultures Coloniales*, I(1897), 237-239.

3492 · Bovy, Joseph. "Lettres," *Précis Historiques*, XLIII(1894), 449-454, 530-534; XLIV(1895), 28-31, 297-299.

3493 · Bracq, Oscar. "Lettres," *Missions en Chine et au Congo*, XII(1898-1900), 132-136.

3494 · _____. "Lettres," *Mouvement Antiesclavagiste Belge*, XI(1899), 222; XIII (1901), 31

3495 · _____. "Lettres," *Mouvement des Missions Catholique au Congo*, XX(1908), 73, 74.

3496 · _____. "Lettres," *Verslag van het Werk der katholiche zendingen in Congo Vrijstaat*, II(1899), 30-33, 135; III(1900), 176.

3497 Brandsma, Gorgonius. "Lettres," *Annalen*[Roosendaal], X(1899-1900), 1084, 1085; XIII(1902-1903), 410-412.

3498 Brazza: See Savorgnan de Brazzà.

3499 . Breiner, Michel. "Lettres," *Annales Apostoliques*, IX(1894), 107-110.

3500 . Briart, Paul. "L'expedition Delcommune au Katanga," *MG*, IX(1892), 149.

3501 . _____. *Les fortifications indigènes au Congo*. Brussels: Weissenbruch, 1895. 30p. Also, *CIL*, IV(1895), 12-14, 22-24, 28-30.

3502 . Brielman, Arthur. *Congo Belge. Mission du Kwango, confiée aux Pères Jésuites*. Mont-St. Armand: A. Descheemaecker, 1901. 16p.

3503 . Brielman, Arthur. "Lettres," *Bode van het H. Hart*, XXX(1898-1899), 221-223, 347, 348; XXXI(1899-1900), 187-190.

3504 . _____. "Lettres," *Missions Belges de la Compagnie de Jésus*, I(1899), 10, 167, 365, 366, 405, 406, 409-414; II(1900), 297, 302, 423-428, 451-456; III(1901), 59-65, 108-112.

3505 . _____. "Lettres," *Précis Historiques*, XLV(1896), 196, 197, 422, 423; XLVI (1897), 340-342, XLVII(1898), 513-518, 519-521.

3506 . Brusseaux, E. "Mutilations ethniques observées au Congo," *Anthropologie*, II(1891), 150-154.

3507 . Büchner, Max. "Afrikanische Komplimente und Ceromonien," *Westermanns Monatshefte*, LXIII(1888), 323-327.

3508 . _____. "Afrikanische Waldteufel," *Schorers Familienblatt*, V(1884), 168.

3509 . _____. "Beiträge zur Ethnographie der Bantu," *Ausland*, LVI(1883), 23-27, 107-110, 442-449.

3510    _____. "Die Büchnersche Expedition," *MAGD*, I(1878-1879), 222-246; II(1880-1881), 44-51.

3511    ·_____. "Durch das Land der Songo," *Allgemeine Zeitung*[Munich], July 7, 1883.

3512    ·_____. "Das Ende von Dr. M. Büchner's Reise im südlichen Kongo-Gebiet," *Globus*, XXXIX(1881), 366-368.

3513    ·_____. "Grausamkeit des Muatiamwo," *Vom Fels zum Meer*[Stuttgart], IV (1884).

3514    ·_____. "Die Kioko," *Allgemeine Zeitung*[Munich], Sept. 14-17, 1883.

3515    ·_____. "Kunstgewerbe bei den Negern," *Westermanns Monatshefte*, LXI (1886-1887), 384-396, 514-525.

3516    ·_____. "Kunst und Witz der Neger," *Ausland*, LVII(1884), 9-14.

3517    ·_____. "Die Lukokessa, die gynokratische Köningin des Lunda-Reiches," *Globus*, LI(1887), 135-137.

3518    ·_____. "Meine Sklaven. Ein afrikanisches Stimmungsbild," *Ausland*, LX(1887), 781-786.

3519    ·_____. "Metamorphosen des Christenthums bei den Negern," *Nord und Süd* [Berlin], XLVII(1888), 110-117.

3520    ·_____. "Das Recht in Afrika," *Gegenwart*[Berlin], XXX(1886), 81.

3521    ·_____. "Das Reich des Muatiamvo und seine Nachbarlander," *Deutsche Geographische Blatter*[Bremen], XVII(1893), 56-67.

3522    ·_____. "Seine Expedition," *MAGD*, I(1878-1879), 12, 82, 133, 150, 222, 232, 235, 239; III(1882-1883), 1, 82-88, 224-246.

3523    ·_____. "Eine Totenfeier in Innerafrika," *Ausland*, LX(1887), 340-345.

3524    ·_____. "Über afrikanische Reisetechnik," *Ausland*, LV(1882),

3525    ·_____. "Über den Bau von Hütten und Häusern im tropischen Afrika," *DK*, IV(1887), 382-385.

3526 . _____. "Über den Umgang mit Negern," *DK*, III(1886), 220-221.

3527 . _____. "Über einige Fertigkeiten der Bantu-Neger," *Österreichische Monatschrift für den Orient*[Vienna], X(1884), 103-106.

3528 . _____. "Von Dr. M Büchner's Expedition im Kongo Gebiet," *Globus*, XXXIX(1881), 187-189, 201-202.

3529 . _____. "Vortrag über seine Reise in dem Lunda-Reich," *VGE*, IX(1882), 77-103.

3530 . _____. "Wie lebt man auf einer Afrikareise ?" *Schorers Familienblatt*, V(1884), 232-235.

3531 . _____. "Zur Charakteristik der Bantu-Neger," *Österreichische Monatschrift für den Orient*[Vienna], XIII(1887), 76.

3532 . Büttner, C. G. [*Dr.*]. "Die Bantu-Völker," *Export*[Berlin], X(1888).

3533 . Büttner, Richard. [*Dr.*]. "Die Congo-Expedition," *MAGD*, IV(1884-1885), 309, 314, 369; V(1886-1889), 2-12.

3534 . _____. "Einige Ergebnisse meiner Reise in Westafrika, 1884-86, insbesondere des Landmarsches von San-Salvador über den Quango nach dem Stanley-Pool," *MAGD*, V(1886-1889), 168-271.

3535 . _____. "Die Eroffnung der Kongobahn," *DK*, XV(1898), 248-251.

3536 . _____. "Ethnographische Ergebnisse seiner Reise," *MAGD*, V(1886-1889),

3537 . _____. "In der Residenz des Muene Putu Kassongo," *Vossische Zeitung*[Berlin], 1886, Sonntagsbeilage, n. 45.

3538 . _____. "Reise nach dem Congo, S. Salvador, Stanley Pool, 1885," *MAGD*, V(1886-1889),

3539 . _____. "Reiseberichte," *MAGD*, IV(1884-1885),

3540 . _____. *Reisen im Kongolande*. Leipzig: Hinrichs, 1890. 283p.

3541 . _____. "Über seine Reise von Salvador zum Quango und zum Stanley-Pool," *VGE*, XIII(1886), 300.

3542 . _____. "Von der deutschen Expedition zur Erforschung des südlichen Kongobeckens," *Tägliche Rundschau*[Berlin], 1886, nos. 192-194, 199, 248.

3543 . _____and others. "Berichte über die Kongo-Expedition," *MAGD*, IV(1884-1885), 309.

3544 . Buléon. "Les Pygmées en Afrique," *Mouvement anti-esclavagiste belge* [Brussels], VII(1894), 427.

3545 . Burdo, Adolphe. *Les Arabes dans l'Afrique centrale*. Paris: Dentu, 1885. 48p.

3546 . _____. *Les Belges dans l'Afrique centrale, leurs voyages, aventures et découvertes*. 3 vols. Brussels: Maes, 1884.

3547 . _____. "Rapports des voyageurs de l'Association," *BSBG*, IV(1880), 498. Also, *Association Internationale Africaine*, III(1880), 155-205.

3548 . Burrows, Guy. *The Curse of Central Africa, with Which Is Incorporated a Campaign amongst Cannibals by Edgar Canisius*. London: Everett, 1903. 276p.

3549 . _____. *The Land of Pygmies*. London: Pearson; New York: Crowell, 1898. 299p.

3550 . _____. "On the Natives of the Upper Welle District of the Belgian Congo," *JAI*, XXVIII(1898), 35-47.

3551 . Burton, Richard Francis. *Two Trips to Gorilla Land and the Cataracts of 
3552   the Congo*. 2 vols. London: Sampson Low, 1876.

. _____. "The Upper Congo Versus Europe," *Academy*[London], XXVIII(1883), 239-241.

3553 . Butaye, Achiel. "Lettres," *Missiën der Witte Paters*, XXI(1900), 229, 230, 307-309; XXII(1901), 300-303.

3554 . Buyle, Fréderic. "Lettres," *Missions en Chine et au Congo*, (1892-1894), 347-350, 461, 462. See also, *Missiën in China en Congo*, same period.

3555 . Caldeira, C. J. *Apontamentos d'uma viagem de Lisboa á China*. Vol. II: *Congo*. Lisbon, 1883.

3556 . Callewaert, Emiel. "Lettres," *Portugal em Africa*, VII(1900), 190, 191.

3557 . Calon, Eugène. "Lettres," *Missions en Chine et au Congo*, XII(1898-1900), 399, 400; XIV(1902), 74-76.

3558 . Cambier, Emeri. "Culture en collaboration avec les indigènes," *Bulletin Agricole du Congo Belge*, XXI(1930), 225-234.

3559 . _____. "Lettere," *MCM*, XIX(1890), 4-6; XX(1891), 45-48; XXI(1892), 435-439; XXIII(1894), 238-240, 262-264.

3560 . _____. "Lettres," *Annales Oeuvre Ste Enfance*, XLII(1891), 47-52, 93-97.

3561 . _____. "Lettres," *APFL*, LXII(1890), 144.

3562 . _____. "Lettres," *Belgique Coloniale*, III(1897), 236, 237; V(1899), 260, 292-294, 305, 306.

3563 . _____. "Lettres," *BSBG*, XIX(1895), 636-640.

3564 . _____. "Lettres," *Congo Belge*, V(1900), 140-142.

3565 . _____. "Lettres," *MCL*, XXI(1889), 567-569.

3566 . _____. "Lettres," *MG*, X(1893), 38.

3567 . _____. "Lettres," *Missions en Chine et au Congo*, (1889-1891), 12 -14,25-30, 42-47, 92-96, 110-112, 123-128, 156-159, 176, 204-206, 239, 285-287, 345-351, 362-368, 412-415, 429-431; (1892-1894), 124-128, 234-239, 441-446, 509, 510; (1895-1897), 42-44, 120-123, 169-172, 173, 202-207, 294-299, 434, 435; (1898-1900), 486-489. See also, *Missiën in China en Congo*, same period.

3568 . _____. "Lettres," *Mouvement Antiesclavagiste*, III(1891), 199-203.

3569 ———————. "La tribu des Zappo-Zappo," in *La vérité sur la civilisation au Congo par un Belge* [de Hauleville]. Brussels: Lebègue, 1903. 178-184.

3570 Cambier, Ernest François.[*Capt.*]. *Conférence sur l'Afrique centrale.* Brussels: Cnophis fils, 1881. 31p.

3571 ———————. "Études du chemin de fer du Congo," *MG*, V(1888), 99.

3572 ———————. "Die Expeditionen der Internationalen Afrikanischen Association," *MAGD*, II(1880-1881).

3573 ———————. "Rapports sur les marches de la première expedition," *BSBG*, II (1878), 472-484. Also, *Association internationale africaine*, I(1879), 21-55, 65-84, 103-106, 113-115.

3574 ———————and others. "Le chemin de fer du Congo," *BSRGA*, XIII(1888-1889).

3575 Cameron, Verney Lovett. "Le commerce de l'Afrique," *BSRGA*, XVI(1891), 261-280.

3576 Cammaert. "De Bangasso à Kinshassa," *MG*, XI(1894), 77.

3577 Campana, Pascal. "Cartas," *Portugal em Africa*, VII(1900), 340.

3578 ———————. "Lettere," *MCM*, XXVIII(1899), 329; XXIX(1900), 388.

3579 ———————. "Lettres," *Annales Apostoliques*, XVI(1900-1901), 42, 43, 286, 287.

3580 ———————. "Lettres," *Annales Oeuvre Ste-Enfance*, XLIV(1893), 44-51.

3581 ———————. "Lettres," *APFL*, LXI(1889), 203-216; LXXII(1900), 472, 473.

3582 ———————. "Lettres," *MCL*, XXXI(1899), 306; XXXII(1900), 362.

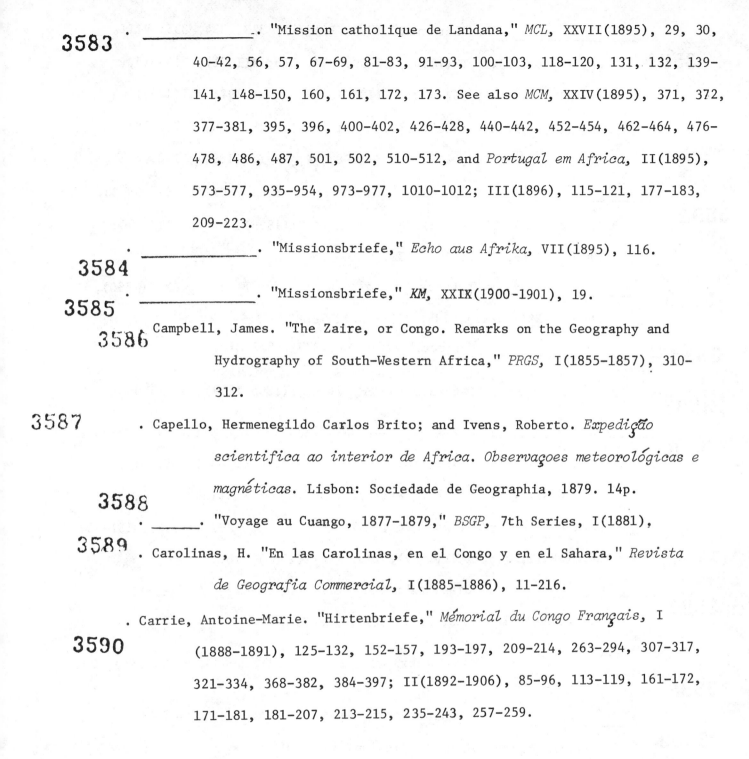

3583 . _____. "Mission catholique de Landana," *MCL*, XXVII(1895), 29, 30, 40-42, 56, 57, 67-69, 81-83, 91-93, 100-103, 118-120, 131, 132, 139-141, 148-150, 160, 161, 172, 173. See also *MCM*, XXIV(1895), 371, 372, 377-381, 395, 396, 400-402, 426-428, 440-442, 452-454, 462-464, 476-478, 486, 487, 501, 502, 510-512, and *Portugal em Africa*, II(1895), 573-577, 935-954, 973-977, 1010-1012; III(1896), 115-121, 177-183, 209-223.

3584 . _____. "Missionsbriefe," *Echo aus Afrika*, VII(1895), 116.

3585 . _____. "Missionsbriefe," *KM*, XXIX(1900-1901), 19.

3586 Campbell, James. "The Zaire, or Congo. Remarks on the Geography and Hydrography of South-Western Africa," *PRGS*, I(1855-1857), 310-312.

3587 . Capello, Hermenegildo Carlos Brito; and Ivens, Roberto. *Expedição scientifica ao interior de Africa. Observaçoes meteorológicas e magnéticas*. Lisbon: Sociedade de Geographia, 1879. 14p.

3588 . _____. "Voyage au Cuango, 1877-1879," *BSGP*, 7th Series, I(1881),

3589 . Carolinas, H. "En las Carolinas, en el Congo y en el Sahara," *Revista de Geografia Commercial*, I(1885-1886), 11-216.

3590 . Carrie, Antoine-Marie. "Hirtenbriefe," *Mémorial du Congo Français*, I (1888-1891), 125-132, 152-157, 193-197, 209-214, 263-294, 307-317, 321-334, 368-382, 384-397; II(1892-1906), 85-96, 113-119, 161-172, 171-181, 181-207, 213-215, 235-243, 257-259.

3591 . "Lettere," *MCM*, VI(1877), 323, 334, 335; VIII (1879), 340, 341; IX(1880), 97-99, 592, 616; X(1881), 313-315, 349-351, 469-474, 567-570; XI(1882), 147, 148, 292; XII(1883), 517-519; XVI(1887), 585, 586, XVIII(1889), 229, 230, 277, 278; XXV(1896), 205-208, 411; XXVII(1898), 4; XXVIII(1899), 148.

3592 . "Lettres," *Annales Apostoliques*, III(1888), 36-38, 151; V(1890), 118; VIII(1893),76, 110, 111; XI(1896), 41-50; XVI(1900-1901), 52-56, XVII(1901), 22.

3593 . "Lettres," *Annales Oeuvre Ste-Enfance*, XXXI(1880), 35-37; XXXII(1881), 136, 137; XXXIII(1882), 316-319.

3594 . "Lettres," *APFL*, LI(1879), 372-375.

3595 . "Lettres," *BGCSS*, VI(XIX)(1898-1899), 520-530.

3596 . "Lettres," *MCL*, IX(1877), 197-199; XI(1879), 333-335; XII(1880), 85-87; XIII(1881), 217-219, 435, 436, 447, 448, 517; XIV(1882), 134, 135, 279; XV(1883), 505, 506; XIX(1887), 565, 566; XXI(1889), 217-219, 265, 266;,XXIII(1891), 23; XXVIII(1896), 181-184; XXIX(1897), 566; XXXI(1899), 125; XXXII(1900), 76.

3597 . "Missionsbriefe," *Echo aus Afrika*, VII(1895), 5; VIII(1896), 125, 126; XIII(1901), 208-210.

3598 . "Missionsbriefe," *KM*, X(1882), 89-95; XXIV(1896), 234.

3599 . *Organisation de la Mission du Congo Français.* Loango: Imprimerie de la Mission, 1898. 109p.

3600 _____. "Une visite à Saint-Antoine de Sogno (Congo)," *MCL*, X(1878), 472-474, 485, 486, 496-498, 524-526, 536-538. See also, *MCM*, VII(1878), 500-502, 523, 524, 586-588, 609-611, and *KM*, VII(1879), 65-71, 98-102.

3601 _____. "Voyage dans le Haut-Congo à l'Oubanghi[Afrique equatoriale]," *MCL*, XX(1888), 342-345, 353-356. See also, *MCM*, XVIII(1889), 154, 155, 176-178.

3602 _____. "Voyage de Mgr. Carrie dans le Haut-Congo," *Bulletin de la Congrégation*, I(XIV)(1887-1888), 482-492.

3603 · Carvalho, Henrique de. "Expedição ao Muata Yanvo," *BSGL*, V(1885), 476.

3604 · _____. *Expedição portugueza ao Muatianvua, 1884-1888*. 4 vols. Lisbon: Imprensa naçional, 1890.

3605 · _____. *O Lubuco. Algumas observaçoes sobre o livro do Sr. Latrobe Bateman, intitulado: The First Ascent of the Kasai*. Lisbon: Imprensa naçional, 1889. 59p.

3606 · _____. *A Lunda ou os Estados do Muatianvua, dominios da soberania de Portugal*. Lisbon, 1890. 422p.

3607 · Casman, W. "Journal d'un voyage entre Léopoldville et l'équateur," *MG*, II(1885), 38.

3608 · Castellani, Charles Jules. *Les femmes au Congo*. Paris: Flammarion, 1899. 307p.

3609 · Castro, A. J. de. [*Major da provincia*]. "O Congo em 1845. Roteiro da viagem ao reino do Congo. . .em Junho de 1845," *BSGL*, II(1880-1881), 53-67.

3610 · Cattier and Wodon. "Enquête sur les coutumes des peuplades congolaises," *Bulletin de la Société d'études coloniales*, I(1894),

3611 · Cauderlier, E. *Le gin et le Congo*. Brussels: Lefebvre, 1895. 24p.

3612 · Cauteren, Willem van. *Trente histoires de congolais, scènes vécues en Afrique*. Brussels: Maison du Jass, n.d.. 168p.

3613 · _____. *Vers le Katanga de Banana à Pweto*. Brussels: Publications de la Société d'Études Coloniales de Belgique, 1904. 43p.

3614 · Cerisier, Charles. *Le Congo français en 1892. Éléments de statistique et d'appréciation du pays*. Nancy: Berger-Levrault, 1892. 16p.

3615 · Chaillé-Long, Charles. "Note sur les Pygmées de l'Afrique," *BSKG*, 1891.

3615 . Chalot, Charles. *Le Cacaoyer et sa culture*. Libreville: Imprimerie du Gouvernement, 1895. Also, Paris: G. Carré et C. Naud, 1897. 121p.

3617 . _____. *Notice sur la concession de M. Hallez d'Arros dans le Como*. Paris: Challamel, 1898. 23p.

3618 . _____. "La région équatoriale," *Revues des cultures coloniales*, I (1897), 202-205.

3619 . Chaltin. [*Capt.*]. "De Bazolo a l'Uellé. Exploration de la rivière Lulu," *MG*, IX(1892), 58.

3620 . _____. "Le Congo au point de vue physique, politique et économique," *BSRGA*, X(1885), 450-478.

3621 . _____. "Le district de l'Aruwimi-Uellé. Aperçu économique sur les régions de l'Aruwimi de la Lulu, du Rubi, de la Tele, du Bas-Lomami et de la partie du Congo comprise entre Isangi et le confluent de l'Itimbiri," *CIL*, IV(1895), 108-110, 114-116, 122-123.

3622 . _____. "Exploration de la Lulu et de l'Aruwimi," *CIL*, III(1894), 105-108.

3623 . _____. "La question arabe au Congo," *Bulletin de la Société belge d'études colonials*, I(1894), 163-196.

3624 . _____. "Rapport sur la révolte des Arabes du Lualaba et du Lomami," *MG*, IX(1892), 92.

3625 . Charmanne, H. "Le chemin de fer du Congo de Matadi à Léopoldville," *BSRGA*, XIV(1889), 375-390. Also, *BSBG*, XIII(1889), 149-183.

3626 . _____. "Conférence," *MG*, IX(1892), 119.

3627 . _____. "L'expédition du chemin de fer," *MG*, V(1888), 90.

3628 . Chavanne, Josef. [*Dr.*] "Die Handelsverhältnisse im Kongo-Staate und dem benachbarten Freihandels-Gebiete," *Österreichische Monatsschrift für den Orient*[Vienna], Das Handels-Museum, beilage, XII(1886),

3629    . _____. "Die Kongobahn," *Deutsche Rundschau für Geographie und Statistik*
              IX(1886), 241.

3630    . _____. *Reisen und Forschungen im alten und neuen Kongo-Staate in den*
              *Jahren 1884 und 1885.* Jena: H. Costenoble, 1887. 508p.

3631    . Chavannes, Charles de. *Mission de Brazza au Congo. Exposé sommaire de*
              *voyage dans l'Ouest africain.* Lyon: Mougin-Rusand, 1886. 39p.

3632    Cholet, J. "L'exploration de la Sangha," *MG*, VII(1890), 112.

3633    . Claeys, Adolf. "Lettres," *Maandelijksch Verslag der Afrikaansche Missiën,*
              XVIII(1897), 73-75; XIX(1898), 47-50.

3634    . _____. "Lettres," *Missions d'Afrique*, XIX(1898), 51-54.

3635    Clark, H. F. "The Congo Missions," *Missionary Review of the World*, XIII
              (1890), 826-833.

3636    . Claver, Pierre. "Lettres," *Annalen der Afrikaansche Missiën*, XIV(1897-1898),
              147-151; XVI(1899-1900), 362, 363.

3637    . Clément de Saint-Marcq. "De l'alimentation des noirs entre les falls
              et Kassongo," *MG*, VII(1890), 42.

3638    . Cneut, Camille. "Lettres," *Congo Belge*, II(1897), 236.

3639    . _____. "Lettres," *Missions en Chine et au Congo*, (1895-1897), 293, 294,
              521, 522; (1898-1900), 30-32, 170-172, 402-403; (1901), 160-165,
              238, 239; (1902), 93. See also, same period, *Missiën in China en*
              *Congo.*

3640    . _____. "Lettres," *Mouvement Antiesclavagiste Belge*, XI(1899), 94; XII
              (1900), 51; XIII(1901), 174, 175; XIV(1902), 16-19.

3641    . _____. "Lettres," *Verslag van het Werk der katholiche zendingen in*
              *Congo Vrijstaat*, III(1900), 34; IV(1901), 117-119.

3642    . Cocheteux. "Contribution à l'étude de l'anthropologie du Congo,"
              *Bulletin de la Société d'anthropologie de Bruxelles*, VIII
              (1889-1890), 75-106.

3643 Colle, Pierre. "Lettres," *Missions d'Afrique*, XX(1899), 161-165, 257-263, 377-380; XXII(1901), 10-17, 65-69, 123, 124.

3644 ———. "Lettres," *Missien der Witte Paters*, XX(1899), 278-283; XXI(1900), 123, 124; XXII(1901), 42-48.

3645 . Comber, T. J. "A Boat Journey Round Stanley Pool," *PRGS*, New Series, VI(1884), 71-75.

3646 . ———. "Brief Account of Recent Journeys in the Interior of the Congo," *PRGS*, New Series, III(1881), 20-26.

3647 . ———. "The Congo Mission," *MH*, LXXVIII(1882).

3648 . ———. "Explorations Inland from Mount Cameroons and Journey through the Congo to Makuta," *PRGS*, New Series, I(1879), 225-240.

3649 . ———. "Explorations Round Congo," *MH*, LXXVI(1880), 401-404.

3650 . ——— and Grenfell, George. "The Congo Mission: Tidings from the Interior," *MH*, LXXXI(1885), 6.

3651 . Comte, Paul. *Les N'Sakkaras, leur pays, leurs moeurs, leurs coutumes, leurs croyances, etc., avec un glossaire N'Sakkara, par un membre de la mission française du Haut-Oubangui(1893-1895).* Bar-le-Duc: Comte-Jacquet, 1895. 136p.

3652 . Coquilhat, Camille. "Le Capitaine Hanssens en Afrique," *BSBG*, X(1886), 5.

3653 . ———. "Le Congo et la tribu des Bangalas," *BSBG*, IX(1885), 625-647.

3654 . ———. "Le Haut-Congo," *BSRGA*, X(1885-1886), 231-248.

3655 . ———. "Rapport sur l'évacuation de la station des Stanley-Falls," *MG*, III(1886), 107.

3656 . ———. "Les rites funéraires et la cannibalisme au Congo," *Bollettino Società africana d'Italia. Sezione fiorentina*[Florence], V (1889).

3657       . _____. *Sur le Haut-Congo*. Brussels: Office de publicité, 1888. 535p.

3658       Paris: Lebèque, 1888. 533p.

     . Cordeiro, Luciano. "Lettre sur le pays du Muata Jamvo," *JMGS*, IV(1888), 182.

3659       . _____. *Portugal and the Congo*. London: Stanford, 1883. 104p.

3660       . _____. "Les premières explorations de l'Afrique centrale," *Bulletin de la Société de Géographie de Lyon*, II(1876).

3661       . _____. *La question de Zaire. Lettre à Behaghel*. Lisbon, 1883.

3662      . Corio, L. *I commerci dell'Africa*. Milan: Bellini & Co., 1890. 468p.

3663      . Cornet, Jules. *Observations sur les terrains anciens du Katanga faites au cours de l'expédition Bia-Francqui (1891-93)*. Liège: Vailant-Carmanne, 1897. 170p.

3664      . Costermans. [*Lt.*]. "Le district de Stanley-Pool," *Bulletin de la Société Belge d'Études Coloniales*, II(1895), 24-76.

3665      . Coullous. [*Père*]. "Les missions de Kibonga et de Mpala," *MCL*, XX(1888), 325.

3666      . Crampel, Paul. "Congo français: au pays des M'fans," *Journal des Voyages*, XXVII(1890), 321.

3667      . _____. "Notes sur les conditions climatologiques du Congo français au-dessus et au-dessous de l'équateur," *CRSG*, X(1891), 307.

3668      . Crawford, Daniel. *Back to the Long Grass. My Link with Livingstone*. London: Hodder and Stoughton, 1922. 373p. New York: Doubleday, 1923.

3669      . _____. *Thinking Black. Twenty-Two Years without a Break in the Long Grass of Central Africa*. London: Morgan & Scott, 1912. 485p. New York: Doran, 1913. 485p.

3670 . Croonenberghs, Eugenius. "Lettres," *Missiën in China en Congo*, (1898-1900), 169; XIV(1902), 93, 281-286.

3671 . Crudgington, Henry E. and Bentley, W. Holman. "The Recent Journey of Messrs Crudgington and Bentley to Stanley Pool, on the Congo," *PRGS*, New Series, III(1881), 553-560.

3672 . Cureau, A. [*Dr.*]. "Congo: Les états Zandés," *Revue Coloniale* [Paris: Ministre des colonies], V(1899), 707-713; VI(1900), 766-772.

3673 . Cus, Alphonse. "Lettres," *Missions Belges de la Compagnie de Jésus*, II(1900), 418-423, 460-462; III(1901), 74-77, 115-118, 273-275; IV(1902), 194-197, 221-229, 361, 362, 415-419, 429-437.

3674 . Daenen. [*Capt.*]. "Les sacrifices humains dans le Bas-Congo," *MG*, IV(1887), 83-84.

3675 . Danckelman, Alexander Sylvester Flavius Ernst. [*Freiherr von*]. "Bemerkungen zu den Höhenmessungen der Ostafrikanischen Expedition," *MAGD*, V(1886-1889), 78.

3676 . _____. "Brief vom Kongo," *PM*, XXIX(1883), 388.

3677 . _____. *Das Congo-Gebiet*. Elberfeld: Asher, 92p.

3678 . _____. "Kalamba. Negercharacter. Ackerbau. Landwerke. Religionsitten. Gebraüche," *MAGD*, IV(1884-1885), 242-262.

3679 . _____. "Die Pogge-Wissmansche Expedition. Mit aus Pogges Tagebüchern," *MAGD*, IV(1884-1885), 228.

3680 . Daniel, P. *Meine Brüder, die Neger in Afrika. Ihr Wesen, ihre Befähigung, ihre jetzige traurige Lage, ihre Hoffnungen. Ein ernstes Wort . . .von einem Neger, früher Sklave, jetzt Missionar.* Münster: W. W. Helms, 1892.

3681 . Dannfelt. [*Lt.*]. "Les indigènes du Bas-Congo," *MG*, V(1888), 1; VII(1890), 19.

3682 . Dean, John M. *Cross of Christ in Bolo-Land*. Edinburgh: Oliphant, Anderson, and Ferrier, 1902. 233p. New York: Revell, 1902.

3683 . De Backer, Albertus. "Lettres," *Missions en Chine et au Congo,* (1889-1891), 300-303, 457-462, 544. See also, *Missiën in China en Congo,* same period.

3684 . _____. "Lettres," *Mouvement Antiesclavagiste,* IV(1892), 149.

3685 . De Beerst, Gustave. "Lettres," *Annalen der Afrikaansche Missiën,* XI (1894-1895), 130-134.

3686 . _____. "Lettres," *Maandelijksch Verslag der Afrikaansche Missiën,* XII (1891), 259-264, 306-314; XV(1894), 119-123, 211-217, 248-252, 283-287, 311-315, 337-341; XVI(1895), 8-11, 243-246; XVIII(1897), 184-188.

3687 . _____. "Lettres," *Missions d'Afrique,* (1895-1897), 98-101, 516-523, 542-545.

3688 . _____. "Lettres," *Missions d'Alger,* (1893-1894), 257-260.

3689 . Decazes. "Notes sur quelques peuplades de l'ouest Africain, Mfans, Bateke," *Bulletin de Géographie Historique et Descriptive,* II(1887), 150-156, 195.

3690 . De Cleene, Natalis. "Lettres," *Missions en Chine et au Congo,* (1898-1900), 451-462; (1901), 19-24, 240; (1902), 30, 95, 128-131. See also, *Missiën in China en Congo,* same period.

3691 . _____. "Die Schülerkolonien in Belgisch-Kongo," KM, XXVII (1898-1899), 78-81, 104-107. See also, *Missions en Chine et au Congo,* (1898-1900), 87-96, 97-103, and *Missiën in China en Congo,* same period.

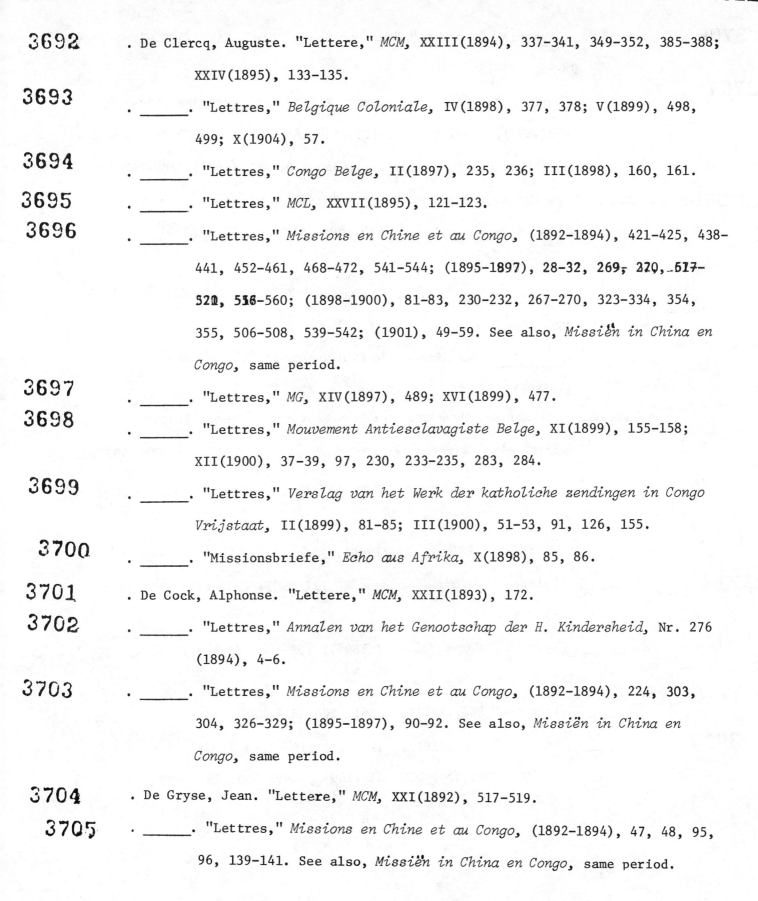

3692　. De Clercq, Auguste. "Lettere," *MCM*, XXIII(1894), 337-341, 349-352, 385-388; XXIV(1895), 133-135.

3693　. _____. "Lettres," *Belgique Coloniale*, IV(1898), 377, 378; V(1899), 498, 499; X(1904), 57.

3694　. _____. "Lettres," *Congo Belge*, II(1897), 235, 236; III(1898), 160, 161.

3695　. _____. "Lettres," *MCL*, XXVII(1895), 121-123.

3696　. _____. "Lettres," *Missions en Chine et au Congo*, (1892-1894), 421-425, 438-441, 452-461, 468-472, 541-544; (1895-1897), 28-32, 269, 270, 517-520, 558-560; (1898-1900), 81-83, 230-232, 267-270, 323-334, 354, 355, 506-508, 539-542; (1901), 49-59. See also, *Missiën in China en Congo*, same period.

3697　. _____. "Lettres," *MG*, XIV(1897), 489; XVI(1899), 477.

3698　. _____. "Lettres," *Mouvement Antiesclavagiste Belge*, XI(1899), 155-158; XII(1900), 37-39, 97, 230, 233-235, 283, 284.

3699　. _____. "Lettres," *Verslag van het Werk der katholiche zendingen in Congo Vrijstaat*, II(1899), 81-85; III(1900), 51-53, 91, 126, 155.

3700　. _____. "Missionsbriefe," *Echo aus Afrika*, X(1898), 85, 86.

3701　. De Cock, Alphonse. "Lettere," *MCM*, XXII(1893), 172.

3702　. _____. "Lettres," *Annalen van het Genootschap der H. Kindersheid*, Nr. 276 (1894), 4-6.

3703　. _____. "Lettres," *Missions en Chine et au Congo*, (1892-1894), 224, 303, 304, 326-329; (1895-1897), 90-92. See also, *Missiën in China en Congo*, same period.

3704　. De Gryse, Jean. "Lettere," *MCM*, XXI(1892), 517-519.

3705　. _____. "Lettres," *Missions en Chine et au Congo*, (1892-1894), 47, 48, 95, 96, 139-141. See also, *Missiën in China en Congo*, same period.

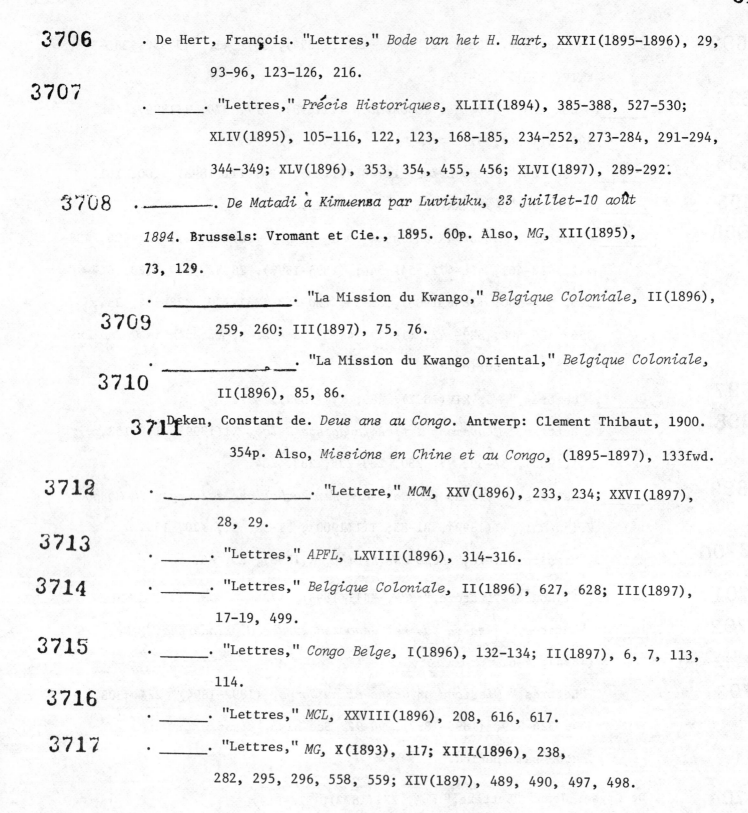

3706 . De Hert, François. "Lettres," *Bode van het H. Hart*, XXVII(1895-1896), 29, 93-96, 123-126, 216.

3707 . _____. "Lettres," *Précis Historiques*, XLIII(1894), 385-388, 527-530; XLIV(1895), 105-116, 122, 123, 168-185, 234-252, 273-284, 291-294, 344-349; XLV(1896), 353, 354, 455, 456; XLVI(1897), 289-292.

3708 . _____. *De Matadi à Kimuensa par Luvituku, 23 juillet-10 août 1894*. Brussels: Vromant et Cie., 1895. 60p. Also, *MG*, XII(1895), 73, 129.

3709 . _____. "La Mission du Kwango," *Belgique Coloniale*, II(1896), 259, 260; III(1897), 75, 76.

3710 . _____. "La Mission du Kwango Oriental," *Belgique Coloniale*, II(1896), 85, 86.

3711 . Deken, Constant de. *Deus ans au Congo*. Antwerp: Clement Thibaut, 1900. 354p. Also, *Missions en Chine et au Congo*, (1895-1897), 133fwd.

3712 . _____. "Lettere," *MCM*, XXV(1896), 233, 234; XXVI(1897), 28, 29.

3713 . _____. "Lettres," *APFL*, LXVIII(1896), 314-316.

3714 . _____. "Lettres," *Belgique Coloniale*, II(1896), 627, 628; III(1897), 17-19, 499.

3715 . _____. "Lettres," *Congo Belge*, I(1896), 132-134; II(1897), 6, 7, 113, 114.

3716 . _____. "Lettres," *MCL*, XXVIII(1896), 208, 616, 617.

3717 . _____. "Lettres," *MG*, X(1893), 117; XIII(1896), 238, 282, 295, 296, 558, 559; XIV(1897), 489, 490, 497, 498.

3718 . Delcommune, A. *Alexandre Joseph Philippe.* "Les affluents du Congo debouchant près de la station de l'équateur," *MG*, VII(1890), 108.

3719 . _____. "Exploration de la Lulonga," *MG*, VI(1889), 61.

3720 . _____. "Exploration de Luaba et de Katanga. Decouverte du lac Kassali et du gorges de Nzilo. Rapport," *MG*, IX(1892), 139-142.

3721 . _____. "L'exploration du Lomami," *MG*, VI(1889), 29, 59.

3722 . _____. "Les explorations du steamer (*Le Roi des Belges*) dans le district de Tippo-Tip," *MG*, VI(1889), 65.

3723 . _____. "Rapport sur la region des chutes," *MG*, V(1888), 24.

3724 . _____. "Relation du voyage de Mpala à Luzambo," *MG*, X(1893), 39.

3725 . _____. "Voyage au Katanga," *BSRGA*, XVIII(1893), 236-241.

3726 . _____. "Exploration du Ruki et du Lac Matumba," *CIL*, I(1892), 197-199, 205-207, 214-215.

3727 . _____. *Vingt anneés de vie africaine. Récits de voyages d'aventures et d'exploration au Congo belge, 1874-1893.* 2 vols. Brussels: Larcier, 1922.

3728 . Deligne, Erneste. "Coutumes nègres," *CIL*, II(1893), 122.

3729 . _____. "Quelques légendes bangala," *CIL*, II(1893), 82.

3730 . _____. "La tribu des Banza," *CIL*, III(1894), 68.

3731 . Delisle, F. [*Dr.*]. "La mission Dybowski. Parure et industries diverses," *Nature*, XXI(1893), 55-58.

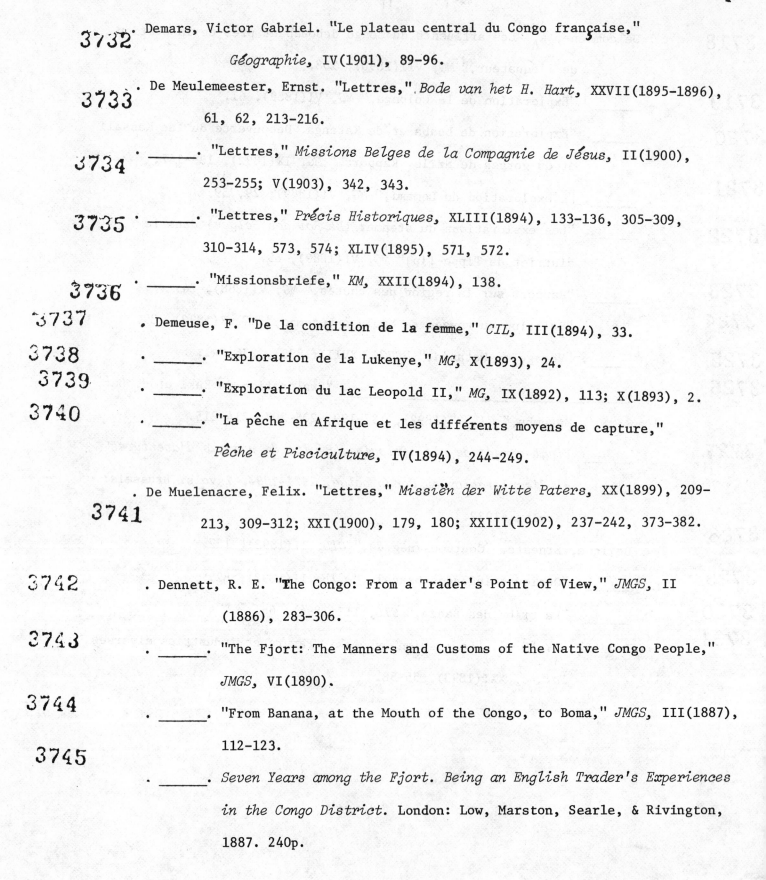

3732 . Demars, Victor Gabriel. "Le plateau central du Congo française," *Géographie*, IV(1901), 89-96.

3733 . De Meulemeester, Ernst. "Lettres," *Bode van het H. Hart*, XXVII(1895-1896), 61, 62, 213-216.

3734 . _____. "Lettres," *Missions Belges de la Compagnie de Jésus*, II(1900), 253-255; V(1903), 342, 343.

3735 . _____. "Lettres," *Précis Historiques*, XLIII(1894), 133-136, 305-309, 310-314, 573, 574; XLIV(1895), 571, 572.

3736 . _____. "Missionsbriefe," *KM*, XXII(1894), 138.

3737 . Demeuse, F. "De la condition de la femme," *CIL*, III(1894), 33.

3738 . _____. "Exploration de la Lukenye," *MG*, X(1893), 24.

3739 . _____. "Exploration du lac Leopold II," *MG*, IX(1892), 113; X(1893), 2.

3740 . _____. "La pêche en Afrique et les différents moyens de capture," *Pêche et Pisciculture*, IV(1894), 244-249.

3741 . De Muelenacre, Felix. "Lettres," *Missiën der Witte Paters*, XX(1899), 209-213, 309-312; XXI(1900), 179, 180; XXIII(1902), 237-242, 373-382.

3742 . Dennett, R. E. "The Congo: From a Trader's Point of View," *JMGS*, II (1886), 283-306.

3743 . _____. "The Fjort: The Manners and Customs of the Native Congo People," *JMGS*, VI(1890).

3744 . _____. "From Banana, at the Mouth of the Congo, to Boma," *JMGS*, III(1887), 112-123.

3745 . _____. *Seven Years among the Fjort. Being an English Trader's Experiences in the Congo District.* London: Low, Marston, Searle, & Rivington, 1887. 240p.

3746 . Derikx, Leo. "Lettres," *Het H. Misoffer*, III(1900), 94-98, 166, 167, 222-224, 237-240; IV(1901), 40-43, 55-58, 77-79, 104, 148, 171-173, 188-191; V(1902), 38-41, 110-112, 117-121, 160-164.

3747 . Destrain, E. "Productions et négoce du bassin du Kwilou-Niadi," *BSBG*, X(1886), 115-123.

3748 . De Vulder, Gustaaf. "Lettres," *Missiën der Witte Paters*, XXII(1901), 294-299.

3749 . De Winton, Francis. "The Congo Free State," *PRGS*, New Series, VIII(1886), 609-624.

3750 . Dhanis, Francis. [*Baron*]. *Le baron Francis Dhanis au Kwango et pendant la campagne Arabe*. Antwerp: J. B. van Caneghem, 1910. 32p.

3751 . _____. "La campagne Arabe du Manyema," *CIL*, IV(1895), 25-27, 33-35, 41-43, 60-63, 68-70, 77-79.

3752 . _____. "Le district d'Upoto et la fondation du camp de l'Arouwimi," *BSBG*, XIV(1890), 5-45. See also, same title, *Publications de l'Etat indépendant du Congo*, No. 3, 44p.

3753 . _____. "La région au Sud du Stanley-Pool de Lutete au Kwango," *Annales de Géographie*, IV(1894), 227. See also, *MG*, XI(1894).

3754 . Dierkes, Bernard. "Lettres," *Mouvement Antiesclavagiste Belge*, XI(1899), 93; XII(1900), 98, 275-277; XIII(1901), 146.

3755 . _____. "Lettres," *Verslag van het Werk der katholiche zendingen in Congo Vrijstaat*, II(1899), 51; III(1900), 109-112.

3756 . Donckier de Donceel, F. "Les productions végétales et animales de consommation et d'exportation dans le bassin du Congo," *Journal de l'Association des anciens élèves de l'Institut agricole de Gemblous* [Gembloux, Belgium], VI(1895), 391.

3757 . Doppler, Alphons. "Lettres," *MCL*, XXXII(1900), 266; XXXV(1903), 400.

3758 . Douville, Jean-Baptiste. *Trente mois de ma vie, quinze mois avant et quinze mois après mon voyage au Congo, ou, ma justification des infamies débitées contre moi.* Paris: The author, 1833. 399p.

3759 . _____. *Voyage au Congo et dans l'intérieur de l'Afrique Équinoxiale, fait dans les années 1828, 1829 et 1830.* 3 vols. Paris: Redouard, 1832. Spanish translation, 4 vols., Madrid: Tomás Jordán, 1833.

3760 . Droogmans, Hubert. *Notices sur le Bas-Congo.* Brussels: Vanlurggenhandt, 1901.

3761 . Du Couret, L. [Hadji-abd-el-Hamid Bey, *pseud.*]. *Voyage au pays des Niam-Niam ou hommes à queue.* Paris: Martimon, 1854. 105p.

3762 . Duloup, G. "Huit jours chez les Mbenga," *Bulletin de la Société de Géographie de Lille*, III(1884), 39-53.

3763 . Duparquet, Charles-Victor-Albert. "Lettres," *BSGP*, Sixth Series, VII(1874), 530-532; XII(1876), 412-426.

3764 . Dupont, Édouard François. *Compte rendu sommaire de la conférence donnée par M. Ed. Dupont sur les résultats de ses exploitations géologiques au Congo.* Brussels: Polleunis, 1888. 28p.

3765 . _____. *Conference donnée, le 29 février 1888, à la Société belge des Ingénieurs et des Industriels sur les resultats de l'exploration scientifique qu'il a faite au Congo en juillet-décembre 1887.* Brussels: Imprimerie des Travaux publics, 1888. 18p.

3766 . _____. "Les cultures au Stanley-Pool," *MG*, IV(1887), 109.

3767 . _____. *Lettres sur le Congo. Récit d'un voyage scientifique entre l'embouchure du fleuve et le confluent du Kassai.* Paris: C. Reinwald, 1889. 724p.

3768 . _____. "Die Oberflächenbildungen des Kongo-Beckens," *VGE*, XV(1888), 490.

3769    . Dutrieux. [*Dr.*]. "Notes d'anthropologie," *Association Internationale Africaine*, I(1879), 85-98. Also, *BSBG*, IV(1880), 102-114.

3770    . _____. "La question africaine au point de vue commercial(Conférences données à l'Union syndicale les 9 et 23 mars 1880)," *Bulletin de l'Union Syndicale de Bruxelles*, 1880.

3771    . _____. "Rapports sur les marches de la première expédition," *Association Internationale Africaine*, I(1879), 5-20, 57-60.

3772    . Dybowski, Jean. "L'agriculture et l'industrie chez les noirs du Congo," *MG*, X(1893), 26.

3773    . _____. "Exploitation des produits du Congo," *Nouvelle Revue*, 1893, p.663.

3774    . _____. "La route de Brazzaville," *Nature*[Paris], XX(1892), 119-122.

3775    . _____. "Mission au Congo français," *CRSG*, XIII(1894), 220-221.

3776    . _____. "Pygmées du Congo," *Nature*[Paris], XXII(1894), 305.

3777    . Ekhoff, Emil. *Om en samling af etnog. föremäl, hemförda af Svenska Kongofarare*. **Ymer**, 1886. 308p.

3778    . Ellitoo, Grant. "Exploration et organisation de la province du Kwilou-Niadi," *BSBG*, X(1886), 101-122.

3779    . Engels, Alfons. "Lettere," *MCM*, XXI(1892), 63, 64.

3780    . _____. "Lettres," *Maandelijksch Verslag der Afrikaansche Missiën*, XVIII (1897), 70-73; XIX(1898), 374-379.

3781    . _____. "Lettres," *Missions d'Afrique*, XIX(1898), 227-231.

3782    . Eucher, Roy. *Le Congo. Essai sur l'histoire religieuse de ce pays depuis sa découverte (1484) jusqu'a nos jours.* Huy [Belgium]: Charpentier & Emond, 1894. 264p.

3783    . Eyers, Georges. "La factorerie de la Société Belge du Haut-Congo près de Matadi," *CIL*, IV(1895), 170-171.

3784 . Faes, Jozef. "Lettres," *Maandelijksch Verslag van de Afrikaansche Missiën,*
XIX(1898), 15-18.

3785 . _____. "Lettres," *Missiën der Witte Paters,* XXIII(1902), 149-154, 159, 160;
XXV(1904), 255-256.

3786 . Falkenstein, J. *Die Loango-Küste.* Berlin: J. F. Stiem, 1876.

3787 . _____. "Reiseberichte," *Correspondenzblatt der Afrikanischen Gesellschaft,*
I(1873), 76, 110, 124, 144.

3788 . Fièvez. [*Capt.*]. "Le district de l'équateur," *CIL,* IV(1895), 73-75, 84-
87, 92-95, 97-99.

. Fitzer, Elpide. "Lettres," *Annales Apostoliques,* IX(1894), 143-146.

3789 . _____. "Missionsbriefe," *Echo aus Afrika,* V(1893), 17-19; VI(1894), 92, 93.

3790 . Flapper, Lodewijk [*Fr. Willibrord*]. "Lettres," *Annalen der Afrikaansche
3791 Missiën,* XI(1894-1895), 161-165; XII(1895-1896), 14, 15; XIII
(1896-1897), 111-118; XIV(1897-1898), 225-230.

3792 _____. "Lettres," *Maandelijksch Verslag der Afrikaansche Missiën,* XVI
(1895), 269-271; XVII(1896), 331-338.

3793 . _____. "Lettres," *Missions d'Afrique,* XIX(1898), 149-152.

3794 . Fleuriot de Langle. "L'empire du Congo," *TM,* XXXI(1876), 289.

3795 . Foa, Édouard. *Chasses aux grands fauves dans l'Afrique centrale pendant
la traversée du continent noir du Zambéze au Congo français.*
Paris: Plon, 1899. 352p.

. Foncé, Antonius. "Lettres," *Missions en Chine et au Congo,* (1898-1900), 441,
3796 442; (1904), 245-248.

3797 . Fonck, H. "Über Waffen, Geräte, Trachten usw. in Urundi und Ruanda," *MDS*, XIII(1900).

3798 . Fourneau, Alfred L. *Au vieux Congo, notes de route. (1884-1891).* Paris: Comité de l'Afrique française, 1932. 323p.

3799 . _____. "Mission Fourneau. Rapport du chef de mission," *Revue Coloniale* [Paris: Ministère des colonies], V(1899), 681-707.

3800 . Franciscus, Emiel Delhaye. "Lettres," *Maandelijksch Verslag der Afrikaansche Missiën*, XII(1891), 265, 266.

3801 . François, Curt Carl [*Lt.*]. *Die Erforschung des Tschuapa und Lulongo. Reisen in Central-Afrika.* Leipzig: Brockhaus, 1888. 220p.

3802 . _____. "Ein Fahrt auf dem Lulua: Erlebnisse aus dem centralafrikanischen Forschungsleben," *Ausland*, LXI(1888).

3803 . _____. "Geschichtliches über die Bangala, Lunda und Kioko," *Globus*, LIII(1888), 273-276.

3804 . _____. "Reisen im südlichen Kongo-Becken," *PM*, XXXII(1886), 271-276, 322-326. Also, *VGE*, XIII(1886), 151.

3805 . Francqui. [*Lt.*]. "Le bassin supérieur du Congo," *BSBG*, XVII(1893), 543-564.

3806 . _____. "Historique du service des transports à dos d'homme," *MG*, V(1888), 39.

3807 . _____. "Le lac Moero," *MG*, X(1893), 75.

3808 . _____. "De Lusambo aux lacs Moero et Bangwelo. Le bassin supérieur du Lualaba et du Luapula," *BSBG*, XVII(1893), 141-153.

3809 . _____. "Voyage au Katanga," *BSRGA*, XVIII(1893), 241-251.

3810 · _____ and Cornet. "L'exploration du Lualaba depuis ses sources jusqu'au lac Kabele," *MG*, X(1893), 87-91, 101-102.

3811 · _____ _____. "L'exploration du Lubudi," *MG*, XI(1894), 31.

3812 · _____ _____. "Le plateau des Sambas. Sources du Sankuru, du Lomami, du Luemme et de la Luime," *MG*, XI(1894), 63.

3813 · Franke, G. A. J. *Over de belangrijkste tochten in het Congogebied.* Groningen, 1883.

3814 · Frick. *Mittheilungen über das Congo-Gebiet.* Gotha, 1873. 4p.

3815 · Frobenius, Leo V. "Die Ba Tshonga," *Globus*, LXV(1894), 206-210.

3816 · _____. "Die Fensterthüren im Congo-Becken," *Globus*, LXIV(1893), 326-328.

3817 · _____. "Die Keramik und ihre stellung zur Holzschnitzerei im südlichen Kongobecken," *Internationales Archiv für Ethnographie*, VII(1894).

3818 _____. "Staatenentwicklung und Gattenstellung im südlichen Kongobecken," *Deutsche Geographische Blätter*, XVI(1893).

3819 · Froment, E. "Trois affluents du Congo français," *Bulletin de la Société de Géographie de Lille*, VII(1887), 458-474.

3820 · Fuchs, F. "L'exploration du Mayombe (Bas-Congo)," *Mouvement Anti-Esclavagiste Belge* [Brussels], VI(1893), 33.

3821 · _____. "Le Mayombe," *BSBG*, XIX(1895), 1-23. Also, Publication de l'État indépendant du Congo, No. 10, 1893.

3822 · _____. "Moeurs congolaises," *Société Nouvelle: Revue Internationale* [Brussels], X(Oct., 1889).

3823 · Futterer, Karl Joseph. *Kongostaat.* Berlin: D. Reimer, 1895.

3824 Galinand, Joseph. *Le R.P. Allaire missionnaire au Congo d'après ses écrits et sa correspondance.* Paris: H. Oudin, 1899. 155p.

3825 . Gaillard, G. "Exploration de la Haute-Sangha et du Haut-Ubangi," *BSGP*, Seventh Series, XV(1893), 224-238. Also, *MG*, VIII(1891),91.

3826 24543. Garnier, Alfred. *Une excursion au pays des Noirs.* Lons-le-Saunier: C. Martin, 1896. 48p.

3827 . _____ . "Lettere," *MCM*, XXIII(1894), 520, 521.

3828 . _____ . "Lettres," *Annales Apostoliques*, V(1890), 52-59; XI(1896), 51-57;
3829 XVI(1900-1901), 197-202.

. _____ . "Lettres," *MCL*, XXV(1893), 580; XXVI(1894), 428.

3830 . _____ . "Missionsbriefe," *KM*, XXIII(1895), 19.

3831 . Geens, Emile. "Lettres," *Missions en Chine et au Congo*, (1901), 212-215; (1902), 27-29, 94-95.

3832 . Gèle, A. van. [*Capt.*]. "Die Fahrt des *En Avant* auf dem Ubangi," *PM*, XXXIV(1888), 145-148.

3833 . Gerboin, François. "Les nouvelles fondations de l'Ounyanyembé (Afrique Équatoriale)," *MCL*, XLIII(1910), 9-11, 21-23, 33-35, 45-47, 53-57, 68-70, 77-81, 90-94, 102-104.

3834 Gillain. [*Capt.*]. "Sankuru. Luemi. Lomani," *MG*, XII(1895), 159.

3835 . Gillet, Justin. "Lettres," *Bode van het H. Hart*, XXVII(1895-1896), 27, 28.
3836 . _____ . "Lettres," *Précis Historiques*, XLV(1896), 127, 128, 198-200, 350-352, 419-422; XLVII(1898), 98, 99.

3837 . Giron, Emmanuel. "Lettres," *Annales Apostoliques*, I(1886), 29-36, 114-118.
3838 . _____ . "Lettres," *Echo des Missions d'Afrique*, II(1885), 80, 81, 110-113, 193, 194.

3839 . Glave, E. J. "The Congo River Today," *Century*, XXXIX(1889-1890), 618-620.

3840 . _____. "Cruelty in the Congo State," *Century*, LIV(1897), 699-715.

3841 . _____. "Le fétishisme au Congo," *Société Nouvelle: Revue Internationale*[Brussels], XIV(1891), 518. SEE ALSO, CENTURY, XLI (1890-1891), 825-836.

3842 . _____. "Letters," *Century*, L(1895), 867, 868; LIV(1897), 796-798.

3843 . _____. "New Conditions in Central Africa: the Dawn of Civilization between Lake Tanganyika and the Congo: Extracts from the Journal of the Late E. J. G.," *Century Illustrated Monthly Magazine*, LIII(1897), 900-915.

3844 . _____. *Six Years of Adventure in Congo-Land*. London: Sampson Low, 1893. 247p.

3845 . _____. "The Slave Trade in the Congo Basin," *Century*, XXXIX (1889-1890), 824-838.

3846 . Goblet d'Alviella. [*Comte*]. "Croyances religieuses des peuples du Congo," *BSBG*, VIII(1884),

3847 . Gochet, F. Alexis M. *La barbarie africaine et l'action civilisatrice des missions catholiques au Congo et dans l'Afrique équatoriale.* Liège: Dessain, 1889. 208p.

3848 . _____. *Le Congo belge illustré ou l'État indépendant du Congo (Afrique centrale) sous la souveraineté de S.M. Leopold II, roi des Belges.* Liège: Dessain, 1888. 360p.

3849 . _____. *Le Congo français illustré, géographie, ethnographie et voyages.* Paris: Procuré générale, 1892. 232p.

3850 . _____. *Les Congolais, leurs moeurs et usages: histoire, géographie et ethnographie de l'État indépendant du Congo.* Liège: Dessaim, 1890. 192p.

3851 Goedleven, Isidore. "Lettres," *Voix du Rédempteur*, IX(1900), 243-246, 281-283, 359, 360; XIII(1904), 198.

3852 . Goerke, Melchior. "Lettres," *Règne du Coeur de Jésus*, XIII(1901), 237-240; XIV(1902), 80-84, 138-143, 202-207, 250-255, 306-311.

3853 . Goetz, Joseph. "Lettres," *Annales Apostoliques*, New Series, (1897-1898), 331-334.

3854 . Götzen, von. [*Graf*]. "Über seine Reise quer durch Central Afrika," *VGE*, XXII(1895), 102-119.

3855 . Goldsmid, F. J. [*Maj.Gen.*]. "My Recent Visit to the Congo," *PRGS*, New Series, VI(1884), 177-183.

3856 . Gorin. [*Lt.*]. "Kwango et Lunda. Peuplades de la frontière portugaise," *CIL*, III(1894), 2-3, 10-11.

3857 . Gourdy, Jean. "Lettere," *MCM*, XXIX(1900), 609.

3858 . _____. "Lettres," *MCL*, XXXII(1900), 582; XXXVI(1904), 460.

3859 . Grandy, W. G. [*Lt.*]. "Report of the Proceedings of the Livingstone Congo Expedition," *PRGS*, XIX(1874-1875), 78-104.

3860 . Grenfell, George. "Discoveries on the Kassai River," *MH*, LXXXII(1886), 321.

3861 . _____. "Exploration of the Tributaries of the Congo, between Leopoldville and Stanley Falls," *PRGS*, New Series, VIII(1886), 627-634.

3862 . _____. "Letters on the Journey on the Congo," *MH*, LXXXI(1885).

3863 . _____. "Our Congo Mission Work," *MH*, LXXVIII(1882), 281-290.

3864 . _____. "The Upper Congo as a Waterway," *GJ*, XX(1902), 485-498.

3865 . _____. "Voyages of the *S.S. Peace* on the Congo and Affluents," *JMGS*, II(1886), 87-94. Also, *MH*, LXXXII(1886), 110.

3866 . _____ and Comber, T. J. "Explorations on the Congo, from Stanley Pool to Bangala, and up the Bochini to the Junction of the Kwango," *PRGS*, New Series, VII(1885), 353-369.

3867 . Greshoff. "Congo: I. Van Ango-Ango naar Salvador; II. Van Ango-Ango naar Leopoldville; III. Langs den Kassai," *Tijdschrift van het Nederlandsch Aardrijkskundig Genootschap* [Amsterdam], III(1886).

3868
· Gueluy, Albert. "Lettres," *Missions en Chine et au Congo*, (1889-1891), 72-74, 206-208; (1892-1894), 92-94, 246-248. See also, *Missiën in China en Congo*, same period.

3869
· Guessfeldt, Paul. "Ansichten von der Loango küste, aufgenommen von Mitgliedern der Deutschen Güssfeldtschen Expedition nach west Afrika," *PM*, XXIII(1877), 107-108.

3870
· _____. "Bericht über die von ihn geleitete expedition an der Loango-küste," *VGE*, II(1875), 195-225.

3871
· _____. "Die grundlages der karte von der Loangoküste," *PM*, XXII(1876), 41-42.

3872
Guillemé, Mathurin. "Haut-Congo; les Wabembés; la mission de Kibanga," *MCL*, XXI(1889), 73-76.

3873
· _____. "Lettere," *MCM*, XVIII(1889), 21-24, 85-89, 553-556; XXI(1892), 481, 482; XXV(1896), 445-447; XXVII(1899). 300.

3874
· _____. "Lettres," *Annalen der Afrikaansche Missiën*, III (1886-1887), 144-149, 162-176; VI(1889-1890), 35-37, 259-263, 290-293, 318-321; VII(1890-1891), 18-21, 48-51, 73-81, 118-122, 141-146; VIII(1891-1892), 65-72, 176-179, 311-313; XII(1895-1896), 221-228, 289-297, 350-354; XIII(1896-1897), 76-83, 128-135, 200-205.

3875
· _____. "Lettres," *APFL*, LIX(1887), 176-181; LX(1888), 230-258, 374-394; LXIX(1897), 115-122.

3876
· _____. "Lettres," *Maandelijksch Verslag der Afrikaansche Missien*, XII(1891), 378-381; XVI(1895), 166-170; XVII(1896), 235-241, 306-310, 338-342, 375-379.

3877 ————————. "Lettres," *MCL*, XX(1888), 608-612; XXI(1889), 491-494; XXVIII(1896), 421-424; XXX(1898), 287, 288.

3878 ————————. "Lettres," *Missions d'Afrique*, XIX(1898), 186-191, 209-217, 235-238; XX(1899), 19-27, 140-148.

3879 ————————. "Lettres," *Missions d'Alger*, (1883-1886), 234-236, 330-334, 424-437; (1887-1890), 193-197, 471-479; (1891-1892), 18-25; (1893-1894), 363-365; [title changes to *Missions d'Afrique*(Paris)]. (1895-1897), 58-64, 363-369.

3880 ————————. "Missionsbriefe," *Afrika-Bote*, I(1895), 87-91; II (1896), 170-174; III(1897), 15, 16, 29-32.

3881 ————————. "Missionsbriefe," *KM*, XVI(1888), 63; XVII(1889), 22.

3882 ————————. "Les premieres religieuses missionaires dans le Haut-Congo belge," *Missions d'Afrique*[Paris], (1895-1897), 402-406, 454-458.

3883 ————. "Voyage d'exploration dans le Marungu," *Mouvement Anti-Esclavagiste Belge*[Brussels], V(1892), 229.

3884 . Guiness, Fanny E. [Mrs. H. Grattan]. *The First Christian Mission on the Congo*. 4th Ed. London: Hodder and Stoughton, 1882. 116p.

3885 . ————. *The New World of Central Africa. With a History of the First Christian Mission on the Congo*. London: Hodder and Stoughton, 1890. 510p. New York: Revell, 1890. 535p.

3886 . Guiral, Léon. *Les Batékés*. Paris: Leroux, 1886. 32p. See also, Ch. 10 of authors *Le Congo français du Gabon à Brazzaville*.

3887 . ————. *Le Congo français du Gabon à Brazzaville*. Paris: Plon-Nourrit, 1889. 322p.

3888 . Hallez d'Arros, Hippolyte. *Colonisation du Congo français*. Paris: Challamel, 1899.

3889 . Hambursin, F. "Au Congo," *Journal de l'Association des anciens élèves de l'Institut agricole de Gembloux* [Gembloux, Belgium], VI (1895), 325.

3890 . Hanquet, Jean-Baptiste. "Lettres," *Missions Belges de la Compagnie de Jésus*, I(1899), 271-274, 366; II(1900), 269; III(1901), 38-40, 158.

3891 . Hanssens. [*Capt.*]. "Les Bayanzi, moeurs et coutumes," *MG*, I(1884), 6, 10, 14.

3892 . _____. "Au Stanley Pool. Lettres inédites du capitaine Hanssens," *CIL*, I(1892), 5-7, 13-15, 22-23, 29-31, 37-39, 45-47.

3893 . _____. "Le service des transports entre Matadi et Manyanga," *MG*, VIII (1891), 128.

3894 . Harou. [*Lt.*]. "Souvenirs de voyage dans l'Afrique centrale," *Revue Artistique* [Antwerp], III(1880-1881).

3895 . Hendrickx, François Xavier. "Lettres," *Missions Belges de la Compagnie de Jésus*, I(1899), 287, 288; II(1900), 37, 230, 231, 327-329; IV (1902), 312.

3896 . Henricy, Michel. "Lettres," *Précis Historiques*, XLIV(1895), 429-433.

3897 . Herr. [*Dr.*]. "Mission Clozel dans le nord du Congo français (1894-1895)," *AG*, V(1895-1896), 309-317.

3898 . Herrebaut, Eduard. "Lettres," *Maandelijksch Verslag der Afrikaansche Missiën*, XI(1890), 3-11, 41-44, 100-106, 173-176; XII(1891), 13-18, 41-43; XVIII(1897), 213-216.

3899 . Hert, de. "De Matadi à Kimuenza par Luvituku," *Précis Historiques* [Brussels], XLIV(1895), 105, 168, 234. Also, *MG*, XII(1895), 73.

3900 . Hinde, Sidney Langford. *The Fall of the Congo Arabs*. London: Methuen; New York: Whittaker, 1897. 308p. French Translation, *La chute de la domination arabe au Congo*. Brussels: Société d'Études coloniales, 1897. 170p.

3901 . _____. "Three Years' Travel in the Congo Free State," *GJ*, V(1895), 426-442. Also, *MG*, XII(1895), 148.

3902 . Hodister, A. "Les Arabes sur le Haut-Congo," *MG*, VIII(1891), 83.

3903 . _____. *Au Congo*. Ghent: Leliaert and Siffer, 1888. 12p.

3904 . _____. "De Bangala à Nyangwe," *MG*, VII(1890), 119.

3905 . _____. "L'exploration de la Mongala," *MG*, VII(1890).

3906 . _____. "Exploration des branches supérieures de la Mongala," *MG*, VII(1890), 103.

3907 . _____. "Landana à Boma," *MG*, V(1888), 86.

3908 . _____. "Les trois dernières lettres," *MG*, IX(1892), 82.

3909 . Homeyer, A. von. "Reiseberichte," *Correspondenzblatt der Afrikanischen Gesellschaft*, I(1877), 258, 292.

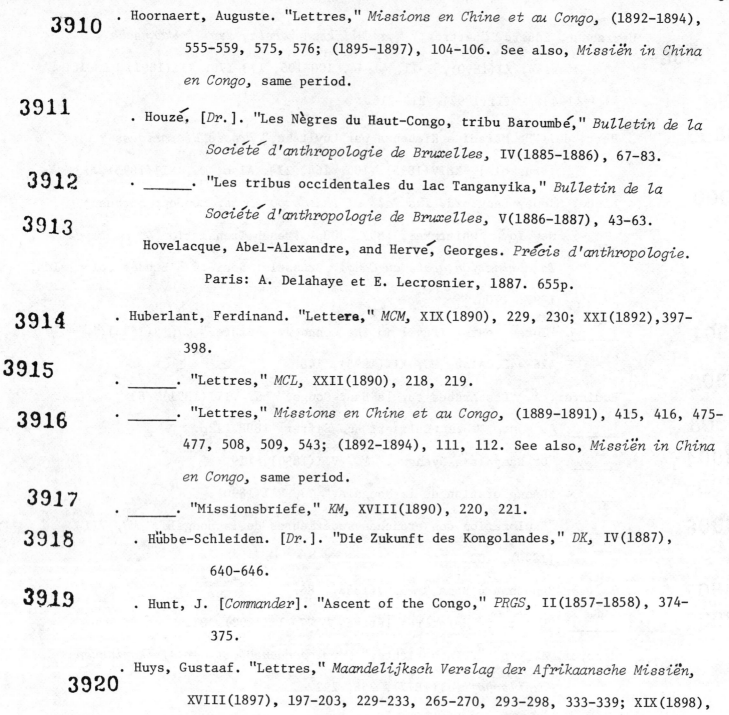

3910 . Hoornaert, Auguste. "Lettres," *Missions en Chine et au Congo*, (1892-1894), 555-559, 575, 576; (1895-1897), 104-106. See also, *Missiën in China en Congo*, same period.

3911 . Houzé, [*Dr.*]. "Les Nègres du Haut-Congo, tribu Baroumbé," *Bulletin de la Société d'anthropologie de Bruxelles*, IV(1885-1886), 67-83.

3912 . _____. "Les tribus occidentales du lac Tanganyika," *Bulletin de la Société d'anthropologie de Bruxelles*, V(1886-1887), 43-63.

3913 Hovelacque, Abel-Alexandre, and Hervé, Georges. *Précis d'anthropologie*. Paris: A. Delahaye et E. Lecrosnier, 1887. 655p.

3914 . Huberlant, Ferdinand. "Lettere," *MCM*, XIX(1890), 229, 230; XXI(1892),397-398.

3915 . _____. "Lettres," *MCL*, XXII(1890), 218, 219.

3916 . _____. "Lettres," *Missions en Chine et au Congo*, (1889-1891), 415, 416, 475-477, 508, 509, 543; (1892-1894), 111, 112. See also, *Missiën in China en Congo*, same period.

3917 . _____. "Missionsbriefe," *KM*, XVIII(1890), 220, 221.

3918 . Hübbe-Schleiden. [*Dr.*]. "Die Zukunft des Kongolandes," *DK*, IV(1887), 640-646.

3919 . Hunt, J. [*Commander*]. "Ascent of the Congo," *PRGS*, II(1857-1858), 374-375.

3920 . Huys, Gustaaf. "Lettres," *Maandelijksch Verslag der Afrikaansche Missiën*, XVIII(1897), 197-203, 229-233, 265-270, 293-298, 333-339; XIX(1898), 50-54, 72-76, 113-117, 170-173, 174-181, 196-201, 240-244, 275-279.

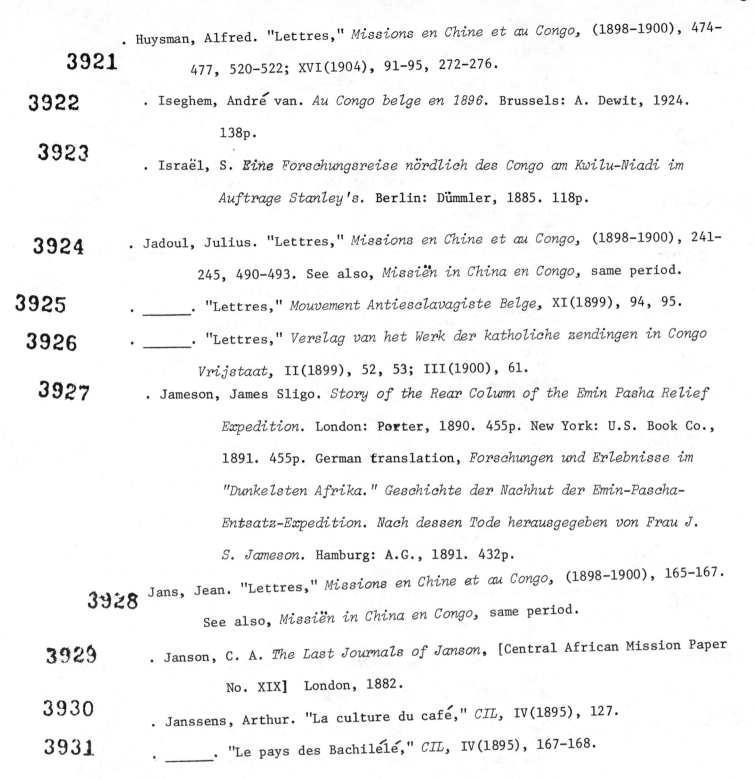

3921   . Huysman, Alfred. "Lettres," *Missions en Chine et au Congo*, (1898-1900), 474-477, 520-522; XVI(1904), 91-95, 272-276.

3922   . Iseghem, André van. *Au Congo belge en 1896*. Brussels: A. Dewit, 1924. 138p.

3923   . Israël, S. *Eine Forschungsreise nördlich des Congo am Kwilu-Niadi im Auftrage Stanley's*. Berlin: Dümmler, 1885. 118p.

3924   . Jadoul, Julius. "Lettres," *Missions en Chine et au Congo*, (1898-1900), 241-245, 490-493. See also, *Missiën in China en Congo*, same period.

3925   . _____. "Lettres," *Mouvement Antiesclavagiste Belge*, XI(1899), 94, 95.

3926   . _____. "Lettres," *Verslag van het Werk der katholiche zendingen in Congo Vrijstaat*, II(1899), 52, 53; III(1900), 61.

3927   . Jameson, James Sligo. *Story of the Rear Column of the Emin Pasha Relief Expedition*. London: Porter, 1890. 455p. New York: U.S. Book Co., 1891. 455p. German translation, *Forschungen und Erlebnisse im "Dunkelsten Afrika." Geschichte der Nachhut der Emin-Pascha-Entsatz-Expedition. Nach dessen Tode herausgegeben von Frau J. S. Jameson*. Hamburg: A.G., 1891. 432p.

3928    Jans, Jean. "Lettres," *Missions en Chine et au Congo*, (1898-1900), 165-167. See also, *Missiën in China en Congo*, same period.

3929   . Janson, C. A. *The Last Journals of Janson*, [Central African Mission Paper No. XIX] London, 1882.

3930   . Janssens, Arthur. "La culture du café," *CIL*, IV(1895), 127.

3931   . _____. "Le pays des Bachilélé," *CIL*, IV(1895), 167-168.

3932 . Janssens, Augustinus. "Lettres," *Missions en Chine at au Congo*, (1898-1900), 438-440. See also, *Missiën in China en Congo*, same period.

3933 . _____. "Lettres," *Mouvement Antiesclavagiste Belge*, XI(1899), 38, 39, 170-171; XIII(1901), 146, 147; XIV(1902), 271, 272.

3934 . _____. "Lettres," *Verslag van het Werk der katholiche zendingen in Congo Vrijstaat*, II(1899), 97.

3935 . _____. "Missionsbriefe," *Annalen der Missionarissen*, VII(1907), 167-170.

3936 . Jardin, E. "Le Congo, souvenir d'un voyage en 1885," *Bulletin de la Société de Géographie de Rochefort*, IV(1884),

3937 . Jeannest, Charles. *Quatre années au Congo*. Paris: Charpentier et Cie, 1883. 327p.

3938 . Jehoul, Gerardus. "Lettres," *Mouvement Antiesclavagiste Belge*, XII(1900), 189, 190.

3939 . Joalland, Paul Lules, and Meynier, O. [*Général*]. "Les missions du Chari et de l'Afrique centrale," *Afrique Française*, XI(1901), 184-197.

3940 . Jobit, Eugene, and Loefler, Charles. "Mission Gendron au Congo française," *Géographie*, III(1901), 181-196.

3941 . Johnston, Harry Hamilton. "An Artist's Visit to the River Congo," *Graphic* [London], Oct. 13, 27; Nov. 3,17, 1883.

3942 . _____. *George Grenfell and the Congo; a History and Description of the Congo Independent State and Adjoining Districts of Congoland*,

Together with Some Account of the Native Peoples and Their Languages, the Fauna and Flora; and Similar Notes on the Cameroons and the Island of Fernando Po, the Whole Founded on the Diaries and Researches of the Late Rev. George Grenfell, B.M.D, F.R.G.S.; and on the Records of the British Baptist Missionary Society; and on Additional Information Contributed by the Author, by the Rev. Lawson Forfeitt, Mr. Emil Torday, and Others._ 2 vols. London: Hutchinson, 1908.

3943 . _____. *Der Kongo; Reise von seiner Mündung bis Bolobo.* Leipzig: Brockhaus, 1884. 437p.

3944 . _____. "The River Congo, from Its Mouth to the Bóloboʹ; with Notes on the Physical Geography, Natural History, Resources, and Political Aspect of the Congo Basin," *PRGS,* New Series, V(1883), 692-710.

3945 . _____. "A Visit to Mr. Stanley's Stations on the River Congo," *PRGS,* New Series, V(1883), 569-581.

3946 . Julien. [*Capt.*]. "Du Haut-Oubangui vers le Chari par le bassin de la rivière Kota," *BSGP,* Seventh Series, XVII(1877), 129-178, 340-384.

3947 . _____. "Exploration de la Haute Banghi à la Yeouka et le long de l'Oubangui," *Géographie,* V(1902), 216-218.

3948 . Jungers. [*Capt.*]. "le Bas Congo," *BSBG,* XIII(1889), 385-414.

3949 . Junker, Wilhelm Johann. "Explorations et découvertes dans les bassins de l'Uellé et du Bomu," *CIL,* I(1892), 157, 165, 173, 181, 189.

3950 _____. "Kartenskizze der Gebiete im Süden des Uellé," *PM*, XXX(1884), 96-100.

3951 _____. "Land und Leute auf der Grenze des Nil- und Uellé-Systems," *Globus*, XLIV(1883), 41-44.

3952 _____. "Reise am Uëlle und Majo, Dezember 1881 bis Februar 1882, und Touren im Momvú-Lande, März 1882, Erkundigungen über die Flüsse im Süden des Uëlle," *PM*, XXVIII(1882), 441-443.

3953 _____. "Über seine dreijährigen Reisen in den äquatorialen Provinzen Central-Afrika's," *VGE*, VI(1879), 204-217.

3954 _____. "Voyages dans l'Afrique équatoriale," *BSKG*, 1880, No.7, pp.19-36.

3955 Kade, von [*Major*]. *Mission und Kolonisation*. Aschaffenburg: Weiland, 1892.

3956 Kaeckenbeeck, F. *L'état indépendant du Congo et le commerce*. Brussels: Weissenbruch, 1892. 16p.

3957 Kayser, Johann. "Lettres," *Règne du Coeur de Jésus*, XIV(1902), 46-48, 84-86.

3958 _____. "Lettres," *Sacré Coeur au Centre de l'Afrique*, I(1901-1902), 1-3, 3-5.

3959 _____. "Missionsbriefe," *Echo aus Afrika*, XII(1900), 91, 92.

3960 Kethulle de Ryhove, de la [*Lt.*]. "Le Sultanat de Rafaï," *CIL*, IV(1895), 149.

3961 Kindt, Joseph. "Lettres," *Belgique Coloniale*, VIII(1902), 452.

3962 _____. "Lettres," *Missiën der Witte Paters*, XXII(1901), 218-220, 249, 250; XXIII(1902), 339-342.

3963 _____. "Lettres," *Missions d'Afrique*, XXII(1901), 248.

3964 Klink, Hendrik. *Het Kongo-land en zijn bewoners in betrakking tot de europeesche staakkunde en den handel*. Haarlem: Tjeenk Willink, 1891. 195p.

3965 . Koffel, Alphons. "Lettres," *Lis de St-Joseph*, VI(1895), 202, 203; VII (1896), 379-382.

3966 . Koller, C. S. "Die Giftprobe (Nkassa) und die Zauberer (Ndotschi) der Kongo-Neger," *KM*, XX(1892), 161-166.

3967 . _____ ____. "Der Lukullafluss im Kongogebiet," *KM*, XVII(1889), 181-186, 209-215, 234-239.

3968 . Kollmann, J. "Die Pygmäen und ihre systematische Stellung innerhalb des Menschengeschlechtes," *Verhandlungen des Naturforschenden Gesellschaft, Basel*, XVI(1902).

3969 . Krafft, Georg. "Cartas," *Portugal em Africa*, I(1894), 25-28, 57-60, 104-110; II(1895), 499-504, 623-625; IV(1897), 354-356, 455-456.

3970 . _____. "Lettres," *Annales Apostoliques*, VI(1891), 27-29, 107-109.

3971 . _____. "Lettres," *Annales Oeuvre Ste-Enfance*, XXXVII(1886), 28-45.

3972 . _____. "Lettres," *Echo des Missions d'Afrique*, I(1884), 25-33.

3973 . _____. "Missionsbriefe," *Echo aus Afrika*, IV(1892), 129-131; V(1893), 66-67; VI(1894), 37-38; VII(1895), 5-7, 43.

3974 . Kund. "Bericht über die von der Afrikanischen Gesellschaft in Deutschland entsandte Expedition," *VGE*, XIII(1886), 313.

3975 . _____. "Bericht von der Kongo-Expedition," *MAGD*, IV(1884-1885),

3976 . _____. "Fahrt auf dem Congo von Stanley-Pool bis Bangala," *MAGD*, IV (1884-1885), 379.

3977 . _____. "Recent Explorations in the Southern Congo Basin," *PRGS*, New Series, VIII(1886), 725.

3978 . _____. "Reiseberichte," *MAGD*, IV(1884-1885), 313-372.

3979 . _____. "Vortrag über seine Forschungsreise in Afrika," *DK*, IV(1887), 69-70.

3980 . Landbeck, Paul. *Kongoerinnerungen: Zwölf Jahre Arbeit und Abenteurer im Innern Afrikas*. Berlin: A. Scherl, [1923]. 196p.

3981 . _____. *Malu Malu: Erlebnisse aus der Sturm und Drangperiode des Kongo-staates*. Berlin: A. Scherl, [1930]. 193p.

3982 . Lapsley, Samuel Norvell. *Life and Letters of Samuel Norvell Lapsley*. n.p., n.p., 1893.

3983 . Laurent, Émile. *Conferences sur le Congo*. Gembloux: Berce-Hettick, 1900. 67p.

3984 . Laurent, Raphael. "Lettres," *Annales Apostoliques*, XV(1899-1900), 274.

3985 . _____. "Lettres," *Lis de St-Joseph*, VIII(1897), 136-138; X(1899), 80, 81.

3986 . Lauwers, Auguste. "Lettres," *Missions Belges de la Compagnie de Jésus*, III(1901), 457-460; V(1903), 100-103, 341, 342. VI(1904), 280.

3987 . Lechartraire, A. "Les Missions au Congo Belge," *RHM*, VIII(1931), 182-196.

3988 . Lecomte, Raoul. "Lettere," *MCM*, XVI(1887), 193, 194.

3989 . _____. "Lettres," *MCL*, XIX(1887), 169, 170.

3990 Ledien, F. "Exploration des bords du Congo et de ses affluents entre Vivi et Lukungu," *MG*, III(1886), 21.

3991 . Lejeune, Charles. "Les Inkimbas," *CIL*, III(1894), 59-61.

3992 . _____. "Les Tombes," *CIL*, III(1894), 4.

3993 . Lejeune, Leon. "La Femme et la famille au Congo," *MCL*, XXXII(1900), 172-174, 190-192, 202-204, 209-211, 221-223, 236-237, 247-249, 259-260. See also *MCM*, XXX(1901), 203-204, 212-215, 227-228, 239-240, 250-252, 261-264, 276, 287-288.

. Le Louët, Georges. "Lettres," *Annales Oeuvre Ste-Enfance,* XL(1889), 398-412.

3994

3995 . Lemaire, Charles François Alexandre.[Lt.]. *Au Congo. Comment les noirs travaillent.* Brussels: Bulens, 1895. 139p.

3996 . _____. "Le camp d'instruction de l'équateur," *CIL,* I(1892), 186-187.

3997 . _____. "Les communications entre la Belgique et le Congo," *CIL,* IV(1895), 9, 20, 28, 37.

3998 . _____. *Congo et Belgique.* Brussels: Bulens, 1894. 253p.

3999 . _____. "Dans la région des cataractes. Aperçus ethnographiques," *MG,* VII(1890), 103; VIII(1891), 28, 70; IX(1892), 53.

4000 . _____. "Dans la région des cataractes. Le portage à dos d'homme entre Matadi et le Stanley-Pool," *MG,* VIII(1891), 109. Also, *CIL,* IV(1895), 4.

4001 . _____. "De la toilette," *CIL,* II(1893), 8.

4002 . _____. "Une exploration dans le Ruki," *CIL,* III(1894), 14-15, 28-30.

4003 . _____. "Une forge à l'équateur," *CIL,* I(1892), 167.

4004 . _____. "Les marchés publics," *CIL,* I(1892), p.114.

4005 . _____. "La numération parlée," *CIL,* III(1894), 146, 162, 171, 192.

4006 . _____. "On the Congo: the Belgian Scientific Expedition to Ka-Tanga," *SGM,* XVII(1901), 526-556.

4007 . _____. "La pêche," *MG,* IX(1892), 25.

4008 . _____. "Quelques pratiques superstitieuses," *CIL,* I(1892), 202.

4009 . _____. "Scènes d'Afrique," *CIL,* III(1894), 102, 126.

4010 . _____. "Les tatouages," *CIL,* I(1892), 155.

4011 . _____. "Vers le Congo. Souvenirs d'escale," Supplement de *l'Indépendance Belge,* 1894, Nos. 25 mars; 8, 22 avril; 13, 27 mai; 17 juin; 8, 15, 29 juillet.

4012 . _____. *Voyage au Congo.* Brussels: Bulens, 1895.

4013     . Le Marinel, Georges. [*Capt.*]. "Exploration du Kotto," *MG*, VIII(1891), 144.

4014     . _____. "De Nyangoué à Loulouabourg," *MG*, V(1888), 55.

4015     . _____. "Les rapides de l'Ubangi," *Bulletin officiel de l'État indépendant du Congo*, 1894, pp.167-171. Also, *MG*, XI(1894), 2.

4016     . _____. "La région du Haut-Ubangi," *BSBG*, XVII(1893), 5-42.

4017     . Le Mintier, Joseph. "Lettres," *Annales Apostoliques*, XV(1899-1900), 275; XX(1904), 167.

4018     . Le Monnier, F. "Die Österreichische Kongo-Expedition," *MKKG*, XXVIII (1885), 225.

4019     . _____. "Die Rückkehr der Österreichische Kongo-Expedition," *MKKG*, XXX (1887), 1-5.

4020     . Lempereur, Louis. "Lettres," *Echo aus Knechtsteden*, II(1900-1901), 22-25, 37-40, 57-60, 72-74; III(1901-1902), 171-173.

4021     . Lenz, Oscar. [*Dr.*]. "Die Arbeiterverhältnisse in den Handels-Factoreien West Afrikas," *Österreichische Monatsschrift fur den Orient* [Vienna], V(1879), 8-9.

4022     . _____. "Ein Besuch bei den Cannibalen West-Afrikas," *Gegenwart*, XI (1877), 214-216, 232-234.

4023     . _____. "L'expédition autrichienne au Congo," *BSGP*, Seventh Series, XIII (1887), 209-245.

4024     . _____. "Die Handelsverhaltnisse im äquatorialen Theile West-Afrika's," *Deutsche Geographische Blätter* [Bremen], II(1878), 37-84.

4025     . _____. "Islam und Afrikaforschung," *Aus allen Weltteilen*, XIV(1883), 289-292.

4026     . _____. "Die Österreichische Kongo-Expedition," *PM*, XXXII(1886), 121-123.

4027 .\_\_\_\_\_. "Österreichische Kongo-Expedition Briefe," *MKKG*, XXVIII(1885), 348, 402, 503, 557; XXIX(1886), 26, 102, 257, 337, 575; XXX(1887), 86.

4028 .\_\_\_\_\_. "Über die sogenannten Zwergvölker Afrikas," *Vorträge des Vereines zur Verbreitung naturwissenschaftlicher Kenntnisse in Wien*, XXIV(1894), 1-38.

4029 .\_\_\_\_\_. "Über Zwergvölker in West-Afrika," *MKKG*, XXI(1877), 28.

4030 .\_\_\_\_\_. "Vom Kongo zum Zambesi," *Fernschau*[Aarau, Switzerland], 1889, pp. 91-121.

4031 .\_\_\_\_\_. "Zwergvölker und Anthropophagen in West-Afrika," *Jahresbericht der Geographische Gesellschaft in Bern*, IV(1881-1882), 125-132.

4032 . Leray, François. "Lettres," *Annales Apostoliques*, New Series (1897-1898), 24.

4033 . Le Roy, Alexandre. *Les pygmées. Négrilles d'Afrique et Negritos de l'Asie.* Tours: Alfred Mame et fils, 1899. 364p.

4034 Levadoux, Antoine. "Lettres," *Annales Apostoliques*, I(1886), 104-110.

4035 . Lewis, Thomas. "The Ancient Kingdom of Kongo: Its Present Position and Possibilities," *GJ*, XIX(1902), 541-558.

4036 .\_\_\_\_\_. "Itineraries in Portuguese Congo," *SGM*, XVII(1901), 572-582.

4037 .\_\_\_\_\_. "Life and Travel among the People of the Congo," *SGM*, XVIII(1902), 358-369.

4038 .\_\_\_\_\_. "The Old Kingdom of Kongo," *GJ*, XXXI(1908), 589-611.

4039 . Liebrechts, Charles. *Congo. Suite à mes souvenirs d'Afrique. Vingt années a l'administration centrale de l'État indépendant du Congo, 1889-1908.* Brussels: Office de publicité, 1920. 336p.

4040 . _____. "Léopoldville," *BSBG*, XIII(1889), 501-537. See also, same title, *Publications de l'État indépendant du Congo*, No. 2, 1889, 40p.

4041 . _____. *Souvenir d'Afrique, Congo, Léopoldville, Balolo, Équateur.*

4042 Brussels: Office de publicité, 1909. 266p.

. Liénart, V. "Exploration de l'Oubanghi," *BSBG*, XII(1888), 374-398.

4043 . Lindegaard, A. E. A. *Soldaterliv i Congo, 1897-1900*. Copenhagen: Busck, 1928. 199p.

4044 . Loriot, F. *Explorations et missions dans l'Afrique équatoriale*. Paris:

4045 Gaum et Cie., 1890. 375p.

. Lotens, Joseph M. G. *L'État indépendant du Congo. Notice descriptive.* Alost: De Seyn-Verhougstraete, 1899. 1102p.

4046 . Luec, Mathurin. "Lettres," *Annales Apostoliques*, VIII(1893), 107-110.

4047 . Luschan, Felix von. "Bogen und Pfeile der Watwa vom Kiwu-See," *ZE*, XXXI(1899).

4048 . Lux. [*Lt.*]. "Unter der Bangelas in Westafrika," *Globus*, XXXV(1879),

4049 . Macar, Ghislain de [*Capt.*]. "À Loulouabourg," *MG*, V(1888), 59.

4050 . _____. "Chez les Bakubas," *CIL*, IV(1895), 172-174.

4051 . _____. *Le Kassaï et ses affluents*. Liège: Renard, 1889. 44p.

4052 . _____. "La tribu des Bakuba," *MG*, X(1893), 103, 109.

4053 . Mackay, A. M. [*Rev.*]. "Africa as a Source of Cotton Supply," *The Textile Mercury* [Manchester], I(1889).

4054 . Magalhães, Carlos de. "O Zaire e a Guine portugueza," *BSGL*, V(1885), 132-145.

4055 . Maistre, M. Casimir. "Journey from the Congo to the Shari and Benue," *GJ*, II(1893), 323-325.

4056 . Mandat-Grancey, Edmond de [*Baron*]. *Au Congo, 1898. Impressions d'un touriste*. Paris: Plon, 1900. 299p.

4057 Maonde, Charles. "Lettres," *Lis de St-Joseph*, X(1899), 172-174.

4058 Marichelle, Christophe. "Une école rurale au Congo français," *MCL*, XXX
(1898), 570-574, 582-585, 593, 594, 606-609, 616, 617. Also, *MCM*,
XXVIII(1899), 415-418, 428-430, 439-441, 448-450, 462, 463.

4059 . Marno, Ernst. "Ein Akka-Weib und ein Akka-Mädchen," *Mitteilungen der
Anthropologische Gesellschaft in Wien*, V(1875), 157, 366.

4060 . Marquer, E. "L'aviso le *Talisman* au Congo," *Bulletin de la Société Bretonne
de Géographie*, XI(1892), 150-160.

4061 Marquès, Leo. "Lettres," *Maandelijksch Verslag der Afrikaansche Missiën*,
XII(1891), 313-317.

4062 _____. "Lettres," *Missions d'Alger*, (1891-1892), 480, 481.

4063 . Martini, Christian. *To danske Kongofarere. Erindringer fra vort første
Ophold i Kongostaten*. Copenhagen: Pontoppidun, 1890. 92p.

4064 . Massenza, Jean-Baptiste. "Lettere," *MCM*, XXV(1896), 363-365.

4065 _____. "Lettres," *APFL*, LXVIII(1896), 363-366.

4066 _____. "Lettres," *MCL*, XXVIII(1896), 339, 340.

4067 . Masui, Theodore. *D'Anvers à Banzyville*. Brussels: Bulens, 1894. 144p.
Also, *CIL*, III(1894), 82-84, 92-95.

4068 . Matos e Silva, João de. "Cabinda: Algumas palavras acerca da emigração,"
*BSGL*, X(1891), 195-201.

4069 . Mechow, von. "Bericht über die von ihm geführte Expedition zur Aufklärung
des Kuango-Stromes 1878-1881," *VGE*, IX(1882), 475-489.

4070 . _____. "Die Quango-Expedition," *MAGD*, II(1880-1881), 155-156.

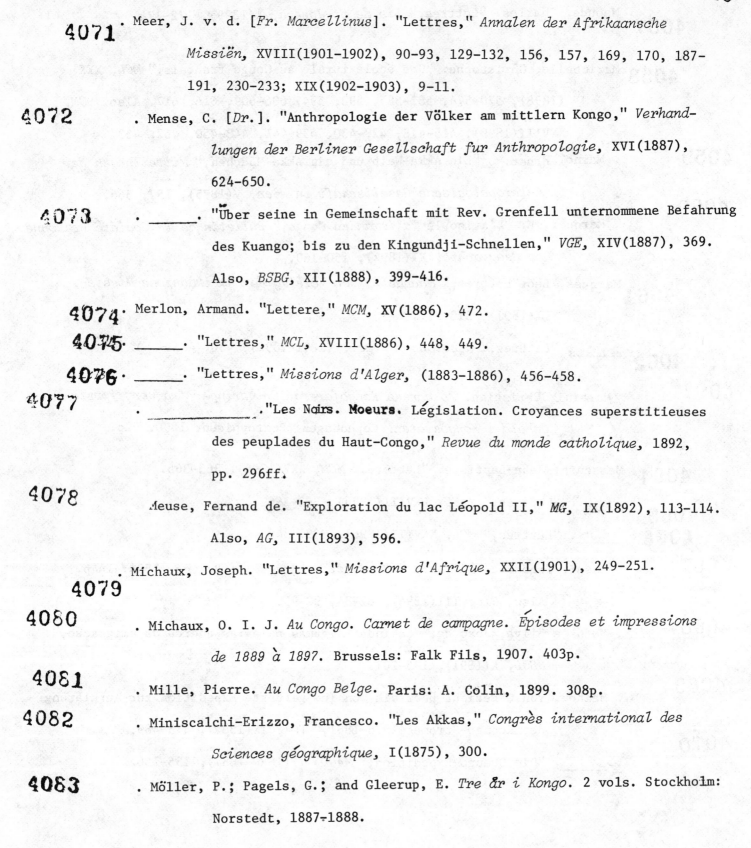

4071. Meer, J. v. d. [*Fr. Marcellinus*]. "Lettres," *Annalen der Afrikaansche Missiën*, XVIII(1901-1902), 90-93, 129-132, 156, 157, 169, 170, 187-191, 230-233; XIX(1902-1903), 9-11.

4072. Mense, C. [*Dr.*]. "Anthropologie der Völker am mittlern Kongo," *Verhand-lungen der Berliner Gesellschaft für Anthropologie*, XVI(1887), 624-650.

4073. _____. "Über seine in Gemeinschaft mit Rev. Grenfell unternommene Befahrung des Kuango; bis zu den Kingundji-Schnellen," *VGE*, XIV(1887), 369. Also, *BSBG*, XII(1888), 399-416.

4074. Merlon, Armand. "Lettere," *MCM*, XV(1886), 472.

4075. _____. "Lettres," *MCL*, XVIII(1886), 448, 449.

4076. _____. "Lettres," *Missions d'Alger*, (1883-1886), 456-458.

4077. _____. "Les Noirs. **Moeurs**. Législation. Croyances superstitieuses des peuplades du Haut-Congo," *Revue du monde catholique*, 1892, pp. 296ff.

4078. Meuse, Fernand de. "Exploration du lac Léopold II," *MG*, IX(1892), 113-114. Also, *AG*, III(1893), 596.

4079. Michaux, Joseph. "Lettres," *Missions d'Afrique*, XXII(1901), 249-251.

4080. Michaux, O. I. J. *Au Congo. Carnet de campagne. Épisodes et impressions de 1889 à 1897*. Brussels: Falk Fils, 1907. 403p.

4081. Mille, Pierre. *Au Congo Belge*. Paris: A. Colin, 1899. 308p.

4082. Miniscalchi-Erizzo, Francesco. "Les Akkas," *Congrès international des Sciences géographique*, I(1875), 300.

4083. Möller, P.; Pagels, G.; and Gleerup, E. *Tre år i Kongo*. 2 vols. Stockholm: Norstedt, 1887-1888.

4084   . Mönkemeyer, W. "Kritische Bemerkungen zu L. Haneufe's Ackerbaukolonie-
Projekt am Congo," *Globus*, IL(1886), 73-74.

4085   . _____. "Das Sanitarium zu Boma und die Klimatischen Verhältnisse des
Unter-Congo-Gebietes," *Globus*, L(1886), 171-173.

4086   . _____. "Die Vegetation des unteren Congo," *Globus*, XLVIII(1885), 330-333.

4087   . _____. "Vom Kongo, persönliche Eindrücke und Erfahrungen," *DK*, II(1885),
19ff.

4088   . _____. "Die Zukunst des Plantagenbaues am untern Kongo," *DK*, III(1886),
711-713.

4089   . Mohun. "Sur le Congo, de Kassongo au confluent de la Lukuga," *AG*, IV
(1894), 228.

4090   Moinet, Isaac. "Lettere," *MCM*, XIII(1884), 354.

4091   . _____. "Lettres," *Annalen der Afrikaanschen Missiën*, III(1886-1887), 68-
70; V(1888-1889), 61-67.

4092   . _____. "Lettres," *APFL*, LVI(1884), 166-185.

4093   . _____. "Lettres," *MCL*, XII(1880), 386; XVI(1884), 340.

4094   . _____. "Lettres," *Missiën der Witte Paters*, XX(1899), 318-320, 368-377;
XXI(1900), 310-315.

4095   . _____. "Lettres," *Missions d'Afrique*, XIX(1898), 171-175, 304-309; XX
(1899), 248-255, 288.

4096   . _____. "Lettres," *Missions d'Algers*, (1879-1882), 470-473, 500-502;
(1883-1886), 44-48, 141-143, 178, 179, 275-280; (1887-1890), 299-305,
642-644; (1891-1892), 174, 175, 430, 431, 480; (1893-1894), 72-74;
(1897-1900), 562-568, 826-833.

4097   . _____. "Missionsbriefe," *Afrika-Bote*, V(1899), 183-188.

4098   . _____. "Missionsbriefe," *KM*, XI(1883), 222, 223; XII(1884), 134, 135;
XVI(1888), 218-221.

4099. Moleyre, L. "Les flèches des Batékés," *Nature* [Paris], XI(1883), 127.

4100. Moloney, Joseph Augustus. "The Stairs Expedition to Katangaland," *GJ*, II (1893), 238-244.

4101. _____. *With Captain Stairs to Katanga*. London: Sampson Low, 1893. 280p.

4102. Monet, Henri. "Le commerce du Congo," *BSRGA*, XI(1886), 265.

4103. Moraes Sarmento, Favio P. "Communicação feita á direcção das obras publicas de Angola, pelo conductor de primeira classe, major João Carlos Ribeiro, ácerca do serviço que lhe foi incumbido extraordinariamente, para dirigir a armação de uma casa de Madeira destinada a missão portugueza em S.S. do Congo," *BSGL*, III(1882), 209-222.

4104. Moreau, Joseph. "Lettres," *Annales Apostoliques*, XV(1898-1899), 4-6.

4105. _____. "Lettres," *APFL*, LXX(1898), 26-35.

4106. _____. "Lettres," *Lis de St-Joseph*, II(1891), 40-44.

4107. _____. "Missionsbriefe," *Echo aus Afrika*, XII(1900), 121-125.

4108. _____. "Missionsbriefe," *Echo aus Knechtsteden*, X(1908-1909), 35.

4109. Morgan, E. D. "The Free State of the Congo," *PRGS*, New Series, VII(1885), 223-236.

4110. _____. "Notes on the Lower Congo, from Its Mouth to Stanley Pool," *PRGS*, New Series, VI(1884), 183-193.

4111 . Murard, Claude. "Lettres," *MCL*, XXXII(1900), 242.

4112 . Musy, Maurice. "Correspondance de M. Musy, chef de poste à Bangui (Oubangui), *Revue de géographie*[dirigée par M.L.Drapeyron], XIV(1890-1891).

4113 . Niesten, L. "Une éclipse de soleil au Congo," *MG*, III(1886), 17.

4114 . Nipperdey, H. "Der Fetisch und Fetisch-Glaube in West-Afrika," *Ausland*, LIX(1886), 712.

4115 . _____. "The Industrial Products and Food-Stuffs of the Congo," *SGM*, II (1886), 482-487.

4116 . _____. "Von Loango nach Majombe am Kwilu-Niadi," *Ausland*, LIX(1886), 587.

4117 . _____. "Zur Bedeutung der Wochenmärkte am Kongo," *Revue Coloniale Internationale*, V(1887).

4118 Notte, Charles Joseph. *Document Notte: Stanley au Congo, 1879-1884.* Brussels: Ministère du Congo belge et du Ruanda-Urundi, Archives, 1960. 206p.

4119 . Overman, Hubert. "Lettres," *Missions en Chine et au Congo,* (1898-1900), 136-139.

4120 . Page. "Les Stanley-Falls," *MG*, X(1893), 3.

4121 . Pagels, G. "Några ord om seder och bruk bland vildarna vid öfre Kongo," *Ymer*, VI(1886), 238.

4122 . Pahde, P. "Die Erforschung des Kongo-Systems," *Geographische Zeitschrift,* I(1895), 516.

4123 . Paiva Manso. [*Visconde de*]. *Historia do Congo.* Lisbon: Academia, 1877. 369p.

4124 Paquay. *Le chemin de fer du Congo.* Brussels: Brismée, 1895. 16p.

4125 . Paris, Victor. "Lettere," *MCM*, XIII(1884), 262.

4126 . _____. "Lettres," *Echo des Missions d'Afrique*, I(1884), 150-155.

4127 . _____. "Lettres," *MCL*, XVI(1884), 245.

4128 . Parke, Thomas Heazle. *My Experiences in Equatorial Africa as Medical Officer of the Emin Pasha Relief Expedition.* London: Sampson Low; New York: Scribner's, 1891. 526p.

4129 . Parminter. "Sur le Kassai et le Sankuru," *MG*, X(1893), 80.

4130 . Pauli. [*Dr.*]. "Am Ogowe," *Globus*, LII(1887), 42-46, 55-58.

4131 . Pauly, Dionysius. "Lettres," *Het H. Misoffer*, I(1898), 122, 123, 158, 159, 173-175.

4132 . Pauwels. *Aux Belges! Vérités sur le Congo par un échappé au massacre de l'expédition Hodister.* Antwerp: Reynart-Corewijn, 1893. 32p.

4133 . Pechuel-Loesche, Eduard. [*Dr.*]. "Bericht über die zweite Kwilu-Reise," *Correspondenzblatt der Afrikanischen Gesellschaft*, I(1873), 271.

4134 . _____. "Besitz, Recht, Hörigkeit unter Afrikanern," *Deutsche Rundschau für Geographie und Statistik*, XII(1889).

4135 . _____. "Das Centralafrikanische Problem," *Österreichische Monatsschrift für den Orient*, X(1884), 33-39, 153-158, 173-176.

4136 . _____. "Handel und Produkte der Loango Küste," *Geographische Nachrichten für Welthandel und Volkswirtschaft*, I(1879), 273.

4137 . _____. *Herrn Stanley's Partisane und meine offiziellen Berichte vom Kongolande.* Leipzig, 1886. 31p.

4138 . _____. "Ein Hexenprocess in Loango," *Gartanlaube*, XXV(1877), 177-180.

4139 . _____. "Kongoforschung und Kongofrage," *VGE*, XI(1884), 184-211.

4140 . _____. "Das Kongogebiet," *DK*, I(1884), 257-264.

4141     . _____ . *Kongoland. I. Amtliche Berichte und Denkschriften über das belgische Kongo-Unternehemen. II. Unterguinea und Kongostaat als Handels- und Wirtschaftsgebiet, nebst einer Liste der Faktoreien bis zum Jahre 1887.* Jena: Costenoble, 1887. 522p.

4142     . _____ . "Das Kuilu-Gebiet," *PM*, XXIII(1877), 10.

4143     . _____ . "Ein Palaver in Loango," *Gartenlaube*, XXVI(1878), 627-632.

4144     . _____ . "Ruder und Canoes in West-Afrika," *Globus*, L(1886), 74-77.

4145     . _____ . "Schwimmende Factoreien in Westafrika," *Natur*[Halle], XXVI(1877), 157.

4146     . _____ . *Volkskunde von Loango.* Stuttgart: Strecker and Schröder, 1907. 482p.

4147     . _____ . "Westafrikanischer Leben," *Aus allen Weltteilen*, IX(1878),302, 321; X(1879), 75.

4148     . _____ ; Güssfeldt, Paul; and Falkenstein, J. *Die Loango-Expedition, ausgesandt von der deutschen Gesellschaft zur Erforschung Äquatorial Afrika's, 1873-1876.* 3 vols. Leipzig: Frohberg, 1879. Also, 3 vols., Stuttgart: Strecker and Schroder, 1907.

4149     Peeters, Paul. *Henry Beck de la Compagnie de Jésus, missionnaire au Congo belge.* Brussels: Société de Saint-Augustin, 1898. 211p. 2nd edition, Brussels: Société de Saint-Augustin, 1899. 238p.

4150 . Pelleman, Amandus. "Lettres," *Maandelijksch Verslag der Afrikaansche Missiën*, XII(1891), 139-141.

4151 . Pereira, Sebastião José. "Breve noticia de uma viagem ao Rio Lunda em agosto de 1883," *BSGL*, V(1885), 56-61.

4152 . Petitbois, G. *Quelques semaines au Congo*. Liège: C.A. Desoer, 1896. 152p.

4153 . Pfeil, Joachim. [*Graf*]. "Die Erforschung des Ulanga-Gebietes," *PM*, XXXII (1886), 353-363.

4154 . Phillips, Richard Cobden. "The Lower Congo; a Sociological Study," *JAI*, XVII(1887), 214-233.

4155 . _____. "The Social System of the Lower Congo," *JMGS*, III(1887), 154-169.

4156 . _____. "Volksstämme am Kongo. Eine sociologische Studie," *Deutsche Geographische Blätter*, VIII(1884), 313.

4157 . Picard, Edmond. "Aryens et Sémites au Congo," *Nouvelle Revue Internationale*, XII(1894), 98-102.

4158 . _____. *En Congolie*. Brussels: Larcier, 1896. 232p.

4159 . Piessens, Albijn. "Lettres," *Missions en Chine et au Congo*, (1892-1894), 576. See also, *Missien in China en Congo*, same period.

4160 . Pieton, T. S. "From Lukungu to Palaballa," *Baptist and Missions Magazine*, LXV(1885), 324.

4161 . Pinaud, A. and Chalot, C. *Petit traité de culture potagère à l'usage des postes et stations du Congo français*. Libreville: Imprimerie du Gouvernement, 1895.

4162 . Pogge, Paul. "Aufzeichnungen über das Reich und den Hof des Muatiamvo, Notizen über die Regierungsweise, die Haupstadt, die Sitten, etc.," *Globus*, XXIII(1873).

4163 . _____. "Berichte," *MAGD*, III(1881-1883), 79-146, 216.

4164 . _____. "Brief des Reisender," *MAGD*, II(1880-1881), 251.

4165 . _____. "Itinerar von Kimbundo bis Quizimeme, dem Mussumba oder der Residenz der Muata-Jamvo, und weiter östlich bis Inchibaraka vom 16 september 1875 bis 28 februar 1876," *ZGE*, XII(1877), 199.

4166 . _____. "Das Reich und der Hof des Muata-Jamvo," *Globus*, XXXII(1877), 14-28.

4167 . _____. "Reiseberichte," *VGE*, III(1876), 183-237.

4168 . _____. "Über die in Mussumba zu begründende deutsche Station," *MAGD*, II(1880-1881), 134-140.

4169 . Ponthier. [*Capt.*]. "Rapport sur le combat du Bomokandi," *Indépendance Belge*, March 25, 1892.

4170 . Potagos, Papagiotis [*Dr.*]. *Voyage à l'ouest du Haut-Nil en 1876-1877.* Paris: Delagrave, 1880. Also, *BSGP*, Sixth Series, XX(1880), 5.

4171 . Poussot, Jean-Joseph. "Voyage dans le Zaire," *BGCSS*, V(1866-1867), 777-795.

4172 . Prager, Erich. "Spiele der Eingeborenen im Kongostaate," *DK*, XVI(1899), 322-324.

4173 . Prévers, Joseph. "Lettres," *Bode van het H. Hart*, XXXII(1900-1901), 151-155.

4174 . _____. "Lettres," *Missions Belges de la Compagnie de Jésus*, I(1899), 11, 12, 27-31, 68-75, 241-244, 315-318, 414, 415; II(1900), 60-66, 77-81, 82-87, 128-131, 157-163, 262, 263, 371-378; III(1901), 176-184.

4175 . _____. "Lettres," *Précis Historiques*, XLVI(1897), 531, 532; XLVII(1899), 104-109, 259-268, 313-317, 587-589.

4176 . _____. "Missionsbriefe," *Echo aus Afrika*, XIII(1901), 65-70.

4177 Prévers, Joseph. "Superstitions indigènes au Kwango," *Belgique Coloniale*, V(1899), 271 fwd.

4178 . Probert, Herbert. *Life and Scenes in Congo*. Philadelphia: American Baptist Publication Society, 1889. 192p.

4179 . Ratzel, F. [Dr.]. *Die Afrikanischen Bögen, ihre Verbreitung und Verwandtschaften*. Leipzig: Hirzel, 1891.

4180 . _____. "Einige Bemerkungen zur Skizze der staatenbildenden Völker und der Eingebornenstaaten von Afrika," *PM*, XXXI(1885), 249.

4181 . _____. "Die geographische Verbreitung des Bogens und der Pfeile in Afrika," *Berichte der Philologisch-historische Klasse der Koenigliche Sächsische Gesellschaft der Wissenschaften*, XXXIX(1887), 233.

4182 . _____. *Die Naturvölker Afrikas*. Leipzig: Bibliographisches Institute, 1887-1888. 660p.

4183 . _____ _____ "Versuch einer Zusammen fassung der wissenschaftlichen Ergebnisse der Stanleyschen Durchquerung," *PM*, XXXVI(1890), 257, 281.

4184 . Reelick, Willibrord. "Lettres," *Messager des Ames du Purgatoire*, IV (1900-1901), 732, 733.

4185 . _____. "Lettres," *Règne du Coeur de Jésus*, XII(1900), 150; XIII(1901), 201-203; XV(1903), 197-199.

4186 . Reichard, Paul. "Bericht über die Reise nach Urna und Katanga," *Globus*, XLVIII(1885), 23-26. Also, *MAGD*, IV(1883-1885), 303.

4187 . Reichelmann, G. *Meine Erlebnisse in den Wissmann-Truppe*. Magdeburg: Creutz, 1892. 232p.

4188 . Reichelt, G. T. "Kongoland und Kongostaat, wie sie sind und sein werden," *Ausland*, LXI(1888).

4189 . Remy, Jules. *Le Catholicisme et la vapeur au centre de l'Afrique*. Poitiers: Imprimerie du "Courrier de la Vienne," 1901. 155p.

4190 . _____. "Lettres," *Annales Apostoliques*, XI(1896), 63-66; XVI(1900-1901), 286.

4191 . _____. "Les Soeurs missionnaires au centre de l'Afrique," *MCL*, XXV(1893), 416, 417, 427-429, 440-443.

4192 . Renard, A. "Les insectes [animaux] nuisibles dans les missions," *Missions Belges de la Compagnie de Jésus*, I(1899), 118-123, 194-199, 277-285, 389-397; II(1900), 28-35, 132-138, 170-174, 330-335; III(1901), 34-37, 145-148, 219-222, 303-305, 464-467; IV(1902), 155-158, 365-369.

4193 . Renier, Arsenius. "Lettres," *Missions en Chine et au Congo*, (1898-1900), 413-416.

4194 . Roelens, Victor. "Lettere," *MCM*, XXVI(1897), 194, 195; XXXII(1903), 590-592.

4195 . _____. "Lettres," *Annalen der Afrikaansche Missiën*, X(1893-1894), 129-139, 331-338; XIX(1902-1903), 103-105, 221-223.

4196 . _____. "Lettres," *Maandelijksch Verslag der Afrikaansche Missiën*, XV (1894), 6-20, 20, 21, 22-25, 82-92, 167-174, 202-211, 324-337; XVI (1895), 35-43, 88-92; XVIII(1897), 227, 228; XIX(1898), 35-42, 101-106, 106-109, 131-139, 140-146, 227-229, 323-327, 356-367.

4197 . _____. "Lettres," *Missiën der Witte Paters*, XX(1899), 3-12, 42-50, 69-79, 131, 132, 146-160, 183-188, 238-249, 346-348, XXI(1900), 23-32, 77-81, 127-134, 165-168, 228, 229, 255-258, 299-306; XXII(1901), 30-32, 331-333.

4198 . _____. "Lettres," *Missions d'Afrique*[Malines], XIX(1898), 36-43, 195-197, 323-327, 362-372; XX(1899), 3-7, 58-64, 97, 98, 156-160, 193-203, 204, 205, 211-221, 225-235, 263-270, 289-299, 340-346.

4199 . _____. "Lettres," *Missions d'Afrique*[Paris], (1895-1897), 320-322; (1897-1900), 418-425, 661-665, 817-825.

4200    . _____. "Lettres," *Missions d'Alger*, (1891-1892), 431; (1893-1894), 182-184, 223-227, 391-395.

4201    . _____. "Missionsbriefe," *Afrika-Bote*, II(1896), 135-137; IV(1898), 164, 165; V(1899), 101-105.

4202    . _____. "Missionsbriefe," *Echo aus Afrika*, VII(1895), 103-105; XVIII(1906), 129-133.

4203    . _____. "Les missions de Baudouinville," *Belgique Coloniale*, V(1899), 377, 378, 388, 389, 412, 413, 424, 425.

4204    . Roger, Oscar. "Le Congo," *BSBG*, IX(1884), 651-670.

4205    . Rogers, J. L. [*Rev.*]. "Stanley-Pool," *MH*, LXXXVI(1890).

4206    . Roget, L. "Le district de l'Arouwimi-et-Ouellé," *BSBG*, XV(1891), 97-128. Also, *Publications de l'État du Congo*, No. 5, 1891, 39p.

4207    . _____. "Le sultanat de Djabbir," *MG*, VII(1890), 101.

4208    . Rohlfs, Gerhard. [*Dr.*]. "Die Brusseler Conferenz zur Erforschung und Regeneration Afrika's im palais des Konigs der Belgen, Leopold II, 12 September 1876," *PM*, XXII(1876), 388-393.

4209    . Roskoschny, H. *Das Kongogebiet und seine Nachbarländer*. Leipzig: Gressner, 1885. 240p.

4210    . Rosseel, Joseph. "Lettres," *Missiën der Witte Paters*, XXII(1901), 294-299, 364-368; XXIII(1902), 28-32, 70-76, 116-118.

4211. Rotsaert, Karel. "Lettres," *Missiën der Witte Paters*, XX(1899), 332–336; XXII(1901), 27–29, 33–41, 254–256, 340–344; XXIII(1902), 214–217.

4212. Rouvre, Charles de. "La Guinée méridionale indépendante; Kongo, Kacongo, Ngogo et Loango de 1870 à 1877," *BSGP*, Sixth Series, XX(1880).

4213. _____. "Huit ans au Congo," *Exploration*, III(1879), 372.

4214. Saegher, De. "Les coutumes des indigenes de l'Etat indépendant du Congo," *Bulletin de la Société Belge d'Études coloniales*, I(1894).

4215. Saillens, R. *Au pays des ténèbres. Histoire de la première mission chrétienne au Congo.* Paris: Fischbacher, 1890. 116p.

4216. Sauter, Karl. *Des Leben am Kongo.* Bern, 1886. 24p.

4217. Savorgnan de Brazzà, Pierre Paul François Camille. *Conférences et lettres ...sur les trois explorations dans l'Ouest Africain, de 1875 à 1886.* Paris: Dreyfous, 1887. 463p.

4218. _____. "De l'Atlantique à Congo interieur," *Bulletin de la Société de Géographie Commerciale de Paris*, IV(1882), 271–277.

4219. _____. *Lettre à M. Paul Bourde, écrite de Brazzaville, à la veille de son retour en France, sur les impressions et les conclusions de l'enquête qu'il vient de terminer au Congo.* Paris: L. de Soye et fils, 1906. 8p.

4220. _____. "Lettere del Conte G. di Brazza," *BSGI*, XIX(1886), 114, 204, 406.

4221. _____. "Voyage dans l'Ouest africain," *TM*, LIV(1887), 1400ff.

4222. Scheymans, Jean. "Lettres," *Missions d'Afrique*, XXII(1901), 275–281; XXIV(1903), 212–224.

4223 . Schmitz, Bruno. "Lettres," *APFL*, LXXII(1900), 263-277.

4224 . _____. "Lettres," *Belgique Coloniale*, VII(1901), 15, 173, 174.

4225 . _____. "Lettres," *Maandelijksch Verslag der Afrikaansche Missiën*, XVII (1896), 187-189, 241-244, 261-264, 265-271, 298-302, 328, 349-350; XVIII(1897), 75-81, 367-372; XIX(1898),165-170.

4226 . _____. "Lettres," *Missiën der Witte Paters*, XXI(1900), 40-47, 201-204, 224-227, 231-232; XXII(1901), 65-71, 268-272.

4227 . _____. "Lettres," *Missions d'Afrique*[Malines], XIX(1898), 167-171, 244-247; XX(1899), 12-15, 271-274; XXII(1901), 122, 123, 252-255.

4228 . _____. "Lettres," *Missions d'Afrique*[Paris], (1897-1900), 743-745; (1901-1902), 16-21.

4229 . Schoutens, Etienne. "Le Congo et les Franciscains," *Messager de St. François*, XI(1885-1886), 49-56. Also, *Bode van den H. Franciskus*, XI(1885-1886), 1-8; XII(1886-1887), 94.

4230 . Schutt, O. "Begräbnissgebraüche in West-Afrika," *Natur*, XXX(1881), 317-318.

4231 . _____. "Ethnographische Bemerkungen," *MAGD*, I(1879), 200.

4232 . _____. "Geographische und naturwissenschaftliche Bemerkungen," *MAGD*, I (1879), 193-198.

4233 . _____. "Im Reich der Bangala," *Ausland*, LIV(1881), 381-384.

4234 . _____. *Reise in südwestlichen Becken des Congo*. Berlin: Reimer, 1881. 180p.

4235 . _____. "Reiseberichte," *MAGD*, I(1879), 64-110, 173.

4236 . Schweinfurth, Georg August. "The Wellé Problem," *SGM*, IV(1888), 149-152.

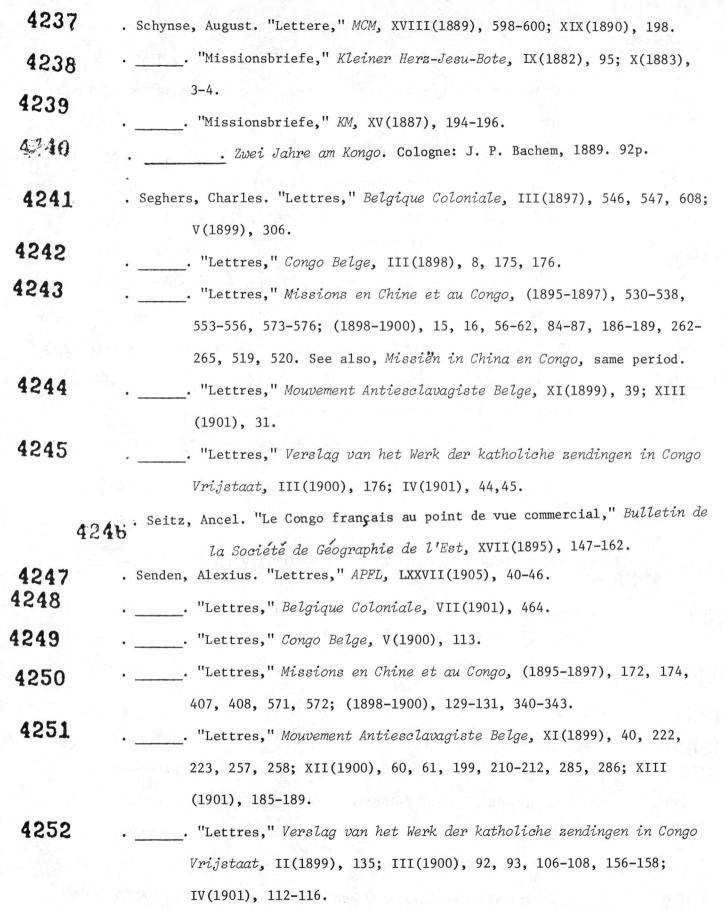

4237    . Schynse, August. "Lettere," *MCM*, XVIII(1889), 598-600; XIX(1890), 198.

4238    . _____. "Missionsbriefe," *Kleiner Herz-Jesu-Bote*, IX(1882), 95; X(1883),

3-4.

4239    . _____. "Missionsbriefe," *KM*, XV(1887), 194-196.

4240    . _____. *Zwei Jahre am Kongo*. Cologne: J. P. Bachem, 1889. 92p.

4241    . Seghers, Charles. "Lettres," *Belgique Coloniale*, III(1897), 546, 547, 608;

V(1899), 306.

4242    . _____. "Lettres," *Congo Belge*, III(1898), 8, 175, 176.

4243    . _____. "Lettres," *Missions en Chine et au Congo*, (1895-1897), 530-538,

553-556, 573-576; (1898-1900), 15, 16, 56-62, 84-87, 186-189, 262-

265, 519, 520. See also, *Missiën in China en Congo*, same period.

4244    . _____. "Lettres," *Mouvement Antiesclavagiste Belge*, XI(1899), 39; XIII

(1901), 31.

4245    . _____. "Lettres," *Verslag van het Werk der katholiche zendingen in Congo*

*Vrijstaat*, III(1900), 176; IV(1901), 44,45.

4246    . Seitz, Ancel. "Le Congo français au point de vue commercial," *Bulletin de*

*la Société de Géographie de l'Est*, XVII(1895), 147-162.

4247    . Senden, Alexius. "Lettres," *APFL*, LXXVII(1905), 40-46.

4248    . _____. "Lettres," *Belgique Coloniale*, VII(1901), 464.

4249    . _____. "Lettres," *Congo Belge*, V(1900), 113.

4250    . _____. "Lettres," *Missions en Chine et au Congo*, (1895-1897), 172, 174,

407, 408, 571, 572; (1898-1900), 129-131, 340-343.

4251    . _____. "Lettres," *Mouvement Antiesclavagiste Belge*, XI(1899), 40, 222,

223, 257, 258; XII(1900), 60, 61, 199, 210-212, 285, 286; XIII

(1901), 185-189.

4252    . _____. "Lettres," *Verslag van het Werk der katholiche zendingen in Congo*

*Vrijstaat*, II(1899), 135; III(1900), 92, 93, 106-108, 156-158;

IV(1901), 112-116.

4253 . Serpa Pimentel, Jayme Pereira de Sampaio Forjaz de. "Um anno no Congo, 1 de maio de 1895 a 1 de maio 1896. Apreciações sobre o districto do Congo. Coordenação de alguns Documentos relativos ao Congo. Traços geraes d'una administração ultramarina," *Portugal em Africa*, VI (1899), 85-109, 142-162, 189-206, 240-257, 289-311, 329-344, 381-404, 425-447, 465-497, 529-559, 601-635; VIII(1901), 145-152, 193-207, 346-360, 413-420, 475-482, 535-542, 597-602, 661-683.

4254 . _____. "O Congo portuguez. Relatorios sobre as feitorias do Zaire, seu commercio, trabalhos de Stanley, missões inglezas e Cabinda," *BSGL*, VII(1887), 269-310.

4255 . Sharpe, Alfred. "A Journey to Garenganze," *PRGS*, New Series, XIV(1892), 36-47.

4256 . Silva Porto, Antonio Francisco Ferreira da. "Journey from Bihe (Bié) to the Bakuba Country," *PRGS*, New Series, IX(1887), 753-756.

4257 . Simpelacre, Achiel. "Lettres," *Voix du Rédempteur*, IX(1900), 206-211, 316, 317, 391, 392, 393-395; X(1901), 104-106, 138-141, 358-360.

4258 . Singer, H. "Das Kongoquellgebiet," *PM*, XLV(1899), 19.

4259 . Slosse, Eugene. "En avant avec la brigade d'études," *CIL*, III(1894), 26, 35, 42, 54, 60, 71, 76.

4260 . _____. "La récolte du malafoux," *CIL*, I(1892), 64.

4261 . _____. "La vannerie," *CIL*, II(1893), 66.

4262 . Söllner, Charles. *Un voyage au Congo*. Namur: Godenne, 1895. 234p.

4263 . Sousa, Antonio José de. "No Congo: Trabalhos da missaõ portuguese de Salvador," *BSGL*, V(1885), 36-56.

4264 . Sousa Barroso, Antonio José de. "O Congo: seu passado, presente et futuro," *BSGL*, VIII(1888-1889), 167-235.

4265 . _____. "Trabalhos em Africa: missaõ portugueza do Congo," *BSGL*, VI (1886), 455-498.

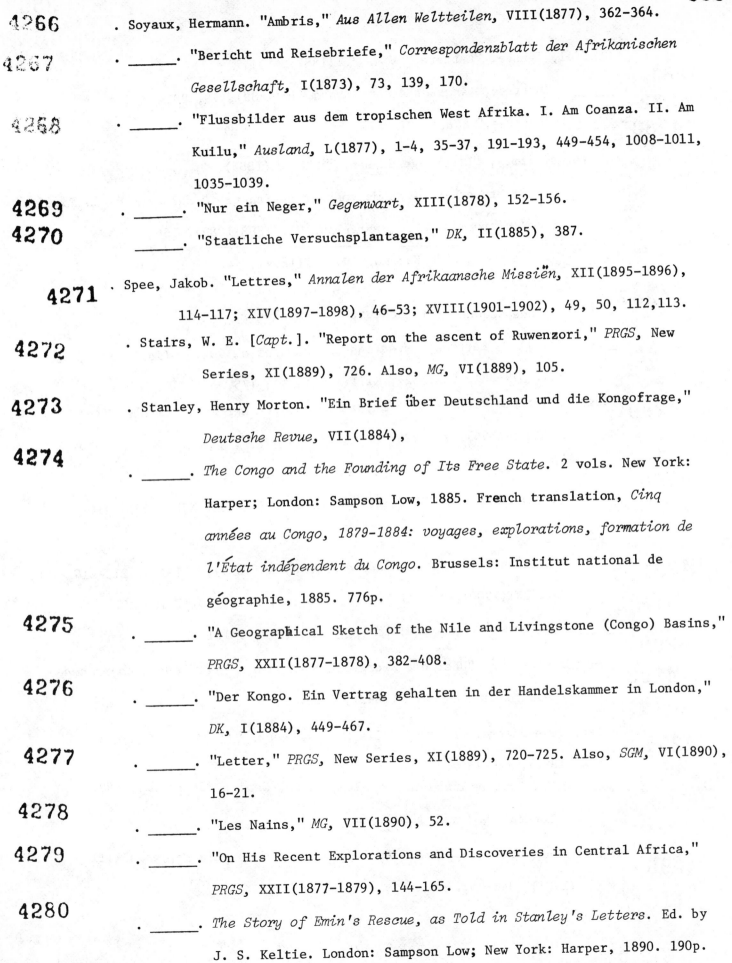

4266 . Soyaux, Hermann. "Ambris," *Aus Allen Weltteilen,* VIII(1877), 362-364.

4267 . _____. "Bericht und Reisebriefe," *Correspondenzblatt der Afrikanischen Gesellschaft,* I(1873), 73, 139, 170.

4268 . _____. "Flussbilder aus dem tropischen West Afrika. I. Am Coanza. II. Am Kuilu," *Ausland,* L(1877), 1-4, 35-37, 191-193, 449-454, 1008-1011, 1035-1039.

4269 . _____. "Nur ein Neger," *Gegenwart,* XIII(1878), 152-156.

4270 _____. "Staatliche Versuchsplantagen," *DK,* II(1885), 387.

4271 Spee, Jakob. "Lettres," *Annalen der Afrikaansche Missiën,* XII(1895-1896), 114-117; XIV(1897-1898), 46-53; XVIII(1901-1902), 49, 50, 112,113.

4272 . Stairs, W. E. [*Capt.*]. "Report on the ascent of Ruwenzori," *PRGS,* New Series, XI(1889), 726. Also, *MG,* VI(1889), 105.

4273 . Stanley, Henry Morton. "Ein Brief über Deutschland und die Kongofrage," *Deutsche Revue,* VII(1884),

4274 . _____. *The Congo and the Founding of Its Free State.* 2 vols. New York: Harper; London: Sampson Low, 1885. French translation, *Cinq années au Congo, 1879-1884: voyages, explorations, formation de l'État indépendent du Congo.* Brussels: Institut national de géographie, 1885. 776p.

4275 . _____. "A Geographical Sketch of the Nile and Livingstone (Congo) Basins," *PRGS,* XXII(1877-1878), 382-408.

4276 . _____. "Der Kongo. Ein Vertrag gehalten in der Handelskammer in London," *DK,* I(1884), 449-467.

4277 . _____. "Letter," *PRGS,* New Series, XI(1889), 720-725. Also, *SGM,* VI(1890), 16-21.

4278 . _____. "Les Nains," *MG,* VII(1890), 52.

4279 . _____. "On His Recent Explorations and Discoveries in Central Africa," *PRGS,* XXII(1877-1879), 144-165.

4280 . _____. *The Story of Emin's Rescue, as Told in Stanley's Letters.* Ed. by J. S. Keltie. London: Sampson Low; New York: Harper, 1890. 190p.

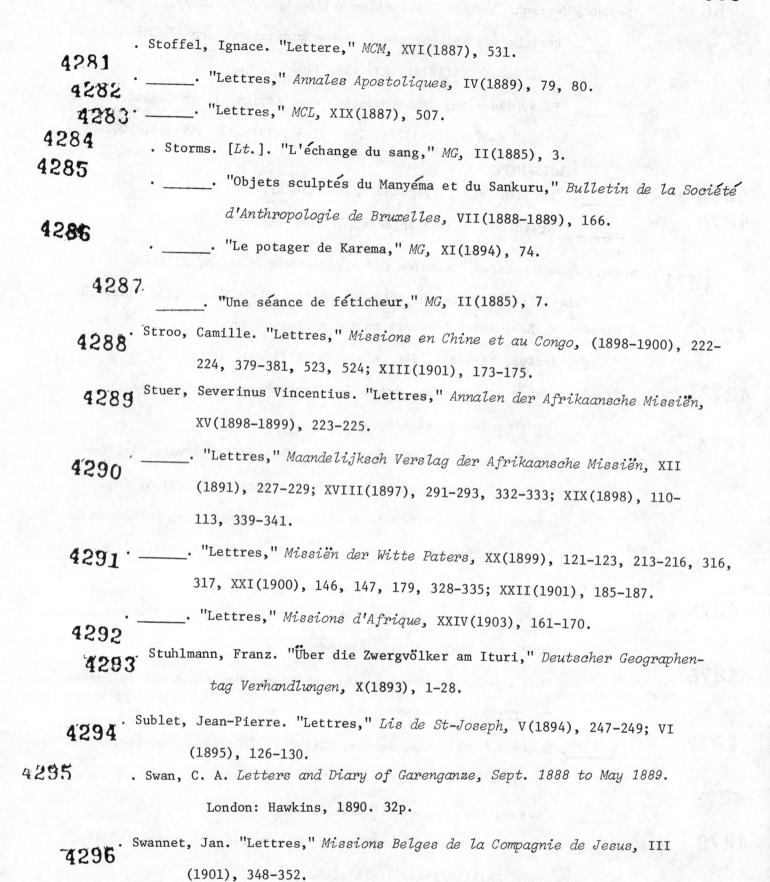

4281 . Stoffel, Ignace. "Lettere," *MCM*, XVI(1887), 531.

4282 . ———. "Lettres," *Annales Apostoliques*, IV(1889), 79, 80.

4283 . ———. "Lettres," *MCL*, XIX(1887), 507.

4284 . Storms. [*Lt.*]. "L'échange du sang," *MG*, II(1885), 3.

4285 . ———. "Objets sculptés du Manyéma et du Sankuru," *Bulletin de la Société d'Anthropologie de Bruxelles*, VII(1888-1889), 166.

4286 . ———. "Le potager de Karema," *MG*, XI(1894), 74.

4287 . ———. "Une séance de féticheur," *MG*, II(1885), 7.

4288 . Stroo, Camille. "Lettres," *Missions en Chine et au Congo*, (1898-1900), 222-224, 379-381, 523, 524; XIII(1901), 173-175.

4289 . Stuer, Severinus Vincentius. "Lettres," *Annalen der Afrikaansche Missiën*, XV(1898-1899), 223-225.

4290 . ———. "Lettres," *Maandelijksch Verslag der Afrikaansche Missiën*, XII (1891), 227-229; XVIII(1897), 291-293, 332-333; XIX(1898), 110-113, 339-341.

4291 . ———. "Lettres," *Missiën der Witte Paters*, XX(1899), 121-123, 213-216, 316, 317, XXI(1900), 146, 147, 179, 328-335; XXII(1901), 185-187.

4292 . ———. "Lettres," *Missions d'Afrique*, XXIV(1903), 161-170.

4293 . Stuhlmann, Franz. "Über die Zwergvölker am Ituri," *Deutscher Geographen-tag Verhandlungen*, X(1893), 1-28.

4294 . Sublet, Jean-Pierre. "Lettres," *Lis de St-Joseph*, V(1894), 247-249; VI (1895), 126-130.

4295 . Swan, C. A. *Letters and Diary of Garenganze, Sept. 1888 to May 1889.* London: Hawkins, 1890. 32p.

4296 . Swannet, Jan. "Lettres," *Missions Belges de la Compagnie de Jesus*, III (1901), 348-352.

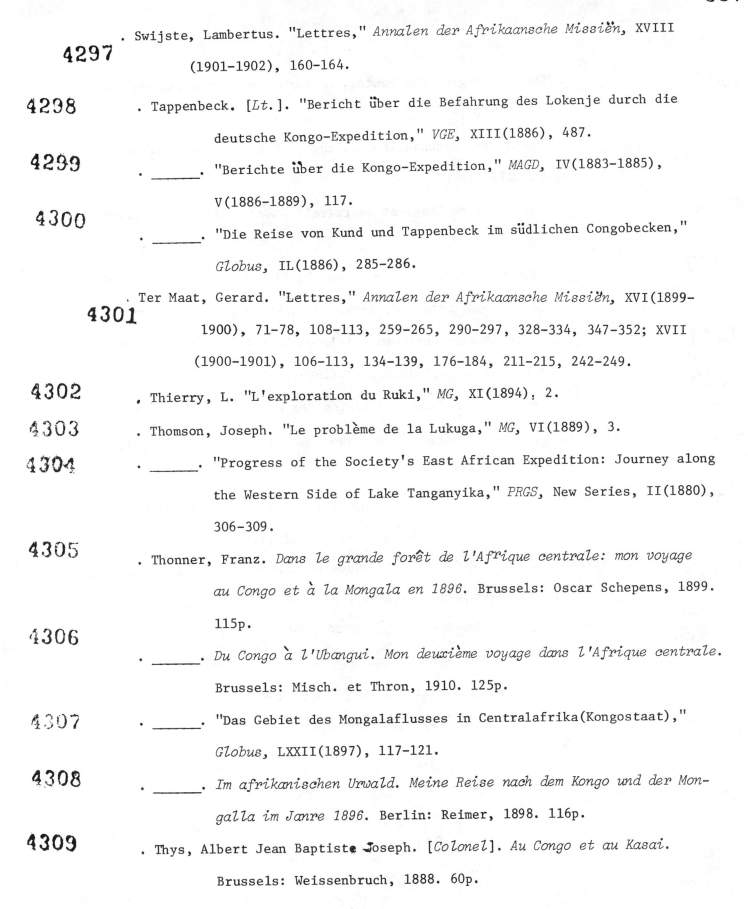

4297 . Swijste, Lambertus. "Lettres," *Annalen der Afrikaansche Missiën*, XVIII (1901-1902), 160-164.

4298 . Tappenbeck. [*Lt.*]. "Bericht über die Befahrung des Lokenje durch die deutsche Kongo-Expedition," *VGE*, XIII(1886), 487.

4299 . _____. "Berichte über die Kongo-Expedition," *MAGD*, IV(1883-1885), V(1886-1889), 117.

4300 . _____. "Die Reise von Kund und Tappenbeck im südlichen Congobecken," *Globus*, IL(1886), 285-286.

4301 . Ter Maat, Gerard. "Lettres," *Annalen der Afrikaansche Missiën*, XVI(1899-1900), 71-78, 108-113, 259-265, 290-297, 328-334, 347-352; XVII (1900-1901), 106-113, 134-139, 176-184, 211-215, 242-249.

4302 . Thierry, L. "L'exploration du Ruki," *MG*, XI(1894), 2.

4303 . Thomson, Joseph. "Le problème de la Lukuga," *MG*, VI(1889), 3.

4304 . _____. "Progress of the Society's East African Expedition: Journey along the Western Side of Lake Tanganyika," *PRGS*, New Series, II(1880), 306-309.

4305 . Thonner, Franz. *Dans le grande forêt de l'Afrique centrale: mon voyage au Congo et à la Mongala en 1896*. Brussels: Oscar Schepens, 1899. 115p.

4306 . _____. *Du Congo à l'Ubangui. Mon deuxième voyage dans l'Afrique centrale*. Brussels: Misch. et Thron, 1910. 125p.

4307 . _____. "Das Gebiet des Mongalaflusses in Centralafrika(Kongostaat)," *Globus*, LXXII(1897), 117-121.

4308 . _____. *Im afrikanischen Urwald. Meine Reise nach dem Kongo und der Mongalla im Janre 1896*. Berlin: Reimer, 1898. 116p.

4309 . Thys, Albert Jean Baptiste Joseph. [*Colonel*]. *Au Congo et au Kasai*. Brussels: Weissenbruch, 1888. 60p.

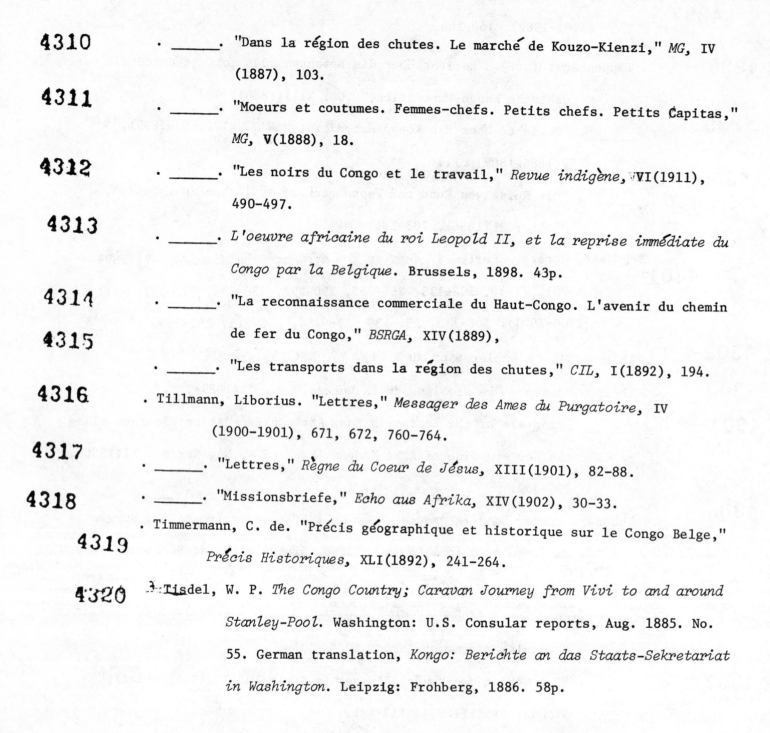

4310 · \_\_\_\_\_ . "Dans la région des chutes. Le marché de Kouzo-Kienzi," *MG*, IV (1887), 103.

4311 · \_\_\_\_\_ . "Moeurs et coutumes. Femmes-chefs. Petits chefs. Petits Capitas," *MG*, V(1888), 18.

4312 · \_\_\_\_\_ . "Les noirs du Congo et le travail," *Revue indigène*, VI(1911), 490-497.

4313 · \_\_\_\_\_ . *L'oeuvre africaine du roi Leopold II, et la reprise immédiate du Congo par la Belgique.* Brussels, 1898. 43p.

4314 · \_\_\_\_\_ . "La reconnaissance commerciale du Haut-Congo. L'avenir du chemin de fer du Congo," *BSRGA*, XIV(1889),

4315 · \_\_\_\_\_ . "Les transports dans la région des chutes," *CIL*, I(1892), 194.

4316 . Tillmann, Liborius. "Lettres," *Messager des Ames du Purgatoire*, IV (1900-1901), 671, 672, 760-764.

4317 · \_\_\_\_\_ . "Lettres," *Règne du Coeur de Jésus*, XIII(1901), 82-88.

4318 · \_\_\_\_\_ . "Missionsbriefe," *Echo aus Afrika*, XIV(1902), 30-33.

4319 · Timmermann, C. de. "Précis géographique et historique sur le Congo Belge," *Précis Historiques*, XLI(1892), 241-264.

4320 · Tisdel, W. P. *The Congo Country; Caravan Journey from Vivi to and around Stanley-Pool.* Washington: U.S. Consular reports, Aug. 1885. No. 55. German translation, *Kongo: Berichte an das Staats-Sekretariat in Washington.* Leipzig: Frohberg, 1886. 58p.

4321 . _____. "My Trip to the Congo," *Century*, XXXIX(1889-1890), 609-618.

4322 . _____and Glave, E. J. "The Realm of Congo," *Century*[U.S.], XXXIX(1889-1890), 609-620, 824-838.

4323 . Tobback. [*Capt.*]. "Rapport sur la révolte des Arabes du Lualaba," *MG*, IX(1892), 83.

4324 . Trilles, H. "Au pays Fan," *Bulletin de la Société de Géographie de Lille*, XLIII(1902),

4325 . _____. *Chez les Fang, ou, quinze années de séjour au Congo français.* Lille: Desclée, De Brouwer et Cie.,1912. 286p. Paris: Desclee, 1913. 386p. Also, *MCL*, XXX(1898), 103ff.

4326 . _____. "Les Fang," *Bulletin de la Société de Géographie de Lille*, XLVI (1906), 360-370; XLVIII(1907), 5-9.

4327 . _____. "Mille lieues dans l'inconnu. A travers les pays fang, de la côte aux rives du Djah, août 1899-avril 1901," *MCL*, XXXIV(1902), 4ff; XXXV(1903), 304ff; XXXVII(1905), 143-144.

4328 . _____. "Monsieur Bébé au pays Fang," *Bulletin de la Société de Géographie de Lyon*, XVII(1891), 518-521.

4329 . _____. "Noirs et blancs (légende Fang)," *Revue indigène*, III(1908), 69-73, 155-157, 180-182, 218-220.

4330 . _____. "Un peuple du Congo français. Les Fang," *Bulletin de la Société de Géographie de Lille*, XLIX(1909),

4331 . _____. "Le peuple Fang," *Revue indigène*, VII(1912), 48-58, 99-106.

4332 . _____. "Proverbes, légendes et contes Fang," *Bulletin de la Société Neuchâteloise de Géographie*, XVI(1905), 49-295.

4333 . _____. "Les rites de la naisance chez les Fang," *Bulletin de la Société Neuchâteloise de Geographie*, XX(1909-1910), 403-411.

4334 . _____. *Le totemisme chez les Fang*. Paris: Picard, 1912. 654p.

4335 . Tristram Pruen, S. *The Arab and the African: Experiences in Eastern Equatorial Africa during a Residence of Three Years*. London: Seeley, 1891. 338p.

4336 . Tritton, J. *Rise and Progress of the Work on the Congo River*. London: Baptist Mission House, 1884. 63p.

4337 . Trouet, Léon. *Le chemin de fer du Congo*. Brussels: Goemaere, 1898. 101p.

4338 . Troup, John Rose. *With Stanley's Rear Column*. London: Chapman & Hall, 1890. 361p.

4339 . Tuckey, James Hingston. *Narrative of an Expedition to Explore the River Zaire, Usually Called the Congo, in South Africa, in 1816. . .to Which Is Added the Journal of Professor Smith*. London: Murray, 1818. 498p. French ed., *Relation d'une expédition entreprise en 1816, sous les ordres du capitaine J. K. Tuckey, pour reconnaitre le Zaïre, suivie du journal du professeur Smith*. 2 vols. Paris: De Gide, 1818.

4340 . Ulff, F. "Les funérailles dans le Bas Congo," *CIL*, III(1894), 44-46.

4341 Ussel, Annet. "Lettres," *Annales Apostoliques,* VI(1891), 52-62.

4342 Uzès, Anne de Rochechouart-Mortemart [*Duchesse d'Uzès*]. *Le voyage de mon fils au Congo.* Paris: Plon, 1894. 342p.

4343 . Valcke, Louis. "Cinq années sur le Congo," *Bulletin de la Société de Géographie Commerciale de Paris,* VIII(1886), 203.

4344 . _____. "D'Anvers au Congo," *MG,* VIII(1891), 73.

4345 . _____. "Matadi-port de mer," *MG,* VI(1889), 65.

4346 . Van Acker, August. "Lettres," *Maandelijksch Verslag der Afrikaansche Missiën,* XVII(1896), 38, 39, 103-108, 183-186, 294-298, 328, 329; XVIII(1897), 19-24, 177-180, 264; XIX(1898), 60, 61.

4347 . _____. "Lettres," *Missions d'Afrique,* XIX(1898), 43, 44; XXII(1901), 170-180.

4348 . _____. "Missionsbriefe," *Afrika-Bote,* VII(1900-1901), 31-34.

4349 . _____. "Missionsbriefe," *KM,* XXVI(1897-1898), 212.

4350 . Van Campenhout, Emile. *Rapport sur lex travaux du laboratoire médicale de Léopoldville, en 1899-1900.* Brussels: Hayez, 1901. 164p.

4351 . Van Damme, Joseph. "Comment les nègres transportent," *CIL,* IV(1895), 129.

4352 . _____. "Lettres," *Missions en Chine et au Congo,* (1895-1897), 92, 93, 124-126, 252-254. See also, *Missiën in China en Congo,* same period.

4353 . Van den Bosch, Alphonse. "Lettres," *Bode van het H. Hart,* XXVII(1895-1896), 209, 297-301.

4354 . _____. "Lettres," *Précis Historiques,* XLIV(1895), 495; XLV(1896), 158, 161; XLVI(1897), 436-438.

4355 . Van den Gheyn, Joseph. "La langue Congolaise et les idiomes Bantous," *Précis Historiques,* XLI(1892), 49-62, 97-110.

4356 Van der Lest, Christiaan [*Fr. Norbertus*]. "Lettres," *Annalen der Afrikaansche Missiën*, XIII(1896-1897), 352-355.

4357 . Van der Meiren, Joseph. "Lettres," *Missiën der Witte Paters*, XXII(1901), 148-154, 315-317; XXIII(1902), 319, 320.

4358 . Van der Molen, Leon. "Lettres," *Missions en Chine et au Congo*, (1898-1900), 71-75, 213,214, XIII(1901), 140-143; XV(1903), 259-261.

4359 . Van der Straeten, Hendrik. "Lettres," *Bode van het H. Hart*, XXIX(1897-1898), 152, 153, 182-184; XXXI(1899-1900), 55, 56.

4360 Vanderyst, H. "L'agriculture au Congo, suivi de remarques de G. de Marneffe," *Journal de l'Association des anciens élèves de l'Institut agricole de Gembloux*, IV(1893), 88.

4361 . Vande Velde, Fritz [*Capt.*]. "Le Bas-Congo," *BSBG*, XII(1888), 521-534.

4362 . Vande Velde, Lievin [*Capt.*]. "Le Bas Congo, lettres inédites," *CIL*, I(1892), 78-79, 85-87, 93-95, 101-103, 109-111, 117-119, 125-127, 133-135, 141-143, 149-151.

4363 . _____. "La région du Bas-Congo et du Kwilou-Niadi. Usages et coutumes des indigènes," *BSBG*, X(1886), 347-412.

4364 . Van de Vliet, Clément. "L'exploration de l'Uellé. De Djabbir à Suruangu," *CIL*, III(1894), 114-117, 121-125, 131-135, 140-143, 147-150, 164-167, 172-175.

4365 . Vandrunen, James. *Heures africaines. Algérie, Sahara, Congo, îles de l'Atlantique*. Brussels: Bulens, 1900. 409p.

4366 . Van Eetvelde, Edmond. "Etablissement de lignes télégraphiques. Rapport et décrets," *Bulletin officiel de l'État indépendant du Congo*, 1893, pp.240-245.

4367 . Van Gele. "L'exploration de l'Oubanghi-Doua-Koyou," *BSBG*, XIII(1889), 5.

4368 . _____. "Explorations on the Welle-Mobangi River," *PRGS*, New Series, XI(1899), 325-341.

4369 Van Genechten, Ludolphus. "Lettres," *Het H. Misoffer*, II(1899), 76, 100, 119, 120, 135, 136, 229-232; III(1900), 20-23, 165, 166; IV(1901), 43, 44, 75-77, 94-96, 119, 120, 133, 134, 151-153, 227-229; V(1902), 17-19, 50-54, 71-73, 86, 87, 140-143.

4370 . Van Hoestenberghe, Eugeen. "Lettres," *Maandelijksch Verslag der Afrikaansche Missiën*, XVI(1895), 324-327; XVII(1896), 39-42.

4371 . Van Hoof, Hieronymus. "Lettres," *Het H. Misoffer*, I(1898), 91-95, 123-126, 185-193; II(1899), 17-22, 22-24, 32-37, 53-56, 67-73, 128-132, 147-149, 159-165, 173-175, 189-192, 207-210, 226-229; III(1900), 35-38, 74-80, 98-104, 113-118, 124-128, 141-147, 160-165, 169-174, 184-188, 235-237; IV(1901), 20-24, 44, 58-60, 114-119, 134-139, 153-156, 166-170, 185-188.

4372 . Van Mons, A. "Conférence et projections de photographies prises au Congo. Résumé," *Bulletin de la Société d'Anthropologie de Bruxelles*, XI(1892-1893), 211.

4373 . _____. "La pêche au Congo," *CIL*, II(1893), 26.

4374 . Van Octroy, F. [*Capt.*]. "Le Katanga, orographie, hydrographie, climat," *Revue des Questions Scientifiques*, XXXVIII(1895).

4375 . _____. "Missions catholiques au Congo," *Revue des Questions Scientifiques*, XIII(1889), 272.

4376 . Van Reusel, Charles. *Notice historique sur le Congo et biographie du capitaine Van Kerckhoven*. Malines: Heymans, 1895. 58p.

4377 . Van Ronslé, Camillus. "De Congo-Missie jubileert 1888-1938. De Terugblik van een baanbreker, Z. H. Exc. Mgr Van Ronslé," *Annalen van Sparrendaal*, XXXVIII(1938), 170-175.

4378 . _____. "Le développement des Missions Catholiques dans la Colonie belge (Vicariat de Léopoldville)," *Revue Illustrée de l'Exposition Missionnaire Vaticane*, II(1925), 626-630.

4379    . _____ _____. "Lettere," *MCM*, XIX(1890), 181-184.

4380    . _____. "Lettres," *Belgique Coloniale*, V(1899), 187, 188.

4381    . _____. "Lettres," *Congo Belge*, IV(1899), 104; VII(1902), 39, 88.

4382    . _____. "Lettres," *MG*, VII(1890), 93, 94, XV(1898), 628; XIX(1902), 61,
        62, 122, 123.

4383    . _____. "Lettres," *Missions en Chine et au Congo*, (1889-1891), 175, 176,
        188-192, 253-256, 269-272, 313-318, 398-400, 524-527; (1892-1894),
        172-174, 253-256, 269-272; (1898-1900), 168, 401, 402. See also,
        *Missiën in China en Congo*, same period.

4384    . _____. "Lettres," *Mouvement Antiesclavagiste*, III(1891), 224-228; IV
        (1892), 187, 188; XI(1899), 221, 222; XII(1900), 97; XIII(1901),
        129-136.

4385    . _____. "Lettres," *Verslåg van he Werk der katholiche zendingen in Congo
        Vrijstaat*, II(1899), 5-13, 134; III(1900), 61.

4386    . _____. "Missionsbriefe," *Echo aus Afrika*, XI(1899), 15-21.

4387    . Van Straelen, C. *Missions Catholiques et Protestantes au Congo*. Brussels:
        Société Belge de Librairie, 1898. 67p.

4388    . Van Tricht, Victor. *Le Congo Belge*. Namur: A. Godenne, 1897. 74p.

4389    . Van Wincxtenhoven. *Exposition universelle d'Anvers de 1894. Les colonies
        de l'État indépendant du Congo. Rapport publié par le Commissariat
        générale du Gouvernement*. Brussels: F. Hayez, 1895. 100p.

4390    . Vasconcellos, Ernesto de. "Rio Zaïre: apontamentos para um roteiro,"
        *BSGL*, III(1882), 734-740.

4391    . Vauthier, G. "Le chemin de fer du Congo de Matadi à Léopoldville. Les
        environs de Matadi et le massif de Palaballa," *BSRGA*, XIV(1889),
        375-390.

4392 . Vauthier, René. *Le Congo belge, notes et impressions.* Brussels: Lebèque, 1900. 237p.

4393 . Vereycken, M. "La région des cataractes," *CIL,* IV(1895), 130-131, 137-139, 145-148.

4394 . Vermeulen, Julien. "Lettres," *Missions Belges de la Compagnie de Jésus,* I(1899), 167, 405, 415-417.

4395 . Veys, Lodewijk. "Lettres," *Voix du Rédempteur,* IX(1900), 430-432; X(1901), 25-28. Also, Supplement for Feb., 1901, 1-4, 242-245, 319-322, 428-431.

4396 . Virchow. [*Dr.*]. "Über die Schädel von Baluba und Kongo-Negern," *Verhandlungen der Berliner Gesellschaft für Anthropologie,* XVI (1886), 752.

4397 . Visseq, Alexandre. "Lettres," *APFL,* LIX(1887), 79-96.

4398 . Voulgre, Joseph Denis Antoine André. *Le Congo français. Le Loango et la vallée du Kouilou.* Paris: J. Andre, 1897. 206p.

4399 . _____. *Quelques mois au Congo français.* Biarritz, 1897.

4400 . Vyncke, Ameet. *Brieven van eenen vlaamschen Missionaris in Midden-Afrika.* Ghent: Lebaert, Siffer, 1888. 148p.

4401 . Wahis. [*Colonel*]. "Extrait d'un rapport du Gouverneur Général. Les établissements religieux du Stanley-Pool," *Précis Historiques*, XLV (1896), 518-520.

4402 . Ward, Herbert. "Ethnographical Notes Relating to the Congo Tribes," *JAI*, XXIV(1894-1895), 285-299.

4403 . _____. *Five Years with the Congo Cannibals*. London: Chatto & Windus, 1890. 308p. German translation, *Fünf Jahre unter den Stämmen des Kongo-Staates*. Leipzig: C.F. Amelang, 1891. 211p.

4404 . _____. *My Life with Stanley's Rear-Guard*. London: Chatto & Windus, 1891. 163p.

4405 . _____. *A Voice from the Congo: Comprising Stories, Anecdotes, and Descriptive Notes*. London: Heinemann, 1910. 299p.

4406 Warlomont, Charles. *Corréspondance d'Afrique. Ouvrage posthume.* Brussels: Monnom, 1888. 143p.

4407 . Waroux, Louis. "Lettres," *Congo-Indië*, (1898), 6, 7.

4408 . _____. "Lettres," *Précis Historiques*, XLIV(1895), 448, 449, 536, 537; XLV(1896), 340, 341.

4409 . Wauters, Alphonse Jules. "Les affluents français de l'Ubangi," *MG*, XII(1895), 157.

4410 . _____. "Les aqueducs," *CIL*, II(1893), 12.

4411 . _____. "Les Arabes dans l'Afrique centrale," *MG*, V(1888), 93.

4412 _____. "Le bassin du Lubudi, d'après les renseignements de MM. Francqui, Cornet, P. Le Marinel et Cameron," *MG*, XI(1894), 32.

4413 . _____. "Les cantines," *CIL*, II(1893), 108.

4414 _____. *Le capitaine Cambier et la première expédition de l'Association internationale africaine*. n.p.: Muquardt, 1880. 30p.

4415 . _____. "Le capitaine Hanssens sur le Haut-Congo. Relation de sa navigation entre le Stanley-Pool et les Stanley-Falls, du 23 mars au 6 août 1884," *MG*, I(1884), 67.

4416 . _____. "Le chemin de fer du Bas-Congo, concédé à la 'Congo Railway Co.' de Manchester," *MG*, II(1885), 111; III(1886), 2, 83.

4417 . _____. *Le chemin de fer du Congo*. Brussels: Institut national de géographie, 1887. 105p. Also, *MG*, III(1886), 2, 87, 94, 99, 104; VI(1889), 37.

4418 . _____. "Les Chinois," *CIL*, II(1893), 100.

4419 . _____. *Le Congo et les Portugais; réponse au mémorandum de la Société de Géographie de Lisbonne*. Brussels: Vanderauwera, 1883. 52p.

4420 _____. "La conquête du Manyeme par le commandant Dhanis," *CIL*, III(1894), 153-160.

4421 . _____. "Les Déclarations de la Conférence de Berlin en faveur de la liberté commerciale au Congo," *MG*, IX(1892), 91.

4422 . _____. "De l'Aruwimi à l'Uellé, d'après le capitaine Becker," *MG*, VII(1890), 60.

4423 . _____. "De l'initiation des nègres aux travaux des Européens," *CIL*, I (1892), 19, 107.

4424 . _____. "L'eléphant d'Afrique est-il domesticable?" *MG*, III(1886), 39.

4425 . _____. "L'elephant d'Afrique et son role dans l'histoire de la civilisation," *BSBG*, V(1880), 150-186.

4426 · _____. "Les entreprises belges au Congo," *MG*, VII(1890), 10.

4427 · _____. "Les événements du Haut-Congo. Relation des aventures de l'expédition Jouret-Doré sur le Lualaba. La revolte arabe. Le mort de m. Hodister. Déposition de M. Doré, agent de l'expédition du syndicat commercial," *MG*, IX(1892), 95.

4428 · _____. "L'expédition Hodister," *MG*, IX(1892), 99.

4429 · _____. "L'expédition Paul Le Marinel, du camp de Lusambo chez Msiri," *MG*, IX(1892), 9, 27.

4430 · _____. "L'expédition Vankerckhoven, De Djabbir à Wadelaï, par la vallée de l'Uellé," *MG*, X(1893), 67.

4431 · _____. *Les expéditions de la Compagnie du Congo.* Brussels: Weissenbruch, 1888. 82p.

4432 · _____. *Les expéditions de la Compagnie du Congo pour le Commerce et l'Industrie. Organisation. Départ. Premiers travaux.* Brussels: Institut national de géographie, 1887. 76p.

4433 · _____. "Exploration de la Djuma-Kwilu par le major Parminter," *MG*, X (1893), 97.

4434 · _____. "Exploration de la Likuala," *MG*, IV(1887), 52.

4435 · _____. "L'exploration de la Lukuga, l'émissaire du lac Tanganika, par l'expédition Delcommune," *MG*, XI(1894), 27.

4436 · _____. "Exploration de l'Oubangi par M. le capitaine Van Gèle," *MG*, V (1888), 27, 37.

4437 · _____. "L'exploration du Kassai et de ses affluents par le steamer *Roi des Belges*," *MG*, VI(1889),

4438 · _____. "L'exploration du Lomami," *MG*, VI(1889), 29.

4439 . _____. "La huitième traversée de l'Afrique centrale, par le lieutenant Gleerup," *MG*, III(1886), 73.

4440 . _____. "L'invasion arabe dans le Haut-Congo. Le désastre de la mission Hodister," *MG*, IX(1892), 79.

4441 . _____. "Karéma, première station de l'Association internationale africaine," *BSBG*, IV(1880),

4442 . _____. "Le Katanga. Interview du R. Swan," *MG*, IX(1892), 27.

4443 . _____. "La liberté commerciale au Congo," *MG*, IX(1892), 61, 68, 85, 97, 117.

4444 . _____. "Le massif de Matadi," *CIL*, I(1892), 116, 213.

4445 . _____. "Le massif de Palaballa," *CIL*, I(1892), 188; II(1893), 4, 156.

4446 . _____. "Matadi," *CIL*, I(1892), 4, 12, 20, 36, 44, 68, 80; II(1893), 140, 172.

4447 . _____. "Les missions catholiques au Congo. Historique," *CIL*, III(1894), 169, 195.

4448 _____. "Monnaies indigènes et introduction de la monnaie européenne," *CIL*, I(1892), 34.

4449 . _____. "La Mpozo," *CIL*, I(1892), 156; II(1893), 52.

4450 . _____. "Les nains du Congo," *MG*, IV(1887), 25. Also, *CIL*, I(1892), 42, 50.

4451 . _____. "Le pays entre Luluabourg et le Lualaba," *MG*, VIII(1891), 32.

4452 . _____. "Le personnel ouvrier," *CIL*, I(1892), 52, 124.

4453 . _____. "Les ponts de la ligne," *CIL*, I(1892), 28, 100, 140, 164, 196; II(1893), 20, 69, 84, 132, 180; III(1894), 52, 101, 118.

4454 . _____. "Le port de Banana," *MG*, II(1885), 21.

4455 · \_\_\_\_\_ · "Production et commerce du Caoutchouc, Statistiques," *MG*, IX(1892), 49. See also, fascicule 14, Compagnie du Congo pour le commerce et l'industrie, pp.62-66. Brussels: Bourland, 1892.

4456 · \_\_\_\_\_ · "La province du Bas-Congo, de Boma jusqu'au Tchiloango. Interview de M. le lieutenant Mikic," *MG*, II(1885), 78.

4457 · \_\_\_\_\_ · "Le ravin du diable," *CIL*, II(1893), 124.

4458 · \_\_\_\_\_ · "Le ravin Léopold," *CIL*, I(1892), 84, 92, 108.

4459 · \_\_\_\_\_ · "Referendum sur la question de la population de l'État indépendant du Congo," *MG*, XII(1895), 91ff.

4460 · \_\_\_\_\_ · "La région au nord du Congo, l'Oubangi, le Rouki et la Mongalla, d'après les récentes explorations de MM. Van Gèle, Le Marinel, Roget et Hodister," *MG*, VIII(1891), 19-23.

4461 · \_\_\_\_\_ · "La région au sud du Stanley-Pool, de Lutete au Kwango, par le commandant Dhanis," *MG*, XI(1894), 91.

4462 · \_\_\_\_\_ · "La réoccupation des Stanley-Falls," *MG*, V(1888), 74, 81.

4463 · \_\_\_\_\_ · *Stanley au secours d'Emin-Pacha*. Paris: Quantin, 1890. 424p.

4464 · \_\_\_\_\_ · "Sur le Congo. De Kassongo au confluent de la Lukuga. Exploration d'une nouvelle section inconnue due fleuve, par le consul Mohun," *MG*, XI(1894), 84.

4465 · \_\_\_\_\_ · "Les travailleurs indigènes," *CIL*, II(1893), 148.

4466 · \_\_\_\_\_ · "Les travaux de la 2e section Kenge-Lufu et les premiers résultats de l'exploitation," *CIL*, III(1894), 119, 161, 193; IV(1895), 36, 76.

4467 · \_\_\_\_\_ · "La treizième traversée de l'Afrique centrale de Pangani à Banana, par le comte von Götzen," *MG*, XI(1894), 109; XII(1895), 43.

4468 . _____. *Voyages en Afrique. De Bruxelles à Karema. Le royaume des éléphants.* Brussels: Office de publicité, 1901. 177p.

4469 . Wauwermans, H. "L'oeuvre africaine dans ses rapports avec les progrès du commerce et de l'industrie," *BSRGA*, II(1877), 349-372.

4470 . _____. "Résumé historique des tentatives coloniales faites par la Belgique et Anvers," *BSRGA*, XX(1895), 435-449.

4471 . Weeks, John H. *Among Congo Cannibals. Experiences, Impressions and Adventures during a Thirty Years' Sojurn amongst the Boloki and Other Congo Tribes, with a Description of Their Curious Habits, Customs, Religions and Laws.* London: Seeley, Service; Philadelphia: Lippincott, 1913. 351p.

4472 . _____. *Among the Primitive Bakongo. A Record of Thirty Years' Close Intercourse with the Bakongo and Other Tribes of Equatorial Africa, with a Description of Their Habits, Customs and Religious Beliefs.* London: Seeley, Service, 1914. 318p.

4473 . _____. *Congo Life and Folklore.* London: Religious Tract Society, 1911. 468p.

4474 . Weghsteen, Joseph. "Lettres," *Missiën der Witte Paters*, XXI(1900), 121-123; XXII(1901), 313-315, 379, 380.

4475 . Weimers, Théodore. [*Colonel*]. *La question militaire et la question congolaise, présentées à la presse, au parlement et au gouvernement belges.* Brussels: Société belge de librairie, n.d.. 60p.

4476 . Wendling, Victor. "Cartas," *Portugal em Africa*, VII(1900), 618-629; VIII
(1901), 421-424, 544, 545.

4477 . _____. "Lettres," *MCL*, XXXII(1901), 28-29.

4478 . Wermuth, Carl. "Von der Südwest=Grenze des Kongobeckens," *DK*, II(1885),
155-159, 217-222.

4479 . Werner, J. R. "The Congo and the Ngala and Aruwimi Tributaries," *PRGS*,
New Series, XI(1889), 342-351.

4480 . _____. *A Visit to Stanley's Rear-Guard at Major Barttelot's Camp on the
Aruwhimi, with an Account of River-Life on the Congo.* Edinburgh:
Blackwood, 1889. 330p.

4481 . Werth, E. "Tumbatu, die Insel der Watumbatu," *Globus*, LXXIV(1898), 169-
173.

4482 . Wester. [*Lt.*]. "Le Cannibalisme," *Ymer*, VI(1886).

4483 . Westmark, T. "Chez les Bangallas," *Bulletin de la Société de Géographie
Commerciale de Paris*, XII(1886), 431.

4484 . _____. "Om de senaste upptäckerna vid öfre Kongo," *Ymer*, V(1885), 122.

4485 . Wèvre. "Voyage scientifique dans le Mayombe," *Belgique Coloniale*, I
(1895-1896), 22-23.

4486 . Wichmann, H. "Der Anfänge der Erschliessung des Congo-Beckens von Western
her," *PM*, **XXV**III(1882).

4487 Wieder, Martin. "Missionsbriefe," *Echo aus Afrika*, IV(1892), 39, 40, 69,
70, 125-128, 139, 140; V(1893), 64-66; VI(1894), 2, 3, 67; VII(1895),
33; VIII(1896), 63, 64, 100, 101; IX(1897), 47, 48, 120, 121, 132-134.

4488 · Wieder, Straton. "Cartas," *Portugal em Africa*, II(1895), 505, 506; III (1896), 447-456; IV(1897), 8-16, 65-71, 113-122, 477-482.

4489 · Wilde, Jules de. "Dans la Mongala," *CIL*, IV(1895), 186, 187.

4490 · _____. "Lettere," *MCM*, XXI(1892), 135-137, 147-150, 541-543; XXII(1893), 61, 62; XXIII(1894), 517-520.

4491 · ____. "Lettres," *Annalen van het Genootschap der H.Kindsheid*, Nr.277(1894), 72-77; Nr. 279(1894), 124-127.

4492 · ____. "Lettres," *APFL*, LXIV(1892), 330-334.

4493 · ____. "Lettres," *MCL*, XXIV(1892), 286.

4494 ____. "Lettres," *MG*, X(1893), 17.

4495 · _____. "Lettres," *Missions en Chine et au Congo*, (1889-1891), 379, 380, 492-496, 508, 554-557, 574-576; (1892-1894), 25-32, 142-144, 156-158, 207, 208, 378-380, 395, 472-474, 525-528; (1895-1897), 106-109, 157-160. See also, *Missiën in China en Congo*, same period.

4496 · _____. "Missionsbriefe," *KM*, XX(1892), 241-242; XXII(1894), 90-91.

4497 · Wills, J. T. "Between the Nile and the Congo: Dr. Junker and the (Welle) Makua," *PRGS*, New Series, IX(1887), 285-304.

4498 · Wilwerth. [*Lt*.]. "La chasse," *CIL*, III(1894), 180.

4499 · ____. "Chez les Mongwandies," *CIL*, III(1894), 175-176.

4500 · ____. "La construction des pirogues," *CIL*, III(1894), 191.

4501 · ____. "Coutumes congolaises," *CIL*, IV(1895), 151.

4502 · ____. "L'esclavage et le cannibalisme," *CIL*, IV(1895), 157-159.

4503 ____. "Les habitations indigènes, des Bangalas, des Upotos et des Mogwandis," *CIL*, IV(1895), 141-142.

4504 ____. "Le travail du cuivre," *CIL*, IV(1895), 7.

4505 · Winz, Bonifatius. "Lettres," *Almanach du Congo,* (1900), 31.

4506 · _____. "Lettres," *Règne du Coeur de Jesus,* XII(1900), 87-91, 123-127.

4507 · Wissmann, Hermann Wilhelm Leopold Ludwig von. [*Lt.*]. "Briefe, Nov. 17, 1881," *MAGD,* IV(1883-1885), 179.

4508 · _____. "Generalbericht," *MAGD,* IV(1883-1885), 37.

4509 · _____. *Hermann von Wissmann, Deutschlands grösster Afrikaner; sein Leben und Werken.* Berlin: A. Schall (Verein der Bücherfreunde), 1907. 580p.

4510 · _____. "In Innerafrika stattgehabte Völkerverschiebungen und der Tanganyika-See," *Verhandlungen der Berliner Gesellschaft für Anthropologie,* XIII(1883), 453-460.

4511 · _____. "Das Land der Baschilange," *PM,* XXXIV(1888), 353-357.

4512 · _____. *Mes appréciations sur les critiques de l'oeuvre du Congo mantenues dans la réplique de M. le Dr. Pechuel-Loesche à M. Stanley.* Brussels: P. Weissenbruck, 1886.

4513 · _____. "On the Influence of Arab Traders in West Central Africa," *PRGS,* New Series, X(1888), 525-530.

4514 · _____. "Reiseberichte," *MAGD,* III(1881-1883), 68, 149, 249; IV(1883-1885), 35-74.

4515 · _____. "Reisebriefe," *MAGD,* III(1881-1883), 149; IV(1883-1885), 319.

4516 · _____, Wolf, Ludwig, and François, Kurt von. *Im Innern Afrikas. Die Erforschung des Kassai während den Jahre 1883, 1884 und 1885.* Leipzig: Brockhaus, 1891. 461p.

4517 · Witte, Jehan de. *Les deux Congo. 35 ans d'apostolat au Congo français. Mgr. Augouard. Les origines du Congo belge. Préface du Comte de Mun.* Paris: Plon, Nourrit, 1913. 408p.

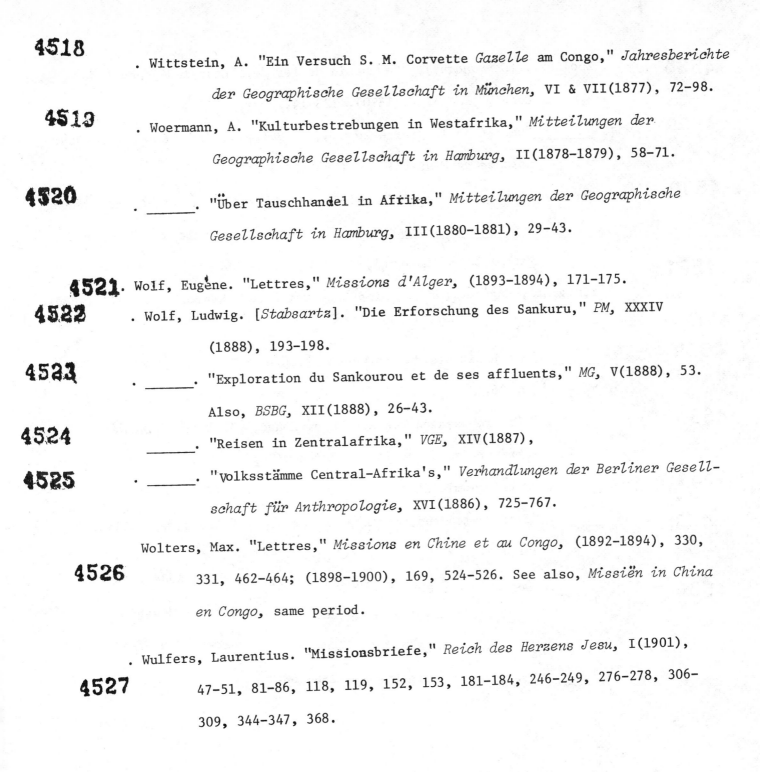

4518 . Wittstein, A. "Ein Versuch S. M. Corvette *Gazelle* am Congo," *Jahresberichte der Geographische Gesellschaft in München*, VI & VII(1877), 72-98.

4519 . Woermann, A. "Kulturbestrebungen in Westafrika," *Mitteilungen der Geographische Gesellschaft in Hamburg*, II(1878-1879), 58-71.

4520 . _____. "Über Tauschhandel in Afrika," *Mitteilungen der Geographische Gesellschaft in Hamburg*, III(1880-1881), 29-43.

4521 . Wolf, Eugene. "Lettres," *Missions d'Alger*, (1893-1894), 171-175.

4522 . Wolf, Ludwig. [*Stabsartz*]. "Die Erforschung des Sankuru," *PM*, XXXIV (1888), 193-198.

4523 . _____. "Exploration du Sankourou et de ses affluents," *MG*, V(1888), 53. Also, *BSBG*, XII(1888), 26-43.

4524 _____. "Reisen in Zentralafrika," *VGE*, XIV(1887),

4525 . _____. "Volksstämme Central-Afrika's," *Verhandlungen der Berliner Gesellschaft für Anthropologie*, XVI(1886), 725-767.

4526 Wolters, Max. "Lettres," *Missions en Chine et au Congo*, (1892-1894), 330, 331, 462-464; (1898-1900), 169, 524-526. See also, *Missiën in China en Congo*, same period.

4527 . Wulfers, Laurentius. "Missionsbriefe," *Reich des Herzens Jesu*, I(1901), 47-51, 81-86, 118, 119, 152, 153, 181-184, 246-249, 276-278, 306-309, 344-347, 368.

4528 . Zboïnski, [*Commandant*]. "Le chemin de fer de l'État indépendant du Congo," *BSRGA*, XV(1890), 123-142.

4529 . _____. "Un age de la pierre au Congo," *Bulletin de la Société d'Anthropologie de Bruxelles*, VI(1887-1888), 56.

4530 . Ziemann, A. "Strömungs- und Schiffartsverhältnisse an der Congo-Mündung und im Banana-Creek," *Annalen der Hydrographie und Maritimen Meteorologie*[Hamburg], XI(1883), 164-166.

4531 . Zintgraff, Eugène. [*Dr.*]. "Eindrücke vom untern Kongo," *VGE*, XIII(1886), 83.

4532 _____. "Les habitants du Bas-Congo. Moeurs et coutumes," *MG*, II(1885), 10, 26.

4533 . _____. "Körpermessengen von Negern am Kongo," *Verhandlungen der Berliner Gesellschaft für Anthropologie*, XVI(1886), 26-33.

4534 . _____. "Physiognomie d'un marché africain," *MG*, I(1884), 66.

4535 . _____. "Über Gesten und Mienenspiel der Neger," *Ausland*, LXIII(1890), 461-464.

4536 . _____. "Der untere Congo von Banana bis Vivi und die Bedeutung des Congo für die Erforschung der Hinterländer des deutschen schutzgebietes Kamerun," *Mitteilungen der Geographische Gesellschaft in Hamburg*, V(1885-1886), 258-268.

MALAWI

4537 . Angus, H. Crawford. "A Trip to Northern Agoniland," *SGM*, XV(1899),

74-79.

4538 . Buchanan, John. *East African Letters*. Edinburgh: Blackwood, 1890. 48p.

4539 _____. "The Industrial Development of Nyasaland," *GJ*, I(1893), 245-253.

4540 . _____. "Industrial Developments of Nyasa," *Journal of the Tyneside Geographical Society*, II(1893), 137-146.

4541 . _____. "Journey along the Southern Frontier of Nyassa-land," *PRGS*, New Series, XIII(1891), 265-273.

4542 . _____. *Shirè Highlands, East Central Africa, As Colony and Mission*. London: Blackwood, 1885. 260p.

4543 . Buchner, C. "Häuserbau am Nyassa," *DK*, X(1893), 71.

4544 _____ and Wangemann. "Die Mission des Superintendent Merensky zum Nyassa-See," *DK*, IX(1892), 33-34.

4545 . Chatouville, Camille de. "Lettres," *Missions d'Afrique*, (1901-1902), 107-108.

4546 . Codrington, Robert. "The Central Angoniland District of the British Central Africa Protectorate," *GJ*, XI(1898), 509-522.

4547 . _____. "A Visit to Lake Chiuta, British Central Africa," *GJ*, VII(1896), 183-186.

4548 . Cotterill, Henry Bernard. "Nyasa—with Notes on the Slave Trade," *JRSA*, XXVI(1878), 678-685.

4549 . _____. "Opening Out of the District to the North of Lake Nyassa," *JRSA*, XXVII(1879), 242-247.

4550 . Crawshay, Richard. "A Journey in Angoni Country," *GJ*, III(1894), 59-60.

4551 . Delamarche, Julien. "Lettere," *MCM*, XXVII(1898), 127.

4552 . _____. "Lettres," *MCL*, XXX(1898), 87-88.

4553 . _____. "Lettres," *Missions d'Afrique*[Malines], XIX(1898), 91-92.

4554 . _____. "Lettres," *Missions d'Afrique*[Paris], (1897-1900), 265-267.

4555 . Dupont, Joseph. "Lettres," *Annalen der Afrikaansche Missiën*, XI(1894-1895), 220-222, 277-278, 344-349; XIV(1897-1898), 318.

4556 . _____. "Lettres," *Annales Oeuvre Ste-Enfance*, XLVI(1895), 401-410.

4557 . _____. "Lettres," *Maandelijksch Verslag der Afrikaansche Missiën*, XV (1894), 295-300; XVI(1895), 117-122, 143-147; XVII(1896), 152-155.

4558 . _____. "Missionsbriefe," *Afrika-Bote*, I(1895), 55-63; II(1896), 84-87; III(1897), 138-139, 149-150, 170-172; IV(1898), 147.

4559 . Elliot, G. F. Scott. "Commercial Prospects of British Central and East Africa," *JRSA*, XLIV(1896), 423-431.

4560 . Elmslie, Walter Angus. *Among the Wild Ngoni*. London: Oliphant; Chicago: Revell, 1899. 320p.

4561 . Forbes, Patrick William. *Blantyre to Tanganyika*. Reading: Beecroft and Alexander, 1896. 16 p. [Reprinted from the *Rhodesia Herald*.]

4562 Fotheringham, L. Monteith. *Adventures in Nyassaland: A Two Year's Struggle with Arab Slave Dealers in Central Africa*. London: Sampson Low & Co., 1891. 304p.

4563 . Fraser, Donald. *African Idylls. Portraits and Impressions of Life on a Central African Mission Station*. London: Seeley, 1923. 229p.

4564 . _____. *Winning a Primitive People. Sixteen Years' Work among the Warlike Tribe of the Ngoni and the Senga and Tumbuka Peoples of Central Africa*. New York: Dutton, 1914. 320p. London: Seeley Service, 1922. 320p.

4565 . Füllerborn, F. "Über die Nyassa-Länder," *Verhandlungen der Abteilungen Berlin-Charlottenburg der Deutsch Kolonial Gesellschaft*, II (1901), 30.

4566 . ———. "Über untersuchungen im Nyassa-See und den Seen im nördlichen Nyassa-Land," *VGE*, XXVII(1900), 332.

4567 . Glave, E. J. "Glave in Nyasaland," *Century*, LII(1896), 589-606.

4568 . Goetstouwers, Cornelius. "Lettres," *Annalen der Afrikaansche Missiën*, XII(1895-1896), 202-209; XIV(1897-1898), 319-325.

4569 . ———. "Missionsbriefe," *Stern der Neger*, I(1898), 14-17, 66-68, 175-178, 267-270.

4570 . Guillé, Raoul. "Lettres," *Missions d'Afrique*, (1895-1897), 545-550.

4571 . ———. "Missionsbriefe," *Afrika-Bote*, III(1897), 145-149.

4572 . Guillerme, Louis. "Lettres," *MCL*, XXXIII(1901), 169-172.

4573 . Guyard, Georges. "Lettres," *Missions d'Afrique*, (1901-1902), 193-199.

4574 . Henderson, James. "Northern Nyasaland," *SGM*, XVI(1900), 82-89.

4575 . Hetherwick, Alexander. [*Rev.*]. "Notes of a Journey from Domasi Mission Station, Mount Zomba, to Lake Namaramba, August 1887," *PRGS*, New Series, X(1888), 25-32.

4576 . ———. "Some Animistic Beliefs among the Yaos of British Central Africa," *JAI*, XXXII(1902), 89-95.

4577 . Hynde, R. S. "Among the Machinga People," *SGM*, VII(1891), 656-662.

4578 . Johnson, William Percival. *Chinyanja Proverbs*. Cardiff: Smith Brothers, 1922. 26p.

4579 . ———. *My African Reminiscences, 1875-1895*. London: Universities Mission to Central Africa, [1926]. 236p.

4580 · _____. *Nyasa, the Great Water; Being a Description of the Lake and the Life of the People.* London: Humphrey Milford, 1922. 204p.

4581 · Johnston, Harry Hamilton. "British Central Africa," *PRGS*, New Series, XII(1890), 713-740.

4582 · _____. *British Central Africa: an Attempt to Give Some Account of a Portion of the Territories under British Influence North of the Zambezi.* London: Methuen, 1897. 544p.

4583 · _____. "The British Central Africa Protectorate," *GJ*, V(1895), 193-218.

4584 · _____. "England's Work in Central Africa," *Proceedings of the Royal Colonial Institute*, XXVIII(1896-1897), 50-75.

4585 Kerr-Cross, David. "Crater-Lakes North of Lake Nyasa," *GJ*, V(1895), 112-124.

4586 · _____. "Dawn in Nyassaland," *Blackwood's Magazine*, Nov., 1891, 657-663.

4587 · Last, J. T. "A Journey from Blantyre to Angoni-Land and Back," *PRGS*, New Series, IX(1887), 177-187.

4588 · _____. "A Journey from Blantyre to the Namuli Hills," *PRGS*, New Series, IX(1887), 42-44.

4589 · _____. "On the Society's Expedition to the Namuli Hills,"East Africa," *PRGS*, New Series, IX(1887), 467-478.

4590 · Laws, Robert. [*Rev.,MD*]. "Journey along Part of the Western Side of Lake Nyassa, in 1878," *PRGS*, New Series, I(1879), 305-321.

4591 · Livingstone, David, and others. "Expedition to Lake Nyassa in 1861-63," *JRGS*, XXXIII(1863), 251-276.

4592 . Lugard, F. *Frederick John DEVRY.* "The Fight against the Slavers on Nyassa," *Contemporary Review*, LVI(1889), 335-345.

4593 . _____. "Lake Nyassa and Central Africa," *JMGS*, V(1889), 347-355.

4594 . McKinnon, Charles. "Journey from Domira Bay, Lake Nyasa, to Fife, on the Tanganyika Plateau," *GJ*, XIX(1902), 603-605.

4595 . Maples, Chauncy. *Journals and Papers of Chauncy Maples, Late Bishop of Likoma.* Ed. by his sister, Ellen Maples. London: Longmans & Co., 1899. 278p.

4596 . _____. "Lukoma: an Island in Lake Nyassa," *JMGS*, V(1889), 59-68. Also, *SGM*, IV(1888), 420-431.

4597 . _____, Kerr Cross, D., and others. "Nyasaland and African Exploration," *JMGS*, VI(1890), 287-296.

4598 . Moggridge, L. T. "The Nyassaland Tribes, Their Customs and Their Poison Ordeal," *JAI*, XXXII(1902), 467=472.

4599 . Money, R. I. and Kellett, S. "Explorations in the West of Lake Nyasa," *GJ*, X(1897), 146-170.

4600 Murray, A. C. *Nyasaland en mijne ondervindingen oldaar.* Amsterdam: Hollandsch-Afrikaansche Uitg.-Mij., [1897]. 313p.

4601 . O'Neill, H. E. "Notes on the Nyassa Region of East Africa," *JMGS*, IV(1888), 87-101.

4602 Richter, J. *Evangelische Mission im Njassaland.* Berlin: Missionsgesellschaft, 1898. 225p.

4603 . Rowley, Henry. *The Story of the Universities' Mission to Central Africa.* London: Saunders, Otley, 1867.

4604 . _____. *Twenty Years in Central Africa.* London: Wells Gardner, 1882. 288p.

4605 . Sclater, B. L. [*Lt.*]. "Routes and Districts in Southern Nyasaland," *GJ*, II(1893), 403-423.

4606 . Sharpe, Alfred. "The Geography and Resources of British Central Africa," *GJ*, VII(1896), 367-387.

4607 . _____. "A Journey through the Country Lying between the Shire and
Loangwa Rivers," *PRGS*, New Series, XII(1890), 150-157.

. _____. "Trade and Colonisation in British Central Africa,"

4608 *SGM*, XVII(1901), 129-148.

4609 . Stevenson, James. *Civilization of South East Africa*. Glasgow: J. Maclehose
and Sons, 1877. 56p.

4610 . Stewart, James. "Observations on the Western Side of Lake Nyassa, and
on the Country Intervening between Nyassa and Tanganyika,"
*PRGS*, New Series, II(1880), 428-431.

4611 . _____. "The Second Circumnavigation of Lake Nyassa," *PRGS*, New Series,
I(1879), 289-305.

4612 . _____. *The Zambesi Journal of James Stewart, 1862-1863.* Edited by J. P.
R. Wallis. London: Chatto & Windus, 1952. 276p.

. Werner, Alice. "African Folk-lore," *Contemporary Review*, LXX(1896),
4613 377-390.

4614 . _____. "Geschichten der Mang'anja," *ZAOS*, III(1897), 353-357.

4615 . _____. "Hair Dressing and Other Customs in Angoniland," *Cape
Illustrated Magazine*, VI(1895), 105-109.

. _____. " A Hundred Miles in a Hammock," *Cape Illustrated
4616 Magazine*, VII(1897), 203-209, 228-234.

4617 . Wiese, Carl. "Beiträge zur Geschichte der Zulu im Norden des Zambesi,
namentlich der Angoni," *ZE*, XXXII(1900), 181-201.

4618 . Young, Edward Daniel. "Lake Nyassa Mission," *PRGS*, XX(1875-1876), 451-
453.

4619 . _____. *Nyassa; a Journal of Adventures Whilst Exploring Lake Nyassa,
Central Africa, and Establishing the Settlement of "Livingstonia."*
London, 1876.

4620 . _____. "On a Recent Sojurn at Lake Nyassa," *PRGS*, XXI(1876-1877), 225-233.

4621 . _____. *The Search After Livingstone.* London, 1868.

MOZAMBIQUE

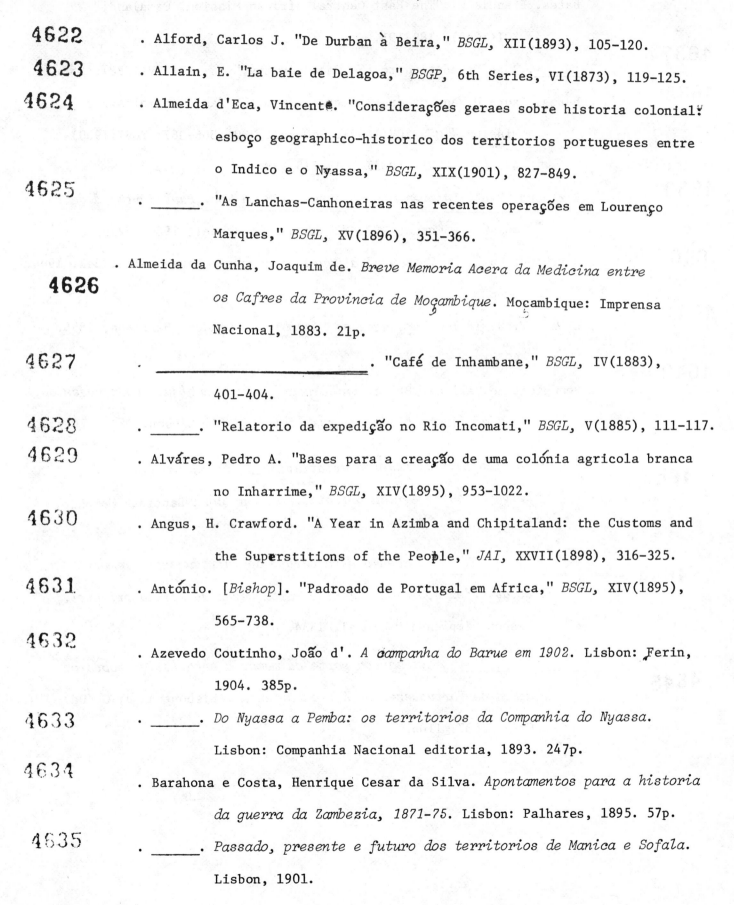

4622 . Alford, Carlos J. "De Durban à Beira," *BSGL*, XII(1893), 105-120.

4623 . Allain, E. "La baie de Delagoa," *BSGP*, 6th Series, VI(1873), 119-125.

4624 . Almeida d'Eca, Vincente. "Considerações geraes sobre historia colonial: esboço geographico-historico dos territorios portugueses entre o Indico e o Nyassa," *BSGL*, XIX(1901), 827-849.

4625 . _____. "As Lanchas-Canhoneiras nas recentes operações em Lourenço Marques," *BSGL*, XV(1896), 351-366.

4626 . Almeida da Cunha, Joaquim de. *Breve Memoria Acera da Medicina entre os Cafres da Provincia de Moçambique*. Moçambique: Imprensa Nacional, 1883. 21p.

4627 . _____ . "Café de Inhambane," *BSGL*, IV(1883), 401-404.

4628 . _____. "Relatorio da expedição no Rio Incomati," *BSGL*, V(1885), 111-117.

4629 . Alváres, Pedro A. "Bases para a creação de uma colónia agricola branca no Inharrime," *BSGL*, XIV(1895), 953-1022.

4630 . Angus, H. Crawford. "A Year in Azimba and Chipitaland: the Customs and the Superstitions of the People," *JAI*, XXVII(1898), 316-325.

4631 . António. [*Bishop*]. "Padroado de Portugal em Africa," *BSGL*, XIV(1895), 565-738.

4632 . Azevedo Coutinho, João d'. *A campanha do Barue em 1902*. Lisbon: Ferin, 1904. 385p.

4633 . _____. *Do Nyassa a Pemba: os territorios da Companhia do Nyassa*. Lisbon: Companhia Nacional editoria, 1893. 247p.

4634 . Barahona e Costa, Henrique Cesar da Silva. *Apontamentos para a historia da guerra da Zambezia, 1871-75*. Lisbon: Palhares, 1895. 57p.

4635 . _____. *Passado, presente e futuro dos territorios de Manica e Sofala*. Lisbon, 1901.

4636 Bates, Francis W. "The East Central African Mission, Gazaland," *MH*, XCI(1895), 189-191.

4637 · _____. "The Expedition to the Gaza Country," *MH*, LXXXIV(1888), 558.

4638 · Bates, Laura H. and others. "Letters from the East Central Africa Mission," *MH*, XCV(1899), 240-241, 290, 366-367; XCVI(1900), 479-481; XCVII(1901), 114-115, 284.

4639 · Berthoud, Paul. *Lettres missionaires de M. & Mme. Paul Berthoud de la mission romande, 1873-79.* Lausanne: Bridel, 1900. 525p.

4640 · Berthoud, Ruth. *Du Transvaal à Lourenço Marques.* Lausanne: Bridel, 1904. 308p.

4641 · · · Bleek, W. H. I. *The Languages of Mozambique.* London: Harrison, 1856. 403p.

4642 · Bonnefont de Varinay, P. de. *La Compagnie de Mozambique, sa concession, son administration, ses résultats (1888).* Lisbon, 1899. 201p.

4643 · Botelho, Sebastião Xavier. *Memoria estatistica sobre os dominos Portuguezes na Africa oriental.* Lisbon: Jose Baptista Morando, 1835. 400p.

4644 · _____. *Resumo para servir de introduccao a memoria estatistica sobre os dominios Portuguezes na Africa oriental.* Lisbon: Imprensa Nacional, 1834. 85p.

4645 · _____. *Segunda parte da memoria estatistica sobre os dominios Portuguezes na Africa oriental.* Lisbon: A. J. C. Da Cruz, 1837. 110p.

4646 . Brandão Cró de Castro Ferreri, Alfredo. *De Lisbao a Moçambique*. Lisbon: Mattos Moreira, 1884. 156p.

4647 . Browne. [*Lt.*], and Owen, W. F. W. "Particulars of an Expedition up the Zambezi to Senna, Performed by Three Officers of His Majesty's Ship *Leven*, When Surveying the East Coast of Africa in 1823," *JRGS*, II(1832), 136-152.

4648 . Bunker, Fred R. and others. "Letters from the East Central African Mission," *MH*, XCI(1895), 17-18, 101-102, 197-198, 240-241, 283-284, 364, 460; XCII(1896), 291-292, 540.

4649 . Caetano da Silva Lima, Manuel. "Expedição de Manica," *BSGL*, V(1885), 496-501.

4650 . Caetano do Rosario e Noronha, D. Isidoro. *Defeza das Immunidades da Santa Igreja de Moçambique (Prelasia mullius Diocesis) e dos Direitos episcopaes e mais preeminencias de seus Prelados, ou a minha Questão exposta em toda a sua luz. Desaggravo de duas affrontas feitas ao Sacerdocio catholico. Refutação das Objecções postas contra a inamobilidade dos Prelados de Moçambique*. Lisbon: Typographia Universal, 1864. 160p.

4651 . Caldas Xavier, Alfred Augusto. "Provincia de Moçambique. Districto de Inhambane: o Inharrime e as guerras Zavallas," *BSGL*, II(1880-1881), 479-528.

4652 . _____. "Reconhecimento do Limpopo: os territorios ao sul do Save e os Vatuas," *BSGL*, XIII(1894), 127-176.

4653 . Camara, Perry da. "Districto de Cabo Delgado," *BSGL*, VI(1886), 67-102

4654 . Campbell, W. *Travellers' Records of Portuguese Nyasaland*. London: King, Sell and Railton, 1899. 318p.

4655 . Carvalho e Menzes, José Guedes de. "Moçambique. Politica indigena,"
BSGL, II(1882), 70-79.

4656 . Carvalho Soveral, Ayres de. *Breve estudo sobre a ilha de Moçambique
acompanhado d'um pequeno vocabulario portuguez-macua*. Porto:
Chadron, 1887. 31p.

4657 . Castilho Barreto e Noronha, Augusto de. "Acerca de Lourenço Marques:
perigos e deveres," BSGL, XIV(1895), 535-563.

4658 . _____. *O districto de Lourenço Marques, no presente e no futuro*. Lisbon:
Mattos Moreira, 1881. 230p.

4659 . _____. *Relatorio da guerre da Zambezia em 1888*. Lisbon: Imprense
Nacional, 1891. 175p.

4660 . _____. *O Zambese: apontamentos de duas viagems*. Lisbon, 1880.

4661 . Churchill, William A. "The Sugar-Loaf Mountain, Mozambique," GJ, IV
(1894), 352-355.

4662 . Cooley, William Desborough. "A Memoir on the Civilization of the Tribes
Inhabiting the Highlands Near Dalagoa Bay," JRGS, III(1833),
310-324.

4663 . Coqui. "Journey from Origstadt to Delagoa Bay, etc.," PRGS, III
(1858-1859), 373-375.

4664 . Costa, Eduardo da. *O districto de Moçambique en 1898*. Lisbon: Livraria
Ferin, 1902.

4665 . Courtois, José Victor. "Relatorio sobre a minha viagem. . .as terras de
Macanga," BSGL, V(1885), 502-520.

**4666** Cowie, Alexander, and Green, Benjamin. "Notice Respecting the Late Expedition Overland to the Portuguese Settlement at Delagoa Bay," *South African Almanack and Directory for the Year 1830*, pp. 262-267.

**4667** . Decle, Lionel. "The Arungo and Marombu Ceremonies amongst the Tshinyungwe," *JAI*, XXIII(1893-1894), 421-422.

**4668** . _____. "The Ma-Goa," *JAI*, XXIII(1893-1894), 422-423.

**4669** . _____. "Funeral Rites and Ceremonies amongst the 'Tshinyai' (or 'Tshin-yungwe')," *JAI*, XXIII(1893-1894), 420-421.

**4670** . Deventer, Marinus Lodewijk van. *La Hollande et la Baie-Delagoa*. The Hague: Nijhoff, 1883. 27p.

**4671** . Doyle, Denis. "A Journey through Gazaland," *PRGS*, New Series, XIII (1891), 588-590.

**4672** . Ennes, Antonio. *A guerra d'Africa em 1895; memorias*. Lisbon, 1898. 631p.

**4673** . Erskine, St. Vincent. "Journey of Exploration to the Mouth of the River Limpopo," *JRGS*, XXXIX(1869), 233-275. Also, *PRGS*, XIII(1868-1869), 320-338.

**4674** . _____. "Journey to Umzila's, South-East Africa, in 1871-1872," *JRGS*, XLV(1875), 45-128. Also, *PRGS*, XIX(1874-1875), 110-132.

**4675** . _____. "Third and Fourth Journeys in Gaza, or Southern Mozambique," *JRGS*, XLVIII(1878), 25-56. Also, *PRGS*, XXII(1877-1878), 127-134.

**4676** . Feio, Bento Cazimiro. "O Inhampallala," *BSGL*, XV(1896), 375-378.

**4677** . Ferreria, José Joaquim. *Recordaçoes de expedição da Zambezia em 1869*. Elvas: Progresso, 1891. 142p.

**4678** . Findlay, Frederick Roderick Noble. *Big Game Shooting and Travel in South-East Africa*. London: Unwin, 1903. 313p.

4679 . Freire de Andrade, Alfredo Augusto. *Colonisaçao de Lourenço Marques: conferencia feita em 13 de Março de 1897*. Oporto: Silva Texeira, 1897. 56p.

4680 . _____and others. "Explorações portuguezas em Lourenço Marques e Inhambane," *BSGL*, XIII(1894), 293-391, 398-476.

4681 . Frewen, R. "Notes on Daka and Pandamatinka, on the Zambesi," *PRGS*, XXII(1877-1878), 223-224.

4682 . Fülleborn, F. "Über die Darstellung der Lebensformen bei den Eingeborenen im süden der Deutsch-Ostafrikanischen Kolonie," *ZE*, XXXII(1900).

4683 . Gillmore, Parker. *On Duty: A Ride through Hostile Africa*. London: Chapman & Hall, 1880. 380p.

4684 . _____. *Through Gasa Land, and the Scene of the Portuguese Aggression; the Journey of a Hunter in Search of Gold and Ivory*. London: Harrison, 1890. 349p.

4685 . Gilson, H. J. and others. "Letters from the East Central African Mission," *MH*, XCIII(1897), 68, 197-198, 511-512; XCIV(1898), 193-194, 400-401, 457.

4686 . Gorjão de Moura, Francisco Izidoro. "Campanha nas terras do Bire," *BSGL*, VIII(1888-1889), 359-389.

4687 . _____. "De villa Gouveia no Gorongoza ao Rio Pungué," *BSGL*, V(1885), 492-496.

4688 . Grove, Daniel. "A Macua," *BSGL*, XVI(1897), 127-145.

4689 . Guyot, Paul. *Le Zambèze*. Paris: Plon, 1898 32p.

4690 . Hamilton, Charles Edward. *Sketches of Life and Sport in South-Eastern Africa*. London, 1870.

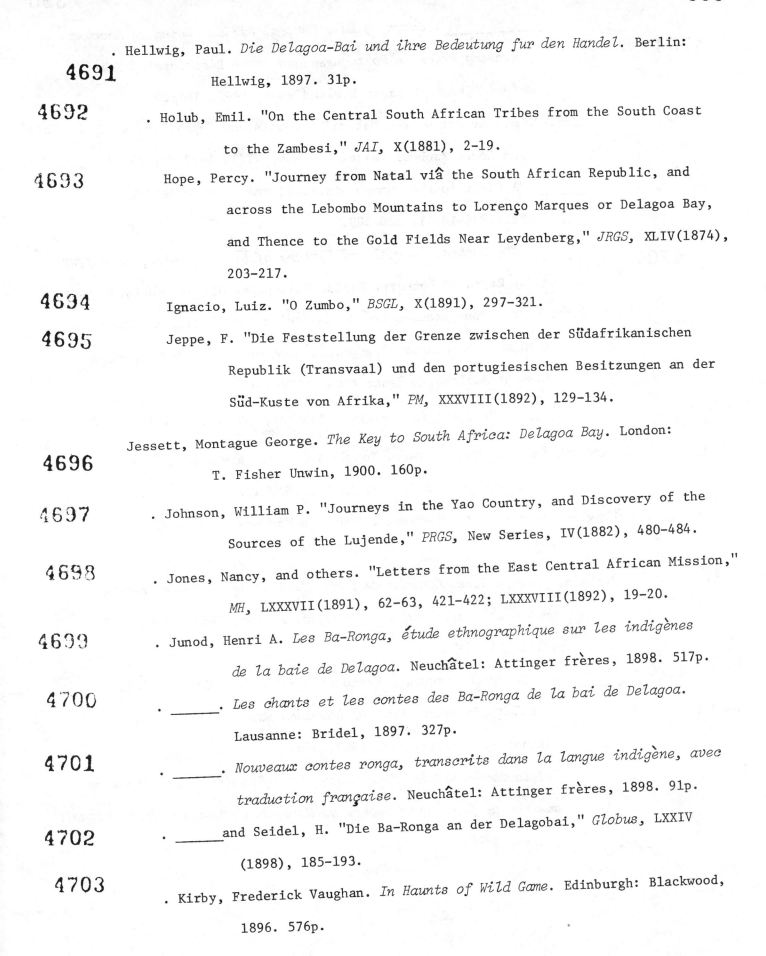

4691 . Hellwig, Paul. *Die Delagoa-Bai und ihre Bedeutung fur den Handel*. Berlin: Hellwig, 1897. 31p.

4692 . Holub, Emil. "On the Central South African Tribes from the South Coast to the Zambesi," *JAI*, X(1881), 2-19.

4693 Hope, Percy. "Journey from Natal viâ the South African Republic, and across the Lebombo Mountains to Lorenço Marques or Delagoa Bay, and Thence to the Gold Fields Near Leydenberg," *JRGS*, XLIV(1874), 203-217.

4694 Ignacio, Luiz. "O Zumbo," *BSGL*, X(1891), 297-321.

4695 Jeppe, F. "Die Feststellung der Grenze zwischen der Südafrikanischen Republik (Transvaal) und den portugiesischen Besitzungen an der Süd-Kuste von Afrika," *PM*, XXXVIII(1892), 129-134.

4696 Jessett, Montague George. *The Key to South Africa: Delagoa Bay*. London: T. Fisher Unwin, 1900. 160p.

4697 . Johnson, William P. "Journeys in the Yao Country, and Discovery of the Sources of the Lujende," *PRGS*, New Series, IV(1882), 480-484.

4698 . Jones, Nancy, and others. "Letters from the East Central African Mission," *MH*, LXXXVII(1891), 62-63, 421-422; LXXXVIII(1892), 19-20.

4699 . Junod, Henri A. *Les Ba-Ronga, étude ethnographique sur les indigènes de la baie de Delagoa*. Neuchâtel: Attinger frères, 1898. 517p.

4700 . _____. *Les chants et les contes des Ba-Ronga de la bai de Delagoa*. Lausanne: Bridel, 1897. 327p.

4701 . _____. *Nouveaux contes ronga, transcrits dans la langue indigène, avec traduction française*. Neuchâtel: Attinger frères, 1898. 91p.

4702 . _____ and Seidel, H. "Die Ba-Ronga an der Delagobai," *Globus*, LXXIV (1898), 185-193.

4703 . Kirby, Frederick Vaughan. *In Haunts of Wild Game*. Edinburgh: Blackwood, 1896. 576p.

4704 _____. *Sport in East Central Africa. Being an Account of Hunting Trips in Portuguese and Other Districts of East Central Africa.* London: Rowland Ward, 1899. 340p.

4705 . Kirk, John. "Report on the Natural Products and Capabilities of the Shiré and Lower Zambesi Valleys," *PRGS*, VI(1861-1862), 25-32.

4706 . _____. "A Visit to the Munego District, near Cape Delgado," *PRGS*, XXI(1876-1877), 588-589.

4707 _____. *The Zambesi Journal and Letters of Dr. John Kirk, 1858-1863.* Ed. by Reginald Foskett. 2vols. Edinburgh: Oliver and Boyd, 1965.

4708 . Lapa, Joaquim José, and Brandão Cró de Castro Ferreri, Alfredo. *Elementos para um diccionario chorographico da provincia de Moçambique.* Lisbon: Adolpho, Modesto & Ca., 1889. 149p.

4709 . Leigh, T. S. "A Visit to the River Zambezi," *JRGS*, XIX(1849), 1-7.

4710 . Lindley, Daniel. "Fort, Trade, Population, and Language at Delagoa. Ltr dated Dec. 31, 1838," *MH*, XXXV(1839), 193-195.

4711 . Longle, Armando. "De Inhambane a Lourenço Marques," *BSGL*, VI(1886), 13-37.

4712 . Machado, Joaquim José. *Caminho de Ferro de Lourenço Marques. Parecer da Comissão africana e informação.* Lisbon, 1882. Also, *BSGL*, III(1882), 5-20.

4713 . _____. "De Lourenço Marques à Pretoria," *BSGL*, V(1885), 645-766.

4714 . _____. *Questões africanas: Maputo, Lourenço Marques, Mossamedes.* Lisbon: Typ. Portuguesa, 1889. 58p.

4715 . _____. *Relatorio acêrca dos Trabalhos para a Fixação da Directriz do caminho de ferro entre Lourenço Marques e Fronteira de Transvaal.* Lisbon, 1884.

4716 . _____. "O territorio de Manica e Sofala sob a administração da companhia de Moçambique," *BSGL*, XIV(1895), 491-533.

4717 . Mackay, Wallis. *The Prisoners of Chiloane or, with the Portuguese in South-East Africa.* London: Trischler, 1890. 184p.

4718 . McLeod, Lyons. *Travels in Eastern Africa; with the Narrative of a Residence in Mozambique.* 2 vols. London: Hurst & Blackett, 1860.

4719 . Mager, E. *Die Auswanderung nach Südostrafrika, mit besonderer Berücksichtigung der von Karl Mauch bereisten Gebiete.* Gmund: Scharpt & Kraus, 1897. 97p.

4720 . Maples, Chauncy. *Chauncy Maples, Pioneer Missionary in East Central Africa for Nineteen Years and Bishop of Likoma, Lake Nyasa. A Sketch of His Life with Selections from His Letters. By His Sister, Ellen G. Maples Cook.* London and New York: Longmans, Green, 1897. 403p.

4721 . _____. "Makua Land, between the Rivers Rovuma and Luli," *PRGS*, New Series, IV(1882), 79-87.

4722 . _____. "Melanesians and Anyanja—a Family Comparison," *Nyasa News*, IV(1894), 112-116.

4723 . _____. "Mtonya (a Stronghold)," *Nyasa News*, I(1893), 192-196.

4724 . _____. "On the Results of the Exploration of the Country Lying between Lake Nyassa and the Indian Ocean, from the Years 1880-1884," *JMGS*, I(1885), 69-85.

4725 . Mártires, Bartolomeu dos. "Descrição dos estabelecimentos religiosos da Cidade de Moçambique, extraida de um manuscrito do Bispo de S. Tomé e Prelado de Moçambique. . .em 1882," in *Almanáque Civil-Ecclesiastico Historico-Administrativo da Provincia de Moçambique para o anno de 1859.* Moçambique, 1859. p.116ff.

4726 . Mendes de Vasconcellos Cirne, Manuel Joaquim. *Memoria sobre a provincia de Moçambique.* Lisbon: Imprensa Nacional, 1890. 47p.

4727
4728
. Miranda, Jose Francisco Barreto. *Manica-Sofala. Guide to the Mozambique Company's Territory*. London: William Clowes & Sons, 1902. 134p.

. Montanha, Joaquim de Santa Rita, and Macqueen, James. "Journey from Inhambane to Zoutpansberg," *JRGS*, XXXII(1862), 63-68.

4729
Monteiro, Rose. *Delagoa Bay, Its Natives and Natural History*. London: G. Philip, 1891. 274p.

4730
. Moraes Pinto, José Xavier de. "Districto de Manica: Gouveia, Serra Gorongosa, séde provisoria do districto de Manica," *BSGL*, VI (1886), 9-13.

4731
. Moraes Sarmento, Affonso de. "Memoria ácerca da defeza do valle do Zambeze na parte que diz respeito á região do litoral," *BSGL*, II(1880-1881), 620.

4732
. Mousinho de Albuquerque, Joaquim Augusto. *Moçambique, 1896-1898*. Lisbon: Gomes, 1899.

4733
. "Naval Officer." "Remarks on Delagoa Bay, a Large Harbour Situated on the South-East Coast of Africa, and on the Country and Nations Adjoining It," *South African Quarterly Journal*, 1st Series, II(1830), 132-144.

4734
. Noronha, Eduardo de. *A rebellão dos indigenas em Lourenço Marques*. Lisbon: Typ. de Jornal, 1894. 110p.

4735
. _____. *Lourenço Marques e as suas relações com a Africa do sul*. Lisbon: Imprensa Nacional, 1896. 52p. Also, *BSGL*, XV(1896), 45-96.

4736    Oliveira, Delphim José de. *A Provincia de Moçambique e O Bonga*. Coimbra: Imprensa Academica, 1879. 42p.

4737    . O'Neill, Henry E. "East Africa between the Zambesi and Rovuma Rivers: Its People, Riches and Development," *SGM*, I(1885), 337-352. Also, *PRGS*, New Series, VII(1885), 430-449.

4738    _____. "Journey from Mozambique to Lakes Shirwa and Amaramba," *PRGS*, New Series, VI(1884), 632-655, 713-741.

4739    _____. "Journey from Quillimane to Blantyre," *PRGS*, New Series, VII(1885), 646-655.

4740    . _____. "Journey in the District West of Cape Delgado Bay, Sept.-Oct., 1882," *PRGS*, New Series, V(1883), 393-404.

4741    . _____. "Journeys in the District of Delagoa Bay, Dec. 1886-Jan.1887," *PRGS*, New Series, IX(1887), 497-504.

4742    . _____. *The Mozambique and Nyassa Slave Trade*. London: British and Foreign Anti-Slavery Society, 1885. 24p.

4743    . _____. "Notes on the Nyassa Region of East Africa," *JMGS*, IV(1888), 87-101.

4744    _____. "Observaçoes acêrca da costa e interior da provincia de Moçambique," *BSGL*, III(1882), 195-208, 259-270.

4745    . _____. "On the Coast Lands and Some Rivers and Ports of Mozambique," *PRGS*, New Series, IV(1882), 595-605.

4746    . _____. "Report on Journey in the District of Delagoa Bay, December, 1886 - January, 1887," *JMGS*, III(1887), 103-109.

4747    . _____. "Some Remarks upon Nakala (Fernão Veloso Bay) and Other Ports on the Northern Mozambique Coast," *PRGS*, New Series, VII(1885), 373-377.

4748 . \_\_\_\_\_. "A Three Months' Journey in the Makua and Lomwe Countries," *PRGS*, New Series, IV(1882), 193-213.

4749 . Ousley, B. F. "A Day at Kambini," *MH*, LXXXIII(1887), 142-143.

4750 . \_\_\_\_\_. "East Central Africa Mission: a New Station," *MH*, LXXXI(1885), 396-397.

4751 . \_\_\_\_\_. "Removal of King Gungunyana's Capital," *MH*, LXXXVI(1890), 19-20.

4752 . \_\_\_\_\_. "The School at Kambini," *MH*, LXXXIV(1888), 69-70.

4753 . \_\_\_\_\_and Richards, E. H. "The Revolt aginast the Portuguese," *MH*, LXXXIII(1887), 58-59, 92-93.

4754 . \_\_\_\_\_and others. "Letters from the East Central African Mission," *MH*, LXXXIV(1888), 256, 351-352, 387-388, 502; LXXXV(1889), 110, 287, 334-335, 495; LXXXVI(1890), 65-66, 237-238, 515.

4755 . \_\_\_\_\_. "Notes on East Central African Mission," *MH*, LXXXIII(1887), 309-310, 529.

4756 . Paiva de Andrada, Joaquim Carlos. [*Major*]. "A Manica e o Musila," *BSGL*, III(1882), 57-64, 67-69.

4757 . \_\_\_\_\_. "Campanhas da Zambezia," *BSGL*, VII(1887), 715-738; VIII(1888-1889), 405-439.

4758 . \_\_\_\_\_. "Journeys to Maxinga and the Mazoe, 1881," *PRGS*, New Series, IV(1882), 417-419.

4759 . \_\_\_\_\_. *Manica: Being a Report Addressed to the Minister of the Marine and the Colonies of Portugal*. London: George Philip and Son, 1891. 63p.

4760 . \_\_\_\_\_. "No caminho de Mussirise," *BSGL*, VII(1887), 356-358.

4761 _____. *Report and Protest of the Affairs Occured at Manica*. Cape Town: Hofmeyr & Regter, 1891. 31p.

4762 . _____. "Zambesi Expedition, 1881," *PRGS*, New Series, IV(1882), 372-374.

4763 . Paiva Manso, Levy María Jordão. [*Visconde*]. *Memoria sobre Lourenço Marques (Delagoa Bay)*. Lisbon: Imprensa Nacional, 1870. 149p.

4764 Parker, Hyde. "On the Quilimane and Zambesi Rivers," *PRGS*, I(1855-1857), 312-315.

4765 . Perry da Camara. [*Major*]. *Africa Oriental: Descripção des Territorios do districto de Cabo Delgado que fazem parte da Concessao Feita a Companhia do Nyassa*. Lisbon: Adolpho Modesto and Co., 1893. 32p.

4766 . Peters, Wilhelm Carl Hartwig. *Naturwissenschaftliche Reise nach Mossambique (1842-1848)*. Berlin: Reimer, 1852. 202p.

4767 . Rankin, Daniel J. "The Chinde River and Zambezi Delta," *PRGS*, New Series, XII(1890), 136-144. Also, *SGM*, V(1889), 475-480.

4768 . _____. "Journey from Blantyre to Quillimane," *PRGS*, New Series, VII (1885), 655-664.

4769 . Renato Baptista, Joaquim. *Africa oriental: caminho de ferro da Beira a Manch, excursões e estudoes effectuados em 1891*. Lisbon: Imprensa Nacional, 1892. 115p.

4770 . Richards, E. H. "An African Prayer Meeting," *MH*, LXXXIV(1888),199-201.

4771 . _____. "East Central African Mission. A Site Secured," *MH*, LXXXI (1885), 23-25.

4772 _____. "Explorations by the East Central African Mission," *MH*, LXXXI (1885), 94-98.

4773 . _____. "A Visit to Baleni," *MH*, LXXXI(1885), 356-359.

4774 . _____. "Work of East Central Africa Mission," *MH*, LXXXI(1885), 239-240.

1775 . Ross, A. Carnegie. "Beira," *SGM*, XI(1895), 180-185.

4776 . Sá da Bandeira. [*Vicomte*]. "Notes sur les fleuves Zambèse et Chiré et sur quelques lacs de l'Afrique orientale," *BSGP*, 5th Series, III(1862), 351-361.

4777 . Sanders, M. J. "Life in Central Africa," *MH*, LXXXI(1885), 375-378.

4778 . Sarmento, Adolpho. *A Morrumbala. Um sanatorium na Zambezia*. Lisbon; 1899. 47p.

4779 . Silva, Antonio. [*Marques*]. "Moçambique," *BSGL*, III(1882), 45-50.

4780 . Smythies. [*Bishop*]. "The Discovery of the Source of the Lugenda River," *JMGS*, I(1885), 302-310.

4781 . Soares, Augusto Estanislau Xavier. *Descripção da villa de Sofalla, de seus principales edificios, população, agricultura, commercio, etc. Seguida do Catalogo de seus Governadores e dos de Moçambique, depois que esta foi separada do Governo da India*. Nova Goa: Imprensa Nacional, 1857. 100p.

4782 . Sousa Barroso, Antonio José de. "Padroado de Portugal em Africa," *BSGL*, XIV(1895), 565-738.

4783 . _____. *Relatório Apresentado a S. Exca o Ministro e Secretário de Estado Dós Negócios de Marinha e Ultramar*. Barcelona: Companhia Editora do Minho, 1931. 60p.

4784 . Stewart, James [*Rev., Dr.*]. "The City of Mozambique," in *The Cape and Its People*, Roderick Noble, Ed., Cape Town: J. C. Juta, 1869.

4785 . _____. "Survey of the Eastern Coast of Lake Nyassa, and Latest News of the 'Lake-Junction Road'," *PRGS*, New Series, V(1883), 689-692.

4786 . Terao. [*Governor of Senna*]. "Memoir Relative to the Captaincy of Rios de Senna, a Portuguese Settlement of the South-East Coast of Africa," *South African Quarterly Journal* (First Series), I(1830), 49-71.

4787 . Torrend, Julius. "Contes en Chwabo ou langue de Quelimane," *ZAOS*, I (1895), 243-249; II(1896), 46-50, 244-248.

4788 . Trindade Coelho, José Francisco. [**Editor**]. *Dezoito annos em Africa; notas e documentos para a biographia do conselheiro José d'Almeida*. Lisbon: de Mendonça, 1898. 539p.

4789 . Warren, C. [*Capt.*]. "From the Gold Region in the Transvaal to Delagoa Bay," *JRGS*, XLVIII(1878), 383-387.

4790 . Wiese, Carl. "Expedição portugueza à M'pesene (1889)," *BSGL*, X(1891), 235-273, 331-430, 465-497; XI(1892), 373-599.

4791 . Wilcox, W. C. "East Central African Mission: A Visit to the Makwakwas," *MH*, LXXXI(1885), 310-311.

4792 . _____. "East Central African Mission: Another New Station," *MH*, LXXXI (1885), 467-468.

4793 . _____. "The Mission Plantation," *MH*, LXXXI(1885), 69-70.

4794 . _____; Ousley, B. F. ; and Richards, E. H. "News from the East Central African Mission," *MH*, LXXXII(1886), 20, 62-63, 107, 144, 181-182, 264-266, 346-347, 381-382.

4795 . Wilder, George A. "The Coronation of a New Chief," *MH*, XCII(1896), 112-114.

4796 . _____. "The Expedition to the Kraal of Gungunyana, Gaza Country," *MH*, LXXXV(1889), 55-58.

4797 . _____ and others. "Letters from the East Central African Mission," *MH*, LXXXIX(1893), 25-26, 410; XC(1894), 158-159, 250-251, 286-287, 385-386, 426-427, 489-490.

4798 . Woodhead, Cawthra. *Natal e a Moçambique*. Oporto, 1895.

4799 . Worsfold, William Basil. *Portuguese Nyasaland*. London: S. Low & Co., 1899. 295p.

RHODESIA

4800 . Alderson, Edwin Alfred Hervey. *With the Mounted Infantry and the Mashona-land Field Force, 1896.* London: Methuen, 1898. 308p.

4801 . Alford, Charles J. *Report of an Expedition in Search of Coal in the Districts Immediately South of the Zambesi, for the British South Africa Company.* n.p., n.p., 1894. 18p.

4802 . Allen, Alfred. "Letters," *Letters and Notices,* (1883), 96-100, 101-104.

4803 . Aloy, Pedro. "Cartas," *Cartas de Filipinas Cuad,* VI(1887), 222-229.

4804 . _____. "Missionsbriefe," *KM,* XXI(1893), 42.

4805 . Apel, Johann. "Letters," *Zambesi Mission Record,* I(1898-1901), 371, 372.

4806 . Baden-Powell, Robert Stephenson Smyth. *The Matabele Campaign, 1896; Being a Narrative of the Campaign in Supressing the Native Rising in Matabeleland and Mashonaland.* London: Methuen, 1897. 500p.

4807 . _____. *Sport in War.* London: Heinemann, 1900. 202p.

4808 . Baecher, Aloysius. "Missionsbriefe," *Echo aus Afrika,* VII(1895), 62-64, 119, 120.

4809 . _____. "Missionsbriefe," *KM,* XXIV(1896), 88-90.

4810 . Bailie, Alex C. "Report on the General Features of the Interior of South Africa, between Barkly and Gubuluwayo, to Accompany Map of the Route," *JRGS,* XLVIII(1878), 287-293.

4811 . Baines, Thomas. *The Gold Regions of South-Eastern Africa*. London: Edward Stanford, 1877. 240p.

4812 . _____. "Letters," *CMM*, 2nd Series, I(1870), 65-81; IV(1872), 28-34, 99-107.

4813 . _____. "The Limpopo, Its Origin, Course, and Tributaries," *JRGS*, XXIV(1854), 288-291.

4814 . _____. *The Northern Goldfields Diaries of Thomas Baines, 1869-1872*. Edited by J. P. R. Wallis. 3 vols. London: Chatto & Windus, 1946.

4815 . _____. *Voyage dans le sud-ouest de l'Afrique*. Paris: Hachette, 1868. 298p.

4816 . _____and Mann, Robert J. "Account of Mr. Baines's Exploration of the Gold-Bearing Region between the Limpopo and Zambesi Rivers," *JRGS*, XLI(1871), 100-131.

4817 . Baldwin, William Charles. *African Hunting, from Natal to the Zambesi, 1852-1860*. London: Bentley; New York: Harper, 1863. 451p. French translation, *Du Natal au Zambesi, 1851-66. Récits de chasses*. Paris: Hachette, 1868. 308p.

4818 . Balfour, Alice Blanche. *Twelve Hundred Miles in a Wagon*. London: Arnold, 1895. 265p. See also, *National Review*, April & May; 1895, 183-206, 351-373.

4819 "Bamangwato". *To Ophir Direct: or the South African Gold Fields, with a Map Showing the Route Taken by Hartley and Mauch, in 1866-67, and an Account of the "Transvaal" or South African Republic: Its Ways and Means; and a Few Words on a Proposed New Port, as the Shortest Road for Diggers*. London: Edward Stanford, 1868. 46p.

4820 . Barthélemy, Marc. "Letters," *Zambesi Missions Record*, I(1898-1901), 19-21.

4821 . Bent, James Theodore. "Mashonaland and Its Inhabitants," *New Review*, VI(1892), 580-592.

4822 . _____. "Mashonaland and Its People," *Contemporary Review*, LXIV(1893), 642-653.

4823 . _____. "On the Finds at the Great Zimbabwe Ruins (with a View to Elucidating the Origins of the Race that Built Them)," *JAI*, XXII(1892-1893), 124-133.

4824 . _____. "On the Origin of the Mashonaland Ruins," *Nineteenth Century*, CCII(1893), 991-997.

4825 . _____. *The Ruined Cities of Mashonaland: Being a Record of Excavation and Exploration in 1891.* London: Longmans, 1892. 376p.

4826 . _____. "The Ruins of Mashonaland," *PRGS*, New Series, XIV(1892), 273-298.

4827 . _____. "The Tribes of Mashonaland and Their Origin," *SGM*, VIII(1892), 534-539.

4828 . Berghegge, Franz. "Missionsbriefe," *KM*, X(1882), 154, 155.

4829 . Bick, Karl. "Letters," *Zambesi Mission Record*, I(1898-1901), 27-34.

4830 . _____. "Lettres," *APFL*, LXIX(1897), 345-367.

4831 . _____. "Missionsbriefe," *KM*, XXII(1894), 65, 66.

4832 . Biehler, Eduard. "Lettere," *MCM*, XXVII(1898), 175.

4833 . Blake, J. Y. F. [*Colonel*]. "Golden Rhodesia - a Revelation," *National Review*, Aug., 1897, 839-851.

4834 . _____. "Native Rhodesians," *National Review*, Oct., 1897, 217-225.

4835 . Blennerhassett, Rose, and Sleeman, Lucy. *Adventures in Mashonaland. By Two Hospital Nurses*. London: Macmillan, 1893. 340p.

4836    . Boggie, A. *From Ox-Wagon to Railway. Being a Brief History of Rhodesia and the Matabele Nation.* Bulawayo: "Times" Printing Office; 1897. 42p.

4837    . Boggie, Jeannie M. *Experiences of Rhodesia's Pioneer Women. Being a True Account of the Adventures of the Early White Women Settlers in Southern Rhodesia . . , Elicited and Arranged by J. M. Boggie.* Bulawayo: Philpott and Collines, 1938. 263p.

4838    . Booms, Heinrich. "Lettres," *Lettres de Jersey*, I(1882), 363-367.

4839    . _____. "Lettres," *Précis Historiques*, XXXIX(1890), 20-22, 130-132.

4840    . _____. "Lettres," *Sommervogel*, I(1890), 1772,1773.

4841    . _____. "Missionsbriefe," *KM*, X(1882), 155; XVIII(1890), 90, 110, 111; XIX(1891), 18, 19.

4842    . Boos, Anton. "Letters," *Zambesi Mission Record*, I(1898-1901), 121-127.

4843    . _____. "Missionsbriefe," *Echo aus Afrika*, X(1898), 145-147; XI(1899), 53, 54.

4844    . _____. "Missionsbriefe," *KM*, XXI(1893), 155, 156, 177, 178; XXII(1894), 18, 19, 264; XXVII(1898-1899), 66, 67.

4845    . Bordeaux, Albert François Joseph. *Rhodésie et Transvaal. Impressions de voyage.* Paris: Plon, 1898. 284p.

4846    . _____. *Les mines de l'Afrique du Sud, Transvaal, Rhodesie, etc.*

4847    . Bottomley, George. *A Journey to the South African Gold Fields.* Durban: Natal Herald Office, 1870. 77p.

4848    . Bourne, Henry Richard Fox. *Matabeleland and the Chartered Company.* London: P. S. King and Son, 1897. 40p.

4849 . Bowler, Louis P. "Addenda to Pamphlet on 'Facts about the Matabele, Mashonas, and the Middle Zambesi," Pretoria, 1889. 4p.

4850 . _____. *Facts about the Matabele, Mashonas, and the Middle Zambesi, Giving a Full Description of the Countries.* Pretoria: B. Gluckstein, 1889. 36p.

4851 . British South Africa Company. *Reports on the Native Disturbances in Rhodesia, 1896-1897.* London, 1898. 160p.

4852 Brou, A. "Zimbabyé, les grandes ruines de l'Afrique du Sud," *Études,* LXVI (1895), 227-249.

4853 Brown, William Harvey. *On the South African Frontier. The Adventures and Observations of an American in Mashonaland and Matabeleland.* New York: Scribners, 1899. 430p.

4854 . Burnham, Frederick Russell. *Scouting on Two Continents.* Garden City, N.Y.: Doubleday, Page, 1928. 370p.

4855 . Caldas Xavier, Augusto. *A Zambezia. Estudos Coloniaes Dedicados a Sociedad de Geografia de Lisboa.* Lisbon: Imprensa nacional, 1888.

4856 . Campbell, A. "Land of the Matabele," *Canadian Monthly,* IX(1876), 18-20.

4857 Carnegie, David. *Among the Matabele; with Portraits of Lobengula and Khama.* London: Religious Tract Society, 1894. 128p.

4858 . _____. "Lobengula and His Times. Some Vivid Reminiscences," *Diamond Fields Advertiser,* Aug. 18, 1906.

4859 . Cecil, Evelyn. *On the Eve of War. A Narrative of Impressions During a Journey in Cape Colony. . .and Rhodesia.* London: John Murray, 1900. 147p.

4860 . Chadwick, J. Cooper. *Three Years with Lobengula and Experiences in South Africa.* London: Cassell, 1894. 160p.

4861 . Chambers, Stracey. *The Rhodesians. Sketches of English South African Life.* London and New York: John Lane, 1900. 153p.

4862 . Coillard, François. "Du pays des Matébéles," *JME,* LIII(1878), 174-179.

4863 . Collings, T. C. "Mashonaland and Rhodesia as a Field for the Settler," *Travel,* I(1896), 54-57.

4864 . Colquhoun, Archibald R. *Dan to Beersheba. Work and Travel in Four Continents.* London: William Heinemann, 1908. 348p.

4865 . _____. "Matabeleland," *Proceedings of the Royal Colonial Institute,* XXV(1893), 44-103.

4866 . _____. *Matabeleland: the War, and Our Position in South Africa.* London: Leadenhall, 1894. 167p.

4867 . Courtois, José Victor. *Notes chronologiques sur les anciennes missions catholiques au Zambèze.* Lisbon: Imprimérie franco-portugaise, 1889. 76p.

4868 . Croonenberghs, Charles. "Coup d'oeil général sur la mission du Haut-Zambèse," *MCL,* XIV(1882), 297, 298, 311, 312, 323, 324.

4869 . _____ "Letters," *Zambesi Mission Record,* IX(1930-1934), 337-344, 471-473.

4870 . _____. "Lettere," *MCM,* VIII(1879), 297; X(1881), 55, 266-268; XI(1882), 230-233, 242-246, 412-414, 479, 480.

4871 . _____. "Lettres," *APFL,* LIII(1881), 250-278.

4872 . _____. "Lettres," *MCL,* XI(1879), 284, 285; XIII(1881), 41, 42, 169-171; XIV (1882), 218-221, 230-235, 389, 390, 431.

4873 . _____. "Lettres," *Précis Historiques,* XXVIII(1879),373-375, 376, 377, 380, 381, 504-510, 516-519, 618-621, 623-627, 630-636; XXIX(1880),129-140, 182-190, 291-299, 385-409, 657-677; XXX(1881), 66-69, 74-89, 185-191, 198-220, 417-419; XXXI(1882), 177-200; XXXIII(1884),537-552, 605-629; XXXIV(1885), 35-53, 84-97, 334-342.

4874 . _____. "Missionsbriefe," *KM,* VIII(1880), 194-197; IX(1881),23, 24, 81-83, 106-108, 126-128; XIII(1885), 175-177.

4875      ———————————. "La mission du Zambese," *MCL.* XIV(1882), 441, 442, 452, 453, 464, 465. Also, *MCM*, XI(1882), 526, 527, 563, 564, 571, 572.

4876     . Czimmermann, Stephan. "Cartas," *Novo Mensageiro do Coração de Jesu*, XI (1891), 664-671; XIV(1894), 513-516.

4877     ———————————. "Letters," *Letters and Notices*, (1888), 493-497, 575-578.

4878     . ———————————. "Lettres," *Lettres de Jersey*, VII(1888), 120-123, 207-209.

4879     . ———————————. "Missionsbriefe," *Echo aus Afrika*, III(1891), 53, 54, 60-62; IV(1892), 93, 94, 101, 102; V(1893), 27-31, 55-57, 96-98; VI(1894), 3, 27, 33-36.

4880     . ———————————. "Missionsbriefe," *Echo z Afrijki*, II(1894), 14-16, 45, 46.

4881     ———————————. "Missionsbriefe," *Gott will es*, III(1891), May.

4882     ———————————. "Missionsbriefe," *KM*, XV(1887), 49-51; XVI(1888), 19-22, 172-175; XVII(1889), 89-91, 154-156; XVIII(1890), 240-242; XIX(1891), 42-44, 218-220; XXI(1893), 22, 23, 119, 130, 131, 178; XXII(1894), 135-137.

4883     ———————————. "Missionsbriefe," *Sendbote des göttlich Herzens Jesu*, XXV(1889), 344-346; XXVII(1891), 218-220; XXVIII(1892), 314-316.

4884     . Daignault, Alphonse. "Lettres," *Précis Historiques*, XXXIX(1890), 125.

4885     . ——————. "Missionsbriefe," *KM*, XIX(1891), 218.

4886     . Davidson, H. Frances. *South and Central Africa; a Record of Fifteen Years' Missionary Labors among Primitive Peoples*. Elgin, Ill.: Brethern Publishing House, 1915. 481p.

4887 . Davis, Alexander. *Davis' Directory of Bulawayo and Handbook to Matabeleland.* London: Cooper and Budd, 1898. 234p.

4888 . _____. *The Directory of Bulawayo and Handbook to Matabeleland, 1896.* Capetown: W. A. Richards, 1896. 220p.

4889 . Dawkins, Charles Tyrwhitt. *Précis of Information Concerning Southern Rhodesia.* London: War Office, 1899. 55p.

4890 . Dawson, May M. *Veld and Heather. Memories of Home and Sketches of Life from the Land of Lobengula.* London: J. M. Dent, 1902. 140p.

4891 . Day, Arthur. "Letters," *Zambesi Mission Record,* I(1898-1901), 296-300.

4892 . Decle, Lionel. "On Some Matabele Customs," *JAI,* XXIII(1894), 83-88.

4893 . _____. "Two Years in Rhodesia," *National Review,* Apr., 1896, 531-545.

4894 . Dejoux, Jean-Baptiste. "Lettere," *MCM,* XI(1882), 73-75.

4895 . _____. "Lettres," *MCL,* XIV(1882), 38, 39.

4896 . _____. "Missionsbriefe," *KM,* XII(1884), 190, 207-209.

4897 . De Moura, Johann Joseph. "Missionsbriefe," *Echo aus Afrika,* V(1893),116; VI(1894), 113, 114; VII(1895), 51; VIII(1896), 88.

4898 . Depelchin, Henri. "Lettere," *MCM,* IX(1880), 517-520; X(1881), 572; XI (1882), 229-232.

4899 . _____. "Lettres," *APFL,* LIV(1882), 90-120, 245-252.

4900 . _____. "Lettres," *BSBG,* IV(1880), 737-743.

4901 . _____. "Lettres," *MCL,* XI(1879), 285; XII(1880), 493-496; XIII(1881), 558; XIV(1882), 73-75, 461, 593, 594.

4902   . \_\_\_\_. "Lettres," *Précis Historiques,* XXVII(1878),728; XXVIII(1879), 372, 373, 377, 378, 380, 381, 385-395, 402, 496-503, 511-516, 519-526, 611-617, 622, 623, 627, 628, 636; XXIX(1880), 45-74, 111-128, 164-182, 286-291, 604-611; XXX(1881), 419-421, 496-522, 600-624, 648-667; XXXI (1882), 5-15, 554-556, 693, 694; XXXII(1883), 79-97, 176-188, 193-203, 264-282, 305-327.

4903   . \_\_\_\_. "Missionsbriefe," *KM,* X(1882), 20-22, 217-219; XI(1883), 42.

4904   . _____. "Reise nach dem Zambesi," *PM,* XXV(1879), 435.

4905   . _____. "Zambesi-Mission," *PM,* XXVIII(1882), 277.

4906   . Deplace, Edmond. "Lettres," *Précis Historiques,* XXXIX(1890), 23-32.

4907   . \_\_\_\_. "Missionsbriefe," *KM,* XVIII(1890), 195-198.

4908   . De Sadeller, Frans. "The Expedition to Umzila's Kraal in 1880: Brother De Sadeller's Narrative," *Zambesi Mission Record,* V(1914-1917), 135-140, 179-182, 217-221, 248-250, 289-293, 317-320, 359-361.

4909   . _____. "Lettere," *MCM,* XI(1881), 172-175.

4910   . \_\_\_\_. "Lettres," *MCL,* XIV(1882), 109-112.

4911   . \_\_\_\_. "Lettres," *Précis Historiques,* XXX(1881), 335-343, 409-416; XXXI (1882), 87-96; XIII(1894), 390, 391.

4912   . Desmaroux, Felix. "Missionsbriefe," *KM,* XX(1892), 107; XXVI(1897-1898), 68.

4913   . Dickins, Vincent. "Journeys in South-Eastern Mashonaland," *GJ,* XXIX(1907), 15-23.

4914   . Diesterweg, Moritz. *Aus dem Pionier-Leben wahrend Meines 20 jährigen Aufenthaltes in Süd-Afrika.* Burg: A. Hopfer, 1903. 227p.

4915   . Donovan, Charles Henry Wynne. *With Wilson in Matabeleland, or, Sport and War in Zambesia.* London: Henry, 1894. 322p.

4916 . Doyle, Denis. *The Rise and Fall of the Matabele Nation*. Grahamstown: Gregory and Sherry, 1893. 16p.

4917 . Dupeyron, Pierre. "Missionsbriefe," *KM*, XXII(1894), 162, 163; XXIII(1895), 235-238.

4918 . Durand, E. *Une explorer française au Zambèze*. Paris, n.p., 1888. 116p.

4919 . Du Toit, Stephanus Jacobus. *Rhodesia, Past and Present*. London: Heinemann, 1897. 218p.

4920 . _____. *Sambesia, of Salomo's Goudmijnen Bezocht in 1894*. Paarl: D. K. Du Toit, 1895. 226p.

4921 . Eckersley, W. Alfred. "Notes in Eastern Mashonaland," *GJ*, V(1895), 27-46.

4922 . Enderlin, Isidor. "Missionsbriefe," *KM*, XXVII(1898-1899), 186.

4923 . Engels, Ferdinand. "Missionsbriefe," *KM*, X(1882), 219, 220; XI(1883), 107-110, 127-133; XII(1884), 20-23; XXVIII(1899-1900), 184, 185.

4924 . Erlington. *Erlington's Handbook on Mashonaland. The Country and How to Reach It*. London: Erlington & Co., 1892. 87p.

4925 . Etterle, Joseph. *Les Maladies de l'Afrique tropicale*. Brussels: Société Belge de Librairie, 1892. 192p.

4926 . Fairbridge, W. E. "Some Home Truths about Rhodesia," *National Review*, March, 1897, 30-41.

4927 . Finlason, C. E. *A Nobody in Mashonaland: or, the Trials and Adventures of a Tenderfoot*. Cape Town: J. C. Juta & Co., 1893. 330p.

4928 ., Fitzpatrick, James Percy. *Through Mashonaland with Pick and Pen.*
Johannesburg: Argus, 1892. 64p.

4929 . Foa, Édouard. "Travels in the Basin of the Zambesi," *JRSA*, XLII(1894),
338-344.

4930 . Fraser, George. "Letters," *Letters and Notices*, (1881), 317-328.

4931 . _____. "Lettres," *Précis Historiques*, XXXI(1888), 568.

4932 . _____. "Missionsbriefe," *KM*, XVI(1888), 257.

4933 . Friedrich, Karl. "Missionsbriefe," *Echo aus Afrika*, VIII(1896), 55-57;
XI(1899), 145.

4934 . Fritsch, Gustav. *Süd Afrika bis zum Zambesi.* Leipzig: G. Freytag, 1885.
233p.

4935 Frobenius, Herman. "Rhodesia," *DK*, XVI(1899), 351-353.

4936 . Fry, J. W. Ellerton. "The March of the British into Mashonaland. The Route
by the Healthy Highlands," in R. W. Murray, Ed., *South Africa
from Arab Domination to British Rule*, London: E. Stanford, 1891.

4937 Gabriel, Emanuel. "Letters," *Letters and Notices*, (1882), 159; (1885),
39, 40.

4938 . _____. "Lettres," *Lettres de Jersey*, IV(1885), 145, 146.

4939 . _____. "Missionsbriefe," *KM*, XI(1883), 151-153; XII(1884), 102, 103,
162, 187, 188; XIII(1885), 22.

4940 . Gell, Philip Lyttelton. *Rubber Industry in the British South Africa
Company's Territory.* Salisbury, n.p., 1900. 28p.

4941 . Gilbert, Sharrad H. *Rhodesia—and After. Being the Story of the 17th and 18th Battalions of Imperial Yeomanry in South Africa*. London: Simpkin Marshall, Hamilton, Kent, & Co., Ltd., 1901. 350p.

4942 . Goy, Mathilde Keck. *Alone in Africa. Or, Seven Years on the Zambesi*. London: J. Nisbet & Co., 1901. 78p.

4943 . Green, Elsa Goodwin. *Raiders and Rebels in South Africa*. London: George Newnes, 1898. 208p.

4944 . Hall, Richard Nicklin. "Great Zimbabwe," *Report of the South African Association for the Advancement of Science*, I(1903), 304-315.

4945 . _____ and Neal, W. G. *The Ancient Ruins of Rhodesia-Monomotapa Imperium*. London: Methuen & Co., 1902. 396p. 2nd Ed., 1904.

4946 . _____ and Neal, W. G. "Architectual Construction of Ancient Ruins in Rhodesia," *Proceedings of the Rhodesian Scientific Association*, II(1901), 5-28.

4947 . Hammond, John Hays. *The Autobiography of John Hays Hammond*. 2 vols. New York: Farrar & Rinehart, 1935.

4948 . _____. *The Truth about the Jameson Raid*. Boston: Marshall Jones, 1918. 50p.

4949 Harding, Colin. *Frontier Patrols. A History of the British South African Police and Other Rhodesian Forces*. London: Bell, 1937. 372p.

4950 Harris, William Cornwallis. *The Wild Sports of Southern Africa, Being the Narrative of a Hunting Expedition from the Cape of Good Hope through the Territories of the Chief Moselekatse to the Tropic of Capricorn*. n.p., 1839. Reprinted, Cape Town: C. Struik, 1964. 359p. *Africana Collectanea*, VI.

4951 . Hartmann, Andre M. [*Missionary*]. "The Mashonas: By One Who Knows Them," *South African Catholic Magazine*, III(1893), 477-482.

4952 . _____. "Letters," *Zambesi Mission Record*, I(1898-1901), 128-133, 244-247, 334-339, 453-455.

4953 . _____. "Missionsbriefe," *Echo aus Afrika*, IV(1892), 102, 103; VII(1895), 15-19, 105-108; VIII(1896), 101-103; IX(1897), 18, 19, 91-93; X(1898), 64, 144, 145; XII(1900), 52; XIII(1901), 141-144.

4954 . _____. "Missionsbriefe," *KM*, XVIII(1890), 88-90.

4955

. Haynes, C. E. [*Capt.*]. "Matabeleland and the Country between the Zambesi and Limpopo Rivers: a Gold Country," *JMGS*, III(1887), 244-252.

4956 . Heep, Ferdinand. "Letters," *Letters and Notices*, (1881), 269-273.

4957 . _____. "Missionsbriefe," *KM*, XII(1884), 74, 75, 162, 163, 187.

4958 . Hiller, Johannes. "Lettere," *MCM*, XXVII(1898), 542, 543.

4959 . _____. "Lettres," *MCL*, XXX(1898), 529, 530; XXXII(1900), 616, 617.

4960 . _____. "Missionsbriefe," *Echo aus Afrika*, VII(1895), 76-80; IX(1897), 20, 21, 140, 141; X(1898), 24, 25, 95, 96; XI(1899), 5-7, 83-85; XII (1900), 103-106, 172, 173; XIII(1901), 83, 84.

4961 . _____. "Missionsbriefe," *KM*, XIV(1886), 45-47, 131, 132; XXVI(1897-1898), 67; XXIX(1900-1901), 182.

4962 . Hintze, H. "Ancient Ruins in Rhodesia," *Science of Man*, II(1899), 466-468.

4963 . Hole, Hugh Marshall [*Lt. Col.*]. "Native Rhodesians: a Rejoiner," *National Review*, Nov., 1897, 354-359.

4964 _____. "Rhodesia," in J. Scott Keltie, Ed., *British Africa.* London: Kegan Paul, Trench, Trubner & Co., 1899, pp. 27-36.

4965 Holland, F. Catesby. "The Prospects of Rhodesia," *Contemporary Review,* LXXII(1897), 470-481.

4966 Holub, Emil. "Die Ma-Atebele," *ZE,* XXV(1893), 177-206.

4967 _____. *The Victoria Falls. A Few Pages from the Diary of Emil Holub, M.D., Written during His Third Trip into the Interior of Southern Africa.* Grahamstown: T. & G. Sheffield, 1879. 16p.

4968 Hornig, Joseph. "Letters," *Zambesi Mission Record,* I(1898-1901), 58-59, 379-382.

4969 _____. "Lettres," *Précis Historiques,* XXXVI(1887), 31-45; XXXIX(1890), 121-126; XLI(1892), 267-275.

4970 _____. "Missionsbriefe," *Echo aus Afrika,* XIII(1901), 188-192, 206-208.

4971 _____. "Missionsbriefe," *KM,* XIII(1885), 177, 178.

4972 Hübner, Adolf. [*Freiherr von*]. "Über alte Befestigungen im Reich der Matabelen (Masili Katses Reich) in Süd-Ost-Afrika," *ZE,* III(1871), 53-56.

4973 Janssens, Jean [*Abbé*]. "Lettres," *Précis Historiques,* XLII(1893), 409-412.

4974 Johnson, Frank W. F. "Rhodesia: Its Present and Future," *Proceedings of the Royal Colonial Institute,* XXXIII(1901), 1-33.

4975 _____. *Great Days: The Autobiography of an Empire Pioneer.* London: Bell, 1940. 366p.

4976 Kerr, Henry. "Missionsbriefe," *KM,* XIX(1891), 240, 241; XXI(1893), 176, 177.

4977 . _____. "The Zambesi Mission," *Month*, LXXVII(1893), 16-32, 196-212, 394-406, 519-531.

4978 . Knight, Edward Frederick. *Rhodesia of Today: a Description of the Present Condition and the Prospects of Matabeleland and Mashonaland*. London: Longmans, 1895. 151p.

4979 . _____. "Rhodesia: Some Personal Recollections," in *South Africa and Its Future*. Cape Town: D. E. M'Connell, 1903, pp. 55-71.

4980 . Knight-Bruce, George Wyndham Hamilton. *Gold and Gospel in Mashonaland, 1888, Being the Journals of the Mashonaland Mission of Bishop Knight-Bruce and the Concession Journey of Charles Dunell Rudd*. Edited by C. E. Fripp and V. W. Hiller. London: Chatto & Windus, 1949. 246p.

4981 . _____. *Journals of the Mashonaland Mission, 1888 to 1892*. London: Society for the Propagation of the Gospel in Foreign Parts, 1892. 99p.

4982 . _____. *Memories of Mashonaland*. London and New York: Arnold, 1895. 242p.

4983 . _____. "Notes of a Journey through Mashonaland in 1889," *PRGS*, New Series, XII(1890), 346-352.

4984 . Kroot, Bartholomeus. "Letters," *Letters and Notices*, (1885), 221, 222.

4985 . _____. "Lettres," *Lettres de Jersey*, I(1882), 367-369.

4986 . _____. "Missionsbriefe," *KM*, XIII(1885), 177-263.

4987 . Laing, D. Tyrie. *The Matabele Rebellion, 1896; with the Belingwe Field Force*. London: Dean, 1897. 327p.

4988 . Lallemand, A. "Lettres," *Précis Historiques*, XLI(1892), 203-225, 265-276, 362-381.

4989        _____. "La mission du Zambèse en 1885," *Précis Historiques*, XXXV (1886), 32-44, 74-86, 136-157.

4990   . Law, Augustus Henry. "Letters," *Letters and Notices*, (1879), 311-313, 319-321, 335-338, 340-342; (1880), 89-102, 181-206, 255-263; (1881), 1-3, 76-82,

4991   . _____. "Letters," *Précis Historiques*, XXVIII(1879), 381, 403.

4992   . _____. *A Memoir of the Life and Death of the Reverend Father Augustus Henry Law, S.J.* 3 vols. London: Burns & Oates, 1882-1893.

4993   . _____. "Missionsbriefe," *KM*, IX(1881), 171, 172.

4994   . _____ *Notes in Remembrance and Last Relics of Augustus Law, S.J.* London: Burns and Oates, 1886. 116p.

4995   . Lawson, H. W. L. "South Africa: 1 - Rhodesian Affairs," *Fortnightly Review*, May, 1896, 704-715.

4996   Leboeuf, Louis. "Letters," *Zambesi Mission Record*, I(1898-1901), 373-378.

4997   . _____. "Missionsbriefe," *Echo aus Afrika*, XIII(1901), 195-197.

4998   . Le Chartrain, Alexandre. "Sud-Afrique et Mashonaland," *Etudes*, LVIII (1893), 239-263; LIX(1893), 282-303, 466-488.

4999   Leonard, Arthur Glyn. *How We Made Rhodesia*. London: Kegan Paul, 1896. 356p.

5000   . Liagre, Edouard. "Lettres," *Bode van het H. Hart*, XXX(1898-1899), 348.

5001   . _____. "Lettres," *Missions Belges de la Compagnie de Jésus*, I(1899), 12-14, 86, 87, 125, 286, 287.

5002   . _____. "Lettres," *Précis Historiques*, XLII(1893), 223-225, 270-275, 319-324, 357-366, 422-426, 472-475, 512-520; XLIII(1894), 37-44, 65-84, 133, 166-173, 315-326, 534-536, 570-573, 576, 577; XLIV(1895), 23-27, 117-122, 350-359, 384-389, 433-437, 567-571; XLV(1896), 128-131, 194-196, 247-256, 337-340, 412, 413, 535-537; XLVI(1897), 50, 51, 113-115, 392-394; XLVII(1898), 465, 466.

5003   _____. "Missionsbriefe," *KM*, XXII(1894), 42, 43.

5004 . Lindley, Augustus F. *After Ophir; or a Search for the South African Gold Fields.* 2nd Ed. London: Cassal, Petter and Galpin, [1870]. 312p.

5005 . Lindlohr, Georg. "Missionsbriefe," *KM*, XXI(1893), 115, 116, 119.

5006 . Lippert, Marie. *The Matabeleland Travel Letters of Marie Lippert, Sept. 21 - Dec. 23, 1891.* Cape Town: Friends of the South African Public Library, 1960. 56p.

5007 . Lombary, Edmond. "Lettres," *Bode van het H. Hart,* XXVII(1895-1896), 212, 213, 333-336, 365-367; XXIX(1897-1898), 245-247.

5008 . _____. "Lettres," *Précis Historiques,* XLII(1893), 312, 355-357, 413-415; XLVI(1897), 145-147, 339, 340.

5009 . Mackenzie, John. "The Chartered Company in South Africa: A Review and Criticism," *Contemporary Review,* March, 1897, 305-328.

5010 _____. *Day-Dawn in Dark Places: a Story of Wanderings and Work in Bechwanaland.* London: Cassell, 1883. 278p.

5011 _____. *Ten Years North of the Orange River. A Story of Everyday Life and Work among the South African Tribes, from 1859 to 1869.* Edinburgh: Edmonston & Douglas, 1871. 523p.

5012 . Maguire, James Rochfort. *The Pioneers of Empire. Being a Vindication of the Principle, and a Short Sketch of the History of Chartered Companies, with Special Reference to the British South Africa Company.* London: Methuen, 1896. 139p.

5013 . Mandy, Frank. "Golden Mashonaland," *Scribner's Magazine,* XI(1892), 455-470.

5014 Manheimer, Émile. *Le nouveau monde Sud-Africa: la vie au Transvaal.* Paris, n.p., 1896. 349p.

5015 . Marquez. "Missionsbriefe," *KM*, XXII(1894), 40, 41.

5016 Martin, Richard Ernest Rowley. *Report on the Native Administration of the British South Africa Company.* [C.8547]. London: Her Majesty's Stationery Office, 1897. 28p.

5017 . Mathers, Edward Peter. *Zambesia, England's El Dorado in Africa, Being a Description of Matabeleland and Mashonaland and the Less-Known Adjacent Territories, and an Account of the Gold Fields of British South Africa.* London: King & Sell, 1891. 480p.

5018 . Mauch, Carl. *Carl Mauch's Reisen in Inneren von Süd-Afrika, 1865-1872.* Gotha: Justus Perthes, 1874. 52p.

5019 . Maund, Edward Arthur. "Mashonaland and Its Development," *Proceedings of the Royal Colonial Institute,* XXIII(1891-1892), 248-270.

5020 . _____. "On Matabele and Mashona Lands," *PRGS*, New Series, XIII (1891), 1-18.

5021 . _____. "Our New Colonies—Zambesia, Matabele, and Mashonaland," *Journal of the Tyneside Geographical Society,* I(1891), 45-60.

5022 . _____. "Zambezia, the New British Possession in Central South Africa," *PRGS*, New Series, XII(1890), 649-655.

5023 . Mennell, Frederick Philip. "Zimbabwe Ruins," *Rhodesia Science Association,* III(1902), 69-84. Also, *Special Report of Rhodesia Museum,* Bulawayo, 1903. 16p.

5024 . Moffat, John, and others. *The Matabele Mission, a Selection from the Correspondence of John and Emily Moffat, David Livingstone and Others, 1858-1878.* Edited by J. P. R. Wallis. London: Chatto & Windus, 1945. 268p.

5025 . Moffat, Robert. *The Matabele Journals of Robert Moffat, 1829-1860.* Edited by J. P. R. Wallis. 2 vols. London: Chatto & Windus, 1945.

5026 . _____. "Visit to Moselekatse, King of the Matabele," *JRGS,* XXVI(1856), 84-109.

5027 . Montagu, John Walter Edward Douglas Scott [*Lord Montagu*]. "Nature versus the Chartered Company," *Nineteenth Century,* Aug., 1896, 194-198.

5028 . Moreau, Joseph. "Lettere," *MCM,* XXVIII(1899), 193, 194, 270, 304.

5029 . _____. "Lettres," *MCL,* XXXI(1899), 169-171, 257, 281.

5030 . _____. "Missionsbriefe," *KM,* XXVII(1898-1899), 279.

5031 . Muller, Hendrik Pieter Nicolaas. *Land und Leute zwischen Zambesi und Limpopo.* Giessen: Roth, 1896. 165p.

5032 . _____. *De Zuid-Afrikaansche Republick en Rhodesia.* Gravenhage, 1896. 66p.

5033 . Nadaillac, Jean-François-Albert. *Le Mashonaland.* Paris: De Soye & Fils, 1894. 42p.

5034 . Nagel, Emil. "Die nördlichen Goldfelder des Matabili-Landes. Aus den Tagebuche eines Afrikareisenden," *PM,* XXVIII(1882), 342-347.

5035 . Nesser, Jakob. "Letters," *Zambesi Mission Record*, I(1898-1901), 268-270.

5036 . Newman, Charles L. Norris [Capt.]. *Matabeleland, and How We Got It*. London: T. Fisher Unwin, 1895. 241p.

5037 . Newton, Francis James. *Matabeleland. Report upon the Circumstances Connected with the Collision between the Matabele and the Forces of the British South Africa Company at Fort Victoria in July 1893, and Correspondence Connected Therewith*. London: H.M.S.O., 1894. 61p.

5038 . Nicot, Victor. "Lettere," *MCM*, XXV(1896), 373, 374.

5039 . _____. "Letters," *Zambesi Mission Record*, I(1898-1901), 59-61, 87-89, 150, 263, 317, 378, 452.

5040 . _____. "Lettres," *MCL*, XXVIII(1896), 326, 327.

5041 _____. "Missionsbriefe," *KM*, XXIV(1896), 209, 210.

5042 . Norris, S. C. "Rhodesia and Northwards," *Macmillan's Magazine*, Feb., 1901. 272-279.

5043 . Oates, Frank. *Matabele Land and the Victoria Falls. A Naturalist's Wanderings in the Interior of South Africa*. London: Kegan Paul, 1889. 383p.

5044 . O'Neil, Joseph. "Letters," *Zambesi Mission Record*, I(1898-1901), 64-68, 167-174, 232-235, 271-278, 309-315, 410-415, 447-451, 478-482, 488-493.

5045 . Orpen, Joseph Millerd. "The God Who Promised Victory to the Matabele," *Nineteenth Century*, Aug., 1896, 187-193.

5046 · Orr, Claire A. "England's Latest Conquest in Africa," *Cosmopolitan*, May, 1894, 35-45.

5047 Patterson, R. R. [*Capt.*]. "Notes on Matabeli-Land," *PRGS*, New Series, I(1879), 509-512.

5048 · Peters, Carl. "Discovery of Ophir," *Harper's Magazine*, Dec., 1900, 115-124.

5049 · _____. *Das Goldene Ophir Solomo's. Eine Studie zur Geschichte der Phönikischen Weltpolitik.* Munich and Leipzig: R. Oldenburg, 1895. 64p. English translation, *King Solomon's Golden Ophir. A Research into the Most Ancient Gold Production in History.* London: Leadenhall Press; New York: Scribner's Sons, 1899. 177p.

5050 · _____. *Im Goldland des Altertums. Forschungen zwischen Zambesi und Sabi.* Munich: J. F. Lehmann, 1902. 408p. English translation, *The Eldorado of the Ancients.* London: C. Arthur Pearson, 1902. 447p.

5051 _____. "Macombe's Country (South of the Zambesi), Its Ancient Goldfields and Industrial Resources," *JMGS*, XVI(1900), 48-56.

5052 · Platzer, Joseph. "Missionsbriefe," *Echo aus Afrika*, VI(1892), 67, 68, 107, 108; VII(1893), 64, 65.

5053 · Plumer, Herbert Charles Onslow. *An Irregular Corps in Matabeleland.* London: Kegan Paul, 1897. 250p.

5054 · Prestage, P^eter. "Bulawayo," *South African Catholic Magazine*, IV(1894), 517-522.

5055 · _____. "Letters," *Zambesi Mission Record*, I(1898-1901), 15-18, 89-94, 442-446.

5056 · _____. "Missionsbriefe," *KM*, XIV(1886), 86, 87; XVI(1888), 256, 257.

5057 . Prihoda, Franz. "Missionsbriefe," *KM*, XIV(1886), 46.

5058 . Puff, Anton. "Missionsbriefe," *KM*, XXII(1894), 279, 280.

5059 . Quicke, F. C. [*Capt.*]. "Supplementary Journeys by Captain F. C. Quicke," in Major A. St. H. Gibbons, "Explorations in Marotseland and Neighbouring Regions," *GJ*, XVII(1901), 106-134.

5060 . Ramone, Léonce de. "Lettres," *Annales Franciscaines*, XVIII(1892-1894), 315-317.

5061 . _____. "Lettres," *Echo de St. François*, II(1895), 196-198; IV(1897), 503, 504.

5062 . Rand, Frank R. [*Dr.*]. "Wayfaring Notes in Rhodesia," in British South Africa Company, *Reports on the Administration of Rhodesia, 1897-1898*, pp. 389-397.

5063 . Randall-MacIver, David. " The Rhodesia Ruins: Their Probable Origin and Significance," *GJ*, XXVII(1906), 325-336.

5064 . Richartz, Franz. "Letters," *Zambesi Mission Record*, I(1898-1901), 53-55, 61-63, 127, 128, 474-477.

5065 . _____. "Missionsbriefe," *Echo aus Afrika*, VII(1895), 51, 52; VIII(1896), 42; IX(1897), 8-12; XII(1900), 148-150.

5066 . _____. "Missionsbriefe," *KM*, XX(1892), 198-200; XXI(1893), 90, 91, 243-246; XXIII(1895), 188-190, 277, 278; XXIV(1896), 67, 90, 91, 255, 278, 279; XXV(1897), 59-61; XXVI(1897-1898), 46-48, 90, 91; XXVII(1898-1899), 214.

5067 . Rieder, Josef. "Lettres," *Lettres de Mold*, I(1883), 642-645; II(1884), 541-544; IV(1886), 270, 271, 495, 496.

5068 . Romilly, Hugh H. *Letters from the Western Pacific and Mashonaland, 1878-1891.* Edited by Samuel H. Romilly. London: David Nott, 1893. 384p.

5069 Rugg, Roland (Ed.). *Matabeleland: Its Gold Fields, Boundaries, Geology, Mineral and Other Resources, History, and Armed Strength.* London: E. Forster Groom, 1890. 136p.

5070 . Ryan, John. "Letters," *Zambesi Mission Record,* I(1898-1901), 262, 263.

5071 . Sauer, Hans [Dr.]. *Legislative Council Election. To the Electors of Matabeleland.* Bulawayo: Argus, 1899. 18p.

5072 . Sawyer, Arthur Robert. *The Goldfields of Mashonaland.* Manchester: John Heywood, 1894. 99p.

5073 Schlichter, Dr. Heinrich G. "Die Ruinen von Simbabye," *PM,* XXXVIII(1892), 283-286.

5074 _____. "Travels and Researches in Rhodesia," *GJ,* XIII(1899), 376-391.

5075 . Scott, E. D. *Some Letters from South Africa, 1894-1902.* Manchester and London: Sherratt and Hughes, 1903. 183p.

5076 . Selous, F. Frederick Courtenay. "Cause and Effect of the Matabele War," *National Review,* April, 1894, pp. 250-272. Also, *Journal of the Tyneside Geographical Society,* II(1894), 230-254.

5077 . _____. "The Economic Value of Rhodesia," *SGM,* XIII(1897), 505-514.

5078 . _____. "Further Explorations in Matabele-Land," *PRGS,* New Series, X (1888), 293-296.

5079 . _____. "Further Explorations in the Mashuna Country," *PRGS,* New Series, V(1883), 268-271

5080 _____. "Mashunaland and the Mashunas," *Fortnightly Review*, New Series, XLV(1889), 661-676.

5081 . _____. "Recent Explorations in Mashuna-Land," *PRGS*, New Series, III (1881), 352-358.

5082 . _____. "A Recent Journey in Eastern Mashona Land," *PRGS*, New Series, XII(1890), 146-150.

5083 . _____. *Sunshine and Storm in Rhodesia. Being a Narrative of Events in Matabeleand, Both before and during the Recent Native Insurrection, Up to the Date of the Disbandment of the Bulawayo Field Force.* London: Ward, 1896. 290p.

5084 _____. *Travel and Adventure in South-East Africa. Being the Narrative of the Last Eleven Years Spent by the Author on the Zambesi and Its Tributaries; with an Account of the Colonisation of Mashunaland and the Progress of the Gold Industry in That Country.* London: Ward, 1893. 503p.

5085 . _____. "Travel and Sport in South Africa," *JMGS*, IX(1893), 45-48.

5086 _____. "Twenty Years in Zambezia," *GJ*, I(1893), 289-322.

5087 . Smith, Ronald. *The Great Gold Lands of South Africa. A Vacation Run in Cape Colony. . . .to which Are Added Narratives of Adventures in Matabeleland, and an Account of the Expedition to Mashonaland.* London: Ward, Lock & Co., 1891. 296p.

5088 . Spillman, Joseph. *Vom Cap zum Sambesi.* Freiburg im Breisgau: Herder'sche Verlagshandlung, 1882. 432p.

5089 . Statham, Francis Reginald. "Chartered Company: the Other Side," *National Review*, March, 1896, 33–50.

5090 . Stempfel, Anton. "Letters," *Zambesi Mission Record*, I(1898–1901), 493–496.

5091 . Stevenson, Rennie. *Through Rhodesia with the Sharpshooters*. London: John MacQueen, 1901. 199p.

5092 . Strasheim, P. A. [*Rev*.]. *In the Land of Cecil Rhodes*. Cape Town: J.C. Juta & Co., 1896. 122p.

5093 . Stuart, J. M. *The Ancient Gold Fields of Africa*. London: Express Printing Co., 1891. 312p.

5094 . Surridge, Frank Harold [*Rev*.]. "Matabeleland and Mashonaland," *Proceedings of the Royal Colonial Institute*, XXII(1890–1891), 305–331.

5095 . Swan, Robert M. W. "The Geography and Meteorology of Mashonaland," *PRGS*, New Series, XIV(1892), 299–302.

5096 . _____. "List of Stations in Mashonaland," *PRGS*, New Series, XIV(1892), 303–304.

5097 . _____. "The Orientation of the Buildings at Zimbabwe," *PRGS*, New Series, XIV(1892), 306–309.

5098 . _____. "Some Features of the Ruined Temples of Mashonaland," *SGM*, VIII (1892), 539–544.

5099 . _____. "Some Notes on Ruined Temples in Mashonaland," *JAI*, XXVI(1896–1897), 2–12.

5100 . Sykes, Francis William. *With Plumer in Matabeleland Relief Force during the Rebellion of 1896*. Westminster: Constable, 1897. 296p.

5101 . Sykes, Richard. "Letters," *Zambesi Mission Record*, I(1898-1901), 11-15, 330-333, 365-370, 406-410, 456-459.

5102 . Tangye, Harold Lincoln. *In New South Africa: Travels in the Transvaal and Rhodesia*. London: Cox, 1896. 431p.

5103 . Terorde, Anton. "Letters," *Letters and Notices*, (1881), 153-163, 256, 257.

5104 . _____. "Lettres," *Précis Historiques*, XXVIII(1897), 399-402.

5105 . _____. "Missionsbriefe," *KM*, VII(1879), 132-134, 152-159, 194-199, 212-216, 236-240; VIII(1880), 16-18, 36-40, 104-109, 130; IX(1881), 201-206; XI(1883), 69-77.

5106 . Thomson, H~ENRY CRANFUIRD~. *Rhodesia and Its Government*. London: Smith, Elder, 1898. 352p.

5107 . _____. "Rule of the Chartered Company," *National Review*, Feb., 1899, 895-908.

5108 . Thomson, J. Mudie. *Political Reorganisation: A Study Towards Rhodesian Self-Government*. Bulawayo, 1898. 30p. Rhodesian Problems, No. 1.

5109 . Torrend, Jules. "Colonisation et Missions," *Études*, LXXIV(1898), 265-268.

5110 . _____. "Lettere," *MCM*, XXIV(1895), 205-208; XXV(1896), 253-255; XXVI(1897), 438, 439; XXVII(1898), 376-378; XXX(1901), 173, 174, 185.

5111 . _____. "Lettres," *APFL*, LXVI(1894), 155, 156, 472; LXXIII(1901), 310, 311.

5112 . _____. "Lettres," *MCL*, XXV(1893), 233, 593; XXVI(1894), 356; XXVII(1895), 193-196; XXVIII(1896), 230-232; XXIX(1897), 413; XXX(1898), 364; XXXI(1899), 556; XXXIII(1901), 160, 173.

5113 . _____. "Missionsbriefe," *KM*, XV(1887), 154, 155; XXVI(1897-1898), 189, 190.

5114     . _____. "Mission du Zambèse," *Études*, LXXII(1897), 530-536.

5115     . Van Henexthoven, Emiel. "Lettres," *Bode van het H. Hart*, XXVII(1895-1896), 61; XXVIII(1896-1897), 223, 314-316; XXIX(1897-1898), 318; XXXI (1899-1900), 190; XXXII(1900-1901), 91, 92, 127, 128; XXXIII(1901-1902), 91-93.

5116     . _____. "Lettres," *MCL*, XXV(1893), 448, 533.

5117     . _____. "Lettres," *Missions Belges de la Compagnie de Jésus*, I(1899), 11, 86, 123, 124, 205, 244-246, 326, 327, 365, 444, 445; II(1900), 75, 150, 268, 269, 298, 299, 325, 351, 352; III(1901), 78, 79, 118, 119, 227, 437, 438, 471.

5118     . _____. "Lettres," *Précis Historiques*, XLII(1893), 217-222, 266-270, 310-319, 416-422, 467-472, 501-512, 537-540; XLIII(1894), 24-37, 84, 85, 118-132, 173-179, 218-226, 226-237, 388, 389, 439-442, 578-584; XLIV(1895), 19-23, 57-67, 379-384, 389-391; XLV(1896), 124, 125, 157, 158, 347-349, 418, 419, 533-535; XLVI(1897), 19, 20, 49, 50, 241-245. 337, 338, 435, 436, 529, 530; XLVII(1898), 33-35, 49-51, 97, 98, 104, 109, 158, 159, 161-163, 585.

5119     . _____. "Missionsbriefe," *KM*, XXII(1894), 19-22, 41, 42, 211, 212; XXIII (1895), 159-162.

5120     . Vesteneck, Moritz. "Missionsbriefe," *KM*, XII(1884), 258, 259.

5121     . Vierin, Guillaume. "Lettres," *Lettres de Mold*, I(1882), 645-649; II(1883), 133-136.

5122     . _____. "Missionsbriefe," *KM*, XII(1884), 208.

5123 . Vollers, Johannes. "Missionsbriefe," *Echo aus Afrika*, XI(1899), 72-76.

5124 . _____. "Missionsbriefe," *KM*, XXIII(1895), 66, 67.

5125 . Waal, David Christian de. *With Rhodes in Mashonaland*. Cape Town: Juta, 1896. 351p.

5126 . Webb, Allan B. [*Rev.*]. "From Bloemfontein to the Zambesi; a Great Missionary Journey by the Bishop of Bloemfontein," *Mission Field*, XXXIV(1889).

5127 . Wernsdorff, Fritz Wolf von. *Ein Jahr in Rhodesia*. Berlin: Otto Janke, 1899. 168p.

5128 . White, Franklin. "On the Khami Ruins, Near Bulawayo," *Rhodesia Science Association*, I(1900), 11-18.

5129 _____. "On the Ruins of Dhlo-Dhlo, in Rhodesia," *JAI*, XXXI (1901), 21-28.

5130 . Wilkinson, J. Fenwick. "Journey through the Gold Country of South Africa," *PRGS*, XIII(1868-1869), 134-137.

5131 . Wilkinson, William Fischer. "On Gold Mining in Rhodesia," *JRSA*, XLIV (1896), 687-694.

5132 . Williams, Herbert Wynne Vaughan. *A Visit to Lobengula in 1889*. Pietermaritzburg: Shuter & Shooter, 1947. 191p.

5133 . Willoughby, John Christopher. "Alarm in Matabeleland," *New Review*, June, 1896, 703-712.

5134 . _____. "How We Occupied Mashonaland," *Fortnightly Review*, CCXCII, New Series, XLIX(1891), 513-532.

5135 . _____. *A Narrative of Further Excavations at Zimbabye, Mashonaland*. London: Philip, 1893. 43p.

5136 . Wills, Walter H. and Hall, J. *Bulawayo Up-to-Date. Being a General Sketch of Rhodesia.* London: Simpkin, Marshall, Hamilton, Kent, and Co., 1899. 320p.

5137 . Wills, William Arthur; Collingridge, Leonard Thomas; and others. *The Downfall of Lobengula: the Causes, History and Effect of the Matabeli War.* London: African Review Offices, 1894. 335p.

5138 . Wilmot, A. *Monomotapa (Rhodesia), Its Monuments, and Its History from the Most Ancient Times to the Present Century.* London: T. Fisher Unwin, 1896. 260p.

5139 . Witt, Robert Clinton. "Personal Recollections of Cecil Rhodes. . .as Peacemaker on the Matoppo Hills," *Nineteenth Century and After,* CCCIII(1902), 841-848.

5140 . Wood, Joseph Garbett. *Through Matabeleland: the Record of a Ten Months' Trip in an Ox-Waggon through Mashonaland and Matabeleland.* Cape Town: J. C. Juta & Co., 1893. 198p.

5141 . Woon, Harry Vernon [*Capt.*]. *Twenty-Five Years' Soldiering in South Africa.* London: Andrew Melrose, 1909. 447p.

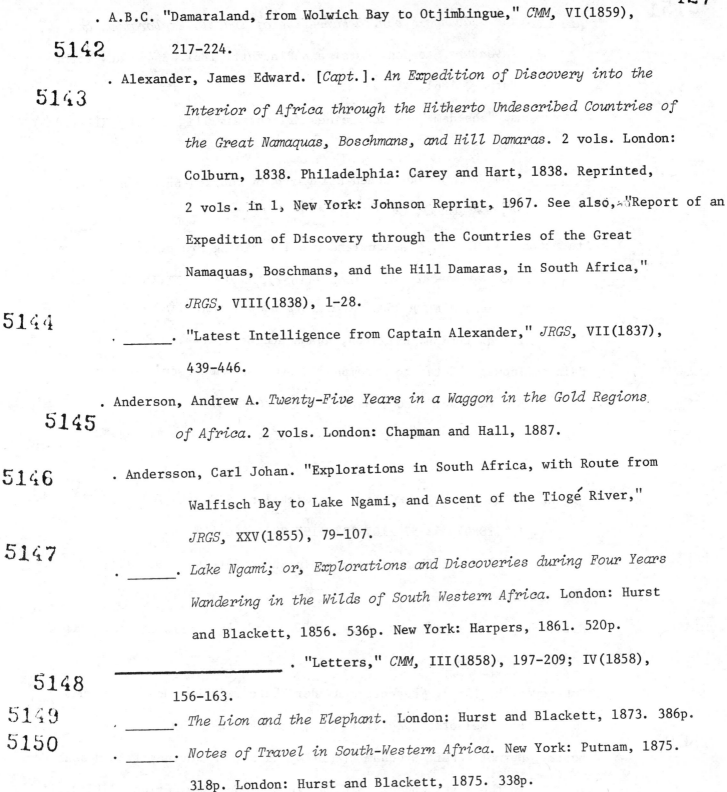

5142 . A.B.C. "Damaraland, from Wolwich Bay to Otjimbingue," *CMM*, VI(1859), 217-224.

5143 . Alexander, James Edward. [*Capt.*]. *An Expedition of Discovery into the Interior of Africa through the Hitherto Undescribed Countries of the Great Namaquas, Boschmans, and Hill Damaras*. 2 vols. London: Colburn, 1838. Philadelphia: Carey and Hart, 1838. Reprinted, 2 vols. in 1, New York: Johnson Reprint, 1967. See also, "Report of an Expedition of Discovery through the Countries of the Great Namaquas, Boschmans, and the Hill Damaras, in South Africa," *JRGS*, VIII(1838), 1-28.

5144 . _____. "Latest Intelligence from Captain Alexander," *JRGS*, VII(1837), 439-446.

5145 . Anderson, Andrew A. *Twenty-Five Years in a Waggon in the Gold Regions of Africa*. 2 vols. London: Chapman and Hall, 1887.

5146 . Andersson, Carl Johan. "Explorations in South Africa, with Route from Walfisch Bay to Lake Ngami, and Ascent of the Tiogé River," *JRGS*, XXV(1855), 79-107.

5147 . _____. *Lake Ngami; or, Explorations and Discoveries during Four Years Wandering in the Wilds of South Western Africa*. London: Hurst and Blackett, 1856. 536p. New York: Harpers, 1861. 520p.

5148 . _____. "Letters," *CMM*, III(1858), 197-209; IV(1858), 156-163.

5149 . _____. *The Lion and the Elephant*. London: Hurst and Blackett, 1873. 386p.

5150 . _____. *Notes of Travel in South-Western Africa*. New York: Putnam, 1875. 318p. London: Hurst and Blackett, 1875. 338p.

5151  . _____. *The Okavango River; a Narrative of Travel, Exploration and Adventure*. London: Hurst and Blackett, 1861. 364p. New York: Harper, 1861. 414p.

5152  . Anonymous. "Aus dem Tagebuche eines Kriegsfreiwilligen," *DK*, XIII(1896), 334-335.

5153  . _____. "Vom Letzten Deutschen kriegszug in Deutsch-Südwestafrika," *DK*, XVI(1899), 84-87.

5154  . Atherstone, W. Guyon. "Namaqualand and Its Mining Prospects," *Eastern Province Monthly Magazine*, I(1857), 642-651; II(1857), 1-8.

5155  . Backhouse, James. *A Narrative of a Visit to the Mauritius and South Africa*. London: Hamilton, Adams and Co., 1844. 648p.

5156  . Baines, Thomas. "Notes to Accompany Mr. C. J. Andersson's Map of Damara Land," *JRGS*, XXXVI(1866), 247-248.

5157  . Baum, H. *Kunene-Sambesi Expedition*. Berlin: Verlag des Kolonial-Wirtschaftlichen Komitees, 1903. 593p.

5158  . Belck, Waldemar. "Die koloniale Entwickelung Südwest-Afrikas," *DK*, III(1886), 52-57, 107-111, 197-202, 456-462.

5159  . Biehe, G. "Die deutschen Missionare in Südwestafrika," *DK*, IV(1887), 110-112.

5160  . Bittrolff, R. *Der Krieg in Deutsch-Südwestafrika*. Karlsruhe: J. Reiffs, 1895. 52p.

5161  . Bokemeyer, H. [*Dr.*]. "Beschreibung der Küste zwischen Mossamedes und Port Nolloth," *DK*, VII(1890), 282-285, 296-299.

5162  . Bourke, Dermot Robert Wyndham [*Earl of Mayo*]. "A Journey from Mossamedes to the River Cunéné, S.W. Africa," *PRGS*, New Series, V(1883), 458-470.

5163  . _____. *Proposed Expedition to Ovampo-Land, Landing at Mossamedes, S.W. Coast of Africa*. London: Privately printed, 1882. 64p.

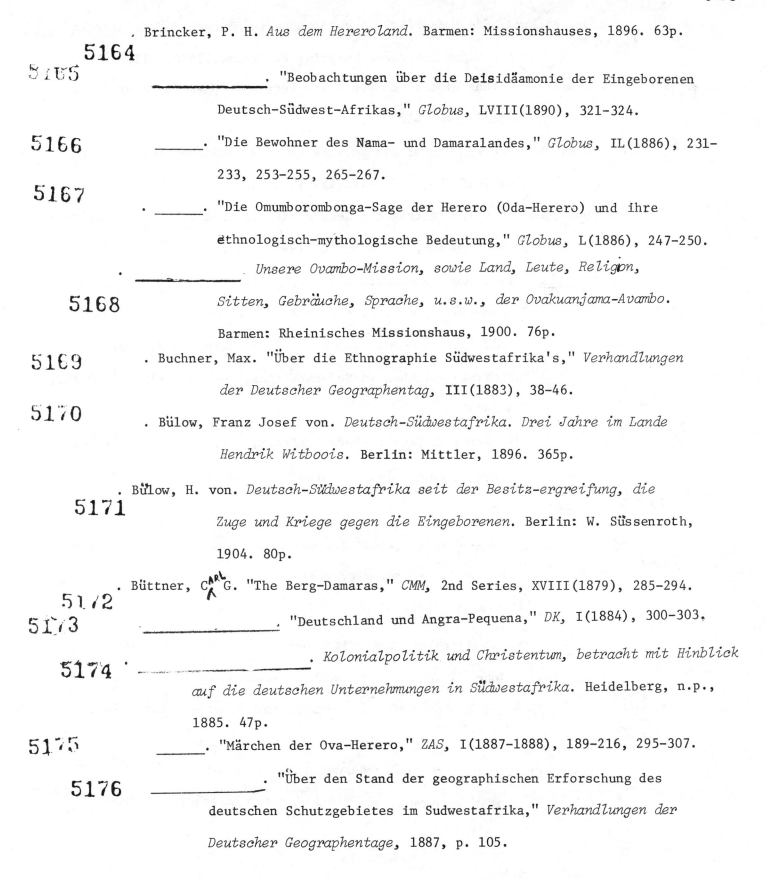

5164 . Brincker, P. H. *Aus dem Hereroland*. Barmen: Missionshauses, 1896. 63p.

5165 _____. "Beobachtungen über die Deisidäamonie der Eingeborenen Deutsch-Südwest-Afrikas," *Globus*, LVIII(1890), 321-324.

5166 _____. "Die Bewohner des Nama- und Damaralandes," *Globus*, IL(1886), 231-233, 253-255, 265-267.

5167 . _____. "Die Omumborombonga-Sage der Herero (Oda-Herero) und ihre ethnologisch-mythologische Bedeutung," *Globus*, L(1886), 247-250.

5168 . _____ *Unsere Ovambo-Mission, sowie Land, Leute, Religion, Sitten, Gebräuche, Sprache, u.s.w., der Ovakuanjama-Avambo.* Barmen: Rheinisches Missionshaus, 1900. 76p.

5169 . Buchner, Max. "Über die Ethnographie Südwestafrika's," *Verhandlungen der Deutscher Geographentag*, III(1883), 38-46.

5170 . Bülow, Franz Josef von. *Deutsch-Südwestafrika. Drei Jahre im Lande Hendrik Witboois*. Berlin: Mittler, 1896. 365p.

5171 . Bülow, H. von. *Deutsch-Südwestafrika seit der Besitz-ergreifung, die Zuge und Kriege gegen die Eingeborenen*. Berlin: W. Süssenroth, 1904. 80p.

5172 . Büttner, Carl G. "The Berg-Damaras," *CMM*, 2nd Series, XVIII(1879), 285-294.

5173 _____. "Deutschland und Angra-Pequena," *DK*, I(1884), 300-303.

5174 . _____ *Kolonialpolitik und Christentum, betracht mit Hinblick auf die deutschen Unternehmungen in Südwestafrika.* Heidelberg, n.p., 1885. 47p.

5175 . "Märchen der Ova-Herero," *ZAS*, I(1887-1888), 189-216, 295-307.

5176 _____. "Über den Stand der geographischen Erforschung des deutschen Schutzgebietes im Sudwestafrika," *Verhandlungen der Deutscher Geographentage*, 1887, p. 105.

5177 . Carow, Richard. *Die Kaiserliche Schutztruppe in Deutsch-Südwest-Afrika unter Major Leutwein*. Leipzig: E. Freund, 1898. 113p.

5178 . Conradt, L. "Das Hinterland von Angra-Pequena und Walfischbay," *DK*, IV(1887), 407-410.

5179 . Dominikus, Ludwig. "Über die Entwicklung des südlichen Theiles von Südwestafrika," *DK*, VIII(1891), 17-20.

5180 . Dove, Karl [*Dr.*]. "Beiträg zur Geographie von SW-Afrika," *PM*, XL(1894), 60-64, 100-106, 172-175; XLI(1895), 92-96.

5181 . _____. "Bilder aus Südwestafrika," *DK*, XVI(1899), 33-34.

5182 . _____. *Deutsch-Südwestafrika. Ergebnisse einer wissenschaftlichen Reise im südlichen Damaraland*. Gotha: J. Perthes, 1898. 93p.

5183 _____. "Koloniale Aufgaben in Südwestafrika," *DK*, XII(1895), 250-253, 258-259.

5184 _____. "Der Krieg in Deutsch-Südwestafrika," *DK*, XIII(1896), 155-156.

5185 . _____. "Mitteilungen über das südliche Damaraland," *VGE*, XX(1893), 399.

5186 . _____ _____. *Süd-West-Afrika: Kriegs- und Friedensbilder aus der ersten deutschen Kolonie*. Berlin: Verein für Deutsche Litteratur, 1896. 348p.

5187 _____. "Von Walfischbai nach Otjimbingue," *DK*, IX(1892), 151-153.

5188 . Dunn, Edward John. *Report on the Country Traversed by the Gold Prospecting Expedition in Namaqualand*. Capetown: n.p., 1872. 11p.

5189 . Duparquet, P. "Le Damaraland. Résumé de deux lettres du P. Duparquet à M. l'abbé Durand", *BSGP*, 6th Series, XX(1880), 459-462.

5190    Eden, T. E. *The Search for Nitre, and the True Nature of the Guano. Being an Account of a Voyage to the South-West Coast of Africa; also, a Description of the Minerals Found There, and of the Guano Islands in That Part of the World.* London: R. Groombridge & Sons, 1846. 133p.

5191    . Eggers.[*Lt.*]. "Bericht über eine Reise nach dem Okavangogebiet," *MDS,* XIII(1900), 185-189.

5192    . Einwald, August. *Zwanzig Jahre in Süd-Afrika.* Hannover: Gebrüder Janecke, 1901. 136p.

5193    . Elffers, Hubertus. *Through the Thirst Land. A Story of the Kalahari.* Cape Town: J. C. Juta, 1902. 38p.

5194    . Esser, Max. *An der Westküste Afrikas; Wirtschaftliche und Jagd Streifzüge.* Berlin: A. Ahn, 1898. 225p.

5195    . _____. "Meine Reise nach dem Kunene im Grenzgebiet von Deutsch Südwest Afrika," *VGE,* XXIV(1897), 103-113.

5196    . _____. "Sitten der Hereros," *DK,* XIV(1897), 193-194.

5197    . Falkenhausen, Helene von. *Ansiedlerschicksale; Elf Jahre in Deutsch-Südwestafrika, 1893-1904.* Berlin: D.Reimer, 1906. 260p.

5198    . Fleck, E. [*Dr.*]. "Meine Reise in die Tauschabschlucht (Deutsch-Südwestafrika)," *PM,* XLV(1899), 281-282.

5199    . François, Curt Carl von. [*Major*]. *Deutsch-Südwest-Afrika. Geschichte der Kolonisation bis zum Ausbruch des Krieges mit Witbooi, April 1899.* Berlin: D. Reimer, 1899. 223p.

5200    . _____. *Kriegführung in Süd-Afrika.* Berlin, n.p., 1900. 57p.

5201 François, Hugo von. *Nama und Damara. Deutsch-Süd-West-Afrika.* Magdeburg: E. Baensch, 1896. 334p.

5202 Fritsch, Gustav. "Uber die Ova-Herero," *Globus*, XXVIII(1875), 245-247.

5203 Gadow, G. [*Dr.*]. *Zehn Jahre in alten Südafrika, 1892-1901. Berufliche, Sociale, und Politische Bilder aus den Errinerungen eines deutschen Artes.* Königsberg: W. Koch, 1903. 115p.

5204 Galton, Francis. *Memories of My Life.* 2nd Ed. London: Methuen, 1908. 339p.

5205 _____. *The Narrative of an Explorer in Tropical South Africa; Being an Account of a Visit to Damaraland in 1851.* London: J. Murray, 1853. 314p. London and New York: Ward, Lock, 1889.

5206 _____. "Recent Expedition into the Interior of South-Western Africa," *JRGS*, XXII(1852), 140-163.

5207 Gerstenhauer, M. R. "Deutsch-Südafrika und die Buren," *DK*, XVI(1899), 151-152.

5208 Gessert, Ferdinand. "Die Bewässerungsfrage in Namaland," *Globus*, LXXIII(1898), 217-218.

5209 _____. "Reise von Bethanien nach Garis im Namaland," *Globus*, LXXIV (1898), 249-251.

5210 Gibson, Alan G. S. *Between Capetown and Loanda: a Record of Two Journeys in South West Africa.* London: Gardner, 1905. 203p.

5211 Gill, David. *Report on the Boundary Survey between British Bechuanaland and German S.W. Africa,* Berlin, 1906. 162p.

5212 Green, Frederick J. "Narrative of a Journey to Ovampoland," *CMM*, VII(1860), 302-307, 353-363.

5213 . _____. "Narrative of an Expedition to the North-West of Lake Ngami, Extending to the Capital of Debabe's Territory, *via* Souko River, Hitherto an Enexplored Portion of Africa," *Eastern Province Monthly Magazine*, I(1857), 252-267, 316-323, 385-392, 533-543, 595-601, 661-669.

5214 . Grundemann, R. "Die Mission in Südwestafrika," *DK*, V(1888), 99-101.

5215 . Gurich, Georg. *Deutsch Südwest-Afrika. Reisebilder und Skizzen aus den Jahren 1888 und 1889 mit eineim original-Routenkarte.* Hamburg: L. Friederichsen & Co., 1891. 216p.

5216 . Hahn, Carl Hugo Luisingen. "Damaraland and the Berg Damaras," *CMM*, New Series, XIV(1877), 218-230, 289-297.

5217 . _____. "Reise im Lande der Hereró und Bergdamara in Sudwest-Afrika, 1871," *PM*, XIX(1873), 95-101.

5218 . Hahn, J. "Das Land der Ovaherero," *ZGE*, 1868, pp. 193, 493.

5219 . _____. "Die Ovahereró," *ZGE*, IV(1869).

5220 . Hahn, Theophilus. "Ein Bruderkrieg in Südwestafrika," *Globus*, XVI (1869-1870), 236-238, 246-249.

5221 . _____. "Die Nama-Hottentoten," *Globus*, XII(1867), 238-242, 275-279, 304-307, 332-336.

5222 . _____. "Ein Racenkampf im nordwestlichen Theile der Cap-Region. Ein Bild aus dem Volkerleben Südwest-Afrikas," *Globus*, XIV(1868), 202-207, 245-248, 270-272.

5223 . _____. "Sagen und Märchen der Ova-Hereró in Südafrika," *Globus*, XIII (1868), 268-270, 308-311.

5224 . Hartmann, Georg [Dr.]. *Deutsch Südwest Afrika im Zusamenhang mit Süd-Afrika.* Berlin: W. Süsserott, 1899. 20p.

5225 . _____ "Das Kaoko-Gebiet in Deutsch-Südwest-Afrika auf Grund eigener Reisen und Beobachtungen," *VGE*, XXIV(1897), 113.

5226 . Hermann, F. "Gross Namaland," *DK*, VII(1890), 156-159.

5227 . Hindorf, R. *Der landwirtschaftliche Wert und die Besiedlungsfähigkeit Deutsch-Südwest-Afrikas.* Berlin: Mittler & Sohn, 1895. 88p.

5228 . Hoepener. "Über seiner Reise an der Westküste Süd-Afrika," *VGE*, X (1883),

5229 . Hollway, Henry Charles Schunken. "Geography of South West Africa," *South African Philosophical Society*, II(1881), 1-6.

5230 . Irle, J. *Die Herero. Ein Beitrag zur Landes-, Volks- und Missionskunde.* Gütersloh: G. Bertelsmann, 1906. 352p.

5231 . Israël, Siegmund. [Lt.]. "Land und Leute im Damara- und Namaqua-Gebiet," *Globus*, XLVIII(1885), 186-189, 202-206.

5232 . Jacobowski, Ludwig. [Dr.]. "Das Weib in der Poesie der Hottentotten," *Globus*, LXX(1896), 173-176.

5233 . Jordan, W. W. "From Damaraland to the Nhemba Country; Extract from the Diary of W. W. Jordan," *Cape Quarterly Review*, II(1883), 519-539.

5234 . Judt. [Missionar]. "Deutsche Kolonisation an der Südwestküste Afrikas," *DK*, I(1884), 187-188.

5235 . Kleinschmidt. "Hendrik Witbooi," *Globus*, LXVI(1894), 149-153.

5236 . _____ "Die Lage in Deutsch-Südwestafrika," *Globus*, LX(1891), 161-163.

5237 . Knop. "Die Kupfererzlagerstatten von Klein-Namaqualand und Damaraland," *Neues Jahrbuch fur Mineralogie, Geologie, und Palaontologee,* 1861, p. 513.

5238 Krebs, Wilhelm. "Klima und Landwirtschaft in Deutsch-Südwestafrika," *DK,* IX(1892), 63-65, 81-83.

5239 . Ku'Eep [*Pseudonym*]. "Sketches and Recollections of Great Namaqualand," *CMM,* I(1857), 365-369.

5240 . Leutwein, Theodore [*Major*]. *Elf Jahre Gouverneur in Deutsch-Südwest-Afrika.* Berlin: E. S. Mittler, 1907. 589p.

5241 . _____ . *Die Kampfe der Kaiserlichen Schutztruppe in Deutsch-Südwest-Afrika in den Jahren 1894-1896, sowie die sich Heraus fur uns ergeben Lehren.* Berlin: E. S. Mittler, 1899. 30p.

5242 . Lewis, Robert. *The Germans in Damaraland.* Cape Town: Townshend and Son, 1889. 31p.

5243 . Ludloff, R. F. [*Dr.*]. "Ein Besuch auf Hornkranz," *DK,* VIII(1891), 173-175.

5244 . _____ . *Nach Deutsch-Namaland(Südwestafrika). Reisebrief.* Coburg: Dietzsche, 1891. 136p. Berlin: Luckhardt's, 1891. 136p.

5245 . Lübbert, A. "Über die Heilmittel und Heilmethoden der Eingeborenen in Deutsch-Südwest-Afrika," *MDS,* XIV(1901).

5246 . Lüderitz, C. A. (Ed.). *Die Erschliessung von Deutsch-Südwestafrika durch Adolf Lüderitz; Akten, Briefe und Denkschriften.* Oldenburg: G. Stalling, 1945. 166p.

5247 . Lunay, J. B. *Voyage dans le Sud-ouest de l'Afrique.* Paris, 1868.

5248 . McKiernan, Gerald. *The Narrative and Journal of Gerald McKiernan in South West Africa, 1874-1879.* Edited by P. Serton. Cape Town: Van Riebeeck Society, 1954. 197p.

5249 Mertens, W. "Eisenbahnbau in Südwestafrica," *DK,* XVI(1899), 138-139, 217-218.

5250 Meyer, W. von. *Reisen in Süd-Afrika während der Jahre 1840 und 1841.* Hamburg: J. P. Erie, 1843. 221p.

5251 . Moffat, Robert. "Journey from Colesberg to Steinkopf and from Little Namaqualand Eastward, along the Orange River, the Northern Frontier of the Colony, etc. etc.," *JRGS*, XXVIII(1858), 153-187.

5252 . Nolte, Karl. "Krankheiten und Heilmittel der Nama und Buschmänner," *DK*, III(1886), 629-632.

5253 . _____. "Zur Wasserfrage in Südwestafrika," *DK*, V(1888), 37-39, 45-47.

5254 . Olpp, F. *Aus dem Missionsleben in Südwestafrika.* Barmen: Missionshauses, 1896. 30p.

5255 . _____. *Bilder aus dem Missionsarbeit unter dem Namas in Südwestafrika.* Barmen: Missionshauses, 1893. 46p.

5256 . Olpp, Johannes. *Angra Pequena und Gross-Nama-Land.* Elberfeld: R. L. Friedrichs, 1884. 41p.

5257 . _____. *Erlebnisse im Hinterlande von Angra-Pequena.* Barmen: Rheinischen Missions-Gesellschaft, 1886. 218p.

5258 . P. "Aus den Briefen eines Kriegsfreiwilligen," *DK*, XIII(1896), 291-293, 300.

5259 . Palgrave, William Coates. "Damaraland and Great Namaqualand," *CMM*, XV(1877), 59-64.

5260 . _____. "Report of W. C. Palgrave, Special Commissioner to the Tribes North of the Orange River, of His Mission to Damaraland and Great Namaqualand in 1876," *Cape Paper*, Appendix 2, 1877, pp. 117-141.

5261 . Pechuel-Lösche, Eduard. "Zur Kenntnis des Herero Landes," *Ausland*, LIX(1886), Nrs. 42-45, pp. 821, 849, 869.

5262 Petersen, Heinrich. "Eine deutsche Niederlassung am Oranienflusse," *DK*, VI(1889), 90-92, 98-100.

5263 Pfeil, Joachim. [*Grafen*]. "Skizze von Südwestafrika," *PM*, XL(1894), 1-11, 42-44.

5264 . _____. "South-West Africa, English and German," *GJ*, II(1893), 29-43.

5265 . _____. "Studien in Südwestafrika," *DK*, X(1893), 95-98, 112-113.

5266 . Pilgram, B. "Handel und Dampferverbindungen mit Deutsch-Südwestafrika," *DK*, IV(1887), 676-682.

5267 Pohle, H. "Bericht über die von Herrn Lüderitz ausgerüstete Expedition nach Südwestafrika, 1884-85," *PM*, XXXII(1886), 225-238.

5268 . Rehbock, Theodor. "Die Anlage einer landwirtschaftlichen Kolonie in Deutsch-Südwestafrika," *DK*, XV(1898), 252-253.

5269 . _____. *Deutschlands Pflichten in Deutsch-Südwestafrika*. Berlin: Reimer, 1904. 43p.

5270 . _____. *Deutsch-Südwest-Afrika. Seine wirtschaftliche Erschliessung, unter besonderer Berücksichtigung der Nutzbarmachung des Wassers*. Berlin: Reimer, 1898. 237p.

5271 . _____ *Reisebilder aus Deutsch-Süd-West-Afrika*. Berlin: D. Reimer, 1898. 37p.

5272 . _____. "Die Standämme des Südlichen Namalanders," *DK*, XVII(1900), 262-263.

5273 . Reid, Percy C. "Journeys in the Linyanti Region," *GJ*, XVII(1901), 573-585.

5274 · Ridsdale, Benjamin [*Rev.*]. *Scenes and Adventures in Great Namaqualand.* London: T. Woolmer, 1883. 293p.

5275 · Ritter, Karl. "Reisebriefen vom Nama- und Damaraland," *DK*, III(1886), 541-544.

5276 · Rohlfs, Gerhard. *Angra Pequena. Die erste deutsche Kolonie in Afrika.* Bielefeld: Velhagen and Klasing, 1884. 16p.

5277 · Schenk, A. "Bewässerungsanlagen und Landwirtschaftliche Kolonien in Deutsch-Südwestafrika," *Geographische Zeitschrift*, V(1899), 705.

5278 · _____ . "Das Gebiet zwischen Angra Pequena und Bethanien," *PM*, XXXI(1885), 132-136.

5279 · Schinz, Hans. *Deutsch-Südwest-Africa. Forschungsreisen durch den deutsche Schutzgebiet Gross-Nama und Hereroland, nach dem Kunene, dem Ngami-See und der Kalaxari.* Leipzig: A. Schwartz, 1891. 568p.

5280 · _____ · "Die jüngsten Vorgänge in Deutsch-Südwest-Afrika," *DK*, VI (1889), 6-7.

5281 · _____ · "Vorgänge in unserem südwestafrikanischen Schutzgebiet," *DK*, V(1888), 156-157.

5282 · Schwabe, Kurd. [*Lt.*]. "Einiges über die Küste des südwestafrikanischen Schutzbebiet und den Verkehr an der Selben," *DK*, XI(1894), 165-166.

5283 · _____ · *Im deutschen Diamantenlande. Deutsch-Südwestafrika von der Errichtung der deutschen Herrschaft bis zur Gegenwart (1884-1910).* Berlin: F.S. Mittler & Sohn, 1909. 443p.

5284 · _____ · *Mit Schwert und Pflug in Deutsch-Südwestafrika. Vier Kriegs- und Wanderjahrs.* Berlin: Mittler, 1899. 448p.

5285 · _____ · "Von der südwestafrikanischen Eisenbahn," *DK*, XIV(1897), 497-499; XV(1898), 35-36; Beilage Nr.8 (24 Feb. 98), 73.

5286 · Schwarz, Bernard. "Ein Besuch bei Hendrik Wittboy, dem Messias der Hottentotten, im Sommer 1888," *DK*, VI(1889), 43-46, 50-51.

5287 _____. *Im deutschen Goldlande*. Berlin: Hermann
    Peters, 1889. 199p.

5288 . _____. "Otnimbingue: ein Städtebild aus Damaraland," *DK*, VI(1889),
    124-127, 130-132.

5289 . Spengler, Hermann. "Das Hinterland der Walfischbay," *DK*, IV(1887), 434-436.

5290 . Sydenfaden. "First Visit to the Great Namaquas," *MH*, VI(1810-1811),
    465-468.

5291 Tindall, Henry [*Rev.*]. *Two Lectures on Great Namaqualand and Its
    Inhabitants*. Cape Town: G.T. Pike's Machine Printing Office, 1856.
    47p.

5292 . Tindall, Joseph. *The Journal of Joseph Tindall, Missionary in South
    West Africa, 1839-1855*. Edited by B. A. Tindall. Cape Town:
    Van Riebeeck Society, 1959. 221p.

5293 Üchtritz, C. von. [*Baron*]. "Bericht aus Windhoek, Nov. 20, 1891," *DK*,
    IX(1892), 17-19.

5294 . _____. "Bericht von Windhoek," *DK*, VIII(1891), 175-180.

5295 . _____. "Einem Privatbriefe aus Südwestafrika," *DK*, X(1893), 6-7.

5296 . Vedder, Heinrich. *Das alte Südwestafrika. Südwestafrikas Geschichte bis
    zum Tode Mahareros, 1890*. Berlin: Warneck, 1934. 666p. English Ed.
    *South West Africa in Early Times*. London: Oxford, 1938. 525p.

5297 . Viehe, G. "Die Ovaherero," in S. R. Steinmetz (Ed.), *Rechtsverhältnisse
    vor eingeborenen Völker in Afrika und Ozeanien*. Berlin: J. Springer,
    1903. 455p.

5298 . Warncke, W. "Südwestafrikanisches," *DK*, XV(1898), 118-119.

5299 . _____. "Zum Erwerb von Regierungsfarmen in Deutsch-Südwestafrika," *DK*,
    XVI(1899), 35-36.

5300 . Watermeyer, J. C. *Deutsch-Südwestafrika. Seine landschaftlichen Verhältnisse.* Berlin: D. Reimer, 1899. 25p.

5301 ————. "Notes on a Journey in German South West Africa," *South African Philosophical Society,* XI(1899), 19-33.

5302 . Weiss, K. "Der Baiweg," *DK,* XII(1895), 314-315.

5303 . Witbooi, Hendrik. "Zwei Briefe, 1892," *DK,* IX(1892), 165-166.

5304 ————. *Die Dagboek van Hendrik Witbooi, Kaptein van die Witbooi-Hottentotte, 1884-1905, bewerk na die oorspronklike dokumente in die Regeringsargief, Windhoek.* Cape Town: The Van Riebeeck Society, 1929. 244p.

ZAMBIA

5305 . Berghegge, F. *Verslag eener reis in Midden-Afrika (Zambesie-Missie).* The Hague: T. C. B. ten Hagen, 1882. 28p.

5306 Bertrand, Alfred J. *Alfred Bertrand, Explorer and Captain of Cavalry.* (Selections from Diaries, Compiled by His Wife.) London: Religious Tract Society, 1926. 238p.

5307 . _____. *Au pays des Ba-Rotsi, Haut-Zambèse. Voyage d'exploration en Afrique.* Paris: Hachette, 1898. 331p. English translation, *The Kingdom of the Barotsi, Upper Zambesia.* London: Unwin, 1899. 304p.

5308 . _____. *En Afrique avec le missionaire Coillard.* Geneva: Eggimann, 1899. 203p.

5309 . _____. "From the Machili to Lialui," *GJ*, IX(1897), 145-147.
5310 . Blair-Watson, A. "Kilwa Island in Lake Mweru," *GJ*, VI(1895), 458-460.

5311 . Blanca, Salvatore. "Lettere," *MCM*, IX(1880), 334.

5312 . _____. "Lettres," *MCL*, XII(1880), 299, 300.

5313 . _____. "Missionsbriefe," *KM*, IX(1881), 255.

5314 . Butt, G. E. *My Travels in North West Rhodesia, or, a Missionary Journey of Sixteen Thousand Miles.* London: Dalton, c. 1910. 283p.

5315 . Chesnaye, C. P. "A Journey from Fort Jameson to the Kafue River," *GJ*, XVII(1901), 42-48.

5316 . Codrington, Robert. "A Journey from Fort Jameson, to old Chitambo and the Tanganyika Plateau," *GJ*, XV(1900), 227-232.

5317    Coillard, François. "Expédition du Zambèze," *JME*, LIX(1884), 31-33, 46-55,
103-106, 137-151, 188-189, 278-282, 356, 363, 442-445, 465-474;
LX(1885), 104-116, 133-162, 187-202, 254-259, 339-350, 376-385,
421-431; LXI(1886), 14-27, 60-63, 132-133, 165-180, 229, 266-271,
346-348, 392-400, 478-482; LXII(1887), 19-28, 140-152, 165-191,
215-218, 303-311, 384-387, 448-450, 462-465; LXIII(1888), 12-19,
63-69, 99-101, 103-107, 188-197, 339-348, 383-385.

5318    _____. "Une expédition guerrière des Barotsis," *JME*, LXIII(1888),
370-383.

5319    _____. *On the Threshold of Central Africa. A Record of Twenty Years'
Pioneering among the Barotse of the Upper Zambesi.* London:
Hodder & Stoughton, 1897. 663p.

5320    _____. *Sur le Haut-Zambèze. Voyages et travaux de mission.* Paris:
Berger-Levrault, 1898. 590p. 2nd Ed. Paris: Berger-Levrault, 1899. 694p.

5321    Croad, Hector. "The Choma Division of the Mweru District," *GJ*, XI(1898),
617-624.

5322    Davey, T. G. *The Northern Copper (B.S.A.) Company, Limited. Report on the
Company's Properties.* London: W. W. Sprague, 1902. 49p.

5323    Finaughty, William. *The Recollections of William Finaughty, Elephant
Hunter, 1864-1875.* Philadelphia: Lippincott, 1916. 242p. Cape
Town: Balkema, 1957.

5324    Gibbons, Alfred St. Hill. *Africa from South to North through Marotseland.*
2 vols. London: Lane, 1904.

5325    _____. *Exploration and Hunting in Central Africa, 1895-1896.* London:
Methuen, 1898. 408p.

5326 . _____. "A Journey in the Marotse and Mashikolumbwe Countries," *GJ*, IX (1897), 121-143.

5327 . _____. "Marotseland and the Tribes of the Upper Zambezi," *Proceedings of the Royal Colonial Institute*, XXIX(1897-1898), 260-276.

5328 _____ and Quicke, F. C. [*Capt.*]. "Explorations in Marotseland and Neighbouring Regions," *GJ*, XVII(1901), 106,133. Also, *JMGS*, XVII(1901), 29-32, a.C JOURNAL OF THE TYNESIDE GEOGRAPHICAL SOCIETY, IV (1902) 403-422.

5329 . Goy, A. "Les débuts de M. Goy à Séfula," *JME*, LXIII(1888), 428-429.

5330 . Grey, George. "The Kafue River and Its Headwaters," *GJ*, XVIII(1901), 62-77.

5331 . Hamilton, James Stevenson. *The Barotseland Journal of James Stevenson-Hamilton, 1898-1899*. Edited by J. P. R. Wallis. London: Chatto & Windus, 1953. 246p.

5332 . Harding, Colin. [*Colonel*]. *In Remotest Barotseland. Being an Account of a Journey of Over 8,000 Miles through the Wildest and Remotest Parts of Lewanika's Empire*. London: Hurst & Blackett, 1905. 413p.

5333 . Hartert, Heinrich. "Ein Besuch bei den M'pangwes am Muni," *Globus*, LX (1891), 209-212.

5334 Holub, Emil. *Eine Culturskizze des Marutse-Mambunda-Reiches in Süd-Central-Africa*. Vienna: K.K. Geographische Gesellschaft, 1879. 210p.

5335 . Hoste, Cyril D. "Explorations West of the Loangwa River," *GJ*, XI(1898), 624-628.

5336 . Jacottet, Édouard. *Études sur les langues du Haut-Zambèze*. 2 vols. Paris: Leroux, 1896-1901.

Jalla, Adolphe. *Pionniers parmi les Ma-rotse*. Florence: Impr. claudienne,

5337    1903. 359p.

5338    Keck, Mathilde. *Allen in Afrika, of, Zeven Jaren aan de Zambezi*.

        Neerbosch: Typ. der Weesinrichting, [1902]. 70p.

5339    . Lawley, Arthur. [*Capt*.]. "From Bulawayo to the Victoria Falls: a Mission

        to King Lewanika," *Blackwood's Magazine*, CLXIV(1898), 739-759.
        SEE ALSO, BRITISH SOUTH AFRICA COMPANY, REPORTS ON THE ADMINISTRATION

5340    . Livingstone, Charles. "On the Batoka Country," *PRGS*, VI(1861-1862), 32-36.

5341    Luck, Reginald A. *Visit to Lewanika, King of Barotse*. London: Marshall,

        1902. 86p.

5342    . MacLeod, Norman. *Trade and Travel in Early Barotseland: the Diaries of

        George Westbeech, 1885-1888, and Captain Norman MacLeod, 1875-

        1876*. Edited by E. C. Tabler. Berkeley: University of California,

        1963. 125p. London: Chatto & Windus, 1963.

5343    Reid, Percy C. "A Journey up the Machili," *GJ*, IX(1897), 143-145.

5344    . Selby, P. H. "Journey to the Kafue and Zumbo Districts," *GJ*, XIX(1902),

        605-607.

5345    . Selous, Frederick Courtenay. "Letters on His Journeys to the Kafue

        River, and on the Upper Zambesi," *PRGS*, New Series, XI(1889),

        216-224.

5346    . Sharpe, Alfred. "A Journey from Lake Nyassa to the Great Loangwa and

        Upper Zambezi Rivers," *PRGS*, New Series, XII(1890), 744-751.

5347    . Singer, H. "Der Bangueolo-See," *PM*, XLIV(1898), 259-260.

5348    . Thomson, Joseph. "To Lake Bangweolo and the Unexplored Regions of

        British Central Africa," *GJ*, I(1893), 97-118.

5349 . Torrend, Jules. *Specimens of Bantu Folk-Lore from Northern Rhodesia.* London: Kegan Paul, Trench, Trübner & Co., 1921. 187p.

5350 . Wallace, L. A. "North-Eastern Rhodesia," *GJ*, XXIX(1907), 369-395.

5351 . Weatherley, Poulett. "Circumnavigation of Lake Bangweolo," *GJ*, XII (1898), 241-259.

WESTERN AFRICA

5352   . Abu Tālib ibn Muḥammad Khan, Iṣfahānī. *The Travels of Abu Talib ibn Muhammad Khan in Asia, Africa and Europe during the Years 1799 to 1803.* 2 vols. London: Longman, 1810. French ed., Paris, 1811; German ed., Vienna, 1813.

5353   . Adams, John [*Captain*]. *Remarks on the Country Extending from Cape Palmas to the River Congo.* London: Whittaker, 1823. 265p.

5354   . Adams, Robert. *The Narrative of Robert Adams, a Sailor, Who Was Wrecked on the Western Coast of Africa, in the Year 1810, Was Detained Three Years by the Arabs of the Great Desert, and Resided Several Months in the City of Tombuctoo.* London : Murray, 1816. 213p.

5355   . ..lexander, James Edward. *Narrative of a Voyage of Observation among the Colonies of Western Africa in the Flagship Thalia and of a Campaign in Kaffir Land in 1835.* 2 vols. London: Colburn, 1837.

5356   . Allen, W. [*Capt.,R.N.*]. "Excursions up the River of Cameroons and to the Bay of Amboises," *JRGS*, XIII(1843), 1-17.

5357   . _____. "On a New Construction of a Map of a Portion of Western Africa, Showing the Possibility of the Rivers Yeú and Chadda Being the Outlet of the Lake Chad," *JRGS*, VIII(1838), 289-307.

5358   . Ancelle, J. [*Capt.*], and others. *Le Soudan français.* 1 vol. in 6 parts. Lille: Danel, 1881-1888.

5359 . Andry. [*Commandant*]. "Etude sur le chemin de fer de Kayes à Bamakou, du Sénégal au Niger," *Bulletin de la Société de Géographie Commerciale de Paris*, XV(1893), 321-354.

5360 . Arlett, W. [*Lt., R.N.*]. "Survey of Some of the Canary Islands, and of Part of the Western Coast of Africa, in 1835," *JRGS*, VI(1836), 285-310.

5361 . Aube, Theodore [*Admiral*]. "L'île d'Arguin et les pêcheries de la côte occidentale d'Afrique," *RMC*, XXXIII(1872), 240.

5362 . Avézac-Macaya, Marie Armand Pasçal d'. *Études de géographie critique sur une partie de l'Afrique septentrionale. Itinéraires de Hhagy Ebn-el-Dyn el-Aghouathy*. Paris: Renouard, 1836. Also published as, "Relation d'un voyage dans l'intérieur de l'Afrique septentrionale," in *BSGP*, 2nd Series, vols. I(1834) through V(1836).

5363 . Badgley, James. *Memoir on the Navigation of the Western Coast of Africa from Cape Bojador to Mount Souzos*. London, 1827.

5364 . Baillaud, E. "Les territories française du Niger, leur valeur économic," *Géographie*, II(1900), 9-24.

5365 . Barre, Paul. "La pénétration du Soudan par le Sénégal et le Niger," *Revue de Géographie*, VIII(1894), 134-146.

5366 . _____. *Sénégambie et Guinée; la région gabonaise*. 2 vols. Paris: Challamel, 1888.

5367 . Barrow, A. H. *Fifty Years in Western Africa. Being a Record of the Work of the West Indian Church on the Banks of the Rio Pongo*. London: Society for Promoting Christian Knowledge, 1900. 157p.

5368 . Barth, Heinrich. "Account of Two Expeditions in Central Africa by the Furnays," *JRGS*, XXIII(1853), 120-122.

5369 . _____. "Chronologische Tabelle aus dem Tarikh-es-Sudan," *PM*, I(1855), 97.

5370 . _____. "A General Historical Description of the State of Human Society in North Central Africa," *JRGS*, XXX(1860), 112-128.

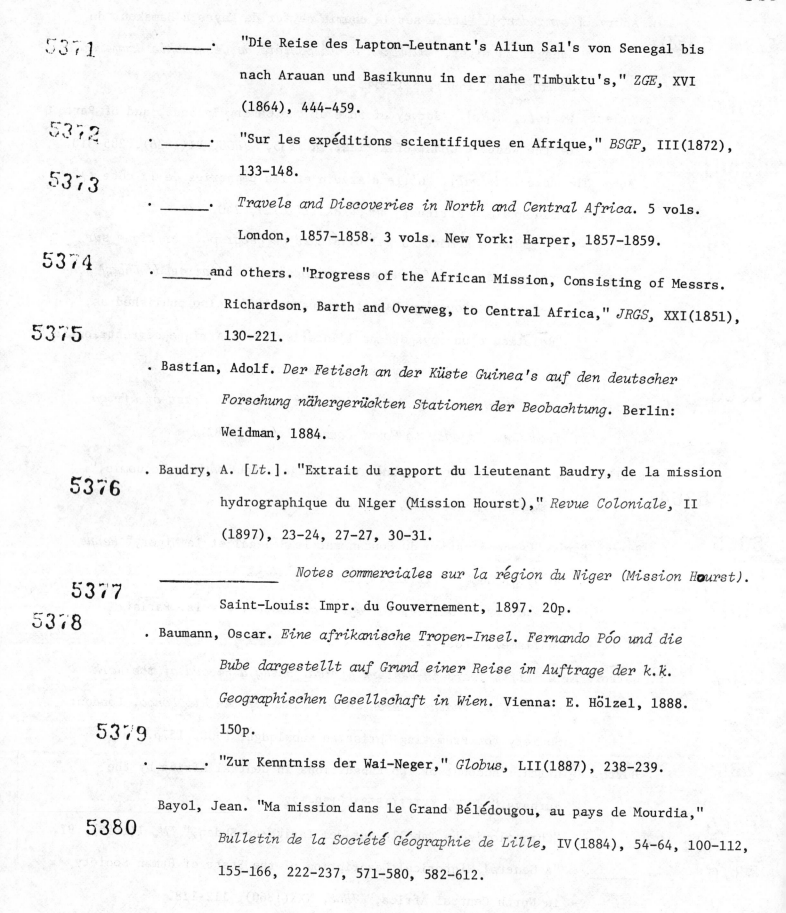

5371       \_\_\_\_\_. "Die Reise des Lapton-Leutnant's Aliun Sal's von Senegal bis nach Arauan und Basikunnu in der nahe Timbuktu's," *ZGE*, XVI (1864), 444-459.

5372      \_\_\_\_\_. "Sur les expéditions scientifiques en Afrique," *BSGP*, III(1872), 133-148.

5373      \_\_\_\_\_. *Travels and Discoveries in North and Central Africa*. 5 vols. London, 1857-1858. 3 vols. New York: Harper, 1857-1859.

5374      \_\_\_\_\_and others. "Progress of the African Mission, Consisting of Messrs. Richardson, Barth and Overweg, to Central Africa," *JRGS*, XXI(1851), 130-221.

5375      Bastian, Adolf. *Der Fetisch an der Küste Guinea's auf den deutscher Forschung nähergerückten Stationen der Beobachtung*. Berlin: Weidman, 1884.

5376      Baudry, A. [*Lt.*]. "Extrait du rapport du lieutenant Baudry, de la mission hydrographique du Niger (Mission Hourst)," *Revue Coloniale*, II (1897), 23-24, 27-27, 30-31.

5377      _____ *Notes commerciales sur la région du Niger (Mission Hourst)*. Saint-Louis: Impr. du Gouvernement, 1897. 20p.

5378      Baumann, Oscar. *Eine afrikanische Tropen-Insel. Fernando Póo und die Bube dargestellt auf Grund einer Reise im Auftrage der k.k. Geographischen Gesellschaft in Wien*. Vienna: E. Hölzel, 1888. 150p.

5379      \_\_\_\_\_. "Zur Kenntniss der Wai-Neger," *Globus*, LII(1887), 238-239.

5380      Bayol, Jean. "Ma mission dans le Grand Bélédougou, au pays de Mourdia," *Bulletin de la Société Géographie de Lille*, IV(1884), 54-64, 100-112, 155-166, 222-237, 571-580, 582-612.

5381 . _____ "Voyage au Soudan, au Bambouk et au Fouta-Djallon," *Bulletin de la Société de Géographie de Lille*, I(1882), 167-170, 195-218.

5382 . _____. "Voyage dans le Fouta-Djallon et le Bambouk," *Bulletin de la Société de Géographie Commercial de Bordeaux*, 2nd Series, VI(1883), 106-110, 135-146.

5383 _____ *Voyage en Sénégambie: Haut-Niger, Bambouck, Fouta-Djallon et Grad-Bélédougou, 1880-1885*. Paris: Baudoin, 1888. 230p. Also, *RMC*, XCIV(1887), 441-473; XCV(1887), 72-104, 256-281, 438-466; XCVI(1888), 155-181, 492, 559.

5384 . Beau de Rochas, Alphonse. *Oasis et Soudan. La pénétration du Soudan, considérée dans ses rapports avec la création des grandes oasis sahariennes*. Paris: Fischbacher, 1888. 64p.

5385 . Beecham, John. *The Claims of the Missionary Work in Western Africa, and the Importance of Training a Native Ministry*. London: Mason, 1842. 16p.

5386 . Belcher. [*Captain*, Royal Navy]. "Extracts from Observations on Various Points of the West Coast of Africa, Surveyed by His Majesty's Ship "Aetua" in 1830-32," *JRGS*, II(1832), 278-303.

5387 Benezis. [*Sergeant*]. "La religion Musulmane au Soudan française d'apres le texte du sergeant Benezis," [Translated by Marchand] *Renseignements Coloniaux*, (1897), 91-111.

5388 Benitez, Cristobal. *Mi viaje por el interior del Africa*. Tanger: Mission Catholic Español, 1899. 206p.

5389 _____. "Notas tomadas por...en sul viaje por Marruccos, el desierto de Sahara y Sudan a Senegal," *BSGM*, 1886, June, 337-362; July-Aug., 7-24; Sept.- Oct., 176-199.

5390 Berthelot, Sabin. *De la pêche sur la côte occidentale d'Afrique, et des établissements les plus utiles au progres de cette industrie.* Paris: Bertrand, 1840. 302p.

5391 Binger, Louis-Gustave. "Au fond du golfe de Guinée," *Nature*, XII(1892), 22-26.

5392 _____. *Esclavage, islamisme, et christianisme.* Paris: Societe d'editions scientifiques, 1891. 112p.

5393 _____. *Du Niger au Golfe de Guinée par le pays de Kong et le Mossi, 1887-1889.* 2 vols. Paris: Hachette, 1892.

5394 _____. "Transactions objets de commerce, monnaies des contrées d'entre le Niger et la côte d'Or," *Bulletin de la Société de Géographie Commerciale de Paris*, XI(1889-1890), 77.

5395 _____. *Une vie d'explorateur. Souvenirs extraits des carnets de route ou notes sous la dictee par son fils Jacques Binger.* Paris: Sorlot, 1938. 287p

5396 Bissuel, Henri. *Les Touareg de l'ouest.* Algiers: Jourdan, 1888. 210p.

5397 Blaise, Eugene. "La côte occidental d'Afrique; du Gabon jusqu'a Angra-Pequeña," *Bulletin Société Bretonne de Géographie*, IV(1885), 569-590.

5398 Blyden, Edward Wilmot. *From West Africa to Palestine.* Freetown: Sawyer, 1873. 201p.

5399 _____. *West Africa before Europe, and Other Addresses, Delivered in England in 1901 and 1903.* London: Phillips, 1905. 158p.

5400 _____ and others. *The People of Africa.* New York: Randolph, 1871. 157p.

5401 Bodichon, Eugene. *Étude sur l'Algérie et l'Afrique.* Paris and Algiers: the author, 1847. 256p.

5402 _____. *Projet d'une exploration politique, commerciale, et scientifique d'Alger à Tombouctou par le Sahara.* Paris: Martinet, 1849 56p.

5403 . Bohner, H. *Im Lande des Fetischs*. Basel: Missionsbuchhandlung, 1890. 287p.

5404 . Bois. [*Commandant*]. "De la conquête industrielle et commerciale du Soudan et des contrées intertropicales au moyen de voies de communication rapides," *Bulletin de la Société de Géographie Commerciale de Paris*, IX(1886-1887), 154-165.

5405 . Bonnetain, P. *Dans la brousse. Sensations du Soudan*. Paris: A.Lemerre, 1895. 260p.

5406 . Bossi, Giacomo. *I negri della Nigrizia occidentale e della interna, e i Mori e Arabi erranti del Saara e del deserto di Libia*. 3 vols. Turin: Fodratti, 1849.

5407 . Boteler. [*Captain*, Royal Navy]. "Memoir Descriptive of Prince's Island and Anna Bom, in the Bight of Biafra," *JRGS*, II(1832), 274-278.

5408 . Boudyck Bastiaanse, J.H. van. *Voyage a la côte de Guinée, dans le golfe de Biafra, a l'île de Fernando po*. . . .The Hague, 1853. 451p.

5409 . Bouët-Willaumez, Louis-Edouard. *Description nautique des côtes de l'Afrique occidentale comprises entre le Sénégal et l'Équateur*. Paris: Imprimerie, royale, 1846. 216pp. 2d ed. Paris: Dupont, 1849. 323p.

5410 . _____. *Commerce et traite des noirs aux côtes occidentales d'Afrique*. Paris: Imprimerie nationale, 1848. 230p.

5411 . Bourne, Henry Richard Fox. *Blacks and Whites in West Africa; An Account of the Past Treatment and Present Condition of West African Nations under European Influence or Control*. London: P. S. King & Son, 1902. 88p.

5412 . Bowdich, Thomas Edward. *An Essay on the Geography of North-Western Africa*. Paris: Cellot, 1821. 96p.

5413 . _____. *An Essay on the Superstitions, Customs, and Arts, Common to the Ancient Egyptians, Abyssinians, and Ashantees*. Paris: Smith, 1821. 69p.

5414 . _____. *Excursions in Madeira and Porto Santo, during the Autumn of 1823, while on His Third Voyage to Africa; to which Is Added, by Mrs. Bowdich, I. A Narrative of the Continuance of the Voyage to Its Completion. . .II. A Description of the English Settlements on the River Gambia. . .III. Appendix: Containing Zoological and Botanical Descriptions, and Translations from the Arabic.* London: Whittaker, 1825. 278p.

5415 . Boyle, James. *A Practical Medico-Historical Account of the Western Coast of Africa. . . .together with the Causes, Symptoms, and Treatment of the Fevers of West Africa.* London: S. Highley, 1831. 423p.

5416 . Brally, J. "Sur la côte occidentale d'Afrique, de Grand Bassam a Porto Novo," *Bulletin de la Société de Géographie Commerciale de Paris,* XV(1894-1895), 395-409.

5417 . Bridge, Horatio. *Journal of an African Cruiser; Comprising Sketches of the Canaries, the Cape de Verde, Liberia, Madeira, Sierra Leone, and Other Places of Interest on the West Coast of Africa.* Ed. by Nathaniel Hawthorne. New York and London: Wiley and Putnam, 1845. 179p. New York: Putnam, 1853.

5418 . Briot, Ernest-H.-E.-A. "Journal relatant le voyage de M. Ernest-Hyacinthe-Erasme-Ange Briot de Gorée au Gabon, commencé le 16 Janvier 1846," in *Notes et Documents relatifs à la vie et à l'oeuvre du Vén. F.-M.-P. Libermann,* V(1936), 347-355.

5419 . Brosselard-Faidherbe, Henri François. *Casamance et Mellacorée. Pénétration au Soudan.* Paris, 1893. 106p.

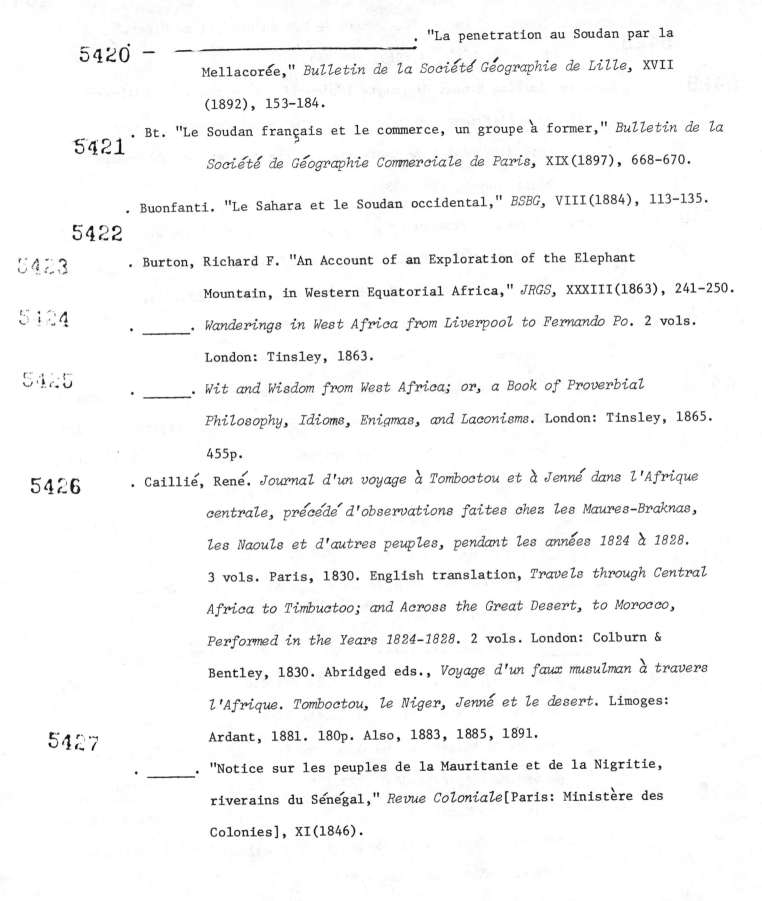

5420 — ———————————————. "La penetration au Soudan par la
Mellacorée," *Bulletin de la Société Géographie de Lille*, XVII
(1892), 153-184.

5421 . Bt. "Le Soudan français et le commerce, un groupe à former," *Bulletin de la Société de Géographie Commerciale de Paris*, XIX(1897), 668-670.

5422 . Buonfanti. "Le Sahara et le Soudan occidental," *BSBG*, VIII(1884), 113-135.

5423 . Burton, Richard F. "An Account of an Exploration of the Elephant Mountain, in Western Equatorial Africa," *JRGS*, XXXIII(1863), 241-250.

5424 . ———. *Wanderings in West Africa from Liverpool to Fernando Po*. 2 vols. London: Tinsley, 1863.

5425 . ———. *Wit and Wisdom from West Africa; or, a Book of Proverbial Philosophy, Idioms, Enigmas, and Laconisms*. London: Tinsley, 1865. 455p.

5426 . Caillié, René. *Journal d'un voyage à Tomboctou et à Jenné dans l'Afrique centrale, précédé d'observations faites chez les Maures-Braknas, les Naouls et d'autres peuples, pendant les années 1824 à 1828*. 3 vols. Paris, 1830. English translation, *Travels through Central Africa to Timbuctoo; and Across the Great Desert, to Morocco, Performed in the Years 1824-1828*. 2 vols. London: Colburn & Bentley, 1830. Abridged eds., *Voyage d'un faux musulman à travers l'Afrique. Tomboctou, le Niger, Jenné et le desert*. Limoges: Ardant, 1881. 180p. Also, 1883, 1885, 1891.

5427 . ———. "Notice sur les peuples de la Mauritanie et de la Nigritie, riverains du Sénégal," *Revue Coloniale*[Paris: Ministère des Colonies], XI(1846).

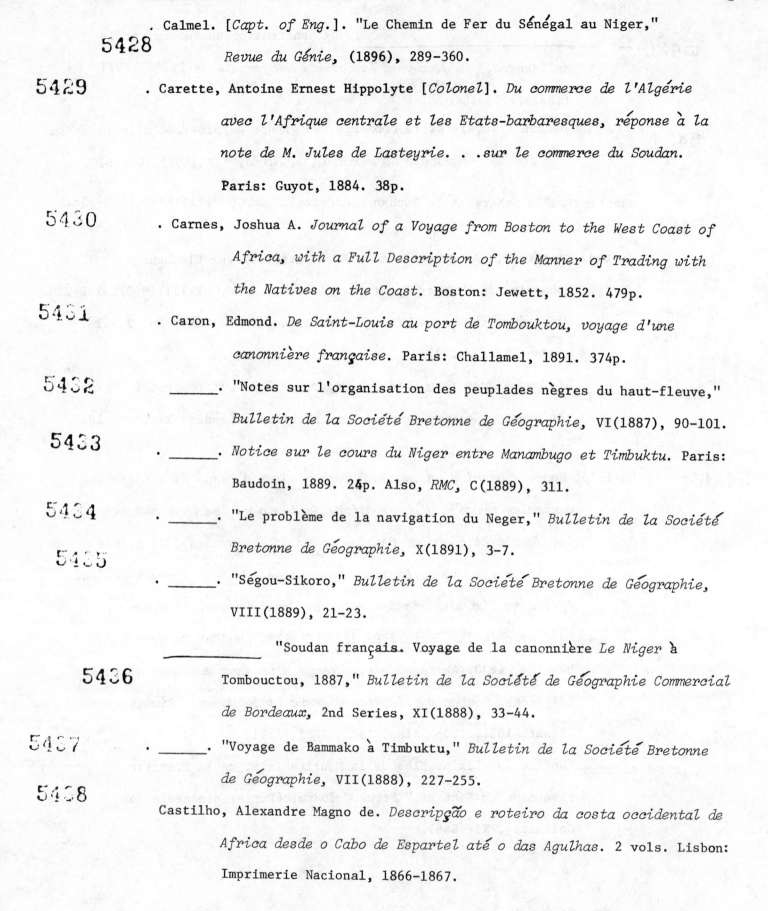

5428 . Calmel. [*Capt. of Eng.*]. "Le Chemin de Fer du Sénégal au Niger," *Revue du Génie*, (1896), 289-360.

5429 . Carette, Antoine Ernest Hippolyte [*Colonel*]. *Du commerce de l'Algérie avec l'Afrique centrale et les Etats-barbaresques, réponse à la note de M. Jules de Lasteyrie. . .sur le commerce du Soudan.* Paris: Guyot, 1884. 38p.

5430 . Carnes, Joshua A. *Journal of a Voyage from Boston to the West Coast of Africa, with a Full Description of the Manner of Trading with the Natives on the Coast.* Boston: Jewett, 1852. 479p.

5431 . Caron, Edmond. *De Saint-Louis au port de Tombouctou, voyage d'une canonnière française.* Paris: Challamel, 1891. 374p.

5432 _____. "Notes sur l'organisation des peuplades nègres du haut-fleuve," *Bulletin de la Société Bretonne de Géographie*, VI(1887), 90-101.

5433 . _____. *Notice sur le cours du Niger entre Manambugo et Timbuktu.* Paris: Baudoin, 1889. 24p. Also, *RMC*, C(1889), 311.

5434 . _____. "Le problème de la navigation du Neger," *Bulletin de la Société Bretonne de Géographie*, X(1891), 3-7.

5435 . _____. "Ségou-Sikoro," *Bulletin de la Société Bretonne de Géographie*, VIII(1889), 21-23.

5436 _____ "Soudan français. Voyage de la canonnière *Le Niger* à Tombouctou, 1887," *Bulletin de la Société de Géographie Commercial de Bordeaux*, 2nd Series, XI(1888), 33-44.

5437 . _____. "Voyage de Bammako à Timbuktu," *Bulletin de la Société Bretonne de Géographie*, VII(1888), 227-255.

5438 Castilho, Alexandre Magno de. *Descripção e roteiro da costa occidental de Africa desde o Cabo de Espartel até o das Agulhas.* 2 vols. Lisbon: Imprimerie Nacional, 1866-1867.

5439. Castilho Barreto e Noronha, Augusto de. "A provincia de S. Thomé e o Golfo de Benin," *BSGL*, XIV(1895), 777-819.

5440. Cervera, Julio. "Conferencia dada por el Señor Don Cervera en la reunión ordinaria de 2 de noviembre de 1886, acerca de su viaje de exploración por el Sáhara Occidental," *Boletín de la Sociedad Geográfica de Madrid*, XXII(1887), 7-20.

5441. Chanoine, Julien. *Itinéraire de la mission du Tchad*. Paris: Société de Géographie, 1899. 21p.

_____. "Mission Voulet-Chanoine, itinéraire du capitaine Chanoine de Dienné a Sansanne-Haoussa," *BSGP*, 7th Series, XX (1899), 220-235.

5442. Chevalier, A. "Lettre," *Bulletin du Museum National d'Histoire Naturelle*, II(1899), 325-326.

5443. Christian Traveller. *Western Africa; Being an Account of the Country and Its Products; of the People and Their Condition; and of the Measures Taken for Their Religious and Social Benefit*. London: L. Knight & Co., 1841. 208p.

5444. Clarke, John. "On the Mouths of the Jamoor River, Western Africa," *JRGS*, XVI(1846), 255-258.

5445. _____. *Specimens of Dialects, Short Vocabularies of Languages, and Notes of Countries and Customs in Africa*.n.p., n.p., 1849. 104p.

5446. Clozel, Marie François Joseph. "Le groupe occidental des Bantous," *TM*, LXXII(1896).

5447. _____. *Haute-Sangha. Bassin du Tchad. Les Bayas, notes ethnographiques et linguistics*. Paris: Andre, 1896. 48p.

5448.

5449 . Cochelet, Charles. *Naufrage du brick français la Sophie, perdu le 30 mai 1819, sur la côte occidentale d'Afrique, et captivité d'une partie des naufragés dans le désert de Sahara; avec de nouveaux renseignements sur la ville de Timectou.* 2 vols. Paris: P. Monge aîné, 1821. English translation, *Narrative of the Shipwreck of the Sophia on the 30th of May 1819, on the Western Coast of Africa, and of the Captivity of a Part of the Crew in the Desert of Sahara.* London: Phillips, 1822. 130p.

5450 . Cole, J. Augustus. *A Revelation of the Secret Orders of Western Africa.* Dayton, Ohio: United Brethren, 1886. 99p.

5451 Colin, G. "Le Soudan occidental," *RMC*, LXXVIII(1885), 5-32.

5452 ──────── . "Voyage au Bambouk et au Fouta-Djallon," *CRSG*, VIII(1889), 42-46.

5453 Collier, George Ralph. *West Africa Sketches.* London: Seeley, 1824. 273p.

5454 . Compiègne, Victor D. "Escales de deux voyageurs français à la côte occidentale d'Afrique," *BSGP*, 6th Series, VI(1873), 404-422.

5455 . Cons, H. "Le bassin du Niger," *Bulletin de l'Union Géographique du Nord de la France*, VIII(1887), 128-143.

5456 . Cooper, H. T. H. "On a Proposed Trade Route from the Gambia to Timbuctoo," *PRGS*, XX(1875-1876), 78-79.

5457 . Corry, Joseph. *Observations upon the Windward Coast of Africa, the Religion, Character, Customs of the Natives Made in the Years 1805 and 1806.* London: Nicol, 1807. 163p.

5458 . Crean, J. F. "On Service in West Africa," *Canadian Military Institute*, No. 12 (1896-1902), 28-38.

5459 . Crouch, Archer Philip. *Glimpses of Feverland; or, a Cruise in West African Waters.* London: Sampson Low, 1889. 323p.

5460 . Crow, Hugh. *Memoirs of the Late Capt. Hugh Crow of Liverpool, Comprising a Narrative of His Life Together with Descriptive Sketches of the West Coast of Africa.* London: Longman, Rees, 1830. 316p.

5461 . Crozals, Jacques Marie Ferdinand Joseph de. *Les Peulhs, étude d'ethnologie africaine.* Paris: Maisonneuve, 1883. 271p.

5462 . Cruickshank, B. *Missions to the King of Dahomey. Copy of Dispatches from the Lieut. Governor of the Gold Coast, Giving an Account of Missions to the King of Ashantee and Dahomey.* London: H.M.S.O., 1894.

5463 . Daniell, William Freeman. *Sketches of the Medical Topography and Native Diseases of the Gulf of Guinea, Western Africa.* London: Highley, 1849. 200p.

5464 . Darondeau. *Instructions nautiques sur les côtes occidentales d'Afrique comprises entre le détroit de Gibraltar et le golfe de Bénin.* Paris: Ledoyen, 1852.

5465 . Daumas, Melchior Joseph Eugène. *Le grand désert, ou, itinéraire d'une caravane du Sahara au pays des Nègres, royaume de Haoussa.* Paris: Chaix, 1848. 445p.

5466 . Deburaux, Édouard Léopold Joseph. *Au pays des Touaregs.* Paris: Delagrave, 1901. 303p.

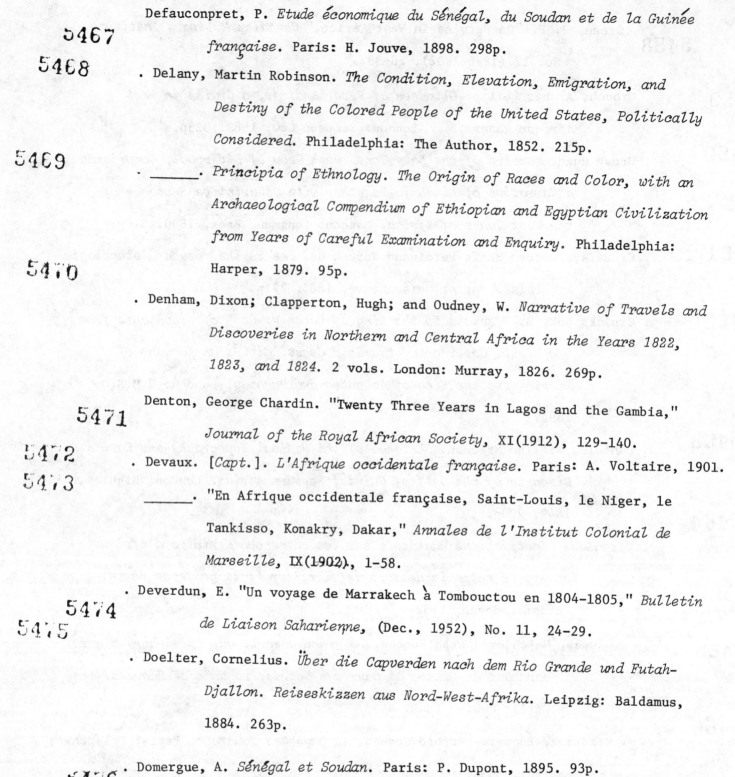

5467 Defauconpret, P. *Etude économique du Sénégal, du Soudan et de la Guinée française.* Paris: H. Jouve, 1898. 298p.

5468 . Delany, Martin Robinson. *The Condition, Elevation, Emigration, and Destiny of the Colored People of the United States, Politically Considered.* Philadelphia: The Author, 1852. 215p.

5469 . _____. *Principia of Ethnology. The Origin of Races and Color, with an Archaeological Compendium of Ethiopian and Egyptian Civilization from Years of Careful Examination and Enquiry.* Philadelphia: Harper, 1879. 95p.

5470 . Denham, Dixon; Clapperton, Hugh; and Oudney, W. *Narrative of Travels and Discoveries in Northern and Central Africa in the Years 1822, 1823, and 1824.* 2 vols. London: Murray, 1826. 269p.

5471 Denton, George Chardin. "Twenty Three Years in Lagos and the Gambia," *Journal of the Royal African Society,* XI(1912), 129-140.

5472 . Devaux. [*Capt.*]. *L'Afrique occidentale française.* Paris: A. Voltaire, 1901.

5473 _____. "En Afrique occidentale française, Saint-Louis, le Niger, le Tankisso, Konakry, Dakar," *Annales de l'Institut Colonial de Marseille,* IX(1902), 1-58.

5474 . Deverdun, E. "Un voyage de Marrakech à Tombouctou en 1804-1805," *Bulletin de Liaison Saharienne,* (Dec., 1952), No. 11, 24-29.

5475 . Doelter, Cornelius. *Über die Capverden nach dem Rio Grande und Futah-Djallon. Reiseskizzen aus Nord-West-Afrika.* Leipzig: Baldamus, 1884. 263p.

5476 . Domergue, A. *Sénégal et Soudan.* Paris: P. Dupont, 1895. 93p.

5477 . Dubarry, A. *Le rachat de l'honneur. Aventures d'un soldat français au Soudan.* Paris: Chavaray, Mantoux, Martin, 1895. 2nd Ed., 1897.

5478 . Duclot, N. *Contribution à la géographie médicale. Haut-Sénégal et Haut-Niger.* Bordeaux: Olivier-Louis Favraud, 1886. 111p.

5479 . Du Couret, Louis. [Colonel]. *Mémoire à S.M. Napoléon III, empéreur des Français, sur lés résultats de la mission officielle que ce voyageur vient de remplier en Afrique.* Paris: Pommeret et Moreau, 1853. 16p.

5480 . Duncan, John. "Note of a Journey from Cape Coast to Whyddah, on the West Coast of Africa," *JRGS*, XVI(1846), 143-153.

5481 . _____. "Notice of a Journey from Whyddah on the W. Coast of Africa to Adofoodiah in the Interior," *JRGS*, XVI(1846), 154-162.

5482 . Durand, F. "Campagne du Soudan 1889-1890. Histoire médicale," *Archives de Médicine et de Pharmacie Navales*, LVI(1891), 7-39.

5483 . Dyer, Hugh McN. *The West Coast of Africa, As Seen from the Deck of a Man-of-War.* London: Griffin, 1876. 151p.

5484 . Elliott, G. F. Scott. "Some Notes on Native West African Customs," *JAI*, XXIII(1893-1894), 80-83.

5485 . Ellis, Alfred Burdon. *The Land of Fetish.* London: Chapman & Hall, 1883. 316p.

5486 . _____. *West African Islands.* London: Chapman & Hall, 1885. 352p.

5487 . _____. *West African Sketches.* London: Tinsley, 1881. 326p.

5488 . _____. *West African Stories.* London: Chapman & Hall, 1890. 278p.

5489 . Escayrac de Lauture, Pierre-Henri-Stanislas. *Le desert et le Soudan.* Paris: Dumaine, 1853. 631p.

5490 _____. *Mémoire sur l'état social de l'Afrique intérieure.* Paris, 1856. 50p.

5491 . _____. *Mémoire sur le Soudan, géographie naturelle et politique, histoire et ethnographie, moeurs et institutions de l'empire des Fellatas, du Bornou, du Baguermi, du Wadt, du Dar-Four, rédigé, d'apres des renseignements entièrement nouveaux et accompagné d'une esquisse du Soudan oriental.* Paris: Bertrand, 1855-1856. 184p.

5492 Faidherbe, Louis L. C. *L'avenir du Sahara et du Soudan.* Paris: Challamel aîne, 1863. 28p. See also, *RMC*, VIII(1863), 221.

5493 _____. "Populations noires des Bassins du Sénégal et du Haut-Niger," *Revue Coloniale*, 2nd Series, XVI(1856), 328-341.

5494 . _____. *Le Soudan français; Chemin de Fer de Medine au Niger.* Lille: L. Danel, 1883. 19p. Also, *Bulletin de la Société de Géographie de Lille*, II(1883), 225-244; IV(1885), 83, 170; V (1886), 17-36; and *Bulletin de l'Union Géographique du Nord de la France*, II(1881), 487-505.

5495 . Falkenstein, Julius August Ferdinand. *Afrikas Westküste vom Ogowe bis zum Darira-Land.* Leipzig: Freytag, 1885. 241p.

5496 . Fennekol, Frederik Willim. *Proeve over de kust van Guinea; houdende eene poging tot onderzoek, hoc, en in hoeverre, dat land tot eene ware volkplanting zou kunnen gevormd worden.* The Hauge: Immerzeel, 1831. 154p.

5497 . Feris. [Dr.]. "Études sur les climats équatoriaux en géneral," *Archives de Médecine Navale*, IX(1879).

5498 . Fitzau, August. "Die Nordwestküste Afrikas von Agadir bis St. Louis," *Deutsche Geographische Blätter*, XI(1888).

5499 . Flickinger, Daniel Kumler. *Off Hand Sketches of Men and Things in Western Africa.* Dayton, Ohio, 1857.

5500 . Foote, Andrew Hull. *Africa and the American Flag.* New York: Appleton, 1854. 390p.

5501 . Foote, Henry Grant [Mrs.]. *Recollections of Central America and the West Coast of Africa.* London: n.p., 1869. 221p.

5502 . Forbes, Frederick E. [Lt., Royal Navy]. "Despatch Communicating the Discovery of a Native Written Character at Bohmar, on the Western Coast of Africa, Near Liberia, Accompanied by a Vocabulary of the Vahie or Vei Tongue," *JRGS*, XX(1850), 89-101.

5503 _____. *Six Months' Service in the African Blockade, from April to October 1848, in Command of H. M. S. Bonetta.* London, 1849.

5504 Ford, Henry A. *Observations on the Fevers on the West Coast of Africa.* New York: Jenkins, 1856. **48**p.

5505 . Freeman, J. J. "Afrique occidentale," *JME*, XX(1845), 256-273.

5506 . Freeman, Thomas Birch. *Journal of Various Visits to the Kingdoms of Ashanti, Aku and Dahomi, in West Africa.* London: Mason, 1844. 298p.

5507 . Frey, Henry Nicolas. *Côte occidentale d'Afrique.* Paris: Marpon et Flammarion, 1890. 543p.

5508 . Frobenius, Leo V. "Holzwaffen und Industrieformen Afrika," *Globus*, LXVIII(1895), 218-221.

5509 _____. "Hühner im Kult. Studie aus West-Afrika," *MDS*, VII (1894).

5510 _____. "Der Westafrikanische Kulturkreis," *PM*, XLIII(1897), 225-236, 262-267; XLIV(1898), 193-204, 265-271.

5511 Froment, Edouard. "Deux ans au Sénégal et au Soudan. Souvenirs d'un soldat d'infanterie de marine (1884-1886)," *Bulletin de la Société de Géographie de Lille*, XIV(1890), 34-47, 121-135, 184-196, 225-233, 296-304, 362-370.

5512 . Fuller, J. and others. "Letters from West Africa," *BM*, XLIV(1852), 185-186, 250-251, 454-455, 519-522, 654-656; XLV(1853), 124-125, 725-726, 830.

5513 . Gaffarel, P. "Le Soudan français," *Revue de Géographie*, XXII(1888), 321-330, 422-435.

5514 . Galliéni, Joseph Simon [*Commandant*]. "Exploration du haut Niger," *TM*, XLIV(1882), 257-320; XLV(1883), 113-208.

5515 . _____. *Mission d'exploration du Haut-Niger. Voyages au Soudan français, Haut-Niger et pays de Ségou, 1879-1881*. Paris: Hachette, 1885. 632p.

5516 . Garner, R. O. "Superstitions of the West African Tribes," *Australian Association for the Advancement of Science*, VI(1895), 589-595.

5517 . Girard, H. "Notes anthropométriques sur quelques Soudannaia occidentaux (Malinkés, Bambaras, Foulahs, Soninkés, etc.)," *Anthropologie*, XIII(1902), 41-56, 167-181, 329-347.

5518 . Glover, John. "Geographical Notes on the Country Traversed between the River Volta and the Niger," *PRGS*, XVIII(1873-1874), 286-292.

5519 . Goldberry, S. M. X. *Fragments d'un voyage dans les contrées occidentales de ce continent compris entre le Cap Blanc et le Cap des Palmes*. 2 vols. Paris: Treuttel and Wurz, 1802.

5520 . Gollmer, Charles Henry Vidal. *Charles Andrew Gollmer, His Life and Missionary Labours in West Africa, Compiled from His Journals and the Church Missionary Society's Publications*. London: Hodder & Stoughton, 1889. 220p.

5521 . Gouraud. [*Lt.*]. "Soudan française," *CRSG*, XVI(1897), 238-245.

5522 . Gramberg, Jan Simon Gerardus. *Schetsen van Afrika's Westkust*. Amsterdam: Weijtingk & Brave, 1861.

**5523** . Grant, Charles Scovell. *West African Hygiene; or, Hints on the preservation of Health, and the Treatment of Disease on the West Coast of Africa.* London: Colonial Office, 1882. 36p.

**5524** . Gray, William [*Major*]. *Travels in Western Africa, in the Years 1818-21.* London: Murray, 1825. 413p. French translation, *Voyage dans l'Afrique occidentale, pendant les années 1818-21.* Paris: A. de Gastel, ]826. 392p.

**5525** . Greff, Richard. "Die Angolares-Neger der Insel São Thomé," *Globus*, XLII (1882), 362-364, 376-378.

**5526** . _____. "Der Insel São Thomé," *PM*, XXX(1884), 121-132.

**5527** . Grover, John. [*Capt.*]. "An Account of the Island of Arguin, on the Western Coast of Africa," *JRGS*, XVI(1846), 162-167.

**5528** . Grundemann, R. "Die Mission in den deutschen Schutzgebieten in West Afrika," *DK*, V(1888), 129-131, 140-141, 227-229.

**5529** . Gruner. [*Dr.*]. "Die Franzosischen Ansprüche auf das hinterland von Togo," *DK*, XII(1895), 377-378.

**5530** . Güssfeldt, Paul. "Voyage à la côte occidentale d'Afrique," *BSKG*, No. 3, 1876.

**5531** . _____. "Briefe von Mitgleidern der deutschen westafrikanischen Expedition," *ZGE*, VIII(1873), 471-496.

**5532** . Guillaumet, Édouard. "Le Soudan français," *Bulletin de la Société Normande de Géographie*, XVIII(1896), 197-217.

**5533** . Guilleux, Charles. *Journal de route d'un caporal de tirailleurs de la Mission Saharienne (Mission Foureau-Lamy), 1898-1900.* Belfort: Spitzmuller, 1904. 398p.

5534 . H., R. "Le Soudan français, ce qu'il vaut," *Bulletin de la Société de Géographie Commerciale de Paris*, XII(1889), 165-167.

5535 . Hartert, Ernst. "Reise im westlichen Sudan, mit besonderer Berücksichtigung der pflanzlichen Reichtümer," *PM*, XXXIII(1887), 172-183.

5536 . Hautefeuille, Laurent Basile. *Plan de colonisation des possessions françaises dans l'Afrique occidentale, au moyen de la civilisation des nègres indigènes, précédé d'un examen critique des essais de défrichements faits jusqu'a ce jour*. Paris: Levavasseur, 1830. 200p.

5537 . Hay, J. S. "On the District of Akém, in West Africa," *JRGS*, XLVI(1876), 299-308. Also, *PRGS*, XX(1875-1876), 475-482.

5538 . Hecquard, Louis Hyacinthe. *Voyage sur la côte et dans l'intérieur de l'Afrique occidentale*. Paris: de Bénard, 1855. 409p.

5539 . Heinzelmann. *Reisen in Afrika durch die Lander der Nord Küste und die Sahara, Senegambien dem Sudan*. Leipzig, 1852.

5540 Hennessy, John Pope. "British Settlements in West Africa," *JRSA*, XXI(1837), 436-449.

5541 . Henric. [*Dr.*]. "Rapport médical sur les colonnes du Dakol et la mission du Mossi (Soudan français) du 25 février 1896 au 16 avril 1897," *Archives de Médicine et de Pharmacie Navales*, LXIX(1898), 321-339.

5542 Hodgson, William Brown. *The Foulads of Central Africa, and the African Slave Trade*. New York, 1843. 24p.

5543 ____. *Notes on Northern Africa, the Sahara and Soudan, in Relation to the Ethnography, Languages, History, Political and Social Condition, of the Nations of Those Countries*. New York: Wiley, and Putnam, 1844. 107p.

5544 . Holman, James. *Travels in Madeira, Sierra Leone, Teneriffe, St. Jago, Cape Coast, Fernando Po, Princess Island, etc. etc.* London: Routledge, 1840.

5545 . Hornberger, C. "Das Ewe-Gebiet an der Sklavenküste von West-Afrika," *PM*, XIII(1867), 48-54.

5546 . Horton, James Africanus Beale. *Physical and Medical Climate and Meteorology of the West Coast of Africa, with Valuable Hints to Europeans for the Preservation of Health in the Tropics.* Edinburgh, n.p., 1867. 321p.

5547 _____. *West African Countries and Peoples, British and Native.* London, 1868.

5548 . Hubler, T. "Quelques notes sur la côte occidentale d'Afrique. De Dakar au Gabon," *Bulletin de la Société de Géographie Commerciale de Bordeaux*, XI(1888), 44.

5549 . Humbert. [Colonel]. *La France au Soudan.* Paris: Paul Stock, 1891. 30p. Also, *Bulletin de la Société Bretonne de Géographie*, XI(1892), 1-31.

5550 . Huntley, Henry Veel. *Seven Years' Service on the Slave Coast of Western Africa.* 2 vols. London: Newby, 1860.

5551 . Hutchinson, Thomas Joseph. *Impressions of Western Africa, with Remarks on the Diseases of the Climate and a Report on the Peculiarities of Trade up the Rivers in the Bight of Biafra.* London: Longmans, Brown, Green, Longmans, & Roberts, 1858. *313p.*

5552 . _____. *Ten Years' Wanderings among the Ethiopians; with Sketches of Manners and Customs of the Civilized and Uncivilized Tribes, from Senegal to Gabon.* London: Hurst & Blackett, 1861.

5553 . Hutter. [*Hauptmann*]. "West-Afrikanisches Reiseleben," *DK*, XV(1898), 282-285, 290-292, 298-300, 306-307, 314-315, 350-353, 362-364.

5554 . Iradier y Bulfy, Manuel. *Africa, viaje y trabajos de la Asociación Euskara la Exploradora.* 2 vols. Victoria: Iturbe, 1887.

5555 . "J. S." "Einiges über St. Thomé," *Globus*, XXXIX(1881), 219-220.

5556 . Jackson, James Grey. *An Account of the Empire of Morocco and the Districts of Suse and Tafilelt, Compiled from Miscellaneous Observations Made during a Long Residence in, and Various Journies through These Countries. To which Is Added an Account of Ship Wrecks on the Western Coast of Africa and an Account of Timbuctoo.* London: G.& W. Nicol, 1809. 288p. 2nd ed., 1811, 3rd ed., London: Cadell & Davies, 1814

5557 . _____. *An Account of Timbuctoo and Hausa, Territories in the Interior of Africa, by El Hage Abd Salam Shabeeny; with Notes, Critical and Explanatory. To Which Is Added Letters, Descriptive of Travels through West and South Barbary, and across the Mountains of Atlas; Also Fragments, Notes, and Anecdotes, Specimens of the Arabic Epistolary Style, etc.* London: Hurst, Rees, Orme and Brown, 1820.

5558 . Jacolliot, Louis. *La Côte d'Ébène. Le dernier des négriers.* Paris: Librairie illustrée, 1876. 329p.

5559 . Jaubert, Alfred. *La côte occidentale d'Afrique. Création de comptoirs belges.* Antwerp: L. Legros, 1880. 71p.

5560 . Johnston, Harry Hamilton. "Bantu Borderland in Western Africa," *PRGS,* New Series, X(1888), 633-637.

5561 _____. "British West Africa and the Trade of the Interior," *Proceedings of the Royal Colonial Institute,* XX (1888-1889), 90-128.

5562 . ____. "The Portuguese Possessions in West Africa," *SGM,* I(1885), 465-482.

5563 . Kerhallet, Charles Phillippe de. [*Captain*]. *Instructions nautiques sur la côte occidentale d'Afrique, comprenant le Maroc, le Sahara et la Sénégambie.* Paris: Lainé et Havard, 1867. 334p.

5564 . ____. *Manuel de la navigation à la côte occidentale d'Afrique.* 3 vols. Paris: P. Dupont, 1851-1852.

5565 . Kieffer. [*Dr.*]. "Hôpitaux. Morbidité et mortalité en 1899. Sénégal et Soudan," *Annales d'Hygiene et de Médecine Coloniales,* IV(1901), 248-258.

5566 . King, W. J. Harding. "A Visit to the Hoggar Tuaregs," *GJ,* XX(1902), 507-517.

5567 . Kingsley, George Henry. *Notes on Sport and Travel.* London: Macmillan, 1900. 544p.

5568 . Kingsley, Mary H. "Development of Dodos," *National Review,* XXVII(March, 1896), 66-79.

5569 _____. "Liquor Traffic with West Africa," *Fortnightly Review,* April, 1898, pp. 537-560.

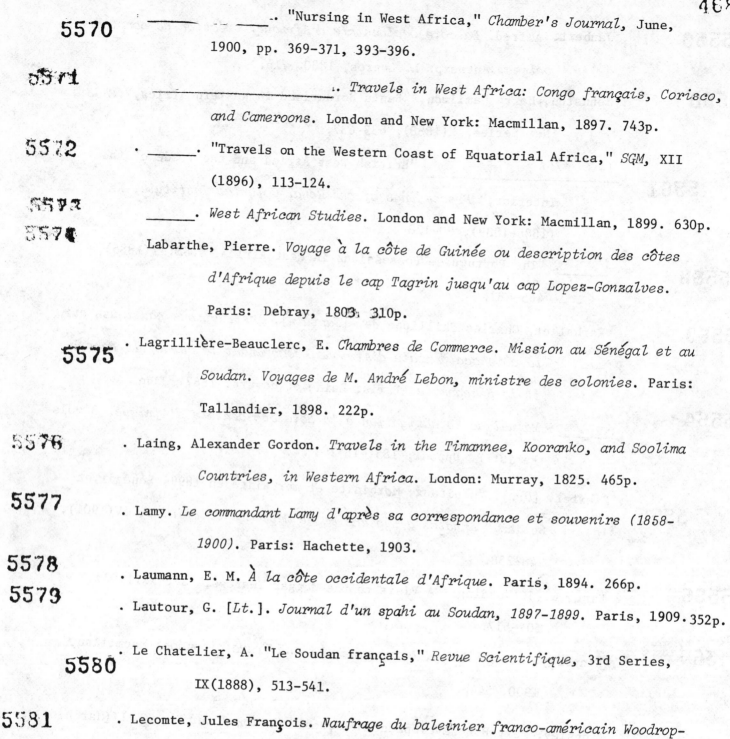

5570 _____ _____. "Nursing in West Africa," *Chamber's Journal*, June, 1900, pp. 369-371, 393-396.

5571 _____. *Travels in West Africa: Congo français, Corisco, and Cameroons*. London and New York: Macmillan, 1897. 743p.

5572 . _____. "Travels on the Western Coast of Equatorial Africa," *SGM*, XII (1896), 113-124.

5573 _____. *West African Studies*. London and New York: Macmillan, 1899. 630p.

5574 Labarthe, Pierre. *Voyage à la côte de Guinée ou description des côtes d'Afrique depuis le cap Tagrin jusqu'au cap Lopez-Gonzalves*. Paris: Debray, 1803. 310p.

5575 . Lagrillière-Beauclerc, E. *Chambres de Commerce. Mission au Sénégal et au Soudan. Voyages de M. André Lebon, ministre des colonies*. Paris: Tallandier, 1898. 222p.

5576 . Laing, Alexander Gordon. *Travels in the Timannee, Kooranko, and Soolima Countries, in Western Africa*. London: Murray, 1825. 465p.

5577 . Lamy. *Le commandant Lamy d'après sa correspondance et souvenirs (1858-1900)*. Paris: Hachette, 1903.

5578 . Laumann, E. M. *À la côte occidentale d'Afrique*. Paris, 1894. 266p.

5579 . Lautour, G. [*Lt.*]. *Journal d'un spahi au Soudan, 1897-1899*. Paris, 1909. 352p.

5580 . Le Chatelier, A. "Le Soudan français," *Revue Scientifique*, 3rd Series, IX(1888), 513-541.

5581 . Lecomte, Jules François. *Naufrage du baleinier franco-américain Woodrop-Sims sur la côte occidentale d'Afrique*. Paris: Les Libraires du Palais-Royale, 1833. 56p.

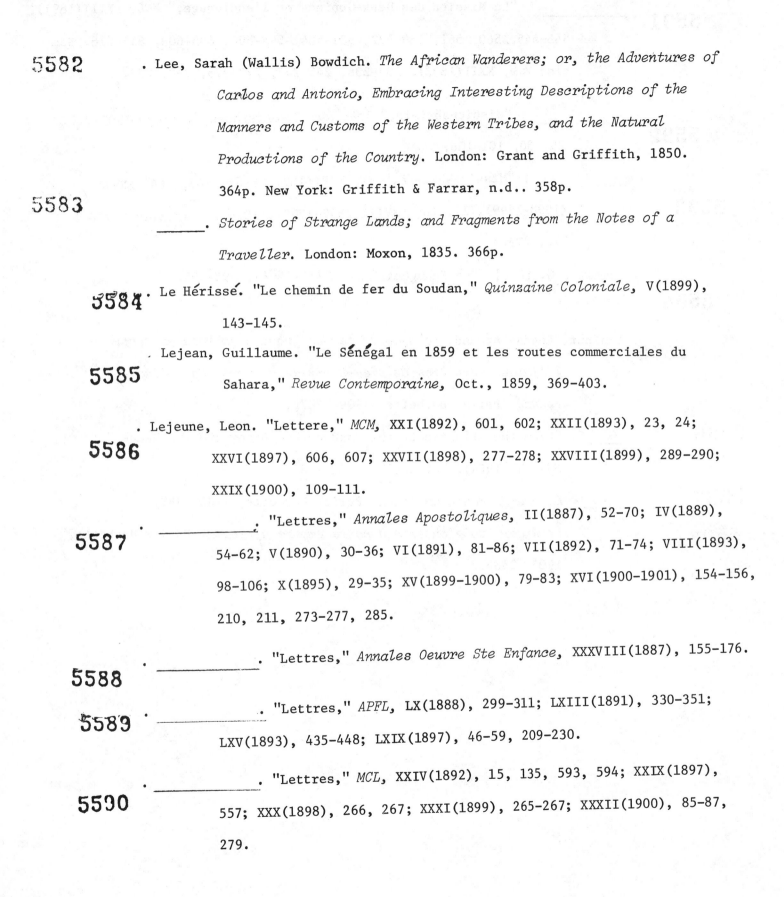

5582     . Lee, Sarah (Wallis) Bowdich. *The African Wanderers; or, the Adventures of Carlos and Antonio, Embracing Interesting Descriptions of the Manners and Customs of the Western Tribes, and the Natural Productions of the Country.* London: Grant and Griffith, 1850. 364p. New York: Griffith & Farrar, n.d.. 358p.

5583     _____. *Stories of Strange Lands; and Fragments from the Notes of a Traveller.* London: Moxon, 1835. 366p.

5584     . Le Hérissé. "Le chemin de fer du Soudan," *Quinzaine Coloniale,* V(1899), 143-145.

5585     . Lejean, Guillaume. "Le Sénégal en 1859 et les routes commerciales du Sahara," *Revue Contemporaine,* Oct., 1859, 369-403.

5586     . Lejeune, Leon. "Lettere," *MCM,* XXI(1892), 601, 602; XXII(1893), 23, 24; XXVI(1897), 606, 607; XXVII(1898), 277-278; XXVIII(1899), 289-290; XXIX(1900), 109-111.

5587     . _____. "Lettres," *Annales Apostoliques,* II(1887), 52-70; IV(1889), 54-62; V(1890), 30-36; VI(1891), 81-86; VII(1892), 71-74; VIII(1893), 98-106; X(1895), 29-35; XV(1899-1900), 79-83; XVI(1900-1901), 154-156, 210, 211, 273-277, 285.

5588     . _____. "Lettres," *Annales Oeuvre Ste Enfance,* XXXVIII(1887), 155-176.

5589     . _____. "Lettres," *APFL,* LX(1888), 299-311; LXIII(1891), 330-351; LXV(1893), 435-448; LXIX(1897), 46-59, 209-230.

5590     . _____. "Lettres," *MCL,* XXIV(1892), 15, 135, 593, 594; XXIX(1897), 557; XXX(1898), 266, 267; XXXI(1899), 265-267; XXXII(1900), 85-87, 279.

5531 ————————. "La Mission des Deux-Guniees et l'esclavage," *MCL*, XXIII(1891), 543-545, 560, 561, 569-572, 581-584, 594-596, 605-608, 615-616. See also *MCM*, XXII(1893), 233-236, 245-247, 272-275, 298, 299.

5592 . ————————. "Missionsbriefe," *Echo aus Knechtsteden*, II(1900-1901), 29, 30, 101-106.

5593 . ————————. "Missionsbriefe," *KM*, XXVI(1897-1898), 263, 264; XXVII (1898-1899), 17, 18; XXVIII(1899-1900), 203-205, XXIX(1900-1901), 278, 279.

5594 . Lemaire, C. [*Lt.*]. "Le Sohnghoï," *MG*, XIII(1896), 594-596.

5595 . Lenfant, Eugène Armand. *Le découverte des grandes sources du centre de l'Afrique. Rivières de vie—Rivières de mort. Nana—Ouam— Penndé*. Paris: Hachette, 1909. 287p.

5596 . ————. "From the Atlantic to the Chad by the Niger and the Benue," *SGM*, XX(1904), 306-316.

5597 . ————. *La grande route du Tchad*. Paris: Hachette, 1905. 288p.

5598 . ————. *Le Niger, voie ouverte à notre empire africain*. Paris: Hachette, 1903. 256p.

5599 . Lenz, Oscar. *Skizzen aus Westafrika.* Berlin: Hofmann, 1878. 346p.

5600 . _____. *Timbuctu. Reise durch Marokko, die Sahara und den Sudan ausgeführt im Auftrage der Afrikanischen Gesellschaft in Deutschland in den Jahren 1879 und 1880.* 2 vols. Leipzig: Brockhaus, 1884. French edition, 2 vols., Paris: Hachette, 1886.

5601 . Leonard, Peter. *Records of a Voyage to the West Coast of Africa, in H.M.'s Ship Dryad, and of the Service of That Station for the Suppression of the Slave Trade.* Edinburgh, 1833. American edition, *The Western Coast of Africa; Journal of an Officer under Captain Owen. Records of a Voyage in the Ship Dryad, in 1830, 1831 and 1832.* Philadelphia: Mielke, 1833. 177p.

5602 . Le Prédour, Fortuné Joseph Hyacinthe. *Description de la côte occidentale d'Afrique depuis le cap de Naze, jusqu'au cap Roxo.* Paris: Depôt des Cartes et Plans de la Marine, 1828. 31p. See also, *Annales Maritimes,* XXXV(1828), 920.

5603 . _____. *Résumé des operations hydrographiques faites sur la côte occidentale d'Afrique dans les années 1826 et 1827 à bord de la frégate la Flore et de la goëlette la Dorade.* Paris: Huzard-Courcien, 1828. 15p.

5604 . Libermann, François-Marie-Paul. *Notes et documents relatifs à la vie et à l'oeuvre du vénérable François-Marie-Paul Libermann, Supérieur général de la Congrégation du Saint-Esprit.* 13 vols. Paris: Maison-Mère, 1927-1941.

5605 . Loomis, Eben Jenks. *An Eclipse Party in Africa; Chasing Summer across the Equator in the U.S. Pensacola.* Boston: Roberts Brothers, 1896. 218p.

5606 . Lugard, Frederick John Dealtry. "A Journey in West Africa and Some Points of Contrast with East Africa," *SGM*, XI(1895), 609-625.

5607 . Lynch, William F. *Report to the U. S. Navy Department in Relation to His Mission to the Coast of Africa. (House of Representatives Document)*. Washington: G. P. O., 1853. 64p.

5608 . Lyon, G. F. *A Narrative of Travels in Northern Africa, in the Years 1818, 19 and 20, Accompanied by Geographical Notices of Soudan, and of the Courses of the Niger*. London: Murray, 1821. 383p.

5609 . Mackenzie, Donald. *The Flooding of the Sahara: an Account of the Proposed Plan for Opening Central Africa to Commerce and Cultivation from the Northwest Coast with a Description of Soudan and Western Sahara*. London: Low, Marston, Searle & Rivington, 1877.

5610 . MacQueen, James. *Geographical and Commercial View of North Central Africa: Containing a Particular Account of the Course and Termination of the Great River Niger in the Atlantic Ocean*. Edinburgh, n.p., 1821. 288p.

5611 Madrolle, Claudius. *En Guinée: Côte occidentale d'Afrique, Casamance, Guinée portugaise, Guinée française, Fouta-Djallon, Sierra-Leone, Soudan français et Haut Niger*. 2nd ed. Paris: La Soudier, 1895. 407p.

5612 . Mage, Abdon Eugene. [*Capt.*]. "Auf dem Marktplatze in Yamina am obern Niger," *Globus*, XII(1867), 89-91.

5613 _____. "Aufenthalt beim König Ahmadu zu Segu am obern Niger," *Globus*, XIV(1868), 225-234, 257-266.

5614 _____. "Reise vom Senegal bis an den obern Niger," *Globus*, XIV(1868), 1-11, 33-44, 65-73.

5615

_____. *Voyage dans le Soudan occidental, Sénégambie-Niger. . .1863-1866.* Paris: Hachette, 1868. 693p. Also, *TM*, XVII(1868), 1-112, and, *RMC*, XX(1867), 26-88, 395-424, 620-659, 895-932; XXI(1867). 134-151, 367-405, 626-663, 803-853; XXII(1868), 766-796; XXIII(1868), 163-206, 463-492, 719-751, 1007-1049.

5616

. Mahistre. *Le Soudan français.* Foix: Gadrat, 1890. 46p.

5617

. Marchand. [*Lt.*]. "Renseignements sur la situation des colonies. Soudan français. Mission militaire de Bakhounou (1890-1891)," *JORF*, Jan. 11, 13, 1892, 153-156, 240-244.

5618

. Marriott, H. P. Fitzgerald. "The Secret Societies of West Africa," *JAI*, XXIX(1899), 21-24.

5619

. Marshall, James [*Sir*]. *Handbook to the West African Court.* London: W. Clowes & Sons, 1886. 37p.

5620

. Martínez y Sanz, Miguel. *Breves apuntes sobre la Isla de Fernando Po en el Golfo de Guinea.* Madrid: Reneses, 1859. 104p.

5621

. Mattei, Antoine [*Commandant*]. *Bas-Niger, Bénoué, Dahomey.* Grenoble: Vallier, 1890. 199p.

5622

. Mauléon, De. "Le cap des Palmes, le Dahomey, Fernando Po et l'Île du Prince," *Revue Coloniale*, VI(1845), 69.

5623

. Menvielle. [*Capt.*]. "Le Soudan français," *Bulletin de la Société de Géographie de Toulouse*, XVIII(1890), 229-260.

5624

. Merrick, J. and others. "Letters from West Africa," *BM*, XLI(1849), 53-54, 181-183, 458, 591-593, 657-660, 722; XLII(1850), 120-121, 242-243, 506-510, 647-649; XLIII(1851), 51-52, 463-468, 662-663, 730-732.

5625 . Mévil, Andre. *Samory. Préface du Général de Trentinian.* Paris: Flammarion, 1899. 267p.

5626 . Michel. "Notes sur le Sénégal et le Soudan français," *Bulletin de la Société de Géographie Commercial de Bordeaux,* 2nd Series, X(1887), 597-613.

5627 . Miller, Thomas [*Commander, Royal Navy*]. "Western Africa: Its Coast, Resources, and Trade," *Nautical Magazine and Naval Chronicle,* 1855, pp. 291-296, 345-355.

5628 . Moḥammad ibn ʿOmar al Tounisī ibn Solaimān. *Voyage au Ouadây.* Translated by A. Perron. 2 vols. Paris: Duprat, 1851.

5629 . Moister, William. *Memorials of Missionary Labours in Western Africa and the West Indies; with Historical and Descriptive Observations.* London, 1850. New York: Lane & Scott, 1851. 348p. 3d Ed. London, 1866. 592p

5630 . Moloney, A. "On the Melodies of the Volof, Mandingo, Ewe, Yoruba, and Houssa People of West Africa," *JMGS,* V(1889), 277-298.

5631 . Moloney, Cornelius Alfred. *Sketch of the Forestry of West Africa, with Particular Reference to Its Present Principal Commercial Products.* London: Sampson Low, 1887. 533p.

5632 . Monnier, Marcel. "De la côte d'Ivoire au Soudan méridional: mission de M. le capitaine Binger," *CRSG,* XI(1892), 499-529.

5633 . _____. *France noire. Côte d'Ivoire et Soudan. Mission Binger.* Paris: Plon, 1893. 299p.

5634 . Monrad, Hans Christian. *Gemälde der Kuste von Guinea, und der Einwohner derselben, wie auch der dänischen Colonien auf dieser Küste; entworfen . . .in den Jahren, 1805 bis 1809. Aus Dänischen ubersetz von H. E. Wolf.* Weimar: Landes-Industrie, 1824. 388p.

5635 . Monteil, Parfait-Louis. *De Saint-Louis à Tripoli par le lac Tchad, voyage au travers du Sudan et du Sahara accompli pendant les annees 1890-91-92.* Paris: Alcan, 1895. 462p.

5636 . _____. "Sénégal et Soudan," *BSGP,* 7th Series, VIII(1886), 101-115.

5637 _____. *Souvenirs vécus. Quelques feuillets de l'histoire coloniale. Les rivalités internationales.* Preface de M. le Géréral Mangin. Paris, 1924. 157p.

5638 . Morrell, Benjamin. *Narrative of a Voyage to the South and West Coast of Africa: Containing the Information from Whence Originated the Present Trade in Guano, Founded on Certain Islands on the Coast.* London: Whittaker, 1844. 144p.

5639 _____. *A Narrative of Four Voyages to the South Sea, North and South Pacific Ocean, Chinese Sea, Ethiopic and Southern Atlantic Ocean, Indian and Antartic Ocean, from the Year 1822 to 1831; Comprising Critical Surveys of Coasts and Islands, with Sailing Directions and an Account of Some New and Valuable Discoveries, etc.* New York: J. & J. Harper, 1832. 492p.

5640 Muḥammad Bartā. *Appendix to Benjamin Anderson's Journey to Musadu. An Exact Facsimile of a Letter from the King of Musadu to the President of Liberia Written by a Young Mandingo at Musadu, in Arabic, in the Latter Part of 1868.* Translated by E. W. Blyden. New York, 1870. 14p.

5641 . Muteau, A. *De Paris à Paris, par Lisbonne, le Sénégal et le Soudan.* Paris: La Nouvelle Revue, 1898. 76p.

5642 . Nachtigal, Gustav [Dr.]. "Journey to Lake Chad and Neighbouring Regions," *JRGS,* XLVI(1876), 396-411.

5643 . _____. "Neueste Nachrichten von Dr. Nachtigal in Kuka (bis januar 1871). Ethnographie von Wadai," *PM,* XVII(1871), 326-334.

5644 _____. "Reise von Kanem nach Borku," *ZGE,* VIII(1873), 141-158.

5645 _____. "Voyage du Bornou au Baguirmi," *TM,* XL(1880), 337-416.

5646 . "Naval Officer." "Life in a Gunboat on the West Coast of Africa," *United Service Magazine*, July, 1849, pp. 344-349.

5647 . Nogueira, A. F. "A ilha de S. Thomé," *BSGL*, V(1885), 401-455.

5648 Oberlander, R. *West Afrika, vom Senegal bis Benguela*. Leipzig: O. Spanner, 1878. 464p.

5649 . O'Connor, L. Smyth [*Colonel*]. "Notes on an Expedition down the Western Coast of Africa to the Bijuga Islands, and the Recently Discovered River Kittaniny," *PRGS*, III(1858-1859), 379-385.

5650 . Olivier, E. "Les routes commerciales du Soudan," *Revue Coloniale*, II (1897), 69-70.

5651 Ollone, Hestains d'. *De la côte d'Ivoire au Soudan et à la Guinée, 1898-1900*. Paris: Hachette, 1901.

5652 . _____. "Côte d'Ivore et Liberia. Variations cartographiques relatives à ces contrées et état actuel de nos connaissances," *AG*, XII (1903), 130-144.

5653 . Ord, Harry St. George [*Maj. Gen.*]. *Report of Colonel Ord, the Commissioner Appointed to Inquire into the Condition of the British Settlements on the West Coast of Africa*. London: Colonial Office, 1865. 51p.

5654 Park, Mungo. *Journal of a Mission to the Interior of Africa in the Year 1805. Together with Other Documents. . .Relating to the Same Mission*. London: Murray, 1815. 219p.

5655 _____. *Travels in the Interior Districts of Africa: Performed under the Direction and Patronage of the African Association, in the Years 1795, 1796 and 1797*. Edited by Bryan Edwards. London, 1799.

5656 . Peney, Alfred. "Études sur l'ethnographie, la physiologie, l'anatomie, et les maladies des races du Soudan," *BSGP*, 4th Series, XVII (1859), 321-355.

5657 . Pereira Carneiro, Don Jacinto. "Memoir on the Trade to the West Coast of Africa Northward of the Equator," *Nautical Magazine and Naval Chronicle*, 1855, pp. 407-415.

5658 Péroz, Marie Étienne. *Au Niger. Récits de Campagnes, 1891-1892*. Paris: Lévy, 1894. 426p.

5659 _____. *Par vocation. Vie et aventures d'un soldat de fortune, 1870-1895*. Paris: Calmann-Lévy, 1905. 533p.

5660 Philebert, Charles. *La conquête pacifique de l'intérieur africain, nègres, musulmans et chretiens*. Paris: Leroux, 1889. 376p.

5661 . Plouzanne, E. F. *Contribution à l'étude de l'hygiène des troupes européennes en campange dans les pays intertropicaux, Haut-Sénégal et Haut-Niger*. Bordeaux: Impr. Cadoret, 1887. 53p.

5662 . Pouyer. [*Lt.*]. "Le commerce Européen a la côte occidentale d'Afrique depuis le Sénégal jusqu'à Saint Paul de Loanda," *Revue Maritime et Coloniale*, XXXIX(1874), 225-238.

5663 . Prax. [*Vice-Consul de France*]. *Le commerce de l'Algérie avec la Mecque et le Soudan; routes suivies par les caravanes*. Paris: Rouvier, 1849. 32p.

5664 Quinquandon, F. [*Capt.*]. "Mission du Dr. Tautain et du capitaine Quinquandon dans le Bélédougou et le pays au Nord de cette région," *Bulletin de la Société de Géographie Commercial de Bordeaux*, 2nd Series, XI(1888), 1-13.

5665 _____. "Rapport...par le capitaine Quinquandon...sur sa Mission auprès Tiéba, roi de Kénédougou," *Bulletin de la Société Bretonne de Géographie,* XI(1892), 31-74, 95-132.

5666 . Rabenhorst, Rudolf. "Beobachtungen in Westafrika," *DK,* III(1886),498-503.

5667 . \_\_\_\_\_. "Die Katholische Mission in Westafrika," *DK,* III(1886), 344-347.

5668 . Rackow, Hermann. "Pflanzerleben in Westafrika," *DK,* XV(1898), 206-208.

5669 . Raffenel, "Divers itinéraires de la Sénégambie et du Soudan," *BSGP,* 3rd Series, XII(1849), 303.

5670 _____. "Exploration du pays de Galam, du Bondou et du Bambouk, et retour par la Gambie," *Revue Coloniale,* 1st Series, IV(1844), 136-218.

5671 . \_\_\_\_\_. *Rapport sur le pays de Galam, le Bondou et le Bambouk, addressé le 17 mars 1844 au gouverneur du Sénégal.* Paris: Impr. Royale, 1844.

5672 . \_\_\_\_\_ "Second voyage d'exploration dans l'intérieur de l'Afrique, entrepris par M. A. Raffenel," *Revue Coloniale,* 1st Series, XI (1847), 296-304; XIII(1847), 1-47; 2nd Series, III(1848), 217-276. Also published as an extract, Paris: P. Dupont, 1850. 90p.

5673 . Ramsay, T. W. *Costumes on the West Coast of Africa, by an Officer of the Commisariat.* n.p., n.p., c.1830. 11p.

5674 . Reade, W. Winwood. "Extracts of Letters from W. Winwood Reade, Esq., to Andrew Swanzy, Esq., F.R.G.S, Relating to His Journeys in Western Africa," *PRGS,* XIII(18 8-1869), 353-359.

5675 . \_\_\_\_\_. "Report on a Journey to the Upper Waters of the Niger from Sierra Leone," *PRGS,* XIV(1869-1870), 185-188.

5676 . Reading, Joseph Hankinson. *A Voyage along the Western Coast: or, Newest Africa, a Description of Newest Africa, or, the Africa of To-day and the Immediate Future.* Philadelphia: Reading, 1901. 211p.

5677 . Reibell, Eugène. "La compagne contre Rabah," *Renseignements Coloniaux*, 1901, pp. 15-23.

5678 . Rey, H. "Notes sur la géographie médicale de la côte occidentale d'Afrique," *BSGP*, 6th Series, XVI(1878), 229.

5679 . Richardson, James. *Narrative of a Mission to Central Africa, Performed in the Years 1850-51*. 2 vols. London: Chapman and Hall, 1853.

5680 . _____. *Travels in the Great Desert of Sahara, in 1845 and 1846; Including a Description of the Oases and Cities of Ghat, Ghadames, and Mourzuk*. 2 vols. London: R. Bentley, 1848.

5681 . Riley, James. *An Authentic Narrative of the Loss of the American Brig Commerce, Wrecked on the Western Coast of Africa in the Month of August, 1815*. New York: T.W.W. Mercein, 1817. 554p.

5682 . Robbins, Archibald. *A Journal Comprising an Account of the Loss of the Brig Commerce, of Hartford, Conn.; James Riley, Master: upon the Western Coast of Africa, August 28, 1815; Also of the Slavery and Sufferings of the Author and the Rest of the Crew, upon the Desert of Zahara, in the Years 1815, 1816, 1817*. Hartford, Conn.: Andrus & Son, 1851. 275p.

5683 . Robert, Maurice. *Du Sénégal au Niger*. Paris: Challamel aîné, 1879.

5684 . Robertson, G. A. *Notes on Africa, between Cape Verde and the River Congo*. London: Sherwood, Neeley, and Jones, 1819. 460p. Also, *Walckenaer's Voyages*, XI(1842), 408-483.

5685 . Robinson, C. H. "Hausa Pilgrimages from the Western Sudan, Together with a Native Account of the Death of General Gordon," *GJ*, II (1893), 451-454.

5686 _____. "The Slave Trade in the West African Hinterland," *Contemporary Review*, LXXIII(1898), 698-705.

5687 Rohlfs, Friedrich Gerhard. *Beiträge zur Entdeckung und Erforschung Afrika's. Berichte aus den Jahren 1870-1875.* Leipzig: Dürr'sche, 1876. 266p.

5688 _____. *Land und Volk in Africa. Berichte aus dem Jahren 1865-1870.* Bremen: J. Kuhtmann, 1870. 240p.

5689 _____. "Letters from Mr. Gerhard Rohlfs to Sir R. I. Murchison," *PRGS*, XI(1866-1867), 33-35.

5690 _____. *Quer durch Afrika. Reise von Mittelmeer nach dem Tschad-See und zum Golf von Guinea.* 2 vols. Leipzig: Brockhaus, 1874.

5691 _____. *Reise durch Nord-Afrika vom mittelländischen Meere bis zum Busen von Guinea 1865 bis 1867.* 2 vols. Gotha: Perthes, 1868-1872.

5692 Roussin, Albin René [*Baron*]. "Voyage d'Albert Roussin, capitaine de vaisseau, en 1817 et 1818: navigation aux côtes occidental d'Africa depues le cap Bojador jusqu'à mont Souros," *Walckenaer's Voyages*, VI(1842), 297-354.

5693 Ruxton, W. F. "Extracts from Commander W. F. Ruxton's Report on Various Rivers on the West Coast of Africa," *PRGS*, X(1865-1866), 66-69.

5694 Saker, A.; Prince, C. K.; and others. "Letters from West Africa," *BM*, XXXIX(1847), 590-593, 663-664, 730-731; XL(1848), 52-53, 114, 441-443, 507-509, 634-635, 701-702.

5695 Salesses, Pierre-Eugène-Mathurin. [*Lt.Col.*]. "Le chemin de fer de Conakry au Niger navigable (Mission 1898)," *Renseignements Coloniaux* [du Comite de l'Afrique française], 1898, 225-240.

5696 _____. "Les chemins de fer de l'Afrique occidentale française," *Bulletin de la Société de Géographie Commerciale de Paris*, XXXI (1909), 47-63.

5697 _____. "De Conakry au Niger," *BSGP*, 7th Series, XX(1899), 365-411.

5698 . _____. "Les voies de pénétration dans les pays tropicaux," Bulletin du Comite de l'Afrique Française, (1897), 337-341.

5699 . Sanderval, A. O. Le Niger et le Soudan, projet de chemin de fer de la côte Niger par le Foutah-Djallon. Paris: Pillet et Dumoulin, 1881. 4p.

5700 . Sarrazin, Henri-Étienne-Gaston. Races humaines du Soudan français. Chambéry: Impr. Générale de Savoie, 1901. 306p.

5701 . Schlechter, Friedrich Reichardt Rudolph. Westafrikanische Kautschuk-Expedition. . .1899-1900. Berlin: Deutsche Kolonialblatt, 1900. 326.

5702 . Seeger. "Die Sklaverei im Togolande und der englischen Goldküstenkolonie," DK, IX(1892), 54-56.

5703 . Seidel, H. "Islam und Moscheen im Westlichen Sudan," Globus, LXI(1892), 328-331.

5704 . Sevin-Desplaces. "Soudan et Dahomey," Nouvelle Geographie, V(1892), 67-68.

5705 . Smith, John. Trade and Travels in the Gulph of Guinea, Western Africa, with an Account of the Manners, Habits, Customs, and Religion of the Inhabitants. London: Simpkin & Marshall, 1851. 223p.

5706 . Smith, Robert. "Trials of the Converts in Africa," BM, LV(1863), 804.

5707 . Soleillet, Paul. Les voyages et découvertes de Paul Soleillet dans le Sahara et dans le Soudan, en vue d'un projet d'un chemin de fer transsaharien. Paris: M. Dreyfous, 1881. 241p.

5708 . Soleillet, J.J.M.M.P. Voyage d'Alger à Saint-Louis du Sénégal par Tombouctou. Avignon: François Seguin, 1875. 33p.

5709 . Soller, C. "Les caravanes du Soudan occidental et les pêcheries d'Arguin," *Bulletin de la Société de Géographie Commerciale de Paris*, X(1888), 280-297.

5710 . Sorela, Luis. *Les possessions espagnoles du Golfe de Guinée, leur présent et leur avenir*. Paris: Lahure, 1884. 46p.

5711 Soyaux, Herman *Aus West-Afrika, 1873-76. Erlebnisse und Beobachtungen*. 2 vols. Leipzig: Brockhaus, 1879.

5712 . Spilsbury, Francis B. *Account of a Voyage to the Western Coast of Africa*. London, 1807.

5713 . Staudinger, P. "Kano im Vergleich zu Timbuktu," *DK*, XI(1894), 37-38.

5714 . Steiner, P. "Die religiösen Vorstellungen von Gott bei den Westafrikanern," *Globus*, LXV(1894), 52-55.

5715 . Stokes, Robert. *Regulated Slave Trade: Reprinted from the Evidence. . . Given before the Select Committee of the House of Lords in 1849*. London: Ridgeway, 1850.

5716 . Stopford, J. G. B. "Glimpses of Native Law in West Africa: the Law of Inheritance, the Law of Breach of Promise, the Law of Slander, Secret Societies," *Journal of the Royal African Society*, I(1901), 80-97.

5717 . Tautain, L. [*Dr.*]. "Contribution a l'étude de la pathologie des Mandingues," *Bulletin et Mémoires de la Société d'Anthropologie de Paris*, VII(1884), 532-540.

5718 . _____. "Le domaine géographique des Mandingues," *Revue d'Ethnographie*, V(1886), 545-547.

5719 . _____. "Légendes et traditions des Soninké relatives à l'empire de Ghanata, d'après des notes recueilles pendant une tournée de Bamako à Sokoto, Gumba, etc., en 1887," *Bulletin de Géographie Historique et Descriptive*, (1895), 472-480.

5720 . Thomas, Charles W. *Adventures and Observations on the West Coast of Africa and Its Islands, Historical and Descriptive Sketches of Madeira, Canary, and Cape Verd Islands.* New York: Derby & Jackson, 1860. 479p. London, 1864.

5721 . Thompson, George. *The Palm Land; or West Africa, Illustrated. Being a History of Missionary Labors and Travels, with Descriptions of Men and Things in Western Africa.* Cincinnati: Moore, Wilstach, Keys, 1859. 456p.

5722 . _____. *Thompson in Africa: or, an Account of the Missionary Labors, Sufferings, Travels and Observations of George Thompson in West Africa at the Mendi Mission.* New York: George Thompson, 1852. 356p.

5723 . Thompson, William Cooper. "Narrative of a Journey from Sierra Leone to Timbu, Capital of Fútah Jállo, in Western Africa," *JRGS*, XVI (1846), 106-138.

5724 . Thomson, Joseph. "Mohammedanism in Central Africa," *Contemporary Review*, L(1887), 876-883.

5725 . Toutée, Georges Joseph [*Général*]. *Dahomé, Niger, Touareg. Récit de Voyage.* Paris: Colin, 1897. 370p.

5726 _____. *Du Dahomé au Sahara. La nature et l'homme.* Paris: Colin, 1899. 272p.

5727 . _____. "Les essences forestières dans la zone équatoriale," *Académie d'Agriculture de France*, VI(1921), 545-554.

5728 . Travassos Valdez, Francisco. *Six Years of a Traveller's Life in Western Africa*. 2 vols. London: Hurst & Blackett, 1861. Portuguese Ed., *Africa occidental: noticias e consideraçoes*. Lisbon: da Silva, 1864.

5729 . Trentinian, De. [*Général*]. "Extraits du compte rendu de la situation commerciale du Soudan français, région Sénégal et région Sud, à la fin de l'année 1898," *Revue Coloniale*, V(1899), 537-551.

5730 . Trew, J. M. [*Rev.*]. *Africa Wasted by Britain, and Restored by Native Agency, in a Letter to the Bishop of London*. London: J. Hatchard and Son, 1843. 61p.

5731 . Valbert, G. "Le chemin de fer du Soudan et les trois campagnes du colonel Borgnis-Desbordes," *Revue des deux Mondes*, (Oct., 1883), 681-692.

5732 . Vallière, J. [*Capt.*]. "Situation politique des états situés entre le Sénégal et le Niger," *Bulletin de la Société Géographie Commerciale de Bordeaux*, IV(1881), 451-468.

5733 . Venn, Henry [*Rev.*]. *West African Colonies. Notices of the British Colonies on the West Coast of Africa*. London, n.p., 1865. 39p.

5734 . Venture de Paradis. "Itinéraires sur les pays compris entre le Maroc, Tombouctou et le Sénégal," *BSGP*, 3rd Series, XI(1849), 100-105.

5735 . Vigne d'Octon, Paul. *Terre de mort—Soudan et Dahomey*. Paris: Marpon, 1892. 285p.

5736 . Vincent. [*Capt.*]. "Extrait d'un voyage exécuté, en 1860, dans le Sahara occidental," *BSGP*, 5th Series, I(1861), 5-37.

5737 . _____. "Voyage dans l'Adrar et retour à Saint-Louis," *TM*, III(1861).

5738 . Virchow, R. "Über Akka," *ZE*, XIX(1887).

5739 . Vischer, Hanns. "A Journey from Tripoli across the Sahara to Lake Chad," *GJ*, XXXIII(1909), 241-264.

5740 . Vogel, Edward. "Mission to Central Africa," *JRGS*, XXV(1855), 237-245.

5741 . _____. "Notes from the Mission to Central Africa," *PRGS*, II(1857-1858), 30-35.

5742 . _____ and others. "Mission to Central Africa," *JRGS*, XXIV(1854), 276-283.

5743 . Vohsen, Ernst. "Eine Reise durch das Timméné-Land," *PM*, XXIX(1883), 373-376.

5744 . _____. "Der Tschadsee," *DK*, XVII(1900), 186.

5745 . Walckenaer, Charles Athanase. *Recherches géographiques sur l'intérieur de l'Afrique septentrionale, comprenant l'histoire des voyages entrepris ou exécutés jusqu'à ce jour pour pénétrer dans l'intérieur du Soudan; l'exposition des systèmes géographiques qu'on à formés sur cette contrée; l'analyse de divers itinéraires Arabes pour déterminer la position de Timbouctou; et l'examen des connaissances des anciens relativement a l'intérieur de l'Afrique: suivies d'un appendice, contenant divers itinéraires, traduits de l'Arabe.* Paris: Didot, 1821. 526p.

5746 . Walker, S. A. *Missions in Western Africa, among the Soosoos, Bulloms, etc., Being the First Undertaken by the Church Missionary Society for Africa and the East.* Dublin: Curry, 1845.

5747 . Welty, Aloyse. "Lettre," *BGCSS*, III(1862-1863), 509-510.

5748 Whitford, John. *Trading Life in Western and Central Africa*. Liverpool: "Porcupine" Office, 1877. 335p.

5749 Whiton, Samuel J. *Glimpses of West Africa, with Sketches of Missionary Labor*. Boston: American Tract Society, 1866. 208p.

5750 Wilson, John Leighton. [Rev.]. *Western Africa, Its History, Condition, and Prospects*. New York: Harper; London: Sampson, Low, 1856. 527p.

5751 . Zahn, F. M. *Vier Freistätten im Sclavenlande; Nochmals sechs Jahre Missions-Arbeit in Westafrika*. Bremen: Rilgerloch, 1870. 104p.

5752 . Zöller, Hugo. *Die deutschen Besitzungen an der westafrikanischen Küste*. Berlin: Spimann, 1885.

5753 . Zündel, G. "Land und Volk der Eweer auf der Sklavenküste in Westafrika," *ZGE*, 1877, pp. 376, 401.

5754 . Autenrieth, F. R. *Der Anbruch e. neuen Zeit in Deutsch-Kamerun.* Stuttgart: Holland & Josenhans, 1900. 130p.

5755 . _____ *Ins Inner-Hochland von Kamerun.* Stuttgart: Holland & Josenhans, 1900. 160p.

5756 . Bachmaier, Sebastian. "Missionsbriefe," *Echo aus Afrika,* VI(1894), 78, 94-96.

5757 . _____. "Missionsbriefe," *Stern von Afrika,* I(1894), 22, 46.

5758 . Bancken, Friedrich. "Missionsbriefe," *Stern von Afrika,* I(1894), 12, 91; VIII(1901), 75.

5759 . Bernstorff. [*Graf von*]. "Ein 'Trade'," *DK,* XVI(1899), 369-370.

5760 . Betz, R. "Die Trommelsprache der Duala," *MDS,* XI(1899), 1-86.

5761 . Böckner, C. "Streifzüge in Kamerun," *DK,* X(1893), 7-9, 35-37, 74-75.

5762 . Bohner, Heinrich. "Sklaverei und Sklavenhandel in Kamerun," *Evangelisch Missions Magazine,* 1893, pp.16-29.

5763 . Borchert, Wilhelm. "Missionsbriefe," *Stern von Afrika,* I(1894), 68.

5764 . Brockmann, Paul. "Missionsbriefe," *Stern von Afrika,* VII(1900), 43-46, 59-61.

5765 . Büchner, Max. *Kamerun. Skizzen und Betrachtungen.* Leipzig: Deniker, 1887. 259p.

5766 . _____. "Kamerun-Englisch," *DK,* II(1885), 676-678.

5767 . Burton, Richard Francis. *Abeokuta and the Camaroons Mountains. An Exploration.* 2 vols. London: Tinsley, 1863.

5768 . _____. "Account of the Ascent of the Camaroons Mountain, in Western Africa," *PRGS,* VI(1861-1862), 238-248.

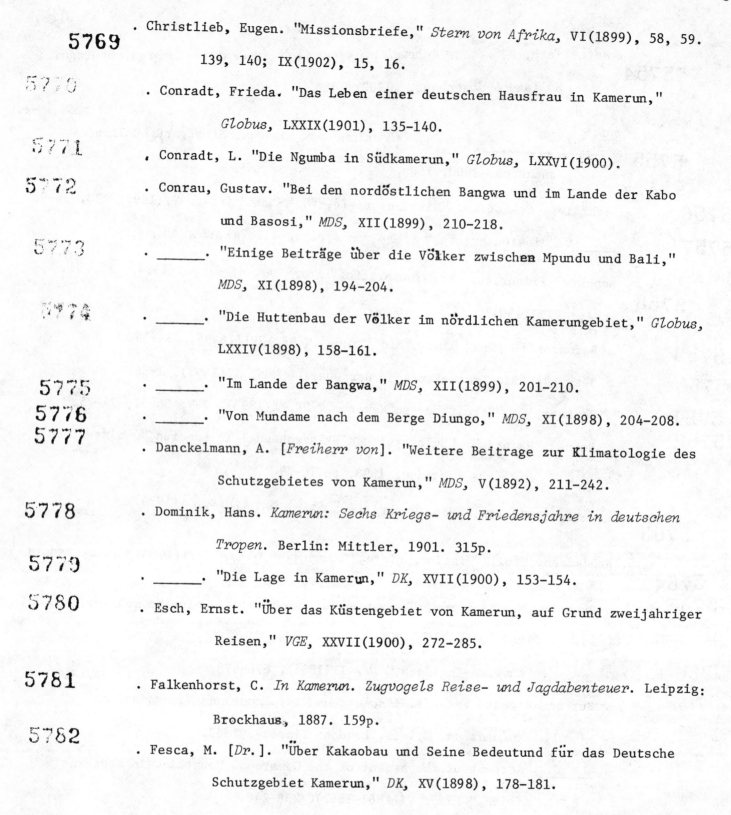

5769 · Christlieb, Eugen. "Missionsbriefe," *Stern von Afrika*, VI(1899), 58, 59. 139, 140; IX(1902), 15, 16.

5770 · Conradt, Frieda. "Das Leben einer deutschen Hausfrau in Kamerun," *Globus*, LXXIX(1901), 135-140.

5771 · Conradt, L. "Die Ngumba in Südkamerun," *Globus*, LXXVI(1900).

5772 · Conrau, Gustav. "Bei den nordöstlichen Bangwa und im Lande der Kabo und Basosi," *MDS*, XII(1899), 210-218.

5773 · _____. "Einige Beiträge über die Völker zwischen Mpundu und Bali," *MDS*, XI(1898), 194-204.

5774 · _____. "Die Huttenbau der Völker im nördlichen Kamerungebiet," *Globus*, LXXIV(1898), 158-161.

5775 · _____. "Im Lande der Bangwa," *MDS*, XII(1899), 201-210.

5776 · _____. "Von Mundame nach dem Berge Diungo," *MDS*, XI(1898), 204-208.

5777 · Danckelmann, A. [*Freiherr von*]. "Weitere Beitrage zur Klimatologie des Schutzgebietes von Kamerun," *MDS*, V(1892), 211-242.

5778 · Dominik, Hans. *Kamerun: Sechs Kriegs- und Friedensjahre in deutschen Tropen*. Berlin: Mittler, 1901. 315p.

5779 · _____. "Die Lage in Kamerun," *DK*, XVII(1900), 153-154.

5780 · Esch, Ernst. "Über das Küstengebiet von Kamerun, auf Grund zweijahriger Reisen," *VGE*, XXVII(1900), 272-285.

5781 · Falkenhorst, C. *In Kamerun. Zugvogels Reise- und Jagdabenteuer*. Leipzig: Brockhaus, 1887. 159p.

5782 · Fesca, M. [*Dr.*]. "Über Kakaobau und Seine Bedeutund für das Deutsche Schutzgebiet Kamerun," *DK*, XV(1898), 178-181.

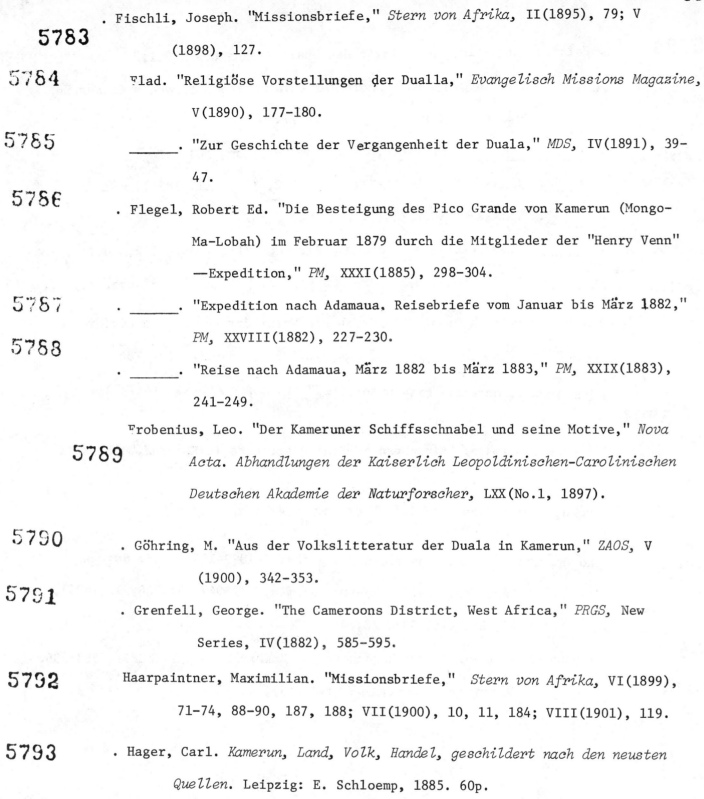

5783 . Fischli, Joseph. "Missionsbriefe," *Stern von Afrika*, II(1895), 79; V (1898), 127.

5784 Flad. "Religiöse Vorstellungen der Dualla," *Evangelisch Missions Magazine*, V(1890), 177-180.

5785 _____. "Zur Geschichte der Vergangenheit der Duala," *MDS*, IV(1891), 39-47.

5786 . Flegel, Robert Ed. "Die Besteigung des Pico Grande von Kamerun (Mongo-Ma-Lobah) im Februar 1879 durch die Mitglieder der "Henry Venn"—Expedition," *PM*, XXXI(1885), 298-304.

5787 . _____. "Expedition nach Adamaua. Reisebriefe vom Januar bis März 1882," *PM*, XXVIII(1882), 227-230.

5788 . _____. "Reise nach Adamaua, März 1882 bis März 1883," *PM*, XXIX(1883), 241-249.

5789 Frobenius, Leo. "Der Kameruner Schiffsschnabel und seine Motive," *Nova Acta. Abhandlungen der Kaiserlich Leopoldinischen-Carolinischen Deutschen Akademie der Naturforscher*, LXX(No.1, 1897).

5790 . Göhring, M. "Aus der Volkslitteratur der Duala in Kamerun," *ZAOS*, V (1900), 342-353.

5791 . Grenfell, George. "The Cameroons District, West Africa," *PRGS*, New Series, IV(1882), 585-595.

5792 Haarpaintner, Maximilian. "Missionsbriefe," *Stern von Afrika*, VI(1899), 71-74, 88-90, 187, 188; VII(1900), 10, 11, 184; VIII(1901), 119.

5793 . Hager, Carl. *Kamerun, Land, Volk, Handel, geschildert nach den neusten Quellen*. Leipzig: E. Schloemp, 1885. 60p.

5794 . Halbing, Augustin. "Genealogie des Duala, sohns des Mbêdi,"

Mitteilungen des Seminars für Orientalische Sprachen zu Berlin,

IX(1906), Abtlg. III. pp. 259-277.

5795 . _____. "Lettere," MCM, XX(1891), 55, 543.

5796 . _____. "Lettres," APFL, LXIII(1891), 152, 153; LXIV(1892), 74, 75.

5797 . _____. "Lettres," MCL, XXIII(1891), 481, 482.

5798 . _____. "Missionsbriefe," Echo aus Afrika, XVIII(1906), 159, 160.

5799 . _____. "Missionsbriefe," Stern von Afrika, VIII(1901), 37, 55, 71, 88,

5800 . Hammerstein, A. von. "Die Gegebenen Vorbilder für den Landbau im

Camerun-Gebiet," Globus, IL(1886), 169-172, 184-186.

. Hanewinkel, Martin. "Missionsbriefe," Stern von Afrika, II(1895), 92.

5801

5802 . Hesse, Hermann. "Eingebornen—Schiedsgerichte in Kamerun," DK, XIII

(1896), 299-300.

. Högn, Karl. "Missionsbriefe," Stern von Afrika, VII(1900), 25, 58, 140.

5803

5804 . Höver, Joseph. "Missionsbriefe," KM, XXVIII(1899-1900), 87, 88;

"Missionsbriefe," Stern von Afrika, I(1894), 35, 36; II(1895),

38-40, 66; VI(1899), 23, 41.

5805 . Hübbe-Schleiden. "Frohe Botschaft aus Kamerun," DK, IV(1887), 583-586.

5806 . _____. "Kameruns Zukunft," DK, IV(1887), 429-432.

5807 . Hübler, Michael. *Zur Klimatographie von Kamerun.* Munich, 1896. 88p. *Münchener Geographische Studien,* Vol. I.

5808 . Hutter, Franz Karl. [*Hauptmann*]. "Der Abschluss von Blutsfreundschaft und Verträgen bei den Negern des Graslandes in Nordkamerun," *Globus,* LXXV(1899), 1-4.

5809 . _____. "Mein Aufenthalt bei den Balis, 1891-93," *DK,* X(1893), 99-101.

5810 . _____. "Politische und Sociale Verhältnisse bei den Graslandstämmen Nordkameruns," *Globus,* LXXVI(1899), 284-289, 303-309.

5811 . _____. "Die Völkerstämme an der Südgrenze Adamauas (Nordkamerun)," *Globus,* LXXV(1899), 377-382.

5812 . _____. *Wanderungen und Forschungen im Nord-hinterland von Kamerun.* Braunschweig: Vieweg, 1902. 578p.

5813 . _____. "Die Zeichensprache bei den Negern des Wald- und Graslandes in in Nordkamerun," *Globus,* LXXIV(1898), 201-204.

5814 _____. "Zeremonien beim Schliessen von Blutfreundschaft bei den Graslandstämmen im Kamerun-Hinterland," *MDS,* V(1892), 176-178.

5815 . Imhof, Johann. "Missionsbriefe," *Echo aus Afrika,* VI(1894), 4, 5.

5816 . _____. "Missionsbriefe," *Stern von Afrika,* I(1894), 31.

5817 . Jäger, Johann. "Missionsbriefe," *Stern von Afrika,* I(1894), 77.

5818 . Johnston, Harry Hamilton. "Explorations in the Cameroons District of Western Equatorial Africa," *SGM,* IV(1888), 513-536.

5819 . Kingsley, Mary H. *The Ascent of Cameroon's Peak and Travels in French Congo.* Liverpool: Liverpool Geographical Society, 1896. 20p.

5820 . Kirchoff, Alfred. "Aus dem Süden der Kamerun-Kolonie," *PM,* XXXII(1886), 144-146.

5821 · Klosterknecht, Joseph. "Missionsbriefe," *Echo aus Afrika*, III(1891), 12, 13, 19, 20, 41, 42.

5822 · _____. "Missionsbriefe," *KM*, XIX(1891), 110, 111.

5823 · König, Franz. "Missionsbriefe," *Echo aus Afrika*, IX(1897), 94-98.

5824 · _____. "Missionsbriefe," *Stern von Afrika*, II(1895), 45, 70, 71, 76; III (1896), 23-28, 30, 31; IV(1897), 8, 15, 23, 32, 69, 79, 80, 86, 94; V(1898), 41, 58, 86, 105; VI(1899), 13, 14, 107, 108; VII(1900), 184-186; VIII(1901), 42, 150, 174, 188.

5825 · Kohler, J. *Über das Negerrecht, namentlich in Kamerun.* Stuttgart: F. Enke, 1895. 64p.

5826 · Kopf, Vinzenz. "Missionsbriefe," *Stern von Afrika*, VIII(1901), 119.

5827 · Kreuzkamp, Joachim. "Missionsbriefe," *Stern von Afrika*, VI(1899), 123-125.

5828 · Kuentz, Joseph. "Missionsbriefe," *Lis de St-Joseph*, XII(1901), 341, 342.

5829 · Kugelmann, Max. "Missionsbriefe," *KM*, XX(1892), 15, 16, 67, 68; XXIV(1896), 235.

5830 · Langhans, Paul. "Das Kamerun-Gebirge," *PM*, XXXI(1885), 421.

5831 · Matzat, H. "Regenmessungen aus Kamerun," *PM*, XLVI(1900), 21.

5832 · Mayer, Jakob. "Missionsbriefe," *Stern von Afrika*, III(1896), 5, 12.

5833 · Meinhof, Carl. "Benga und Dualla," *ZAS*, II(1888-1889), 190-208.

5834 · Merrick, J. "A Visit to the Camaroon Mountains," *BM*, XXXVII(1845), 98-108.

5835 · Milligan, Robert H. *The Fetish Folk of West Africa.* New York: Revell, 1912. 328p.

5836 · Morgen, Curt von. *Durch Kamerun von Süd nach Nord. Reisen und Forschungen im Hinterlande 1889 bis 1891.* Leipzig: Brockhaus, 1893. 390p.

5837     Müller, Joseph. "Missionsbriefe," *Stern von Afrika*, IV(1897), 7, 64, 82, 89, 94; V(1898), 9, 29, 43, 59, 73, 88, 139, 171; VI(1899), 10-12, 30-32, 42-44, 61-63, 76, 77, 92-95, 108-111, 125, 156, 157, 174, 175, 190, 191; VII(1900), 7-10, 13, 14, 28-31, 46-48, 61-63.

5838     Münch, Friedrich. "Missionsbriefe," *Stern von Afrika*, VII(1900), 168-170; VIII(1901), 140, 174.

5839     Otto, Ludwig. "Lettere," *MCM*, XXV(1896), 172, 173, 469-472; XXVI(1897), 208; XXVII(1898), 78; XXVIII(1899), 148, 149.

5840     . _____. "Missionsbriefe," *Stern von Afrika*, III(1896), 46, 52-55, 71; IV (1897), 56, 72; V(1898), 7, 26.

5841     . Passarge, Siegfried. *Adamaua. Bericht über die Expedition des Deutschen Kamerun-Komitees in den Jahren 1893-1894*. Berlin: Reimer, 1895. 573p. Also, *DK*, XIII(1896), 11-12, and *VGE*, XXI(1894), 369-378.

5842     . _____. "Die Besitzergreifung des Hinterlanders von Kamerun," *DK*, XVI (1899), 69-72.

5843     . _____. "Garua," *DK*, XIII(1896), 121-124.

5844     . _____. "The German Expedition to Adamawa," *GJ*, V(1895), 50-53.

5845     . _____. "Gold im Hinterland von Kamerun," *DK*, XVI(1899), 21-22.

5846     . _____. *Kamerun*. Leipzig, 1910.

5847     . _____; Warburg, D.; and Wohltmann, F. "Die Zukunft unserer Kolonie Kamerun," *DK*, XVI(1899), 309-312.

5848 . Pauli. "Kamerun," *PM*, XXXI(1885), 13.

5849 . Plehn, Frederick. *Die Kamerun-Küste. Studien zur Zlimatologie, Physiologie und Pathologie in den Tropen*. Berlin: A. Hirschwald, 1898. 363p.

5850 . Prager, Erich. "Die Neue Station am Sanga-Ngoko," *DK*, XVI(1899), 271-272.

5851 Puttkamer, Jesko Albert Eugen von. *Gouverneursjahre in Kamerun*. Berlin: G. Stilke, 1912. 331p.

5852 . Rabenhorst, Rudolf. "Aus der Kamerunkolonie," *DK*, II(1885), 411-413.

5853 . Rackow, Herman. "Die Anwendung der Wechselwirtschaft im Tropischen Ackerbau," *DK*, XIII(1896), 114-116.

. Reichenow. "Über die deutsche Kolonie Kamerun," *VGE*, XI(1884), 358.

5854

5855 . Riebe, Otto. *Drei Jahre unter deutscher Flagge im Hinterland von Kamerun*. Berlin: Hayn, 1897. 102p.

5856 . Rieder, Michael. "Missionsbriefe," *Stern von Afrika*, VI(1899), 22, 23, 36, 37.

5857 . Rogozinski, Stefan. "Expedition nach dem Camerons," *PM*, XXIX(1883), 366-373.

5858 . _____. "Reisen im Kamerun-Gebiete," *PM*, XXX(1884), 132-139.

5859 . Ross, Alexander, and Langhans, Paul. "Vergessene Reisen in Kamerun. I. Reisen des Missionars Alexander Ross von Alt-Kalabar nach Efut, 1877 und 1878," *PM*, XLVIII(1902), 73-78.

5860 Saker, A. "Cameroons," *BM*, XXXVIII(1846), 123.

5861 . _____. "Letter from West Africa, Sept., 1856," *BM*, XLVIII(1856), 768-769.

5862 _____ and others. "Letters from Amboises Bay," *BM*, LI(1859), 583-585, 715-716; LII(1860), 50-53, 257-259, 530-532.

5863 . Schäfer, Johann. "Missionsbriefe," *Stern von Afrika*, VI(1899), 23-26; VII (1900), 122, 123; VIII(1901), 12.

5864 . Scheve, E. *Die Mission der deutschen Baptisten in Kamerun von 1884 bis 1901.* Berlin: F. G. Oncken, 1901. 126p.

5865 . Schickle. [*Missionary*]. "Missionsbriefe," *Stern von Afrika,* VI(1899), 26.

5866 . Schilitz, Alfons. "Missionsbriefe," *Echo Aus Afrika,* XIII(1901), 225-228.

5867 . _____. "Missionsbriefe," *Stern von Afrika,* II(1895), 92; IV(1897), 7; VI(1899), 155, 156, 164, 165; VIII(1901), 111, 119-121.

5868 Schoeller, Michael. "Missionsbriefe," *Stern von Afrika,* VII(1900), 110, 111.

5869 Schwab, *Gustav.* "Aus Unserem Schutzgebiet Kamerun," *DK,* XVI(1899), 476-496.

5870 _____. "Missionsbriefe," *Stern von Afrika,* V(1898), 157; VI(1899), 37-41, 162, 163.

5871 . Schwarz, Bernhard Wilhelm. *Kamerun: Reise in die Hinterlande der Kolonie.* Leipzig: Baldamus, 1888. 357p.

5872 . _____. "Rekognoszierungszug durch die Hinterlande von Kamerun," *DK,* III(1886), 260-270.

5873 . Seidel, August. *Deutsch-Kamerun.* Berlin: H. F. Meidinger, 1906. 367p.

5874 . Smith, Robert. "A Scene in African Missionary Life," *BM,* LV(1863), 122-123.

5875 . Stang, Peter. "Missionsbriefe," *KM,* XXIII(1895), 92, 93.

5876 . Staudinger, Paul. "Zu dem Metallvorkommen in Adamaua und Südkamerun," *DK,* XVI(1898), 34-35.

5877 . Stein. "Anthropologisches in Kamerun," *ZE,* XXIX(1897), 602-603.

5878 _____. "Erlaüterungen zu meinen Reisen in Süd Kamerun 1895-1899," *MDS,* XIII(1900), 93-108.

5879 _____. "Über den Ossa-(Lungas-)See, Kamerungebiet," *MDS,* X(1897), 155-164.

5380      . ————— "Über die geographischen Verhältnisse des Bezirks Lolodorf (Sud-Kamerun), Speziell die dort wohnenden Volksstämme," *MDS*, XII(1899).

5381      . Stenzel, Gregor. "Missionsbriefe," *Stern von Afrika*, VII(1900), 76-79; VIII(1901), 77, 92.

5382      Thormählen, Johannes. "Land und Leute in Kamerun," *DK*, I(1884), 417-420.

5383      . Valdan, Georg. "Schilderungen aus Kamerun," *DK*, VII(1890), 108-109. 123-126, 134-137, 146-149, 159-161, 171-172, 194-195.

5384      . Vierkandt, A. [*Dr.*]. *Die Volksdichte im westlichen Central=Afrika*. Leipzig: Duncker et Humblot, 1895. 110p.

5385      . Virchow, R. "Bagelli-Zwerge in Kamerun," *ZE*, XXV(1893).

5386      . Vohsen, Ernst. "Gando," *DK*, XVI(1899), 465-466.

5387      . Walter, Fritz. "Missionsbriefe," *Echo aus Afrika*, VII(1895), 109.

5388      ————— . "Missionsbriefe," *Stern von Afrika*, I(1894), 61; II(1895), 60; III(1896), 6, 13, 14.

5389      . Walter, Georg. "Missionsbriefe," *KM*, XX(1892), 255,256.

5390      . ————— . "Missionsbriefe," *Stern von Afrika*, I(1894), 11, 44, 45, 51-54, 62, 67, 69; III(1896), 45; IV(1897), 7, 16, 62, 71; VI(1899), 6, 7, 90-92, 103-107, 120-122, 138, 139, 171-174, 188-190.

5391      . Wheeler, John A. "Clarence Peak, from Bimbia," *BM*, XLVI(1854), 450-451.

5392      . ————— . "King Aqua's Town," *BM*, XLVI(1854), 50.

5393      . Wittum, Johanna. *Unterm Roten Kreuz in Kamerun und Togo*. Heidelberg: Evangelischer Verlag, 1899. 160p.

5894 . Wöhrmann, Bernard. "Missionsbriefe," *Stern von Afrika*, II(1895), 47.

5895 . Wohltmann, F. "Die Faktoreien am Wuriflusse in Kamerun," *DK*, XVI(1899), 321.

5896 . _____. *Handbuch der tropischen Agricultur für die deutschen Kolonien in Afrika auf wissenschaftlicher und praktischer Grundlage. Vol. I, Die natürlichen Faktoren der tropischen Agricultur und die Merkmale ihrer Beurteilung.* Leipzig: Duncker und Humblot, 1892. 440p.

5897 . _____. *Der Plantagebau in Kamerun und seine Zukunft. Drei Reiseberichte.* Berlin: E. S. Mitter and Sohn, 1896. 39p.

5898 . _____. *Vortrag . . .über Kamerun.* Berlin, 1900-1901.

5899 . Woitscheck, Paul. "Missionsbriefe," *Stern von Afrika*, IV(1897), 40; V(1898), 127; VII(1900), 13, 43, 79, 80, 91-93, 107, 111, 112, 139, 140; VIII(1901), 10, 175.

5900 . Zimmermann, Oskar. *Durch Busch und Steppe vom Campo bis zum Schari, 1892-1902; ein Beitrag zur Geschichte der Schutztruppe von Kamerun.* Berlin: E. S. Mittler, 1909. 238p.

5901 Zintgraff, Eugen. *Nord-Kamerun. Schilderung der im Auftrage des Auswärtigen Amtes zur Erschliessung des Nördlichen Hinterlandes von Kamerun während der Jahre 1886-1892 unternommenen Reisen.* Berlin: Paetel, 1895. 467p.

5902 . Zöller, Hugo. "Der Batanga—oder Moanja-Fluss," *Deutsche Geographische Blätter*, VIII(1885), 211.

5903 . _____. *Das Flussgebiet von Kamerun. Seine Bewohner und Seine Hinterländer.* Stuttgart: Spemann, 1885. 250p. Vol. III of *Die deutschen Besitzungen an der westafrikanischen Küste.*

5904 . _____. *Forschungsreisen in der deutschen Colonie Kamerun.* Stuttgart: Spemann, 1885. 291p. Vol. II of *Die deutschen Besitzungen etc.*

5905 _____. *Das südlich Kamerun Gebiet.* Stuttgart: Spemann, 1885.234p. Vol. IV of *Die deutschen Besitzungen etc.*

5906 . Brunache, Paul. *Le centre de l'Afrique. Autour du Tchad*. Paris: F. Allan, 1894. 340p.

5907 . Cazemajou, M. G. "Du Niger vers le lac Tchad. Journal de route," *Bulletin de la Comité de l'Afrique Française*, X(1900), 42-48, 87-91, 172-174, 207-210, 241-244, 301-304, 335-357, 361-362.

5908 . Clozel, F. J. "Du Congo au Niger par le Baghirmi," *Journal de Voyages*, XXXIII, pp.241-244, 262-263, 273-275, 294-295, 305-307, 326-327, 341-342, 353-355, 374-375, 387-388.

5909 . _____. "Sa mission dans la Haute-Sangha," *Bulletin de la Comité de l'Afrique Française*, V(1895).

5910 . Delafosse, Maurice. *Essai sur le people et la langue Sara. Bassin du Tchad*. Paris: André, 1898. 47p.

5911 . Dybowski, Jean. "La mission Jean Dybowski vers le Tchad," *TM*, LXV(1893), 113-176.

5912 . _____. *La route du Tchad. Le Loango au Chari*. Paris: Firmin-Didot, 1893. 380p.

5913 . Lenfant, Eugene. "Opérations de la mission Lenfant dans les bassins du Bahr Sara et du Logone," *Géographie*, XVI(1907), 281-286.

5914 . Nachtigal, Gustav. "Die Abstammung der Könige von Wadaï," *Globus*, XXIV (1873), 335-336.

5915 . _____. "Beschreibung von Wara, der Hauptstadt von Wadaï," *ZGE*, VI (1871), 526-540.

5916 . _____. "Brief von Dr. G. Nachtigal aus Wadaï (12 August 1873); seine Reise nach Dar Runga," *PM*, XX(1874), 261-265.

5917 · _____ · "Der Hofstaat der Köenigs von Baghirmi," *Globus*, XXIV(1873), 119-121, 137-139, 153-155.

5918 · _____ · "Die Länder im Suden Wadaï's," *ZGE*, X(1875), 110-117.

5919 · _____ · "Nachrichten von Dr. G. Nachtigal in Inner Afrika. Die tributären Heidenländer Baghirmis," *PM*, XX(1874), 10-16, 323-331.

5920 _____ · "Nachrichten von Nachtigal aus Wadaï," *VGE*, I(1873), 47-55.

5921 · _____ · "Reise in die südlichen Heidenländer Baghirmis," *ZGE*, VIII(1873), 249-257, 311-374.

5922 · _____ · "Reise nach Tibesti," *ZGE*, V(1870), 69-75.

5923 · _____ · *Résultats d'un voyage dans le Soudan.* Paris, 1875.

5924 · _____ · "Übersicht über die Geschichte Wadaï," *ZGE*, VI(1871), 345-366.

5925 · _____ · "Le voyage de Nachtigal au Ouaddaï," *Renseignements Coloniaux*, IX(1903), 42-72, 104-119, 135-146, 167-173, 180-197, 215-230, 247-255, 268-276.

5926 · _____ · "Zug mit einer Sklavenkarawane in Baghirmi," *Globus*, XXIV(1873), 215-218, 231-233.

5927 · _____ · "Zur Geschichte Baghirmis," *ZGE*, IX(1874), 39-59, 99-132.

5928 · Percher, Jules-Hippolyte [Alis, Harry. *pseud.*]. *À la conquête du Tchad.* Paris: Hachette, 1891. 297p.

5929 · Rohlfs, Gerdard. *À travérs del Sáhara.* Madrid: Bruno del Amo, 1929. 159p.

5930 · Segni, Filippo da. "Viaggio del Padre Filippo da Segni O. F. M. da Tripoli di Barberia al Bournou nel 1850," *BSGI*, IV(1870), 137-150.

5931 . Albéca, Alexandre L. d'. "Au Dahomey," *TM*, LXVII(1894).

5932 . _____ . *Côte occidentale d'Afrique. Les établissements français au golfe de Benin, géographie, commerce, langues.* Paris: Baudoin, 1889.

5933 . _____ . "Le Dahomey en 1894," *CRSG*, XIII(1894), 305-310; XIV(1895), 183-210.

5934 . _____ . *La France au Dahomey.* Paris: Hachette, 1895.

5935 . _____ . "La rivière Mono au Dahomey. Délimitation de la frontière entre les établissements du Bénin et la colonie allemande du Togo," *CRSG*, XII(1893), 250-251.

5936 . Andrés, Marcelino. "Viaje por las costas de Africa, Cuba e isla de Santa Elena (1830-32); viaje al reino de Dahomey. Edited by Augustín Jesús Barreiro," *Boletín de la Sociedad Geografica Nacional*, LXXII(1932), 725-748; LXXIII(1933), 35-54, 238-260.

5937 . Aublet, Edouard [*Capt.*]. *La conquête du Dahomey, 1893-94, d'après les documents officiels.* 2 vols. Paris: Berger-Levrault, 1894-5.

5938 . Avril, Adolphe d'. *La Côte des Esclaves: le Yoruba, le Dahomey.* Paris, 1889.

5939 . Badin, Adolphe. *Jean-Baptiste Blanchard au Dahomey. Journal de la campagne, par un Marsouin.* Paris: A. Colin, 1895. 309p.

5940 . Bartet, A. [*Dr.*]. "Colonne expéditionnaire dans le Haut-Dahomey," *Archives de Médecine Navale*, L(1898).

5941 . Barth, Henry. "Land und Leute in Dahomey," *Jahresbericht der Geographische Gesellschaft in Bern*, II(1879), 149-164.

5942 . Baudin, Nöel. "La guerre civile à Porto-Novo," *MCL*, VII(1875),

5943 . Bayol, Jean. [*Dr.*]. "L'attaque de Kotonou," *Revue Bleue*, XXX(1892).

5944 . _____. *Les Dahoméens au Champ de Mars, moeurs et coutumes (Exposition d'Ethnographie coloniale)*. Paris: A. Herment, 1893. 21p.

5945 . _____. "Les forces militaires du Dahomey," *Revue Scientifique*, XXX (1892), 520-524.

5946 . _____. "Le langage des Dahoméens," *Figaro*, November 13, 1892.

5947 . Bel, Camille. "Lettere," *MCM*, XVIII(1889), 3-5.

5948 . _____. "Lettres," *MCL*, XX(1888), 602, 603.

5949 . Béraud, Médard. "Note sur le Dahomé," *BSGP*, 5th Series, XII(1866), 371-386.

5950 . Bern, J. *L'expédition du Dahomey (août-décembre 1892). Notes éparses d'un volontaire*. Sidi-bel-Abbès: C. Lavenne, 1893. 432p.

5951 . Bertin, Théodule Charles Eugène. *Renseignements sur le royaume de Porto-Novo et le Dahomey*. Paris: Baudoin, 1890. 19p.

5952 . Bettencourt Vasconcellos Corte Real Do Canto, Vital de. *Descripção historica, topographica e ethnographica do dictricto de S. João Baptista d'Ajudá e do reino de Dahomé Costa da Mina.* Lisbon, 1869. 91p.

5953 . _____. *Missionarios francezes propagadores de Fé na Costa da Mina e qual o prestigio portuguez. Considerações e melhoramentos a fazer no Forte de S. João Baptista de Ajudá.* Lisbon: Vicente A. Gomes dos Santos, 1867. 23p.

5954 . Borghero, Francesco Saverio. [*Abbé*]. *Le Dahomey. Géographie, histoire, état religieux, moral et politique.* Paris, 1865. 20p.

5955 . _____. "Lettre à M. d'Avézac au sujet d'une carte de la côte des esclaves," *BSGP*, 5th Series, XII(1866), 73-89.

5956 \_\_\_\_. "Lettres," *APFL*, XXXIII(1861), 78-79, 81-102, 152-158, 257-281, 380-394; XXXIV(1862), 153-156, 209-235, 257-293; XXXV (1863), 8-48, 81-141, 257-277; XXXVI(1864), 82-129, 242-248, 396-416, 419-444; XXXVII(1865), 7-31, 83-116; XXXIX(1867), 23-45, 109-126, 232-249, 267-289, 345-358, 460-485; XL(1868), 73-79, 143-161, 292-306, 363-382.

5957 Bouche, J. E. "La côte des esclaves et les visées de l'Angleterre," *Revue de France*, LII(1875).

5958 \_\_\_\_. "Le Dahomé, son histoire," *Exploration*, I(1876), 581-584.

5959 Bouche, Pierre-Bertrand. [*Abbé*]. "Dahomey," *Revue du Monde Catholique*, April 25, 1877.

5960 \_\_\_\_. *Le Dahomey*. Paris: Martinet, 1874. 24p.

5961 \_\_\_\_. "Dahomey," in *La France coloniale*, Alfred-Nicolas Rambaud, Ed., Paris: Colin, 1886.

5962 \_\_\_\_. "Le Dahomey et Porto-Novo," in *La France coloniale*, Paris: Colin, 1893. (6th ed.)

5963 \_\_\_\_. *Les Noirs peints par eux-mêmes*. Paris: Poussielgue frères, 1883. 144p.

5964 \_\_\_\_. *Sept ans en Afrique occidentale. La Côte des Esclaves et le Dahomey*. Paris: Plon, Nourrit, 1885. 403p.

5965 Bricet, Hyacinthe. *Directoire et coutumier a l'usage de la Prefecture Apostolique du Dahomey*. Ouidah: Imprimerie de la Mission Catholique, 1899. 96p.

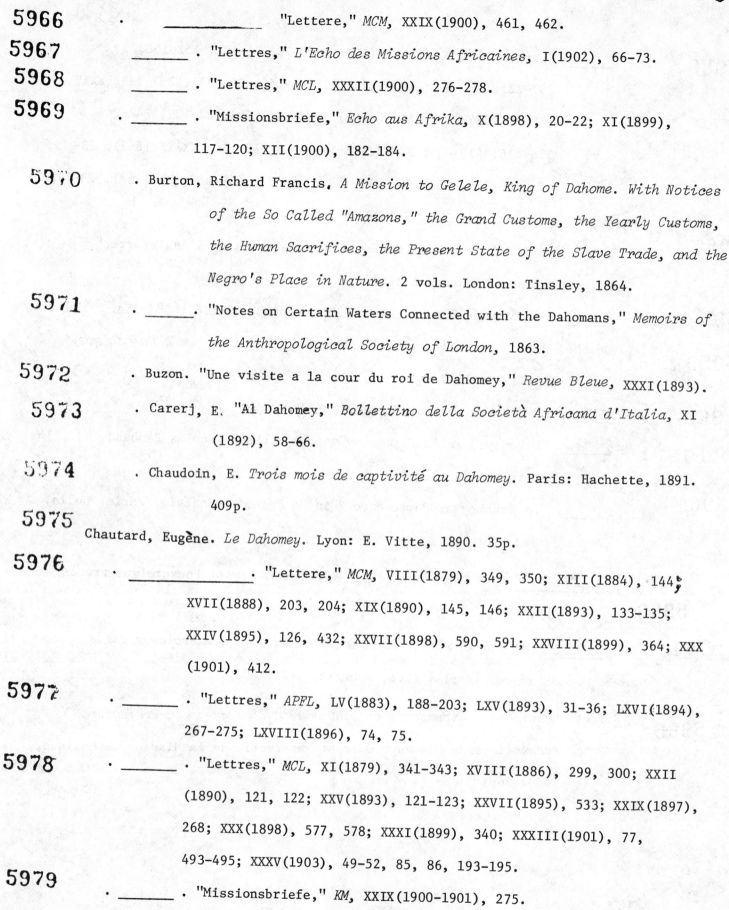

5966     ●———————— "Lettere," *MCM*, XXIX(1900), 461, 462.

5967     ——— . "Lettres," *L'Echo des Missions Africaines*, I(1902), 66-73.

5968     ——— . "Lettres," *MCL*, XXXII(1900), 276-278.

5969     ●——— . "Missionsbriefe," *Echo aus Afrika*, X(1898), 20-22; XI(1899), 117-120; XII(1900), 182-184.

5970     . Burton, Richard Francis. *A Mission to Gelele, King of Dahome. With Notices of the So Called "Amazons," the Grand Customs, the Yearly Customs, the Human Sacrifices, the Present State of the Slave Trade, and the Negro's Place in Nature.* 2 vols. London: Tinsley, 1864.

5971     ●——— . "Notes on Certain Waters Connected with the Dahomans," *Memoirs of the Anthropological Society of London*, 1863.

5972     . Buzon. "Une visite a la cour du roi de Dahomey," *Revue Bleue*, XXXI(1893).

5973     . Carerj, E. "Al Dahomey," *Bollettino della Società Africana d'Italia*, XI (1892), 58-66.

5974     . Chaudoin, E. *Trois mois de captivité au Dahomey*. Paris: Hachette, 1891. 409p.

5975     Chautard, Eugène. *Le Dahomey*. Lyon: E. Vitte, 1890. 35p.

5976     ●———————— . "Lettere," *MCM*, VIII(1879), 349, 350; XIII(1884), 144; XVII(1888), 203, 204; XIX(1890), 145, 146; XXII(1893), 133-135; XXIV(1895), 126, 432; XXVII(1898), 590, 591; XXVIII(1899), 364; XXX (1901), 412.

5977     ●——— . "Lettres," *APFL*, LV(1883), 188-203; LXV(1893), 31-36; LXVI(1894), 267-275; LXVIII(1896), 74, 75.

5978     ●——— . "Lettres," *MCL*, XI(1879), 341-343; XVIII(1886), 299, 300; XXII (1890), 121, 122; XXV(1893), 121-123; XXVII(1895), 533; XXIX(1897), 268; XXX(1898), 577, 578; XXXI(1899), 340; XXXIII(1901), 77, 493-495; XXXV(1903), 49-52, 85, 86, 193-195.

5979     ●——— . "Missionsbriefe," *KM*, XXIX(1900-1901), 275.

5980     _____. "De Porto-Novo à Abéokouta," *MCL*, XV(1883), 281-283, 296-298, 305, 306.

5981     _____. "Saint-Joseph de Tocpo ou Un orphelinat agricole à la Côte des Esclaves," *MCL*, XIII(1881), 442, 443, 466-468, 498-500.

5982     Courdioux, Philibert. "Lettere," *MCM*, I(1872), 205-206; II(1873), 389.

5983     _____. "Lettres," *MCL*, II(1869), 345-347; IV(1871-1872), 466-467; V (1873), 11, 365-366.

5984     Crouch, A. P. "Dahomey and the French," *Nineteenth Century*, Oct. 1890, 601-615.

5985     Demanche, G. "Dahomey," *Revue française de l'étranger et des colonies*, XVIII, pp. 397-406.

5986     Deniker, J. "Les Dahoméens. Étude anthropologique," *Revue générale des sciences pures et appliquées*, II(1891), 374-378.

5987     Dolei.     "Lettere," *MCM*, XXI(1892), 314; XXII(1893), 110, 111.

5988     _____. "Lettres," *MCL*, XXIV(1892), 307, 308; XXV(1893), 98.

5989     Dorgère, Alexandre. "Lettere," *MCM*, XI(1882), 580, 581; XIX(1890), 558; XX(1891), 376, 377, 433-438, 555.

5990     _____. "Lettres," *MCL*, XIV(1882), 568, 569; XXII(1890), 268; XXIII(1891), 421-426.

5991     _____. "Missionsbriefe," *KM*, XVIII(1890), 154.

5992     _____. "Prisonniers au Dahomey," *MCL*, XXIII(1891).

5993     Dubarry, Armand. *Voyage au Dahomey*. Paris: Dreyfous, 1879. 283p.

5994     Duncan, John. *Travels in Western Africa in 1845 and 1846: Comprising a Journey from Whydah, through the Kingdom of Dahomey, to Adofoodia, in the Interior*. 2 vols. London: Bentley, 1847.

5995     Erman, W. [*Dr.*]. "Entdeckung und Aufnahme des Whemi-Flusses in Dahomey," *Globus*, XXXI(1877), 13-15.

5996    Feris. [Dr.]. "La Côte des Esclaves," *Archives de Médicine Navales*, XXXI
        (1879).

5997    _____. "La côte des esclaves et les nouvelles possessions françaises,"
        *Revue Scientifique*, XXI(1883).

5998    Foà, Edouard. "Dahoméens et Egbas," *Nature* [Paris], XIX(1891), 199-202.
        262-266.

5999    . _____. "Le Dahomey et Porto-Novo," *CRSG*, X(1891), 33-35.

6000    . _____. "Le Dahomey et ses habitants," *Revue Scientifique*, XLVII(1895),
        365-368.

6001    _____. *Le Dahomey. Histoire, géographie, moeurs, coutumes, commerce,
        industrie, expéditions françaises (1891-1894)*. Paris: Hennuyer,
        1895. 429p.

6002    . _____. *Sur le fleuve Whémé, limite entre le Porto-Novo et le Dahomey*.
        Paris, 1888.

6003    . Fonssagrives, Jean-Baptiste-Joseph-Marie-Pascal. *Au Dahomey. Souvenirs
        de campagnes (1892-1893)*.

6004    . _____. *Notice sur le Dahomey*. Paris: A. Lévy, 1900. 408p.

6005    . Forbes, Frederick Edyn. *Dahomey and the Dahomans: Being the Journals of
        Two Missions to the King of Dahomey and Residence at His Capital
        in the Years 1849 and 1850*. 2 vols. London: Longmans, Brown, Green
        & Longmans, 1851.

6006    . Forgues, E. D. *Une mission en Dahomey*. Paris, 1864.

6007    . Freeman, Thomas Birch. "Wesleyan Mission in Guinea [Dahomey]," *MH*, XL
        (1844), 63-67.

6008    . Gandoin. "Trois mois de captivité au Dahomey," *Illustration*, XLVIII(1890).

6009    . Garenne, E. "Au Dahomey," *Revue de la France Moderne*, July, 1890.

6010 . Geoffroy, A. "Un drame au Dahomey," *Revue du monde catholique*, Sept.–Oct., 1892.

6011 . Gouzien, Paul. [*Dr.*]. *Notice sur le Dahomey*. Paris: Office colonial, 1900.

6012 . Grandin, C. *À l'assaut du pays des noirs. Le Dahomey*. 2 vols. Paris: Remé Haton, 1895.

6013 . Guillevin. [*Lt.*]. *Voyage dans l'intérieur royaume de Dahomey*. Paris: Bertrand, 1862. 47p.

6014 . Hagen, A. [*Dr.*]. "La colonie de Porto-Novo et le roi Toffa," *Mémoires de la Société d'Ethnographie, Paris* ["*Revue Ethnographie*"], VI (1887), 81–116.

6015 . Ignace, S. "Lettres," *MCL*, XXIV (1892), 612–615.

6016 . Laffitte, J. [*Abbé*]. *Le Dahomé. Souvenirs de voyage et de mission*. Tours: Mame, 1873. 223p. Also, 1874, 252p.

6017 . _____. *Le Pays des Nègres et la Côte des Esclaves*. Tours: Mame, 1876. 238p.

6018 . Lambinet, Édouard. *Notice géographique, topographique et statistique sur le Dahomey*. Paris: Baudoin, 1893. 94p.

6019 . Lecron, Joseph. "Lettere," *MCM*, XIX (1890), 206, 207, 457, 458; XXII (1893), 207, 313, 314.

6020 . _____. "Lettres," *APFL*, LVIII (1886), 177–185; LXI (1889), 107–126; LXII (1890), 267–270, 271–276; LXVII (1895), 289–299.

6021 . _____. "Lettres," *MCL*, XXII (1890), 194, 195, 445, 446; XXIII (1891), 229; XXIV (1892), 273; XXV (1893), 195, 301, 302.

6022 . _____. "Missionsbriefe," *KM*, XVIII (1890), 130, 131.

6023 . Lefebvre, Malo. "Notes sur la barre de Kotonou," *RMC*, 1891, pp.441–453.

6024    Lissner, Ignace. "Lettere," *MCM*, XXVI (1897), 218-220.

6025    _____ . "Lettres," *MCL*, XXIX (1897), 194-196, 448.

6026    . Looy, Hendrik van. *Een Reisje in Dahomey. Naar het verhaal der geloofs-zendelingen en ndre reizigers verzamelt en geranschikt door.* Mechelen: H. Dessain, 1892. 126p.

6027    . McLeod, John. *A Voyage to Africa; with Some Account of the Manners and Customs of the Dahomian People.* London: Murray, 1820. 162p.

6028    . Malavialle, Léon. *Le Dahomey.* Montpellier: Boehm, 1891. 47p.

6029    . Martin. "A travers le Dahomey," *MCL*, XXVIII (1896), 562-564, 568, 569, 581-584, 595-597. See also, *MCM*, XXVI (1897), 334, 335, 355-358, 367-371.

6030    . _____ . "Lettere," *MCM*, XXI (1892), 291, 292.

6031    . _____ . "Lettres," *MCL*, XXIV (1892), 273.

6032    . Massé, D. "Au Dahomey," *Revue de Paris*, VI (1899).

6033    . Mauléon, de. "Voyage au Dahomey," *Annales Maritimes et Coloniales*, III (1845), 504ff.

6034    . Ménager, Ernest. "Lettres," *MCL*, XI (1879), 27-28; XVI (1884), 451; XVIII (1886), 116-119.

6035    . Morienval, Henri. *La guerre du Dahomey, journal de campagne d'un sous-lieutenant d'infanterie de marine.* Paris: Hatier, 1893. 240p.

6036    . Nicolas, Victor. *L'expédition du Dahomey en 1890, avec un aperçu géographique et historique.* Paris, Limoges, 1892. 152p.

6037    . Nuëlito, E. *Au Dahomey, journal d'un officier de spahis.* Abbeville: C. Paillart, 1897. 237p.

6038    . Paimblant du Rouil. "La seconde campagne du Dahomey; rôle et valeur militaire des Haoussas," *Revue du Cercle militaire*, XXVI (1896), Feb. 22 and 29, March 7 and 14.

6039    . Pauli. [*Dr.*]. "Porto Novo," *Globus*, IL (1886), 241-249.

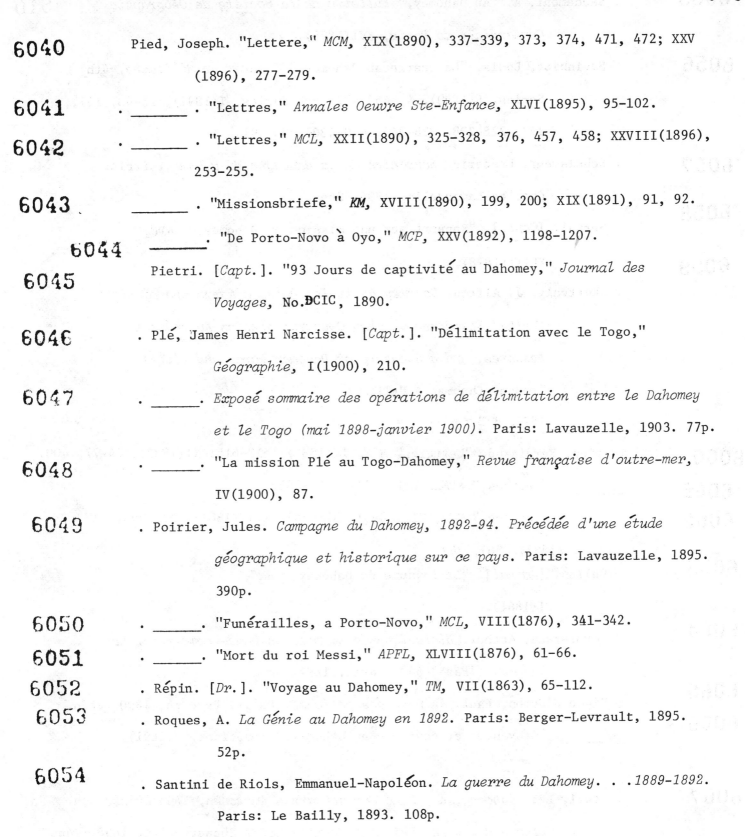

6040    Pied, Joseph. "Lettere," *MCM*, XIX(1890), 337-339, 373, 374, 471, 472; XXV (1896), 277-279.

6041    . _____. "Lettres," *Annales Oeuvre Ste-Enfance*, XLVI(1895), 95-102.

6042    . _____. "Lettres," *MCL*, XXII(1890), 325-328, 376, 457, 458; XXVIII(1896), 253-255.

6043    . _____. "Missionsbriefe," *KM*, XVIII(1890), 199, 200; XIX(1891), 91, 92.

6044    . _____. "De Porto-Novo à Oyo," *MCP*, XXV(1892), 1198-1207.

6045    Pietri. [*Capt.*]. "93 Jours de captivité au Dahomey," *Journal des Voyages*, No.DCIC, 1890.

6046    . Plé, James Henri Narcisse. [*Capt.*]. "Délimitation avec le Togo," *Géographie*, I(1900), 210.

6047    . _____. *Exposé sommaire des opérations de délimitation entre le Dahomey et le Togo (mai 1898-janvier 1900)*. Paris: Lavauzelle, 1903. 77p.

6048    . _____. "La mission Plé au Togo-Dahomey," *Revue française d'outre-mer*, IV(1900), 87.

6049    . Poirier, Jules. *Campagne du Dahomey, 1892-94. Précédée d'une étude géographique et historique sur ce pays*. Paris: Lavauzelle, 1895. 390p.

6050    . _____. "Funérailles, a Porto-Novo," *MCL*, VIII(1876), 341-342.

6051    . _____. "Mort du roi Messi," *APFL*, XLVIII(1876), 61-66.

6052    . Répin. [*Dr.*]. "Voyage au Dahomey," *TM*, VII(1863), 65-112.

6053    . Roques, A. *La Génie au Dahomey en 1892*. Paris: Berger-Levrault, 1895. 52p.

6054    . Santini de Riols, Emmanuel-Napoléon. *La guerre du Dahomey. . .1889-1892*. Paris: Le Bailly, 1893. 108p.

6055 . Saudemont, A. "Au Dahomey," *Bulletin de la Société de Géographie Commerciale de Paris*, XVI(1895).

6056 . Savinhiac, Louis. "La guerre au Dahomey," *Spectateur Militaire*, 4th Series, L(1890), 4, 457-472; 5th Series, I(1891), 33-43, 131, 142, 228-238, 328-343, 420-430, 485-491.

6057 . Schelameur, Frédéric. *Souvenirs de la campagne du Dahomey*. Paris: Charles-Lavauzelle, 1896. 266p.

6058 . Serval. [*Capt.*]. "Rapport sur une mission au Dahomey," *RMC*, XLIII(1878),

6059 . Skertchly, J. Alfred. *Dahomey as It Is; Being a Narrative of Eight Months' Residence in That Country; also an Appendix ir Assantee, and a Glossary of Dahoman Words and Titles*. London: Chapman & Hall, 1874. 537p.

6060 . Terrien, Ferdinand. "Lettere," *MCM*, IX(1880), 613-615; XI(1882), 74-77, 400.

6061 . _____ . "Lettres," *APFL*, LIV(1882), 375-385.

6062 . _____ . "Lettres," *MCL*, XII(1880), 578-581; XIII(1881), 590-593; XIV (1882), 367, 368.

6063 . Vallon. [*Amiral*]. "Le royaume du Dahomey," *RMC*, I(1861).

6064 . Vermeersch, Arthur. *Historique de la mission Baud-Vermeersch. Le Dahomey (1884-1885)*. Paris, 1897.

6065 . Vigné d'Octon, Paul. *Au pays des fétiches*. Paris: Lemerre, 1890. 287p.

6066 . _____ . "Croyances et coutumes au Dahomey," *Tradition*, V(1891).

6067 . Woerl, Leo. *Dahomey, das Land der schwarzen Amazonen. Eine Skizze von Land und Leuten*. Leipzig: Woerl's Reise Bücherverlag, 1898. 24p.

6068 . Wolf, Ludwig. [*Oberstabsartz*]. "Beitrag zur Kilir-Sprache (Sugu)," *ZAS*, III(1889-1890), 293-295.

6069 . Zimmermann, Joseph. "Porto-Novo. Le fetiche onse. Épreuves judiciaires," *APFL*, LIII(1881), 58-66.

EQUATORIAL GUINEA

6070    Almazan, Venancio Ramón. "Geografía médica de las islas de Elobey y Corisco (1890)," *Medicina Colonial*, I(July, 1943), 76.

6071    _____. "La Isla de Elobey. Apuntes para su geografía médica," *Revista General de la Marina*, XXV(1899), 732.

6072    _____. "La Isla de Elobey Chico. Apuntes para su geografía médica," *RGCM*, III(1890), 338-339.

6073    Almonte, Enrique de. *Notas para le descripción física, geológica y agrológica de la zona noroeste de la isla de Fernando Póo y de la Guinea Contenental Española*. Madrid, 1900.

6074    Anton y Ferrandiz, Manuel. "Estudio de un cráneo notable del Golfo de Guinea," *Anâles de la Sociedad Española de Historia Natural*, XVI(1887).

6075    _____. "El Sr. Ossorio en Guinea. Colecciones de la Historia Natural y Etnografía. Antropología," *RGCM*, II(1886), 86-87.

6076    Armengol y Cornet, Pedro. *¿A las islas Marianas o al Golfo de Guinea? Memoria laureada con el primer áccesit por la Real Academia de Ciencias Morales y Políticas*. Madrid: Eduardo Martínez, 1878. 110p.

6077    Arnal y Lapuerta, Manuel de. *Memoria para la fundación de una Colonia agrícola y comercial en la Isla de Fernando Póo*. Madrid: Fortanet, 1884. 50p.

6078    Balmaseda, Francisco Javier. *Los confinados a Fernando Póo e impresiones de un viaje a Guinea*. New York: "La Revolución," 1869. 253p.

6079 . Baumann, Oscar. "Beiträge zur physischen Geographie von Fernando Póo," *BSGM*, XI(1876).

6080 . _____. "La Isla de Fernando Póo," *BSGM*, XXII(1887), 359-365.

6081 . Becker, Jerónimo. "Fernando Póo y la Guinea Española," *Boletín de la Academia de la Historia*, LXIII, p.443.

6082 . Bonnelli, Emilio. "Fernando Póo," *Revista de Geografía Colonial y Mercantil*, I(1897), 502.

6083 . _____. "España en Africa: Golfo de Guinea. Lo que puede hacerse. Cómo hay que colonizar. El clima. Ejército colonial. Trabajos preparatorios. El arroz," *Español*, VII(1900), No.15.

6084 . _____. "Exploraciones en Fernando Póo," *BSGM*, XXXVIII(1896), 49-56.

6085 . _____. "La Guinea Española," *Boletín de las Cámaras de Comercio*, IX(1895), 59.

6086 . _____. *Guinea Española. Apuntes sobre su estado político y colonial.* Madrid, 1887.

6087 . _____. "Guinea Española. Ultimas noticias de Fernando Póo," *Revista de Geografía Colonial y Mercantil*, II(1898).

6088 . _____. "Un viaje al Golfo de Guinea," *BSGM*, XXIV(1888), 291-313.

6089 Bravo Jenties, Miguel. *Revolución bubana: Los confinados a Fernando Póo. Relación que hace uno de los deportados.* New York, 1869. 112p.

6090 Burton, Richard Francis. "Letter from Capt. Richard Burton, F.R.G.S., H.M. Consul to Fernando Po," *PRGS*, VI(1861-1862), 64-66.

6091 . _____. "A Visit to Fernando Poo Peak," *Alpine Journal*, VII(1874), 119.

6092 . Cabello, Pedro. "Apuntes para Fernando Póo. 1898," *Medicina Colonial*, I(July, 1943), 76.

6093 . Clark, John; and Prince, C. K. "Letters," *BM*, XXXIII(1841), 246-249, 358-361, 466-470, 518-520, 578-580, 672-673; XXXIV(1832), 91-94, 148-150, 389-391, 553-558; XXXVII(1845), 46-47, 108-109, 203-207, 429-431.

6094 . Compiègne, de. [*Marquis*]. "Lettre sur le Vieux-Calabar, Fernando Póo," *BSGP*, 6th Series, V(1873), 401-422.

6095 . Diboll, J. "Letters," *BM*, XLVIII(1856), 253-255, 709.

6096 . Donacuige. *Aventuras de un piloto en el Golfo de Guinea*. 2 vols. Madrid: N. Minuesa, 1886.

6097 . Garcia Maraber, Francisco. "Breves consideraciones acerca del clima de la Isla de Fernando Póo [1859]," *Medicina Colonial*, I(July, 1943), 75.

6098 . Hoffmann. [*Capt.*]. "Fernando Póo. Nach dem Berichte. . .Commandant Corvetten, Capitan Hoffmann," *Annalen der Hydrographie*, XIII (1885), 11.

6099 . Ibarra, Jose de. "Guinea española: Agricultura en Fernando Póo; Commercio en Elobey; Necesidad de combinar el comercio con la colonización," *RGCM*, II(1887), 186-191.

6100 . Iglesias y Pardo, Luis. *Observaciones teórico-prácticas sobre las fiebres africanas de Fernando Póo, precidida de una reseña histórico-geográfica de la isla.* Ferrol: Taxonera, 1874. 140p.

6101     . Iradier Bulfy, Manuel. "Descripción de los territorios adquiridos (en el Muni en 1884)," *RGCM*, I(1885-1886), 231-233.

6102     . _____. "España en el Golfo de Guinea," *RGCM*, I(1885-1886), 231-235, 241-245, 252-257, 269-273, 340-345.

6103     . _____. "Exploración en los territorios del Golfo de Guinea," *BSGM*, XXI(1886), 25-36.

6104     . _____. "Memoria de la expedición al Muni en 1884," *RGCM*, I(1885-1886), 121-123, 244-245, 254-257, 269-271.

6105     . _____. "Pruebas de la posedición al Muni en 1884: Situación creada por los alemanes, franceses e ingleses," *RGCM*, I(1885-1886), 242-243.

6106     . _____. "Pruebas de la posesión anterior de Expana en la Cuenca del Muni," *RGCM*, I(1885-1886), 244-245.

6107     . Janikowski, L. "Isla de Fernando Póo. Su estado actual y sus habitantes. Descripción e historia. Población. Salubridad. Temperatura. Santa Isabel: carácter de sus habitantes; mejoras introducidas en esta población; producción, vegetales, etc.," *RGCM*, II(1887-1888).

6108    . Lopez Saccone, Luis. *Apuntes médico-geográficos sobre la isla de Fernando Póo y consideraciones acerca del paludismo como enfermedad predominante del país. Memoria.* Madrid: Fortanet, 1893.

6109    . Mann, Gustav. "Account of an Ascent of Clarence Peak, Fernando Poo," *Journal of Proceedings of the Linnean Society - Botany,* VI(1862), 27.

6110    . Mata, José de. *Memoria de las Misiones de Fernando Póo y sus dependencias, escrita con las licencias oportunas por el Rvdo. P. Procurador de los Misioneros Hijos del Inmaculado Corazón de Maria.* Madrid: A. Perez Dubrull, 1890. 102p.

6111    . Medina, Rafael. "Apuntes de un viaje al Golfo de Guinea [1860]," *Medicina Colonial,* I(July, 1943), 75.

6112    . Merrick, J. and Prince, C. K. [*Dr.*]; and others. "Letters," *BM*, XXXVI (1844), 43-44, 153-159, 374-380, 431-432, 480-487, 539-541, 674-678.

6113    . Monfort, Manuel. *La Guinea Española.* Montevideo: "El Siglo Illustrado", 1901.

6114    . Montaldo y Pero, Federico. *Entretrópicos. Una campaña sanitaria, higénica y médica, en la Estación Naval del Golfo de Guinea en 1896-97.* Madrid: Minuesa, 1899.

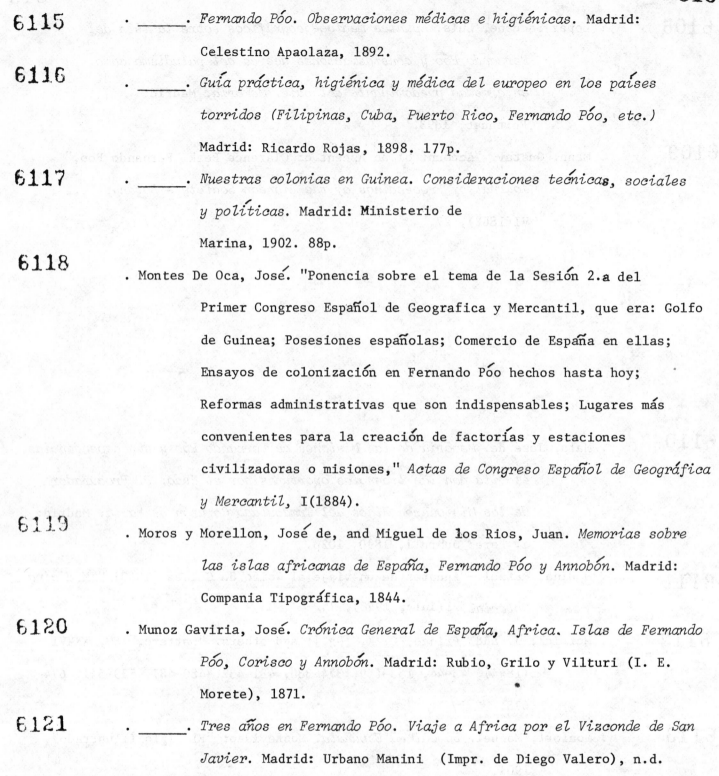

6115 · _____. *Fernando Póo. Observaciones médicas e higiénicas.* Madrid: Celestino Apaolaza, 1892.

6116 · _____. *Guía práctica, higiénica y médica del europeo en los países torridos (Filipinas, Cuba, Puerto Rico, Fernando Póo, etc.)* Madrid: Ricardo Rojas, 1898. 177p.

6117 · _____. *Nuestras colonias en Guinea. Consideraciones tecnicas, sociales y políticas.* Madrid: Ministerio de Marina, 1902. 88p.

6118 . Montes De Oca, José. "Ponencia sobre el tema de la Sesión 2.a del Primer Congreso Español de Geografica y Mercantil, que era: Golfo de Guinea; Posesiones españolas; Comercio de España en ellas; Ensayos de colonización en Fernando Póo hechos hasta hoy; Reformas administrativas que son indispensables; Lugares más convenientes para la creación de factorías y estaciones civilizadoras o misiones," *Actas de Congreso Español de Geográfica y Mercantil,* I(1884).

6119 . Moros y Morellon, José de, and Miguel de los Rios, Juan. *Memorias sobre las islas africanas de España, Fernando Póo y Annobón.* Madrid: Compania Tipográfica, 1844.

6120 . Munoz Gaviria, José. *Crónica General de España, Africa. Islas de Fernando Póo, Corisco y Annobón.* Madrid: Rubio, Grilo y Vilturi (I. E. Morete), 1871.

6121 · _____. *Tres años en Fernando Póo. Viaje a Africa por el Vizconde de San Javier.* Madrid: Urbano Manini (Impr. de Diego Valero), n.d.

6122 . Navarro, Joaquin. "Algunas consideraciones sobre los acuerdos votados y aprobados en Congreso Español de Geografía, relativos a las posesiones españolas del Golfo de Guinea," *Revista General de la Marina*, XIV(1884), 287, 471, 657.

6123 . _____. *Apuntes sobre el estado de la costa occidental de Africa y principalmente de las posesiones españolas d l Golfo de Guinea*. Madrid: Impr. Nacional, 1859.

6124 . Navarro y Canizares, Luis. "Ligeras consideraciones sobre el estado de las posesiones españolas del golfo de Guinea," *BSGM*, XXIV (1888), 157-186.

6125 . Negrin, Ignacio de. "Golfo de Guinea. Servicio prestado por la marina española a Inglaterra en la costa africana," *Crónica Naval de España*, IX(1859), 418-422.

6126 . _____. "Posesiones españolas en el golfo de Guinea. Estracto de un diario de navegación a Fernando Póo y observaciones sobre esta isla, sus producciones y colonización," *Crónica Naval de España*, IX(1859).

6127 . _____. "Posesiones españolas del golfo de Guinea. Fernando Póo. Breves apuntes sobre su pasado, presente y porvenir," *Crónica Naval de España*, IX(1859).

6128 . Ossorio Zabala, Amado. "Condiciones de colonización que ofrecen los territorios españoles del Golfo de Guinea. Conferencia pronunciada en la reunión del 8 de junio de 1887," *BSGM*, XXII(1887), 314-332.

6129 . _____. "España del Golfo de Guinea," *RGCM*, I(1885-1886), 12-15.

6130 . _____. "Españoles y franceses en el Río Muni. Una página del diario," *RGCM*, II(1886), 87.

6131 . _____. "Fernando Póo y el Golfo de Guinea," *BSGM*, V(1878), 182, 289, 348. Also, *Anales de la Sociedad Española de Historia Natural*, XV(1886).

6132 . _____. "Golfo de Guinea. Jefes y pueblos que han reconocido la soberanía de España en las cuencas de los ríos Campo y San Benito," *RGCM*, II(1887-1888), 389-390.

6133 . _____. "Golfo de Guinea. Nuevos atropellos de Francia," *RGCM*, I(1885-1886), 81-82.

6134 . _____. "Le raza blanca en el Golfo de Guinea. Condiciones de vida para el blanco (trabajo alimentación). Causas de la mortalidad en la marinería española. Civilización de Africa por los mestizos. Los negros. El comercio y la religión. Producción actual y porvenir de Fernando Poo," *RGCM*, II(1887-1888), 374-378.

6135 . Parr, Theophilus. "Fernando Po, West Africa," *JMGS*, V(1889), 20-28.

6136 . Paul, Ewald. "Kolonisation von Fernando Po," *DK*, I(1884), 403-405.

6137 . Perez Lasso de la Vega, Jorge. "Fernando Póo. Comercio español en la costa de Africa," *Crónica Naval de Espana*, VI(1858), 470-481.

6138 . _____. "Islas españolas del Golfo de Guinea. Colonización de Fernando Póo," *Crónica Naval de Espana*, XI(1860), 292-297.

6139 . _____. "Islas españolas del Golfo de Guinea. Observaciones sobre la dependencia y relación de estas islas con la Metrópoli, su estado actual y porvenir," *Crónica Naval de España*, V(1857), 314-330.

6140 . _____. "Porvenir de las posesiones y colonias de España en Africa. Isla de Fernando Póo," *Crónica Naval de Espana*, IX(1859), 385-396, 481-495; X(1859), 26-36.

6141      . Roe, Henry. *West African Scenes: Being Descriptions of Fernando Po, Its Climate, Productions, and Tribes: the Cause and Cure of Sickness; with Missionary Works, Trials and Encouragements.* London, 1874.

6142      . Rogozinski, Stefan de. "Une ascension au pic de Santa Isabel, Fernando Po," *Revue de Géographie,* III(1892), 197-203; IV(1893), 287-295; V(1894), 366-372.

6143      . Ruiz y Albaya, José. *Un Larache en Fernando Póo, o tres meses de residencia en la Isla. (Descripción de los cultivos que se practican en las llamadas "fincas" en la Isla de Fernando Póo y otros que se practican en Filipinas y ensayan en dicha Isla, con un proyecto de Secadero-Almacén, Secadero y Lavadero.* Cadiz: "Revista Medica," 1898.

6144      . Saker, Alfred, and Dibull, J. "Letters," *BM,* IL(1857), 55-56, 117-119, 250-251, 653-655, 790-791; L(1858), 122-123, 186.

6145      . _____, and others. "The Descent of a Spanish Armada," *BM,* L(1858), 514-519, 580-585, 714-716; LI(1859), 119-123.

6146      . Soyaux, Hermann. "Auf Fernando Poo," *Aus Allen Weltteilen,* VIII(1877), 1, 159.

6147      . Sturgeon, T. "Letters," *BM,* XXXIV(1842), 452-453; XXXV(1843), 276-282, 434-436; XXXVI(1844), 105.

6148      . _____; Prince, G. K.; and others. "Letters," *BM,* XXXVII(1846), 182-187, 453-455, 516-523, 713-715, 823-827; XXXIX(1847), 53-55, 182-183, 459.

6149 . Usera y Alarcon, Jerónimo Mariano. *Memoria de la isla de Fernando Póo.* Madrid: Tomás Aguado, 1848. 96p.

6150 . _____. *Observaciones al llamado opúsculo sobre la colonización de Fernando Póo.* Madrid: Eusebio Aguado, 1852. 46p.

6151 . Valero Belenguer, José. *Exploraciones recientes en las posesiones españolas del Golfo de Guinea. Conferencia del 18 de junio de 1891, en el Centro del Ejército y de la Armada.* Madrid: Cuerpo Administrativo del Ejército, 1891. 34p.

6152 . _____. "La Guinea Española. En el Contenente y en las islas Corisco y Elobeyes. 1891," *BSGM*, XXXI(1891), 209-234.

6153 . _____. "La Guinea Española. La isla de Fernando Póo," *BSGM*, XXXII(1892), 144-243.

GABON

6154 . Adams, Henry M. "Visit to the Shikani Towns and to the Pangwes," *MH*, LII(1856), 43-45.

6155 . Adams, Martin. "Lettere," *MCM*, XXVI(1897), 271, 625, 626.

6156 . _____ . "Lettres," *Annales Apostoliques*, XII(1897-1898), 325-327.

6157 . _____ . "Lettres,," *APFL*, LXIX(1897), 319.

6158 . _____ . "Lettres," *Lis de St-Joseph*, X(1899), 235.

6159 . _____ . "Lettres," *MCL*, XXIX(1897), 243, 601, 602.

6160 . _____ . "Missionsbriefe," *Echo aus Afrika*, XI(1899), 161, 162.

6161 Amrhein, Andreas. "Le Gabon à vol d'oiseau," *MCL*, XIX(1887), 424-425, 439-441. See also, *MCM*, XVII(1888), 223-225, 238-239; and, *KM*, XVI (1888), 186-190, 206-208.

6162 . _____ . "Excursion au pays des Eshiras," *MCL*, XXVI(1894), 586-588, 596-602, 607-613, 619-625. See also, *MCM*, XXIV(1895), 519-521, 532-537, 546-548, 558-560, 569-574, 580.

6163 . _____ . "Lettere," *MCM*, XVI(1887), 540-541; XXVIII(1899), 438.

6164 . _____ . "Lettres," *Annales Apostoliques*, III(1888), 123-131; IX(1894), 104-106; New Series, (1897-1898), 154-155, 253-256, 305-307; XV (1898-1899), 75-77; XVI(1899-1900), 76-79.

6165 . _____ . "Lettres," *APFL*, LX(1888), 175-182; LXIV(1892), 437-448; LXXI (1899), 471-473.

6166 . _____ . "Lettres," *MCL*, XIX(1887), 520; XXXI(1899), 412.

6167 . _____ . "Missionsbriefe," *KM*, XVI(1888), 22.

6168 . Avézac-Macaya, Marie Armand Pascal d'. *Notice sur le pays et le peuple des Yébous. . .suivi d'un vocabulaire de la langue pongua parlée au Gabon.* 2 vols. Paris: Mémoires de la Société Ethnologique, 1841-1845.

6169 . Aymes, A. "Exploration de l'Ogaway," *RMC*, XXVIII(1870), 525-561; XXIX (1870), 54-75.

6170 . _____. "Recherches géographiques et ethnographiques sur le basin du Gabon," *RMC*, 1870.

6171 . _____. "Resumé de voyage d'exploration de l'Ogôoué entrepris par la 'Pioneer', en ]867 et en ]869," *BSGP*, 5th Series, IX(1869), 417.

6172 . Ballay, Noel. "L'Ogôoué," *Bulletin de la Société de Géographie commerciale de Paris*, I(1879).

6173 . Barrat, Maurice. "Ogôoué et Como," *BSGP*, 7th Series, XVII(1896).

6174 . Barth, Heinrich. "Analyse der Reisebeschreibung du Chaillu's Explorations and Adventures in Equatorial Africa, und genauere Betrachtung des in derselben enthaltenen geographischen materials," *ZGE*, New [2nd] Series, X(1861), 430-467.

6175 . Bastian, Adolf. "Climat du Gabon," *Archives de Médecine Navale*, XXVIII (1881).

6176 . Berton, Jules. "De Lastourville sur l'Ogôoué à Samba sur le N'gounié," *BSGP*, 7th Series, XVI(1895), 211-218. Also, *AG*, V(1895), 215.

6177 . _____. "Les races du Gabon. De Lastourville à Samba," *Bulletin de la Société d'Anthropologie de Paris*, XVI(1895), 212-218.

6178 . Bestion. "Étude sur les eaux potable du Gabón," *RMC*, LXXXVII(1883), 746.

6179 . _____. "Étude sur le Gabon: son sol, son climat, ses habitants et ses maladies," *Archives de Médecine Navale*, XXXVI(1881), 245-401.

6180 . _____. "Rapport sur la colonie du Gabón," *Archives de Médecine Navale*, XXXVI(1881).

6181 . Bizemont, H. de., and **Savorgnan** de Brazza, P. "Sur l'Ogôoué," *Revue Géographique Internationale*, IV(1879).

6182 Bonzon, Charles. *A Lambaréné (lettres et souvenirs de C. Bonzon)*. Nancy: Berger-Levrault, 1897. 152p.

6183 . Bouysson, J. "Mission agricole et scientifique. La région côtière du Nord du Gabon. Région du bas-Ogôoué," *CRSG*, XVI(1897), 425-428.

6184 . _____. "Renseignements sur la région côtière au Nord de Libreville et sur le bas Ogôoué," *CRSG*, XVII(1898), 355-359.

6185 Braouezec. "Notes sur les peuplades riveraines du Gabon, de ses afluents et du fleuve Ogouwaï," *BSGP*, 5th Series, I(1861).

6186 Buléon, Joachim Pierre. *Les peuplades Africaines. Voyage d'exploration au pays des Eshiras*. Lyon: Bureaux des Missions Catholiques, 1895. 71p.

6187 . Burton, Richard Francis. "A Day amongst the Fans," *Anthropological Review*, I(1863), 43-54.

6188 . Bushnell, Albert. "Letters and Journals," *MH*, XLI(1845), 158; XLVII(1851), 218-221; L(1854), 228-231; LI(1855), 35-38, 99-104, 197-198, 325-327; LII(1856), 108-109, 209-212, 339-340, 371-375; LIII(1857), 74-76; LV(1859), 65-67, 129-131, 185-187, 289-291, 353-354; LVI (1860), 111-112, 161-163, 300-301; LVII(1861), 80-81, 311-312; LX (1864), 139-140; LXII(1866), 300-301; LXIII(1867), 367; LXIV(1868), 23-24, 313-314; LXV(1869), 100, 153-154, 203-204.

6189 . Cholet, J. "Missions au Gabon-Congo depuis 1866, avec deux croquis," *CRSG*, IX(1890), 455-463.

6190 . Clozel, F. J. "Les colonies françaises: établissements de la Côte d'Or et du Gabon," *RMC*, IX(1863), 44.

6191 . Coffinières De Nordeck, A. de. *Le Gabon. Souvenirs d'une campagne de 1872*. Paris: Challamel, 1912.

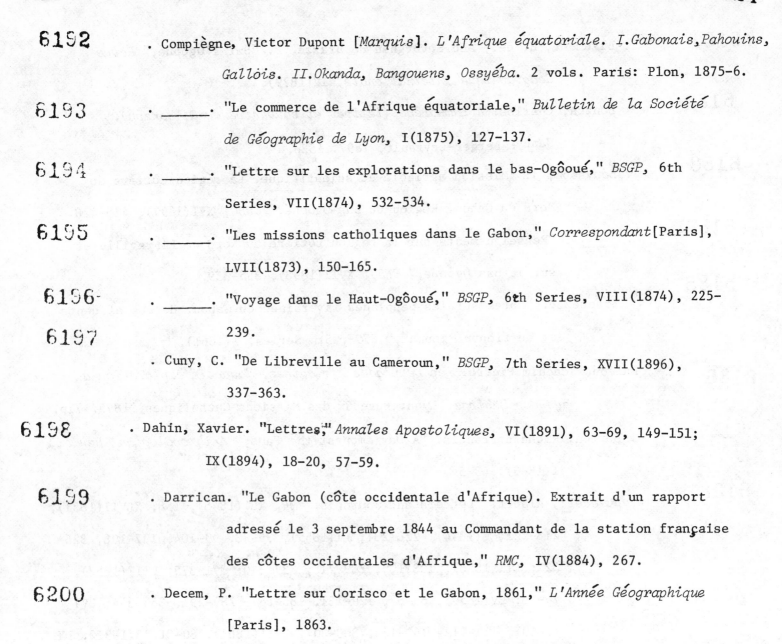

6192 . Compiègne, Victor Dupont [*Marquis*]. *L'Afrique équatoriale. I.Gabonais,Pahouins, Gallois. II.Okanda, Bangouens, Ossyéba.* 2 vols. Paris: Plon, 1875-6.

6193 . _____. "Le commerce de l'Afrique équatoriale," *Bulletin de la Société de Géographie de Lyon,* I(1875), 127-137.

6194 . _____. "Lettre sur les explorations dans le bas-Ogôoué," *BSGP,* 6th Series, VII(1874), 532-534.

6195 . _____. "Les missions catholiques dans le Gabon," *Correspondant*[Paris], LVII(1873), 150-165.

6196- . _____. "Voyage dans le Haut-Ogôoué," *BSGP,* 6th Series, VIII(1874), 225-239.

6197 . Cuny, C. "De Libreville au Cameroun," *BSGP,* 7th Series, XVII(1896), 337-363.

6198 . Dahin, Xavier. "Lettres," *Annales Apostoliques,* VI(1891), 63-69, 149-151; IX(1894), 18-20, 57-59.

6199 . Darrican. "Le Gabon (côte occidentale d'Afrique). Extrait d'un rapport adressé le 3 septembre 1844 au Commandant de la station française des côtes occidentales d'Afrique," *RMC,* IV(1884), 267.

6200 . Decem, P. "Lettre sur Corisco et le Gabon, 1861," *L'Année Géographique* [Paris], 1863.

6201 . Delisle, F. "La fabrication du fer dans le Haut-Ogôoué," *Revue d'Ethnographie*, 1884, pp. 465-473.

6202 . _____. "Notes sur quelques pièces ethnographiques du Haut-Ogôoué," *Bulletin de la Société d'Anthropologie de Paris*, IV(1883).

6203 . Dorlhac de Borne. "Notes sur le Gabon," *Bulletin de la Société d'Anthropologie de Paris*, XI(1890).

6204 . Du Bellay, Griffon. [*Dr.*]. "Le Gabon," *TM*, XII(1865), 273-320. See also, *Illustrated Travels*, I(1869), 289-297, 321-334, 353-366.

6205 Du Chaillu, Paul Belloni. *Adventures in the Great Forest of Equatorial Africa and the Country of the Dwarfs*. London: Murray, 1890. 476p.

6206 _____. *L'Afrique sauvage*. Paris: Michel Lévy, 1868. 412p.

6207 . _____. *The Country of the Dwarfs*. London: Low & Marston, 1872. 374p.

6208 . _____. *Explorations and Adventures in Equatorial Africa; with Accounts of Manners and Customs of the People, and of the Chase of the Gorilla, Crocodile, Leopard, Elephant, Hippopotamus and Other Animals*. New York: Harper, 1861. 479p. London: J. Murray, 1861. French edition, *Voyages et aventures dans l'Afrique équatoriale*. Paris: Michel Levy, 1863. 547p.

6209 . _____. "Extracts from Private Letters Received from M. Du Chaillu," *PRGS*, VIII(1863-1864), 52.

6210 . _____. "Géographie physique et climat de l'Afrique équatoriale," *Annales des Voyages*, I(1868), 95-111.

6211 . _____. "The Great Equatorial Forest of Africa," *Fortnightly Review*, VI(1890).

6212 . _____. *In African Forest and Jungle*. London: Murray, 1903. 193p. New York: Scribner's, 1909.

6213 . _____. *A Journey to Ashango-Land and Further Penetration into Equatorial Africa*. London: J. Murray, 1867. 501p. New York: Harper, 1871.

6214 . _____. *King Mambo*. London: John Murray, 1912. 225p. New York: Scribner's, 1902.

6215 . _____. *Lost in the Jungle*. New York: Harper, 1870. 260p. London: J. Murray, 1870.

6216 _____. *My Apingi Kingdom: with Life in the Great Sahara and Sketches of the Ostrich, Hyena, etc*. New York: Harper, 1871. 254p. London: J. Murray, 1871.

6217 . _____. "On the Physical Geography and Tribes of Western Equatorial Africa," *Athenaeum*, IX(1866), 341.

6218 . _____. "Le pays Aschango," *Annales des Voyages*, II(1867), 257-290.

6219 . _____. "Second Journey into Equatorial Western Africa," *JRGS*, XXXVI (1866), 64-76. Also, *PRGS*, X(1865-1866), 71-80, and *Annales des Voyages*, II(1866), 56-71.

6220 . _____. *Stories of the Gorilla Country*. New York: Harper, 1868. 292p. London: J. Murray, 1868.

6221 . _____. *Wild Life under the Equator*. New York: Harper, 1869. 231p. London: J. Murray, 1869.

6222 Du Quillo. "Voyage dans l'Ogoway, 20 juillet 1873," *RMC*, IV(1874).

6223 . Duron, Adolphe. "Lettre," *Lis de St-Joseph*, VIII(1897), 309-311.

6224 . Fleuriot de Langle. [*Vicomte*]. "Aperçu historique sur les reconnaissances faites par les officiers de la marine française au Gabon de 1843 à 1868," *Annales des Voyages*, III(1868), 256-270.

6225 . _____. "Exploration de l'Ogoway (Afrique occidentale). Recherches géographiques et etnographiques sur le bassin du Gabon. Avant propos," *RMC*, XXVIII(1870), 525.

6226 . _____. "Notes sur le Gabon," *BSGP*, 5th Series, XVII(1869), 462-465.

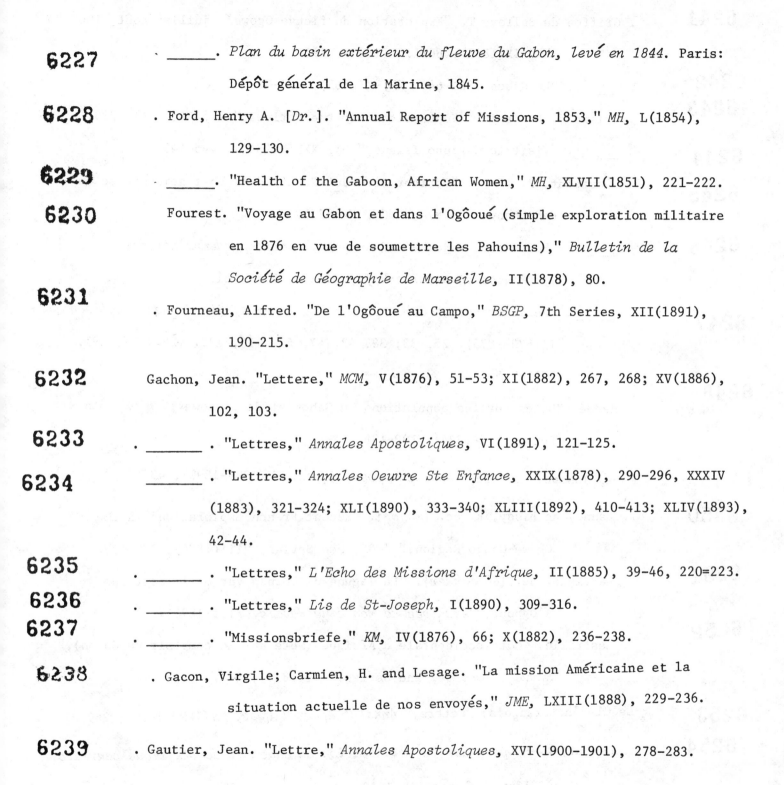

6227      _____. *Plan du basin extérieur du fleuve du Gabon, levé en 1844.* Paris: Dépôt général de la Marine, 1845.

6228      . Ford, Henry A. [*Dr.*]. "Annual Report of Missions, 1853," *MH*, L(1854), 129-130.

6229      _____. "Health of the Gaboon, African Women," *MH*, XLVII(1851), 221-222.

6230      Fourest. "Voyage au Gabon et dans l'Ogôoué (simple exploration militaire en 1876 en vue de soumettre les Pahouins)," *Bulletin de la Société de Géographie de Marseille*, II(1878), 80.

6231      . Fourneau, Alfred. "De l'Ogôoué au Campo," *BSGP*, 7th Series, XII(1891), 190-215.

6232      Gachon, Jean. "Lettere," *MCM*, V(1876), 51-53; XI(1882), 267, 268; XV(1886), 102, 103.

6233      . _____. "Lettres," *Annales Apostoliques*, VI(1891), 121-125.

6234      _____. "Lettres," *Annales Oeuvre Ste Enfance*, XXIX(1878), 290-296, XXXIV (1883), 321-324; XLI(1890), 333-340; XLIII(1892), 410-413; XLIV(1893), 42-44.

6235      . _____. "Lettres," *L'Echo des Missions d'Afrique*, II(1885), 39-46, 220=223.

6236      . _____. "Lettres," *Lis de St-Joseph*, I(1890), 309-316.

6237      . _____. "Missionsbriefe," *KM*, IV(1876), 66; X(1882), 236-238.

6238      . Gacon, Virgile; Carmien, H. and Lesage. "La mission Américaine et la situation actuelle de nos envoyés," *JME*, LXIII(1888), 229-236.

6239      . Gautier, Jean. "Lettre," *Annales Apostoliques*, XVI(1900-1901), 278-283.

6240 . Girod, Léon. "Lettre," *Annales Apostoliques*, XVI(1900-1901), 203-208.

6241 . Griffon du Bellay, T. "Exploration du fleuve Ogowaï, juillet août, 1862," *RMC*, IX(1863), 66ff; X(1863), 296ff.

6242 . _____. "Le Gabon 1861-64," *TM*, X(1865), 273-320.

6243 . Griswold, Benjamin. "Superstition of the Natives," *MH*, XL(1844), 239.

6244 . _____. "Visit to Corisco Island," *MH*, XXXIX(1843), 445-449.

6245 . Güssfeldt, P. [*Dr.*]. "Bericht Dr. Paul Gussfeldt's über seine Reise an den Nhanga in 1874," *ZGE*, X(1875).

6246 . _____. "Reise nach Majombe und Jangela," *Correspondenzblatt der Afrikanischen Gesellschaft*, I(1873-1875), 81.

6247 . _____. "Reiseberichte," *Correspondenzblatt der Afrikanischen Gesellschaft*, I(1873-1875), 25, 33, 38, 43, 47, 61, 115, 122, 129, 137, 191, 199, 215.

6248 . Hedde. "Notes sur les populations du Gabon et de l'Ogoway," *BSGP*, 6th Series, II(1874), 193-198.

6249 . Kowé, Joseph. "Lettre," *Annales Apostoliques*, XV(1898-1899), 43-45.

6250 . Lannoy de Bissy, R. de. [*Major*]. "Recent French Explorations in the Ogowe-Congo Region," *PRGS*, New Series, VIII(1886), 770-779.

6251 . Lartigue, de. [*Commander*]. "La lagune de Fernan Vaz et le delta de l'Ogôoué," *Archives de Médecine Navale*, XIII(1870).

6252 . Lastrille. "Côte occidentale d'Afrique (Note sur le comptoir du Gabon)," *Revue Coloniale*, 2nd Series, XVI(1856), 424.

6253 . Le Clec'h, François. "Lettre," *Annales Apostoliques*, XV(1899-1900), 269-271.

6254 . Lecour, A. *Rapport sur la colonisation du Gabon et de l'Afrique centrale.* Nantes: W. Busseuil, 1848. 16p.

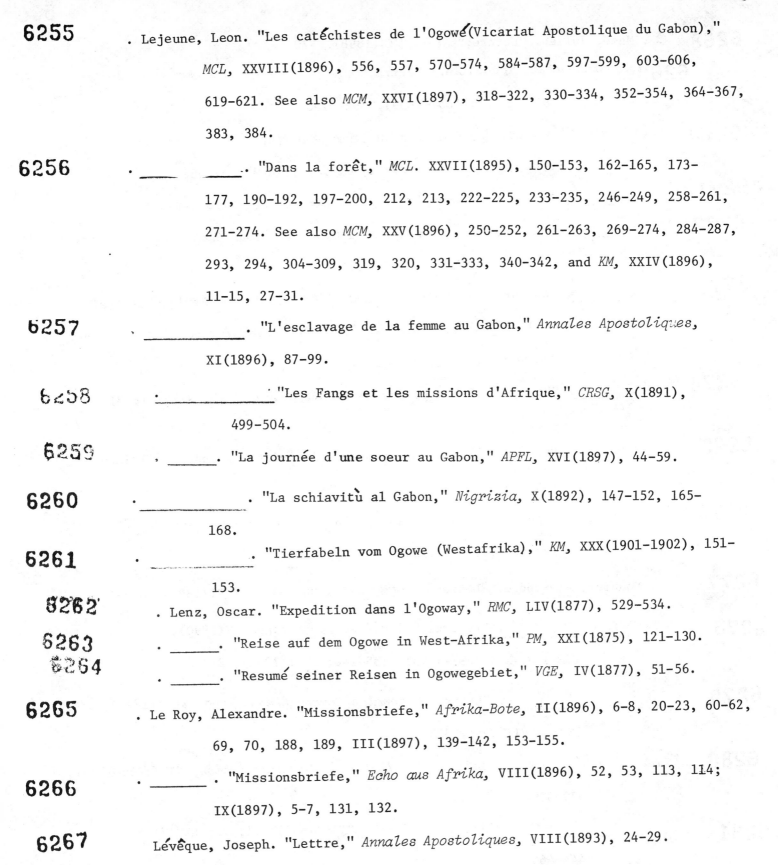

6255      . Lejeune, Leon. "Les catéchistes de l'Ogowe (Vicariat Apostolique du Gabon),"
*MCL*, XXVIII(1896), 556, 557, 570-574, 584-587, 597-599, 603-606,
619-621. See also *MCM*, XXVI(1897), 318-322, 330-334, 352-354, 364-367,
383, 384.

6256      . ___ ___. "Dans la forêt," *MCL*. XXVII(1895), 150-153, 162-165, 173-
177, 190-192, 197-200, 212, 213, 222-225, 233-235, 246-249, 258-261,
271-274. See also *MCM*, XXV(1896), 250-252, 261-263, 269-274, 284-287,
293, 294, 304-309, 319, 320, 331-333, 340-342, and *KM*, XXIV(1896),
11-15, 27-31.

6257      . _____. "L'esclavage de la femme au Gabon," *Annales Apostoliques*,
XI(1896), 87-99.

6258      . _____. "Les Fangs et les missions d'Afrique," *CRSG*, X(1891),
499-504.

6259      . _____. "La journée d'une soeur au Gabon," *APFL*, XVI(1897), 44-59.

6260      . _____. "La schiavitù al Gabon," *Nigrizia*, X(1892), 147-152, 165-
168.

6261      . _____. "Tierfabeln vom Ogowe (Westafrika)," *KM*, XXX(1901-1902), 151-
153.

6262      . Lenz, Oscar. "Expedition dans l'Ogoway," *RMC*, LIV(1877), 529-534.

6263      . _____. "Reise auf dem Ogowe in West-Afrika," *PM*, XXI(1875), 121-130.

6264      . _____. "Resumé seiner Reisen in Ogowegebiet," *VGE*, IV(1877), 51-56.

6265      . Le Roy, Alexandre. "Missionsbriefe," *Afrika-Bote*, II(1896), 6-8, 20-23, 60-62,
69, 70, 188, 189, III(1897), 139-142, 153-155.

6266      . _____. "Missionsbriefe," *Echo aus Afrika*, VIII(1896), 52, 53, 113, 114;
IX(1897), 5-7, 131, 132.

6267      Lévêque, Joseph. "Lettre," *Annales Apostoliques*, VIII(1893), 24-29.

6268  . Macé, Julien. "Lettre," *APFL*, LXX(1898), 470-471.

6269 . Marchandeau, Théophile. "Lettre,"

*BGCSS*, I(1857-1859), 368-379.

6270  . Marche, Alfred. "Le commerce du Gabon," *Bulletin de la Société de Géographie Commerciale de Paris*, I(1879), 52-56.

6271  . _____. "Notes sur Gabon," *BSGP*, 6th Series, X(1877), 393-404.

6272  . _____. "Les peuples riverains de l'Ogôoué," *Revue Géographique Internationale*, XI(1877), 273-276.

6273  . _____. "Rapport sur l'expédition de l'Ogôoué dans l'Afrique centrale en 1875-77," *Archives des Missions Scientifiques et Litteraires*, 3rd Series, VII(1879), 1-14.

6274  . _____. "Voyage au Gabon et sur le fleuve Ogôoué," *TM*, XXXVI(1878), 369-416.

6275  . _____. "Voyage dans le Haut-Ogôoué de la pointe Fetiche à l'Ivindo," *BSGP*, 6th Series, IX(1874), 369-416.

6276  . Mequet. "Excursion dans le haut de la rivière du Gabon," *Revue Coloniale*, 1st Series, XIII(1846), 55.

6277  . Monnier, Alexandre. "Lettere," *MCM*, XIX(1890), 447; XXVI(1897), 409-411.

6278  . _____. "Lettres," *Annales Apostoliques*, V(1890), 119, 120, 138-144; XII(1897-1898), 135-140; XVII(1901), 21, 22.

6279  . _____. "Lettres," *Annales Oeuvre Ste-Enfance*, XLII(1891), 376-383; XLVI(1895), 393-401.

6280  . _____. "Lettres," *Bulletin de la Congrégation*, VII(1899-1900), 379-386.

6281  _____. "Lettres," *APFL*, LXIII(1891), 71, 72; LXVII(1895), 444-465.

6282 . _____ "Lettres," *MCL*, XXII(1890), 447; XXIX(1897), 385-387.

6283 . Monnier, Marcel. "La femme au Gabon," *APFL*, XIV(1895), 443-465.

6284 . Nassau, Robert Hamill. *Africa, an Essay*. Philadelphia: Allen, Lane & Scott, 1911. 35p.

6285 . _____. *Corisco Days; the First Thirty Years of the West Africa Mission*. Philadelphia: Allen, Lane & Scott, 1910. 192p.

6286 . _____. *Crowned in Palmland. A Story of African Mission Life*. Philadelphia: Lippincott, 1874. 390p.

6287 . _____. *Fetichism in West Africa. Forty Years' Observation of Native Customs and Superstitions*. New York: Young People's Missionary Movement, 1904. London: Duckworth, 1904. 389p.

6288 . _____. *In an Elephant Corral, and Other Tales of West African Experiences*. New York: Neale, 1912. 180p.

6289 . _____. *My Ogowe; Being a Narrative of Daily Incidents during Sixteen Years in Equatorial West Africa*. New York: Neal, 1914. 708p.

6290 . _____. *Tales Out of School*. Philadelphia: Allen, Land & Scott, 1911. 153p.

6291 _____. *Where Animals Talk: West African Folk Lore Tales*. Boston: Badger, 1912. 250p. London: Duckworth, 1914. 250p.

6292 . Neu, Henri-Joseph. "Études Gabonnaises. Le pays et les habitants," *Annales Apostoliques*, I(1886), 125-141.

6293 . _____. "Lettres," *Annales Oeuvre Ste-Enfance*, XXXIV(1883), 52-59;

XXXV(1884), 259-265.

6294 . _____. "Lettres," *APFL*, LV(1883), 365-395; LVI(1884), 229-246.

6295 . _____. "Lettres," *L'Echo des Missions d'Afrique*, I(1884), 21, 22; II

(1885), 129-138.

6296 . _____. "Lettres," *MCL*, XVI(1884), 399; XVII(1885), 411.

6297 . _____. "Les Pahouins," *Annales Apostoliques*, II(1887), 86-102.

6298 . _____. "Simbaloba. Scenes de l'esclavage au Gabon," *Annales

Apostoliques*, II(1887), 139-152.

6299 . O'Rorke. "Note sur le pain de Dika du Gabon," *Revue Coloniale*, 2nd Series,

XVII(1857), 495.

6300 . Pechuel-Loesche, Eduard. [*Dr.*]. "Aus dem Leben der Loango-Neger," *Globus*,

XXXII(1877), 10-14, 237-239, 247-251.

6301 . Pecile, A. "Sulla vita delle tribù selvagge nella regione dell'Ogove e

del Congo," *BSGI*, XII(1879), 432.

6302 . Peureux, Nicolas-Joseph. "Lettres," *APFL*, XXXII(1860), 18-33, 356-365.

6303 . _____. "Lettres," *BGCSS*, I

(1857-1859), 214-216, 252-255.

6304 . Pierce, E. J. and Jack, A. D. "Death of Messrs. Herrick and Ford," *MH*,

LIV(1858), 192-194.

6305 . Porter, Rollin. "An Excursion up the Gaboon," *MH*, XLVIII(1852), 83-86.

6306 . Poussot, Jean-Joseph. "Lettres," *Annales Oeuvre Ste-Enfance*, XIII(1861),

251-256.

6307 . Presset, Émile; Gacon, Virgile; and Lesage. "Mission du Gabon," *JME*,

LXIII(1888), 309-311, 353-355, 398-400.

6308 . Preston, Ira M. "Letters and Journals," *MH*, XLIX(1853), 13-18, 225-227;

LIII(1857), 59-62; LXI(1865), 143-146, 389-390.

6309     Pringault, Arthur. "Lettres," *Annales Apostoliques*, VIII(1893), 15-19, 113-116.

6310     . _____ . "Lettres," *Lis de St-Joseph*, IV(1893), 204-207.

6311     Reading, Joseph Hankinson. *The Ogowe Band; a Narrative of African Travel.* Philadelphia: Reading, 1890. 278p.

6312     . Reeb, Anton. "Lettres," *Annales Apostoliques*, IV(1889), 104-114; V(1890), 21-29; VI(1891), 87-96; VIII(1893), 129-136; XII(1897-1898), 327, 328.

6313     _____ . "Missionsbriefe," *Echo aus Afrika*, XI(1899), 162-164; XIII(1901), 45-48.

6314     . _____ . "Missionsbriefe," *KM*, XXII(1894), 163-165.

6315     . Roullet, G. "Les Pahouins, les Bakalais, les Boulons, et les Gabonais," *Annales des Voyages*, IV(1867), 279-286.

6316     . Savorgnan de Brazza. "Expedition sur l'Ogôoué," *Exploration*, III(1878), Nos. 52, 54, 63, 70, 71, 78.

6317     . _____ . "Ses voyages d'exploration dans l'Ogôoué et au Congo," *RMC*, 1883.

6318     . _____ and Bailly, N. "Expédition sur les cours supérieures de l'Ogôoué, de l'Alima et de la Licona," *RMC*, 1879, p.245.

6319     . Serval. "Le Gabon: description de la rivière Rhamboé et de ses affluents," *RMC*, III(1861), 401-404.

6320     . _____ . "Reconnaissance d'une des routes qui mènent du Rhamboé à l'Ogo-Wai," *RMC*, IX(1863), 309-315.

6321     . Soyaux, Hermann. "Nachrichten vom Gabon," *PM*, XXV(1879), 344-347.

6322     . Sutter, E. "Le Gabon," *Revue de Géographie*, II(1879), 217.

6323  Tanguy, Joseph. "Lettre," *Annales Apostoliques*, XV(1898–1899), 36, 37.

6324  . Touchard. "Notice sur le Gabon (côte occidentale d'Afrique)," *RMC*, III
(1861), 1.

6325  Trilles, Henri. "Dans les rivières de Monda," *MCL*, XXVIII(1896), 4–6, 17–21,
31–34, 41–45, 56–58, 66–69, 79–81, 89–93, 103–105, 113–117, 126–128,
140–142. See also, *MCM*, XXV(1896), 443–444, 449–451, 460–462, 476–480,
495–499, 508–514, 522–524.

6326  . _____. "Missionsbriefe," *Echo aus Afrika*, IX(1897), 80; XI(1899),
58–61; XIII(1901), 132–134.

6327  . Tristan, Ange. "Lettres," *Annales Apostoliques*, VIII(1893), 116–118; IX
(1894), 130–135.

6328  . _____ . "Lettres," *MCL*, XXVII(1895), 125, 126.

6329  . Walker, R. B. N. "Journey up the Ogowé River, West Africa," *PRGS*, XVII
(1872–1873), 345–355.

6330  _____ . "Notizen über den Ogowe," *PM*, XXI(1875), 11.

6331  . _____ . "Relation d'une tentative d'exploration en 1866 de la rivière
de l'Ogowé et de la recherche d'un grand lac devant se trouver
dans l'Afrique Centrale," *Annales des Voyages*, 1870, pp. 59–80,
120–144.

6332  . _____ . "M. Skertchley on the Ogowe," *Geographical Magazine* [London], II
(1875), 244–282.

6333  . _____ . "Sur l'Ogôoué et le Ngounié," *PM*, XVIII(1872), 51–57.

6334  . Walker, William. "Letters and Reports," *MH*, XL(1844), 351; XLIV(1848),
195–196; XLV(1849), 120–123; LIV(1858), 311–313; LVII(1861),
257–258; LIX(1863), 178–179; LX(1864), 228, 383; LXVI(1870), 49–
50, 218–219.

6335    _____and Pierce, E. J. "Annual Report, 1856," *MH*, LIII(1857), 201-205.

6336    . Wilson, J. L. "Letters and Reports," *MH*, XXXIX(1843), 229-240; XL(1844), 112-113, 183-186, 381; XLI(1845), 157-158, 217-218; XLII(1846), 24-31, 157-158; XLIII(1847), 251-261; XLV(1849), 208-210, 219-221; XLVII(1851), 257-258.

6337    . _____and Bushnell, Albert. "Opposition Subsiding, Additions to the Church, and the Death of Prince Glass," *MH*, XLVI(1850), 37-38.

6338    . _____and Griswold, Benjamin. "A New Station Selected," *MH*, XXXVIII (1842), 497-500; XXXIX(1843), 156-157.

6339    . _____and Walker, William. "Letters from Gabon," *MH*, XLI(1845), 27-28.

6340    . _____and others. "Eight Annual Report of the Gabon Mission, 1849," *MH*, XLVI(1850), 225-226.

6341 . Allen, Marcus. *The Gold Coast; or, a Cruise in West African Waters.*
London: Hodder & Stoughton, 1874. 183p.

6342 . Annear, S. "Letter," *MH*, XLI(1845), 58-62.

6343 . Armand, P. "Note sur les établissements français de la Côte d'Or,"
*Journal Officiel*, 4 août 1891.

6344 Armitage, C. H. and Montanaro, A. F. *The Ashanti Campaign of 1900.*
London: Sands & Co., 1901. 278p.

6345 . Baden-Powell, Robert Stephenson Smyth. *The Downfall of Prempeh; a Diary
of Life with the Native Levy in Ashanti, 1895-96.* London:
Methuen, 1898. 198p.

6346 . Barter, Charles St. L. "Notes on Ashanti," *SGM*, XII(1896), 441-458.

6347 . Barth, Heinrich. "Volkssagen aus dem Akwapim-Lande, ein Beitrag zur
ethnographischen Kunde Afrika's," *PM*, II(1856), 465-471.

6348 . Beaton, Alfred Charles. *The Ashantee: Their Country, History, Wars,
Government, Customs. . .with a Description of the Neighbouring
Territories.* London: Blackwood, 1877. 140p.

6349 . Beecham, John. *Ashantee and the Gold Coast: Being a Sketch of the History,
Social State, and Superstitions of the Inhabitants of Those
Countries: with a Notice of the State and Prospects of Christianity
among Them.* London: Mason, 1841. 376p.

6350 . Bell, Henry Hesketh Joudou. "The Fetish-Mountain of Krobo," *Macmillan's
Magazine*, July, 1893, pp. 210-219.

6351 . _____. *History, Trade, Resources, and Present Condition of the Gold Coast Settlement.* Liverpool: "Journal of Commerce," 1893. 46p.

6352 . _____. *Outline of the Geography of the Gold Coast Colony and Protectorate.* London: Sampson, Low & Co., 1894. 69p.

6353 . Bliss, Harold C. J. *Relief of Kumasi.* London: Methuen, 1901. 315p.

6354 . Bonnat, J. "Le pays des Achantis et le fleuve Volta," *Explorateur,* 1877-1878.

6355 . Bowdich, Thomas Edward. *Mission from Cape Coast to Ashantee; with a Statistical Account of That Kingdom, and Geographical Notices of Other Parts of the Interior of Africa.* London: Murray, 1819. 512p.

6356 . Boyle, Frederick. *Through Fanteeland to Coomassie. A Diary of the Ashantee Expedition.* London: Chapman & Hall, 1874. 411p.

6357 . Brackenbury, Henry. *The Ashanti War.* 2 vols. Edinburgh and London: Blackwood, 1874.

6358 . _____and Huyshe, George Lightfoot. *Fanti and Ashanti. Three Papers Read on Board the S. S. Ambriz on the Voyage to the Gold Coast.* London: Blackwood, 1873. 131p.

6359 . Burgeat, Emile. "Lettres," *APFL,* LXIII(1891), 425-451.

6360 . Burton, Richard F. "Gold on the Gold Coast," *JRSA,* XXX(1882), 785-794.

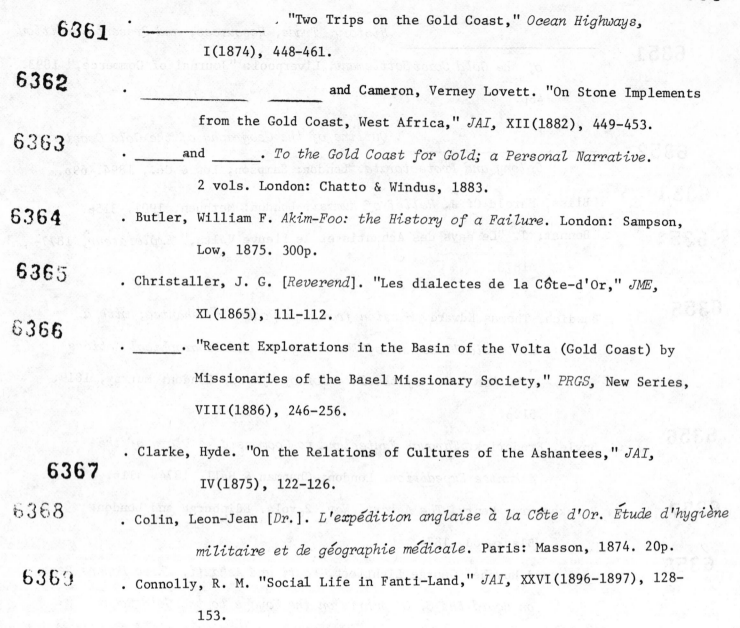

6361 . —————————. "Two Trips on the Gold Coast," *Ocean Highways*, I(1874), 448-461.

6362 . ——————— ————— and Cameron, Verney Lovett. "On Stone Implements from the Gold Coast, West Africa," *JAI*, XII(1882), 449-453.

6363 . ————and ————. *To the Gold Coast for Gold; a Personal Narrative.* 2 vols. London: Chatto & Windus, 1883.

6364 . Butler, William F. *Akim-Foo: the History of a Failure.* London: Sampson, Low, 1875. 300p.

6365 . Christaller, J. G. [*Reverend*]. "Les dialectes de la Côte-d'Or," *JME*, XL(1865), 111-112.

6366 . ——————. "Recent Explorations in the Basin of the Volta (Gold Coast) by Missionaries of the Basel Missionary Society," *PRGS*, New Series, VIII(1886), 246-256.

6367 . Clarke, Hyde. "On the Relations of Cultures of the Ashantees," *JAI*, IV(1875), 122-126.

6368 . Colin, Leon-Jean [*Dr.*]. *L'expédition anglaise à la Côte d'Or. Étude d'hygiène militaire et de géographie médicale.* Paris: Masson, 1874. 20p.

6369 . Connolly, R. M. "Social Life in Fanti-Land," *JAI*, XXVI(1896-1897), 128-153.

6370 . Croft, James A. "Exploration of the River Volta, West Africa," *PRGS*, (1873-1874), 183-193.

6371 . Crooks, John Joseph. *Records Relating to the Gold Coast Settlements, from 1750-1874.* Dublin: Browne & Nolan, 1923. 557p.

6372 . Cruickshank, Brodie. *Eighteen Years on the Gold Coast of Africa, Including an Account of the Native Tribes and Their Intercourse with Europeans.* 2 vols. London: Hurst & Blackett, 1853.

6373 . Dalgleish, W. Scott. "Ashanti and the Gold Coast," *SGM*, XII(1896), 10-21.

6374 . Desnouy. [*Lt.*]. "Les établissements français de la Côte d'Or," *RMC*, 1866.

6375 Dieterle, J. C. "Gebräuche beim Sterben eines Königs in den Tschiländern der Gold Küste," *Ausland*, LVI(1883).

6376 . Dobson, George. "The River Volta, Gold Coast, West Africa," *JMGS*, VIII (1892), 19-25.

6377 . Douchez, F. *Causeries, sur la côte de Guinée á propos de l'expedition de général-mayor Verveer, pendant l'été de 1838; révélées.* The Hague, 1839.

6378 . Duncan, John. "Extract of a Letter to the Librarian of the Royal Geographical Society," *JRGS*, XV(1845), 346-351.

6379 . Dupuis, Joseph. *Journal of a Residence in Ashantee. . .Comprising Notes and Researches Relative to the Gold Coast, and the Interior of Western Africa: Chiefly Collected from Arabic MSS.* London: Colburn, 1824. 264p. Second edition, edited by W. E. F. Ward, London: Cass, 1966. 520p.

6380      . Eiloart, Ernest. *The Land of Death (the Gold Coast Colony). A Pamphlet Addressed to the Members of both Houses of Parliament; with Some Observations on the Present Mode of Making Selections for Colonial Appointments.* London: Hatchards, 1887. 21p.

6381      . Eliot, Edward Carlyon. *Gold Coast Colony: Hints to District Commissioners.* n.p., n.p., 1908. 25p.

6382      . Ellis, Alfred Burdon. *The Ewe-Speaking Peoples of the Slave Coast of West Africa. Their Religion, Manners, Customs, Laws, Language, etc.* London: Chapman & Hall, 1890. 331p. Photomechanical reprint of original, The Netherlands: Anthropological Publications, 1966.

6383      . _____. *A History of the Gold Coast of West Africa.* London: Chapman & Hall, 1893. 400p.

6384      . _____. *The Tshi-Speaking Peoples of the Gold Coast of West Africa; Their Language, Religion, Manners, Customs, Laws, etc.* London: Chapman & Hall, 1887. 343p.

6385      . Freeman, Richard Austin. *Travels and Life in Ashanti and Jaman.* London: Constable; New York: Stokes, 1898. 559p. Also, "Interior of the Gold Coast," *Macmillan's Magazine,* June, 1897, pp. 107-113.

6386      . Freeman, Thomas Birch. "Commencing a Station at Kumasi," *MH*, XXXIX(1843), 37-40.

6387      . _____. *Extracts from a Journal of Various Visits to the Kingdoms of Ashanti, Yourba, and Dahomi in West Africa to Promote the Objects of the Wesleyan Missionary Society.* London: Nichols, 1844. 298p.

6388 . French, George K. "The Gold Coast, Ashanti, and Kumassi," *National Geographic Magazine,* VIII(1897), 1-15.

6389 . Gallaud, Jean. "Lettere," *MCM,* XIII(1884), 317.

6390 . _____ . "Lettres," *APFL,* LVI(1884), 398; LXIV(1892), 147-148.

6391 . _____ . "Lettres," *MCL,* XVI(1884), 92, 304, 399; XXIII(1891), 579.

6392 . Gaudeul, Ange. "Lettere," *MCM,* III(1874), 51, 129-130, 178-179; VI (1877), 170-171.

6393 . _____ . "Lettres," *APFL,* XLVI(1874), 51-67.

6394 . _____ . "Lettres," *Annales Salésiennes,* XLIII(1939), 52-53.

6395 . _____ . "Lettres," *MCL,* V(1873), 603-604; VI(1874), 78-80, 93-94; IX (1877), 157.

6396 . _____ . "Missionsbriefe aus Afrika," *KM,* II(1874), 67.

6397 . Gordon, Charles Alexander. *Life on the Gold Coast.* London: Bailliere, Tindall, 1874.

6398 . Grundy, P. "A Short Account of My Adventures in Ashanti during the Rebellion of 1900," *JMGS,* XVII(1901), 222-229.

6399 . Hay, John Charles Dalrymple [*Bart.*]. *Ashanti and the Gold Coast; and What We Know of It.* London: Stanford, 1874. 82p.

6400 . Hodgson, Mary Alice. *The Siege of Kumassi.* New York: Longmans, Green, 1901. 365p.

6401 . Horton, James Africanus Beale. *Letters on the Political Condition of the Gold Coast Since the Exchange of Territory between the English and Dutch Governments, together with a Short Account of the Ashantee War, 1862-1864, and the Awoonah War, 1866.* London: W.J. Johnson, 1870. 179p.

6402 . Houckgeest, F. A. van Braam. *De expeditie naar de kust van Guinea in het jaar 1869.* Nieuwediep, 1870.

6403   Huppenbauer, D. *Von Khebi nach Kumase. Eine Reise ins Hinterland der Goldküste.* Basel: Missionsbuchhandlung, 1888. 64p.

6404   . Hutton, William. *A Voyage to Africa; Including a Narrative of an Embassy to One of the Interior Kingdoms, in the Year 1820.* London: Longmans, 1821. 488p.

6405   . Irvine, John. "Gold Mines of West Africa," *JRSA,* IL(1899), 305–313.

6406   . Jeekel, C. A. *Onze Bezittingen of de Kuste van Guinea.* Amsterdam, n.p., 1869. 83p.

6407   . Kemp, Dennis. *Nine Years at the Gold Coast.* London and New York: Macmillan, 1898. 279p.

6408   . _____. *Sunny Fountains and Golden Sands.* London: C. H. Kelly, 1898. 32p.

6409   . Kirby, Brandon [*Capt.*]. "A Journey into the Interior of Ashanti," *PRGS,* New Series, VI(1884), 447–452.

6410   . Köppen, W. "Die Regenarmuth der Goldküste," *MDS,* IV(1891), 24.

6411   . Krause, Gottlieb Adolf, and Steiner, Paul. "Von der Goldküste," *DK,* IV (1887), 159–160.

6412   . Lee, Sarah Wallis Bowdich. *Adventures in Fanti-Land.* London: Farrar, 1886. 190p. New York: Dutton, n.d.. 190p.

6413   . Legeay, Pierre. "Lettere," *MCM,* XII(1883), 376.

6414   . _____. "Lettres," *MCL,* XV(1883), 363, 364.

6415   . MacDonald, George. *The Gold Coast, Past and Present; a Short Description of the Country and Its People.* New York: Longmans, 1898. 352p.

6416   . Mähly, E. "Studien von der Goldküste," *Globus,* LXVIII(1895), 149–151, 169–172, 189–191.

6417 ．＿ ＿＿ "Zur Geographie und Ethnographie der Goldküste," *Verhandlungen der Naturforschenden Gesellschaft, Basel,* VII(1885).

6418 Marree, J. A. de. *Reizen op en Beschrijving van de Goldkust van Guinea, voorzien met de noodige ophelderingen, journalen, kaart, platen en bewijzen.* 2 vols. Le Havre, 1817-1818.

6419 Marshall, James. "On the Natives of the Gold Coast," *JAI,* XVI(1886-1887), 180-182.

6420 ．Maximilian, Albert. "Missionsbriefe," *Echo aus Afrika,* VIII(1896), 42-44; IX(1897), 45-47, 145-147; X(1898), 74, 75; XI(1899), 36-38; XII (1900), 106-108; XV(1903), 19-21.

6421 ．＿＿＿＿ . "Missionsbriefe," *KM,* XIX(1891), 111, 112; XXVI(1897-1898), 235, 260-262; XXVIII(1899 -1900), 88, 89, 279, 280; XXIX(1900-1901), 159-161.

6422 ．＿＿＿＿＿＿ *Missionsgrüsse von der Goldküste. Ein Stück Kultur- und Kirchengeschichte aus West-Afrika.* Münster i. W.: "Kreuz und Schwert", 1898. 70p.

6423 ．Maxwell, William Edward. *Affairs of the Gold Coast and Ashanti.* Liverpool, n.p., 1896. 36p.

6424 ．＿＿＿＿＿ . "Results of the Ashanti Expedition, 1895-96," *JMGS,* XII (1896), 37-54.

6425 ．Meredith, Henry. *An Account of the Gold Coast of Africa: with a Brief History of the African Company.* London: Longman, Hurst, Rees, Orme and Brown, 1812. 264p.

6426 . Moloney, Cornelius Alfred. *West African Fisheries, with Particular Reference to the Gold Coast Colony.* London, n.p., 1883. 79p.

6427 . Mondières, A. T. "Les nègres chez eux: ethnographie sur les populations de la Côte d'Or," *Revue d'Anthropologie,* 2nd Series, III(1880), 621-650.

6428 . Musgrave, George Clarke. *To Kumassi with Scott: a Description of a Journey from Liverpool to Kumassi with the Ashanti Expedition, 1895-1896.* London: Wightman, 1896. 216p.

6429 . Noché. "Lettre," *APFL,* XXXVI(1864), 242-248.

6430 . Northcott, H. P. *Report on the Northern Territories of the Gold Coast.* London: War Office, Intelligence Division, 1899.

6431 . Perregaux, W. "A Few Notes on Kwahu, 'Quahoe', a Territory on the Gold Coast Colony, *Journal of the Royal African Society,* II(1903), 444-450.

6432 . Ramseyer, Friedrich Auguste, and Kühne, Johannes. *Four Years in Ashantee.* London; 1875. New York: Carter, 1875. 320p.

6433 . Reade, William Winwood. "La Côte d'Or," *BSGP,* Fifth Series, XVII(1869), 383-392.

6434 . _____. *The Story of the Ashantee Campaign.* London: Smith, Elder, 1874. 434p.

6435 . Reindorf, Carl Christian. *History of the Gold Coast and Ashante, Based on Traditions and Historical Facts, Comprising a Period. . . from About 1500 to 1860.* Basel: Missionsbuchhandlung, 1895. 356p.

6436 . Richards, Thomas Henry Hatton. "The Gold Coast Colony," *Proceedings of the Royal Colonial Institute,* XXIX(1897-1898), 31-35.

6437 . Riche, Alexandre. "D'Elmina à Saltpond ou visite apostolique dans quelques-unes de nos stations de la Côte d'Or," *MCL*, XXVII(1895), 294-297, 304-306, 320-323, 329, 330, 341-343. See also *MCM*, XXV(1896), 345-348, 359, 360, 371, 372, 378-382, and *KM*, XXIV(1896), 199-202, 222-224, 246-248.

6438 . Ricketts, H. I. *Narrative of the Ashantee War; with a View of the Present State of the Colony of Sierra Leone*. London: Simpkin & Marshall, 1831.

6439 . Rogers, Ebenezer. *Campaigning in Western Africa and the Ashantee Invasion*. London, 1874.

6440 . Sarbah, John Mensah. *Fanti Customary Laws. A Brief Introduction to the Principles of the Native Laws and Customs of the Fanti and Akan Sections of the Gold Coast, with a Selection of Cases thereon Decided in the Law Courts*. London: Clowes & Sons, 1897. 295p. 2nd Ed., 1904. 317p.

6441 . _____. *Fanti Law Report of Decided Cases on Fanti Customary Laws. Second Selection*. London: William Clowes & Sons, 1904. 189p.

6442 . _____. *Fanti National Constitution: A Short Treatise on the Constitution and Government of the Fanti, Asanti and Other Akan Tribes of West Africa*. London: William Clowes & Sons, 1906. 273p.

6443 . Skertchly, J. Alfred. *Sport in Ashanti*. London and New York: Warne, 1896. 358p.

6444 . _____. "A Visit to the Gold Fields of Wassaw, West Africa," *JRGS*, XLVIII(1878), 274-283.

6445 . Stanley, Henry Morton. *Coomassie and Magdala: the Story of Two British Campaigns in Africa*. London, 1874. New York: Harper, 1874. 510p.

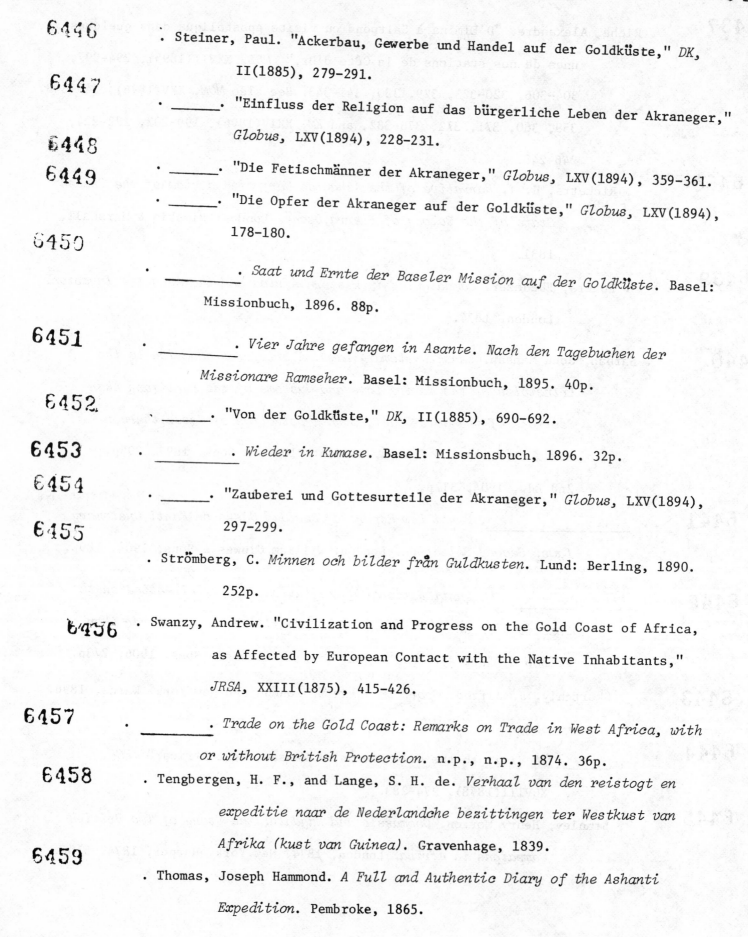

6446 . Steiner, Paul. "Ackerbau, Gewerbe und Handel auf der Goldküste," *DK*,
II(1885), 279-291.

6447 . _____. "Einfluss der Religion auf das bürgerliche Leben der Akraneger,"
*Globus*, LXV(1894), 228-231.

6448
6449 . _____. "Die Fetischmänner der Akraneger," *Globus*, LXV(1894), 359-361.

. _____. "Die Opfer der Akraneger auf der Goldküste," *Globus*, LXV(1894),
178-180.

6450
. _____. *Saat und Ernte der Baseler Mission auf der Goldküste*. Basel:
Missionbuch, 1896. 88p.

6451 . _____. *Vier Jahre gefangen in Asante. Nach den Tagebuchen der
Missionare Ramseher*. Basel: Missionbuch, 1895. 40p.

6452 . _____. "Von der Goldküste," *DK*, II(1885), 690-692.

6453 . _____. *Wieder in Kumase*. Basel: Missionsbuch, 1896. 32p.

6454 . _____. "Zauberei und Gottesurteile der Akraneger," *Globus*, LXV(1894),
297-299.

6455
. Strömberg, C. *Minnen och bilder från Guldkusten*. Lund: Berling, 1890.
252p.

6456 . Swanzy, Andrew. "Civilization and Progress on the Gold Coast of Africa,
as Affected by European Contact with the Native Inhabitants,"
*JRSA*, XXIII(1875), 415-426.

6457 . _____. *Trade on the Gold Coast: Remarks on Trade in West Africa, with
or without British Protection*. n.p., n.p., 1874. 36p.

6458 . Tengbergen, H. F., and Lange, S. H. de. *Verhaal van den reistogt en
expeditie naar de Nederlandche bezittingen ter Westkust van
Afrika (kust van Guinea)*. Gravenhage, 1839.

6459 . Thomas, Joseph Hammond. *A Full and Authentic Diary of the Ashanti
Expedition*. Pembroke, 1865.

6460     . Ulrich, Georges. "Lettre," *MCL.* XXIII(1891), 40.

6461     . Wade, Michel. "Lettere," *MCM,* XXV(1896), 217-219.

6462     _____ . "Lettres," *MCL,* XXVIII(1896), 193-195.

6463     . West, W. [*Reverend*]. "Reprise des travaux missionnaires à Kumasi, capitale du pays des Achantis," *JME,* XXXVII(1862), 381-395.

6464     . Wharton, Henri. "Progrès de l'évangile sur la Côte-d'Or," *JME,* XXXII (1857), 75-77.

6465     . Willcocks, James. *From Kabul to Kumassi. Twenty-Four Years of Soldiering and Sport.* London: Murray, 1904. 440p.

6466     . Wood, Evelyn. *The Ashanti Expedition of 1873-4.* London: Mitchell, 1874. 23p.

6467     . Zahn, F. M. *Von der Elbe bis zum Volta. Sechs Jahre Missions-Arbeit in Westafrika.* Bremen: Valett & Co., 1867. 40p.

6468 . Anderson, Benjamin. *Narrative of a Journey to Musardu, the Capital of the Western Mandingoes.* New York: Green, 1870. 118p.

6469 . Andre. [*Sous-lieutenant*]. "Rapport sur son excursion à Kouniakari," *Moniteur Sénégal et Dépendances,* (1865), 34-35, 38-39, 43-44.

6470 . Aspe-Fleurimont. *La Guineé française, Conakry et les rivières du Sud.* Paris: Challamel, 1899.

6471 . Bayol, Jean [*Dr.*]. "La France au Fouta Djallon," *Revue des Deux-Mondes,* Sept., 1882.

6472 . Béraud et Bouche. *La Guinee française et ses dépendances.* n.p., n.p., 1885.

6473 . Berthier, P. "Examen du fer forgé par les nègres du Fouta-Djallon," *Annales des Mines*[Paris], 1820, pp.129-134.

6474 . Bichet, Georges. "Lettere," *MCM,* XII(1883), 176-178, 187, 188, 189, 190, 500-502, 512, 513; XVI(1887), 269, 270.

6475 . _____. "Lettres," *APFL,* LV(1883), 132-140.

6476 . _____. "Lettres," *L'Echo des Missions d'Afrique,* I(1884), 34, 35, 121-127; II(1885), 196-208.

6477 . _____. "Lettres," *MCL,* XIV(1882), 581-585; XV(1883), 125-131; XIX(1887), 245.

6478 . Bonnat, J. "La côte de Guinée," *Explorateur,* IV(1876), Nos. 73-75.

6479 . Bouteiller, J. [*Capt.*]. *De Saint-Louis à Sierra-Leone; huit ans de navigation dans les rivières du Sud.* Paris: Challamel, 1891. 332p.

6480 . Bowdich, Thomas Edward. *The British and French Expedition to Teembo, with Remarks on Civilization in Africa.* Paris: Smith, 1821. 90p.

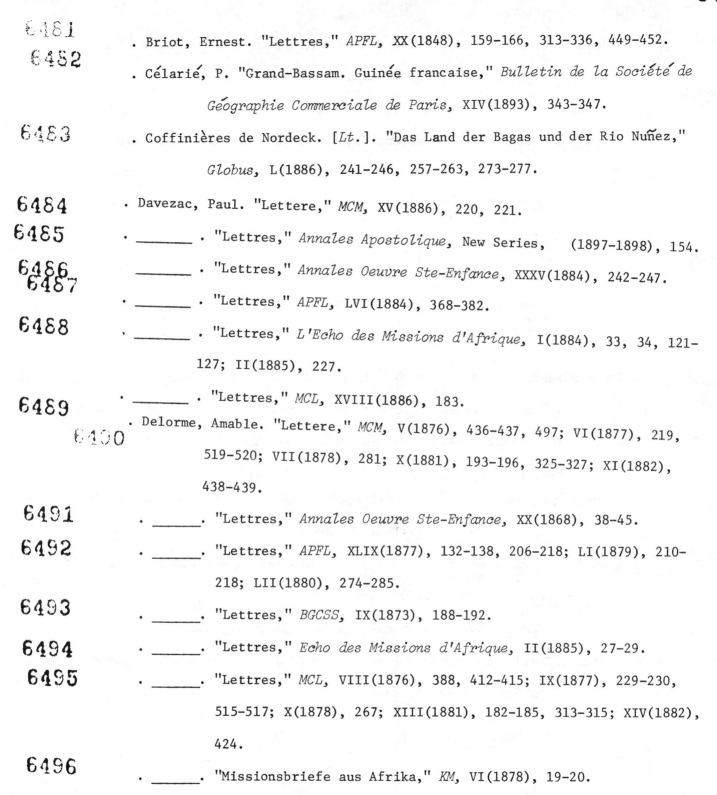

6481 . Briot, Ernest. "Lettres," *APFL*, XX(1848), 159-166, 313-336, 449-452.

6482 . Célarié, P. "Grand-Bassam. Guinée francaise," *Bulletin de la Société de Géographie Commerciale de Paris*, XIV(1893), 343-347.

6483 . Coffinières de Nordeck. [*Lt.*]. "Das Land der Bagas und der Rio Nuñez," *Globus*, L(1886), 241-246, 257-263, 273-277.

6484 . Davezac, Paul. "Lettere," *MCM*, XV(1886), 220, 221.

6485 . _____ . "Lettres," *Annales Apostolique*, New Series, (1897-1898), 154.

6486
6487 . _____ . "Lettres," *Annales Oeuvre Ste-Enfance*, XXXV(1884), 242-247.

. _____ . "Lettres," *APFL*, LVI(1884), 368-382.

6488 . _____ . "Lettres," *L'Echo des Missions d'Afrique*, I(1884), 33, 34, 121-127; II(1885), 227.

. _____ . "Lettres," *MCL*, XVIII(1886), 183.

6489
6490 . Delorme, Amable. "Lettere," *MCM*, V(1876), 436-437, 497; VI(1877), 219, 519-520; VII(1878), 281; X(1881), 193-196, 325-327; XI(1882), 438-439.

6491 . _____ . "Lettres," *Annales Oeuvre Ste-Enfance*, XX(1868), 38-45.

6492 . _____ . "Lettres," *APFL*, XLIX(1877), 132-138, 206-218; LI(1879), 210-218; LII(1880), 274-285.

6493 . _____ . "Lettres," *BGCSS*, IX(1873), 188-192.

6494 . _____ . "Lettres," *Echo des Missions d'Afrique*, II(1885), 27-29.

6495 . _____ . "Lettres," *MCL*, VIII(1876), 388, 412-415; IX(1877), 229-230, 515-517; X(1878), 267; XIII(1881), 182-185, 313-315; XIV(1882), 424.

6496 . _____ . "Missionsbriefe aus Afrika," *KM*, VI(1878), 19-20.

6497 . Devaux. [Capt.]. *Une mission d'études en Guinée française.* Châlons: Imprimerie de l'Union Républicaine, 1900.

6498 . Dubois, Felix. *La vie au continent noir.* Paris: Hetzel, 1894. 330p.

6499 . Fras, P. "Les résultats scientifiques de la mission du Fouta-Djalon (1887-1888)," *Bulletin de la Société de Géographie Commercial de Bordeaux,* 2nd Series, XIV(1891), 161-178, 193, 203, 297, 307, 385-407, 417, 433.

6500 . Gaboriaud. "Mon voyage au Fouta-Djallon," *Bulletin de la Société de Géographie Commerciale de Paris,* IV(1882).

6501 Gallais. "Lettres," *APFL,* XX(1848), 159-166, 313-336, 449-452.

6502 . Gommenginger, Ludwig. "Missionsbriefe," *KM,* XII(1884), 1920.

6503 . _____. "La rivière et le royaume de Porto-Loko (Guinée septentrionale), *MCL,* VI(1874), 548-550, 561-563, 573-575, 596-598, 610, 611, 621, 622. See also *BGCSS,* X(1874-1875), 137-149.

6504 . Guénnégan, Jean-François. "Lettres," *Annales Oeuvres Ste Enfance,* XIII (1861), 29-40; XIV(1862), 348-357.

6505 . Hertz, Charles. *Le paradis des noirs. Excursions sur les côtes de Guinée.* Paris: Tolmer, 1880. 256p.

6506 . _____. *Sur les côtes de Guinee.* Paris: Delagrave, 1885. 252p.

6507 . Jouan, Henri. "La Guinée," *Bulletin de la Société Géographie Commerciale du Havre,* X(1893), 144-175.

6508 . Kobès, Aloys. "Guinée. Extrait d'un mémoire addressé . . .à MM. les Membres des Conseils centraux de Lyon et de Paris," *APFL*, XXVI (1854), 438-452.

6509 . Lambert, M. "Voyage dans le Fouta-Djalon," *TM*, III(1861), 373-400. Also, *RMC*, II(1861).

6510 . Le Berre. "Situation du vicariat des deux Guinées," *APFL*, XLI(1869), 100-114.

6511 . Libermann, François Marie Paul. "L'origine de nos missions de la côte de Guinée," *Annales Apostoliques*, XLIII(1927), 3-6. Also, *Missionary Annals* [Rathmines], XI(1929), 32-34.

6512 . Lysaght, Thomas. [*Lt.Comm.*,R.N.]. "Report on the River Nunez, Its Trade and Resources," *JRGS*, XIX(1849), 29-31.

6513 . Machat, J. "Étude sur la géographie du Fouta-Djallon," *Renseignements Coloniaux* [Supplement to *Bulletin de la Comité de l'Afrique française*.], VI(1900), 124-145.

6514 . _____. *Guinée française: Les rivières du Sud et le Fouta-Djallon.* Paris: Challamel, 1906. 326p.

6515 . _____. "Les ressources économiques du Fouta-Djallon," *Questions Diplomatiques et Coloniales*, V(1899).

6516 . Maclaud, D. [*Dr.*]. "Mission d'étude en Guinée française et Fouta-Djallon," *Revue Coloniale*, V(1899), 437-456.

6517 . Noirot, Ernest. *À travers le Fouta-Djallon et le Bambouk (Soudan occidental) souvenirs de voyage.* Paris: Dreyfous, 1885. 361p.

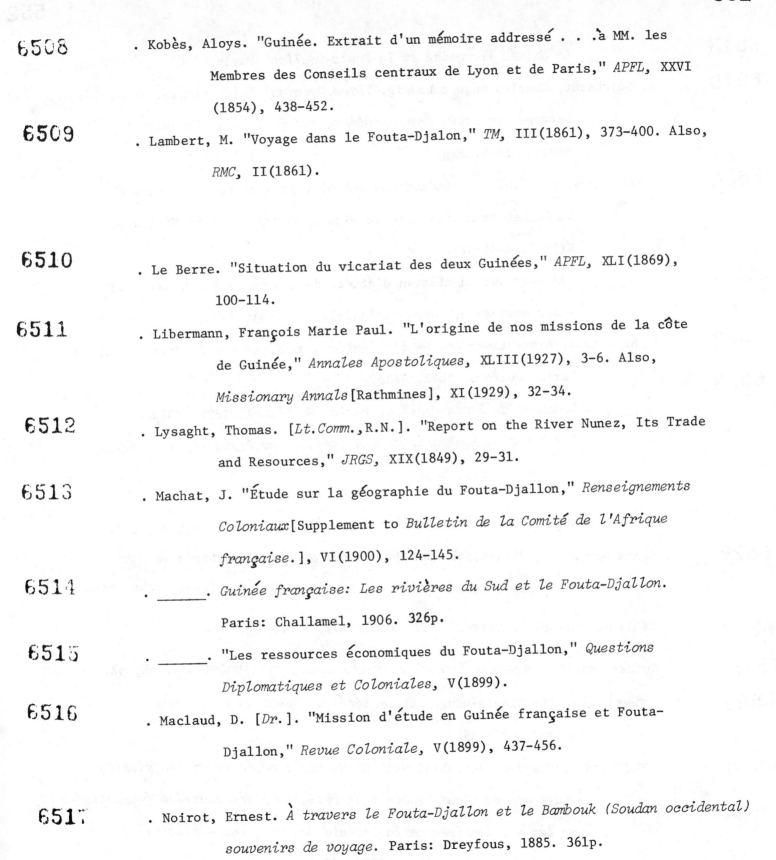

6518 . _____. *La Guinée française et la Fouta-Djallon.* Paris, 1901.

6519 . Reichardt, Charles August Ludwig. *Three Original Fulah Pieces, in Arabic Letters, in Latin Transcription, and in English Translation.* Berlin, 1859. 62p.

6520 . Salesses, E. [*Capt.*]. "Étude d'une nouvelle voie de communication de la Guinée française vers le Niger," *Revue du Génie Militaire,* X(1896), 481-524.

6521 . _____. "Rapport sur la mission d'études du chemin de fer Conakry au Niger navigable," *Revue Coloniale,* V(1899), 1-23.

6522 . Sanderval, Aimé-Oliver de. *De l'Atlantique au Niger par le Foutah-Djallon.*
6523 Paris: Ducrocq, 1882. 411p.

. _____. *Conquête du Fouta-Djallon.* Paris: Challamel, 1899. 338p.

6524 . _____. *Les rives du Konkouré, de l'Atlantique au Foutah-Djalon.* Paris: Challamel, 1900. 30p.

6525 . Ségala, François. "Lettres," *Annales Apostoliques,* XII(1897-1898), 270.

6526 . Senna Barcellos, Christiano José de. *Subsidios para a Historia de Cabo Verde e Guiné.* Lisbon: Academia das Sciencias de Lisboa, 1899. 246p.

6527 . Stalter, Joseph. "Lettres," *APFL,* LIX(1887), 17-23.

6528 . Sutter, Martin. "Lettres," *Annales Apostoliques,* XVI(1900-1901), 41, 42.

6529 . Tautain, L. "Le Dioula-Dougou et le Sénéfo," *Revue de l'Ethnographie,* VI(1887), 395-399.

6530 . Teilhard de Chardin, Joseph-Michel. *La Guinée supérieure et ses missions. Études géographique, sociale et religieuse des contrées évangelisées par les Missionaires de la Société des Missions Africaines de Lyon.* Tours: A. Cattier, 1889. 239p.

6531 . Vigné d'Octon, Paul. "Les pays des Soussoux," *Bulletin de la Société de Géographie Commercial de Bordeaux,* 2nd Series, IX(1886).

IVORY COAST

6532     Audebert, Marie-Louis-Emile. "Journal. Commencé à la Neuville le 31 août 1843, terminé le 12 juin 1844 à Grand-Bassam," *Notes et Documents relatifs à la vie et à l'oeuvre du Vén. F. M. P. Libermann,* Paris, 1936. Vol. 5, pp.181-248.

6533     . Bonhomme, Emile. "Lettere," *MCM,* XXV(1896), 340.

6534     . _____ . "Lettres," *L'Echo des Missions Africaines,* II(1903), 33,34.

6535     . _____ . "Lettres," *MCL,* XXVIII(1896), 305.

6536     . _____ . "Missionsbriefe," *KM,* XXIV(1896), 212, 213.

6537     . Bonhoure, M. "Rapport sur la situation agricole de la Côte d'Ivoire," *Revue Coloniale,* V(1899), 24-28, 79-97.

6538     . Burton, Richard F. "The Kong Mountains," *PRGS,* New Series, IV(1882), 484-486.

6539     . Chaper. "Rapport sur une mission scientifique dans le territoire d'Assinie," *Archives des Missions Scientifiques et Littéraires,* 3rd Series, XII(1885).

6540     . Clozel, Marie François Joseph. "La Côte d'Ivoire," *Notice Historique,* 1899.

6541     . _____ . "Côte d'Ivoire, l'Indénié," *CRSG,* XVI(1897), 260-262.

6542     . _____ . *Les coutumes indigènes de la Côte-d'Ivoire, documents publiés.* Paris: Challamel, 1902. 539p.

6543     . _____ . *Dix ans à la Côte d'Ivoire.* Paris: Challamel, 1906. 350p.

6544     . Cornet, Charles Joseph Alexandre. [Lt.]. *Notes sur la Côte d'Ivoire.* Paris: Charles-Lavauzelle, 1904. 36p.

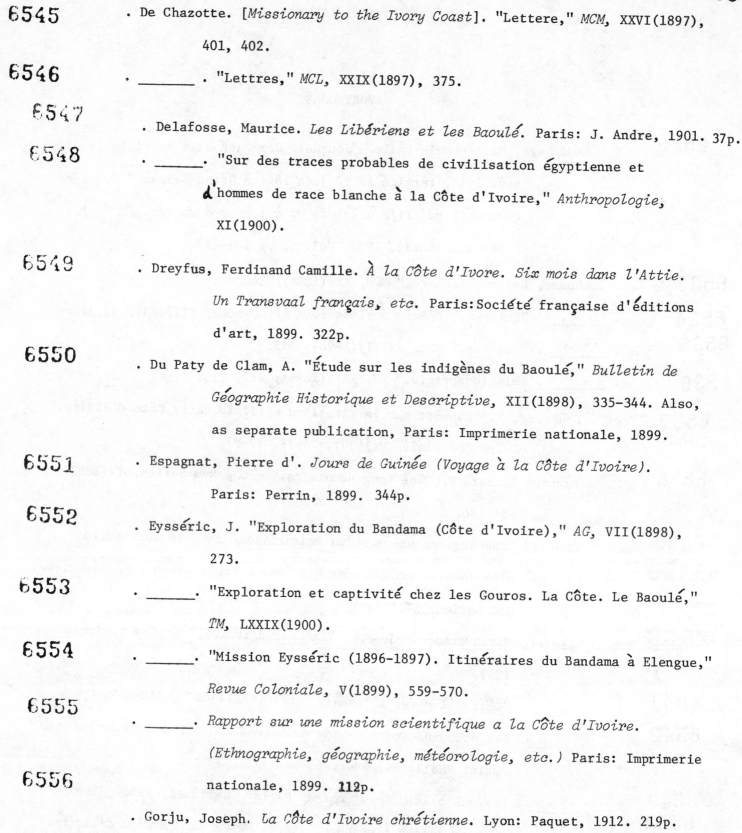

6545   . De Chazotte. [*Missionary to the Ivory Coast*]. "Lettere," *MCM*, XXVI(1897), 401, 402.

6546   . _____. "Lettres," *MCL*, XXIX(1897), 375.

6547   . Delafosse, Maurice. *Les Libériens et les Baoulé*. Paris: J. Andre, 1901. 37p.

6548   . _____. "Sur des traces probables de civilisation égyptienne et d'hommes de race blanche à la Côte d'Ivoire," *Anthropologie*, XI(1900).

6549   . Dreyfus, Ferdinand Camille. *À la Côte d'Ivore. Six mois dans l'Attie. Un Transvaal français, etc.* Paris: Société française d'éditions d'art, 1899. 322p.

6550   . Du Paty de Clam, A. "Étude sur les indigènes du Baoulé," *Bulletin de Géographie Historique et Descriptive*, XII(1898), 335-344. Also, as separate publication, Paris: Imprimerie nationale, 1899.

6551   . Espagnat, Pierre d'. *Jours de Guinée (Voyage à la Côte d'Ivoire)*. Paris: Perrin, 1899. 344p.

6552   . Eysséric, J. "Exploration du Bandama (Côte d'Ivoire)," *AG*, VII(1898), 273.

6553   . _____. "Exploration et captivité chez les Gouros. La Côte. Le Baoulé," *TM*, LXXIX(1900).

6554   . _____. "Mission Eysséric (1896-1897). Itinéraires du Bandama à Elengue," *Revue Coloniale*, V(1899), 559-570.

6555   . _____. *Rapport sur une mission scientifique a la Côte d'Ivoire. (Ethnographie, géographie, météorologie, etc.)* Paris: Imprimerie nationale, 1899. 112p.

6556   . Gorju, Joseph. *La Côte d'Ivoire chrétienne*. Lyon: Paquet, 1912. 219p.

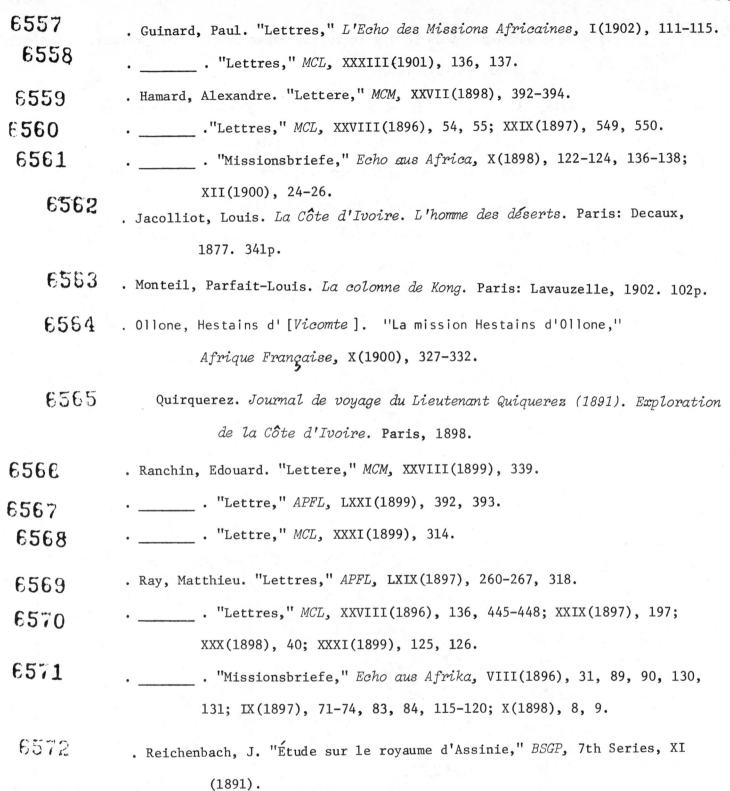

6557      . Guinard, Paul. "Lettres," *L'Echo des Missions Africaines*, I(1902), 111-115.

6558      . _____ . "Lettres," *MCL*, XXXIII(1901), 136, 137.

6559      . Hamard, Alexandre. "Lettere," *MCM*, XXVII(1898), 392-394.

6560      . _____ ."Lettres," *MCL*, XXVIII(1896), 54, 55; XXIX(1897), 549, 550.

6561      . _____ . "Missionsbriefe," *Echo aus Africa*, X(1898), 122-124, 136-138; XII(1900), 24-26.

6562      . Jacolliot, Louis. *La Côte d'Ivoire. L'homme des déserts*. Paris: Decaux, 1877. 341p.

6563      . Monteil, Parfait-Louis. *La colonne de Kong*. Paris: Lavauzelle, 1902. 102p.

6564      . Ollone, Hestains d' [*Vicomte*]. "La mission Hestains d'Ollone," *Afrique Française*, X(1900), 327-332.

6565      Quirquerez. *Journal de voyage du Lieutenant Quiquerez (1891). Exploration de la Côte d'Ivoire*. Paris, 1898.

6566      . Ranchin, Edouard. "Lettere," *MCM*, XXVIII(1899), 339.

6567      . _____ . "Lettre," *APFL*, LXXI(1899), 392, 393.

6568      . _____ . "Lettre," *MCL*, XXXI(1899), 314.

6569      . Ray, Matthieu. "Lettres," *APFL*, LXIX(1897), 260-267, 318.

6570      . _____ . "Lettres," *MCL*, XXVIII(1896), 136, 445-448; XXIX(1897), 197; XXX(1898), 40; XXXI(1899), 125, 126.

6571      . _____ . "Missionsbriefe," *Echo aus Afrika*, VIII(1896), 31, 89, 90, 130, 131; IX(1897), 71-74, 83, 84, 115-120; X(1898), 8, 9.

6572      . Reichenbach, J. "Étude sur le royaume d'Assinie," *BSGP*, 7th Series, XI (1891).

6573   . Thomann, Georges. "À la Côte d'Ivory: la Sassandra," *Renseignements Coloniaux*, 1901, pp. 113-144.

6574   . Verdier, A. *Blocus du territoire d'Assinie (Possession française) par le gouvernement anglais.* La Rochelle: Siret, 1876.

6575   . _____. *Questions coloniales. Côte d'Ivoire. La vérité à propos de l'expédition Monteil.* Paris, 1895. 14p.

6576   . _____. *Trente-cinq années de lutte aux colonies, côte occidentale d'Afrique.* Paris, 1896. 360p.

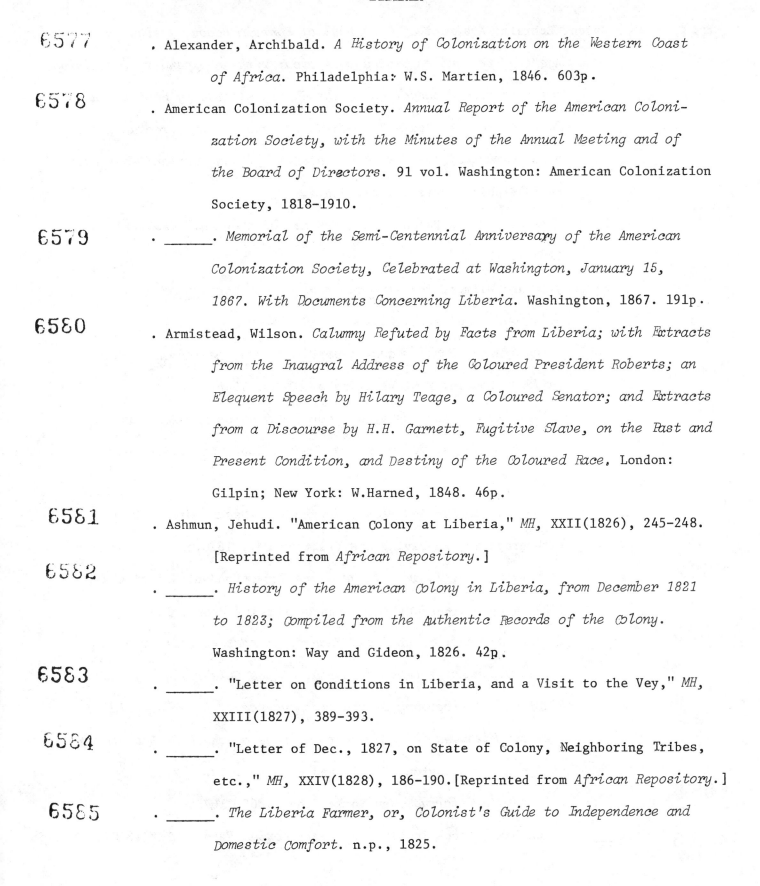

6577    . Alexander, Archibald. *A History of Colonization on the Western Coast of Africa.* Philadelphia: W.S. Martien, 1846. 603p.

6578    . American Colonization Society. *Annual Report of the American Colonization Society, with the Minutes of the Annual Meeting and of the Board of Directors.* 91 vol. Washington: American Colonization Society, 1818-1910.

6579    . _____. *Memorial of the Semi-Centennial Anniversary of the American Colonization Society, Celebrated at Washington, January 15, 1867. With Documents Concerning Liberia.* Washington, 1867. 191p.

6580    . Armistead, Wilson. *Calumny Refuted by Facts from Liberia; with Extracts from the Inaugral Address of the Coloured President Roberts; an Elequent Speech by Hilary Teage, a Coloured Senator; and Extracts from a Discourse by H.H. Garnett, Fugitive Slave, on the Past and Present Condition, and Destiny of the Coloured Race.* London: Gilpin; New York: W.Harned, 1848. 46p.

6581    . Ashmun, Jehudi. "American Colony at Liberia," *MH*, XXII(1826), 245-248. [Reprinted from *African Repository*.]

6582    . _____. *History of the American Colony in Liberia, from December 1821 to 1823; Compiled from the Authentic Records of the Colony.* Washington: Way and Gideon, 1826. 42p.

6583    . _____. "Letter on Conditions in Liberia, and a Visit to the Vey," *MH*, XXIII(1827), 389-393.

6584    . _____. "Letter of Dec., 1827, on State of Colony, Neighboring Tribes, etc.," *MH*, XXIV(1828), 186-190.[Reprinted from *African Repository*.]

6585    . _____. *The Liberia Farmer, or, Colonist's Guide to Independence and Domestic Comfort.* n.p., 1825.

6586 . Bacon, Ephraim. *Abstract of a Journal of Ephraim Bacon, Assistant Agent of the United States to Africa: with an Appendix, Containing Extracts from Proceedings of the Church Missionary Society in England, for the Years 1819-1820. To Which is Prefixed an Abstract of a Journal of the Rev. J.B. Cates. . .in an Overland Journey.* Philadelphia: Potter, 1821. 96p.

6587 . Bacon, Francis. "Cape Palmas and the Mena, or Kroomen," *JRGS*, XII (1842), 196-206.

6588 . Blyden, Edward Wilmot. *The African Problem, and the Method of Its Solution.* Washington: Gibson, 1890. 24p.

6589 . _____. *The African Problem and Other Discourses, Delivered in America in 1890.* London: W.B. Whittingham, 1890. 104p.

6590 . _____. *The Aims and Methods of a Liberal Education for Africans. Inaugral Address, Delivered January 5, 1881.* Cambridge: Wilson, 1882. 30p.

6591 . _____. *Appendix to Ben Anderson's Journey to Musadu.* New York: Lithographing, Engraving and Printing Co., 1870. 14p.

6592 . _____. *Christianity, Islam and the Negro Race.* London: Whittingham, 1887. 432p. Edinburgh: Edinburgh University Press, 1967.

6593 . _____. *Liberia: Past, Present and Future. An Address Delivered July 26, 1866, on Mount Lebanon, Syria, at the Celebration of the Nineteenth Anniversary of the Independence of Liberia, Held by American Missionaries and Other Citizens of the U.S. Residing in Syria.* Washington: M'Gill and Witheraw, 1869. 27p.

6594 . _____. *Liberia's Offering.* New York: Gray, 1862. 167p.

6595 . _____. "On Mixed Races in Liberia," *Smithsonian Report*, XXV(1870), 386-389.

6596 . _____. *Our Origin, Dangers, and Duties. The Annual Address before the Mayor and Common Council of the City of Monrovia, July 26, 1865.* New York: Gray and Green, 1865. 42p.

6597 . _____. *The Problems before Liberia. A Lecture Delivered in the Senate Chamber in Monrovia, July 18, 1909.* London: Phillips, 1909. 32p.

6598 . _____. *The Three Needs of Liberia. A Lecture Delivered at Lower Buchanan, Grand County, Liberia, January 26, 1908.* London: Phillips, 1908. 36p.

6599 . _____. *A Voice from Bleeding Africa, on Behalf of Her Exiled Children.* Monrovia: Killian, 1856. 33p.

6600 . Bourzeix, Pierre. *La République de Libéria.* Paris: Revue Diplomatique, 1887. 88p.

6601 . Brittan, Harriet G. *Scenes and Incidents of Every-Day Life in Africa.* New York: Pudney and Russell, 1860. 353p.

6602 . Brown, George S. *Brown's Abridged Journal: Containing a Brief Account of the Life, Trials, and Travels of George S. Brown, Six Years a Missionary in Liberia, West Africa.* Troy, New York: Prescott and Wilson, 1849. 389p.

6603 . Büttikofer, Johann. [*Conservator*, Reich's Museum, Leyden.] "Bericht über Liberia," *Globús*, XLVI(1884), 40-43, 57-60,75-77,87-93.

6604 . _____. "Einiges über die Eingeborenen von Liberia," *International Archiv für Ethnographie*, I(1888), 33-48,77-91. Reprinted in English translation in *Liberia Bulletin*, No.10, 1897, pp.57-66.

6605 . _____. *Reisebilder aus Liberia. Resultate geographischer, natur-wissenschaftlicher und ethnographischer Untersuchungen während der Jahre 1879-1882 und 1886-1887.* Leiden: Brill, 1890. 440pp.

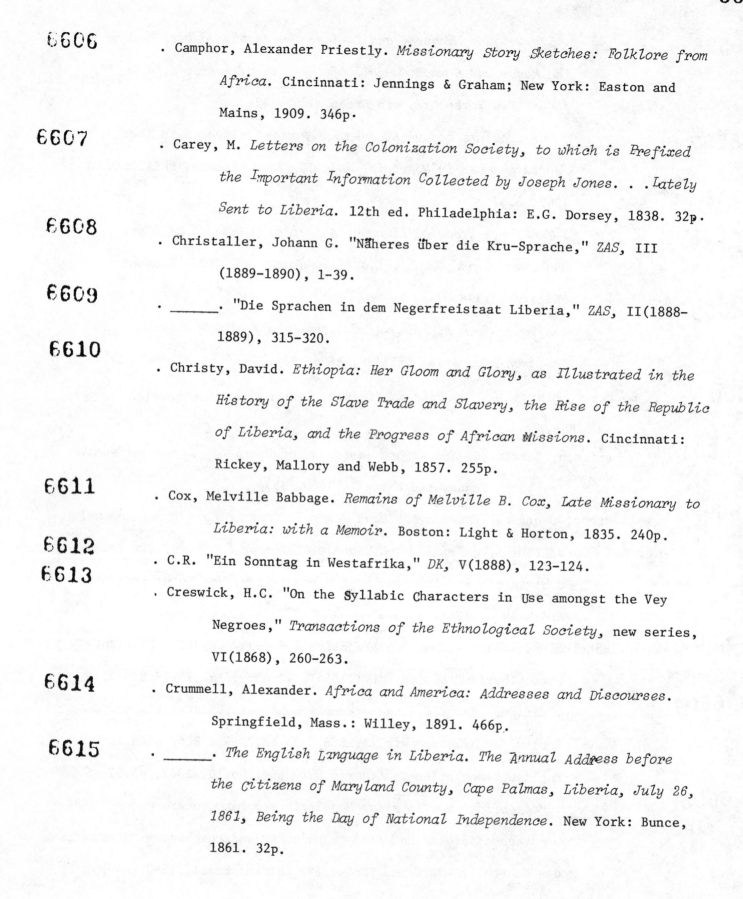

6606
. Camphor, Alexander Priestly. *Missionary Story Sketches: Folklore from Africa*. Cincinnati: Jennings & Graham; New York: Easton and Mains, 1909. 346p.

6607
. Carey, M. *Letters on the Colonization Society, to which is Prefixed the Important Information Collected by Joseph Jones. . .Lately Sent to Liberia*. 12th ed. Philadelphia: E.G. Dorsey, 1838. 32p.

6608
. Christaller, Johann G. "Näheres über die Kru-Sprache," *ZAS*, III (1889-1890), 1-39.

6609
. _____. "Die Sprachen in dem Negerfreistaat Liberia," *ZAS*, II(1888-1889), 315-320.

6610
. Christy, David. *Ethiopia: Her Gloom and Glory, as Illustrated in the History of the Slave Trade and Slavery, the Rise of the Republic of Liberia, and the Progress of African Missions*. Cincinnati: Rickey, Mallory and Webb, 1857. 255p.

6611
. Cox, Melville Babbage. *Remains of Melville B. Cox, Late Missionary to Liberia: with a Memoir*. Boston: Light & Horton, 1835. 240p.

6612
. C.R. "Ein Sonntag in Westafrika," *DK*, V(1888), 123-124.

6613
. Creswick, H.C. "On the Syllabic Characters in Use amongst the Vey Negroes," *Transactions of the Ethnological Society*, new series, VI(1868), 260-263.

6614
. Crummell, Alexander. *Africa and America: Addresses and Discourses*. Springfield, Mass.: Willey, 1891. 466p.

6615
. _____. *The English Language in Liberia. The Annual Address before the Citizens of Maryland County, Cape Palmas, Liberia, July 26, 1861, Being the Day of National Independence*. New York: Bunce, 1861. 32p.

6616 . _____. *The Future of Africa: Being Addresses, Sermons, Delivered in the Republic of Liberia.* New York: Scribner, 1862. 372p.

6617 . Downing, Henry Francis. *A Short History of Liberia (1816-1908) with Descriptive Addenda in Four Parts, for Schools and General Reading.* New York: Gailliard, c.1908. 27p.

6618 . Drayton, B.J. "Letter to the Baptist Missionary Society, London, Feb. 13, 1849," *BM*, XLI(1849), 590-591.

6619 . Dyer, Alfred Stace. *Christian Liberia, the Hope of the Dark Continent. With Special Reference to the Work and Mission of E.S. Morris of Philadelphia.* London, 1879.

6620 . Flickinger, Daniel Kumler. *Ethiopia: or, Twenty Years of Missionary Life in Western Africa.* Dayton: United Brethern, 1877.

6621 . Gudgeon, E.B. "Liberia," *JMGS*, IV(1888), 233-248.

6622 . Hall. "Tour of Doctor Hall up the Cavally River," *MH*, XXXII(1836), 312-314.

6623 . Hartert, Heinrich. "Die Veys," *Globus*, LIII(1888), 236-237.

6624 . Heard, William H. *The Bright Side of African Life.* Philadelphia: A.M.E. Publishing House, 1898. 184p.

6625 , Hening, Mrs. E. F. *History of the African Mission of the Protestant Episcopal Church in the United States with Memoirs of Deceased Missionaries, and Notices of Native Customs.* New York: Stanford and Swords, 1850. 300p.

6626 . Hindorf. "Liberia-Kaffee," *DK*, IX(1892), 112-114.

6627 . Hodgkin, Thomas. *An Inquiry into the Merits of the American Colonization Society. A Reply to the Charges Brought Against It.* London: Watts, 1833.

6628 . Hoffman, C.C. "A Missionary Journey up the Cavalha River, and the Report of a Large River Flowing near the Source of the Former," *PRGS*, VI(1861-1862), 66-67.

6629 . Innes, William. *Liberia: or, the Early History and Signal Preservation of the American Colony of Free Negroes on the Coast of Africa.* Edinburgh: Waugh & Innes, 1831. 2d ed., Edinburgh, 1833.

6630 . Johnson, W. "Letter to the Church Missionary Society, Regeant's Town, April 27, 1821," *MH*, XVIII(1822), 25-27.

6631 . Johnston, Harry Hamilton. "Liberia," *GJ*, XXVI(1905), 131-151.

6632 . _____. *Liberia. . .with an Appendix on the Flora of Liberia by Dr. Otto Stapf*. 2 vol. London: Hutchinson, 1906.

6633 . Kelly, John. "Journal of John Kelly, Catholic Mission SS. Peter and Paul, Cape Palmas, W. Africa, 1842," in *Notes et documents relatifs à la vie et à l'oeuvre du Vén. F.-M.-P. Libermann*, V(1936), 145-180.

6634 . Koelle, Sigismund W. *Narrative of an Expedition into the Vy Country of West Africa and the Discovery of a System of Syllabic Writing*. London, 1849. 34p.

6635 . Kurz. [*Königl. Ober-Grenzkontroleur*]. "Aus Liberia," *DK*, X(1893), 77-78.

6636 . Latrobe, John Hazelhurst Boneval. *Liberia: Its Origin, Rise, Progress and Results. An Address Delivered before the American Colonization Society, January 20, 1880*. Washington, 1880. 11p.

6637 . _____. *Maryland in Liberia. A History of the Colony Planted by the Maryland State Colonization Society under the Auspices of the state of Maryland. . .at Cape Palmas, 1833-1853*. Baltimore: Maryland Historical Society, 1885. 138p.

6638 . Lugenbeel, James Washington. *Sketches of Liberia; Comprising a Brief Account of the Geography, Climate, Productions and Diseases of the Republic of Liberia*. Washington: Alexander, 1850. 43p.

6639 . Mechlin, Joseph. "Letter to a Friend in the United States, 1831," *BM*, XXIII(1831), 556-557.

6640 . Miller, Armistead. *Liberia Described*. Philadelphia: Wilson, 1859. 18p.

6641 . Morris, Edward S. *The Golden Day, an Address Delivered at Monrovia, in the Republic of Liberia, January 1, 1863*. Philadelphia: Young, 1863. 16p.

6642 . M.S. "Der Krustamm in Westafrika und die Sklaverei," *DK*, X(1893), 75-77.

6643 . Nipperdey, Heinrich. "Der Kruboy als Arbeiter und seine Geschichte," *DK*, III(1886), 411-412.

6644 . Norris, Edwin. "Notes on the Vei Language and Alphabet," *JRGS*, XX (1850), 101-113.

6645 . Officer, Morris. *A Plea for a Lutheran Mission in Liberia*. Springfield, Ohio: Nonpareil Office, 1855. 24p.

6646 . Rammstedt, K. "Bilder aus Liberia," *DK*, IV(1887), 78-83, 118-120.

6647 . Ritter, K. "Begründung und gegenwartige Zustände der Neger-Republik Liberia an der Westküste Afrika's," *Zeitschrift für Allgemeine Erdkunde*, I(1853), 5.

6648 . Roberts. "Histoire d'une Négresse et de ses trois fils," *JME*, XLI(1866), 426-429.

6649 . Savage. [*American Episcopal missionary*]. "Death of a Chief—letter, May 5, 1838," *MH*, XXXV(1839), 111-113.

6650 . Schlagintweit-Sakülünski, Hermann von. "Zur Charakteristik der Kru-Neger, nebst allgemeinen anthropologischen Daten," *Ausland*, IL(1876), 668-671, 685-689.

6651 . Schönlein, Philip. "The Cape Palmas Settlement of Liberated Negroes," *PRGS*, I(1885-1857), 98-100.

6652 . Schwarz, B. "Einiges über da interne Leben der Eingeborenen Liberias," *DK*, IV(1887), 737-745.

6653 . Scott, Mrs. Anna M. *Day Dawn in Africa: or, Progress of the Protestant Episcopal Mission at Cape Palmas, West Africa*. New York: Protestant Episcopal Society for the Promotion of Evangelical Knowledge, 1858. 35p.

6654 . _____. *Glimpses of Life in Africa*. New York: American Tract Society, 1857. 64p.

6655 . Smith, Amanda. *An Autobiography; the Story of the Lord's Dealings with Mrs. Amanda Smith, the Coloured Evangelist.* Chicago, 1893. London: Hodder and Stoughton, 1894. 255p.

6656 . Sorela, Luis. *Notas de una misión en la República de Liberia.* Madrid: Huérfanos, 1893. 39p.

6657 Spring, Gardiner. *Memoirs of the Rev. Samuel J. Mills, Late Missionary to the Southwestern Section of the United States, and Agent of the American Colonization Society, Deputed to Explore the Coast of Africa.* New York: Evangelical Missionary Society, 1820. 247p.

6658 . Stetson, George Rochford. *The Liberian Republic as It Is.* Boston: Williams, 1881. 28p.

6659 . Stewart, Thomas McCants. *Liberia: the Americo-African Republic. Being Some Impressions of the Climate, Resources, and People, Resulting from Personal Observations and Experiences in West Africa.* New York: Jenkins' Sons, 1886. 107p.

6660 . Waring, C.M. "Letter, Waring to the Rev. Cornelius Elven, Bury St. Edmunds, Jan. 17, 1833," *BM*, XXV(1833), 249-250.

6661 . Wells, J.M. "Letter from Liberia," *JME*, XXXVIII(1863), 392-396.

6662 . Wilkeson, Samuel. *Concise History of the Commencement, Progress and Present Condition of the American Colonies in Liberia.* Washington: Madisonian, 1839. 88p.

6663 . Williams, Samuel. *Four Years in Liberia.* Philadelphia: King & Baird, 1857. 66p.

6664 . Wilson, J. Leighton. "Annual Report of the Mission, Dec. 28, 1840," *MH*, XXXVII(1841), 350-357.

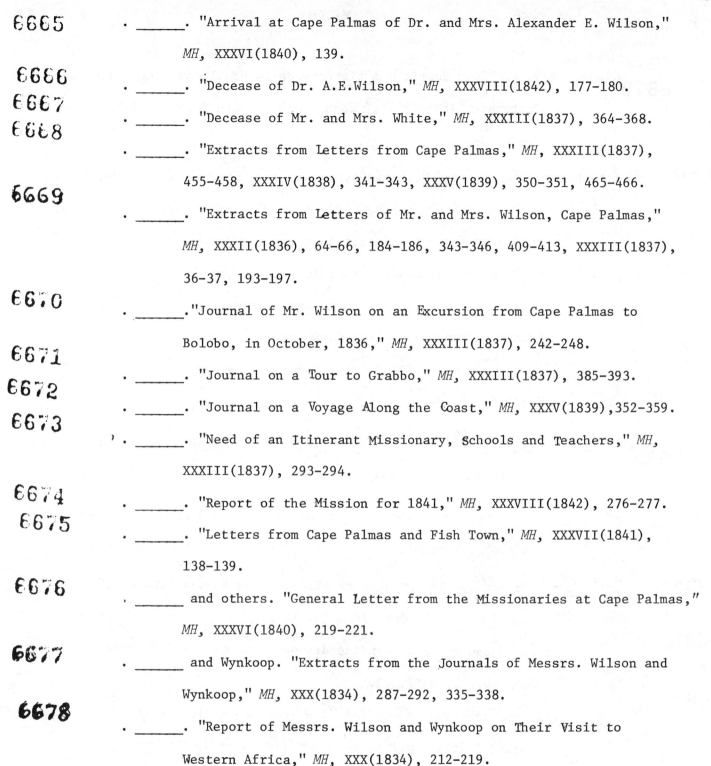

6665 . _____. "Arrival at Cape Palmas of Dr. and Mrs. Alexander E. Wilson," *MH*, XXXVI(1840), 139.

6666 . _____. "Decease of Dr. A.E.Wilson," *MH*, XXXVIII(1842), 177-180.

6667 . _____. "Decease of Mr. and Mrs. White," *MH*, XXXIII(1837), 364-368.

6668 . _____. "Extracts from Letters from Cape Palmas," *MH*, XXXIII(1837), 455-458, XXXIV(1838), 341-343, XXXV(1839), 350-351, 465-466.

6669 . _____. "Extracts from Letters of Mr. and Mrs. Wilson, Cape Palmas," *MH*, XXXII(1836), 64-66, 184-186, 343-346, 409-413, XXXIII(1837), 36-37, 193-197.

6670 . _____."Journal of Mr. Wilson on an Excursion from Cape Palmas to Bolobo, in October, 1836," *MH*, XXXIII(1837), 242-248.

6671 . _____. "Journal on a Tour to Grabbo," *MH*, XXXIII(1837), 385-393.

6672 . _____. "Journal on a Voyage Along the Coast," *MH*, XXXV(1839),352-359.

6673 . _____. "Need of an Itinerant Missionary, Schools and Teachers," *MH*, XXXIII(1837), 293-294.

6674 . _____. "Report of the Mission for 1841," *MH*, XXXVIII(1842), 276-277.

6675 . _____. "Letters from Cape Palmas and Fish Town," *MH*, XXXVII(1841), 138-139.

6676 . _____ and others. "General Letter from the Missionaries at Cape Palmas," *MH*, XXXVI(1840), 219-221.

6677 . _____ and Wynkoop. "Extracts from the Journals of Messrs. Wilson and Wynkoop," *MH*, XXX(1834), 287-292, 335-338.

6678 . _____. "Report of Messrs. Wilson and Wynkoop on Their Visit to Western Africa," *MH*, XXX(1834), 212-219.

6679 · Abbatucci, S. "Pour servir à l'histoire de la boucle du Niger (Mission Destenave, 1896-1898)," *Ethnographie*, 11th Series, (1938), Nos. 35-36, 3-13.

6680 · Anthonay, Léon d', and Valran, Gaston. *Essai d'économie coloniale. De la préparation méthodique d'une mission coloniale; Le caoutchouc au Soudan français.* Paris: Rousseau, 1900. 88p.

6681 Archinard, L. "A propos du Soudan français (Préface du General Archinard au volume du lieutenant de vaisseau Hourst: *Sur le Niger et au pays des Touaregs*)," *Renseignements Coloniaux*, IV(1898), 47.

6682 · _____. "La campagne de 1892-1893 au Soudan," *Renseignements Coloniaux*, II(1896), 1- 36.

6683 · _____. "Fabrication de la poudre à tirer par les Malinké du pays de Kita et du Fouladougou," *Revue Ethnographique*, I(1882), 526-527.

6684 · _____. "La fabrication du fer dans le Soudan," *Revue Ethnographique*, III(1885), 249-255.

6685 · _____. "Rapport sur la campagne de 1890-1891 au Soudan français," *Journal Officiel*, Oct. 10 & 29, 1891.

6686 · _____. "Le Soudan en 1893, considérations commerciales," *Renseignements Coloniaux*, I(1895), 43.

6697 · _____. *Le Soudan français en 1888-1889.* Paris: Imprimerie national, 1890. 28p. Extracted from *Memorial de l'Artillerie de la Marine.*

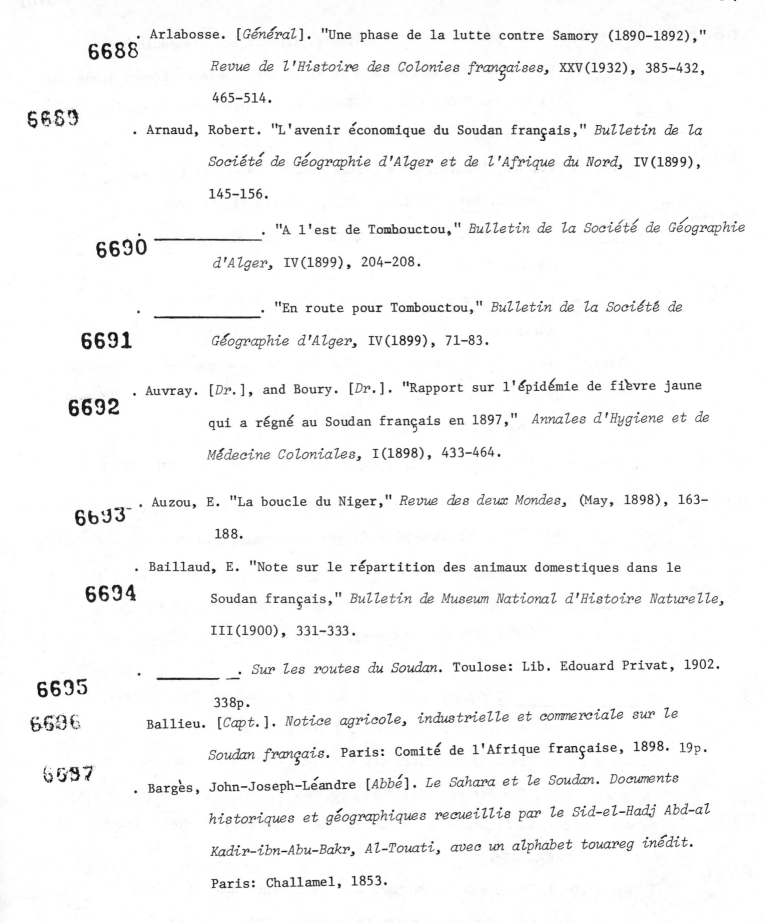

6688 . Arlabosse. [*Général*]. "Une phase de la lutte contre Samory (1890-1892)," *Revue de l'Histoire des Colonies françaises*, XXV(1932), 385-432, 465-514.

6689 . Arnaud, Robert. "L'avenir économique du Soudan français," *Bulletin de la Société de Géographie d'Alger et de l'Afrique du Nord*, IV(1899), 145-156.

6690 . _____. "A l'est de Tombouctou," *Bulletin de la Société de Géographie d'Alger*, IV(1899), 204-208.

6691 . _____. "En route pour Tombouctou," *Bulletin de la Société de Géographie d'Alger*, IV(1899), 71-83.

6692 . Auvray. [*Dr.*], and Boury. [*Dr.*]. "Rapport sur l'épidémie de fièvre jaune qui a régné au Soudan français en 1897," *Annales d'Hygiene et de Médecine Coloniales*, I(1898), 433-464.

6693 . Auzou, E. "La boucle du Niger," *Revue des deux Mondes*, (May, 1898), 163-188.

6694 . Baillaud, E. "Note sur le répartition des animaux domestiques dans le Soudan français," *Bulletin de Museum National d'Histoire Naturelle*, III(1900), 331-333.

6695 . _____. *Sur les routes du Soudan*. Toulose: Lib. Edouard Privat, 1902. 338p.

6696 . Ballieu. [*Capt.*]. *Notice agricole, industrielle et commerciale sur le Soudan français*. Paris: Comité de l'Afrique française, 1898. 19p.

6697 . Bargès, John-Joseph-Léandre [*Abbé*]. *Le Sahara et le Soudan. Documents historiques et géographiques recueillis par le Sid-el-Hadj Abd-al Kadir-ibn-Abu-Bakr, Al-Touati, avec un alphabet touareg inédit*. Paris: Challamel, 1853.

6698 . Baril, C. "Une page d'histoire médicale. Rapport sur l'expedition militaire du Logo (Soudain 1878) et l'epidemie de fievre jaune qui la termina," *Annales de Medecine et de Pharmacie Coloniales,* XXXIV(1935).

6699 Barth, Heinrich. "Extract of a Letter from Dr. Barth to Dr. Beke, Timbuctu, Sept. 7, 1853," *JRGS,* XXIV(1854), 283-288.

6700 . _____. "Lettres sur son voyage à Tombouctou," *BSGP,* 4th Series, X (1855), 301-313.

6701 . _____ "Reise von Kuka nach Timbuctu," *PM,* I(1855), 3.

6702 . _____ "Rückreise von Timbuctu nach Kano," *PM,* I(1855), 85.

6703 . Bary, Erwin de. *Le dernier rapport d'un Europeen sur Ghât et les Touaregs de l'Aïr (journal de voyage d'Erwin de Bary, 1876-1877.)* Paris: Fischbacher, 1898. 221p.

6704 . Bastard, G. "Une ville du Niger, Dienné," *TM,* (1900), 129-132, 137-140.

6705 . Bayol, Jean [*Dr.*]. "L'inauguration du chemin de fer dans le Haut-Sénégal," *Bulletin de la Société de Géographie Commerciale de Paris,* IV (1881-1882), 387-389.

6706 . _____. "Mission du Dr. Bayol sur le Haut-Niger," *Bulletin de la Société de Géographie Commercial de Bordeaux,* 2nd Series, III (1880), 481-483.

6707 _____. *Voyage au pays de Bamako sur le Haut Niger.* Paris, 1881. **Also,** *BSGP,* 7th Series, I(1881), 25-61, 123-163.

6708 . Beaumier, A. "Premier établissement des Israelites à Tombouctou," *BSGP,* 5th Series, XX(1870), 345-370.

6709 . Béchet, Eugene. *Cinq ans de séjour au Soudan français.* Paris: Plon, Nourrit, 1889. 270p.

6710 . Beck. [*Dr.*]. "Eine neue Route nach dem Obern Niger und dem Sudan. (Voyage des missionnaires Aschantee et Buss à Salaga),"

6711  *Jahresbericht der Geographische Gesellschaft, Bern,* III(1880).

. Béliard, L. "Extrait du rapport de M. Béliard, chirurgien du poste de Médine, à la suite du voyage qu'il fait à Nioro avec M. Perraud," *Moniteur Sénégal et Dépendances,* (1865), 159-160, 171-172.

6712  Ben Said, M. "Les Touareg de la région de Tombouctou. Leur exode vers le Nord-Est," *Revue Tunisienne,* X(1903), 34-49, 116-123, 209-214.

6713  . Bigrel, Charles. "Le Haut-Sénégal," *Bulletin de la Société de Etudes Coloniales et Maritimes,* VI(1884), 468-474.

6714  . Binger, Louis-Gustave. "Les routes commerciale du Soudan occidental," *Gazette Géographique,* New Series, XXI(1886).

6715  . Blanc, L. *Livre de lecture et d'instruction à l'usage des élèves des écoles du Soudan français.* Paris: A. Colin, 1899. 142p.

6716  . Blot. [*Vétérinaire*]. "La farine au Soudan," *Revue des Cultures Coloniales,* III(1898), 172-173.

6717  . _____ . "Soudan français. La situation agricole," *Revue des Cultures Coloniales,* I(1897), 63-65.

6718  Blutzet, R. [*Lt.*]. "La région de Tombouctou," *BSGP,* 7th Series, XVI(1895), 374-388.

6719  . Bois, Alexis. [*Commandant*]. *Sénégal et Soudan. De Dakar au Niger.* (Conference du 6 nov. 1866 a la Société de Géographie Commerciale.) Paris: Challamel, 1887. 21p.

6720  . _____ . *Sénégal et Soudan. Travaux publics et chemins de fer.* Paris: Challamel, 1886. 75p.

6721  . Boiteux, G. [*Lt.*]. "Tombouctou," *CRSG,* XIII(1894), 394-395, 416-417.

6722 . Bonhomme, Emile. "Lettres," *APFL*, LXII(1890), 205-209.

6723 . Bonnetain, Mme P. *Une Française au Soudan*. Paris: Librairies-Imprimeries reunies, 1894. 377p.

Bonnier, François-Xavier

6724 . "Campagne topographique 1882-1883 dans le Soudan. Aperçu général du pays, moeurs et coutumes des Bambara," *Bulletin de l'Union Géographique du Nord de la France*, IV(1883), 577-589.

6725 _____. *Mission au pays de Ségou (Soudan français). Campagne dans le Gueniékalary et le Sansanding en 1892*. Paris: Berger-Levrault, 1898. 89p.

6726 Bonnier, Gaetan. *L'occupation de Tombouctou*. Paris: Librairie militaire Fournier, 1931. 290p.

6727 . Borgnis-Desbordes [*Général*]. "Au vieux Soudan. Lettres inédites du général Borgnis-Desbordes," *Renseingements Coloniaux*, (1910), 81-94, 145-150, 159-168.

6728 . _____. "Un cinquantenaire. L'arrivée des Français au Niger," *Revue Military, A.O.F.*, April, 1935, 33-41.

6729 . Bourgès, J. *Notice sur le Soudan français et le Tonkin*. Paris: Asselin et Houzeau, 1893. 162p.

6730 . Bouton, Eugène [*Under pseud. J.Rodes*]. "Un regard sur le Soudan," *Revue Blanche*, XX(1899), 321-330.

6731. Bréchet, E. *Cinq ans de séjour au Soudan français*. Paris: Plon, 1889.

6732 . Brosselard, Charles. *Tlemcen et Tombouctou*. Alger: A. Bourget, 1861. 21p.

6733 . Broussais, Émile. *De Paris au Soudan. Marseille-Alger-Transsaharien*. Alger: de Casabianca,1891. 296p.

6734 . C, B. "Au Bambouk, notes de voyage," *Bulletin de la Société de Géographie Commerciale de Paris,* XII(1889), 686-690.

6735 . Caltelneau, F. de. *Renseignements sur l'Afrique centrale et sur une nation d'hommes à queue qui s'y trouverait d'après le rapport des nègres du Soudan esclaves à Bahia.* Paris, 1851. 48p.

6736 . Caron, Edmond. "Conférence sur la pénétration au Soudan. Voyage de Bamako à Timbuktu," *Bulletin de la Société Bretonne de Géographie,* VII (1889), 227-255.

6737 . _____ . *Le marine au Niger.* Paris: L. Baudoin, 1888. 35p. See also, *RMC,* XCIX(1888), 504.

6738 . _____ . "Voyage de la canonnière *Le Niger* à Tombouctou, 1887," *Bulletin de la Société de Géographie Commerciale de Bordeaux,* 2nd Series, XI(1888), 33.

6739 . Castonnet des Fosses. "Tombouctou, son passé, son présent et son avener," *Bulletin de la Société de Géographie Commerciale de Paris,* XVI (1894-1895), 66-70.

6740 . Cazalbou, L. "Les jardins d'essais au Soudan," *Revue des Cultures Coloniales,* III(1898), 55-58, 116-118; IV(1899), 86-87.

6741 . Cherbonneau, A. "Gadamès et le commerce soudanien," *Revue de Géographie,* IV(1881).

6742 . _____ . "Itinéraire de Tombouctou aux monts de la Lune," *Recueil de la Société Archeologique de la province de Constantine,* I(1853).

6743 . Chevalier, A. "L'exploration agricole et forestière du Soudan français," *Bulletin de la Société des Etudes Coloniales et Maritimes,* XXVI (1901), 363-377.

6744 . Colin, G. [*Dr.*]. "Le Bambouk," *Bulletin de la Société languedocienne de Géographie*, VIII(1885), 640-645.

6745 . _____ . "Le Diébédougou," *RMC*, LXXXI(1884), 501-503.

6746 . _____ . "Haut-Sénégal. Exploration sur la Falémé," *RFEC*, I(1885), 45-49.

6747 . _____ . "La population du Bambouk," *Revue d'Anthropologie*, 3rd Series, I(1886), 432-447.

6748 . _____ . "Resultats de sa mission dans la région de la Falémé," *CRSG*, III(1884), 490.

6749 _____ . *Soudan français, étude politique.* Paris, 1889.

6750 . Collomb. [*Dr.*]. "Contribution à l'étude de l'éthnologie et de l'anthropologie des races du Haut-Niger," *Bulletin de la Société d'Anthropologie de Lyon*, V(1885), 145-170.

6751 . _____ . "Les populations du Haut-Niger," *Bulletin de la Société d'Anthropologie de Lyon*, VI(1886), 2.

6752 _____ "Les races du Haut-Niger," *Bulletin de la Société d'Anthropologie de Lyon*, V(1885), 207-237.

6753 . _____ . "Sur les moeurs de la race bambara," *Bulletin de la Société d'Anthropologie de Lyon*, I(1885), 10-18.

6754 . Conrard. [*Capt.*]. "Sur Bammako (Haut-Niger) et les pays environmants," *CRSG*, VII(1888), 466-472.

6755 . Coppolani, Xavier. *Rapport d'ensemble sur ma mission au Soudan français (1er partie): Chez les Maures.* Paris: Levee, 1899. 34p.

6756 . Coutant. *Le Soudan et la France. Les habitants des rives du Niger.* Paris: Challamel, 1879.

6757 . Coviaux, L. "Notes sur les principaux produits du Moyen-Niger,"
*Agriculture Pratique des Pays Chauds*, I(1901-1902), 442-471, 608-615.

6758 . _____ . "Les produits du cercle de Ségou et des territories de
Sansanding," *Revue des Cultures Coloniales*, VIII(1901), 177-179,
234-236, 299-303.

6759 . Crozais, J. de. "Le commerce du sel du Sahara au Soudan," *Revue de
Géographie*, 1886.

6760 . David, Louis. "Lettres," *Missions d'Afrique*, (1901-1902), 106, 107.

6761 . Decazes. "Travers le Soudan français. La pénétration par le Niger,"
*Bulletin de la Société Normande de Géographie*, XII(1890), 362-
382.

6762 . Delafosse, M. and Hubert, L. *Tombouctou, son histoire, sa conquête*. Paris:
Guillaumin, 1894. 28p.

6763 . Delanneau. [*Capt.*]. "Exploration du cours du Bakhoy (Soudan)," *Bulletin
de la Société de Géographie Commerciale de Bordeaux*, 2nd Series,
V(1882), 516.

6764 . _____ . "Haut-Sénégal. Expédition du colonel Borgnes-Desbordes.
Extrait du rapport du capitaine Delanneau," *Bulletin de ls Société
de Géographie de Bordeaux*, 2nd Series, VI(1883), 178-180.

6765 . _____ . "Le pays de Bammako," *Bulletin de la Société de
Géographie commercial de Bordeaux*, VI(1883), 373-375.

6766 . _____ . "Rapport de reconnaissance sur l'itinéraire de Kita au Niger
et à Keniéra," *Bulletin de la Société Géographie Commerciale de
Bordeaux*, V(1882), 330-333.

6767 . Demanche, G. "Soudan français. Le pénétration par le Niger," *RFEC*, XIV
(1895), 113-125.

6768 . _____. "Le Soudan française et la campagne contre Samory," *RFEC*, XVII
(1898), 189-295

6769 . Derrien. [*Commandant*]. "Mission topographique du Haut-Niger," *Bulletin de
la Société de Géographie et d'Archeologie d'Oran*, IV(1881), 8, 44,
80, 141.

6770 . Descostes, François. *Au Soudan (1890-1891). Souvenirs d'un tirailleur
sénégalais d'après sa correspondance intime.* Paris: Picard, 1893. 69p.

6771
6772 . _____. *Des Alpes au Niger. Souvenirs d'un Marsouin.* Paris: Juven, 1898. 270p.

. Dubois, Félix. *Tombouctou la mystérieuse.* Paris: Flammarion, 1897. 420p.

English edition, London: Heinemann, 1896. 377p.

6773 Duchêne, Lucien. "Lettres," *Annalen der Afrikaansche Missiën*, X(1893-
1894), 32-37, 59-65; XVIII(1901-1902), 4-6.

6774 . _____. "Lettres," *Maandelijksch Verslag der Afrikaansche Missiën*, XV
(1894), 42-47, 68-72, 101-105, 150-154, 187-190.

6775 . _____. "Lettres," *Missiën der Witte Paters*, XXII(1901), 113-123, 169-180.

6776 . _____. "Lettres," *Missions d'Afrique*, XXII(1901), 101-113, 339-346, 363-
374.

6777 . _____. "Lettres," *Missions d'Alger*, (1891-1892), 491-496; (1897-1900),
635-641, 695-706; (1901-1902), 102-106.

6778 . _____. "Missionsbriefe," *Afrika-Bote*, VI(1899-1900), 266-272.

6779 . Dumas, P. "Jardin d'essai de Kati. Essays sur les cultures potagères,"
*Agriculture Pratique des Pays Chauds*, I(1901-1902), 416-421.

6780     . Duponchiec, A. "Exploitation agricole et coloniale du Soudan nigérien,"

        *Bulletin de la Société Languedocienne de Geographie*, XXIII(1900),

        15-21, 169-189, 291-307. Also, *Revue Coloniale*, VI(1900), 949-974,

        1026-1034, 1083-1095, 1101-1124.

6781     . Dupouy, Edouard. [*Dr.*]. *Les chasses au Soudan*. Paris: Challamel, 1894. 357p.

6782     . _____. "Le Korté, poison d'épreuve au Soudan," *Archives de*

        *Médicine et de Pharmacie Navales*, XLIII(1885), 153-154.

6783     . Dupuis, Auguste. "La coiffure nationale des Tombouctiens," *MCL*, XXXI

        (1899), 283-286. Also, *MCM*, XXIX(1900), 197-200.

6784     . Duranton. "Extrait d'un mémoire de M. Duranton sur son voyage au Rocher

        de Félou," *BSGP*, 1st Series, (1824), No. 17, 178-180.

6785     . Duveyrier, Henri. *Exploration du Sahara. Les Touareg du Nord*. Paris:

        Challamel aîné, 1864. 499p.

6786     Elteil, A. d'. "Du Sénégal au Niger," *Exploration*, VI(1878), 340.

6787     . Emily, J. "Souvenirs d'un Soudanais. La fin d'Hamadou Schecou," *Académie*

        *des Sciences coloniales - Comptes Rendus - Communications*, VIII

        (1926-1927), 225-237.

6788     . F. "De Kayes à Tombouctou," *Bulletin de la Société de Géographie de l'Est*,

        XVIII(1896), 55-85.

6789     Faidherbe, Louis L. C. "La question du Niger," *Revue Scientifique*, XXIII

        (1885), 65-68.

6790     . _____. "Tombouctou et les grandes voies commerciales du nord-ouest de

        l'Afrique," *Revue Scientifique*, XXII(1884), 609-613.

6791     · _____ . "Un vapeur français à Tombouctou,"
*Bulletin de la Société de Géographie de Lille*, VIII(1887), 193-199.

6792     · Faucon. [*Lt.*]. *L'Occupation de Tombouctou*. Brest: Presse régimentaire,
1896. 44p.

6793     · Ficheux, Victor. "Lettres," *Annalen der Afrikaansche Missiën*, XII
(1895-1896), 34-37.

6794     · _____ . "Lettres," *Missions d'Afrique*, (1895-1897), 369, 370; (1897-
1900), 557-560.

6795     · _____ . "Récit de la fondation de la mission de Soungobougou,"
*Bulletin de la Missions d'Afrique des Pères Blancs*, (1899), No. 136,
557-560.

6796     · Figeac, T. [*Capt.*]. "Au Soudan," *Bulletin de la Société de Géographie de
Rochefort*, XXIV(1902), 37-44.

6797     · Forêt, Auguste. *Aux bords du Niger. Relation de voyage*. Paris: Challamel,
1888. 37p.

6798     · Gall, Eugen. "Missionsbriefe," *Afrika-Bote*, VI(1899-1900), 164, 165, 189,
190, 207, 208.

6799  Galliéni, Joseph-Simon. "La conquête commerciale du Soudan français," *Bulletin de la
Société de Géographie Commerciale de Paris*, X(1888), 288-294.

6800     · _____ . [*Général*]. *Deux campagnes au Soudan français 1886-
1888*. Paris: Hachette, 1891. 638p.

6801     · _____ . "La France au Soudan," *MG*, IX(1892), 81-84.

6802     · _____ . *Une colonne dans le Soudan français (1886-1887)*. Paris: L.Baudoin,
1888. 68p.

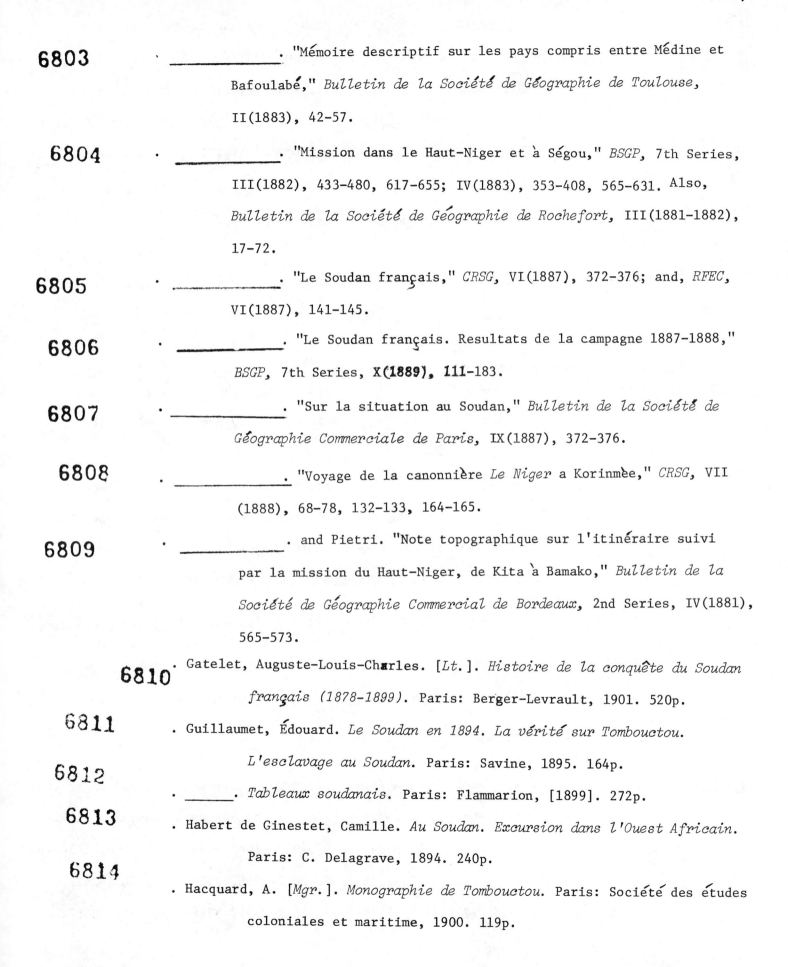

6803     _____. "Mémoire descriptif sur les pays compris entre Médine et Bafoulabé," *Bulletin de la Société de Géographie de Toulouse*, II(1883), 42-57.

6804     _____. "Mission dans le Haut-Niger et à Ségou," *BSGP*, 7th Series, III(1882), 433-480, 617-655; IV(1883), 353-408, 565-631. Also, *Bulletin de la Société de Géographie de Rochefort*, III(1881-1882), 17-72.

6805     _____. "Le Soudan français," *CRSG*, VI(1887), 372-376; and, *RFEC*, VI(1887), 141-145.

6806     _____. "Le Soudan français. Resultats de la campagne 1887-1888," *BSGP*, 7th Series, X(1889), 111-183.

6807     _____. "Sur la situation au Soudan," *Bulletin de la Société de Géographie Commerciale de Paris*, IX(1887), 372-376.

6808     _____. "Voyage de la canonnière *Le Niger* a Korinmèe," *CRSG*, VII (1888), 68-78, 132-133, 164-165.

6809     _____. and Pietri. "Note topographique sur l'itinéraire suivi par la mission du Haut-Niger, de Kita à Bamako," *Bulletin de la Société de Géographie Commercial de Bordeaux*, 2nd Series, IV(1881), 565-573.

6810     Gatelet, Auguste-Louis-Charles. [Lt.]. *Histoire de la conquête du Soudan français (1878-1899)*. Paris: Berger-Levrault, 1901. 520p.

6811     Guillaumet, Édouard. *Le Soudan en 1894. La vérité sur Tombouctou. L'esclavage au Soudan*. Paris: Savine, 1895. 164p.

6812     _____. *Tableaux soudanais*. Paris: Flammarion, [1899]. 272p.

6813     Habert de Ginestet, Camille. *Au Soudan. Excursion dans l'Ouest Africain*. Paris: C. Delagrave, 1894. 240p.

6814     Hacquard, A. [Mgr.]. *Monographie de Tombouctou*. Paris: Société des études coloniales et maritime, 1900. 119p.

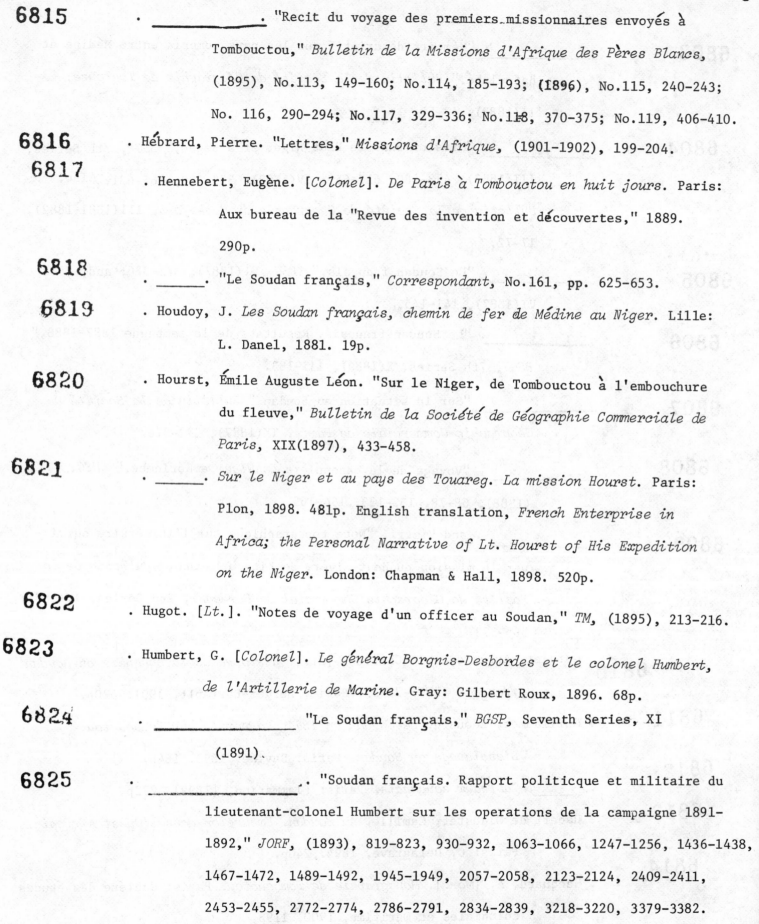

6815 . _____ . "Recit du voyage des premiers missionnaires envoyés à Tombouctou," *Bulletin de la Missions d'Afrique des Pères Blancs,* (1895), No.113, 149-160; No.114, 185-193; (1896), No.115, 240-243; No. 116, 290-294; No.117, 329-336; No.118, 370-375; No.119, 406-410.

6816 . Hébrard, Pierre. "Lettres," *Missions d'Afrique,* (1901-1902), 199-204.

6817 . Hennebert, Eugène. [*Colonel*]. *De Paris à Tombouctou en huit jours.* Paris: Aux bureau de la "Revue des invention et découvertes," 1889. 290p.

6818 . _____ . "Le Soudan français," *Correspondant,* No.161, pp. 625-653.

6819 . Houdoy, J. *Les Soudan français, chemin de fer de Médine au Niger.* Lille: L. Danel, 1881. 19p.

6820 . Hourst, Émile Auguste Léon. "Sur le Niger, de Tombouctou à l'embouchure du fleuve," *Bulletin de la Société de Géographie Commerciale de Paris,* XIX(1897), 433-458.

6821 . _____ . *Sur le Niger et au pays des Touareg. La mission Hourst.* Paris: Plon, 1898. 481p. English translation, *French Enterprise in Africa; the Personal Narrative of Lt. Hourst of His Expedition on the Niger.* London: Chapman & Hall, 1898. 520p.

6822 . Hugot. [*Lt.*]. "Notes de voyage d'un officer au Soudan," *TM,* (1895), 213-216.

6823 . Humbert, G. [*Colonel*]. *Le général Borgnis-Desbordes et le colonel Humbert, de l'Artillerie de Marine.* Gray: Gilbert Roux, 1896. 68p.

6824 . _____ "Le Soudan français," *BGSP,* Seventh Series, XI (1891).

6825 . _____ . "Soudan français. Rapport politicque et militaire du lieutenant-colonel Humbert sur les operations de la campaigne 1891-1892," *JORF,* (1893), 819-823, 930-932, 1063-1066, 1247-1256, 1436-1438, 1467-1472, 1489-1492, 1945-1949, 2057-2058, 2123-2124, 2409-2411, 2453-2455, 2772-2774, 2786-2791, 2834-2839, 3218-3220, 3379-3382.

6826     . _____ . "Le Soudan francais en 1897," *Nouvelle Revue,* (Nov., 1897), 18-37.

6827     . Imbert. [*Commander*]. "La région de Tombouctou," *Bulletin de la Société de Geographie de Aix-Marseille,* XXIV(1900), 172-192.

6828     . Jaime, Jean-Gilbert-Nicomède. [*Lt.*]. *De Koulikoro à Tombouctou à bord du "Mage", 1889-1890.* Paris: Dentu, 1889-1890. 436p.

6829     . _____ . "Notes relatives à la population du Moninfabougou et du Sarro (Haut-Niger)," *Revue mensuelle de l'École d'Anthropologie, de Paris,* I(1891), 107-113.

6830     . Joffre, Joseph-Jacques-Césaire. *My March to Timbuctoo.* London: Chatto and Windus, 1915. 169p.

6831     . _____ . *Operations de la colonne Joffre avant et après l'occupation de Tombouctou, 1893-1894.* Paris: Berger-Levrault, 1895. 76p.

6832     . _____ . "Région de Tombouctou," *Bulletin de la Société languedocienne de Géographie,* XVIII(1895), 171-188.

6833     . Jollet, A. A. *Contribution à la géographie médicale du Soudan occidental: Histoire médicale du poste de Koundou.* Rochefort-sur-Mer: C. Thèze, 1887. 73p.

6834     . Klobb. [*Colonel*]. *Dernier carnet de route. Au Soudan français, suivi du rapport officiel du gouverneur Bergès sur "la fin de la mission Klobb."* Paris: Flammarion, n.d. 293p.

6835     . _____ . *Un drame colonial. À la recherche de Voulet. Mission Klobb-Meynier.* Paris: Nouvelles Editions Argo, 1931. 239p.

6836     . _____ . "La region de Tombouctou. Le dernier repport du colonel Klobb," *Renseingements Coloniaux,* (1899), 157-168.

6837 . Korper, M. *Mission agricole et zootechnique dans le Soudan occidental, 1884-1885.* Paris: Challemel, 1886. 61p.

6838 . Laffont. [*Dr.*]. "Rapport médical de la campagne 1887-1888 dans le Soudan français," *Archives de Médecine Navales,* LI(1889), 161-174, 259-293, 338-354, 426-449; LII(1889), 35-54, 122-143, 225-237. Also, *Bulletin de la Société des Études Coloniales et Maritimes,* XIV (1889), 345. 346.

6839 . La Forest, M. de. *Souvenirs d'une campagne au Soudan, 1892-1893.* Paris, 1898.

6840 . Lamartiny, J. J. de. *Etudes africaines. —Le Bondou et le Bambouk.* Paris: Société Géographie Commerciale, 1884. 72p.

6841 . _____. "Le pays de Bambouk," *Bulletin de la Société de Géographie Commerciale de Paris,* VI(1883-1884), 28-42.

6842 . _____. "Une visite aux chantiers de Kayès," *Bulletin de la Société Géographie Commerciale de Paris,* VI(1883-1884), 222-223.

6843 . Lannegrace. *Rapport sommaire sur les augmentations et les diminutions du trafic au Soudan français en 1898.* Kayes, 1899.

6844 . Lartigue, R. de. [*Commandant*]. "Notice historique sur la région du Sahel," *Renseingements Coloniaux,* (1898), 69-101, 109-135.

6845 . Lavigerie, Charles-Martial Allemand [*Abp.,* later *Cardinal*]. *Recueil de lettres publiées par Mgr. L'Archevêque D'Alder Délégue Apostolique du Sahara et du Soudan sur les Oeuvres et Missions Africaines.* Paris: Henri Plon, 1869. 128p.

6846 . Lécard, T. *Notice sur les vignes du Soudan.* Saint-Louis: Imprimerie du Gouvernement, 1881.

6847 . Le Cerf, Paul-Edmond [*Lt.*]. *Lettres du Soudan.* Paris: Rousseau, 1895. 91p.

6848 . Lenfant, Eugene [*Colonel*]. "La navigation sur le Niger. Rapport sur la flotille du Soudan français," *Renseignements Coloniaux*, V(1899), 174-178.

6849 . L'Orza de Mont-Orso de Reichenberg, Paul-Jean de. [*Capt.*]. "Autour de Nioro (Sénégal)," *Annales de Géographie*, I(1891), 459.

6850 . _____. "De Kayès au Bambouk," *Revue de Géographie*, (1892), 101-112, 161-171.

6851 . _____. *De Marseille au Soudan français en 1889-1891*. Caen: Jouan et Bigot, 1933. 295p.

6852 . _____ _____. *Souvenirs de mission: de Kayès au Bambouk*. Rouen: J. Girieud, 1902. 60p.

6853 . Lota, François-Louis [*Dr.*]. *Contributions à la géographie médicale du Soudan français; deux ans entre Sénégal et Niger*. Paris: Steinheil, 1887. 79p.

6854 . Mage, Abdon-Eugene. "Episode d'un voyage au pays de Ségou," *BSGP*, Fifth Series, XIII(1867), 72-94.

6855 . Mahiet, R. P. "Rapport sur la mission de Banankourou," *Bulletin de la Missions d'Afrique des Pères Blancs*, (1900), No. 143, 801-803.

6856 . _____. "Récit concernant une famine dans la région de Banankourou," *Bulletin de la Missions d'Afrique des Pères Blancs*, (1900), No. 144, 837-847.

6857 . _____. "Récit d'une attaque des Touareg contre Tombouctou," *Bulletin de la Missions d'Afrique des Pères Blancs*, (1897), No. 126, 226-229.

6858 . Mainguy. [*Dr.*]. "L'agriculture dans la région nord du Soudan et les essais du Jardin de Gao," *Agriculture Pratique des Pays Chauds*, II (1902-1903), 302-336.

6859 . Mangin. [*Général*]. "Lettres de Jeunesse," *Revue des deux Mondes*, (Jan, 1930), 102-125.

6860 . ————. *Lettres du Soudan*. Paris: Editions des Portiques, 1930. 255p.

6861 . Marmier, Gaston-Marie-Anastase [*Commandant*]. *La mission du génie au Soudan en 1891-1892*. Paris: Berger-Levrault, 1894. 22p.

6862 . Mazillier. [*Commandant*]. "De l'utilité de doter la région saharienne de Tombouctou d'un atelier de puisatier," *Revue des Troupes Coloniales*, VIII(1909), 21-33.

6863 . Mevil, Andre. *Au pays su soleil et de l'or (récit d'une mission au Soudan français)*. Paris: Firmin-Didot, 1897. 255p.

6864 . Monteil, C. *Les Bambara du Ségou et du Kaarta. Etude historique, ethnographique et littéraire d'une peuplade du Soudan français*. Paris: Emile Larose, 1924. 404p.

6865 . ————. *Monographie de Djenné, cercle et ville*. Tulle: Jean Mazeyrie, 1903. 340p.

6866 . Monteil, Parfait Louis. *Tombouctou et les Touareg*. Paris: Alcan, 1894.

6867 . Mordacq. *Les Spahis soudanais*. Paris: Henri Charles-Lavauzelle, 1912.

6868 . Moreau, J. L. M. [*Capt.*]. "Note sur des haches polies, provenant de la vallée de la Haute Falémé (Senegal), suivie d'observations de M. Hamy," *Bulletin du Museum National d'Histoire Naturelle*, III (1900), 95-96.

6869 . Morisson. [*Capt.*]. "Les écoles au Soudan français," *Renseingements Coloniaux,* (1897), 81–91.

6870 . Muggs, J. W. "Voyage à Tombouctou," *Journal des Voyages,* XXIV(1824), 283–298.

6871 . Nigote. [*Capt.*]. "La mort du colonel Bonnier," *Bulletin du Comité de l'Afrique Française,* (1896), 178–183.

6872 . Pascal. [*Lt.*]. "Voyage d'exploration dans le Bambouk (Haut-Sénégal)," *Revue Algerienne et Coloniale,* III(1860), 137–164.

6873 . Péroz, Marie-Étienne [*Col.*]. "Chez l'Almamy Samory," *Revue Illustrée,* II(June–Dec., 1886), 629–637, 676–684, 706–712.

6874 . _____ . *Au Soudan français. Souvenirs de guerre et de mission.* Paris: Calmann-Lévy, 1899. 467p.

6875 . _____ . *Le Soudan français et son avenir commercial.* Rouen: Espérance-Cagniard, 1890. 44p.

6876 . _____ . *La tactique dans le Soudan, quelques combats et épisodes de guerre remarquables.* Paris: L. Baudoin 1890. 191p.

6877 . Perraud. [*Lt.*]. "Rapport de M. Perraud, lieutenant de Spahis, commandant du cercle de Médine, sur un voyage à Nioro," *Moniteur Sénégal et Dépendances,* (1865), 147–148, 149–152.

6878 . Philebert, Charles [*General*]. *Creation de postes sur la route du Soudan.* Paris: Baudoin, 1890.

6879 . Piétri, Camille [*Capt.*]. *Les Français au Niger, voyages et combats.* Paris: Hachette, 1885. 438p.

6880 . _____ . "Note topographique sur l'itinéraire suivi par la mission du Haut Niger à Kita a Bammako," *Bulletin de la Société de Géographie Commercial de Bordeaux,* 2nd Series, IV(1881), 565.

6881 . _____ . "Rapport sur la raconnaissance du Baoulé," *Bulletin de la Société de Géographie Commercial de Bordeaux*, 2nd Series, IV (1881), 709-717.

6882 . Piguet. [*Capt.*]. *Les routes de l'Algérie au Soudan*. Paris: Chapelot, 1886.

6883 . Quinquandon, F. "Dans la boucle du Niger (1890-1891). Tiéba et le Kénédougou," *Bulletin de la Société de Géographie Commercial de Bordeaux*, 2nd Series, XIV(1891), 433-473.

6884 . _____ . *Rapport adressé a M. le commandant supérieur du Soudan français sur sa mission auprès de Tiéba, roi du Kénédougou*. Paris: Impr. Journ. Off, 1891. Also, *JORF*, (1891), 4636-4640, 4649-4653, 4678=4682, 4691=4694, 4700-4702; and, *Bulletin de la Société Bretonne de Géographie*, X(1892), 31-74, 95-132, 185-197.

6885 . Quintin, L. [*Dr.*]. "Étude ethnographique sur les pays entre le Sénégal et le Niger avec cartes," *BSGP*, 7th Series, II(1881). 177-218, 303-333.

6886 . _____ . *Extrait d'un voyage au Soudan*. Paris: Thèse, 1869.

6887 . Raffenel, A. and Huart. "Exploration de la rivière Falémé et des mines d'or du Bambouk et du Bondou," *Revue Coloniale*, 1st Series, IV(1844), 3-22.

6888 . Raille, M. *Au Soudan, 1893-1894. La colonne Bonnier. Massacre de Dongoi (Tacoubao), 15 janvier 1894 d'après le récit d'un témoin oculaire*. Reims: Imprimerie coopérative, 1894. 23p.

6889 . Rançon, André. "La légende et la fable chez les races primitives et notamment au Soudan française," *Renseignemente Coloniaux*, 1901, pp. 41-45.

6890 . _____ . "Pénétration au Soudan. Konkodougou et Sintedougou," *Bulletin de la Société de Géographie Commercial de Bordeaux*, 2d Series, XVI(1893), 212-221, 225-246.

6891 Rejou. [*Commandant*]. "Huit mois à Tombouctou et dans la région Nord," *TM*, New Series, IV(1898), 409-432.

6892 Rey. "Rapport sur un voyage dans le Khasso en juin-juillet, 1851," *Revue Coloniale*, 2nd Series, IX(1852), 241-275.

6893 Robert, Maurice. "De la Méditerranée au Niger," *Bulletin de la Société de Géographie Commercial de Bordeaux*, III(1880),

6894 Roger, Jacques François [*Baron*]. "Extrait d'une lettre de M. Le Baron Roger, gouverneur du Sénégal, à M. Jomard, membre de l'Institut," *BSGP*, 1st Series, (1826), No. 5, 410-413.

6895 Roques, A. [*Commandant*]. "Le chemin de fer du Soudan français," *Revue Coloniale*, (1896), 753-782.

6896 Sanderval, Aimé Oliver. [*Comte de*]. *Soudan français. Kahel, carnet de voyage*. Paris: Alcan, 1893. 442p.

6897 Sauvant, R. P. "Rapport sur la Mission catholique à Segou-Sikoro," *Bulletin de la Missions d'Afrique des Pères Blancs*, (1897), No. 126, 406-409.

6898 _____. "Rapport sur la mission de Ségou," *Bulletin de la Missions d'Afrique des Pères Blancs*, (1900), No.143, 804-806.

6899 Sevin-Desplaces, L. "Note sur le Soudan français," *CRSG*, VI(1887), 377-383.

6900 Soleillet, J.J.M.M.P. "Exploration dans le royaume de Ségou," *Bulletin de la Société des Etudes Coloniales et Maritimes*, II(1879), 121-135; III(1879), 94-96.

6901 _____. *Voyage au Ségou, 1878-1879*. Paris: Challamel, 1887. 515p.

6902 . _____. "Voyage en Afrique," *Bulletin de la Société*

6903 *languedocienne de Géographie*, II(1879), 275-312.

. Sornin, A. *Un missionnaire vosgien au Soudan*. Saint-Dié: Humbert, 1892.

36p.

6904 . Sugols. [*Lt.*]. "La justice au Soudan français," *Renseignements Coloniaux*,

(1897), 113-129.

6905 . Tautain, L. "Notes sur les castes chez les Mandingues et en particulier

chez les Banmanas," *Revue de l'Ethnographie*, III(1884), 343-352.

6906 . _____. "Notes sur les croyances et pratiques religieuses des Banmanas,"

6907 *Revue de l'Ethnographie*, III(1884), 389.

. Tellier, Louis-Henri-Ernest-Edmond-Gaston. [*Commandant*]. *Autour de Kita,*

*étude Soudanaise*. Paris: H. Charles-Lavauzelle, 1902. 316p.

6908 . Templier, Guillaume. "Lettres," *Missions d'Afrique*, (1901-1902), 345-351.

6909 . Thiriet, E. *Au Soudan français. Souvenirs, 1892-1894, Macina-Tombouctou*.

Paris: Lesot, 1932. 233p.

6910 . Trentinian, Louis-Edgar de. [*Général*]. "Notice sur les tribus nomades

dans la région de Tombouctou," *Renseignements Coloniaux*, II

(1896).

6911 . _____. *Comptes rendu de la situation commerciale du Soudan*. Kayès,

1899.

6912 . _____. *Réformes financières nécessaires dans nos possessions de*

*l'Afrique occidentale. (Le Soudan et nos colonies cotieres.)*

Paris: Hemmerlé, n.d..

6913 . Valbert, G. "Un épisode des campagnes du Soudan," *Revue des deux Mondes*,

(Dec., 1894), 697-708.

6914 . Vallière, J. "Notice géographique sur le Soudan français," *BSGP*,

7th Series, VIII(1887), 486-521.

6915 . Vasco, G. "La boucle du Niger. Population et religion," *RFEC*, XVI(1892), 74-77.

6916 . Verneau, R. "La cynophagie au Soudan," *Anthropologie*, VIII(1897), 742.

6917 . Vignon. [*Capt.*]. "Le Royaume de Ségou et les Bambara," *Nouvelles Annales des Voyages*, 6th Series, I(1857), 139-164.

6918 . Villedeuil, de. "Région du Niger," *CRSG*, XI(1892), 10-11.

6919 . Vincent. [*Capt.*]. "Voyage d'exploration dans l'Adrar (Sahara occidentale)," *Revue Algerienne et Coloniale*, III(1860).

6920 . Vuillet, J. *Etude du Karité, considéré comme producteur de Gutta*. Paris: J. André, 1901. 36p.

6921 . Vuillot, P. *À Tombouctou*. Paris, 1894. 12p.

6922 ————. "La colonne du Soudan, Tombouctou, le Niger," *CRSG*, XIV(1894), 113-115, 171-172, 210-211, 241-243, 337-338, 368-370.

6923 ————. "Dans la région de Tombouctou. Opérations contre les Kel-Antessar," *Bulletin du Comité de l'Afrique Française*, (1895), 328-329.

6924 ————. "Influences des Kel-Antessar et des Kel-Souk auprès des chefs touareg de la région de Tombouctou," *CRSG*, XVI(1897), 370-373.

6925 ————. "La navigabilité du Niger," *CRSG*, XVI(1897), 369-370.

6926 ————. "Sahara occidental, Bassikounou," *CRSG*, XVII(1898), 70-72.

6927 . X. [*Lt.*]. "Soudan français. Campagne 1887-1888," *Bulletin de la Société de Géographie Commercial de Bordeaux*, 2nd Series, XII(1889), 505-532, 537-568, 633-649.

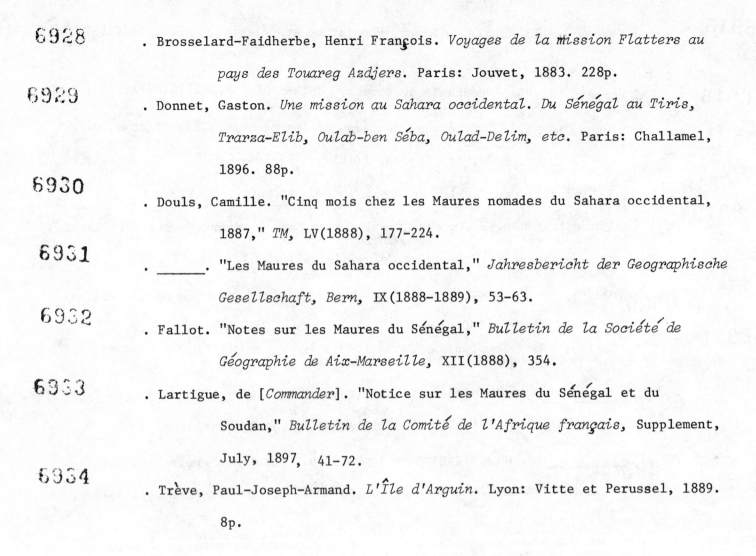

6928     . Brosselard-Faidherbe, Henri François. *Voyages de la mission Flatters au pays des Touareg Azdjers*. Paris: Jouvet, 1883. 228p.

6929     . Donnet, Gaston. *Une mission au Sahara occidental. Du Sénégal au Tiris, Trarza-Elib, Oulab-ben Séba, Oulad-Delim, etc*. Paris: Challamel, 1896. 88p.

6930     . Douls, Camille. "Cinq mois chez les Maures nomades du Sahara occidental, 1887," *TM*, LV(1888), 177-224.

6931     . _____. "Les Maures du Sahara occidental," *Jahresbericht der Geographische Gesellschaft, Bern*, IX(1888-1889), 53-63.

6932     . Fallot. "Notes sur les Maures du Sénégal," *Bulletin de la Société de Géographie de Aix-Marseille*, XII(1888), 354.

6933     . Lartigue, de [*Commander*]. "Notice sur les Maures du Sénégal et du Soudan," *Bulletin de la Comité de l'Afrique français*, Supplement, July, 1897, 41-72.

6934     . Trève, Paul-Joseph-Armand. *L'Île d'Arguin*. Lyon: Vitte et Perussel, 1889. 8p.

## NIGERIA and NIGER

6935    Albéca, Alexandre d'. *Les établissements français du golfe du Bénin,*
        *géographie, commerce, langues, carte.* Paris: L. Daudoin, 1889.

6936    . Allen, William. [*Capt.*]. "Is the Old Calabar a Branch of the River
        Quorra ?" *JRGS*, VII(1837), 198-203.

6937    . _____. *Picturesque Views on the River Niger, Sketched during Lander's*
        *Last Visit in 1832-33.* London: Murray, 1840. 16p.

6938    . _____ _____ _____. "Records of an Expedition up the Quorra
        with Lander," *United Service Journal*, XXX(1838), 310-325.

6939    . _____ and Thompson, Thomas Richard Heywood. *A Narrative of the Expedition*
        *Sent by Her Majesty's Government to the River Niger in 1841.*
        2 vols. London: Bentley, 1848. New York: Barnes and Noble, 1968.

6940    . Anonymous. "Saggio d'una flora medica ed industriale della Costa degli
        Schiavi (Africa occidentale). Per un vecchio missionario. 1873,"
        *MCM*, XIII(1884), 370-372, 379-382, 395-396, 406-408, 439-442,
        454-456, 474-477.

6941    . Bacon, Reginald Hugh Spencer. *Benin, the City of Blood.* London and New
        York: Arnold, 1897. 151p.

6942    . Baikie, William Balfour. "Brief Summary of an Exploring Trip up the
        Rivers Kwòra and Chàdda (or Benué) in 1854," *JRGS*, XXV(1855),
        108-121.

6943    . _____. "Despatch from Dr. Baikie, Commander of the Niger Expedition, to
        Earl Russel, Lukoja, Sept. 10, 1861," *PRGS*, VI(1861-1862), 22-
        23.

6944    . _____. *Narrative of an Exploring Voyage up the Rivers Kwóra and Bínue*
        *in 1854.* London: Murray, 1856. 456p.

6945    . _____. "Notes of a Journey from Bida in Nupe, to Kano in Hausa, Performed
        in 1862," *JRGS*, XXXVII(1867), 92-109. Also, *PRGS*, XI(1866-1867), 49.

6946  .  \_\_\_\_\_and May, Daniel J. "Extracts of Reports from the Niger Expedition,"

6947       *PRGS*, II(1857-1858), 83-98.

      . Ballot. [*Missionaire*]. "Dahomey et golfe de Bénin," *RFEC*, X(1891).

6948  . Barbaglia, Giuseppe. "Lettere," *MCM*, XX(1891), 157-159; XXIV(1895),

6949       579, 580; XXV(1896), 517, 518.

6950  . \_\_\_\_\_. "Lettres," *MCL*, XXVII(1895), 555, 556; XXVIII(1896), 494-496.

      \_\_\_\_\_. "Missionsbriefe," *KM*, XIX(1891), 154, 155.

      . Barth, Heinrich. "Baikies Thaetigkeit am Untern-Niger," *ZGE*, XII(1861),

6951       101.

6952  . \_\_\_\_\_. "Die Imoscharh oder Tuareg, Volk und Land," *PM*, III(1857), 239-

            260.

6953  . \_\_\_\_\_. *The Travels of Abdul Karim in Hausaland and Bornu.* Abridged by

            E. W. Allen. Zaria, Nigeria: North Regional Literature Agency,

            1958. 80p.

6954  . Batty, R. Braithwaite. "Notes on the Yoruba Country," *JAI*, XIX(1899),

6955       160-163.

      . Baudin, Nöel. *Fétichisme et féticheurs.* Lyon: Seminaire des Missions

            africaines, 1884. 112p. English translation, *Fetishism and*

            *Fetish Worshippers.* New York: Benziger Brothers, 1885. 126p.

6956  . \_\_\_\_\_. "Lettere," *MCM*, IV(1875), 183.

6957  . \_\_\_\_\_. "Lettres," *APFL*, XLVIII(1876), 66-76.

6958  . \_\_\_\_\_. "Lettres," *MCL*, VII(1875), 171.

6959     Bazin, Hippolyte. "Lettres," *Annalen der Afrikaansche Missien*, IX

(1892-1893), 70-73.

6960     . _____. "Lettres," *Mission d'Alger*, (1891-1892), 275-277.

6961     . Beaugendre, M. A. "Lettere," *MCM*, III(1873), 177-179.

6962     . _____. "Lettres," *APFL*, XLV(1873), 141-149.

6963     . _____. "Lettres," *MCL*, V(1873), 9-11.

6964     . _____. "Missionsbriefe aus Afrika," *KM*, I(1873), 58-60.

6965     . Becroft, J. [*Capt.*]. "On Benin and the Upper Course of the River Quorra,

or Niger," *JRGS*, XI(1841), 184-192.

6966     . _____. "Substance of a Letter Received from J. Becroft, Esq., Relative

6967     to His Recent Ascent of the Quorra," *JRGS*, VI(1836), 424-426.

Bedingfeld. [*Capt.*, R.N.]. "Narrative of a Journey from Lagos to Odé,

the Capital of the Íjebu Country," *JRGS*, XXXIII(1863), 214-217.

6968     . Berenguer, Vincent. "Lettere," *MCM*, XV(1886), 108.

6969     _____. "Lettres," *MCL*, XV(1882), 622; XVIII(1886), 59.

6970     . Bindloss, Harold. *In the Niger Country*. London: Blackwood, 1898. 338p.

6971     . _____. "An Incident in the Niger Trade," *Chamber's Journal*, II(1899),

154-157.

6972     . Boisragon, Alan M. *Benin Massacre*. New York: New Amsterdam, 1898. London:

Methuen. 1897. 190p.

6973     . Boler, Richard Doubleday, and Knight, Robert. "Notes Accompanying a

Chart of a Portion of the Niger Delta," *JRGS*, XLVI(1876), 411-

412.

6974     . Borghero, Francesco Saverio. "Note géographique sur le delta du Niger,"

*BSGP*, 5th Series, X(1865), 171-176.

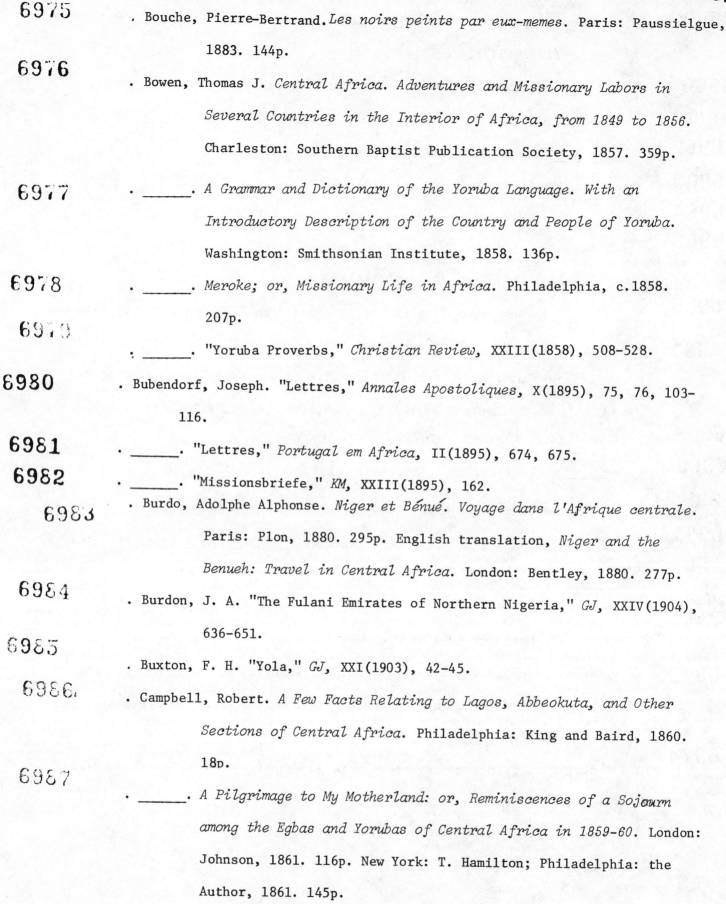

6975 . Bouche, Pierre-Bertrand. *Les noirs peints par eux-memes.* Paris: Paussielgue, 1883. 144p.

6976 . Bowen, Thomas J. *Central Africa. Adventures and Missionary Labors in Several Countries in the Interior of Africa, from 1849 to 1856.* Charleston: Southern Baptist Publication Society, 1857. 359p.

6977 . _____. *A Grammar and Dictionary of the Yoruba Language. With an Introductory Description of the Country and People of Yoruba.* Washington: Smithsonian Institute, 1858. 136p.

6978 . _____. *Meroke; or, Missionary Life in Africa.* Philadelphia, c.1858. 207p.

6979 : _____. "Yoruba Proverbs," *Christian Review,* XXIII(1858), 508-528.

6980 . Bubendorf, Joseph. "Lettres," *Annales Apostoliques,* X(1895), 75, 76, 103-116.

6981 . _____. "Lettres," *Portugal em Africa,* II(1895), 674, 675.

6982 . _____. "Missionsbriefe," *KM,* XXIII(1895), 162.

6983 . Burdo, Adolphe Alphonse. *Niger et Bénué. Voyage dans l'Afrique centrale.* Paris: Plon, 1880. 295p. English translation, *Niger and the Benueh: Travel in Central Africa.* London: Bentley, 1880. 277p.

6984 . Burdon, J. A. "The Fulani Emirates of Northern Nigeria," *GJ,* XXIV(1904), 636-651.

6985 . Buxton, F. H. "Yola," *GJ,* XXI(1903), 42-45.

6986 . Campbell, Robert. *A Few Facts Relating to Lagos, Abbeokuta, and Other Sections of Central Africa.* Philadelphia: King and Baird, 1860. 18p.

6987 . _____. *A Pilgrimage to My Motherland: or, Reminiscences of a Sojourn among the Egbas and Yorubas of Central Africa in 1859-60.* London: Johnson, 1861. 116p. New York: T. Hamilton; Philadelphia: the Author, 1861. 145p.

6988     . Carambauld, Etienne. "Lettere," *MCM*, XI(1882), 512-514; XVII(1888), 419, 420.

6989     . _____. "Lettres," *MCL*, XIV(1882), 329-331; XX(1888), 371, 372.

6990     . Cardi, C. N. de. [*Comte*]. "Ju-Ju Laws and Customs in the Niger Delta," *JAI*, XXIX(1899), 51-61.

6991     . _____. "A Short Description of the Natives of the Niger Coast Protectorate, with Some Account of Their Customs, Religion, Trade, Etc.," in M. Kingsley, *West African Studies*. (London: Macmillan, 1899,) pp.443-566.

6992     . Carter, Gilbert T. "The Colony of Lagos," *Proceedings of the Royal Colonial Institute*, XXVIII(1896-1897), 275-304.

6993     _____. "A Journey in Benin," *PRGS*, New Series, XIV(1892), 457-459.

6994     . Cerminati, Bérenger. "Lettres," *MCL*, XXIX(1897), 135, 221; XXX(1898), 196.

6995     . Chausse, Jean-Baptiste. "Lettere," *MCM*, IX(1880), 522, 523; X(1881), 373-375, 458-462, 470-473; XV(1886), 495, 496; XVI(1887), 561-563; XXII(1893), 8, 9; XXIII(1894), 61-64.

6996     . _____. "Lettres," *APFL*, LVIII(1886), 394; LIX(1887), 57, 58; LXIV(1892), 383; LXV(1893), 150, 151.

6997     . _____. "Lettres," *MCL*, XII(1880), 497, 498; XIII(1881), 41, 230-233, 242-244, 290-292; XVIII(1886), 388, 389, 473; XIX(1887), 541-543; XXIV(1892), 279, 643; XXV(1893), 28; XXVI(1894), 37-40.

6998     . _____. "Missionsbriefe," *KM*, IX(1881), 22, 23; X(1882), 151, 152; XI(1883), 198; XV(1887), 132-134.

6999 . _____, "Voyage à Oyo. Le royaume de l'Ijebu. Avenir de la mission d'Oyo," *APFL*, LX(1888), 395-407.

7000 . \_\_\_\_\_. "Voyage dans le Djébou. I. De Lagos à Ode. II. Visite au roi; III. Confidences royales; IV. Un mot sur le royaume," *APFL*, LIX(1887), 71-78.

7001 . \_\_\_\_\_and Holley, Théodore. "Voyage dans le Yoruba," *MCL*, XVII(1885), 814.

7002 . Clapperton, Hugh. *Journal of a Second Expedition into the Interior of Africa, from the Bight of Benin to Soccatoo, to Which Is Added the Journal of Richard Lander from Kano to the Seacoast, Partly by a More Eastern Route.* London: Murray, 1829. 355p. Philadelphia: Carey, Lee & Carey, 1829.

7003 . Clarke, John, and others. "Calabar," *BM*, XXXVII(1845), 593-596, 676-679, XXXVIII(1846), 188-192.

7004 . Clive, Percy A. "Notes on a Journey to Pali and Mamaidi, in the Kingdom of Bauchi," *GJ*, XIV(1899), 177-183.

7005 . Cole, William. *Life in the Niger, or, the Journal of an African Trader.* London: Saunders, Otley, 1862. 208p.

7006 . Collier, M. A. *Memoir of T. F. Buxton: A Sketch of Emancipation in the West Indies, and of the Niger Expedition for Suppression of the Slave Trade.* Boston: American Tract Society, 1876.

7007 . Colville, Zélia Isabella. "Ten Days on an Oil-River," *Blackwood's Magazine*, CLIII(1893), 372-382.

7008 . Conrau, G. "Leichenfeierlichkeiten bei den Banyang am Oberen Calabar (Crossriver), Nordkamerun," *Globus*, LXXV(1899), 249-251.

7009 . Coquard, Jean-Marie. "Lettere," *MCM*, XXI(1892), 3-5; XXVII(1898), 433,434.

7010 . _____. "Lettres," *APFL*, LXXIII(1901), 28-42.

7011 . _____. "Lettres," *MCL*, XXIII(1891), 340-343, 601-603; XXVI(1894), 414, 415; XXX(1898), 421-424.

7012 . _____. "Missionsbriefe," *KM*, XXVII(1898-1899), 70, 71.

7013 . Crohas, Jean. "Lettere," *MCM*, XXIV(1895), 589-591.

7014 . _____. "Lettres," *MCL*, XXVII(1895), 565-567.

7015 . Crowther, Samuel A. *Journal of an Expedition up the Niger and Tshadda Rivers, Undertaken by Macgregor Laird, Esq., in Connection with the British Government, in 1854*. London: Church Missionary Society, 1855. 234p.

7016 . _____. "La mission du Niger," *JME*, XXXIX(1864), 75-76; XL(1865), 30-33; XLI(1866), 311-314; XLII(1867), 294-297; XLV(1870), 224-228; XLVI(1871), 58-65; XLVIII(1873), 301-309; LIV(1879), 195-199.

7017 . _____. *Niger Mission. Bishop Crowther's Report of the Overland Journey from Lokoja to Bida, on the River Niger, and Thence to Lagos, on the Seacoast*. London: Church Missionary House, 1872. 36p.

7018 . _____. "Notes on the River Niger," *PRGS*, XXI(1876-1877), 481-495.

7019 . _____. *Report of the Overland Journey from Lokoja to Bida, on the River Niger, and Thence to Lagos on the Sea Coast, Nov. 10, 1871 - Feb. 1872*. London: Church Missionary House, n.d..

7020 _____ and Taylor, John C. *Gospel on the Banks of the Niger. No. II. Journals and Notices of the Native Missionaries Accompanying the Niger Expedition of 1857-1859*. London: Church Missionary Society, 1863. 59p.

7021 . _____ and Townsend. "Mission parmi les Yorubas," *JME*, XXV(1850), 241-260.

7022 . Dalton, Ormonde Maddock. "Booty from Benin," *English Illustrated Magazine*, January, 1897, pp. 419-429.

7023 . Delany, Martin Robinson. *Official Report of the Niger Valley Exploring Party*. London: Webb, Millington; Leeds: J. B. Barry, 1861. 64p. New York: Thomas Hamilton, 1861. 75p.

7024 . Deniaud, Toussaint-Donatien. "Lettere," *MCM*, I(1872), 206-207; IX(1880), 184, 409-410, 575-576.

7025 . _____. "Lettres," *MCL*, IV(1871-1872), 467; X(1878), 521; XII(1880), 386-387.

7026 . Dobinson, Henry Hughes. *Letters, with a Prefatory Memoir*. London: Seeley, 1899. 230p.

7027 . Durieux, Antoine. "Lettere," *MCM*, VI(1877), 123-124; IX(1880), 573-575; XII(1883), 99-100.

7028 . _____. "Lettres," *MCL*, IX(1877), 121-122; XII(1880), 418-419, 438-440; XV(1883), 87-88.

7029 . Elliot, G. S. McD. "The Anglo-French Niger-Chad Boundary Commission," *GJ*, XXIV(1904), 505-520.

7030 . Ellis, Alfred Burdon. *The Yoruba-Speaking Peoples of the Slave Coast of West Africa*. London: Chapman & Hall, 1894. 402p.

7031 . Engasser, Jean-Baptiste. "Lettres," *Annales Apostoliques*, XV(1899-1900), 272, 273.

7032 . Ertzscheid, Joseph. "Lettres," *Lis de St-Joseph*, VII(1896), 345-347.

7033 . Fawckner, James. *Narrative of Capt. James Fawckner's Travels on the Coast of Benin, West Africa. Edited by a Friend of the Captain*. London: A. Schloss, 1837. 128p.

Ferryman, Augustus Ferryman Mockler. "Slavery in West Central Africa,"

7034      *Macmillan's Magazine*, July, 1897, pp. 190-198.

. Fiorentini, Filippo. "Lettres," *APFL*, LVII(1885), 237-239, 243-246.

7035

7036    . Flegel, Robert Eduard. "Der Benuë von Djen bis Ribago," *PM*, XXVI(1880),

146.

7037    . _____ . "Der Benuë von Gande bis Djen," *PM*, XXVI(1880), 220-228.

7038    . _____ . "Die Entdeckung des Benuë-Quellgebiets und die Bedeutung des

Benuë fur die Erforschung Afrikas," *Globus*, XLIII(1883), 301-302.

7039    . _____ . "Expedition nach Sokoto," *MAGD*, III(1882), 34.

7040    . _____ . *Lose Blätter aus dem Tagebuche meiner Haussa-Freunde und Reise-*

*gefährten, übersetz, eingeleitet, mit allgemeinen Schilderungen*

*des Volkscharacters und der Socialen Verhältnisse der Haussa's*

*Sowie mit kurzer Lebensgeschichte des Mai gasin baki Versehen.*

Hamburg: Friedericksen, 1895. 47p.

7041    . _____ . "Über seinen Aufenthalt in Westafrika und seine Reisen auf den

Benue," *VGE*, VII(1880), 112.

. _____ . *Vom Niger-Benue. Briefe aus Afrika.* Liepzig: Friedrich, 1890.

7042    125p. Also, *AG*, I(1891), 11.

7043   . François, Charles-Justin. "Lettere," *MCM*, XXI(1892), 445-449.

7044   . _____ ."Lettres," *MCL*, XXIV(1892), 449-452; XXVI(1894), 75,76.

7045   . Friederich, Martin. "Lettere," *MCM*, XXVII(1898), 506.

7046   . _____ . "Lettres," *MCL*, XXX(1898), 495.

7047 . Frigerio, Giovanni. "Lettere," MCMIXXII (1894), 458-460.

7048 . _____. "Lettres," MCL, XXVI (1894), 450, 451.

7049 Gallwey, Henry L. "Journeys in the Benin Country, West Africa," GJ, I (1893), 122-130.

7050 . Ganot, Aimé. "Lettere," MCM, XXX (1901), 601, 602.

7051 . _____. "Lettres," Annales Apostoliques, New Series, (1897-1898), 249-252; XV (1898-1899), 20-22, 78, 79.

7052 . _____. "Lettres," Lis de St-Joseph, IX (1898), 142, 143, 181-185, 208-211, 270-275, 305-309, 335-337; X (1899), 109-111, 141-143, 169-172, 205-207; XI (1900), 53-56, 113-115, 141-144; XII (1901), 339-341, 368-370.

7053 . _____. "Lettres," MCL, XXXII (1900), 89; XXXIII (1901), 589, 590.

7054 _____. "D'Onitsha à Osomari ou quelques pages du journal de la mission du Bas-Niger," MCL, XXXIII (1901), 466-468, 476-479. Also, MCM, XXXI (1902), 418, 419, 426-428.

7055 Glover, John Hawley. The Voyage of the Dayspring, Being the Journal of the Late Sir Hawley Glover, Together with Some Account of the Expedition up the Niger River in 1857. Edited by A. C. G. Hastings. London: John Lane, 1926. 230p.

7056 . Goldie, Hugh. Calabar and Its Mission. Edinburgh: Oliphant Anderson & Co., 1890. 328p.

7057 . _____. "Notes of a Voyage up the Calabar, or Cross River, in November, 1884," SGM, I (1885), 273-283.

7058 . Gollmer, C. A. "On African Symbolic Messages," JAI, XIV (1884), 169-181.

7059 . Gollmer, M., and Hinderer. "Mission d'Abéokouta," JME, XXIX (1854), 338-348, 382-397; XXXIV (1859), 49-51.

7060 . Graff, M. "Mission de l'Eglise d'Angleterre parmi les Yorubas," JME, XXX (1855), 448-464.

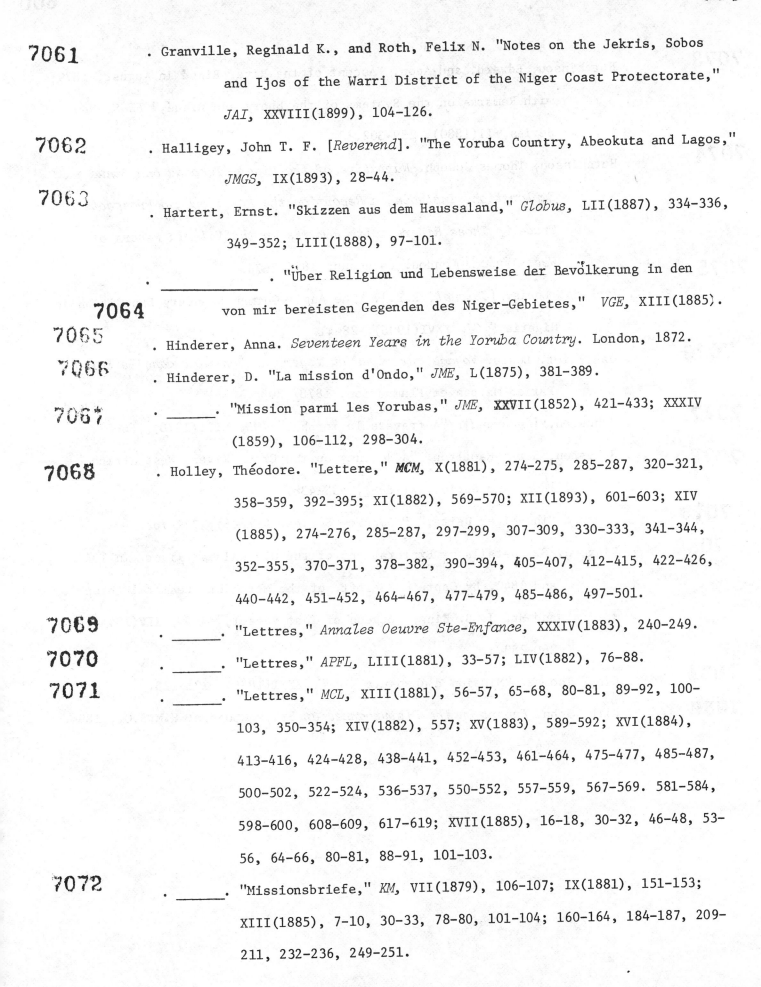

7061 . Granville, Reginald K., and Roth, Felix N. "Notes on the Jekris, Sobos and Ijos of the Warri District of the Niger Coast Protectorate," *JAI*, XXVIII(1899), 104-126.

7062 . Halligey, John T. F. [*Reverend*]. "The Yoruba Country, Abeokuta and Lagos," *JMGS*, IX(1893), 28-44.

7063 . Hartert, Ernst. "Skizzen aus dem Haussaland," *Globus*, LII(1887), 334-336, 349-352; LIII(1888), 97-101.

_____. "Über Religion und Lebensweise der Bevölkerung in den

7064 von mir bereisten Gegenden des Niger-Gebietes," *VGE*, XIII(1885).

7065 . Hinderer, Anna. *Seventeen Years in the Yoruba Country*. London, 1872.

7066 . Hinderer, D. "La mission d'Ondo," *JME*, L(1875), 381-389.

7067 . _____. "Mission parmi les Yorubas," *JME*, XXVII(1852), 421-433; XXXIV (1859), 106-112, 298-304.

7068 . Holley, Théodore. "Lettere," *MCM*, X(1881), 274-275, 285-287, 320-321, 358-359, 392-395; XI(1882), 569-570; XII(1893), 601-603; XIV (1885), 274-276, 285-287, 297-299, 307-309, 330-333, 341-344, 352-355, 370-371, 378-382, 390-394, 405-407, 412-415, 422-426, 440-442, 451-452, 464-467, 477-479, 485-486, 497-501.

7069 . _____. "Lettres," *Annales Oeuvre Ste-Enfance*, XXXIV(1883), 240-249.

7070 . _____. "Lettres," *APFL*, LIII(1881), 33-57; LIV(1882), 76-88.

7071 . _____. "Lettres," *MCL*, XIII(1881), 56-57, 65-68, 80-81, 89-92, 100-103, 350-354; XIV(1882), 557; XV(1883), 589-592; XVI(1884), 413-416, 424-428, 438-441, 452-453, 461-464, 475-477, 485-487, 500-502, 522-524, 536-537, 550-552, 557-559, 567-569. 581-584, 598-600, 608-609, 617-619; XVII(1885), 16-18, 30-32, 46-48, 53-56, 64-66, 80-81, 88-91, 101-103.

7072 . _____. "Missionsbriefe," *KM*, VII(1879), 106-107; IX(1881), 151-153; XIII(1885), 7-10, 30-33, 78-80, 101-104; 160-164, 184-187, 209-211, 232-236, 249-251.

7073 . Hutchinson, Edward, and Anon. "Ascent of the River Binué in August, 1879; with Remarks on the Systems of the Shary and Binué," *PRGS*, New Series, II(1880), 289-302.

7074 . Hutchinson, Thomas Joseph. *Narrative of the Niger, Tshadda and Binue Exploration, Including a Report on the Position and Prospects of Trade up Those Rivers, with Remarks on the Malaria Fevers of West Africa.* London: Longmans, 1855.267p.

7075 . Jackson, Louis. [*Colonel*, R.E.]. "The Anglo-German Boundary Expedition in Nigeria," *GJ*, XXVI(1905), 28-41.

7076 . Jacolliot, Louis. *Voyage aux rives du Niger, au Benin et dans le Borgou.* Paris: Marpan et Flammarion, 1878. 308p.

7077 . Johnston. [*Reverend*]. "A travers le Yoruba," *JME*, LIII(1878), 66-69.

7078 . Johnston, Harry Hamilton. "A Journey up the Cross River, West Africa," *PRGS*, New Series, X(1888), 435-438.

7079 . _____. "The Niger Delta," *PRGS*, New Series, X(1888), 749-763.

7080 . King, J. B. "Details of Explorations of the Old Calabar River, in 1841 and 1842, by Captain Becroft, of the Merchant Steamer 'Ethiope', and Mr. J. B. King, Surgeon of That Vessel," *JRGS*, XIV(1844), 260-283.

7081 . King, Thomas. "Mission d'Abéokuta," *JME*, XXXI(1856), 221-225.

7082 . Kirk, John. *Report on the Disturbances at Brass.* London: H.M.S.O., 1896. 26p.

7083    . Klaus, Isidore. "Lettres," *APFL*, LXX(1898), 356-366.

7084    . Knowles, Charles. "Ascent of the Niger in September and October, 1864," *PRGS*, IX(1864-1865), 72-75.

7085    . Koelle, Sigismund W. *African Native Literature, or Proverbs, Tales, Fables, and Historical Fragments in the Kanuri or Bornu Language.* London: Church Missionary Society, 1854. 434p.

7086    . Krause, Gottlieb A. "Merkwürdige Sitten der Haussa, aus der Haussa-Sprache übersetz," *Globus*, LXIX(1896), 373-375.

7087    Kurtz, Barnabas. "Missionsbriefe," *Echo aus Afrika*, X(1898), 83-85.

7088    Laird, Macgregor, and Oldfield, R. A. K. *Narrative of an Expedition into the Interior of Africa, by the River Niger, in the Steam-Vessels Quorra and Alburkah, in 1832, 1833, and 1834.* 2 **vols.** London: Bentley, 1837.

7089    . Lander, Richard L. *Records of Captain Clapperton's Last Expedition to Africa, with the Subsequent Adventures of the Author.* 2 vols. London: Colburn & Bentley, 1830.

7090    . _____ and Lander, John. *Journal of an Expedition to Explore the Course and Termination of the Niger, with a Narrative of a Voyage down That River to Its Termination.* 3 vols. London: Murray, 1832. New York: Harper, 1832. See also, *JRGS*, I(1832), 179-191.

7091    . Leonard, Arthur Glyn. "Notes of a Journey to Bende," *JMGS*, XIV(1898), 190-207.

7092    . Libs, Jean. "Lettere," *MCM*, XXX(1901), 567, 568.

7093    . _____. "Lettres," *MCL*, XXXIII(1901), 532, 533.

7094   . Lichtenberger, Franz Xaver. "Lettres," *Annales Apostoliques*, XVI(1900-1901), 261, 262.

7095   . Livingstone, Charles. "Discovery of a New Channel through the Forcados River to the Town of Warré," *PRGS*, XIV(1869-1870), 167.

7096   . Lugard, Frederick John Dealtry. "England and France on the Niger: the Race for Borgu," *Nineteenth Century*, XXXVII(1895), 889-903.

7097   . _____. "An Expedition to Borgu, on the Niger," *GJ*, VI(1895), 205-227.

7098   . Macalister, Donald A. "The Aro Country, Southern Nigeria," *SGM*, XVIII (1902), 631-637.

7099   . Macdonald, Claude M. "Exploration of the Benue and Its Northern Tributary, the Kebbi," *PRGS*, New Series, XIII(1891), 449-476.

7100   . Mac Keown, Robert L. *In the Land of the Oil Rivers. The Story of the Qua Iboe Mission.* London: Marshall Brothers, 1902. 164p.

7101   . _____. *Twenty-Five Years in Qua Iboe: the Story of a Missionary Effort in Nigeria.* n.p.: n.p., 1912. 170p.

7102   . MacWilliam, James Ormiston. *Medical History of the Expedition to the Niger, during the Years 1841-42, Comprising an Account of the Fever which Led to Its Abrupt Termination.* London, n.p., 1843. 287p.

7103   . Maigre, E. "De Lagos au Dahomey," *Bulletin de la Société de Géographie de Aix-Marseille*, XIV(1890).

7104   . Mann, Adolphus. "Notes on the Numerical System of the Yoruba Nation," *JAI*, XVI(1887), 59-64.

7105 . Martin, Friedrich. "Lettere," *MCM*, XXVII(1898), 596.

7106 . Mattei, A. "À propos des comptoirs français du Niger," *Bulletin de la Société de Géographie Commerciale de Paris*, VI(1884), 445-446.

7107 . _____. "Cinquante mois au Bas-Niger et dans la Benoue," *MCL*, XX(1888), XXII(1890).

7108 . _____. *Rapports sur le Niger et le Benué*. Paris, 1873. Also, *Archives des Missions Scientifiques et Litteraires*, X(1885), 417.

7109 . May, Daniel J. "Journey in the Yoruba and Nupè Countries in 1858," *JRGS*, XXX(1860), 212-233.

7110 Ménager, Ernest. "La Guinée," *BSGP*, 6th Series, XVI(1878), 151-168.

7111 . _____. "Lettere," *MCM*, VIII(1879), 63; XIII(1884), 459; XV(1886), 297-300.

7112 _____. "Lettres," *Annales de l'Oeuvre Ste-Enfance*, XXXVII(1886), 397-409.

7113 . _____. "Lettres," *BSGP*, 6th Series, XIX(1880), 72-75.

7114 . Mezger, H. "Der Quorra oder Niger [eine geographische Skizze]," *Globus*, VIII(1865), 187-190, 239-241.

7115 . Millson, Alvan. "The Lagoons of the Bight of Benin, West Africa," *JMGS*, V(1889), 333-346.

7116 . _____. "The Yoruba Country, West Africa," *PRGS*, New Series, XIII(1891), 577-587. Also, *JMGS*, VII(1891), 92-104.

7117 . Milum, John [*Reverend*]. "Notes of a Journey from Lagos up the River Niger to Bida, the Capital of Nupè, and Illorin in the Yoruba Country, 1879-80," *PRGS*, New Series, III(1881), 26-37.

7118 . Moloney, Alfred. "Cotton Interests, Foreign and Native, in Yoruba, and Generally in West Africa," *JMGS*, V(1889), 255-276.

7119 . _____. "Notes on Yoruba and the Colony and Protectorate of Lagos, West Africa," *PRGS*, New Series, XII(1890), 596-614.

7120 . Moseley, Lich H. "Regions of the Benue," *GJ*, XIV(1899), 630-637.

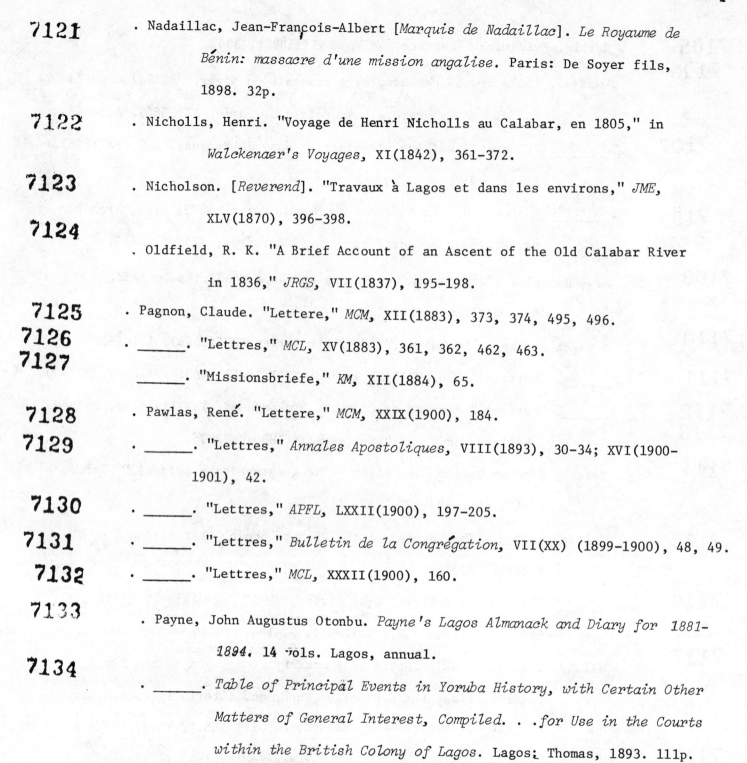

7121 . Nadaillac, Jean-François-Albert [*Marquis de Nadaillac*]. *Le Royaume de Bénin: massacre d'une mission angalise*. Paris: De Soyer fils, 1898. 32p.

7122 . Nicholls, Henri. "Voyage de Henri Nicholls au Calabar, en 1805," in *Walckenaer's Voyages*, XI(1842), 361-372.

7123 . Nicholson. [*Reverend*]. "Travaux à Lagos et dans les environs," *JME*, XLV(1870), 396-398.

7124 . Oldfield, R. K. "A Brief Account of an Ascent of the Old Calabar River in 1836," *JRGS*, VII(1837), 195-198.

7125 . Pagnon, Claude. "Lettere," *MCM*, XII(1883), 373, 374, 495, 496.

7126 . _____. "Lettres," *MCL*, XV(1883), 361, 362, 462, 463.

7127 . _____. "Missionsbriefe," *KM*, XII(1884), 65.

7128 . Pawlas, René. "Lettere," *MCM*, XXIX(1900), 184.

7129 . _____. "Lettres," *Annales Apostoliques*, VIII(1893), 30-34; XVI(1900-1901), 42.

7130 . _____. "Lettres," *APFL*, LXXII(1900), 197-205.

7131 . _____. "Lettres," *Bulletin de la Congrégation*, VII(XX) (1899-1900), 48, 49.

7132 . _____. "Lettres," *MCL*, XXXII(1900), 160.

7133 . Payne, John Augustus Otonbu. *Payne's Lagos Almanack and Diary for 1881-1894. 14 vols*. Lagos, annual.

7134 . _____. *Table of Principal Events in Yoruba History, with Certain Other Matters of General Interest, Compiled. . .for Use in the Courts within the British Colony of Lagos*. Lagos: Thomas, 1893. 111p.

7135 . Pellet, Paul. "Lettere," *MCM*, XXV(1896), 145-148.

7136 _____. "Lettres," *APFL*, LXII(1890), 277-280; LXVIII(1896), 266-274.

7137 . _____. "Lettres," *MCL*, XXVIII(1896), 121-124.

7138 . _____. "Missionsbriefe," *Echo aus Afrika*, XIII(1901), 105-108.

7139 . Pinnock, James. *Benin: Concerning the Country, Inhabitants, Customs and Trade*. Liverpool: "Journal of Commerce", 1897. 54p.

7140 . _____ and Auchterlonie, T. B. "City of Benin: the Country, Customs, and Inhabitants," *Transactions of the Liverpool Geographical Society*, XVI(1898), 5-16.

7141 . _____ and Auchterlonie, T. B. "Personal Experiences in Benin," *Journal of the Tyneside Geographical Society*, III(1897), 392-403.

7142 . Pinnock, Samuel George. *The Romance of Missions in Nigeria*. Richmond, Va.: Educational Department, Foreign Mission Board, Southern Baptist Convention, 1917. 176p.

7143 _____ . *Yoruba Country; Its People, Customs, and Missions*. n.p.: n.p., 1893. 90p.

7144 . Pitt-Rivers, A. *Antique Works of Art from Benin*. London: Printed Privately, 1900. 100p.

7145 . Poirier, Jules. "Lettere," *MCM*, XV(1886), 12; XIX(1890), 147-148; XX (1891), 85-88.

7146 . _____. "Lettres," *APFL*, XLVIII(1876), 61-66; LVII(1885), 239-243; LXII (1890), 304-305.

7147 . _____. "Lettres," *Echo des Mission Africaines*, XXX(1931), 225-226.

7148 . _____. "Lettres," *MCL*, VII(1875), 394-396; XVIII(1886), 35-36.

7149 . Read, C. H., and Dalton, O. M. "Works of Art from Benin City," *JAI*, XXVII(1897-1898), 362-382.

7150    . Reling, Joseph. "Lettres," *Annales Apostoliques*, IX(1894), 127-129; X

(1895), 61-63.

7151    . _____. "Missionsbriefe," *KM*, XXII(1894), 186, 187.

7152    . Ritter, Eugène. "Lettres," *Annales Apostoliques*, XV(1899-1900), 273, 274.

7153    . Robb, M. "Mission du Calabar, mort du roi Eyo-Honesty," *JME*, XXXIV(1859),

148-153.

7154    . Robinson, Charles Henry. "The Hausa Territories. Hausaland," *GJ*, VIII

(1896), 201-211.

7155    . _____. "Hausaland," *SGM*, IX(1893), 643-645; XII(1896), 21-24.

7156    . _____. *Hausaland, or, Fifteen Hundered Miles through the Central Soudan.*

London: Low, Marston, 1896. 304p.

7157    . _____. *Nigeria, Our Latest Protectorate.* London: Marshall, 1900. 223p.

7158    . _____. *Specimens of Hausa Literature.* Cambridge:

University Press, 1896. 112p.

7159    . Robinson, W. "The Work of the Hausa Association," *JMGS*, XII(1896), 60-

64.

7160    . Rohlfs, Gerhard. "Am Benue," *Globus*, XIII(1868), 143-146.

7161    : Roth, Felix N. "A Diary of a Surgeon with the Benin Punitive Expedition,"

*JMGS*, XIV(1898), 208-221.

7162    . Rousselet, Adolphe. "Lettres," *MCL*, XXXI(1899), 485.

7163    _____ "Une révolte d'Indigènes dans la Mission du Niger,"

     *MCL*, XXXI(1899), 400-402, 415-418, 427-429, 436, 437. Also, *MCM*,

     XXIX(1900), 550, 551, 560-563, 586-588, 600.

7164    . Scala, Giambattista. *Memorie di Giambattista Scala, console di S.M.*

     *Italiana in Lagos di Guinéa, intorno ad us suo viaggio in*

     *Abbeockuta, città dell' intermo dell' Africa, fatto nell' anno*

     *1858.* Sampiedarena: Verengo, 1862. 247p.

7165    . Schön, Jacob Friedrich. *Magna Hausa. Native Literature, or, Proverbs and*

     *Historical Fragments. . .in the Hausa Language. To Which Is*

     *Added a Translation in English.* London: Christian Knowledge

     Society, 1885.

7166    . _____and Crowther, Samuel A. *Journals of the Rev. J. F. Schön and Mr.*

     *Samuel Crowther, Who. . .Accompanied the Expedition up the Niger*

     *in 1841, in Behalf of the Church Missionary Society.* London:

     Hatchard, 1842. 393p.

7167    . Schultheiss, G. "Des sociétés secrètes chez les Nègres-Yoruba de la

     Guinée," *Globus*, LXX(1896).

7168    . Séquer, M. A. "Lettera," *MCM*, IV(1875), 54.

7169    . _____. "Lettre," *MCL*, VII(1875), 40-41.

7170    . Simpson, William. *A Private Journal Kept during the Niger Expedition*

     *from May 1841 - June 1842.* London: Shaw, 1843. 139p.

7171    . Staudinger, Paul. "Die Bevölkerung des Haussa-Länder," *Verhandlungen der*

     *Berliner Gesellschaft für Anthropologie*, XXI(1891), 228-237.

7172    . _____. *Im Herzen der Haussaländer. Reise im westlichen Sudan nebst*

     *Bericht über den Verlauf der Deutschen Niger-Benue Expedition.*

     Berlin: Landsberger, 1889. 758p.

7173    . _____. "Todtenbestattung bei den Haussa," *ZE*, XXVIII(1896), 402-405.

7174 . Stone, Richard Henry. [*Reverend*]. *In Africa's Forest and Jungle; or, Six Years among the Yorubans.* New York and Chicago: Revell, 1899. 282p.

7175 . Taubman-Goldie, George D. "Britain's Priority on the Middle Niger," *New Review*, XVI(1897), 687-696.

7176 . _____. *The Future of the Niger Territories.* London: Chamber of Commerce, 1897.

7177 . _____. *Report on the Niger Sudan Campaign (1897) with Miscellaneous Documents, Including the Military Report by Major Arnold.* n.p.: n.p., 1897. 23p.

. Terrier, Auguste. "La pays Zaberma," *Renseignements Coloniaux*, 1901, pp. 25-32.

7179 . Thillier, Joseph. "Lettre," *APFL*, XLIV(1872), 261-270.

7180 . _____. "Lettre," *MCL*, I(1868), 206.

7181 . Thollon, Gonzague. "Lettre," *MCL*, II(1869), 417-419.

7182 . Thomas, W. Nicholas. "On the Oil Rivers of West Africa," *PRGS*, XVII (1872-1873), 148-155.

7183 . Thomson, Joseph. *Mungo Park and the Niger.* London: Phillips, 1890.

7184 . _____. "Niger and Central Sudan Sketches," *SGM*, II(1886), 577-596.

7185 . _____. "Sketch of a Trip to Sokoto by the River Niger," *JMGS*, II (1886), 1-18.

7186 . Townsend. "Abbéokuta et Dahomey," *JME*, L(1875), 338-342.

7187 . Tucker, Charlotte Maris. *Abbeokuta; or, Sunrise within the Tropics; an Outline of the Origin and Progress of the Yoruba Mission.* London: Nisbet, 1853. 278p.

7188 . Vandeleur, C. F. Seymour. "Nupe and Ilorin," *GJ*, X(1897), 349-370.

7189 . Viard, Edouard. *Au Bas-Niger*. Paris: Guérin, 1886. 301p.

7190 . Vischer, Hanns. "Journeys in Northern Nigeria," *GJ*, XXVIII(1906), 368-377.

7191 . Vogel, E. *Niger Flora; or an Enumeration of the Plants of Western Tropical Africa. . .with a Sketch of the Life of Dr. Vogel, and a Journal of the Voyage*. Ed. by W.J.Hooker. London, 1849.

7192 . Vogt, H. "Die Bewohner von Lagos," *Globus*, 1882.

7193 . Walker, James Broom. [*Capt.*]. "Note on the Old Calabar and Cross Rivers," *PRGS*, XVI(1871-1872), 135-137.

7194 _____. "Notes of a Visit, in May 1875, to the Old Calabar and Qua Rivers, the Ekoi Country, and the Qua Rapids," *PRGS*, XX(1875-1876), 224-230.

7195 . _____. "Notes on the Politics, Religion, and Commerce of Old Calabar," *JAI*, VI(1877), 119-124.

7196 . Wallace, William. "The Hausa Territories. Notes on a Journey through the Sokoto Empire and Borgu, in 1894," *GJ*, VIII(1896), 211-219.

7197 . Wilmot. [*Commodore*]. "Resources of the Niger as Regards Legitimate Trade," *PRGS*, VIII(1863-1864), 53-54.

7198 . Wood, J. Buckey. [*Reverend*]. "Die Bewohner von Lagos," *Globus*, XLI (1882), 236-238, 252-254.

7199 . Zappa, Carlo. "Le Bas-Niger," *Bulletin de la Société de Géographie de Lyon*, VI(1886), 335-352; VII(1887), 503-508; XII(1893), 419-426; XIII(1895), 260-267.

7200      . _____ . "Lettere," *MCM*, XVII(1888), 425, 426; XXIII(1894), 100-102, 457, 458; XXVII(1898), 142, 553, 554; XXVIII(1899), 113; XXX(1901), 375, 376, 568.

7201      . _____ . "Lettres," *APFL*, LXVI(1894), 32-43; LXVII(1895), 198-206; LXVIII (1896), 113-129; LXIX(1897), 108-114; LXX(1898), 105-111; LXXI(1899), 152, 459-464; LXXII(1900), 119-134.

7202      . _____ . "Lettres," *MCL*, XXV(1893), 586-588; XXVI(1894), 449, 450; XXX (1898), 112, 541-543; XXXI(1899), 77; XXXIII(1901), 363, 533.

7203      . _____ . "Sur le Niger. De Lokoja à Bida," *MCL*, XXI(1889), 272-275, 285, 286, 293-295. Also, *MCM*, XVIII(1889), 538, 539, 550, 551, 562, 563, 572.

7204    . Almeida, J. B. P. *Exploraçao da Senegambia Portugueza*. Lisbon, 1878.

7205    . Arpoare, Henrique de. "Exploração agronomica em Cabo Verde e Guiné,"
        *BSGL*, III(1882), 362-369.

7206    . Astrié, Max. "La Guinée portugaise," *BSGL*, V(1885), 564-568.

7207    . _____. "Voyage dans l'île d'Orango (Guinée portugaise)," *BSGL*, VI(1886),
        38-55.

7208    . Barros, P. Marcellino [*Marques de*]. "Guiné portugueza," *BSGL*, V(1885),
        117-121.

7209    . _____. "Guiné portugueza: ou breve noticia sobre alguns dos seus usos,
        costumes, linguas e origens de seus povos," *BSGL*, III(1882),
        707-731.

7210    . Bertrand-Bocandé. "Notes sur la Guinée portugaise ou Sénégambie méridionale,"
        *BSGP*, 3rd Series, XI(1849), 265-350; XII(1849), 57-93.

7211    . Brosselard-Faidherbe, Henri François. *La Guinée portugaise et les
        possessions françaises voisines*. Lille: L. Danel, 1889. 116p.

7212    . _____. "Voyage dans la Gambie et la Guinée portugaise," *TM*, LVII(1889).

7213    . Castro e Moraes, Antonio María de Jesús. *Um breve esboço dos costumes de
        S. Thomé e Principe*. Lisbon, 1901.

7214    . Conceição Albano, Antonio [*Marques da*]. "Descripção da Ilha de S. Thomé,"
        *Arquivo das Colonias*, III(1918), 1-5.

7215    . Curado, A. F. *A Ilha de S. Tome*. Lisbon, 1893.

7216    . Da Costa, Aleixo Justiniano Socrates. "Provincia da Guiné portugueza,"
        *BSGL*, III(1883), 94-112, 149-160, 188-203.

7217    . Da Costa Oliveira, E. J. "Guiné portugueza: esboço cartographico," *BSGL*,
        VIII(1888-1889), 297-308.

7218   . \_\_\_\_\_. "Viagem a Guiné portugueza," *BSGL*, VIII(1888-1889), 547-648.

7219   . Geraldes, Francisco Antonio Marques. "Guiné portugueza," *BSGL*, VII(1887), 465-522.

7220   . Peito de Carvalho, Joaquim. "Guiné portugueza. De Geba ao Indornal," *BSGL*, III(1882), 689-694.

7221   . Pereira Baretto, Honorio. *Memoria sobre o estado actual de Senegambia portugueza*. Lisbon, 1843.

7222   . Pinheiro Lobo Machado de Melo e Almada, Vicente. "As Ilhas de S. Tomé e Príncipe. (Notas de una administração colonial. Lugares selectos da biblioteca colonial portuguesa, 1884,)" *Boletim Geral das Colónias*, I(1929), 177-179.

7223   . Stallibras, Edward. "The Bijouga or Bissagos Islands, West Africa," *PRGS*, New Series, XI(1889), 595-601.

7224   . Teixeira da Silva. *Relatorio do governo da Guiné portugueza, 1867-1888*. Lisbon, 1889.

7225   . Teixeira de Barros, Alberto Xavier. "Breves apontamentos sobre a historia politica do Forria," *BSGL*, XV(1896), 339-349.

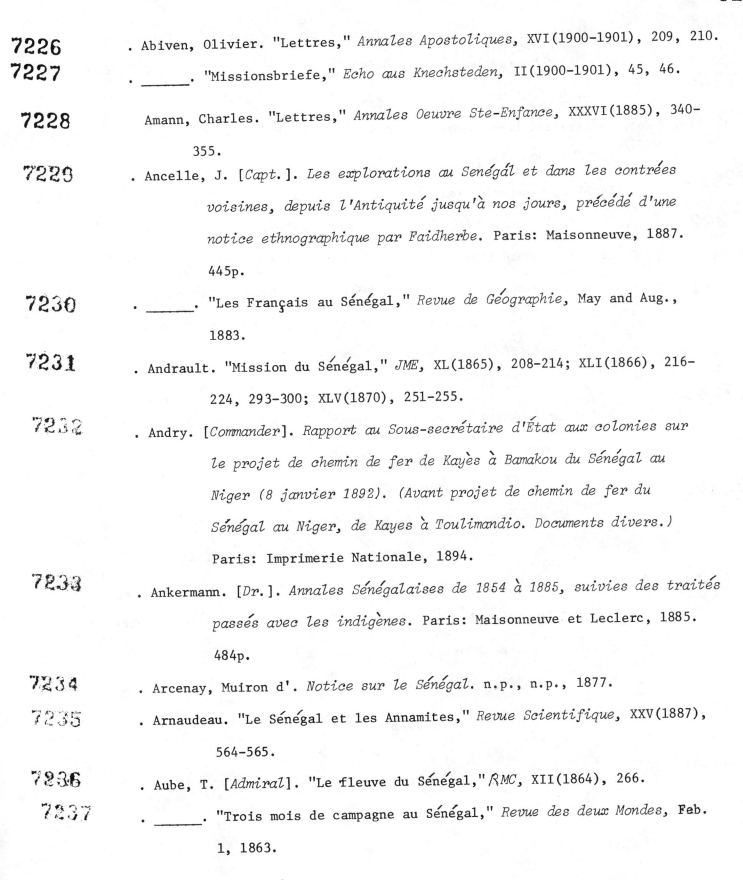

7226 . Abiven, Olivier. "Lettres," *Annales Apostoliques*, XVI(1900-1901), 209, 210.

7227 . _____. "Missionsbriefe," *Echo aus Knechsteden*, II(1900-1901), 45, 46.

7228 Amann, Charles. "Lettres," *Annales Oeuvre Ste-Enfance*, XXXVI(1885), 340-355.

7229 . Ancelle, J. [*Capt.*]. *Les explorations au Sénégal et dans les contrées voisines, depuis l'Antiquité jusqu'à nos jours, précédé d'une notice ethnographique par Faidherbe.* Paris: Maisonneuve, 1887. 445p.

7230 . _____. "Les Français au Sénégal," *Revue de Géographie*, May and Aug., 1883.

7231 . Andrault. "Mission du Sénégal," *JME*, XL(1865), 208-214; XLI(1866), 216-224, 293-300; XLV(1870), 251-255.

7232 . Andry. [*Commander*]. *Rapport au Sous-secrétaire d'État aux colonies sur le projet de chemin de fer de Kayès à Bamakou du Sénégal au Niger (8 janvier 1892). (Avant projet de chemin de fer du Sénégal au Niger, de Kayes à Toulimandio. Documents divers.)* Paris: Imprimerie Nationale, 1894.

7233 . Ankermann. [*Dr.*]. *Annales Sénégalaises de 1854 à 1885, suivies des traités passés avec les indigènes.* Paris: Maisonneuve et Leclerc, 1885. 484p.

7234 . Arcenay, Muiron d'. *Notice sur le Sénégal.* n.p., n.p., 1877.

7235 . Arnaudeau. "Le Sénégal et les Annamites," *Revue Scientifique*, XXV(1887), 564-565.

7236 . Aube, T. [*Admiral*]. "Le fleuve du Sénégal," *RMC*, XII(1864), 266.

7237 . _____. "Trois mois de campagne au Sénégal," *Revue des deux Mondes*, Feb. 1, 1863.

7238 . Audibert, A. A. L. "Rapport adressé à la Commission de l"Exposition Universelle réunie a Saint-Louis," *Revue Coloniale*, XIV(1855).

7239 . Azan, H. "Culture du coton au Sénégal," *RMC*, VIII(1863), 445.

7240 . Bailly-Forfiller, Georges. *À cheval de Dakar à Konakry*. Paris: Lemaire, 1900. 124p.

7241 Barbier, Emmanuel. "Lettres," *APFL*, XXVIII(1856), 5-11.

7242 . _____. "Lettres," *BGCSS*, I(1857-1859), 210-213, 608-613.

7243 . Barron, Edouard [*Mgr.*]. "Lettre," *APFL*, XV(1843), 66-72, 314-330.

7244 . _____. "Relation de la visite faite par M. Edouard Barron, Préfet Ap. de la Guinée, dans sa nouvelle préfecture," in *Notes et Documents relatifs à la vie et à l'oeuvre du Ven. F. M. P. Libermann*, V (1936), 18-81.

7245 . Barthélemy, Adrien. *Guide de voyageur dans la Sénégambie française*. Bordeaux: J. Durand, 1884. 330p.

7246 . Barthet, Désiré. *Ordonnances Synodales de Mgr. Magloire-Désiré Barthet, Vicaire Apostolique de la Sénégambie et Préfet Apostolique du Sénégal*. Dakar: Imprimerie de la Mission, 1893. 232p.

7247 . Basset, René. *Mission au Sénégal*. Algiers: E. Leroux, 1909.

7248 . Baudin. "Naufrage du brick français "Le Courrier-Du-Sénégal" près du Cap Naze à le côte occidentale d'Afrique," *Revue Coloniale*, IV(1844), 403.

7249 . Bayol, Jean [*Dr.*]. *La Sénégambie*. Paris, 1881.

7250 . Beal, B. A. *Quelques considérations sur les maladies observées au Sénégal*. Paris, 1862.

7251 . Beaufort, E. de. "Extrait d'une lettre adressée à M. Jomard par M. de Beaufort, en mission dans le Sénégal," *BSGP*, 1st Series, (1825), No. 25, 332-333.

7252 . Beaufort, P. Grout de. "Expédition dans l'intérieur de l'Afrique par la voie du Sénégal," *Journal des Voyages*, XXIV(1824), 249.

7253 . _____. "Voyage de Grout de Beaufort sur le Sénégal et la Gambie, en 1824 et 1825," *Walckenaer's Voyages*, VI(1842), 355-372.

7254 . Beaumier, August. "Le choléra au Maroc, sa marche au Sahara jusqu'au Sénégal en 1868," *BSGP*, 6th Series, III(1872).

7255 . Bel. "Epidémie de fièvre a Gorée en 1859," *RMC*, I(1861), 194.

7256 . Belcher, Edward. *Directions for the River Gambia*. London, 1835. 12p.

7257 . Bellamy. [*Dr.*]. "Notes ethnographiques recueillies dans le Haut-Sénégal," *Revue d'Ethnographie*, V(1886), 81-84.

7258 . Berchon. "Notes anthropologiques sur le Sénégal," *Bulletin de la Société d'Anthropologie de Paris*, I(1860); II(1861).

7259 . Bérénger-Feraud, Laurent-Jean-Baptiste. *Contes de la Sénégambie*. Paris: Leroux, 1885.

7260 . _____. *De la fièvre bilieuse mélanurique des pays chauds comparée avec la fièvre jaune. Etude clinique faite au Sénégal*. Paris: A. Delahaye, 1874. 442p.

7261 . _____. "Description topographique de l'île de Goree," *RMC*, XXXVI(1873), 885.

7262 . _____. "Etude sur les populations de la Casamance," *Revue d'Anthropologie*, III(1874), 444-461.

7263    • _____. *Étude sur les Ouolofs(Sénégambie)*. Paris: Leroux, 1875. 31p.

7264    • _____. "Étude sur les Sininkés," *Revue d'Anthropologie*, 2nd Series, I(1878), 584-606.

7265    • _____. *Fièvre jaune au Senegal*. Paris: Delahaye, 1874. 440p.

7266    • _____. "Le mariage chez les nègres Sénégambiens," *Revue d'Anthropologie*, 2nd Series, VI(1883).

7267    • _____. *Les Peuls de Sénégambie*. Paris: Leroux, n.d.

7268    • _____. *Les peuples de la Sénégambie; histoire, ethnographie, moeurs et coutumes, légendes*. Paris: Leroux, 1879. 420p.

7269    • _____. *Recueil de contes populaires de la Sénégambie*. Paris: Leroux, 1885. 260p.

7270    • _____. "Le Sénégal (1817-1874)," *RMC*, XXXVI(1873).

7271    • _____. *Traité clinique des maladies des Européens au Sénégal*. 2 vols. Paris: Delahaye, 1875-1878.

7272    • Berthier, P. *Voyage aux sources du Sénégal*. Paris, 1820.

7273    • Blanchet, Edouard [*Rev.*]. "Lettére," *MCM*, VII(1878), 454-455, 457-458,

7274    • _____. "Lettres," *BGCSS*, I(1857-1859), 347-349, 379-384.

7275    • _____. "Lettres," *Echo des Missions d'Afrique*, I(1884), 136-138.

7276    • _____. "Lettres," *MCL*, VIII(1876), 164-165; X(1878), 445-446, 466; XVI(1884), 443-444.

7277    • _____. "Missionsbriefe," *KM*, VI(1878), 238.

7278    • Bocande, B. *Rapport à M. le Ministre de la Marine et des Colonies sur les ressources que présentent les Comptoirs de la Cazamance*. Paris: Dupont, 1856. From *Revue Coloniale*, Oct., 1856.

7279    • Boilat, P. D. [*Abbé*]. "Documents relatifs à la Sénégambie," *BSGP*, 2nd Series, XX(1843), 306-310; 3rd Series, I(1844), 119-121, 343-345, 374-376; XIII(1845), 114-117.

7280    . _____. *Esquisses Sénégalaises, physionomie du pays—peuplades—commerce—religions—passé et avenir—récits et légendes.* Paris: T. Bertrand, 1853.

7281    . Borius, Alfred [Dr.]. *Les maladies au Senegal.* Paris: Baillière, 1882. 363p.

7282    . _____. "Nouvelles recherches sur le climat du Sénégal," *Annales du Bureau central météorologique de France,* 1879.

7283    . _____. *Recherches sur le climat du Sénégal.* Paris: Gauthier-Villars, 1875. 327p.

7284    . _____. *Recherches sur le climat et les établissements français de la côte septentrionale du Golfe de Guinée.* Paris: Gauthier-Villars, 1880.

7285    . Boteler, Thomas, and Hay, R. W. "Supposed Junction of the Rivers Gambia and Casamanza, on the Western Coast of Africa," *JRGS,* III (1833), 72-76.

7286    . Bouchet, Pierre-Marie. "Lettre," *APFL,* XXVIII(1856), 287-295.

7287    . Bou-el-Moghdad. "Voyage par terre entre le Sénégal et le Maroc," *RMC,* I(1861), 417.

7288    . Bouët-Willaumez, Louis Édouard. *Campagnes aux côtes occidentales d'Afrique, 1850.* Paris: Dupont, 1850. 44p.

7289    . Bouquet de la Grye. "Étude sur la barre du Sénégal," *RMC,* LXXXIX(1886), 515.

7290    . Bour, Charles. *Les dépendances du Sénégal. Géographie, population, productions, commerce, colonisation.* Paris: Baudoin, 1885. 89p.

7291    . _____. "Le fleuve Casamance," *Bulletin de la Société de topographie de France,* VII(1882).

7292 . Bourrel. "Voyage dans le pays des Maures Brackna, rive droit du Sénégal, juin-octobre 1860," *RMC*, Sept., Oct., 1861, 511-545.

7293 . Bove, E. *Contributions à la géographie Médicale. Essai sur le poste de Médine (Haut-Sénégal)*. Nancy: Impr. Nancéienne, 1880. 44p.

7294 . Brandt, J. "Sénégal," *JME*, LXIII(1888), 23-26, 70-72, 107-109, 237, 240.

7295 . Brosselard, Charles. *Rapport sur la situation dans la vallée du Sénégal en 1866. Insurrection de Mahmadou-Lamine*. Lille: Danel, 1888.

7296 . Brunner, Samuel. *Reise nach Senegambien und den Inseln des grünen Vorgebirges im Jahre 1838*. Bern: Körber, 1840. 390p.

7297 . Calve. [*Dr.*]. "Description de l'épidémie de fièvre jaune qui a ravagé les etablissements de Gorée et de Saint-Louis du Sénégal, en 1830," *Annales maritimes*, VII(1832).

7298 . Calvet, Adolphe. *Sylves noires*. Paris: Daragon, 1901. 158p.

7299 . Carbonnel, P. F. *De la mortalité actuelle au Sénégal et particulièrement à Saint-Louis*. Paris: Thesis (privately printed), 1873.

7300 . Carlus, J. "Les Sérères de la Sénégambie," *Revue de Géographie*, June, July, Aug., 1880.

7301 . Carrère, Frederick. *Codification des actes qui règlent au Sénégal et dépendances, le service des curatelles aux successions et biens vacants, et celui de la conservation des hypothèques*. Saint-Louis: Imprimerie du Gouvernement, 1862. 122p.

7302 . _____. *Codification des règlements d'administration et de police en vigueur au Sénégal*. Saint-Louis: Imprimerie du Gouvernement, 1865. 239p. Also, *Annuaire du Sénégal*, 1869.

7303 . _____. *Le Sénégal et son avenir*. Bordeaux: A. Pérey, 1870. 15p.

7304 . _____. *Siège par Al Alghi, du Fort de Médine au pays de Kasson. (Haute-Sénégambie)*. n.p., 1858.

7305 . _____, and Holle, Paul. *De la Sénégambie française*. Paris: Didot frères, 1855. 369p.

7306 . Castaing. [Dr.]. *La culture du ricin indigène au Sénégal (textes arabe et français).* Saint-Louis: Imprimerie du Gouvernement, 1889.

7307 . Catel. "Recherches sur les causes de la maladie épidémique qui a ravagé les îles de Saint-Louis et de Gorée pendant l'hivernage de 1830," *Annales maritimes et coloniales,* XLIX(1832), 685.

7308 . César, Louis. "Lettres," *Lis de St-Joseph,* VI(1895), 296, 297.

7309 . _____. "Missionsbriefe," *Afrika-Bote,* V(1899), 169-171.

7310 . Cimbault, Léon. "Lettres," *Annales Apostoliques,* New Series (1897-1898), 147-150.

7311 . Claverie, Paul. *De Dakar à Saint-Louis.* Paris: Plon-Nourrit, 1899.

7312 . _____. *Pages détachées. Notes de voyage, au Sénégal, etc.* Paris: Plon-Nourrit, 1898. 278p.

7313 . Clozel, F. J. *Haut-Sénégal-Niger. Séries d'études publiés sous la direction de M. Le Gouverneur.* 2 vols. Paris: Barnéoud, 1912.

7314 . Colin, G. [Dr.]. *Contribution à la géographie médicale du Haut-Sénégal.* Paris: A. Davy, 1883. 68p.

7315 . _____. "Mes voyages au Sénégal," *Bulletin de la Société de Géographie de Lille,* V(1886), 259-270.

7316 . Collignon and Deniker. "Les Maures du Sénégal," *Anthropologie,* VII (1896), 257-269.

7317 . Coronnat. *La guerre au Sénégal, la colonne du Rip en 1887.* Paris, 1890.

7318 . Corréard, Alexandre. *Naufrage de la frégate la Méduse, faisant partie de l'expédition du Sénégal, en 1816.* Paris: Corréard, 1817. 196p.

7319 . Cros, Pierre. "Lettere," *MCM*, XXIV(1895), 93-95, 102-105.

7320 . _____. "Lettres," *Annales Apostoliques*, IX(1894), 41-57.

7321 . _____. "Lettres," *MCL*, XXVI(1894), 431-433, 440-443.

7322 . Curtis, James. *A Journal of Travel in Barbary in 1801, with Observations on the Gum Trade of Senegal*. London: Longmans & Rees, 1803. 157p.

7323 . Daguerre, Joseph. *Vingt mois au Sénégal (sept. 1879-mai 1881)*. Bayonne: A. Lamaignière, 1881. 57p.

7324 . Dard, Charlotte Adéle Picard. *La chaumière africaine, ou, histoire d'une famille française jetée sur la côte occidentale de l'Afrique, à la suite du naufrage de la Méduse*. Dijon: Noellat, 1824. 313p. Also, "History of the Sufferings and Misfortunes of the Picard Family, after the Shipwreck of the Medusa on the Western Coast of Africa, in the Year 1816," *Constable's Miscellany*, II(1827), 13-197.

7325 . Daunas, Marcel. "Un voyage d'affaires au Sénégal (août-sept. 1898)," *Bulletin de la Société de Géographie Commercial de Bordeaux*, 2nd Series, XXV(1903), 65-72, 113-118, 145-151, 182-187.

7326 . Decressac-Villegrand, Marcel. *Souvenirs du Sénégal. Lettres sur la Gambie et la Casamance*. Guéret: P. Amiault, 1890. 292p.

7327 . Denisart. [*Lt.*]. *Les colonnes du Rip, 1865-1887. (Episodes de la conquête du Sénégal)*. Saint-Louis: Presse regimentaire du 1. er regiment de tirailleurs sénégalais, 1905. 34p.

7328 . Derrien. [*Commandant*]. "Le Haut Sénégal," *Bulletin de la Société Géographie et d'Archéologie d'Oran*, IV(1881), 141-216.

7329 . Dhyèvre, Joseph-Théophile. "Lettre," *BGCSS*, VIII(1870-1872), 570-573.

7330    . Diouf, Léopold. "Excursion dans le Sine et le Saloum," *MCL*, XI(1879), 324-326, 346-349, 360-362, 370-373. Also, *MCM*, VIII(1879), 440-442, 463-466, 475-477, 485-487.

7331    . _____. "Lettre," *Bulletin Mensuel de la Congrégation*, XI(1877), 309.

7332    . Dorlodot-Desessards. "Note sur la navigabilité du fleuve du Sénégal," *RMC*, LXI(1879), 502.

7333    . _____. *Renseignements sur la navigation dans le fleuve du Sénégal.* Paris: Chamerot, 1879.

7334    . Douhaire. "Le Sénégal en 1859," *Correspondant*, XLIX, pp.300-321.

7335    . Duboin, François-Marie [*Mgr.*]. "Lettere," *MCM*, VI(1877), 457-458; VII(1878), 352; X(1881), 287.

7336    . Duby, Martin. "Lettres," *APFL*, XXX(1858), 30-56, 417-426.

7337    . _____. "Lettres," *BGCSS*, I(1857-1859), 484-488; III(1862-1863), 111-112, 374-376, 505-507; IV(1863-1865), 405-411, 625-635.

7338    . _____. "Notes géographiques," *MCL*, IX(1877), 258-259, 270-271, 293-295, 304-307, 354-355, 365-366.

7339    . Duchon-Doris, J. P. *Commerce des toiles bleues dites guinée, de l'industrie française de Pondichéry et de la metropole dans ses rapports avec le Sénégal, l'île de Bourbon et l'étranger.* Paris: de Wittersheim, 1842. 64p.

7340    . Durand, Jean Baptiste Léonard. *Voyage au Sénégal, ou, mémoires ... sur les découvertes, les établissements et le commerce des Européens dans l'Océan Atlantique, depuis le Cap-Blanc jusqu'à la rivière de Sierre-Lionne.* 2 vols. Paris: Agasse, 1803. English translation, *A Voyage to Senegal.* London: Phillips, 1805.

7341 . Du Sorbiers de la Tourasse, Joseph. *De la colonisation du Sénégal.*

Paris: Arthur Savaète, 1897. 76p.

7342 . Enduran, Lodoïx. *La traite des nègres, ou, deux marins au Sénégal.*

Lille: Lefort, 1869. 139p.

7343 . Engel, Léger. "Colonie agricole Ngazobil," *BGCSS,* III(1862-1863), 223-

231, 337-342; IV(1863-1865), 198-204.

7344 . Epinette, Auguste-Marin. "Lettres," *Annales Oeuvre Ste-Enfance,* XXXII

(1881), 326-338; XXXIII(1882), 257-265.

7345 . Esvan, Jean-Marie. "Lettres," *Annales Apostoliques,* XVI(1900-1901), 277,

278.

7346 . Étienne, P. "Sur la nature des terrains traversés par le chemin de fer

de Dakar à Saint-Louis," *Journal Officiel de l'A.O.F.,* May 15,

1897, pp. 194-196.

7347 . Faidherbe, Léon [*General*]. "Des Berbères et les Arabes du bord du Sénégal,"

*BSGP,* 4th Series, VII(1854).

7348 . _____. *Chapitre de géographie sur le Nord-Ouest de l'Afrique à l'usage*

*des écoles de Sénégambie.* Saint-Louis: Imprimerie du Gouvernement,

1864. 40p.

7349 . _____. *Notice sur la colonie du Sénégal et sur les pays qui sont en*

*relation avec elle.* Paris: Bertrand, 1859. 100p.

7350 . _____. "Populations noires des bassins du Sénégal et du Haut-Niger,"

*BSGP,* 4th Series, XI(1856), 281-300.

7351 . _____. *Le Sénégal. La France dans l'Afrique Occidentale.* Paris: Hachette,

1889. 501p.

7352 . Fallot, Ernest. *Histoire de la colonie française du Senegal.* Paris:

Challamel, 1884. 168p.

7353 . Forêt, Auguste. *Un voyage dans le Haut-Sénégal*. Paris: Challamel, 1888. 90p.

7354 . Frey, Henri-Nicolas [*Général*]. *Campagne dans le Haut-Sénégal et dans le Haut-Niger(1885-1886)*. Paris: Plon-Nourrit, 1888. 507p.

7355 . _____. *La Sénégambie*. Paris: Plon-Nourrit, 1898.

7356 . Gael, Vallon. "Le Sénégal, Dakar, Gorée et le colonel Pinet de Laprade," *Marine française*, II(1889), Jan. 31.

7357 . Gallais, Louis-Marie. "Lettres," *APFL*, XXIII(1851), 5-26, 434-456.

7358 . Golaz, G. "Mission du Senegal," *JME*, LVI(1881), 183-188, 228-235, 310-313.

7359 _____. "Voyage et arrivée à Saint-Louis," *JME*, LVI(1881), 140-149.

7360 . Gommenginger, Ludwig. "Le Rio-Pongo (Sénégambie)," *MCL*, VIII(1876), 8-10, 21-23. See also *MCM*, V(1876), 562-564, 574, 575, 611, 612, and *BGCSS*, XII(1876), 656-667.

7361 . Gouldsbury, Valesius Skipton. *Correspondence Regarding Recent Expedition to the Upper Gambia under Administrator V.S.G.* n.p., n.p., 1881. 39p.

7362 . Grimal, T. "Trois ans au Sénégal," *Revue France*, June-Oct., 1874.

7363 . Guérin, Charles. "Excursion à Podor, Dagana et Kouma," *BGCSS*, IX(1873-1874), 132-138.

7364 . _____. "Lettere," *MCM*, X(1881), 535-536.

7365 . _____. "Lettres," *Annales Apostoliques*, III(1888), 110-111.

7366 . _____. "Lettres," *Echo des Missions d'Afrique*, I(1884), 183-187; II(1885), 33-39.

7367 _____. "Lettres," *MCL*, VIII(1876), 417; XIII(1881), 187-188, 510-512.

7368      . Guillet, Edmond. "Lettere," *MCM*, XIV(1885), 325-327.

7369      . _____. "Lettres," *Annales Apostoliques*, IV(1889), 34, 35; V(1890), 103-107.

7370      . _____. "Lettres," *APFL*, LVII(1885), 297-310.

7371      . _____. "Lettres," *MCL*, XVII(1885), 301-303.

7372      . _____. "Missionsbriefe," *KM*, XIII(1885), 195, 196.

7373      . Guillot, E. "La question du Sénégal et les voyages du Dr. Bayol," *Bulletin de la Société de Géographie de Lille*, VIII(1887), 128.

7374      . Guy-Grand, V. L. "La Chrétienté de Fadioute (Sénégambie)," *APFL*, LIII (1881), 76.

7375      . Habert de Ginestet. *Campagnes d'hier et d'aujourd'hui. De Brest au Sénégal, en campagne, en Maraude, une exécution.* Paris: H. Charles-Lavauzelle, 1896. 83p.

7376      . Haurigot, Georges. "Un nouveau fanatique au Sénégal," *Economiste français*, VIII(1869).

7377      . _____. "Quinze mois en Sénégambie," *Nouvelles Annales des Voyages*, I(1869), 5-44.

7378      . _____. *Les pionniers de la France dans l'Afrique occidentale.* Paris, n.d..

7379      . _____. *Quinze mois en Sénégambie.* Paris: Challamel, 1869.

7380      . _____. *Le Sénégal.* Paris: Lecène & Oudin, 1887. 240p.

7381      . Hébert, A. *Une année médicale a Dagana (Sénégal).* Paris, 1880.

7382      . Hecquard, Hyacinthe. *Rapport sur un voyage dans la Casamance.* Paris, 1852.

7383 . Hewett, J. F. Napier. "On the Jolloffs of West Africa," *PRGS*, I(1855-1857), 513-517.

7384 Huard-Baissinère, P. L. "Exploration de la rivière Falémé et des mines d'or du Bambouk et du Bondou, Sénégal," *Annales maritimes et coloniales*, LXXVIII(1844).

7385 . Hubler, T. "De Saint-Louis à Joal par terre," *Bulletin de la Société de géographie commercial de Bordeaux*, 2nd Series, VIII(1885), 294.

7386 . Ingram. "Abridged Account of an Expedition of about 200 Miles up the Gambia," *JRGS*, XVII(1847), 150-155.

7387 . Ingweiler, Georges. "Lettres," *Annales Apostoliques*, I(1886), 142-146.

7388 . Jalabert, Hyacinthe. "Lettres," *Annales Apostoliques*, XVI(1900-1901), 208-209; XVII(1901), 141, 142.

7389 . _____. "Lettres," *Lis de St-Joseph*, VI(1895), 298.

7390 . _____. "Missionsbriefe," *Echo aus Knechtsteden*, II(1900-1901), 30.

7391 . Jaques, L. "Letter from Sénégambie," *JME*, XXXVIII(1863), 210-212; XXXIX, (1864), 417-452.

7392 . _____, Morin, J. , and Mabille, E. "Sénégal," *JME*, LIX(1884), 56-59, 106-108, 189-191, 236-239, 475-480; LX(1885), 162-168, 259-262, 267-273, 446-448; LXI(1886), 28-31, 64-65, 133-134, 302-306, 437-441; LXII(1887), 224-231.

7393 . Joffre. [*Maréchal*]. *Chemin de fer du Sénégal et du Niger. Rapport sur l'avant-projet de la section de Kita-Bammakou, Toulimandio. Avant-projet du chemin de fer du Sénégal au Niger de Kayes à Toulimandio*. Paris: Imprimerie nationale, 1894.

7394     . Jouan, Jean-Marie. "Lettres," *Annales Apostoliques*, IV(1889), 27-34; VIII (1893), 51-60, 88-93.

7395     . _____. "Lettres," *APFL*, LXII(1890), 107-119.

7396     . Kobès, Aloys. "Lettres," *Annales Oeuvre Set-Enfance*, XVI(1864), 183-190; XVIII(1866), 392-402.

7397     . _____. "Lettres," *BGCSS*, III(1862-1863), 90-93, 94-107, 477-478, 511-513; IV(1863-1865), 615-625.

7398     . _____. "Situation de la colonie agricole de Saint-Joseph de Ngazobil," *RMC*, XV(1865), 79ff.

7399     . Kunemann, Alfons. "Missionsbriefe," *Echo aus Knechtsteden*, III(1901-1902), 101-105.

7400     . Lacombe, Jean. "Lettera," *MCM*, IV(1875), 582.

7401     . _____. "Lettre," *Annales Oeuvre Ste-Enfance*, XIV(1862), 52-57.

7402     . _____. "Lettre," *MCL*, VII(1875), 574.

7403     . _____. "Lettres," *BGCSS*, I(1857-1859), 480-484; IV(1863-1865), 412-424; X(1874-1875), 639-641.

7404     . La Feuillade, d'Aubusson. *Memoire sur les moyens d'exploiter par le Senegal les mines d'or de Bambouc*. Paris: Bachelier, 1826. 23p.

7405     . Lamoise, Paul [Rev.]. "Lettre," *APFL*, XXXV(1863), 263-277.

7406     . Lasnet, Alexandre Bernard Étienne Antoine. *Une mission au Sénégal, ethnographie, botanique, zoologie, géologie*. Paris: Challamel, 1900. 348p.

7407     . _____. *Les races du Sénégal: Sénégambie et Casamance*. Paris: Challamel, 1900.

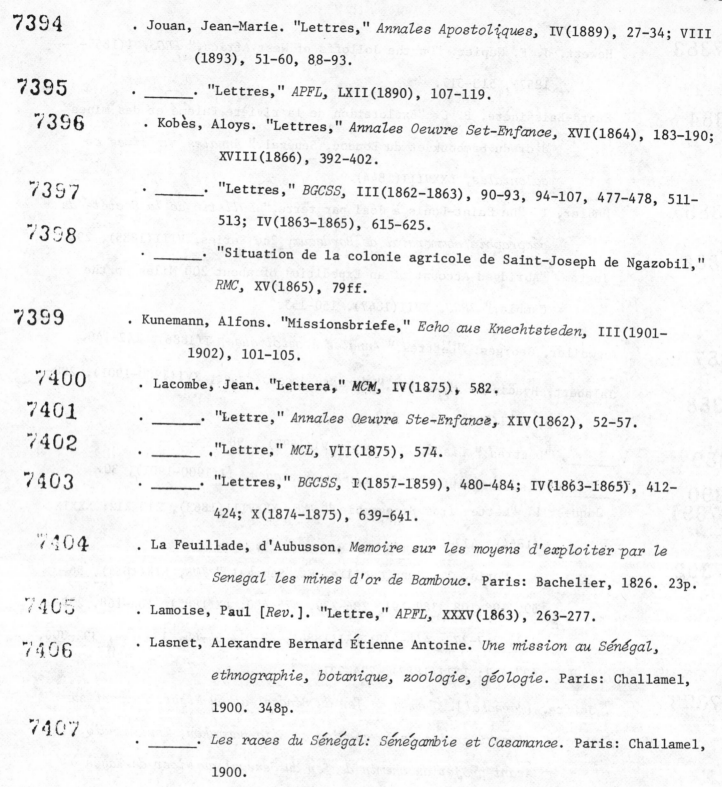

7408 . Le Berre, Jacques. "Lettres," *Annales Apostoliques*, XVI(1900-1901), 209; XVII(1901), 21.

7409 . Lécard, T. *Notice sur les productions de la Casamance, des Sérères et du Oualo. (Documents sur la colonie du Sénégal.)* Saint-Louis: Imprimerie du Gouvernement, 1866.

7410 . Lenz, Oscar. "Die Lenz'sche Expedition. Reise von Tenduf bis Saint Louis," *MAGD*, II(1880-1881), 229, 231.

7411 . Logier, Pierre. "Lettre," *BGCSS*, II(1860-1862), 29-32.

7412 . Lucas, L. "Notice sur le Sénégal," *Bulletin de la Société Bretonne de Géographie*, VI(1887), 208-220

7413 . Mage, Abdon-Eugene. *Du Sénégal au Niger, relation du voyage d'exploration de MM. Mage et Quintin au Soudan occidental, de 1863 à 1866.* Paris: Paul Dupont, 1867. 500p.

7414 . _____. "Les rivières de Sine et Saloum," *RMC*, VII(1863), 673.

7415 . Marchal, Charles-Léopold-Jean-Baptiste. *Voyage au Sénégal.* Paris: Duprat, 1854. 8p.

7416 . Margain, J. P. "Rapport sur le service de santé de l'expédition de Podor," *Revue Coloniale*, XV(1856), 457.

7417 . Marmier. [*Commandant*]. *Rapport sur le prolongement du chemin de fer de Bafoulabe au Niger (1892). Avant-projet du chemin de fer du Sénégal au Niger de Kayes à Toulimandio. Documents divers.* Paris: Imprimerie national, 1894.

7418 . Marree. "Voyage de Saint-Louis à Bakel," *BSGP*, 1st Series, XII(1829).

7419 . Martel, F. A. M. "Salubrité du climat de Gorée," *Annales maritimes et coloniales*, XVI(1828).

7420 . Mercki, Laurent. "Lettres," *Echo des Missions d'Afrique*, II(1885), 192, 193.

7421 . Messager, Yves. "Lettres," *Lis de Saint-Joseph*, VI(1895), 298-300.

7422 . Meyer, Aloys. "Lettera," *MCM*, I(1872), 437.

7423 . _____. "Lettre," *MCL*, II(1869), 340-341.

7424 . _____. "Lettres," *APFL*, XLVI(1874), 104-117.

7425 . _____. "Lettres," *BGCSS*, IX(1873-1874), 712-720.

7426 . Mitchinson, Alex W. *The Expiring Continent; a Narrative of Travel in Senegambia, with Observations on Native Character, the Present Condition and Future Prospects of Africa and Colonisation.* London: Allen, 1881. 469p.

7427 . Mollien, Gaspard T. *Voyage dans l'intérieur de l'Afrique aux sources du Sénégal et de la Gambie, faits en 1818.* 2 vols. Paris: Courcier, 1820. English edition, *Travels in the Interior of Africa to the Sources of the Senegal and Gambia.* Ed. by T. E. Bowdich. London, 1820.

7428 . Monteil, Parfait-Louis. *Une voyage d'exploration au Sénégal, 1879.* Papeete: Imprimerie du Gouvernement, 1882. 84p.

7429 . Montel, Étienne. "Lettere," *MCM*, XVII(1888), 386, 387.

7430 . _____. "Lettres," *Annales Apostoliques*, I(1886), 93-103; II(1887), 125-138.

7431 . _____. "Lettres," *Lis de St-Joseph*, I(1890), 56-62.

7432 . _____. "Lettres," *MCL*, XX(1888), 362, 363.

7433 . _____. "Missionsbriefe," *KM*, XVI(1888), 223.

7434 . Morenas, Joseph Elzéar. *Précis historique de la traite des noirs et de l'esclavage colonial.* Paris: l'auteur, 1828. 424p.

7435 . Morgan. "From the Journal of the Rev. Mr. Morgan, on the River Gambia," *MH*, XX(1824), 89.

7436 Morin, Jean. "Un voyage dans l'intérieur," *JME*, LXI(1886), 307-313.

7437 . Muiron d'Arcenay, L. "Notice sur le Senegal," *BSGP*, XIII(1877).

7438 . Myrgine. [*Lt.*]. *De Saint-Louis au Niger. Souvenirs de campagne.* Laval:
Chailland, 1898. 182p.

7439 . O'Connor, Luke Smyth [*Colonel*]. "Account of a Visit to the King of Bur
Sin, 64 Miles to the North of the Gambia," *PRGS*, III
(1858-1859), 377-379.

7440 . Odin, J. [*Officier*]. *La guerre au Sénégal, la colonne du Rip en 1887.
Leçons à tirer des expéditions du passé.* Paris: E. Dubois, 1890.

7441 . Panet, L. "Relation d'un voyage du Sénégal à Soueira, Mogador,"
*Revue Coloniale*, V(1850). 379-445, 473-563.

7442 . Pascal, Jean-Baptiste. "Lettres," *Annales Oeuvre Ste-Enfance*, XL(1889),
319-335.

7443 . _____. "Lettres," *APFL*, LIX(1887), 379-388.

7444 . _____. "Lettres," *Echo des Missions d'Afrique*, II(1885), 79.

7445 . Pascal, S. L. "Voyage au Bambouk et retour à Bakel," *TM*, III(1861),
39-48.

7446 . Percher, Jules-Hippolyte [**Alis, Harry**, *pseud.*]. "Aliun-Sal's Nachrichten von
dem Ländern zwischen den Senegal und Timbuctu," *Ausland*, XXXVII(1864).

7447 . Pérès, Joseph. "Lettere," *MCM*, XXVIII(1899), 424.

7448 . _____. "Lettres," *MCL*, XXXI(1899), 392.

7449 . Perrottet, George Samuel. *Voyage de Saint-Louis au Sénégal à la presqu'île
du Cap Vert, à Albreda sur la Gambie et à la rivière de Casamance
dans le pays des Feloups-Yola (1829).* n.p.,n.d. 108p.

7450 . Picard. "Voyage de Picard, 1804," *Walckenaer's Voyages*, V(1842), 303-
307.

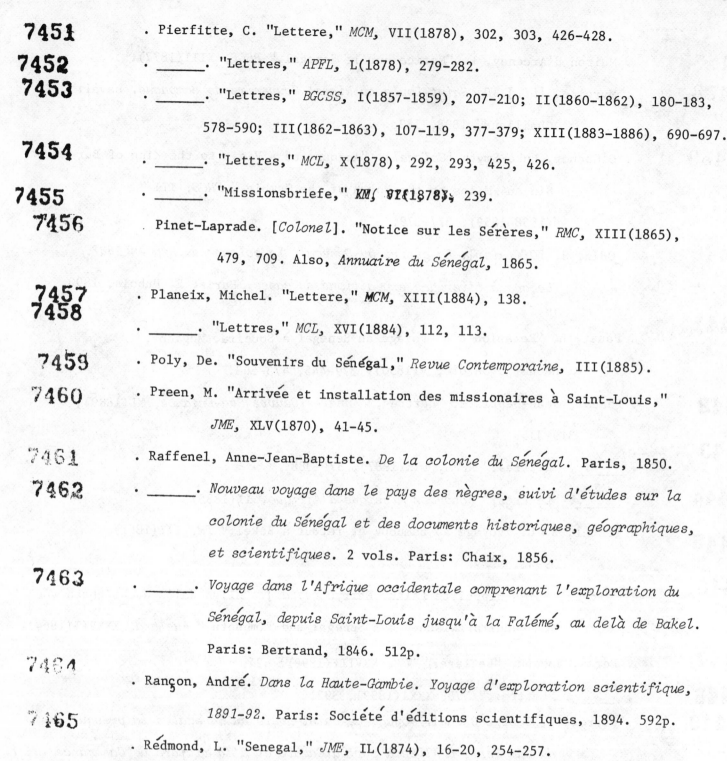

7451 · Pierfitte, C. "Lettere," *MCM*, VII(1878), 302, 303, 426-428.

7452 · _____. "Lettres," *APFL*, L(1878), 279-282.

7453 · _____. "Lettres," *BGCSS*, I(1857-1859), 207-210; II(1860-1862), 180-183, 578-590; III(1862-1863), 107-119, 377-379; XIII(1883-1886), 690-697.

7454 · _____. "Lettres," *MCL*, X(1878), 292, 293, 425, 426.

7455 · _____. "Missionsbriefe," *KM*, VI(1878), 239.

7456 · Pinet-Laprade. [*Colonel*]. "Notice sur les Sérères," *RMC*, XIII(1865), 479, 709. Also, *Annuaire du Sénégal*, 1865.

7457 · Planeix, Michel. "Lettere," *MCM*, XIII(1884), 138.

7458 · _____. "Lettres," *MCL*, XVI(1884), 112, 113.

7459 · Poly, De. "Souvenirs du Sénégal," *Revue Contemporaine*, III(1885).

7460 · Preen, M. "Arrivée et installation des missionaires à Saint-Louis," *JME*, XLV(1870), 41-45.

7461 · Raffenel, Anne-Jean-Baptiste. *De la colonie du Sénégal*. Paris, 1850.

7462 · _____. *Nouveau voyage dans le pays des nègres, suivi d'études sur la colonie du Sénégal et des documents historiques, géographiques, et scientifiques*. 2 vols. Paris: Chaix, 1856.

7463 · _____. *Voyage dans l'Afrique occidentale comprenant l'exploration du Sénégal, depuis Saint-Louis jusqu'à la Falémé, au delà de Bakel*. Paris: Bertrand, 1846. 512p.

7464 · Rançon, André. *Dans la Haute-Gambie. Voyage d'exploration scientifique, 1891-92*. Paris: Société d'éditions scientifiques, 1894. 592p.

7465 · Rédmond, L. "Senegal," *JME*, IL(1874), 16-20, 254-257.

7466      Rémont, Pierre-Marie. "Lettere," *MCM*, XXVI(1897), 439; XXVII(1898), 481-483.

7467      . _____. "Lettres," *Lis de St-Joseph*, VII(1896), 242-246.

7468      . _____. "Lettres," *MCL*, XXIX(1897), 413; XXX(1898), 469-471.

7469      . Renoux, François. "Lettere," *MCM*, VI(1877), 112-113, 217-219.

7470      . _____. "Lettre," *APFL*, L(1878), 269-279.

7471      . _____. "Lettre," *BGCSS*, V(1866-1867), 453-458.

7472      . _____. "Lettres," *Annales Oeuvre Ste-Enfance*, XIX(1867), 317-322; XXIII(1871-1872), 609-612.

7473      . _____. "Lettres," *MCL*, IX(1877), 4-5, 213-216.

7474      . Rey, H. [*Dr.*]. "Note sur les établissements portugais de la Sénégambie," *Archives de Médicine Navale*, XXVIII(1877), 401.

7475      . Rialland, François. "Lettres," *Annales Apostoliques*, XVI(1900-1901), 208.

7476      . Ricard, François-Pierre. *Le Sénégal, étude intime*. Paris: Challamel, 1865. 431p.

7477      . Riehl, François-Xavier. "État. Clergé indigène. Religieuses indigènes. Moyens, obstacles, besoins," *APFL*, XLVI(1874), 436-442.

7478      . _____. "Lettere," *MCM*, IV(1875), 54, 111; VI(1877), 437; X(1881), 172; XIII(1884), 305-307.

7479      . _____. "Lettre," *Annales Apostoliques*, I(1886), 37-38.

7480      . _____. "Lettre," *BGCSS*, XIII(1883-1886), 714-720.

7481      . _____. "Lettre," *Echo des Missions d'Afrique*, I(1884), 160-161.

7482      . _____. "Lettres," *Annales Oeuvre Ste-Enfance*, XXII(1870-1871), 313-316; XXIII(1871-1872), 124-128; XXXVII(1886), 329-336.

7483      . _____. "Lettres," *MCL*, II(1869), 213, 253; IV(1871-1872), 154-155; VII(1875), 41-42, 100; VIII(1876), 569-570; IX(1877), 431-432; XI(1879), 90; XIII(1881), 159-160, 186; XVI(1884), 292.

7484     · _____. "Une première visite pastorale en Sénégambie," *MCL*, XVI(1884), 559-562, 569-572, 584-586, 807.

7485     · Risch, Martin. "Lettres," *BGCSS*, V(1866-1867), 178-185, 449-453.

7486     · Roger, Jacques François. [*Baron*]. *Fables sénégalaises recueillies de l'Ouolof et mises en vers français avec des notes destinées à faire connaître la Sénégambie, son climat, ses principales productions, la civilisation et les moeurs des habitants.* Paris: Neveu, 1828. 288p.

7487     · Rossel, Élisabeth-Paul-Édouard de. [*Admiral*]. *Description nautique de la côte d'Afrique, depuis le cap Blanc jusqu'au Cap Formose.* Paris: Imprimerie royale, 1814.

7488     · Rouvié, E. [*Rev.*]. "Lettre," *BGCSS*, II(1860-1862), 90-97.

7489     · Santamaria, J. C. "Origine des peuples qui habitent le Sénégal français," *BSGP*, 5th Series, V(1863), 169-184.

7490     · Schauenberg, Pierre Reille de. [*Baron*]. "Note sur la Sénégambie," *Bulletin de la Société littéraire de Strasbourg*, 1868.

7491     · Schmaltz. [*Colonel*]. *Sénégal.* Paris: de Goestchy, 1821. 8p.

7492     · Schwindenhammer, Louis-Ignace [*Rev.*]. "Lettre," *APFL*, XXXVI(1864), 119-121.

7493     · Sébire, Albert. "Lettere," *MCM*, XIX(1890), 194, 195; XXI(1892), 614, 615; XXII(1893), 517-519; XXVIII(1899),339-341.

7494     · _____. "Lettres," *Annales Apostoliques*, VI(1891), 97-104; VII(1892), 154, 155.

7495     · _____. "Lettres," *MCL*, XXII(1890), 182, 183; XXIV(1892), 606, 607; XXV(1893), 505, 506; XXXI(1899), 74, 75.

7496     · _____. "Missionsbriefe," *KM*, XVIII(1890), 154, 155.

7497  . _____. "De Thiès à Mbour par le Diobas," *MCL*, XXVI(1894), 541-543, 552-554. Also, *MCM*, XXV(1896), 175-177, 187-190.

7498  . _____. "A travers le Ndoute," *MCL*, XXVI(1894), 564-568, 573-577. Also, *MCM*, XXV(1896), 199-201, 215, 216, 222-226.

7499  . Senè, Gabriel. "Lettere," *MCM*, IV(1875), 565-567; VII(1878), 27-28.

7500  . _____. "Lettres," *MCL*, VII(1875), 558-560; X(1878), 15.

7501  . Stein, Martin. "Lettres," *Lis de St-Joseph*, X(1899), 41, 42.

7502  . Stephen, Henry Lushington. "Judging in the Gambia," *Nineteenth Century*, Nov., 1898, pp. 783-790.

7503  . Strub, Joseph [*Rev.*]. "Lettres," *BSCSS*, III(1862-1863), 218-220, 508-509.

7504  . Tautain, Louis-Frédéric [*Dr.*]. *L'ethnologie et l'ethnographie des pueples du bassin du Sénégal*. Paris: Leroux, 1885. 44p.

7505  . _____. "Études critiques sur l'ethnologie et l'ethnographie des peuples du bassin du Sénégal," *Revue Ethnographique*, IV(1885), 61-80, 137-147, 254-268.

7506  . Taylor, W. "Lettres," *JME*, L(1875), 448-452; LI(1876), 258-259; LII (1877), 211-216; LIII(1878), 377-378, 411-414, 458-461; LIV (1879), 96-97, 348-351, 461-463; LV(1880), 103-107, 216-217, 435-439; LVI(1881), 137-140, 188-189, 226-228, 419-420; LVII (1882), 29-30, 108, 260-261, 376-378; LVIII(1883), 122-128, 170-171, 384-386; LIX(1884), 152-156, 363; LX(1885), 524-527; LXII (1887), 29-31.

7507  . Tellier. [*Commandant*]. "Possessions françaises du Sénégal. Cercle de la Basse-Casamance, poste de Carabane," *Bulletin de l'Union géographique du Nord de la France*, VII(1885), 421.

7508  . Tesseire, Albert. *De la situation actuelle du Sénégal*. Bordeaux, 1870.

7509  . Thaly, J. H. F. "Étude sur les habitants du Haut-Sénégal," *Archives de médicine navales*, VI(1866).

7510 . Thévenot, J. P. F. *Traité des maladies des Européens dans les pays chauds et spécialement au Sénégal, ou essai statistique, médical et hygiénique, sur le sol, le climat et les maladies de cette partie de l'Afrique.* Paris: Baillière, 1840. 399p.

7511 . Tisserand, François. "Lettres," *Annales Apostoliques,* II(1887), 103-106; VIII(1893), 20-23; IX(1894), 35-38.

7512
7513 _____. "Lettres," *MCL,* XXV(1893), 410, 411.

. Vallon. [*Admiral*]. "La Cazamance, dépendance du Sénégal," *RMC,* V(1862), 456.

7514 _____. "Note sur l'origine des noms Sénégal, Galam et Cazamance," *CRSG,* 1888. pp. 142, 187.

7515 . _____. "Le port de Dakar en 1866," *RMC,* XX(1867), 382.

7516 . Verneuil, V. *Mes aventures au Sénégal; souvenirs de voyage.* Paris: Jacottet, Bourdilliat, 1858. 282p.

7517 . Vidal, François. "Lettre," *BGCSS,* V(1866-1867), 459-463.

7518 . Vigne d'Octon, P. "Le port de Dakar. La question du Soudan. Le chemin de fer de Dakar à Saint-Louis," *Bulletin de la Société de Géographie Commercial de Bordeaux,* 2nd Series, X(1887), 449, 481, 486.

7519 . Villéger, F. "L'évangile selon Saint Matthieu traduit en Wolof," *JME,* XLVII(1872), 285-289.

7520 . _____. "Lettres," *JME,* XLVI(1871), 127-132, 166-170; XLVIII(1873), 47-51, 281-286, 361-371, 443-444; IL(1874), 41-47; L(1875), 372-380; LI(1876), 60-62, 168-170, 260-261; LII(1877), 53-55.

7521 . Wahrenhorst. *Côte occidentale d'Afrique: la Cazamance.* Paris, 1891.

7522 . Walter, Louis Philippe. "Lettre," *Annales Apostoliques,* X(1895), 117-120.

7523 . _____. "Lettre," *Annales Oeuvre Ste. Enfance,* XXIII(1871-1872), 544-552.

7524    . _____. "Lettre," *Bulletin de la Congrégation*, III(1891-1893), 864-869.

7525    . _____. "Lettre," *BGCSS*, VII(1869-1870), 158-168.

7526    . Washington. [*Capt.*, *R.N.*]. "Some Account of Mohammed-Sisei, a Mandingo, of Nyáni-Maro on the Gambia," *JRGS*, VIII(1838), 448-454.

7527    . Wendling. [*Colonel*]. "Étude sur le Delta et les Marigots du Sénégal," *Bulletin de la Société de Géographie de Toulon*, 1890.

7528    . Wenger, Antoine. "Lettere," *MCM*, XII(1883), 337-340.

7529    . _____. "Lettres," *MCL*, XV(1883), 265-268.

7530    . Wieder, Joseph. "Lettres," *Annales Apostoliques*, XVI(1900-1901), 209.

7531    . _____. "Lettres," *Lis de St-Joseph*, VIII(1897), 108-110.

7532    . Wintz, Edouard. "Lettres," *Lis de St-Joseph*, VIII(1897), 281, 282.

SIERRA LEONE

7533 . Alldridge, Thomas Joshua. *The Sherbro and Its Hinterland*. London and New York: Macmillan, 1901. 356p.

7534 . _____. *A Transformed Colony. Sierra Leone as It Was and as It Is, Its Progress, Peoples, Native Customs and Undeveloped Wealth*. London: Seeley & Co., 1910. 368p.

7535 . _____. "Wanderings in the Hinterland of Sierra Leone," *GJ*, IV(1894), 123-140.

7536 . Banbury, George Alexander Sethbridge. *Sierra Leone: or, the White Man's Grave*. London: Sonnenschein, 1888. 296p.

7537 . Baumgartner, Etienne [*Rev.*]. "Lettres," *BGCSS*, VI(1867-1869), 894-909.

7538 . _____. "Lettres," *MCL*, II(1869), 59-60, 402.

7539 . Beale, and others. "Lettres," *JME*, XXIV(1849), 47-61.

7540 . Bell, T. M. *Outrage by Missionaries; a Report of the Whole Proceedings on the Trial in Sierra Leone of William Fortunatus John, Phoebe John, John Williams, and Kezia Williams, for the Murder of Amelia John, at Onitsha, River Niger*. Liverpool, n.p., 1883. 136p.

7541 . Betts, and others. "Lettres," *JME*, V(1830), 65-83.

7542 . Blyden, Edward Wilmot. "Report on the Expedition to Falaba, January to March, 1872. (With an Appendix Respecting Dr. Livingstone," *PRGS*, XVII(1872-1873), 117-133.

7543 . _____. *The West African University. Correspondence between E. W. Blyden and . . . J. Pope-Hennessy, C.M.G., Administrator-in-Chief of the West African Settlements*. Freetown: Negro Printing Office, 1872. 17p.

7544 . Bourne, Henry Richard Fox. "Sierra Leone Troubles," *Fortnightly Review*, Aug. 1899, pp. 216-230.

7545 . Bourzeix, Pierre. "Lettere," *MCM*, XIV(1885), 553-556.

7546 . _____. "Lettres," *Echo des Missions d'Afrique*, I(1884), 163-171.

7547 . _____. "Lettres," *MCL*, XVII(1885), 532-535.

7548 . Browne, James. "Lettres," *Annales Apostoliques*, New Series, (1897-1898), 291-293; XVI(1900-1901), 42, 66, 210.

7549 . Bryson, Alexander [*M.D.*]. *An Account of the Origin, Spread, and Decline of the Epidemic Fevers of Sierra Leone*. London: H. Renshaw, 1849. 174p.

7550 . Cardew, Frederic [*Colonel*]. *Railway Schemes, Sierre Leone: An Address Given. . .at a Meeting of the Legislative Council of Sierra Leone . , . .May 1, 1895*. Liverpool, n.p., 1895. 20p.

7551 . Charlesworth, Maria Louisa. *Africa's Mountain Valley; or, the Church in Regent's Town, West Africa*. London; Seeley, 1856. 272p.

7552 . Church, Mary. *Sierra Leone: or the Liberated Africans, in a Series of Letters from a Young Lady to Her Sister, in 1832 and 34*. London: Longman, 1835. 49p.

7553 . Clarke, Robert. *Sierra Leone. A Description of the Manners and Customs of the Liberated Africans; with Observations upon the Natural History of the Colony, and a Notice of the Native Tribes*. London: Ridgway, 1843. 179p.

7554 . Coker, Daniel. *Journal of Daniel Coker, a Descendant of Africa, from the Time of Leaving New York, in the Ship Elizabeth, Capt. Sebor, on a Voyage for Sherbro, in Africa, in Company with Three Agents, and About Ninety Persons of Colour*. Baltimore: Coale, 1820. 52p.

7555 . Cole, J. Augustus. *The Interior of Sierra Leone, West Africa. What Can It Teach Us ?* Dayton, Ohio: United Brethren, 1887. 54p.

7556 . Crooks, John Joseph. *A History of Sierra Leone, Western Africa.* Dublin: Browne & Nolan; London: Simpkin, Marshall, 1903. 375p.

7557 . Cuffee, Paul. *A Brief Account of the Settlement and Present Situation of the Colony of Sierra Leone, in Africa.* New York: Samuel Wood, 1812. 12p.

7558 . Dailey, J. R. *Mal-Administration of Justice in the Colony of Sierra Leone, as Illustrated in the Case of J. R. Dailey.* n.p., n.p., 1857. 102p.

7559 . Davies, William. *Extracts from the Journal of the Rev. W. D. when a Missionary at Sierre Leone, West Africa. Containing Some Account of the Country, Its Inhabitants, the Progress of Religion, among the Negroes, Manner of Government, etc.* Llanidloes, privately printed, 1835. 78p.

7560 . During. "Letter," *MH*, XVIII(1822), 333-334.

7561 . Festing, A. M. *Report on His Mission to Bumban-Limbah, 1887.* London: Her Majesty's Stationery Office, 1892. [C.6687].

7562 . Figaniere e Morão, Joaquim César de. *Descripção de Serra-Leôa e seus contornos; escripta em doze cartas.* Lisbon, 1822.

7563     . Fleck, Joseph. "Lettere," *MCM*, XXX(1901), 133, 134.

7564     . _____. "Lettres," *MCL*, XXXIII(1901), 121-123.

7565     . _____. "Missionsbriefe," *KM*, XXIX(1900-1901), 255.

7566     . Fletcher, Richard. "Letter from Sierra Leone, Dec. 29, 1852," *MH*, XLIX(1853), 119-120.

7567     . Fletcher, W. "Colonie de Sierra Leone: un mouvement religieux, etc," *JME*, XXVIII(1853), 149-156.

7568     . Flickinger, Daniel Kumler. *Fifty-five Years of Active Ministerial Life*. Dayton, Ohio: United Brethren, 1907. 261p.

7569     . Fritsch, Antoine. "Lettres," *BGCSS*, VI(1867-1869), 909-913.

7570     . _____. "Lettres," *MCL*, II(1869), 59.

7571     Garrett, G. H. "Sierra Leone and the Interior, to the Upper Waters of the Niger," *PRGS*, New Series, XIV(1892), 433-453.

7572     : Garride, Manuel. "Un tipo de comercio africano: Sierra Leona. Importancia de este estudio para España. Artículos de importación y de exportación en aquella Colonia inglesa," *Revista de Géografia Commercial*, II(1886-1887), 133.

7573     . Gommenginger, Ludwig. "Lettere," *MCM*, III(1874), 543, 544; V(1876), 173, 174; VI(1877), 124; VIII(1879), 233, 234; XII(1883), 387, 388.

7574     . _____. "Lettres," *Annales Apostoliques*, I(1886), 38-40; II(1887), 118, 119; IV(1889), 85-94.

7575     . _____. "Lettres," *APFL*, LXI(1889), 333-353.

7576     . _____. "Lettres," *Echo des Missions d'Afrique*, I(1884), 114-121.

7577     . _____. "Lettres," *MCL*, VI(1874), 543, 544; VIII(1876), 150; IX(1877), 134; XI(1879), 222, 224, 225; XV(1883), 375, 376.

7578     . Griffith, T. Riseley. "On the Races Inhabiting Sierra Leone," *JAI*, XVI(1886), 300-309.

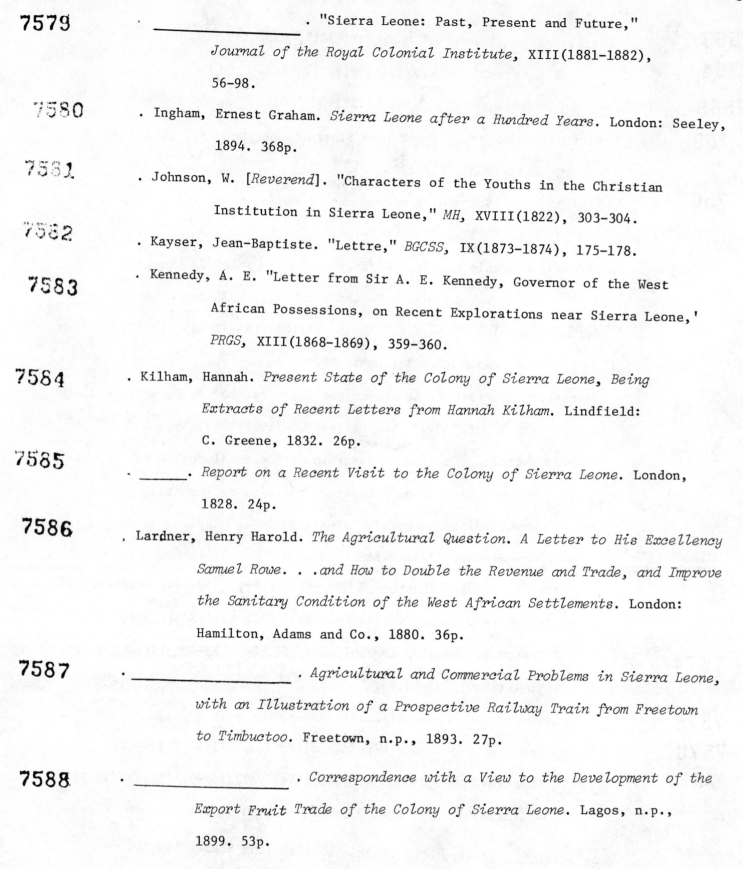

7579 _____. "Sierra Leone: Past, Present and Future," *Journal of the Royal Colonial Institute*, XIII(1881-1882), 56-98.

7580 . Ingham, Ernest Graham. *Sierra Leone after a Hundred Years*. London: Seeley, 1894. 368p.

7581 . Johnson, W. [*Reverend*]. "Characters of the Youths in the Christian Institution in Sierra Leone," *MH*, XVIII(1822), 303-304.

7582 . Kayser, Jean-Baptiste. "Lettre," *BGCSS*, IX(1873-1874), 175-178.

7583 . Kennedy, A. E. "Letter from Sir A. E. Kennedy, Governor of the West African Possessions, on Recent Explorations near Sierra Leone,' *PRGS*, XIII(1868-1869), 359-360.

7584 . Kilham, Hannah. *Present State of the Colony of Sierra Leone, Being Extracts of Recent Letters from Hannah Kilham*. Lindfield: C. Greene, 1832. 26p.

7585 . _____. *Report on a Recent Visit to the Colony of Sierra Leone*. London, 1828. 24p.

7586 . Lardner, Henry Harold. *The Agricultural Question. A Letter to His Excellency Samuel Rowe. . .and How to Double the Revenue and Trade, and Improve the Sanitary Condition of the West African Settlements*. London: Hamilton, Adams and Co., 1880. 36p.

7587 . _____. *Agricultural and Commercial Problems in Sierra Leone, with an Illustration of a Prospective Railway Train from Freetown to Timbuctoo*. Freetown, n.p., 1893. 27p.

7588 . _____. *Correspondence with a View to the Development of the Export Fruit Trade of the Colony of Sierra Leone*. Lagos, n.p., 1899. 53p.

7589 _____. *Manual on Cultivation and Preparation for Export of Some of the Commercial Products Indigenous and Exotic in Sierra Leone and the Reason Why Agriculture Should be Encouraged in the Colony.* London: Davies, Roblin and Pearce, 1890. 109p.

7590 . Lewis, Samuel. *Address to the Sierra Leone Association on Certain Questions Affecting the Interests of the Colony.* Freetown, 1885. 37p.

7591 . _____. *A Few Suggestions of the Wants of Sierra Leone, Written for the Information of a Member of Parliament.* Freetown, 1885. 16p.

7592 . Lutz, Emil. "Lettres," *Annales Apostoliques,* VII(1892), 152-154.

7593 . _____. "Lettres," *Annales Oeuvre Ste-Enfance,* XXXIV(1883), 115-125, 249-256; XXXVI(1885), 132-140; XLII(1891), 98-112, 200, 201; XLIII(1892), 311-313; LI(1900), 22-24.

7594 . _____. "Missionsbriefe," *Echo aus Afrika,* V(1893), 8, 9;

7595 . Lutz, Joseph. "Lettere," *MCM,* XIII(1884), 169-172, 291, 292; XVI(1887), 578; XVII(1888), 461; XX(1891), 541, 542; XXIV(1895), 445-448; XXVI(1897), 535.

7596 . _____. "Lettres," *Annales Apostoliques,* I(1886), 111, 112; II(1887), 81-85; V(1890), 145-151; VI(1891), 147-149; X(1895), 53-61.

7597 . _____. "Lettres," *APFL,* LV(1883), 243-256; LXIV(1892), 248-266.

7598 . _____. "Lettres," *MCL,* XV(1883),400; XVI(1884), 109-112, 270-272; XIX (1887),544; XXIII(1891), 529, 530; XXVII(1895), 423-437; XXIX (1897), 510, 511.

7599 . _____. "Missionsbriefe," *KM,* XI(1883), 256; XX(1892), 67.

7600 . Macaulay. "Colonie de Sierra Leone. Aperçu général, etc.," *JME,* XXIX (1854), 310-317.

7601. Macaulay, Kenneth. *Colony of Sierra Leone Vindicated from the Misrepresentations of Mr. MacQueen of Glasgow.* London, n.p., 1827. 127p.

7602. MacQueen, J. "Letter to R. W. Hay, Under-Secretary of State," *Blackwood's Magazine*, 1826, pp. 871-892.

7603. Marion-Brésillac, Melchior Marie Joseph de. [*Mgr.*]. "Lettre," *APFL*, XXXI(1859), 246-247.

7604. Maxwell, T. "Mission de Sierra-Leone," *JME*, XXVII(1852), 106-108.

7605. Morgan, Thomas. "Letter," *MH*, XVII(1821), 366-367, 398.

7606. Nicol, George Gurney Mather. *Essay on Sierra Leone.* Freetown, n.p., 1881. 20p.

7607. Noirjean, Joseph. "Lettere," *MCM*, XXVIII(1899), 134-136.

7608. _____. "Lettres," *MCL*, XXXI(1899), 111, 112.

7609. Norman. "Letter," *MH*, XX(1824), 219-220.

7610. Norton, Caroline Elizabeth Sarah. *A Residence at Sierra Leone. Described from a Journal Kept on the Spot and from Letters Written to Friends at Home.* London: J. Murray, 1849. 335p.

7611. Parkes, J. C. Ernest. "The Man-Eating People of the Imperri," *Journal of the Liverpool Geographical Society*, (1896), 92-93.

7612. Pearse, Moïse. "Sierra-Leone," *JME*, LI(1876), 176-177.

7613. Poole, Thomas E. *Life, Scenery and Customs in Sierra Leone and the Gambia.* 2 vols. London: Bentley, 1850.

7614. Pringle, George. "White Man's Grave," *Westminster Review*, Nov., 1899, pp. 565-570.

7615 . Raimbault, Jean-Baptiste. "Lettere," *MCM*, XX(1891), 3-5.

7616 . _____. "Lettres," *Annales Apostoliques*, VI(1891), 139-146.

7617 . _____. "Lettres," *APFL*, LVI(1884), 186-202, LXII(1890), 50-56.

7618 . _____. "Lettres," *MCL*, XXII(1890), 613-615.

7619 . Rankin, F. Harrison. *The White Man's Grave; a Visit to Sierra Leone in 1834*. 2 vols. London: Bentley, 1836.

7620 . Raymond, S. [*Abbé*]. "Lettre," *APFL*, XXXI(1859), 248-255.

7621 . Rosenbush, Colin Graham. *Sierra Leone: Its Commercial Position and Prospects*. London: W. Colmer, 1881. 37p.

7622 Ross, D. Palmer. *Medical Notes for Guidance of Junior Medical Officers and Officials (in Sierra Leone) Stationed in the Bush*. n.p., n.p., 1894. 12p.

7623 Ross, Ronald [*Colonel*]. *Report of the Malaria Expedition of the Liverpool School of Tropical Medicine*:Liverpool: Liverpool School of Tropical Medicine, 1900. 58p.

7624 Salesses, E. "Le chemin de fer de la Guinée anglaise," *Revue Coloniale*, V(1899), 203-208.

7625 . Slessor, Arthur K. "A Subaltern in the Bush," *Macmillan's Magazine*, Aug., 1900, pp. 241-253.

7626 . Stoll, Nicolas. "Lettres," *Annales Apostoliques*, I(1886), 147, 148.

7627 . _____. "Lettres," *Echo des Missions d'Afrique*, II(1885), 150-154.

7628 . Trotter, James Keith. "An Expedition to the Source of the Niger," *GJ*, X(1897), 237-259, 386-401.

7629 . _____. *The Niger Sources and the Borders of the New Sierra Leone Protectorate*. London: Methuen, 1898. 238p.

7630    Tuohy, Jérémie. "Lettere," *MCM*, XXVII(1898), 313-315.

7631    _____. "Lettres," *MCL*, XXX(1898), 301-303.

7632    . Vivian, William. "The Mendi Country, and Some of the Customs and
        Characteristics of Its Peoples," *JMGS*, XII(1896), 1-34.

7633    Weeks, John W. "Colonie de Sierra-Leone, ou les nègres affranchis,"
        *JME*, XII(1837), 364-377.

7634    . _____. "Journal, 1843," *JME*, XX(1845), 230-238.

7635    . Wilberforce, D. F. *Sherbro and the Sherbros; or, a Native African's
        Account of His Country and People*. Dayton, Ohio: United
        Brethren, 1886. 37p.

7636    . Wilhelm, Georg. "Sierra-Leone," *JME*, XXXIV(1859), 52-55.

7637    . Wilhelm, J. G. "Letter," *BM*, XI(1819), 404-405.

7638    . Winterbottom, Thomas. *An Account of the Native Africans in the Neighbour-
        hood of Sierra-Leone; to Which Is Added an Account of the
        Present State of Medicine Amongst Them*. 2 vols. London, 1803.

7639    . Young, M. W. and others. "Sierra Leone: vue générale de l'oeuvre,"
        *JME*, XVII(1842), 1-20.

TOGO

7640   Albéca, Alfred B. d'. "Voyage au pays des Éoués," *TM*, New Series, I

(1895), 85-92.

7641   . Anselmann, Georg. "Missionsbriefe," *Kleiner Herz-Jesu-Bote*, XXI(1893-1894),

47-48; XXII(1894-1895), 31, 87-88; XXIII(1895-1896), 78-79; XXIV

(1896-1897), Beilage, 12; XXV(1897-1898), Beilage, 13-14; XXVII

(1899-1900), 49-51.

7642   . Arand, Gregor. "Missionsbriefe," *Kleiner Herz-Jesu-Bote*, XXV(1897-1898),

86-88, and beilage, 26, 27; XXVI(1898-1899), 25, 26, 41, 42, 57,

58, 73, 74, 170.

7643   . Binder, J. *Das Evheland mit dem deutschen Togogebiet in Westafrika.*

Stuttgart: Steinkopf, 1893. 31p.

7644   . Binetsch, G. "Eine Reise durch das Ewegebiet Landeinwärts an der

Sklavenküste," *Mitteilungen der Geographischen Gesellschaft in

Jena*, VIII(1889).

7645   . Bornhaupt, C. von. "Die deutsche Togo-Expedition," *DK*, XII(1895),

329-331; XIII(1896), 81-83.

7646   . Buchner, C. "Das Togogebiet," *DK*, IX(1892), 19-23.

7647 . Bücking, Hermann. "Missionsbriefe," *Kleiner Herz-Jesu-Bote*, XXVI(1898-1899), 136-138; XXVII(1899-1900), 9-10; 25-27; [Title changes to *Steyler Herz etc.*], XXVIII(1900-1901), 58-59, 112-113; XXIX(1901-1902), 118.

7648 . Bürgi, E. "Reisen an der Togoküste und im Ewegebiet," *PM*, XXXIV(1888), 233-237.

7649 Büttner, R. "Die Forschungsstation Bismarckburg in Adeli (Togoland)," *Globus*, LXVI(1894), 1-7.

7650 . Canstatt, D. O. "Die gewerblichen Erzeugnisse des Togogebiets," *DK*, XVII(1900), 551, 578-580.

7651 . Conradt, L. "Das Hinterland der deutschen Kolonie Togo," *PM*, XLII (1896), 11-20, 29-33.

7652 . _____. "Land und Leute des Adelistammes im Hinterlande der Togokolonie," *DK*, XII(1895), 51, 59-60.

7653 . Dier, Matthias. "Missionsbriefe," *Kleiner Herz-Jesu-Bote*, XIX(1891-1892), 94-95; XX(1892-1893), 7, 14-15, 21-22, 28-30, 38-39, 46-50, 53-56, 62-63, 70-71, 78-79, 86-87, 94-95; XXI(1893-1894), 7, 14-15, 23-24, 31-32, 39, 54-56, 63-64, 67-69, 80, 87-88, 92-95; XXII(1894-1895), 6-8, 23, 30-31, 46-48, 54-56, 62-64, 70-71, 79, 86-87, 95; XXIII (1895-1896), 6-7, 14, 23-24, 30-31, 47-48, 55-56, 63-64, 70-71, 94-95. Beilage, 107-108, 110-112. XXIV(1896-1897), 54-55, 86-87; Beilage, 2-4, 8, 11-12, 19-20; XXV(1897-1898), 54-56, 94-95; Beilage, 12, 19-20, 27-28, 29-32, 34-36, 39-40; XXVI(1898-1899), 12-14, 28-29, 45.

7654 _____. *Unter den Schwarzen: Mitteilungen aus Togo über Land und Leute, Sitten und Gebräuche*. Steyl: Missionsdruckeri, 1899. 192p. 2nd Ed., 1901, 397p.

7655 . Dove, Karl. "Otjimbingue," *DK*, XVII(1900), 167-168.

7656      Ewen, Joseph. "Missionsbriefe," *Kleiner Herz-Jesu-Bote*, XXVI(1898-1899), 89-90, 107-109, 187-189, XXVII(1899-1900), 68-69, 80-81; XXVIII (1900-1901), 11-12, 24-26.

7657      . Fies, K. "Der Yamsbau in Deutsch-Togo," *Globus*, LXXXIV(1903), 266-272.

7658      François, D.C. von. "Die wirtschaftliche Tage im Togogebiet," *DK*, XVI(1899), 464, 474-475.

7659      . Grundemann, R. "Das Ewe-Gebiet in West-Afrika," *Ausland*, XLI(1868), 566-569, 590-594.

7660      Grunner and others. "Von der deutschen Togoexpedition," *DK*, XII(1895), 194-197, 202-205, 209-212.

7661      . Härtter, G. "Einige Bausteine zur Geschichte der Ewestämme," *Beiträge zur Kolonialpolitik*, III(1901-1902).

7662      . Heinlein, Adalbert. "Missionsbriefe," *Kleiner Herz-Jesu-Bote*, XXI (1893-1894), 79-80; XXIII(1895-1896), 14-15, 79, 86-87.

7663      . Herold, B. [*Hauptmann*]. "Aneho an der Togoküste," *DK*, XI(1894), 22-23.

7664      _____. "Bericht betreffend religiöse Anschauungen und Gebräuche der deutschen Ewe-Neger," *MDS*, V(1892), 141-160.

7665      · _____. "Die Bewohner des südlichen Togogebiets," *DK*, XII(1895), 282-284.

7666      · _____. "Kannibalismus in Togo," *DK*, XV(1898), 416.

7667      · _____. "Kratschi und Bismarckburg," *DK*, XI(1894), 153-154.

7668      · _____. "Lome an der Togoküste," *DK*, XI(1894), 83-84.

7669      · _____. "Der neue Togo-Grenzvertrag," *DK*, XVI(1899), 451-452.

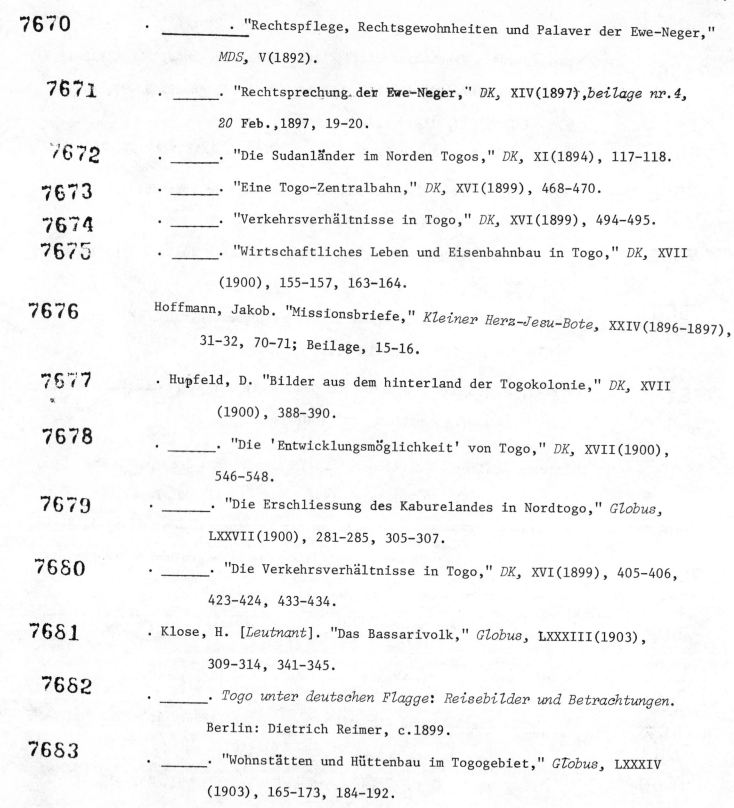

7670    • _____ . "Rechtspflege, Rechtsgewohnheiten und Palaver der Ewe-Neger,"
        *MDS*, V(1892).

7671    • _____ . "Rechtsprechung der Ewe-Neger," *DK*, XIV(1897), *beilage nr.4,*
        *20* Feb.,1897, 19-20.

7672    • _____ . "Die Sudanländer im Norden Togos," *DK*, XI(1894), 117-118.

7673    • _____ . "Eine Togo-Zentralbahn," *DK*, XVI(1899), 468-470.

7674    • _____ . "Verkehrsverhältnisse in Togo," *DK*, XVI(1899), 494-495.

7675    • _____ . "Wirtschaftliches Leben und Eisenbahnbau in Togo," *DK*, XVII
        (1900), 155-157, 163-164.

7676    Hoffmann, Jakob. "Missionsbriefe," *Kleiner Herz-Jesu-Bote*, XXIV(1896-1897),
        31-32, 70-71; Beilage, 15-16.

7677    • Hupfeld, D. "Bilder aus dem hinterland der Togokolonie," *DK*, XVII
        (1900), 388-390.

7678    • _____ . "Die 'Entwicklungsmöglichkeit' von Togo," *DK*, XVII(1900),
        546-548.

7679    • _____ . "Die Erschliessung des Kaburelandes in Nordtogo," *Globus*,
        LXXVII(1900), 281-285, 305-307.

7680    • _____ . "Die Verkehrsverhältnisse in Togo," *DK*, XVI(1899), 405-406,
        423-424, 433-434.

7681    • Klose, H. [*Leutnant*]. "Das Bassarivolk," *Globus*, LXXXIII(1903),
        309-314, 341-345.

7682    • _____ . *Togo unter deutschen Flagge: Reisebilder und Betrachtungen.*
        Berlin: Dietrich Reimer, c.1899.

7683    • _____ . "Wohnstätten und Hüttenbau im Togogebiet," *Globus*, LXXXIV
        (1903), 165-173, 184-192.

7684   . Kost, Theodor. "Missionsbriefe," *Kleiner Herz-Jesu-Bote*, XXVII(1899-1900), 148-150; XXVIII(1900-1901), 144-145; XXIX(1901-1902), 54-55.

7685   . Lauer, Ferdinand. "Missionsbriefe," *Kleiner Herz-Jesu-Bote*, XXVIII(1900-1901), 98-102; XXIX(1901-1902), 38-39.

7686   . Leuschner, Franz. "Negerkunst im deutschen Togogebiet," *Globus*, LXI (1892), 53-57.

7687   . Mertens, Franz. "Missionsbriefe," *Kleiner Herz-Jesu-Bote*, XXIX(1901-1902), 102-103.

7688   . Mischlich, A. "Reisebericht des Missionars A. Mischlich in Bismarck-burg," *MDS*, X(1897), 73-87.

7689   . Müller, Franz. "Missionsbriefe," *Kleiner Herz-Jesu-Bote*, XXIV(1896-1897), 63-64; XXVIII(1900-1901), 59.

7690   . Passarge, Siegfried. "Togo," in *Das deutsche Kolonialreich*, Ed. Hans H.J.Meyer, Leipzig and Vienna: Bibliographische Institut, 1909-1910. vol. 2.

7691   . Plehn, R. "Beiträge zur Völkerskunde des Togo-Gebietes," *Mitteilungen des Seminars für orientalische Sprachen*, II(1899).

7692   . Preil [*Oberleutnant*]. "Eine Otifahrt," *DK*, XVII(1900), 549-550.

7693   . Racklow, Hermann. "Zwei Jahre bei dem Ewevolke," *DK*, VIII(1891),128-131, 147-149.

7694   . Schäfer, Johann. "Missionsbriefe," *Echo aus Afrika*, IV(1892), 73-76, 120-121; V(1893), 21, 47-49, 75-77; VI(1894), 49-50.

7695   . _____. "Missionsbriefe," *Kleiner Herz-Jesu-Bote*, XX(1892-1893), 15-16, 60-61; XXI(1893-1894), 72.

7696   . Schmitz, Peter. "Missionsbriefe," *Echo aus Afrika*, XII(1900), 83-86; XIV(1902), 236-237.

7697   . _____. "Missionsbriefe," *Kleiner Herz-Jesu-Bote*, XXVIII(1900-1901), 126-128.

7698   . _____. "Missionsbriefe," *KM*, XXX(1901-1902), 234-236.

7699   . Seeger, Matthew. "Ein Beitrag zur Eucaluptus-Kultur," *DK*, IX(1892), 10-12.

7700   . Seidel, H. "Bilder aus Togo," *DK*, XVII(1900), 77.

7701   . _____. "Die Ephe-Neger," *Globus*, LXVIII(1895), 313-317, 328-332.

7702   . _____. "Krankheit, Tod und Begräbnis bei den Togonegern," *Globus*, LXXII(1897), 21-25, 40-45.

7703   . _____. "Die Küste und das Vorland der Togo Kolonie, *DK*, XIV(1897), 378-379, 390-393; *beilage nr.20*, p.89.

7704   . _____. *Lome, die Hauptstadt der Togokolonie. Ein Kulturbild aus Westafrika.* Berlin: H. Paetel, 1898. 42p.

7705   . _____. "Die Norddeutsche Missions-Gesellschaft in Togo," *DK*,XVI (1899), 436-437.

7706   . _____. "Salzgewinnung und Salzhandel in Togo," *DK*, XV(1898), 251.

7707   . _____. "Der Sklavenhandel in Togo," *DK*, XVI(1899), 123.

7708   . _____. "System der Fetischverbote in Togo, ein Beitrag zur Volkskunde der Evhe," *Globus*, LXXIII(1898), 340-344, 355-359.

7709   . _____. "Togo im Jahre 1897/98," *Globus*, LXXV(1899), 329-332.

7710   . _____. "Der Yew'e-Dienst im Togolande," *ZAOS*, III(1897), 157-185.

7711   . Spiess, C. [*Missionar - Keta*]. "Die Schmiedekunst im Evhelande," *Globus*, LXXV(1899), 63-64.

7712   , Spieth, J. "Agu," *DK*, XV(1898), 468-470.

7713   . _____. *Die Ewe-Stämme. Material zur kunde des Ewe-Volkes in Deutsch Togo.* Berlin: D. Reimer, 1906. 962p.

7714     . _____. "Der Jehwe-Dienst der Evhe-Neger," *Mitteilungen der Geographischen Gesellschaft in Jena*, XII(1893).

7715     . Thierry, Gaston. [*Oberleutnant, Stationsleiter*]. "Zur Frage der 'Verkehrsverhältnisse' in Togo," *DK*, XVI(1899), 455-456.

7716     . Virchow, R. "Anthropologische Aufnahmen in Togoland," *ZE*, XXVI(1894).

7717     . _____. "Zur Anthropologie der Westafrikaner besonders der Togo-Stämme," *ZE*, XXIII(1891), 44-65.

7718     . Witte, Anton. "Missionsbriefe," *Kleiner Herz-Jesu-Bote*, XXIX(1901-1902), 72-73, 86-87, 146-148.

7719     . Wohltmann, Ferdinand. *Bericht über seine Togo-Reise. Ausgeführt im Auftrage der Kolonial-Abteile des Auswärt Amtes im Dezember, 1899.* Berlin: Mittler & Sohn, 1900. 197pp.

7720     . Wolf, Ludwig. *Letzte Reise nach den Landschaft Barbar (Bariba) oder Borgu.* Berlin, 1890. 24p.

7721     . Zecht, J. von. "Vermischte Notizen über Togo und das Togo-Hinterland," *MDS*, XI(1898), 89-161.

7722     . Zöller, Hugo. "Das Togo-Gebiet," *Globus*, XLVII(1885), 182-185.

7723     . _____. *Das Togogebiet und die Sklavenküste.* Stuttgart: Spemann, 1885. 247pp.

UPPER VOLTA

7724 . Chanoine, Julien. [*Capt.*]. *Documents pour servir à l'histoire de l'Afrique occidentale française de 1895 à 1899*. Paris: Chanoine, n.d.. 302p.

7725 . _____. *Le Gourounsi*. Lille: Danel, 1898. 13p.

7726 . Christaller, Johann G. "Die Volta-Sprachen-Gruppe," *ZAS*, I(1887-1888), 161-188.

7727 . Crozat. [*Dr.*]. "Rapport sur une mission au Mossi (1890)," *Journal Officiel*, Oct. 5-9, 1891.

7728 . François, Kurt von. "Voyage à Salaga et au Mossi," *MDS*, I(1888), 143.

7729 Guignard, A. *Troupes Noires. Premières cartouches*. Paris: Fayard, 1912. 319p.

7730 Ménet, Henri. "Lettres," *Missions d'Afrique*, (1897-1900), 788-791.

7731 . Piguet. [*Capt.*]. *Mission Voulet au Mossi et au Gourounsi*. Paris: Chapelot, 1898. 4pp.

7732 . Tautain, L. "Quelques renseignements sur les Bobo," *Revue Ethnographique*, VI(1887), 228-233.

INDEX OF AUTHORS

A.B.C.  5142

Abargués de Sostén, Juan Víctor. 471 472,473

Abbadie, Antoine Thompson d'. 474-491, 1126

Abbadie, Arnauld d'. 492-494, 1126

Abbate, Onofrio [Pasha]. 1127, 1128

Abbatucci, S.  6679

Abbot, W. L.  1673

Abinal, Antoine.  2585-2587

Abiven, Oliver.  7226, 7227

Abreu e Lima, Luis Antônio de [Viscomde de Carreira].  3136

Abruzzi. [Duke].  3375

Abud, Henry Mallaby.

Abu Tālib ibn Muḥammad Khān, Iṣfahānī.  5352

Achte, Auguste.  2315-2325

Acker, Amand.  1674-1679

Adams, Alfons.  1680

Adams, C.  3376

Adams, Henry M.  6154

Adams, John [Capt.].  5353

Adams, Martin.  6155-6160

Adams, P.  1681

Adams, Robert.  5354

Adler, J. B38

Aga Khan.  1682

Agostini, Domenico. 39

Aigouy, Paul. 2588

Ailloud, Laurent. 2589—2594

Ainsworth, John. 986,987

Airaghi, Cesare. 495

Albéca, Alexandre L. d'. 5931—5935, 6935

Albéca, Alfred B. d'. 7640

Albuquerque, Affonso de. 3137

Alderson, Edwin Alfred Hervey. 4800

Alexander, Archibald. 6577

Alexander, James Edward [Capt.]. 5143,5144,5355

Alexis, F. 3377

Alexis, M. G. 40, 1683, 3378,3379

Alfani, A. 1129

Alford, Charles J. 4622,4801

Alford, Henry Stamford Lewis. 1130

Alis, Harry. See, Percher, Jules-Hippolyte.

Alix, Marie-Bernard. 496

Allain, E. 4623

Allaire, Olivier. 3381—3384

Allart, J. B. 3385,3386

Alldridge, Thomas Joshua. 7533—7535

Allen, Alfred. 4802

Allen, Marcus. 6341

Allen, William [Capt., RN]. 5356,5357, 6936—6939

André, Lourenço.  3139

Andree, R.  499

Andrés, Marcelino.  5936

Andriessen, W. F.  3388

Andry. [Commandant].  5359, 7232

Angus, H. Crawford.  4537, 4630

Ankermann. [Dr.].  7233

Annear, S.  6342

Annoni, Antonio.  3389

"An Officer".  1132

Anonymous.  1690, 3390, 5152, 5153, 6940, 7073

Anselmann, Georg.  7641

Ansorge, William John.  2326

Anthonay, Léon d'.  6680

Antinori, Orazio.  500-506, 1133

Antonelli, Pietro.  507-511

Antoni, Karl.  1134

António. [Bishop].  4631

Anton y Ferrandiz, Manuel.  6074, 6075

Antunez, José Maria.  3140-3143

Apel, Johann.  4805

Arand, Gregor.  7642

Arcenay, Murion d'.  7234

Archinard, L.  6681-6687

Azevedo Coutinho, João d'. 4632,4633

B

Bacheville, Barthélemy. 43

Bachmaier, Sebastian. 5756,5757

Backhouse, James. 5155

Backhove, Hermann. 2335

Bacon, Ephraim. 6586

Bacon, Francis. 6587

Bacon, Reginald Hugh Spencer. 6941

Baden-Powell, George Smyth. 44

Baden-Powell, Robert Stephenson Smyth. 4806,4807,6345

Badgley, James. 5363

Badia y Leyblich, Domingo. 45

Badin, Adolphe. 5939

Baecher, Aloysius. 4808, 4809

Baerts. 3425

Baesten, V. 3426

Bagster, William W. 3147

Baikie, William Balfour. 6942-6946

Bailey, Henry. 3427

Bailie, Alex C. 4810

Baillaud, E. 5364,6694,6695

Bailly, N. 6318

Bailly-Forfiller, Georges. 7240

Baines, Thomas.   2981, 2982, 4811-4816, 5156

Bajard, Joseph.   2336, 2337

Baker.   2601

Baker, Julian A.   176

Baker, Samuel White.   177-182, 529-532, 1139-1141

Balat. [Commandant].   3428

Baldacci, L.   533

Baldwin, William Charles.   2983, 4817

Balfour, Alice Blanche.   4818

Ballay, Noel.   6172

Ballieu. [Capt.].   6696

Ballot. [Missionary].   6947

Balmaseda, Francisco Xavier.   6078

Baltus, Nicolaus.   3429-3431

"Bamangwato."   4819

Banbury, George Alexander Sethbridge.   7536

Bancken, Friedrich.   5758

Banholzer, W.   1142, 1143

Baracho, Dantas.   3148

Baranhona e Costa, Henrique Cesar da Silva.   4634, 4635

Barbaglia, Giuseppe.   6948-6950

Barbe, Firmin.   2602, 2603

Barbier, Emmanuel.   7241, 7242

Barbot, Léon.   2338

Bardon, Louis.   2604—2606

Bareyt, Jean-Baptiste.   2607

Bargès, John-Joseph-Léandre [Abbé].   6697

Baril, C.   6698

Barker. [Lt.].   1067

Barker, E.   2608

Barker, W. C.   534

Barnard, Frederick Lamport.   183

Barrat, Maurice.   6173

Barre, Paul.   5365,5366

Barron, Edouard [Mgr.].   7243,7244

Barros, P. Marcellino.   7208,7209

Barros e Sousa de Mesquita de Macedo Leitão e Carvalhosa, Manoel

   Francisco de [Visconde].   3149

Barros Gomes, Henrique de.   3150

Barrow, A. H.   5367

Barrow, John.   2984, 2985

Barter, Charles St. L.   6346

Bartet, A. [Dr.].   5940

Barth, C. G.   1703

Barth, Heinrich.   3151, 5368—5374, 5941,6174,6347,
   6699—6702, 6951—6953

Barthélemy, Adrien.   7245

Barthélemy, Joseph.   2339

Barthélemy, Marc. 4820

Barthélemy, Paul. 2340

Barthet, Désiré. 7246

Barthez, Xiste. 535-540

Bartholomew. [Capt.]. 46

Barton, George A. 988

Barttelot, Edmund Musgrave. 184

Bary, Erwin de. 6703

Bas, François de. 3432,3433

Baskerville, George Knyton. 2341

Basset, René. 7247

Bast, Joseph. 3152

Bastard, G. 6704

Bastian, Adolf. 3153-3155, 3434- 3439,5375,6175

Bateman, Charles Somerville Latrobe. 3440

Bateman, George W. 1704

Bates, Francis W. 4636,4637

Bates, Laura H. 2986, 4638

Batty, R. Braithwaite. 6954

Batut, Alexandre. 2609, 2610

Batz, Gaston de. 2611

Baudin. 7248

Baudin, Noël. 5942,6955-6958

Baudraz, Claude-Pierre. 541

Baudry, A. [Lt.]. 5376,5377

Baum, H. 5157

Baumann, Oscar. 185-187, 1705-1714, 3441- 3452,5378,5379
Baumgarten, Johannes. 188, 189          6079, 6080
Baumgartner, Etienne [Rev.]. 7537,7538

Baumstark, Paul. 1715

Baur, Étienne.          1716-1722

Bayol, Jean [Dr.]. 5380-5383, 5943- 5946,6471,6705-6707,
Bazin, Hippolyte. 6959,6960          7249

Beal, B. A.   7250

Beale.   7539

Beardall, William.   1723

Beaton, Alfred Charles.   6348

Beau de Rochas, Alphonse.   5384

Beaufort, E. de.   7251

Beaufort, P. Grout de.   7252,7253

Beaugendre, M. A.   6961-6964

Beaumier, August.   6708, 7254

Beaumont, Augustinus.  542-544

Béchet, Eugene.   6709

Bechtinger, J.  545

Beck. [Dr.].  6710

Beck, Henry.  3453

Becker, Jerome Jacques.  3454, 3455,6081

Becroft, J. [Capt.].  6965, 6966

Bedingfeld. [Capt., RN].  6967

Beduschi, Giuseppe. 1144,1145

Beecham, John. 5385, 6349

Beerwald, K. 1724

Behr, H. F. von. 1725-1729

Behrens, T. T. 2342

Beillard, Chauvin. 546-550

Beke, Charles Tilstone. 190-193, 551-560

Bel, Camille. 5947,5948

Bel, Louis. 561-566, 7255

Belcher, Edward [Capt., RN]. 5386, 7256

Belck, Waldemar. 5158

Béliard, L. 6711

Bell, Henry Hesketh Joudou. 6350-6352

Bell, Sarah. 3156

Bell, T. M. 7540

Bellamy. [Dr.]. 7257

Bellefonds, E. L. de. 2343

Bellet, D. 3456

Bellingham, William. 3457

Bellville, Alfred. 1730,1731

Beltrame, Giovanni. 567, 568, 1146-1167

Benezis. [Sergeant]. 5387

Benitez, Cristobal. 5388,5389

Bennett, Albert L. 3458

Bennett, Ernest Nathaniel. 1168, 1169

Benoit, A. 3459

Ben Said, M. 6712

Bent, James Theodore. 569, 570, 1170, 4821-4827

Bentley, H. E. 3465

Bentley, William Holman. 3460-3465, 3671

Béraud, Médard. 3466, 5949, 6472

Berbizier, François. 2612

Berchon. 7258

Bérénger-Féraud, Laurent-Jean-Baptiste. 7259-7271

Berenguer, Vincent. 6968, 6969

Berg. 1732

Berghaus 571

Berghegge, Franz. 4828, 5305

Berghoff, Karl. 1171-1173

Berghold, Kurt. 1068

Beringer, Otto L. 1733

Berlioux, Etienne Felix. 194

Bern, J. 5950

Bernard, V. 3467

Bernhard, Louis. 1734

Bernstorff. [Graf von]. 5759

Berthelot, Sabin. 5390

Berthier, P. 6473, 7272

Berthieu, Jaques. 2613-2616

Berthoud, Paul. 4639

Berthoud, Ruth. 4640

Bertin, Théodule Charles Eugène. 5951

Berton, Jules. 6176,6177

Bertram, Otto. 1735

Bertrand, Alfred J. 5306-5309

Bertrand-Bocandé. 7210

Bertrocchi, Lorenzo. 1174

Bestion. 6178-6180

Béthune, Léon [Baron]. 3468,3469

Bettembourg, Nicholas. 572

Bettencourt Vasconcellos Corte Real do Canto, Vital de. 5952,5953

Betts. 7541

Betz, R. 5760

Biancheri, Lorenzo. 573-582

Bianchi, Gustavo. 583,584

Bichet, Georges. 3470, 6474-6477

Bick, Karl. 4829-4831

Biehe, G. 5159

Biehler, Eduard. 4832

Biermans, Jan. 1175,1176

Bigel, Chrysostome. 585, 586

Bigrel, Charles. 6713

Billiau, Joseph. 3471

Binder, J. 7643

Bindloss, Harold. 6970, 6971

Binetsch, G. 7644

Binger, Louis-Gustave. 5391—5395, 6714

Biron, Jean. 2617

Bissuel, Henri. 5396

Bittrolff, R. 5160

Bizemont, Henri Louis Gabriel de. 1177, 3472, 3473, 6181

Blair-Watson, A. 5310

Blaise, Eugene. 5397

Blake, J. Y. F. [Colonel]. 4833, 4834

Blanc, Henri Jules. 587—590

Blanc, Leonard. 2344, 2345, 6715

Blanca, Salvatore. 5311—5313

Blanchet, Edouard [Rev.]. 7273—7277

Blank, Heinrich. 1178

Blanquart de Bailleul. 3474

Bleek, W. H. I. 4641

Blennerhassett, Rose. 4835

Blinck, H. [Dr.]. 3475

Bliss, Harold C. J. 6353

Blot. [Vétérinaire]. 6716, 6717

Blundell, Herbert Weld. 591, 592

Blutzet, R. [Lt.].  6718

Blyden, Edward Wilmot.  5398—5400, 6588—6599, 7542, 7543

Boavida, António José.  3157

Bocande, B.  7278

Bockelmann, A. von.  1736

Boddaert, Ernest.  1737-1739

Bodeven, Joachim.  3476, 3477

Bodichon, Eugene.  5401, 5402

Bodson, L.  3478

Böcking, G.  1740

Böckner, C.  1741, 5761

Böhm, Richard.  1742-1748, 3479, 3480

Boel, Alphonse.  3481

Boggie, A.  4836

Boggie, Jeannie M.  4837

Boghemans, Audomarus.  3482

Bohe, Jean-Claude.  593, 594

Bohl, J.  3483

Bohm, B.  2004

Bohner, H.  5403

Bohner, Heinrich.  5762

Boilat, P. D. [Abbé].  7279, 7280

Boileau, F. F. R.  1749

Bois, Alexis [Commandant].  5404, 6719, 6720

Boisragon, Alan M.  6972

Boiteux, G. [Lt.].  6721

Bokemeyer, H. [Dr.].  5161

Boler, Richard Doubleday.  6973

Bolognesi, A.  1179

Bonchamps, de.  195

Bonhomme, Emile.  6533—6536, 6722

Bonhoure, M.  6537

Bonnat, J.  6354, 6478

Bonnefont de Varinay, P. de.  4642

Bonnelli, Emilio.  6082—6088

Bonnetain, Mme. Paul.  6723

Bonnetain, Paul.  5405

Bonnier, François-Xavier.  6724, 6725

Bonnier, Gaetan.  6726

Bonola, F.  1180

Bonomi, Luigi.  595, 1181—1186

Bonomi, G.  1187, 1188

Bonzon, Charles.  6182

Booms, Heinrich.  4838—4841

Boos, Anton.  4842—4844

Borchardt, P.  2

Borchert, Wilhelm.  5763

Bordeaux, Albert François Joseph.  4845 4846

Borelli, Jules. 596

Borghero, Francesco Saverio [Abbé]. 5954—5956, 6974

Borgnis-Desbordes, [Général]. 6727 6728

Borius, Alfred [Dr.]. 7281—7284

Bornhak, Conrad. 989

Bornhardt, Friedrich Wilhelm Conrad Eduard. 1750

Bornhaupt, C. von. 7645

Bory de Saint-Vincent, Jean Baptiste Généviève Marcellin. 2618

Bosco, Alessandro dal. 1189

Boshart, August. 47, 3484

Bossi, Giacomo. 5406

Boteler, Thomas [Capt., RN]. 196, 5407, 7285

Botelho, Eduardo Rodrigues Vieira da Costa. 3158—3160

Botelho, Sebastião Xavier. 4643—4645

Bottego, Vittorio. 597, 1069, 1070

Bottomley, George. 4847

Bouchard, Arturo. 1190—1195
Bouche, J. E. 5957, 5958
Bouche, Pierre-Bertrand [Abbé]. 5959—5964, 6472, 6975

Boucher, R. 1071

Boucherie, Nestor. 3485, 3486

Bouchet, Pierre-Marie. 7286

Bouchout, Moretus. 3487

Boudou, Adrien. 2619

Boudyck Bastiaanse, J. H. van. 5408

Bou-el-Moghdad.    7287

Bouët-Willaumez, Louis-Edouard.    5409, 5410, 7288

Bouleuc, Georges.    3488

Bouquet de la Grye.    7289

Bour, Charles.    7290, 7291

Bourdarie, P.    3489

Bourgès, J.    6729

Bourke, Dermot Robert Wyndham [Earl of Mayo].    598, 3490, 5162, 5163

Bourne, Henry Richard Fox.    4848, 5411, 7544

Bourrel.    7292

Boury. [Dr.].    6692

Bourzeix, Pierre.    6600, 7545—7547

Bouteiller, J. [Capt.].    6479

Bouton, Eugène.    6730

Bouysson, J.    3491, 6183, 6184

Bove, E.    7293

Bovy, Joseph.    3492

Bowdich, Thomas Edward.    3161, 5412—5414, 6355, 6480

Bowen, Thomas J.    6976— 6979

Bowler, Louis P.    4849, 4850

Boyer, Adrien.    1751—1753

Boy-Mellis, Andrea.    2620

Boyle, Frederick    6356

Boyle, James.    5415

Brackenbury, Henry.   1196, 6357, 6358

Bracq, Oscar.   3493 − 3496

Braga, Eduardo.   3162

Brally, J.   5416

Brandão Cró de Castro Ferreri, Alfredo.   4646

Brander-Dunbar. [Lt.].   1104

Brandsma, Gorgonius.   3497

Brandt, J.   7294

Braouezac.   6185

Brard,   (Alphonse.)   197, 1754, 2346 − 2355

Brasseur, Paule.   3

Braud, Justin.   2621

Braun, Antoon [Fr. Philippus].   2356

Bravo Jenties, Miguel.   6089

Braz, Manuel Gonçalves.   3163

Brazza: see Savorgnan de Brazzà.

Bréchet, E.   6731

Brégère, Hippolyte.   2622 − 2628

Breher, Xavier.   48

Brehm, A. G.

Brehm, Alfred G.   599, 1197, 1198

Brehme.   1755

Breiner, Michel.   3499

Brenner, Laurentius. 1756

Brenner, Rudolf. 198

Bressers, Richard. 1199

Bressi, Salvatore. 49-51

Bresson, Eugène. 2357, 2358

Briart, Paul. 3500, 3501

Bricet, Hyacinthe. 5965 - 5969

Brichaux, J. B. [Fr. Matthews]. 1757

Bridge, Horatio. 5417

Bridgman, Jon. 4

Bridoux, Léonce [Mgr.] 1758-1766

Brielman, Arthur. 3502 - 3505

Bright, R. G. T. 199, 2359

Brincker, P. H. 5164-5168

Bringuier, Joseph. 1767

Briot, Ernest-Hyacinthe-Erasme-Anga. 5418, 6481

British South Africa Company. 4851

Brittan, Harriet G. 6601

Brockmann, Paul. 5764

Brode, Heinrich. 2987

Brökling, Herman [Fr. Raphael]. 2360

Bronsart von Schellendorff, Fritz. 1768, 1769

Brooke, J. W. 200

Brossard de Corbigny, Charles Paul [Baron]. 2629

Brosse, Max. 6

Brosselard, Charles. 6732, 7295

Brosselard-Faidherbe, Henri François. 5419, 5420, 6928, 7211, 7212

Brou, A. 4852

Broun, W. H. 990

Broussais, Émile. 6733

Brown, George S. 6602

Brown, William Harvey. 4853

Browne. [Lt.]. 4647

Browne, James. 7548

Browne, James Ross. 1770

Broyon-Mirambo, Philippe. 1771

Bruce, Charles. 52

Brucker, Joseph. 2630

Bruel, G. 7

Brunache, Paul. 5906

Brunner, Samuel. 7296

Bruno. 600

Brusseaux, E. 3506

Brutzer, Ernst. 991-993

Bryson, Alexander [M.D.]. 7549

Bt. 5421

Bubendorf, Joseph. 6980-6982

Buchanan, John. 4538-4542

Buchner, C. 4543, 4544, 7646

Buchta, Richard. 201, 1200

Buckley, James Monroe. 53

Buckley, R. B. 994

Büchner, Max. 3164, 3165, 3507—3531, 5169, 5765, 5766

Bücking, Hermann. 7647

Bülow, Franz Josef von. 5170

Bülow, Frieda Friederike Fouise von [Baroness]. 1772

Bülow, H. von. 5171

Bürgi, E. 7648

Büttikofer, Johann. 6603—6605

Büttner, Carl Gotthilf. 202—205, 1773, 3532, 5172—5176


Büttner, Richard [Dr.]. 3166, 3533— 3543, 7649

Buijsrogge, Piet. 1201, 1202

Bulatovich, A. K. 601, 602

Buléon. 3544

Buléon, Joachim Pierre. 6186

Bunker, Fred R. 2988, 4648

Buofanti. 5422

Burchell, William John. 2989

Burdo, Adolphe Alphonse. 3545— 3547, 6983

Burdon, J. A. 6984

Burgeat, Emile. 6359

Burgess, Ebenezer. 206

Burkhardt, John Lewis.   1203

Burlaton, Louis.   2361,2362

Burleigh, Bennet.   1204-1206 , 2631

Burnham, Frederick Russell.   4854

Burrows, Guy.   3548—3550

Burton, Richard Francis.   54,207- 212   603 — 605,1774,1775,
3551, 3552 , 5423—5425,5767,5768 , 5970 , 5971,
6090 , 6091 , 6187,6360—6363,6538

Bushnell, Albert.   6188,6337

Butaye, Achiel   3553

Butler, William Francis.   213,6364

Butt, G. E.   5314

Buxton, Edward North.   55

Buxton, F. H.   6985

Buxton, T. F.

Buyl, A.   36

Buyle, Frédéric.   3554

Buzon.   5972


C., B.   6734

Cabello, Pedro.   6092

Cabon, Alexandre.   2363

Cabrouiller, Vincent.   606-610

Caddick, Helen.   2990

Cadet, Ambroise. 2632 – 2634

Caetano da Silva Lima, Manuel. 4649

Caetano do Rosario e Noronha, D. Isidoro. 4650

Caignard, Pierre. 611–613

Caillaud, Frédéric. 1207, 1208

Caillé, René. 5426, 5427

Caldas Xavier, Alfred Augusto. 4651, 4652, 4855

Caldeira, C. J. 3555

Calemard, François. 2635, 2636

Callet, François. 2637– 2639

Callewaert, Emiel. 3556

Calmel. [Capt. of Eng.]. 5428

Calon, Eugène. 3557

Caltelneau, F. de. 6735

Calve. [Dr.]. 7297

Calvet, Adolphe. 7298

Camara, Perry da. 4653

Cambier, Emeri. 3558– 3569

Cambier, Ernest François [Capt.]. 3570 3574

Camboue, Paul. 2640 – 2648

Cameron, Donald Andreas. 1209

Cameron, James. 2748

Cameron, Verney Lovett. 214–219, 1776, 1777, 2991–2995, 3575 6362, 6363

Cardinall, A. W. 8

Cardoso, F. 3168

Carerj, E. 5973

Carette, Antoine Ernest Hippolyte [Colonel]. 5429

Carey, M. 6607

Carlus, J. 7300

Carmien, H. 6238

Carnegie, David. 4857, 4858

Carneiro, João. 3169

Carnes, Joshua A. 5430

Carol, Jean. 2655

Carolinas, H. 3589

Caron, Edmond. 5431-5437, 6736-6738

Carow, Richard. 5177

Carrère, Frederick. 7301-7305

Carrie, Antoine-Marie[Mgr.]. 3590-3602

Carter, Gilbert T. 6992, 6993

Carvalho, Henrique de. 3603-3606

Carvalho e Menzes, Joaquim Antonio de. 3170

Carvalho e Menzes, José Guedes de. 4655

Carvalho e Menzes, Vasco Guedes de. 3171

Carvalho Soveral, Ayres de. 4656

Casati, Gaetano. 1220

Casman, W. 3607

Cassagne, Pierre.  2656, 2657

Castaing. [Dr.].  7306

Castaing, T. [Abbé].  2658

Castellani, Charles Jules.  3608

Castelyn, Gustave.  1791, 1792

Castilho, Alexandre Magno de.  5438

Castilho Barreto e Noronha, Augusto de.  4657-4660, 5439

Castonnet des Fosses.  6739

Castro, A. J. de [Major].  3609

Castro e Moraes, Antonio María de Jesús.  7213

Catat, Louis.  2659

Catel.  7307

Cattier.  3610

Cauderlier, E.  3611

Caulier, Benoit.  2660, 2661

Causseque, Pierre.  2662—2669

Cauteren, Willem van.  3612, 3613

Cavedon, Emilio.  1221

Cavendish, H. S. H.  220

Cazalbou, L.  6740

Cazeaux, François.  2670 - 2678

Cazemajou, M. G.  5907

Cazet, Jean-Baptiste.  2679 - 2683

Cecchi, Antonio.  621-626

Cecil, Evelyn. 4859

Célarié, P. 6482

Cerisier, Charles. 3614

Cerminati, Bérenger. 6994

Cervera, Julio. 5440

César, Louis. 7308, 7309

Chadwick, J. Cooper. 4860

Chaillé-Long, Charles. 58, 221, 1222, 1223, 2364, 3615

Chalais, Martial. 627-629

Chalot, Charles. 3616-3618, 4161

Chaltin. [Capt.]. 3619-3624

Chambers, Stracey. 4861

Chanler, William Astor. 222

Chanoine, Julien. 5441, 5442, 7724, 7725

Chaper. 6539

Chapman, A. 3103

Chapman, James. 2999, 3000

Charbonnier, Jean-Baptiste. 1793-1796

Charlesworth, Maria Louisa. 7551

Charmanne, H. 3625-3627

Charnay, Désiré. 2684

Chatelain, Aida. 3172

Chatelain, Héli. 3173

Chatouville, Camille de. 4545

Chaudoin, E. 5974

Chausse, Jean-Baptiste [Missionary]. 6995-7001

Chautard, Eugene. 5975-5981

Chavanne, Josef [Dr.]. 59, 3174, 3628-3630

Chavannes, Charles de. 3631

Chenay, Étienne. 2685-2691

Chenivesse, Emile. 1224-1226

Cherbonneau, A. 6741, 6742

Chervalier, Alphonse. 2692, 2693

Chesnais, René de. 1227

Chesnaye, C. P. 5315

Chevalier, A. 5443, 6743

Chevalier, Claude. 2365-2367

Chiesi, Gustavo. 223

Chippindall, William Harold [Lt.]. 2368

Cholet, J. 3632, 6189

Chomérac, Georges. 2369

Christaller, J. G. [Rev.]. 6365, 6366, 6608, 6609, 7726

"Christian Traveller". 5444

Christie, James [M.D.]. 224

Christlieb, Eugen. 5769

Christopher, W. 225

Christy, David. 6610

Church, Mary. 7552

Churchill, William A. **4661**

Churchill, Winston L. S. **1228**

Cimbault, Léon. . **7310**

Claes, Louis Victor [Fr. Victor]. **2370-2372**

Claeys, Adolf. **3633, 3634**

Clapperton, Hugh. **7002**

Clark, David E. **4**

Clark, George Edward. **226**

Clark, H. F.

Clark, John. **6093**

Clarke, Hyde. **6367**

Clarke, John. **5445, 5446, 7003**

Clarke, Robert. **7553**

Classe, Léon. **2373, 2374**

Claver, Pierre. **3636**

Claverie, Paul. **7311, 7312**

Clement, Eugene. **630**

Clément de Saint-Marcq. **3637**

Cleve, G. L. **60, 1797**

Cleveland, Richard Jeffry. **61**

Clinch, B. J. **2694**

Clive, Percy A. **7004**

Clozel, Marie François Joseph. **5447, 5448, 5908, 5909, 6190, 6540-6543, 7313**

Cneut, Camille.    3638—3641

Coccino, Felicissimo da Cortemiglia.  631

Cochelet, Charles.  5449

Cocheteux.    3642

Codrington, Robert.   1798, 4546, 4547, 5316

Coffinières De Nordeck, A. de [Lt.].  6191, 6483

Coignet, F.    2695

Coillard, François.   3001, 3002, 4862, 5317—5320

Coinet, Narcisse.   3175

Coker, Daniel.  7554

Colborne, John [Colonel].  1229

Cole, H.   1799

Cole, J. Augustus.  5450, 7555

Cole, William.   7005

Colin, G. [Dr.].  5451, 5452, 6744—6749, 7314, 7315

Colin, Leon-Jean [Dr.].  6368

Colle, Pierre.   3643, 3644

Collier, George Ralph.  5453

Collier, M. A.   7006

Collignon.   7316

Collingridge, Leonard Thomas.

Collings, T. C.   4863

Collomb. [Dr.].   6750—6753

Colomb, Philip Howard.  227

Colombaroli, Angelo. 1230

Colquhoun, Archibald Ross. 4864-4866

Colrat de Montrozier, Raymond. 3003

Colson, Pierre Louis. 2696

Colston, R. E. [Colonel, R.E.]. 1231-1233

Colville, Henry Edward. 2375

Colville, Zelia Isabella. 62,7007

Comber, T. J. [Rev.] 3645-3650, 3866

Combes, Edmond. 228,632

Combes, Paul. 633

Combet, Joachim. 2697

Comboni, Daniele [Mgr.]. 1234-1242

Compagnie de Madagascar. 2698

Compiègne, Victor Dupont de [Marquis]. 5454, 6094,6192-6196

Comte, Paul. 3651

Conceição Albano, Antonio [Marques]. 7214

Connolly, R. M. 6369

Conrad. [Capt.]. 6754

Conradt, Frieda. 5770

Conradt, L. 1800,5178,5771,7651,7652

Conrau, Gustav. 5772-5776, 7008

Cons, H. 5455

Cook, Albert Ruskin. 2376, 2377

Cook, H. 634

Coulbeaux, Jean-Baptiste.  640

Coulbois, François.  1802-1808

Coullous. [Père].  3665

Courdioux, Philibert.  5982, 5983

Courmont, Raoul, de.  1809-1821

Courtois, José Victor.  4665, 4867

Cousins, G.  2702, 2703

Cousins, William Edward.  2704, 2705

Coutant.  6756

Coviaux, L.  6757, 6758
Cowan, William Deans [Rev.].  2706—2709

Cowie, Alexander.  4666

Cox, E. G.  10

Cox, Melville Babbage.  6611

Cox, Percy Zachariah.  1072

C. R.  6612

Crampel, Paul.  3666, 3667

Crancq, Jean-Marie.  2710, 2711

Crawford, Daniel.  3668, 3669

Crawshay, Richard.  996, 4550

Crean, J. F.  5458

Creswick, H. C.  6613

Crispin, Edward S.  229
Croad, Hector.  5321

Croft, James A. 6370

Crohas, Jean. 7013, 7014

Crombette, Jean-Baptiste. 641,642

Crooks, John Joseph. 6371, 7556

Croonenberghs, Charles. 3008, 4868-4875

Croonenberghs, Eugenius. 3670

Cros, Pierre. 7319-7321

Crosby, Oscar T. 230

Cross, D. Kerr. 1822

Crouch, Archer Philip. 3004, 5459, 5984

Crouzet, Jacques-Jean. 643-649

Crow, Hugh. 5460

Crowther, Samuel A. 7015-7021, 7166

Crozais, J. de. 6759

Crozals, Jacques Marie Ferdinand Joseph de. 5461

Crozat. [Dr.]. 7727

Crudington, Henry E. 3671

Cruickshank, Brodie. 5462, 6372

Crummell, Alexander. 6614-6616

Cruttenden, Charles J. 1073-1075

Cuffee, Paul. 7557

Cunha, P. A. da 3178

Cunningham, James Francis. 2385

Cunninghame, Boyd A. 3179

Cuny, C.   6197

Curado, A. F.   7215

Cureau, A. [Dr.].   3672

Currie, Donald.   3005

Currie, Walter T.   3180-3183

Curtis, James.   7322

Cus, Alphonse.   3673

Czimmermann, Stephan.   4876-4883

## D

Da Costa, Aleixo Justiniano Socrates.   7216

Da Costa Oliveira, E. J.   7217, 7218

Daenen. [Capt.].   3674

Daguerre, Joseph.   7323

Dahin, Xavier.   6198

Dahle, Lars Nielsen.   2712-2714

Dahlgruen, H.   1823

Daignault, Alphonse.   4884, 4885

Dailey, J. R.   7558

Dale, Godfrey.   1824, 1825

Dalgleish, W. Scott.   6373

Dalmond.   2715

Dalton, O. M.   7022, 7149

Danckelman, Alexander Sylvester Flavius Ernst [Freiherr von].   3675-3679, 5777

Daniel, P.   3680

Daniell, William Freeman.   5463

Dannfelt. [Lt.].   3681

Dantas, Gervasio.   3184

Dantin, François-Joseph.   2716

Dantz, K.   1826

Da Offeio, Francesco.   650,651

Dard, Charlotte Adéle Picard.   7324

Darnal, Léon.   3185

Darondeau.   5464

Darrican.   6199

Daull, Emile.   1827-1830

Daumas, Melchior Joseph Eugène.   5465

Daunas, Marcel.   7325

Davey, T. G.   5322

Davezac, Paul.   6484-6489

David, Louis.   6760

Davidson, H. Frances.   4886

Davies, William.   7559

Davis, Alexander.   4887,4888

Davis, Richard Harding.   231

Dawkins, Charles Tyrwhitt.   4889

Dawson, May M.   4890

Day, Arthur.   4891

Dean, John M.   3682

De Backer, Albertus.   3683, 3684

Debaize, Alexandre [Abbé].   1831

De Beerst, Gustave.   3685 — 3688

Debono, Andria.   232

Deburaux, Édouard Léopold Joseph.   1244, 5466

Decazes.   3689, 6761

Decem, P.   6200

De Chazotte. [Missionary].   6545, 6546

Decken, Carl Claus von der [Baron].   233, 234, 1832

Deckert, Emil.   3006

Decle, Lionel.   63, 235, 1833, 4667 — 4669, 4892, 4893

De Cleene, Natalis.   3690, 3691

De Clercq, Auguste.   3692 — 3700

De Cock, Alphonse.   3701 — 3703

De Cosson, Emilius Albert.   652, 1245

Decressac-Villegrand, Marcel.   7326

Defauconpret, P.   5467

Degoutin, A.   653

De Gryse, Jean.   3704, 3705

De Hert, François.   3706 — 3710

Dejoux, Jean-Baptiste.   4894 — 4896

Deken, Constant de.   3711 — 3717

Delafosse, Maurice.   5910, 6547, 6548, 6762

Delamarche, Julien. 4551-4554

Delanneau. [Capt.]. 6763-6766

Delannoy, Charles. 3186

Delany, Martin Robinson. 5468,5469, 7023

Delaunay, Henri. 1834-1837

Delaye. 654

Delbosc, Augustin. 2717- 2726


Delcommune, Alexandre Joseph Philippe. 3718-3727

Delhaise-Arnould, M. L. 3007

Deligne, Erneste. 3728-3730

Delisle, F. [Dr.]. 3731,6201,6202

Delme-Radcliffe, C. [Lt.Col.]. 2386

Delmont, Mamert. 2727, 2728

Delmonte. 655,1246

Delore, Ferdinand d'Hyères. 656

Delorme, Amable. 6490-6496

Delpuech, Emmanuel. 1838

Demanche, G. 5985,6767,6768

Demars, Victor Gabriel. 3732

De Meulemeester, Ernst. 3733-3736

Demeuse, F. 3737-3740

De Moura, Johann Joseph. 4897

De Muelenacre, Felix. 3741

Destrain, E.    3747

Devaux. [Capt.].    5472, 5473, 6497

Deventer, Marinus Lodewijk van.    4670

Deverdun, E.    5474

Devereux, William Cope.    236

De Vulder, Gustaaf.    3748

De Winton, Francis.    3749

Dewitz, Otto von.    3191

Dhanis, Francis [Baron].    3750—3753

Dhyèvre, Joseph-Théophile.    7329

Dias de Carvalho, Henrique Augusto.    3192—3195

Diboll, J.    6095

Dibull, J.    6144

Dichtl, Johann E.    1249—1251

Dickins, Vincent.    4913

Dickson, B.    1000

Dier, P. Matthew.    7653, 7654

Dierkes, Bernard.    3754, 3755

Diesing, Ernst.    1852

Diesterweg, Moritz.    4914

Dieterle, J. C.    6375

Dietlin, Achilles.    1853, 1854

Dimothéos, R. P.    657

Dindinger, J.    33

Douville, Jean-Baptiste.  3758, 3759

Dove, Karl.  64, 658, 5180-5187, 7655

Downing, Henry Francis.  6617

Doyle, Denis.  4671, 4916

Drake, Richard.  65

Drayton, B. J.  6618

Dreyfus, Ferdinand Camille.  6549

Dromaux, Théophile.  1858-1864

(1754),

Drontmann, Herman.  1253, 1254

Droogmans, Hubert.  3760

Drouet, Henri.  3196

Dubarry, Armand.  5477, 5993

Du Bellay, Griffon [Dr.].  6204

Duboin, François-Marie [Mgr].  7335

Dubois, Felix.  6498, 6772

Duby, Martin.  7336-7338

Du Chaillu, Paul Belloni.  6205-6221

Duchêne, Lucien.  6773-6778

Duchon-Doris, J. P.  7339

Duclot, N.  5478

Du Couret, Louis [Colonel].  659, 3761, 5479

Dudon, Paul.  66

Dufey.  660

Duflos, Adéodat. 661,662

Dufton, Henry. 663

Duloup, G. 3762

Dumas, P. 6779

Dumont, Pierre Joseph. 67

Duncan, John. 5480,5481,-5994,6378

Dundas, F. G. 237,1001, 1076

Dunn, Edward John. 5188

Duno, Pasquale da. 664,665

Duparquet, Charles-Victor-Albert. 3197, 3198, 3763, 5189

Duparquet, M. P. 3199

Du Paty de Clam, A. 6550

Dupeyron, Pierre. 4917

Dupoint, Joseph. 2394, 2395

Duponchiec, A. 6780

Dupont. [Mme]. 2735

Dupont, Edouard François. 3764-3768

Dupont, Joseph. 4555 - 4558

Du Pouget, Jean François Albert. See, "Nadaillac."

Dupouy, Edouard [Dr.]. 6781, 6782

Dupré, Marie Jules. 2736

Dupuis, Auguste. 6783

Dupuis, Joseph. 6379

Dupuy, P. J. 2737

Du Quillo.    6222

Durand, E.    4918

Durand, F.    5482

Durand, Jean Baptiste Léonard.    7340

Duranton.    6784

Durieux, Antoine.    7027, 7028

During.    7560

Duron, Adolphe.    6223

Du Sorbiers de la Tourasse, Joseph.    7341

Dutau, P. Adolphe.    1255

Du Toit, Stephanus Jacobus.    4919, 4920

Dutrieux, Pierre Joseph [Dr.].    3010, 3769-3771

Duveyrier, Henri.    6785

Dybowski, Jean.    3772-3776, 5911, 5912

Dye, William M.    666

Dyer, Alfred Stace.    6619

Dyer, Hugh McN.    5483

E

Eberstein, von.    1865

Eckersley, W. Alfred.    4921

Eden, T. E.    5190

Edye, John Simpson.    1077

Eggers. [Lt.].    5191

Ehlers, Otto E.    1866

Enduran, Lodoix.  7342

Engasser, Jean-Baptiste.  7031

Engel, Léger.  7343

Engels, Alfons.  3779-3781

Engels, Ferdinand.  4923

English, George Bethune.  1257

Englund, P.  667

Ennes, Antonio.  4672

Ensor, F. Sidney.  1258

Epinette, Auguste-Marin.  7344

Eppler, Christopher Frederick.  2749

Erhardt, James.  242

Erlanger, Carlo von.  668,669

Erlington.  4924

Erman, W. [Dr.].  5995

Ernst. [Herzog].  670

Erskine, St. Vincent.  3012, 3013, 4673-4675

Ertzscheid, Joseph.  7032

Escamps, Henry d'.  2750

Escayrac de Lauture, Pierre-Henri-Stanislas d'.  5489-5491

Esch, Ernst.  5780

Espagnat, Pierre d'.  6551

Esser, Hubert.  2398

Esser, Max.  5194-5196

671-673

Esteban, Joachim-Marie de Bocequillas.

Esvan, Jean-Marie.    7345

Étienne, P.    7346

Etterle, Joseph.    4925

Eucher, Roy.    3782

Ewald, H.    243

Ewen, Joseph.    7656

Eyers, Georges.    3783

Eysséric, J.    6552-6555

F

F.    6788

Facq, Louis.    2399

Faes, Jozef.    3784, 3785

Faidherbe, Louis Léon César [Général].    5492-5494, 6789-6791
7347-7351

Fairbridge, W. E.    4926

Falcão, Joaquim José,    3200

Falkenhausen, Helene von.    5197

Falkenhorst, C.    1872-1874, 5781

Falkenstein, Julius August Ferdinand.    3786, 3787, 4148, 5495

Falkonberg, B. E.    1259

Fallot, Ernest.    6932, 7352

Farler, John Prediger.    1875-1878

Faucon. [Lt.].    6792

Fauconnier, Ambroise.    2400

Faulkner, Henry. 244

Faure, Joseph. 2751-2753

Faure, Julien. 1879

Faure, Sylvain. 2754, 2755

Fava, M. 1880, 1881

Favitski de Probobysz, de. [Commandant]. 12

Fawckner, James. 7033

Fay, William E. 3201-3204

Fechet, Oscar E. 1260

Feio, Bento Cazimiro. 4676

Felix, Matthieu. 2756

Felkin, Robert William. 245-247, 468, 1261, 1262, 2401, 2402

Fennekol, Frederik Willim. 5496

Ferguson, Robert 69

Feris. [Dr.]. 5497, 5996, 5997

Fernandes das Neves, Diocleciano. 3205

Ferreira, João Antonio da Neves. 3206

Ferreira d'Almeida, J. B. 3138

Ferreira da Silva Porto, Antonio Francisco. 3207

Ferreira do Amaral, Francisco Joaquín. 3208

Ferreria, José Joaquim. 4677

Ferret, Pierre Victor Adolphe. 674, 683

Ferryman, Augustus F. Mockler [Lt.Col.]. 2403, 7034

Ferstl, Basilius. 1882, 1883

Fesca, M. [Dr.]. 5782

Festing, A. M.   7561

Ficheux, Victor.   6793-6795

Fies, K.   7657

Fièvez. [Capt.].   3788

Figaniere e Morão, Joaquim César de.   7562

Figeac, T. [Capt.].   6796

Filliung, Joseph.   3209

Finaughty, William.   5323

Finaz, P.   2757

Findlay, Frederick Roderick Noble.   4678

Finlason, C. E.   4927

Fiorentini, Filippo.   7035

Firminger, Walter Keller.   1884

Fischer, G. A. [Dr.].   248,249, 1004, 1885-1888

Fischer, Nikolaus.   2404

Fischer, Thomas.   3210

Fischli, Joseph.   5783

Fitzau, August.   5498

Fitzer, Elpide.   3789,3790

Fitzgerald, William Walter Augustus.   250

Fitzner, Rudolf.   1889,1890

Fitzpatrick, James Percy.   4928

Flad.   5784,5785

Flad, Johann Martin. 675 — 680

Flapper, Lodewijk. 3791 —3793

Fleck, E. [Dr.]. 5198

Fleck, Joseph. 7563-7565

Flegel, Robert Eduard. 5786-5788, 7036—7042

Fletcher, John Joseph Kilpin. 2758

Fletcher, Richard. 7566

Fletcher, W. 7567

Fleuriot de Langle. [Vicomte]. 70, 251, 3794, 6224—6227

Flick, Jean. 1891

Flickinger, Daniel Kumler. 5499, 6620, 7568

Foa, Édouard. 3014—3019, 3795, 4929, 5998-6002

Förster, B. 1892

Folignet. [Abbé]. 2759, 2760

Foncé, Antonius. 3796

Fonck, H. 3797

Fonssagrives, Jean-Baptiste-Joseph-Marie-Pascal. 6003, 6004

Fontán Lobe, Juan. 13

Fontanié, Victor. 2761—2764

Foot, C. E. 252

Foote, Andrew Hull. 5500

Foote, Henry Grant [Mrs.]. 5501

Forbes, Frederick Edyn [Lt., RN]. 5502, 5503, 6005

Forbes, James. 71

Forbes, Patrick William. 4561

Ford, Henry A. 5504, 6228, 6229

Forêt, Auguste. 6797, 7353

Forgues, E. D. 6006

Forstmann, Henri-Bernard. 681, 682

Foster, Hubert John. 253

Fotheringham, L. Monteith. 4562

Foureau, F. 72

Fourest. 6230

Fourneau, Alfred L. 3798, 3799, 6231

Fraccaro, Giovanni Battista. 1263-1265

Franceschini, Giuseppe Camillo. 1266-1268

Francis, John Cyril. 1078

Franciscus, Emiel Delhaye. 3800

François, Charles Justin. 7043, 7044

François, Curt Carl von [Major]. 3211, 3801-3804, 5199, 5200, 7728

François, D. C. von. 7658

François, Hugo von. 5201

Francqui. [Lt.]. 3805-3812

Franke, G. A. J. 3813

Franzoj, Augusto. 1269-1270

Fras, P. 6499

Fraser, Donald. 4563, 4564

Fraser, George. 4930-4932

Freeman, John D.  2767

Freeman, Joseph John.  2765-2767,5505

Freeman, Richard Austin.  6385

Freeman, Thomas Birch.  5506,6007,6386,6387

Freire de Andrade, Alfredo Augusto.  4679,4680

French, George K.  6388

Frere, Henry Bartle Edward.  254,1893,1894, 3020

Freshfield, Douglas W.  2582

Frewen R.  4681

Frey, Henri Nicolas [Général].  5507,7354,7355

Frick.  3814

Friedrich, Karl.  4933

Friedrich, Martin.  7045, 7046

Frigerio, Giovanni.  7047, 7048

Fritsch, Antoine.  7569, 7570

Fritsch, Gustav.  4934, 5202

Frobenius, Herman.  1271,4935

Frobenius, Leo V.  73 , 3815-3818, 5508-5510,5789

Froment, Edouard.  3819, 5511

Fry, J. W. Ellerton.  4936

Fuchs, F.  3820-3822

Fülleborn, F.  4565,4566,4682

Fuller, J.  5512

Fumagalli, G.  14

Futterer, Karl Joseph.    3823

G

Gaboriaud.    6500

Gabriel, Emmanuel.    4937-4939

Gachet, Célestin.    2768

Gachon, Jean.    6232-6237

Gacon, Jean.    2405, 2406

Gacon, Virgile.    6238

Gadow, G. [Dr.].    5203

Gael, Vallon.    7356

Gaffarel, P.    5513

Gaillard, G.    3825

Galinand, Joseph.    3824

Galinier, Joseph Germain.    674, 683

Gall, Eugen .    6798

Gallais, Louis-Marie.    6501, 7357

Gallaud, Jean.    6389-6391

Gallichet, Henri.    2769

Galliéni, Joseph-Simon [Général].    2770, 2771, 5514, 5515
    6799-6809

Galloway, William.    1272

Gallwey, Henry L.    7049

Galton, Francis F.    5204-5206

Gamble, D. P.    15

Gamitto, Antonio Candido Pedroso. 3021

Gandoin. 6008

Gandon, Antoine. 74

Ganot, Aimé. 7050-7054

Ganzenmüller, Konrad [Dr.]. 1273

Garcia Maraber, Francisco. 6097

Gardes, Henri. 2772-2775

Garenne, E. 6009

Garner, R. O. 5516

Garnier, Alfred. 3826-3830

Garrett, G. H. 7571

Garride, Manuel. 7572

Gatacre, W. [Maj. Gen.]. 1274

Gatelet, Auguste-Louis-Charles [Lt.]. 6810

Gatta, L. 1275

Gattang, Emil. 1895

Gauchy, Louis. 2776-2778

Gaudeul, Ange. 6392-6396

Gaudibert, Henri. 2407-2411

Gautier, E. F. 2779-2781

Gautier, Jean. 6239

Gay, Jean. 16

Geddie, John. 255

Gedge, Ernest. 1001

Geens, Emile.   3831

Geerts, Henri [Fr. Wenceslaus].   2412

Gèle, A. van [Capt.].   3832

Gell, Philip Lyttelton.   4940

Génié, Etienne.   3212-3214

Geoffroy, A.   6010

Geraldes, Francisco Antonio Marques.   7219

Gerard, P. M.   1896

Gerboin, François.   3833

Germain, Adrien.   256

Gerstenhauer, M. R.   5207

Gessert, Ferdinand.   5208, 5209

Gessi, Romolo.   1276, 2413

Geyer, Francis X.   1277-1324


Ghika, Nicolas [Prince].   1079

Giacomelli, Casimiro.   2414-2418

Gibbons, A. St. Hill [Major].   1005, 5324-5328

Gibson, Alan G. S.   5210

Gibson, Henry.   257, 1897, 1898, 2782

Gidrol, Marcellin.   1325-1328

Gilbert, Sharrad H.   4941

Gilbert, Théodore.   684, 685

Gill, David. 5211

Gillain. [Capt.]. 3834

Gillet, Justin. 3835, 3836

Gillmore, Parker. 3022, 4683, 4684

Gilson, H. J. 4685

Gindre, Henri. 2783

Girard, H. 5517

Giraud, Pierre. 1899-1902

Giraud, Victor. 258, 259, 3023, 3024

Giraul. [Visconde de]. 3215

Girault, Ludovic. 2419-2422

Girod, Léon. 6240

Giron, Emmanuel. 3837, 3838

Gissing, C. E. 1906

Glauning, Hans. 1903, 1904

Glave, E. J. 1905, 1906, 3839-3845, 4322, 4567

Gleerup, E. 4083

Gleichen, Albert Edward Wilfred. 686, 1329-1332

Glinskii, D. 687

Glorius, Livinus. 1907

Glover, John Hawley. 5518, 7055

Goarnisson, Jean-Marie. 1908

Gobat, Samuel. 688, 689

Goblet d'Alviella. [Comte]. 3846

Gorges, G. H.  1007

Gorin. [Lt.].  3856

Gorjão de Moura, Francisco Izidoro.  4686, 4687

Gorju, Joseph.  6556

Gorju, Julien-Louis.  2423

Gosseau, Octave.  1911-1913

Gouldsbury, Valesius Skipton.  7361

Gouraud. [Lt.].  5521

Gourdault, Jules.  76

Gourdy, Jean.  3857, 3858

Gouttes, Dominique de Castelnaudary.  691-695, 1080

Gouzien, Paul [Dr.].  6011

Goy, A.  5329

Goy, Mathilde Keck.  4942

Graff, M.  7060

Graham, Douglas Cunninghame.  696

Graham, Gerald.  1341

Gramberg, Jan Simon Gerardus.  5522

Grandidier, Alfred.  17, 2784

Grandidier, G.

Grandin, C.  6012

Grandy, W. G. [Lt.].  3859

Grant, Charles Scovell.  5523

Grant, James Augustus.  266, 267, 420, 421, 1342, 1343

Grover, John [Dr.]. 5527

Grove-Rasmussen, Andreas Christian Ludwig.     2424

Grün, Charles.     1915,1916

Grünenwald, Michel. 270, 271

Grundemann, R.     1917, 5214, 5528, 7659

Grundy, P.     6398

Gruner. [Dr.]. 5529

Grunner.     7660

Gruson, Charles.

Gruson, Edouard. 697-703

Gudgeon, E. B.     6621

Gueluy, Albert.     3868

Guénnégan, Jean-François.     6504

Guérin, Charles. 7363-7367

Guerret. [Abbé].     2786

Guessfeldt, Paul.     3869-3871, 4148, 5530, 5531, 6245-6247

Guignard, A.     7729

Guillain, Charles. 272, 2787

Guillaumet, Édouard.     5532, 6811, 6812

Guillé, Raoul.     4570, 4571

Guillemé, Mathurin [Missionary].     1918-1923     3872-3883

Guillermain, Antonin.     2425-2435

Guillerme, Louis.     4572

Guillet, Alexandre.     1924-1928

Guillet, Edmond.    7368 — 7372

Guilleux, Charles.    5533

Guillevin. [Lt.].    6013

Guillot, E.    7373

Guilmin, H.    3217

Guinard, Paul.    6557, 6558

Guiness, Fanny E.    3884, 3885

Guiral, Léon.    3886, 3887

Guiu, Exupère de Prats-de-mollo.    704

Gunst. [Dr.].    2788

Gurich, Georg.    5215

Gurmie. [Missionary].    1929

Guyard, Georges.    4573

Guy-Grand, V. L.    7374

Guyot, Paul.    3025, 4689

Gwynn, C. W.    273

H

H., R.    5534

Haarpainter, Maximilian.    5792

Habert de Ginestet, Camille.    6813, 7375

Hacquard, A. [Mgr.].    6814, 6815

Häfliger, Johannes.    1930

Härtter, G.    7661

Hagen, A. [Dr.].    6014

Hager, Carl    5793

Hahn, Carl Hugo Luisingen. 5216, 5217

Hahn, Hugo [Rev.].

Hahn, J. 5218, 5219

Hahn, Theophilus. 3026, 5220-5223

Hake, R. von. 1931

Halbing, Augustin. 5794-5799

Halbing, Burchard. 1932

Halévy, Joseph. 705

Hall. [Dr.]. 6622

Hall, J. 5136

Hall, Martin John. 2436

Hall, Richard Nicklin. 4944-4946

Hall, Wilburn 3218

Halle, Ernst von. 3027

Hallez d'Arros, Hippolyte. 3888

Halligey, John T. F. [Rev.]. 7062

Hamard, Alexandre. 6559-6561

Hamberger, Aloys. 1933

Hambursin, F. 3889

Hamilton, A. H. 274

Hamilton, Charles Edward. 706, 4690

Hamilton, James Stevenson. 5331

Hammar, August. 3099

Hammerstein, A. von. 5800

Hammond, John Hays. 4947, 4948

HANBURY, BERNARD. 1653

Hanewinkel, Martin. 5801

[Bishop].

Hanlon, Henry. 1345-1353, 2437

Hannington, James [Bishop]. 2438

Hanquet, Jean-Baptiste. 3890

Hansal, P. M. C. 1354

Hanssens. [Capt.]. 3891-3893

Harding, Colin [Colonel]. 4949 5332

Hardinge, Arthur Henry. 275

Hardwick A. Arkell. 1015

Harou. [Lt.]. 3894

Harris, William Cornwallis. 707, 4950

Harrison, James J. 708

Harrison, Richard. 79

Hartert, Ernst. 5535, 7063, 7064

Hartert, Heinrich. 5333, 6623


Hartmann, Andreas M. 1934, 4951-4954

Hartmann, Georg [Dr.]. 5224, 5225

Hartmann, Maurus. 1935-1938

Hartmann, Robert. 80, 276-278, 709, 1355-1360, 2789

Hasan-Banhasawi. [Colonel]. 1361

Hastie, James. 2790

Haurigot, Georges. 7376-7380

Hautfeuille, Laurent Basile. 5536

Hauttecoeur, Célestin. 1016-1021

Havenith, Gerhard. 3219

Hay, J. S. 5537

Hay, John Charles Dalrymple [Bart.]. 6399

Hay, R. W. 7285

Haynes, C. E. [Capt.]. 4955

Heard, William H. 6624

Hébert, A. 7381

Hébrard, Pierre. 6816

Hecquard, Louis Hyacinthe. 5538, 7382

Hedde. 6248

Hedenborg, Johan. 279

Heep, Ferdinand. 4956, 4957

Heimann, Florinus. 1939

Heimanns, Heinrich. 1362

Heinitz, W. 1081

Heinlein, Adalbert. 7662

Heinrichs, Hubert. 3220

Heinzelmann. 5539

Hellgrewe, Rudolf. 1940

Hellwig, Paul. 4691

Hémery, Alain.   1941,1942

Henderson, James.   4574

Hendle, Innozenz.   1943,1944

Hendrickx, Françoix Xavier.   3895

Hening, E. F. [Mrs.].   6625

Hennebert, Eugène [Colonel].   6817,6818

Hennessy, John Pope.   5540

Henric. [Dr.].   5541

Henricy, Michel.   3896

Henriot, Leone.   1363-1368

Herhallet, C. P.   3028

Hermann, F.   5226

Hermann, Rudolf A.   1945

Herold, B. [Capt.].   7663-7675

Herr. [Dr.].   3897

Herrebaut, Eduard.   3898

Herrman, C.   1946-1949

Hert, de.   3899

Hertz, Charles.   6505,6506

Hervé, Georges.   3913

Hespers, Karl.   2439

Hesse, Hermann.   5802

Hetherwick, Alexander [Rev.].   4575,4576

Heuglin, Martin Theodore von.   280-282,710,711,1082
1369-1371,1950

Hoepner. 5228

Höver, Joseph. 5804

Hofbauer, Severin. 1955

Hofer, Michael. 1956

Hoffman, C. C. 6628

Hoffmann. 1957, 6098

Hofmann, J. 1035

Hoffmann, Jakob. 7676

Holding, John [Rev.]. 2793

Hole, H. Marshall. 4963, 4964

Holland, F. Catesby. 4965

Holland, Trevenen James. 714

Holle, Paul. 7305

Holley, Théodore. 7001, 7068 - 7072

Hollis, Alfred Claud. 287, 288, 1036

Hollway, Henry Charles Schunke. 5229

Holman, James. 5544

Holmwood, Frederick. 289, 1958

Holroyd, Arthur T. 1374

Holst, B. 1037

Holst, Carl. 1959

Holub, Emil. 3029, 3030, 4692, 4966, 4967, 5334

Homeyer, A. von. 3909

Hoornaert, Auguste. 3910

Hope, Percy. 4693

Hopkinson, H. C. B. 1375

Hore, Annie Boyle. 1960

Hore, Edward Coode. 1961-1964

Hornberger, C. 5545

Horne, Johann N. 1965, 1966

Horner, Anton. 1967-1978

Hornig, Joseph. 4968—4971

Horton, James Africanus Beale. 5546, 5547, 6401

Hoskins, George Alexander. 1376


Hoste, Cyril D. 5335

Hotchkiss, Willis R. 1038

Hotten, John Camden. 715

Houckgeest, F. A. van Braam. 6402

Houdoy, J. 6819

Hourst, Émile Auguste Léon. 6820, 6821

Houzé. [Dr.]. 3911, 3912

Hovelacque, Abel-Alexandre. 81, 3913

Hoyos, Ernst [Graf]. 1085

Hozier, Henry Montagne.

Huard-Baissinère, P. L. 7384

Huart. 6887

Huber, Otto. 1377-1383

Huberlant, Ferdinand. 3914—3917

Hubert, L. 6762

Hubler, T. 5548, 7385

Hubrechts, Willem [Fr. Thimotheus]. 1979

Hudt. 3467

Hübbe-Schleiden. [Dr.]. 3918, 5805, 5806

Hübler, Michael. 5807

Hübner, Adolf [Freiherr]. 3031, 4972

Hugot. [Lt.]. 6822

Humbert, G. [Colonel]. 5549, 6823—6826

Hunt, J. [Commander]. 3910

Huntley, Henry Veel. 5550

Hupfeld, D. 7677—7680

Huppenbauer, D. 6403

Hutchinson, Edward. 290-292, 3032, 7073

Hutchinson, George Thomas. 3033

Hutchinson, Thomas Joseph. 5551, 5552, 7074

Hutter, Franz Karl [Capt.]. 5553, 5808—5814

Hutton, William. 6404

Huwiler, Burkhard. 2445

Huys, Gustaaf. 3920

Huyshe, George Lightfoot. 6358

Huysman, Alfred. 3921

Hynde, R. S. 4577

## I

Ibarra, Jose de. 6099

Ibrahim-Effendi. See, Thibaut.

Ibrahim-Hilmy. H. H. Prince. 20

Iglesias y Pardo, Luis. 6100

Ignace, S. 6015

Ignacio, Luiz. 4694

Imbert. [Commandant]. 6827

Imhof, Johann. 5815,5816

Ingham, Ernest Gradam. 7580

Ingram. 7386

Ingweiler, Georges. 7387

Innes, William. 6629

Iradier y Bulfy, Manuel. 5554, 6101-6106

Irby, Charles Leonard. 1384

Irle, J. 5230

Irvine, John. 6405

Iseghem, André van. 3922

Isenberg, Karl Wilhelm. 293, 716, 717,718

Israël, Siegmund. 3923, 5231

Issel, Arturo. 719

Ivens, Roberto. 3167, 3587, 3588

## J

J.S. 5555

Jablonski. 1980

Jack, A. D.   6304

Jackson, Frederick John.   294, 295

Jackson, James Grey.   5556, 5557

Jackson, Louis [Colonel].   7075

Jacobis, Justin de.   720 - 724

Jacobowski, Ludwig [Dr.].   5232

Jacobs, Alfred.   82, 83

Jacobs, Eyries.   83

Jacolliot, Louis.   5558, 6562, 7076

Jacottet, Édouard.   5336

Jacques. [Captain].   1981

Jadoul, Julius.   3924-3926

Jaeger, Franz.   3221, 3222

Jäger, Johann.   5817

Jaime, Jean-Gilbert-Nicomède.   6828, 6829

Jalabert, Emile.   2794, 2795

Jalabert, Hyacinthe.   7388-7390

Jalla, Adolphe.   5337

Jalla, Louis.   3034, 3035

James, Frank Linsly.   1086, 1087, 1385

Jameson, James Sligo.   3927

Jamet, Louis-Hyacinthe.   1982-1986

Janikowski, L.   6107

Jannasch, Robert.   296

Jans, Jean.  3928

Janson, C. A.  3929

Janssens, Arthur.  3930, 3931

Janssens, Augstinus.  3932 - 3935

Janssens, Jean [Abbé].  4973

Jaques, L. =  7391, 7392

Jardin, E.  3936

Jarosseau, André.  725-741

Jaubert, Alfred. - 5559

Jean, Celestin.  2796 - 2798

Jeannest, Charles.  3937

Jedina, Leopold von.  84

Jeekel, C. A.  6406

Jehoul, Gerardus.  3938

Jeppe, F.  4695

Jessen, B. H.  742

Jessett, Montague George.  4696

Joalland, Paul Lules.  3939

Joanne, Adolphe Laurent.  85

Joannis, Joseph de.  2799

Jobit, Eugene.  3940

Joest, Wilhelm.  86

Joffre. [Maréchal].  7393

Joffre, Joseph-Jacques-Césaire.  6830 -6832

Johnson, Frank.

Johnson, Frank William Frederick.  4974,4975

Johnson, W. [Rev.].  6630,7581

Johnson, William Percival [Rev.].  1987 4578-4580,4697

Johnston. [Rev.].  7077

Johnston, Alexander Keith.  1988,1989

Johnston, Charles.  743

Johnston, Harry Hamilton.  87-91, 297,298, 299,1990-1992, 2446,2447, 3036-3039,3941-3945,4581-4584 5560-5562,5818, 6631,6632, 7078,7079

Johnston, James [Dr.].  3040

Johnstone, H. B.  1039

Jollet, A. A.  6833

Jones, Nancy.  4698

Jonveaux, Émile.  300

Jordan, Lewis Garnett.  92,93

Jordan, W. W.  5233

Jorgensen, S. G.  2800

Josset, Jean-Marie.  1993-1997

Jouan, Henri.  6507

Jouan, Jean-Marie.  7394,7395

Joucla, E.  21

Jouen, Louis.  2801-2806

Jouga, Guillaume.  2807,2808

Jougla, Etienne-Sylvain.  744

J. S.

Judt. [Missionary].  5234

Julien. [Capt.].  3946, 3947

Jungers. [Capt.].  3948

Junker, Wilhelm Johann.  301-306, 1386, 1387,  1555, 1998,
3041-3043, 3949-3954

Junod, Henri A.  4699-4702

Kade, von [Major].  3955

Kaeckenbeeck, F.  3956

Kaerger, Karl [Dr.].  1999-2001

Kaiser, E.  1745  2002-2004, 3480

Kallenberg, Friedrich.  2005

Kambo, Charles.  3223

Kan, C. M.  35

Kannenberg, Carl.  2006, 2007

Karr, Heywood Walter Seton-.  1088

Karst, Joseph.  2008

Katte, A. von.  745

Kaufmann, Anton.  1388-1391

Kayser, Gabriel.  22

Kayser, Jean-Baptiste.  7582

Kayser, Johann.  3957-3959

Keane, Henry J.  307

Keck, Daniel. . 2809

Keck, Mathilde. 5338

Keiling, Luiz Alfredo. 94, 3224, 3225

Keller, Conrad [Dr.]. 308, 1089, 2810—2813

Keller, Gherardus. 1392

Kellett, S. 4599

Kelly, John. 6633

Kemp, Dennis. 6407, 6408

Kemp, J. 1393

Kemp, Sam. 3044

Kennedy, A. E. 7583

Kerhallet, Charles Phillippe de [Capt.]. 5563, 5564

Kerivel, Jean de Lannion. 746—750

Kerr, Henry. 4976, 4977

Kerr, Walter Montagu. 3045—3047

Kerr Cross, David. 3048, 4585, 4586, 4597

Kersten, Otto. 2009

Kesten, Gregorius. 1394—1396

Kethulle de Ryhove, de la [Lt.]. 3960

Kieffer. [Dr.]. 5565

Kieffer, André. 3226, 3227

Kieger, Josef. 3228—3231

Kilham, Hannah. 7584, 7585

Kindt, Joseph. 3961—3963

King, J. B.   7080

King, James Stewart [Capt.].   1090

King, Thomas.   7081

King, W. J. Harding.   5566

Kingsley, George Henry.   5567

Kingsley, Mary Henrietta.   5568-5573, 5819

Kipper, Jakob.   3232

Kirby, Brandon [Capt.].   6409

Kirby, Frederick Vaughan.   4703, 4704

KIRCHLECHNER, THEODOR.   309

Kirchoff, Alfred.   5820

Kirk, Christopher.   1397

Kirk, John.   310, 1091, 2010, 2011, 3049, 3050, 4705-4707, 7082

Kirk, R.   751

Klaus, Isidore.   7083

Kleinschmidt.   5235, 5236

Klink, Hendrik.   3964

Klobb. [Colonel].   6834-6836

Klodt, Karl.   1398

Klose, H. [Lt.].   7681-7683

Klosterknecht, Joseph.   5821, 5822

Knight, Edward Frederick.   1399, 2814, 4978, 4979

Knight, Robert.   6973

Knight-Bruce, George Wyndham Hamilton.   4980-4983

Knoblecher, Ignaz.   1400-1404

Knop. 5237

Knowles, Charles. 7084

Kobès, Aloys. 6508, 7396—7398

Kobinger, Johann. 1405

Kocijančič, Johann. 1406

Kock, Hermann. 2448

Koelle, Sigismund W. 6634, 7085

König, Franz. 5823, 5824

Köppen, W. 6410

Koettlitz, Reginald. 311, 312

Koffel, Alphons. 3965

Kohler, J. 2012, 5825

Kohlschütter, E. 1904, 2013

Kolb, George. 313, 1040

Koller, C. S. 3966, 3967

Kollman, J. 3968

Kollmann, Paul. 2014, 2015

Koolen, Petrus. 2016

Kopf, Vinzenz. 5826

Kornmann, Joseph. 2017

Korper, M. 6837

Kost, Theodor. 7684

Kowé, Joseph. 6249

Krafft. [Rev.]. 3233

Krafft, Georg. 3969—3973

Krapf, Johann Ludwig. 314-316, 717, 718, 752, 753, 1041, 1042

Krause, Gottlieb Adolf. 95, 6411, 7086

Krebs, Wilhelm. 5238

Kreijns, Hubert. 2449

Krenzler, Eugen. 2018

Kreuzkamp, Joachim. 5827

Krindach, F. 754

Krockow, Carl von. 317

Kröhling, Mauritius. 2019

Kroot, Bartholomeus. 4984—4986

Ku'Eep. [Pseudonym]. 5239

Kühne, Johannes. 6432

Kuentz, Joseph. 5828

Kugelmann, Max. 5829

Kund. 3974—3979

Kunemann, Alfons. 7399

Kurtz, Barnabas. 7087

Kurz. 6635

L

Laane, Joseph. 2450—2457

Labarthe, Pierre. 5574

Laboucarie, Louis. 2815—2817

Lacerda e Almeida, Francisco José Maria de. 3051—3053, 3234—3236

Lacombe, Auguste.  2818-2821
Lacombe, Jean.  7400-7403
Lacour, A.  96

Lacy, George.  97

Ladislaus, Magyar.

La Feuillade, d'Aubusson.  7404

Laffitte, J. [Abbé].  6016,6017

Laffont. [Dr.].  6838

La Forest, M. de.  6839

Lagardelle.  755

Lagrillière-Beauclerc, E.  5575

Laillet, E.  2822

Laing, Alexander Gordon.  5576

Laing, D. Tyrie.  4987

Laird, Macgregor.  7088

Lallemand, A.  98,4988,4989

Lallemand, M.  1092

Lamaignière. [Abbé].  2823

Lamartiny, J. J. de  6840-6842
Lambert, Henri.  1093

Lambert, M.  6509

Lambinet, Édouard.  6018

Lamoise, Paul [Rev.].  7405

Lamy. [Commandant].  5577

Landbeck, Paul.  3920,3921

Lander, John.  7090

Lander, Richard L.   7089, 7090

Lang, J. C.   3237

Lang, Leo.   2020

Lange, S. H. de.   6458

Langhans, Paul.   2021, 2022, 5830, 5859

Langheld, Wilhelm.   2023, 2024

Lannegrace.   6843

Lannoy de Bissy, R. de [Major].   6250

Lapa, Joaquim José.   4708

Laporte, Francis L. de.   3054

Lapsley, Samuel Norvell.   3982

Lardner, Henry Harold.   7586 - 7589

Lartigue, R. de [Commander].   6251, 6844, 6933

Lasnet, Alexandre Bernard Étienne Antoine.   7406, 7407

Lasserre, Louis de Gonzague de Vézéronce.   756 - 758

Last, J. T.   2025-2027, 2824, 2825, 4587-4589

Lastrille.   6252

Latrobe, John Hazelhurst Boneval.   6636, 6637

Lauer, Ferdinand.   7685

Laumann, Ernst Maurice.   5578

Laurent, Émile.   3983

Laurent, Raphael.   3984, 3985

Lautour, Gaston [Lt.].   5579

Lauwers, Auguste.   3986

La Vaissière, Jules de.    2826—2835

Lavigerie. Charles-Martial Allemand [Cardinal].   99, 6845

Lavigne, Jacques.    2836, 2837

Law, August Henry.    4990—4994

Lawley, Arthur [Capt.].    5339

Laws, Robert [Rev.. MD].    4590

Lawson, H. W. L.    4995

Le Berre.    6510   7408

Le Berre, Jacques.

Leboeuf, Louis.    4996, 4997

Le Brun, J.    2838—2840

Lécard, T.    6846, 7409

Le Cerf, Paul-Edmond [Lt.].    6847

Lechaptois, Adolphe.    2028—2036

Le Chartrain, Alexandre.    4998

Lechartraire, A.    3987

LeChatelier, A.    5580

Le Clech, François.    6253

Leclercq, Jules Joseph.    3055

Lecomte, Ernest [Rev.].    3238—3254

Lecomte, Jules François.    5581

Lecomte, Raoul.    3988, 3989

Leconte, Paul.    2037, 2038

Lecour, A.    6254

Lent, Carl [Dr.]. 2042-2045

Lenz, Oscar. 100, 4021-4031, 5599, 5600, 6262-6264, 7410

Leonard, Arthur Glyn. 4999, 7091

Léonard, Henri. 2046, 2047

Leonard, Peter. 5601

Lepelletier, Ludovic. 2048-2050

Le Prédour, Fortuné Joseph Hyacinthe. 5602, 5603

Lequette, Louise. 764- 767

Leray, François. 4032

Le Roux, Hugues. 768

Le Roy, Alexandre. 320, 1043, 2051-2064, 4033, 6265, 6266

Lesage. 6238

Le Savoureux, M. Joel. 2842

Lesbros, Etienne. 1415

Leue, A. 2065- -2070

Leue, D. 2071, 2072

Leuper, Johann. 3255

Leuschner, Franz. 7686

Leutwein, Theodore [Major]. 5240, 5241

Levadoux, Antoine. 4034

Lévêque, Joseph. 6267

Lévesque, Auguste. 1044, 1045

Lewin, Evans. 23

Lewis, Locke [Capt.]. 2843

Linton, Andrew. 1046

Lippert, Marie. 5006

Lishout, E. van [Fr.Egidius]. 2077

Lissner, Ignace. 6024,6025

Livingstone, Charles. 5340,7095

Livingstone, David. 324-326, 3057-3074, 3256,4591

Livinhac, Léon. 2459-2471

Lloyd, Albert Bushnell. 3075

Locamus, P. 2850

Loefler, Charles.

Logier, Pierre. 7411

Lombard, Joseph-Henri. 2078-2080

Lombary, Edmond. 5007,5008

Longle, Armando. 4711

Loomis, Eben Jenks. 5605

Loonus, Marie Louis. 2472

Looy, Hendrik van. 6026

Lopes, David de Mello. 3257

Lopes de Calheiros e Meneses, Sebastião. 3258

Lopez Saccone, Luis. 6108

Loring, William Wing. 1417

Loriot, F. 4044

L'Orza de Mont-Orso de Reichenberg, Paul-Jean de [Capt.]. 6849-6852

Losi, Giovanni. 1418-1423

Lota, François-Louis [Dr.]. 6853

Lotens, Joseph M. G.    4045

Lourdel, P. Simeon.    2473-2480

Lowther, Henry Cecil [Maj. Gen.].    1094

Lucas, Alexander [Kommerzienrat].    2081

Lucas, Louis.    1424,7412

Luck, Reginald A.    5341

Ludloff, R. F. [Dr.].    5243,5244

Lübbert, A.    5245

Luec, Mathurin.    4046

Lüderitz, C. A.    5246

Lülsdorf, Casimir.    3259

Lugard, Frederick John Dealtry    101,102 327-330, 2481, 2482, 4592, 4593,5606,7096,7097

Lugenbeel, James Washington.    6638

Luke, Harry C.    24

Luna de Carvalho, Joaquim Maria.    3260

Lunay, J. B.    5247

Lupton, Frank [Lupton Bey].    1425,1556

Lur. [Lt.].    3261

Luschan, Felix von.    2082,4047

Lutz, Emil.    7592-7594

Lutz, Joseph.    7595-7599

Lux. [Lt.].    4048

Lux, Anton E.    3262-3264

Lux, Ferdinand.    331

Lynch, Joseph-Antoine.    3265, 3266

Lynch, William F.    5607

Lyon, George Francis.    5608

Lysaght, Thomas [Lt. Comm., RN].    6512

M

Mabille, E.    7392

Macaire, Kyrillos.    772, 773

Macalister, Donald A.    7098

Macar, Ghislain de [Capt.].    4049-4052

Macaulay.    7600

Macaulay, Kenneth.    7601

McClounie, J.    2083

McClure. [Capt.].    3076

McDermott, P. L.    332

Macdonald, Alexander.    1426, 1427

MacDonald, Claude M.    7099

Macdonald, Duff.    333

MacDonald, George.    6415

MacDonald, James Ronald Leslie.    334-336, 1047, 1428

Macé, Julien.    6268

Machado, Joaquim José.    4712-4716

M'Hardy, R. A.    1095

Machat, J.    6513-6515

Machon, Pierre. 2084-2086

Mackay, Alexander Murdoch. 2483, 4053

Mackay, Wallis. 4717

Mackenzie, Donald. 5609

Mackenzie, George Sutherland. 337, 1048, 2484

Mackenzie, John. 3078, 5009-5011

MacKeown, Robert L. 7100, 7101

McKiernan, Gerald. 5248

Mackinder, Halford J. 1049

McKinnon, Charles. 4594

Maclaud, D. [Dr.]. 6516

McLeod, John. 6027

McLeod, Lyons. 4718

MacLeod, Norman. 5342

MacMahon, Edward Oliver. 2851, 2852

MacQueen, James. 4728, 5610, 7602

MacWilliam James Ormiston. 7102

Madinier, Paul. 3079

Madox, John. 1429

Madrolle, Claudius. 5611

Mähly, E. 6416, 6417

Magalhães, Carlos de. 4054

Mage, Abdon Eugene [Capt.]. 5612—5615, 6854, 7413, 7414

Mager, E. 4719

Mager, Henri. 2853, 2854

Maguire, James Rochfort. 5012

Magyar, László. 3077, 3267

Mahiet, R. P. 6855—6857

Mahistre. 5616

Maigre, E. 7103

Mainguy. [Dr.]. 6858

Maistre, Casimir. 103—106, 4055

Malaviallé, Léon. 6028

Malcolm, Neill [Maj. Gen.]. 2485

Manceau, Jean-Baptiste. 2486

Mandat-Grancey, Edmond [Baron]. 2855, 4056

Mandy, Frank. 5013

Mangin. [Général]. 6859—6860

Mangles, James.

Manheimer, Émile. 3080, 5014

Manifatra, Venance. 2856, 2857

Mann, Adolphus. 7104

Mann, Gustav. 6109

Mann, Robert J. 4816

Manning, Edward. 107

Maonde, Charles. 4057

Maples, Chauncy. 2087, 3081, 4595-4597, 4720-4724

Marchal, Charles-Léopold-Jean-Baptiste. 7415

Marchand. [Lt.]. 5617

Marchandeau, Theophile. 6269

Marche, Alfred. 108, 6270-6275

Marcou, Jean. 2487-2494

Margain, J. P. 7416

Marichelle, Christophe. 4058

Marie. [Sister]. 774

Marion-Brésillac, Melchior Marie Joseph de [Mgr.]. 7603

Markham, C. R. 775

Marmier, Gaston-Marie-Anastase [Commandant]. 6861, 7417

Marno, Ernst. 338, 1430-1435, 2088, 4059

Marquer, E. 4060

Marques, Agostinho Sisenando. 3268

Marquès, Leo. 4061, 4062

Marquez. 5015

Marree, J. A. de. 6418, 7418

Marriott, H. P. Fitzgerald. 5618

Marryat, Frederick. 109

Marseille, Eugène. 2858-2860

Marsh, Howard R. 3044

Marshall, James. 5619, 6419

Martel, F. A. M. 7419

Martin. 6029 — 6031

Martin, Ernst. 2089, 2090

Martin, Friedrich. 7105

Martin, Richard Ernest Rowley. 5016

Martínez y Sanz, Miguel. 5620

Martini, Christian. 4083

Martini, Ferdinando. 776 — 778

Martini, Gennaro. 339, 1436-1439

Martinis, Raffael de. 779

Mártires, Bartolomeu dos. 4725

Martonne, Edward Guillaume de. 1440

Mary, G. T. 25

Marzano, Vincenzo. 1441-1444

Mason, Alexander McComb [Mason Bey]. 1445, 2495

Massaia, Guglielmo. 780-793

Massari, A. 110

Massé, D. 6032

Massenza, Jean-Baptiste. 4084-4086

Masui, Theodore. 4087

Mata, José de. 6110

Matasse, Basile. 3269, 3270

Mathers, Edward Peter. 5017

Matos e Silva, João de. 4088

Mattei, Antoine [Commandant]. 5621, 7106—7108

Matteucci, Pellegrino. 340—342, 794—797

Matthews, Thomas. 1446—1448

Matthews, Thomas Trotter. 2861, 2862

Matthias, Nicolaus. 2091

Matzat, H. 5831

Mauch, Carl. 5018

Maude, Francis Cornwallis. 2863

Mauléon, de. 5622, 6033

Maund, Edward Arthur. 5019—5022

Maundrell, H. [Rev.]. 2864

Maupoint, Armand-René. 2865

Mauro, Salvatore. 1449, 1450

Maximilian, Albert. 6420—6422

Maximini, Wunibald. 2092

Maxse, F. I. [Colonel]. 1451, 2496

Maxwell, T. 7604

Maxwell, William Edward. 6423, 6424

May, Daniel A. J. 343, 6946, 7109

Mayer, Ambrosius. 2093

Mayer, Jakob. 5832

Maynard, J. Howard. 2866

Mayo. See Bourke, D. R. W.

Mayr, Heinrich von. 1452

Meyer, W. von.   5250

Meynier, O. [Général].

Mezger, H.   7114

Mezzabotta, Ernesto.   798

Michaux, Joseph.   4079

Michaux, O. I. J.   4080

Michel.   5626

Michel, Antonin.   2868

Michel, Louis.   2869

Middletown, W. H.   3083

Miguel de los Rios, Juan.   6119

Miles, Samuel Barrett.   1101

Millais, J. G.   3103

Mille, Pierre.   4081

Miller, Armistead.   6640

Miller, Samuel T.   3275

Miller, Thomas [Commander, RN].   5627

Milligan, Robert H.   5835

Mills, Samuel J. [Rev.]

Millson, Alvan.   7115, 7116

Milne, Arthur Dawson.   1459, 1460

Milum, John [Rev.].   7117

Miniscalchi-Erizzo, Francesco.   4082

Miramont, J. T. de.   2870

Miranda, José Francisco Barreto.   4727

Mischlich, A.   7688

Mitchell, Libbeus H.   799

Mitchinson, Alex W.   7426

Mitterrutzner, Johann Chrysostomus.   1461-1464

Möller, P.   3276, 3277, 4083

Mönkemeyer, W.   4084-4088

Moffat, Hilda V.   2500
Moffat, John.   5024
Moffat, Robert.   3084 , 5025, 5026, 5251

Moggridge, L. T.   4598

Mohammad ibn 'Omar al Tounisī ibn Solaimān.   5628

Mohr, Eduard.   3085, 3086

Mohun, Richard Dorsey.   347, 2131, 4089

Moinet, Isaac.   4090-4098

Moir, Frederick L. Maitland.   348

Moir, Jane.   3087

Moister, William.   112, 5629

Moleyre, L.   4099

Molinier, Louis.   2501-2503

Mollien, Gaspard T.   7427

Moloney, Alfred.   5630, 7118, 7119

Moloney, Cornelius Alfred.   5631, 6426

Moloney, Joseph Augustus.   4100, 4101

Moncet, Auguste.   2132-2134

Mondières, A. T.  2135, 6427

Monet, Henri.  4102

Money, R. I.  4599

Monfort, Manuel.  6113

Monnier, Alexandre.  6277—6282

Monnier, Jean Marie Albért Marcel.  5632, 5633, 6283

Monrad, Hans Christian.  5634

Montagu, John Walter Edward Douglas Scott [Lord Montagu].  5027

Montaldo y Pero, Federico.  6114—6117

Montanha, Joaquim de Santa Rita.  4728

Montanaro, A. F.  6344

Montaut, Victor.  2871, 2872

Monteil, C.  6864, 6865

Monteil, Parfait-Louis.  5635—5637, 6563, 6866, 7428

Monteiro, A. C. P  3278

Monteiro, Joaquim John.  3088, 3279

Monteiro, Rose.  4729

Montel, Étienne.  7429—7433

Montes De Oca, José.  6118

Montgomery.  2873

montuori.  1465

Moore, John Edward S.  349—351, 2136

Moraes, J. A. da Cunha.  3280

Moraes Pinto, José Xavier de.  4730

Moraes Sarmento, Affonso de.   4731

Moraes Sarmento, Favio P.   4103

Mordacq.   6867

Moreau, J. L. M. [Capt.].   6868

Moreau, Joseph.   4104-4108, 5028-5030

Morenas, Joseph Elzeár.   7434

Morgan.   7435

Morgan, E. D.   4109, 4110

Morgan, Thomas.   7605

Morgen, Curt von.   5836

Morienval, Henri.   6035

Morin, Jean.   7392, 7436

Morlang, F.   1466

Moros y Morellon, José de.   6119

Morphy, Michel.   113

Morrell, Benjamin.   5638, 5639

Morris, Edward S.   6641

Morisson. [Capt.].   6869

Morvan, Yves-Marie.   3281

M. S.   6642

Moschonas, Demetrius.   1467

Moseley, Lich H.   7120

Motta Feo, Luiz da.   3282-3284

Moullée, Simon.   2504-2508

Mounteney Jephson, A. J.   1468

Mountnorris, George Annesley.   800

Mousinho de Albuquerque, Joaquim Augusto.   4732

Müller, Auguste.   3285

Müller, David Heinrich.   801

Müller, Franz.   2137, 2138, 7689

Müller, John B.   114

Müller, John W. von [Baron].   1469, 1470

Müller, Joseph.   5837

Münch, Friedrich.   5838

Münch, Josef.   1471-1474

Muggs, J. W.   6870

Muhammad Bartā.   5640

Muhammad ibn 'Umar, Al-Tūnusī.   1475

Muiron d'Arcenay, L.   7437

Mulders, Gerard [Fr.Jacobus].   2509

Mullens, Joseph.   2874-2877, 3089

Muller, Hendrik Pieter Nicolaas.   5031, 5032

Munoz Gaviria, José.   6120, 6121

Munro, William.   115

Munsch, Aloysius.   352

Munzinger, Johann Albert Werner.   353, 354, 802-806, 1476, 1477

Murard, Claude.   4111

Murat, Chanoine.   2878-2880

Muraton, Louis.     3286 — 3292

Murray, A. C.    4600

Murray, John.    116

Murrer, Lucien.    2510

Musgrave, George Clarke.    6428

Musy, Maurice.    4112

Muteau, A.    5641

Myers, Arthur Bowen Richards.    1478

Myrgine. [Lt.].    7438

### N

N. [Sister].    807

Nachtigal, Gustav.    117, 118, 1479-1481, 5642-5645,
    5914 — 5927

Nadaillac, Jean-François-Albert.    5033, 7121

Nagel, Emil.    5034

Nassau, Robert Hamill.    6284 — 6291

"Naval Officer."    4733, 5646

Navarro, Joaquin.    6122, 6123

Navarro y Canizares, Luis.    6124

Neal, W. G.    4945, 4946

Negrin, Ignacio de.    119, 6125 — 6127

Nesser, Jakob.    5035

Neu, Henri-Joseph.    6292 — 6298

Neufeld, Carl A.    1482

Neuling. [Dr.].    2881

Neumann, Arthur. 1050

Neumann, Oskar. 355 — 357

New, Charles. 358 — 360, 1051

Newman, Charles L. Norris [Capt.]. 5036

Newman, Henry Stanley. 2139

Newton, Francis James. 5037

Nicholls, Henri. 7122

Nichols, Francis O. 3275, 3293

Nicholson. [Rev.]. 7123

Nicol, George Gurney Mather. 7606

Nicolas, Victor. 6036

Nicot, Victor. 5038 — 5041

Nicq, Chanoine Augustin [Abbé]. 2511

Niesten, L. 4113

Nigote. [Capt.]. 6871

Nikolaev, L. 808

Nipperdey, Heinrich. 4114 — 4117, 6643

Noché. 6429

Nogueira, Antonio Francisco. 3294, 5647

Noirjean, Joseph. 7607, 7608

Noirot, Ernest. 6517, 6518

Nolte, Karl. 5252, 5253

Norman. 7609

Noronha, Eduardo de. 4734, 4735

Norris, Edwin. 6644

Norris, S. C. 5042

Northcott, H. P. 6430

Norton, Caroline Elizabeth Sarah. 7610

Notte, Charles Joseph. 4118

Noufflard, C.

Nuëlito, E. 6037

Nurse, Charles G. 1102

O

Oates, Frank. 5043

Oberlander, Richard. 120, 5648

O'Connor, L. Smyth [Colonel]. 5649, 7439

Odin, J. [Officer]. 7440

Oechelhaeuser, Wilhelm. 2140

Officer, Morris. 6645

Ohrwalder, Joseph. 1483-1488

Oldfield, R. A. K. 7088, 7124

Oliphant, Laurence. 1489

Oliveira, Delphim José de. 4736

Oliver, Samuel Pasfield. 2882-2885

Olivier, E. 5650

Ollone, Hessains d'. 5651, 5652, 6564

Olpp, F. 5254, 5255

Olpp, Johannes. 5256, 5257

O'Neill, Henry Edward. 361, 4601, 4737—4748

O'Neill, Joseph. 5044

Oppel, A. 2886

Ord, Harry St. George [Maj. Gen.]. 5653

Orleans, Henri Philippe Marie [Prince d']. 809, 2887

O'Rorke. 6299

Orpen, Joseph Millerd. 5045

Orr, Claire A. 5046

Osgood, Joseph B. T. 362

Osio, Egidio. 810

Oudney, W.

Ossorio Zabala, Amado. 6128—6134

Otto. Ludwig. 5839, 5840

Ousley, B. F. 4749—4755, 4794

Overman, Hubert. 4119

Ovir, Ewald. 2141

Owen, William FitzWilliam. 121, 4647

P

P. 5258

Padrel, Lourenco Justiniano. 3295

Page. 4120

Pagels, G. 4083, 4121

Pagès, Jean-Baptiste. 2888

Pagnon, Claude. 7125—7127

Pahde. P. 4122

Paillard, Julien. 811-816

Paimblant du Rouil. 6038

Paiva, Artur de. 3296 - 3298

Paiva Couceiro, Henrique de. 3299

Paiva de Andrada, Joaquim Carlos [Major]. 4756-4762

Paiva Manso, Levy María Jordao [Visconde]. 4123, 4763

Palgrave, William Coates. 5259, 5260

Pallme, Ignatius. 1490

Panet, Léopold. 7441

Pankow, H. 122

Paquay. 4124

Paré, C. du. 1103

Paris, Victor. 4125 - 4127

Park, Mungo. 5654, 5655

Parke, Thomas Heazle. 123, 2512, 4128

Parker, George Williams. 2889-2891.

Parker, Hyde. 4764

Parkes, J. C. Ernest. 7611

Parkinson, F. B. 1104

Parkyns, Mansfield. 817, 1491

Parminter. 4129

Parr, Theophilus. 6135

Parry, Francis. 1521

Pascal, Jean-Baptiste.  7442—7444

Pascal, Joachim.  2142, 2143

Pascal, S. L. [Lt.].  6872, 7445

Passarge, Siegfried.  5842—5847, 7690

Patterson, R. R. [Capt.].  5047

Paul.  2144

Paul, Ewald.  6136

Pauli. [Dr.].  4130, 5848, 6039

Pauly, Dionysius.  4131

Paulitschke, Philipp Viktor.  818—824, 1105, 1492

Pauwels.  4132

Pawlas, René.  7128—7132

Payeur-Didelot.  124

Payne, John Augustus Otonbu.  7133, 7134

Pearce, Francis Barrow.  363, 1106, 2145

Pearce, Nathaniel.  825

Pearse, Moïse.  7612

Pease, Alfred E.  364, 365

Pechuel-Loesche, Eduard [Dr.].  4133—4148, 5261, 6300

Pecile, A.  6301

Pedroso, Antunes a Fernando de Almeida.  3300

Peel, Charles Victor Alexander.  1107

Peeters, Paul.  4149

Peito de Carvalho, Joaquim.  7220

Pelleman, Amandus.    4150

Pellerin, Anastase de Pisotte.    826, 827

Pellet, Paul.    7135–7138

Peney, Alfred.    366, 5656

Percher, Jules-Hippolyte [Pseud. "Harry Alis"].    3380, 5928, 7446

Perciballi, Giovanni. 125

Percy, Algernon [Duke].    1493

Pereira, Carlos Augusto.    3301

Pereira, Sebastião José.    3347, 4151

Pereira Baretto, Honorio.    7221

Pereira Carneiro, Don Jacinto.    5657

Pereira de Sampaio Forjas de Serpa Pimentel, J.    3302

Pereira do Nascimento, José.    3303, 3304

Pérès, Joseph.    7447, 7448

Perez Lasso de la Vega, Jorge.    6137–6140

Perger, August.    2892

Perini, Rufillo. 828, 829

Péron, François. 126

Péroz, Marie Étienne [Colonel].    5658, 5659, 6873–6876

Perraud. [Lt.].    6877

Perregaux, W.    6431

Perron, Nicoles [Dr.].    1494

Perrottet, George Samuel.    7449

Perry da Camara [Major].    4765

Peters, Karl Friedrich Hubert. 367-369, 2146-2156, 5048-5051

Peters, Wilhelm Carl Hartwig. 4766

Petersen, Heinrich. 5262

Petherick, John. 1495 - ~~1496~~ 1500

Petherick, Katherine.

Petit, Antoine. 830

Petitbois, G. 4152

Peureux, Nicolas-Joseph. 6302, 6303

Peyrilhe, Léon. 2893 - 2895

Pfeiffer, Ida Laura Reyer. 2896

Pfeil, Joachim [Graf]. 370, 2157-2160, 4153, 5263-5265

Phalip, Victor. 2513-2516

Phelps, John Wolcott [General]. 2897

Philebert, Charles [General]. 5660, 6878

Philippe, Jean-Damascène de Pont-de-l'Arche. 831-835

Phillips, Richard Cobden. 4154-4156

Piaggia, Carlo. 371

Picard. 7450

Picard, Edmond. 4157, 4158

Picard, Pierre. 836-842

Picardo, Cado. 2161-2166

Pied, Joseph. 6040-6044

Pierce, E. J. 6304, 6335

Pierfitte, C. 7451-7455

Piessens, Albijn. 4159

Pieton, T. S. 4160

Pietri, Camille [Capt.]. 6045, 6809, 6879-6881

Pignol, Léon. 3305

Pigott, J. R. W. 1052

Piguet. [Capt.]. 6882, 7731

Pilgram, B. 5266

Pilkington, G. L.

Pimazzoni, Francesco. 1501-1504

Pinaud, A. 4161

Pinet-Laprade. [Colonel]. 7456

Pinheiro Lobo Machado de Melo e Almada, Vicente. 7222

Pinnock, James. 7139-7141

Pinnock, Samuel George. 7142, 7143

Pinto, Francisco Antonio. 3306

Piolet, Jean-Baptiste. 127, 128, 2898-2905

Pitt-Rivers, A. 7144

Planeix, Michel. 7457, 7458

Platzer, Joseph. 5052

Plé, James Henri Narcisse [Capt.]. 6046-6048

Plehn, Frederick. 5849

Plehn, R. 7691

Plouzanne, E. F. 5661

Plowden, Walter Chichele. 843

Poussou. 1509

Pouyer. [Lt.]. 5662

Power, Frank. 1510

Powell-Cotton, P. H. G. [Major]. 2520

Pra, François. 2910

Prager, Erich. 4172, 5850

Prager, M. [Capt.]. 2169

Prax. [Vice-Consul de France]. 5663

Pree, H. de. 1054

Preen, M. 7460

Preil. [Lt.]. 7692

Prendergast, James. 1511, 1512

Presset, Émile. 6307

Prestage, Peter. 5054-5056

Preston, Ira M. 6308

Prévers, Joseph. 4173-4177

Préville, de. 2170

Price, Roger. 374

Price, William Salter. 1055

Prideaux, William Francis. 375, 847

Prihoda, Franz. 5057

Prince, C. K. 6093, 6112, 6148

Pringault, Arthur. 6309, 6310

Pringle, George. 7614

Pringle, J. W.   1056

Pringle. M. A. [Mrs.].   1057

Probert, Herbert.   4178

Proctor, John.   1513

Prost. [Sister].   848

Prout, Henry G. [Major].   1514

Prudhoe, Algernon Percy [Duke of Northumberland].   1515

Pruen, Septimus Tristan.   376

Puff, Anton.   5058

Purvis, John Bremmer.   377, 2521

Puts, Hroznata.   3308

Puttkamer, Jesko Albert Eugen von.   5851

### Q

Quass, E.   2171

Quenedey, L.   1516

Quicke, F. C. [Capt.].   5059, 5328

Quinquandon, F. [Capt.].   5664, 5665, 6883, 6884

Quintin, L. [Dr.].   6885, 6886

Quirquerez.   6565

### R

Rabenhorst, Rudolph.   1058. 5666, 5667, 5852

Rackow, Hermann.   5668, 5853, 7693

Raffenel, Anne-Jean-Baptiste.   5669-5672, 6887, 7461-7463

Raffray, Achille.   849, 850, 2172

Ragazzi, Vicenzo.   851

Rahidy, Basilide-Marie.    2911,2912

Raille, M.            6888

Raimbault, Jean-Baptiste.    7615—7618

Rammstedt, K.    6646

Ramone, Leonce de.        (5060,5061
Ramsay, S. [Capt.].    2173

Ramsay, T. W.    5673

Ramseyer, Friedrich Auguste.    6432
Ranchin, Edouard.    6566—6568
Rançon, Andre.
            6889, 6890, 7464
Rand, Frank R.    5062

Randabel, Camille.    2174—2178

Randall-MacIver, David.    5063

Rankin, Daniel J.    3092—3094,4767,4768

Rankin, F. Harrison.    7619

Rankin, L. K.    2179

Ransome, L. H.    2913

Rascalou, Camille.    3309

Rassam, Hormuzd.    852,853

Ratzel, F. [Dr.].    4179—4183

Raum, Johannes.    2180—2183

Ravenstein, E. G.    295
Ray, Matthieu.    6569—6571
Raymond, S. [Abbé.].    7620

Read, C. H.    7149

Read, Frank W.        3310

Reade, William Winwood.    130—132, 5674, 5675,6433,6434

Reading, Joseph Hankinson. 5676, 6311

Rédmond, L. 7465

Reeb, Anton. 6312 -6314

Reelick, Willibrord. 4184, 4185

Regnon, P. de. 2914

Rehbock, Theodor. 5268- 5272

Reibell, Eugène. 5677

Reichard, Paul 1746, 2003, 2004, 2184-2199, 2522, 3480, 4186

Reichardt, Charles August Ludwig. 6519

Reichelmann, G. 4187

Reichelt, G. T. 4188

Reichenbach, J. 6572

Reichenow. 5854

Reid, Percy C. 5273, 5343

Reindorf, Carl Christian. 6435

Reinecke, Paul. 133

Rejou. [Commandant]. 6891

Reling, Joseph. 7150, 7151

Rémont, Pierre-Marie. 7466-7468

Remy, Jules. 4189-4191

Renard, A. 4192

Renato Baptista, Joaquim. 4769

Renier, Arsenius. 4193

Renoux, François. 7469-7473

Répin. [Dr.]. 6052

Resener, Hans. 1517, 1518

Révoil, Georges. 378, 1110-1113, 1519

Rey, 6892

Rey, H. [Dr.]. 5678, 7474

Reybaud, Marie Roch Louis. 854

Reygasse. [Sister]. 855

Rialland, François. 7475

Ricard, François-Pierre. 7476

Richard, Victor. 3311, 3312

Richards, E. H. 4753, 4770-4774, 4794

Richards, Thomas Henry Hatton. 6436

Richardson. 2915

Richardson, James. 5679, 5680

Richartz, Franz. 5064-5066

Riche, Alexandre. 6437

Richter, Franz. 2200, 2201

Richter, Julius. 2523, 4602

Ricketts, H. I. 6438

Ridsdale, Benjamin [Rev.]. 5274

Riebe, Otto. 5855

Rieder, Josef. 5067

Rieder, Michael. 5856

Riedlinger, Emile.    3313 — 3317

Riehl, François-Xavier.    7477—7484

Rigby, C. P.    2202

Riley, James.    5681

Rindermann, Josef.    2203, 2204

Rippon, Joseph.    3318

Risch, Martin.    7485

Ritter, Carl.    379, 6647

Ritter, Eugène.    7152

Ritter, Karl.    5275

Rivalta, Gabriele da.    856

Rivoyre, Barthélémy Louis Denis de.    857—859

Robb, M.    7153

Robbins, Archibald.    5682

Robecchi-Brichetti, Luigi.    860, 861, 1114—1116

Robert, Fritz.    134

Robert, Maurice.    5683, 6893

Roberts,    6648

Robertson, G. A.    5684

Robertson, Patrick.    3095

Robinson, A. M. Lewin.    27

Robinson, Charles Henry.    5685, 5686, 7154 —7158

Robinson, Phil.    1520

Robinson, W.    7159

Roos, Joseph. 2205

Roques, A. 6053, 6895

Roscoe, John. 384, 2527, 2528

Rose, Cowper. 3097

Rosel, G. 140

Rosenbush, Colin Graham. 7621

Rosignoli, P. 1529

Roskoschny, H. 4209

Ross, A. Carnegie. 4775

Ross, Alexander. 5859

Ross, D. Palmer. 7622

Ross, Ronald [Colonel]. 7623

Rosseel, Joseph. 4210

Rossel, Elisabeth-Paul-Édouard de [Admiral]. 7487

Rossetti, Carlo. 880

Rossi, Giacinto. 881, 882

Roth, Felix N. 7061, 7161

Roth, Johann R. 883

Rothbletz, Adelhard. 2206

Rotsaert, Karel. 4211

Roullet, G. 6315

Roupnel, Julien. 3321—3323

Rousseau, Alexis de Bief-du-Four. 884—887

Rousselet, Adolphe. 7162, 7163

Saillens, R.    4215

Saint Johnston, Alfred. 142

Saker, Alfred.    5694, 5860-5862, 6144, 6145

Saldanha da Gama, Antonio de.    3324, 3325

Salesses, Pierre-Eugène-Mathurin [Lt.Col.].    5695-5698, 6520, 6521, 7624

Salle, Antoine.    2531-2533

Salles, A.    890

Salt, Henry.    891, 892

Salvatore, Mauro.    1541, 1542

Salvayre.    893-896

Samassa, Paul [Dr.].    2212

Sanders, Mary J.    3181, 3326, 3331, 4777

Sanders, W. H.    3204, 3327-3332, 3362

Sanderval, Aimé-Oliver [Comte].    5699, 6522-6524, 6896

Santa Brigida de Sousa, Rodolpho de.    3333

Santamaria, J. C.    7489

Santandrea, P. Stefano.    30

Santini de Riols, Emmanuel-Napoléon.    2919, 6054

Santos, Ignacio dos.    3334

Sapelli, Alessandro.    385

Sapeto, Giuseppe.    897-909

Sarbah, John Mensah.    6440-6442

Sarmento, Adolpho.    4778

Sarmento, Alfredo de. 3335

Sarrazin, Henri-Étienne-Gaston. 5700

Sartorius, Ernestine 1543

Sarzeau, J. [Commandant]. 143

Saudemont, A. 6055

Sauer, Hans [Dr.]. 5071

Sauter, Karl. 4216

Sauvant, R. P. 6897, 6898

Savage. 6649

Savinhiac, Louis. 6056

Savorgnan de Brazza, Pierre Paul Francois Camille. 4217-4221
6316-6318

Sawyer, Arthur Robert. 5072

Scala, Giambattista. 7164

Schäfer, Johann. 5863, 7694, 7695

Schaller. [Rev.]. 3336

Schanz, Moritz. 386

Schauenberg, Pierre Reille de [Baron]. 7490

Schelameur, Frédéric. 6057

Schellendorff, F. Bronsart von. 2213

Schenk, Adolf [Dr.]. 5277, 5278

Scheuermann, Antoine. 2214-2216

Scheve, E. 5864

Scheymans, Jean. 4222

Schickle. [Missionary]. 5865

Schilitz, Alfons. 5866, 5867

Schimper, Wilhelm. 910- 913

Schinz, Hans. 5279-5281

Schlagintweit-Sakülünski, Hermann von. 6650

Schlauch, Lorenzo. 144

Schlechter, Friedrich Reichardt Rudolph. 5701

Schleicher, A. W. 914

Schlichter, Henry G. [Dr.]. 387, 3098, 5073, 5074

Schlobach, Gaston. 2217

Schloifer, Otto. 2218, 2219

Schmaltz. [Colonel]. 7491

Schmarda, Ludwig Karl. 145

Schmidt, A. K. [Lt.]. 1059, 1060

Schmidt, Karl Wilhelm. 388, 2220

Schmidt, Rochus. 2221-2224

Schmier, Louis. 2534

Schmit, S. 1544 2539

Schmitt, Seraphim. 2535-

Schmitz, Bruno. 4225-4228

Schneider, Dekan. 2225

Schneider, Gebhard. 2226

Schneider, Jean. 3337

Schneider, Theophil. 2227

Schmitz, Peter. 7696- 7698

Schnitzer, Eduard.  389—393  1545-1555

Schoeller, Max.  394—397

Schoeller, Michael.  5868

Schönlein, Philip.  6651

Schön, Jacob Friedrich.  7165, 7166

Schoutens, Etienne.  4229

Schreiber, Julius.  915

Schroer, C.  1556, 1557

Schütt, Otto.  3338, 3339, 4230-4235

Schufeldt, Mason A.  2920, 2921

Schultheiss, G.  7167

Schulz, Aurel.  3099

Schulze.  2228

Schuver, Juan María.  1558, 1559

Schwab, Gustav.  5869, 5870

Schwabe, Kurd [Lt.].  5282-5285

Schwarz, Bernard Wilhelm.  5286-5288, 5871, 5872, 6652

Schweiger, Ivo.  2229

Schweinfurth, Georg August.  146, 398, 399, 916, 1560-1567, 4236

Schweinitz, Hans Hermann.  400, 401

Schwindenhammer. Louis-Ignace [Rev.].  7492

Schynse, August.  402, 403, 2230, 4237-4240

Sclater, B. L. [Lt.].  4605

Scott, Anna M. [Mrs.].  6653, 6654

Scott, E. D.  5075

Scott, Laurence. [Rev.].  404

Scott, Percy Moreton.  147

Sébire, Albert.  7493—7498

Seckendorff, Goetz Burkhard [Graf].  917

Seeger, M.  5702, 7699

Ségala, François.  6525

Seghers, Charles.  4241—4245

Segni, Filippo da.  5930

Seidel, August.  405, 406, 2231, 5873

Seidel, H.  4702, 5703, 7700—7710

Seiner, Heinrich.  918, 1568—1571

Seitz, Ancel.  4246

Seixas, Antonio José de.  148

Selby, P. H.  5344

Selous, Frederick Courtenay.  3100—3103, 5076—5086, 5345


Sembiante, Giuseppe.  1572—1575

Semler, H.  2232, 2233

Senden, Alexius.  4247—4252

Sené, Gabriel.  7499, 7500

Senkovsky, Joseph De.  407

Senna Barcellos, Christiano Jose de.  6526

Séquer, M. A.  7168, 7169

Serpa Pimental, Antonio de.  3340

Serpa Pimental, Jayme Pereira de Sampaio Forjaza de.  4253, 4254

Serpa Pinto, Alexandre Alberto da Rocha de.  3104, 3105

Serpa Pinto da Ruy, Alexandre Alberto.  3341

Serval. [Capt.].  6058, 6319, 6320

Sevin-Desplaces, L.  5704, 6899

Sewell, M.  2922

Sharpe, Alfred.  3106-3108, 4255, 4606-4608, 5346

Shaw, Flora.  1671

Shaw, George A.  2923, 2924

Shchusev, P. V.  919

Sheldon, Mary French.  408, 1061, 1062

Sibree, James Jr.  2925-2941

Sigiez, Jean.  2234, 2235

Silva, Antonio [Marques].  4779

Silva, José Severino da.  3342

Silva Gil, Francisco da.  3343

Silva Leitão e Castro, António Tomás da.  3344

Silva Porto, Antonio Francisco Ferreira da.  3109, 3110, 4256

Sim, Arthur Fraser.  409

Simar, T.  31

Siméon, Jules.  3345

Simonin, Louis-Laurent.  2942

Simpelacre, Achiel.  4257

Simpson, William. 7170

Singer, H. 4258, 5347

Sinner, Franz. 410

Skertchly, J. Alfred. 6059, 6443, 6444

Slatin, Rudolph Carl. 1576

Sleeman, Lucy. 4835

Slessor, Arthur K. 7625

Slosse, Eugene. 4259-4261

Smith, Alfred Charles. 1577

Smith, Amanda. 6655

Smith, Andrew. 3111, 3112

Smith, Arthur Donaldson. 411-413 , 1117, 1118

Smith, C. S. 414

Smith, Charles Spencer. 149

Smith, F. C. 2540, 2541

Smith, G. E. 1063, 2236

Smith, Horace Francis Harrison. 920

Smith, John. 5705

Smith, John [MD]. 2237

Smith, Robert. 5706, 5874

Smith, Ronald. 5087

Smoor, Corneille. 2238, 2239

Smythies. [Bishop]. 4780

Soares, Augusto Estanislau Xavier. 4781

Söllner, Charles. 4262

Sogaro, Francesco. 1578-1586

Soleillet, Jean Joseph Marie Michel Paul. 921,922 5708,6900-6902
Soleillet, Paul. 5707

Soller, C. 5709

Sorela, Luis. 5710,6656

Sornin, A. 6903

Sorrentino, Giorgio. 1119

Soubiranne. 923

Sousa, Antonio José de. 4263

Sousa, Manuel José de. 3346

Sousa Barroso, Antonio José de. 4264,4265,4782,4783

Sousa Brum, A. J. de. 3347

Southon, Ebenezer J. 2240

Southworth, Alvan S. 1587

Soyaux, Herman. 150, 3348,4266-4270,5711,6146,6321

Spee, Jakob. 4271

Speedy, Cornelia Mary. 1588

Speke, John Hanning. 415-421

Spengler, Hermann. 5289

Spiess, C. [Missionary]. 7711

Spieth, J. 7712-7714

Spillman, Joseph. 5088

Spilsbury, Francis B. 5712

Spiss, Cassian. 2241,2242

Spring. **422**

Spring, Gardiner. **6657**

Squaranti, Antonio. **1589**

Stadlbaur. [Lt.]. **2243**

Staff Officer. **924**

Stairs, W. E. **2244, 2542**

Stairs, William Grant. **423, 4272**

Stallibras, Edward. **7223**

Stalter, Joseph. **6527**

Stang, Peter. **5875**

Stanley, Henry Morton. **151-158, 424-428, 2543, 3113-3116 4273-4280, 6445**

Statham, Francis Reginald. **5089**

Staudinger, Paul. **159, 5713, 5876, 7171-7173**

Stecker, Anton. **429, 925**

Steere, Edward. **430**

Steevens, George Warrington. **1590**

Stein. **5877-5880**
Stein, L.

Stein, Martin. **7501**

Steiner, Paul. **5714, 6411, 6446-6454**

Stella, Giovanni. **926-928**

Stempfel, Anton. **5090**

Stenzel, Gregor. **5881**

Stephen, Henry Lushington. **7502**

Strömberg, C.    6455

Stroo, Camille.    4288

Strub, Joseph [Rev.].    7503

Stuart, J. M..    5093

Stuer, Severinus Vincentius.    4289-4292

Stuhlmann, Franz [Dr.].    438,439    2247-2250, 2546, 4293

Sturgeon, T.    6147,6148

Sturz, J.    2296

Stutfield, Hugh E. M.    1594

Sublet, Jean-Pierre.    4294

Sugols. [Lt.].    6904

Sullivan, George L.    2251

Surridge, Frank Harold [Rev.].    5094

Sutter, E.    6322

Sutter, Martin.    6528

Swan, C.A.    4295

Swan, Robert M. W.    5095-5099

Swann, Alfred James.    3118

Swannet, Jan.    4296

Swanzy, Andrew.    6456,6457

Swayne, Harald George Carlos.    1120

Sweens, Joseph.    2547

Swijste, Lambertus.    4297

Sword, William Dennistoun.    1130

Sydenfaden.  5290

Sykes, Clement Arthur [Brig. Gen.].  1595

Sykes, Francis William.  5100

Sykes, Richard.  5101

Sykes, William Henry.  440

Sylvester. [Missionary].  2548

## T

Taix, Alphonse.  2943-2948

Taix, Henri.  2949-2953

Talazac, Stanislas.  2954-2956

Tamisier, Maurice. 632

Tams, Georg.  3355

Tanguy, Joseph.  6323

Tangye, Harold Lincoln.  5102

Tappenbeck. [Lt.].  4298-4300

Tappi, C.  1596-1616

Taubman-Goldie, George D.  7175-7177

Taurin de Heubécourt Cahagne.  932-947

Tautain, Louis-Frédéric [Dr.].  5717-5719, 6529, 6905-6906, 7504, 7505, 7732

Tauzin, J. M. [Fr. Thimothée].  2549-2551

Taylor, Bayard.  1617

Taylor, John C.  7020

Taylor, W. 7506

Teilhard de Chardin, Joseph-Michel. 6530

Teixeira da Silva. 7224

Teixeira de Barros, Alberto Xavier. 7225

Teixeira de Vasconcellos, Antonio Augusto. 3356

Teleki, Samuel.

Tellier, Louis-Henri-Ernest-Edmond-Gaston [Commandant]. 6907,7507

Templier, Guillaume. 6908

Tenbergen, H. F. 6458

Terao. 4786

Ter Maat, Gerard. 4301

Terorde, Anton. 5103-5105

Terrien, Ferdinand. 6060-6062

Terrier, Auguste. 7178

Tesseire, Albert. 7508

Teyssier, Eustache. 1121

Thaly, J. H. F. 7509

Thede, Julien. 948-950

Thévenot, J. P. F. 7510

Thibaut. ["Ibrahim Effendi"]. 1618

Thiénard, Albert. 2957

Thierry, Gaston [Lt.]. 7715

Thierry, L. 4302

Thillier, Joseph. 7179,7180

Thiriet, E.    6909

Thollon, Gonzague.    7181

Thomann, Georges.    6573

Thomas, Charles W.    5720

Thomas, Joseph Hammond.    6459

Thomas, Thomas Morgan.    3119

Thomas, W. Nicholas.    7182

Thomé, Anton.    2252, 2253

Thome, P.

Thompson, George.    5721, 5722

Thompson, Thomas Richard Heywood.    6939

Thompson, William Cooper.    5723

Thomson, Harry Cranfuird.    5106, 5107

Thomson, J. Mudie.    5108

Thomson, Joseph.    160, 161, 441-446, 2254-2258, 2552, 4303, 4304, 5348, 5724, 7183-7185

Thonner, Franz.    4305-4308

Thormahlen, Johannes.    5882

Thornton, Richard.    2259, 2260, 3120

Thuet, Joseph.    2553, 2554

Thurston, Arthur Blyford.    2555

Thys, Albert Jean Baptiste Joseph [Colonel].    4309-4315

Tiedemann, Adolf von.    447, 1619

Tillman, Liborius.    4316-4318

Trémaux, Pierre. 450,1624-1626

Trentinian, Louis-Edgar De [Général]. 5729,6910-6912

Trève, Paul-Joseph-Armand. 6934

Trew, J. M. [Rev.]. 5730

Trilles, Henri. 4324-4334, 6325,6326

Trindade Coelho, José Francisco. 4788

Tristan, Ange. 6327, 6328

Tristram Pruen, S. 4335

Tritton, J. 4336

Trivier, E. 3121

Trossmann, Simon. 2264

Trotha, L. von. 2265

Trotter, James Keith. 7628,7629

Trouet, Léon. 4337

Troup, John Rose. 4338

Tuaillon, J. L. G. 34

Tucker, Alfred Robert. 451 2559-2561

Tucker, Charlotte Maris. 7187

Tuckey, James Hingston. 4339

Tuohy, Jérémie. 7630, 7631

Twyford, A. W. 1627

U

Üchtritz, C. von [Baron]. 5293-5295

Ulff, F. 4340

Ulrich, Georges. 6460

Ursel, H. d'. 2266

Usera y Alarcon, Jerónimo Mariano. 6149, 6150

Ussel, Annet. 4341

Uzès, Anne de Rochechouart-Mortemart [Duchesse d'Uzès]. 4342

V

Valbert, G. 5731, 6913

Valcke, Louis. 4343-4345

Valdan, Georg. 5883

Valero Belenguer, José. 6151-6153

Vallière, J. [Capt.]. 5732, 6914

Vallon. [Admiral]. 6063, 7513-7515

Valran, Gaston. 6680

Van Acker, August. 4346-4349

Van Agt, Frans. 1628-1629

Van Aken, Antoon. 2267

Van Campenhout, Emile. 4350

Vandaele, Arsenius. 2562

Van Damme, Joseph. 4351, 4352

Vandeleur, Cecil Foster Seymour. 168, 2563, 7188

Van den Bergh, Leonard. 1630-1632

Van den Biesen, Joseph. 2268-2271

Van den Bosch, Alphonse. 4353, 4354

Van den Eynde, Felix. 2272

Van den Gheyn, Joseph. 4355

Van Oost, Achille.  2564-2566

Van Reusel, Charles.  4376

Van Ronslé, Camillus.  4377-4386

Van Straelen, C.  4387

Van Term, Antonius.  1635-1637

Van Thiel, Henri.  2567

Van Tricht, Victor.  4388

Van Waesberghe, August.  2285-2288

Van Wees, Pierre.  2568, 2569

Van Wincxtenhoven.  4389

Varangot, Adolphe.  2570-2572

Vasco, G.  6915

Vasconcellos, Ernesto de.  4390

Vauthier, G.  4391

Vauthier, Rene.  4392

Vayssière, A.  967

Vedder, Heinrich.  5296

Veitch, Sophie Frances Fane.  968

Vekemans, Piet.  2573

Velten, Carl.  452-454

Venn, Henry [Rev.].  5733

Venture de Paradise.  5734

Verdier, A.  6574-6576

Vereycken, M.  4393

Vignon. [Capt.]. 6917

Vigroux, Germain. 2958-2962

Villedeuil, de. 6918

Villéger, F. 7519,7520

Villèle, Joseph de. 2963,2964

Villiers, Frederick. 1648

Vincent. [Capt.]. 5736, 5737, 6919

Vincent, Frank. 169

Vinco, Angelo. 1649-1652

Vinson, Auguste. 2965

Virchow, R. [Dr.]. 4396,5738,5885,7716,7717

Vischer, Hanns. 5739, 7190

Visseq, Alexandre. 4397

Vivell, Coelestin. 2289

Vivian, Herbert. 972

Vivian, William. 7632

Voeltzkow, Alfred. 455, 2966-2969

Vogel, Edward. 5740-5742, 7191

Vogt, H. 7192

Vohsen, Ernst. 5743,5744,5886

Volkens, Georg. 2290,2291

Vollers, Johannes. 5123,5124

Voltz, Joseph. 2292

Voulgre, Joseph Denis Antoine André.  4398,4399

Vuillet, J.  6920

Vuillot, P.  6921-6926

Vyncke, Ameet.  4400

W

Waal, David Christian de.  5125

Waddell, Hope Masterton.  3123

Waddington, G.  1653

Wade, Michel.  6461,6462

Wagner, J.  170

Wahis. [Colonel].  4401

Wahrenhorst.  7521

Wainright, Jacob.  456

Wakefield, Thomas [Rev.].  457-459,1065,2293

Walckenaer, Charles Athanase.  5745

Waldmeier, Theophilus.  973, 974

Walker, James Broom [Capt.].  7193-7195

Walker, R. B. N.  6329-6333

Walker, S. A.  5746

Walker, William.  6334, 6335, 6339

Wall, Alfred H.  2973

Wallace, L. A.  1749,5350

Wallace, William.  7196

Walmsley. [Capt.].  3124

Walmsley, Hugh Molleneux.    3124
Walter, F. A.    3332
Walter, Fritz.    5887, 5888

Walter, Georg.    5889, 5890

Walter, Louis Philippe.    7522, 7525

Walter, Ludwig.    2294, 2295

Walter, Margaret D.    3362

Wangemann, J.    2296, 4544

Warburg, D.

Ward, Gertrude.    460

Ward, Herbert.    4402-4405

Waring, C. M.    6660

Warlomont, Charles.    4406

Warncke, W.    5298, 5299

Waroux, Louis.    4407, 4408

Warren, C. [Capt.].    4789

Washington. [Capt., RN].    7526

Watermeyer, J. C.    5300, 5301

Watkins, Owen Spencer.    1654

Watson, A. Blair.    3125

Watson, C. M. [Lt., RE].    1655-1657

Wauters, Alphonse Jules.    36, 3126, 3127, 4409- 4468

Wauwermans, H.    4469, 4470

Weatherley, Poulett.    5351

Webb, Allan B. [Rev.].    5126

Webster, A. H.    3363

Weeks, John H.    4471—4473

Weeks, John W.    7633, 7634

Weghsteen, Joseph.    4474

Weiler, Josef.    2574—2579

Weimers, Théodore [Colonel].    4475

Weiss, Kurt.    461, 2297, 2298, 5302

Weld, Alfred.    3128, 3129

Wellby, Montagu Sinclair.    462, 975

Welles, C. M.    171

Wellman, F. C.    3364, 3365

Wells, J. M.    6661

Welty, Aloyse.    5747

Welwitsch.    3366

Wendling. [Colonel]    7527

Wendling, Victor.    4476, 4477

Wenger, Antoine.    7528, 7529

Wermuth, Carl.    4478

Werne, Ferdinand.    1658—1660

Werner, Alice.    4613—4616

Werner, J. R.    4479, 4480

Wernsdorff, Fritz Wolf von.    5127

Werth, E.    4481

Werther, C. Waldemar [Lt.].    2299-2302

West, W. [Rev.].    6463

Westbeech, George.

Wester. [Lt.].    4482

Westmark, T.    4483,4484

Wetten, Franciscus van [Fr.Wiro].    2303

Weule, K.    2304

Wèvre.    4485

Wharton, Henri.    6464

Wheeler, John A.    5891,5892

White, Franklin.    5128,5129

Whitford, John.    5748

Whiton, Samuel J.    5749

Wichmann, H.    976, 2305,4486

Wickenburg, Eduard von.    463

Widenmann, A.    2306, 2307

Wieder, Joseph.    7530, 7531

Wieder, Martin.    4487

Wieder, Straton.    4488

Wiener, J.    2308

Wiese, Carl.    4617, 4790

Wilberforce, D. F.    7635

Wilcox, W. C.    4791-4794

Wilde, Jules de.    4489-4496

Wilder, George A. 4795–4797

Wilhelm, Georg. 7636

Wilhelm, J. G. 7637

Wilkes, Charles. 172

Wilkeson, Samuel. 6662

Wilkins, Henry St. Clair. 977

Wilkinson, Edward. 3130

Wilkinson, G. 464

Wilkinson, F. Fenwick. 5130

Wilkinson, J. Gardner. 978

Wilkinson, T. 2970

Wilkinson, William Fischer. 5131

Willcocks, James. 6465

Williams. [Capt.,RE]. 2580

Williams, Herbert Wynne Vaughan. 5132

Williams, Josiah. 1661
Williams, Samuel. 6663
Willoughby, John Christopher. 465,5133–5135

Wills, J. T. 466,1662,4497

Wills, Walter H. 5136

Wills, William Arthur. 5137

Wilmot. [Commodore]. 7197

Wilmot, A. 5138

Wilson. 467

Wilson, Charles Thomas. 468,2309,2581

Wilson, Charles William.    1663,1664

Wilson, H. H.    1665

Wilson, J. C. [Capt., RN].    2971

Wilson, John Leighton [Rev.].    5750, 6336— 6340, 6664—6678

Wilwerth. [Lt.].    4498—4504

Wingate, Francis Reginald.    1666

Winstanley, William.    979

Winterbottom, Thomas.    7638

Wintz, Edouard.    7532

Winz, Bonifatius.    4505, 4506

Wissmann, Hermann Wilhelm Leopold Ludwig von [Lt.].    2310, 3131—3134, 4507—4516

Witbooi, Hendrik.    5303, 5304

Witt, Robert Clinton.    5139

Witte, Anton.    7718

Witte, Jehan de.    4517

Wittstein, A.    4518

Wittum, Johanna.    5893

Wodon.    3610

Wöhrmann, Bernard.    5894

Woerl, Leo.    6067

Woermann, A.    4519, 4520

Wohltmann, Ferdinand.    2311, 5895—5898, 7719

Woitscheck, Paul.    5899

Woldt, A. 173

Wolf, Eugéne. 4521

Wolf, Ludwig [Stabsartz]. 4522-4525, 6068, 7720

Wolff, Willy. 3367-3370

Wollaston, A. F. R. 2582

Wolters, Max. 4526

Wolverton, Frederick Glyn. 1123

Wood, Evelyn. 6466

Wood, J. Buckley [Rev.]. 7198

Wood, Joseph Garbett. 5140

Woodhead, Cawthra. 4798

Woodside, Thomas W. 3182, 3371-3374

Woodward, Edward Mabbott [Maj. Gen.]. 2583

Woon, Harry Vernon [Capt.]. 5141

Woosnam, R. B. 2584

Work, M. N. 37

Worsfold, William Basil. 4799

Wortley, Edward James Montagu Stuart. 1667

Wouters, Willem. 1668

Wright, H. C. Seppings. 1669

Würtz, Ferdinand. 469, 1066

Wulfers, Laurentius. 4527

Wylde, Augustus Blandy. 980, 1670

Wynkoop. 6677-6678  x

x. [Lt.]. 6927

X. Y. Z.   1124

## Y

You, Basile.   981-983

Young, Edward Daniel.   470, 4618-4621

Young, M. W.   7639

Younghusband, Francis [Capt.].   3135

## Z

Zache, H.   2312

Zaghi, Carlo.   984

Zahn, F. M.   5751, 6467

Zappa, Carlo.   7199-7203

Zaytoun, Fred S.   1125

Zboïnski. [Commandant].   4528, 4529

Zebehr Pasha.   1671

Zech, Victor von [Graf].   2313

Zecht, J. von.   7721

Zichy, W. von.   985
Ziegenkorn.   2314
Ziemann, A.   4530

Zimmermann, Joseph.   6069

Zimmermann, Oskar.   5900

Zintgraff, Eugène [Dr.].   4531-4536, 5901

Zöller, Hugo.   5752, 5902-5905, 7722, 7723

Zündel, G.   5753

Zurbuchen, J. [Dr.].   1672